Ancient France

6000–2000

bc

British Museum Society

Ancient France

NEOLITHIC SOCIETIES AND THEIR LANDSCAPES 6000–2000 bc

Edited by CHRISTOPHER SCARRE *with a preface by* GLYN DANIEL

The University Press
Edinburgh

22 George Square, Edinburgh

Set in Linoterm Plantin by
Speedspools, Edinburgh, and
printed in Great Britain by
Alden Press Ltd, Oxford

British Library Cataloguing
in Publication Data
Scarre, Christopher
Ancient France, 6000–2000 bc
1. France—History—to 987
I. Title
944′.01 DC61

ISBN 0 85224 441 X

British Museum Society

Contents

Preface

GLYN DANIEL

WHILE MANY people, from Mercati onwards, set out in Renaissance Europe the idea that there had been a Stone Age in the past of man it was not until the French, in the Somme gravels and the rock-shelters of southern France, demonstrated its existence that prehistoric archaeology came into being. The pre-Roman past of man, hitherto a muddle of Ancient Britons, Gauls, and Goths, was seen in terms of a new technological model of the three ages of Stone, Bronze and Iron by the Danish archaeologist C. J. Thomsen who opened the galleries of the Danish National Museum in 1819, based on this three-age system.

France was rich in the Stone Age from the work of Boucher de Perthes in the north to Lartet and Christy and many another in the south. But was the French Stone Age the same as that defined in Denmark? It was not, and soon it was clear that there were several kinds of stone ages, that of the gravels and rock-shelters of France, that of the kitchen-middens of Denmark, and that of the megaliths and lake-dwellings. It was an Englishman, Sir John Lubbock (later Lord Avebury), who saw these differences clearly and proposed the word Palaeolithic for the *période de la pierre taillée*, and Neolithic for the *période de la pierre polie*. Lubbock did not appreciate the place of the Danish kitchen-middens, and the Mesolithic was a post-Lubbock phrase, which does not appear in his *Prehistoric Times* (1865).

From then on research into the Palaeolithic of France has been vigorously pursued, whereas the prehistory of France from the Mesolithic onwards has not, until recently, received comparable attention. A country which had the Somme gravels and the rock-shelters of Dordogne and the Pyrenees, and the art of Font-de-Gaume, Lascaux and Niaux, and the Abbé Breuil, can be forgiven for finding the Old Stone Age the most exciting part of its pre-Roman past. The study of the French Neolithic lagged behind that of the Palaeolithic. The terms of reference were hard to define; there were megaliths and pottery and lake-dwellings. De Mortillet, Cartailhac and Déchelette were unable to come to terms with the French Neolithic, and an impartial observer might have thought in the years following the 1914–18 war that archaeologists would never get to grips with the French Neolithic, as we in England seemed unable to get to grips with the Neolithic of the British Isles.

It was foreign scholars who made the breakthrough and made us look again at the French material of the *période de la pierre polie*. The Spaniards,

Bosch-Gimpera and Serra-Rafols, began with their creation of the Seine-Oise-Marne culture – a wonderful breakthrough from the megalith-lake-dwellings-*fonds de cabane* muddle. Then English scholars began and the contributions of Childe, Piggott, J. Hawkes, and N. Sandars started off a native French study of the Neolithic. From the end of the 1939–45 war onwards we have seen remarkable and often brilliant surveys, mainly on a regional basis, of the French Neolithic and names such as Bailloud, Burnez, Giot, L'Helgouach, and Guilaine, to mention invidiously only a few, crowd the pages of this book.

Still, British archaeologists have turned to work in France, not only because in France are the origins of some of our own neolithic societies, but because of the intrinsic interest of France in the neolithic polity of prehistoric western Europe. In this book, which I welcome with enthusiasm, a small group of young British archaeologists, who have for years been studying aspects of the French Neolithic, have come together to pool their work. It gives us a detailed regional and synthetic picture which is not obtainable elsewhere. All these writers belong to a generation which is moving away from the culture-historical approach of Childe, as his generation moved away from the geological-period approach of De Mortillet. They want to see their sites and artifacts in terms of environment and ecology; they are prehistoric human geographers, and as such they provide us with a new and refreshing view of Neolithic France as it seems to many in the 1980s. They are up-to-date and have taken full account of the new C 14 chronology. Indeed one of the many values of this book will be the tables of C 14 dates at the end of each chapter. No one working on the prehistory of Europe between 6000 and 2000 bc can be without these tables.

Dr Ilett says in his chapter that it is 'not unfair to conclude that early neolithic research in north-eastern France has only just begun'. It has more than begun; it is well on its way all over France and the work summarised here, carried out in close co-operation with French workers, will prove a new starting point. It records achievement and points to problems. We all tend to be chauvinistic in our history and archaeology, and when the British write about the archaeology of France they are sometimes sneered at by their French colleagues as portraying 'la préhistoire de France outre-manche'. This book cannot be so described except as a compliment. It is the Neolithic of France seen by eight young British archaeologists who have for long worked on both sides of the Channel to the benefit of British and French.

Introduction

CHRIS SCARRE

Aims of the book o period covered o area covered o British archaeologists and the French Neolithic o the concept of 'culture' o settlement and society o the shortage of data o the plan of the book.

BRITAIN IS separated from France by only twenty miles of sea, yet English accounts of the French Neolithic have been few and there is no book on the subject in print, other than this. Piggott, Daniel and McBurney's *France Before the Romans*, which made its appearance in 1974, devoted relatively little space to the neolithic period, since it had to cover the Palaeolithic, Mesolithic and Bronze and Iron Ages as well. Phillips' *Early Farmers of West Mediterranean Europe* (1975) gave a detailed account of the Neolithic of southern France but without much social or economic analysis, or attempt to link events in the south with those in northern and western France. Nor is there any good recent French account to which reference can easily be made. *La Préhistoire Française* (1976) describes in outline the material culture of the different areas, but does not try to interpret them or to provide a coherent survey of the principal developments of the period. Guilaine's more general account, *La France d'avant la France* (1981), gives only a relatively superficial coverage. The present volume is intended to fill the gap, and to serve as a sourcebook for archaeology students and teachers; as a survey for the general reader; and as a demonstration of the relevance of some recent approaches to the interpretation of this material.

The book covers the prehistory of mainland France, the Channel Islands and Corsica from the beginning of the neolithic period to the end of the 3rd millennium bc. For convenience' sake the Neolithic has been assumed to start with the appearance of pottery, an arbitrary but conventional marker. This criterion gives different dates for the beginning of the Neolithic in different parts of France – late 7th millennium bc in the south; middle or later 5th millennium in the west and the north-east. Pottery is not however the sole indicator of the Neolithic considered in the chapters that follow, and attention is also paid to the evidence for the development of an agricultural economy, of village settlements, and of megalithic tombs. The last part of the period falls under what French archaeologists have termed the Chalcolithic, named after the appearance of the first copper objects but before the full Early Bronze Age. There is much continuity between the late neolithic and chalcolithic periods in

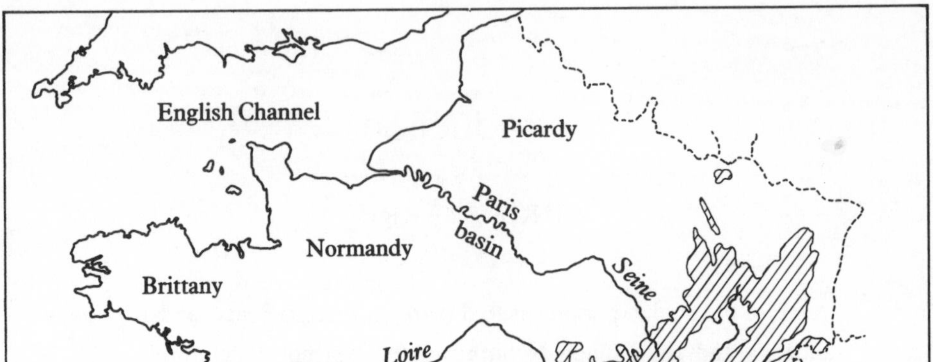

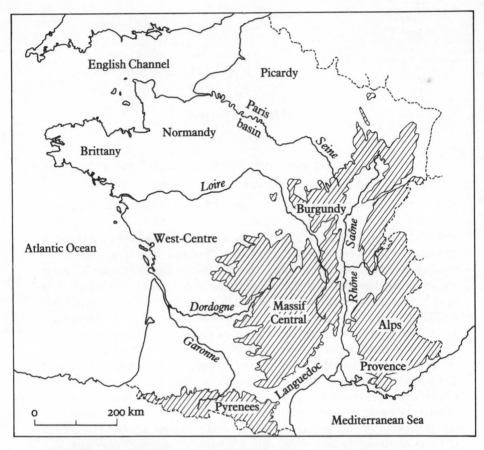

FIGURE 1.1. Map of France, showing the principal rivers and mountains and some of the major regions. Land over 400m is shaded.

many parts of France, and it has seemed logical to include it in this account as the culmination of the developments of the preceding millennia. The traditional terminology, which in most regions recognises a Neolithic divided into Early, Middle and Late, followed by a Chalcolithic, has been retained, despite its limitations; and a list of radiocarbon dates has been attached to each chapter to provide the basis for an absolute chronology.

The frontiers and coasts of France provide a convenient but by no means natural unit for the study of prehistory (Fig. 1.1). The concept of an integral France does not antedate the Middle Ages and it is unsatisfactory and potentially misleading to deal with prehistoric material in terms of political boundaries which are relatively modern, though there are of course strong practical reasons why this must be so. The greatest difficulty is met in north-east France, where the European lowlands sweep uninterruptedly into the Paris basin and beyond; on the north, west and south there is sea, while in the south-west and south-east, natural frontiers are defined by the Pyrenees and the Alps respectively. Yet neither the seas nor the mountains have proved impassable barriers. For much of the period, the south of France appears to have formed a unit with adjacent parts of Spain and Italy, linked by sea and across mountain, and had much less in common with neolithic northern and eastern France. In contrast, the evidence for cross-Channel contact in the neolithic period is slight – not much more than occasional imports into Britain of Grand Pressigny flint and Plussulien dolerite axes; and a few pottery parallels. No *Bandkeramik* or *Cerny* material has been found in Britain, and contact does not seem to have been continuous or significant. On the north-eastern boundary of France there are no sea or mountain barriers and the French neolithic traditions merge with those of the Low Countries, Germany and Switzerland. So, for instance, the Paris basin Bandkeramik belongs to a tradition of central European origin, well represented in Belgium, Dutch Limburg and the Rhineland; the *Chasséen* of north-eastern France is related to the *Michelsberg* of the Low Countries and to the *Cortaillod* of Switzerland; and the late neolithic *Seine-Oise-Marne* group is represented in Belgium and finds a close parallel in Switzerland in *Horgen* material. It is therefore important when considering the French Neolithic to keep in mind that the pattern of developments may not have conformed to the modern political boundaries and that material from adjacent territories should always be taken into account.

The work described in these pages is only the most recent in a long tradition of British research on the French Neolithic. One of the first British prehistorians to turn his attention to the Neolithic of France was Gordon Childe, who around 1930 defined the middle neolithic Chasséen culture on the basis of material from the site of Chassey-le-Camp in Burgundy and from the Abbé Philippe's excavations at Fort Harrouard in Normandy. British prehistorians were also responsible for some of the subsequent refinement of the Chasséen culture concept (Hawkes, 1934; Piggott, 1953). At about the same time, the late neolithic/chalcolithic channelled wares of southern and western France formed part of a study by J. Hawkes (Hawkes, J., 1938). This research was undertaken principally in search of continental parallels and progenitors for British neolithic material, in the light of the diffusionist paradigm then popular. The inter-war period also saw the first of Glyn Daniel's publications on the megalithic tombs (1939a, b), though the culmination of this research came only in 1960 with the appearance of his general survey *The Prehistoric Chamber Tombs of France*.

Since 1945 there has been a steady increase in British research on the French Neolithic. Childe and Sandars' definitive account of the Seine-Oise-Marne culture (1950) and Piggott's studies of the pottery (1953, 1954) are among the more important contributions, and there was further work by Daniel on the megaliths (1955, 1958, 1960). The west of France was especially favoured in the 1950s, with excavations by Sieveking at the flint mines of Le Grand Pressigny (results unpublished), and by Case at the late neolithic enclosure of Les Matignons (Burnez and Case, 1966). The quest for continental parallels, which had dominated earlier British work, began at this time to be replaced by an interest in the French Neolithic for its own sake. The consequences may be seen in the regional studies by Bender on north-western France and by Phillips on the south (Bender and Phillips, 1972; Phillips, 1975, 1982). There was a parallel increase in French interest, with many new excavations in the 1950s and 1960s, and with some areas being studied for the first time. A series of valuable regional syntheses resulted (Bailloud, 1964; Burnez, 1976; Courtin, 1974). The present volume shows that the level of British interest in the French Neolithic has been sustained throughout the last decade. Thanks for this must go in part to those French neolithic specialists whose fieldwork and ready co-operation have encouraged the application of a variety of new approaches to the material.

It has become customary to interpret the French Neolithic in terms of a series of 'cultures', most of which have their basis in pottery types. Prehistorians have in the past devoted considerable time and energy to the definition and study of such cultures, which many thought to be a direct material manifestation of prehistoric social groupings. Recent work has called this assumption into question, by showing that the relationship between material culture and social organisation is more complex than had commonly been supposed and that many archaeological cultures are not valid entities and probably did not correspond to prehistoric social units (Hodder, 1982; Renfrew, 1977). For these reasons the use of the term 'culture' has as far as possible been avoided in this volume, though most work continues to be carried out within the traditional framework.

The decline and fall of the culture concept has been accompanied in British archaeology by an increased interest in the diachronic development of settlement patterns, agricultural strategies, social organisation and trade, and it is approaches of these types which predominate in the present volume. Several of the chapters discuss the significance of settlement expansion in relation to economy and population, and the relationship between settlement patterns and the changing landscape. These studies represent the application to French neolithic data of approaches and attitudes which have not hitherto been common among French prehistorians, though there have been notable exceptions (e.g. Lorblanchet's account of the settlement of the Grands Causses (Lorblanchet, 1965); and the admirable interdisciplinary research, including a site locational assessment, carried out by Guilaine and his colleagues at the Abri Jean Cros (Guilaine, 1979a)). The artefactual evidence has not been ignored in these pages, however, as it is essential for chronology and for the definition of regional groups, and contains important clues about social and economic organisation.

A difficulty which besets all the analyses offered in this volume is the inadequacy of the evidence to answer the questions asked. The last twenty years have seen a considerable advance in knowledge and understanding of the French Neolithic, but in archaeology as in so many fields the existing state of knowledge can never be satisfactory and one must always be seeking more information and fresh hypotheses. A particular difficulty is the partial nature of many of the samples of sites and artefact assemblages upon which we are obliged to base our theories. Any account of the French Neolithic must therefore be by nature only an interim statement, and we await with eagerness the results of further fieldwork which might allow some of the ideas put forward in these chapters to be substantiated and a new set of hypotheses to be formulated.

The treatment of the French Neolithic which follows is arranged by region, starting in the north-east and moving in a clockwise direction to the south, west and north-west. The format of the chapters is similar and broadly as follows:

1) an introductory section gives a brief geographical account of the particular region and a short history of previous research;
2) a central section describes the material culture and chronology;
3) in a final section, each author presents an interpretation of some or all of this material in the light of his own research.

The lists of radiocarbon dates which accompany each chapter are not comprehensive but are designed to document the basic sequences of cultural material. In the case of regions for which many radiocarbon dates are available only a selection of the more important is given. (The by now usual bc/BC convention has been used throughout the book, 'bc' for uncalibrated radiocarbon dates, 'BC' for calibrated or historical dates.) To complement the region-by-region arrangement a final chapter is devoted to a discussion of some of the principal strands in the development of the French Neolithic and a consideration of changing configurations at a wider geographical scale.

The Early Neolithic of North-Eastern France

MIKE ILETT

The land o history of research o MATERIAL CULTURE o *Late Bandkeramik* o Cuiry-lès-Chaudardes o *Epi-Bandkeramik* o Villeneuve-Saint-Germain o Cerny o *Late Rössen* o Berry-au-Bac o burial and ritual o SETTLEMENT in the Early Neolithic o the macro-regional pattern o the micro-regional pattern in the Aisne valley o the role of defence.

NORTH-EASTERN FRANCE is defined as the region north and east of the River Seine and its southernmost tributary, the Yonne (Fig. 2.1). Bordered by the Ardenne massif in the east, and in the south-east by the low Jurassic hills separating the Seine and the upper Meuse-Moselle-Saône drainage networks, the region constitutes the western boundary of Bandkeramik expansion in the later fifth millennium bc.

There is relatively little land above 200m, but the landscape is not flat and featureless. The two major geological characteristics of the Paris basin are a central area of Tertiary limestone and a surrounding band of Cretaceous chalk, and they show considerable variation in relief, drainage, and superficial deposits. These factors certainly influenced the pattern of early neolithic settlement.

The central limestone plateaux are cut through, from N to S, by the alluvial valleys of the Oise, Aisne, Marne, Seine and Yonne. To the south and east of the limestone deposits, valley relief is less marked, as the rivers flow through rolling chalk landscape. Their middle and lower reaches are flanked by gravel terraces of varying extent. To the north, much of the landscape between the Oise and the coast consists of dissected chalk plateaux; and relief is quite varied. The Rivers Somme, Authie, and Canche, which flow through this area, have been much affected by post-glacial sea-level rise. Their narrow, poorly drained valleys are filled with layers of peat and alluvium, within which neolithic material has occasionally been found (Agache *et al.*, 1963, figs 15 and 16). Further north still, in the Escaut drainage basin, the chalk grades into Tertiary sand deposits.

Here the flatter landscape, masked with loess and coversands (Paepe and Sommé, 1970, fig. 17), is artificially divided by the political frontier between France and Belgium. Extensive loess deposits also occur on the dissected chalk

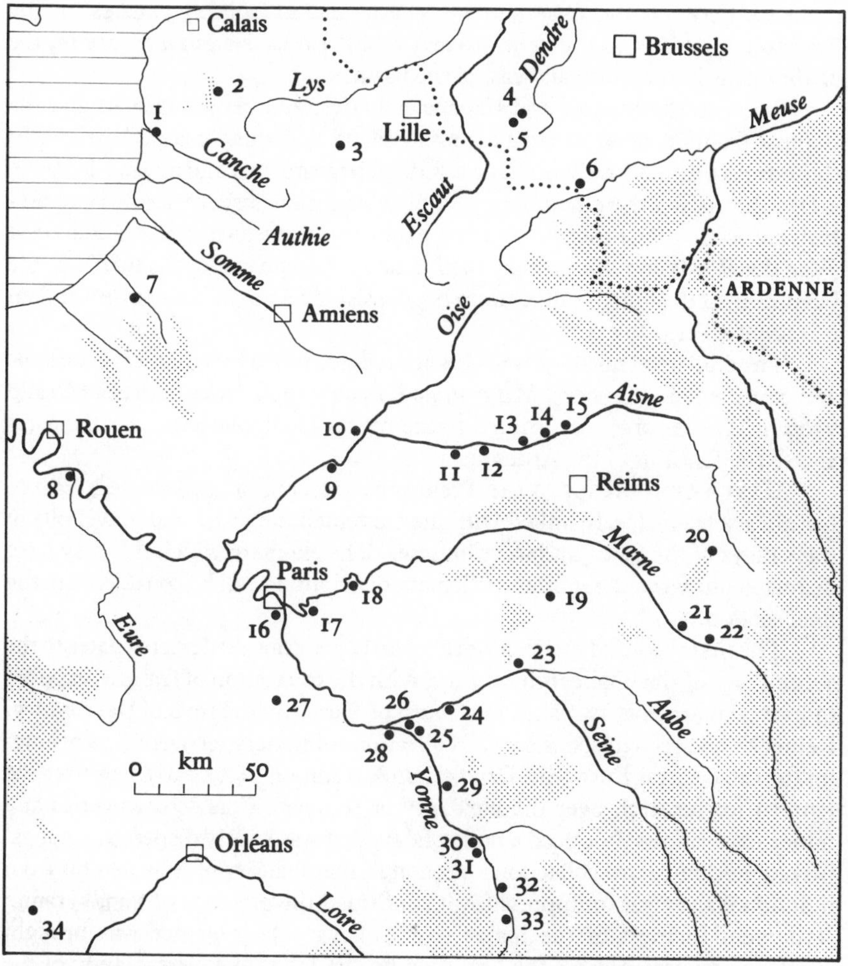

FIGURE 2.1. North-eastern France (land over 200m shaded), showing sites mentioned in text.
1 Etaples (Pas-de-Calais); 2 Montagne de Lumbres (Pas-de-Calais); 3 Sailly-Labourse (Pas-de-Calais); 4 Blicquy (Belgian Hainaut); 5 Aubechies (Belgian Hainaut); 6 Givry (Belgian Hainaut); 7 Blangy-sur-Bresle (Seine-Maritime); 8 Léry (Eure); 9 Pontpoint (Oise); 10 Jonquières (Oise); 11 Villeneuve-Saint-Germain (Aisne); 12 Cys-la-Commune (Aisne); 13 Cuiry-lès-Chaudardes (Aisne); 14 Berry-au-Bac (Aisne); 15 Menneville (Aisne); 16 Villejuif (Val-de-Marne); 17 Champigny (Val-de-Marne); 18 Jablines (Seine-et-Marne); 19 Vert-la-Gravelle (Marne); 20 Ante (Marne); 21 Frignicourt (Marne); 22 Larzicourt (Marne); 23 Barbuise-Courtavant (Aube); 24 Noyen (Seine-et-Marne); 25 Misy-sur-Yonne (Seine-et-Marne); 26 Marolles (Seine-et-Marne); 27 Cerny (Essonne); 28 Cannes-Ecluse (Seine-et-Marne); 29 Armeau (Yonne); 30 Charmoy (Yonne); 31 Chichery (Yonne); 32 Augy (Yonne); 33 Sainte-Pallaye (Yonne); 34 Marcilly (Loir-et-Cher).

plateaux between the Oise and the coast, and in isolated patches on the limestone plateaux in the central Paris basin. Loess is relatively rare on the chalk plains in the south and east of the basin.

Between the Somme and Canche estuaries, and between Calais and the Belgian frontier, areas of reclaimed marshland lie behind coastal barriers. In these areas the neolithic landscape is hidden beneath peat and marine deposits, a fact that is worth remembering in view of recent discoveries of later prehistoric occupation in similar, if more extensive, deposits near the Dutch coast (Van der Waals and Waterbolk, 1976; Louwe Kooijmans, 1976, 1980). At the beginning of the fourth millennium bc, the sea-level was at least 8m lower than it is today (Ters, 1973).

The climate of north-eastern France is determined by a mixture of oceanic and continental influences. Mean annual precipitation varies between 600 and 750mm. Wetter areas are limited to the higher chalk plateaux near the coast and to the foothills of the Ardenne.

HISTORY OF RESEARCH. Prehistoric research in north-eastern France has always been closely linked with the surveillance of sand and gravel pits in the valleys of the Seine and its tributaries. The extent to which this may have distorted our view of neolithic settlement distribution will be considered in the final section.

The first recorded modern work on early neolithic settlements dates to the second half of the nineteenth century, with the excavation of features exposed in gravel quarries at two sites just south of Paris. By the turn of the century, Reinecke had recognised the small collections of pottery recovered, as belonging to the Central European Bandkeramik tradition. This early work set the pattern for research over the next fifty or so years. Chance discoveries and minor excavations produced a body of data that was widely dispersed amongst private and museum collections. Although the quantity of information from individual sites was unimpressive, it confirmed the presence of Bandkeramik settlement in most of the major river valleys. The evidence was brought together and assessed for the first time by Bailloud, in a classic study of the Paris basin Neolithic (1964). The *Rubané Récent du Bassin Parisien* (Paris Basin Late Bandkeramik) was distinguished from other neolithic ceramic groups in the study area, one of which had been associated with an incomplete and atypical houseplan excavated in the Yonne valley in 1957 (Carré *et al.*, 1958). None of the nineteen Bandkeramik settlements listed by Bailloud had been excavated on any scale, and none had produced the characteristic buildings that were by then well known outside France.

As the pace of gravel extraction increased in the 1960s, more rescue activity took place, and the first definite Bandkeramik houseplans were discovered. The excavation of two poorly preserved buildings in 1965 and 1966 at Cys-la-Commune (Aisne; m.r.12) (Boureux and Coudart, 1978, figs 4 and 5) was rapidly followed by the recovery, in remarkably extensive rescue operations, of the first complete houseplans from the middle Seine and Yonne valleys (Joly 1968, 403; Mordant and Mordant, 1970, fig.1).

PLATE 2.1. Aerial view of two longhouses on the western edge of the Bandkeramik settlement at Cuiry-lès-Chaudardes (1976 excavations). The house on the lower left is 39m long; its groundplan is partially disturbed by First World War trenches. The other house is 28m long. Lateral construction pits are being investigated in metre squares. (Photo: Michel Boureux.)

A current Paris University and CNRS project in the Aisne valley marks a clear break with earlier research traditions in northern France. Instigated by the Czech Neolithic specialist, Bohumil Soudsky, on his arrival to teach in Paris in 1971, the project aims to carry out a systematic regional study of later prehistoric settlement, combining large-scale excavation with specific research objectives. Its main excavations so far have taken place at the Bandkeramik settlement of Cuiry-lès-Chaudardes (Aisne) (Plate 2.1; m.r.13) and at the multi-period site at Berry-au-Bac (Aisne; m.r.14), with an important mid-fourth-millennium bc occupation. As a result of this project, a considerable mass of new information about both the material culture and settlement structure of the earlier neolithic is now available, and this forms the basis of much of this chapter.

MATERIAL CULTURE

The early neolithic cultural sequence in north-eastern France can be conveniently divided into three periods: *Late Bandkeramik* c.4100–3900bc, *Epi-Bandkeramik* c.3900–3600bc, and *Late Rössen* c.3600–3300bc. Many of the finer details of the sequence continue to pose problems (Bailloud, 1971, 1974,

1976; Constantin, 1982). Whilst the first and last periods can be broadly related to the well-established Rhineland sequence (Meier-Arendt, 1975, Abb.25), the middle period undergoes independent developments, grouped together here under the rather unsatisfactory term 'Epi-Bandkeramik'. The ceramics of the Epi-Bandkeramik bear little or no resemblance to those of the *Grossgartach*/earlier Rössen complex, its chronological equivalent in West Germany and Alsace (Jürgens, 1979; Lichardus-Itten, 1980). Furthermore, much of the information currently available for the Epi-Bandkeramik is restricted to small assemblages of decorated pottery, and it is very difficult to formulate a clear picture of regional and chronological variation.

The following discussion treats the material culture of the three periods in turn. Rather more attention is paid to the Late Bandkeramik as it is relatively well-documented. A short summary of the evidence for burial in all three periods concludes the discussion.

LATE BANDKERAMIK. The qualitative and quantitative composition of Late Bandkeramik material culture assemblages has emerged only with the large-scale excavations in the Aisne valley.

Pottery. Most of the pottery occurs in a very fragmentary state, together with other kinds of domestic refuse, in the construction pits flanking longhouses (Fig.2.11; Plate 2.1). It is probable that the sherds originate from pots that were broken in and around the houses to which the pits belong. In fact, sherds belonging to the same vessel are often widely scattered amongst the various pits on either side of a building, and it is reasonable to assume that the material from these pits reflects the range of pottery that was used by the occupants in the course of its lifetime. A typical assemblage associated with one of the larger houses at Cuiry-lès-Chaudardes represented the remains of at least one hundred and sixty vessels. It can be divided into small fine-ware and larger, more coarsely-made vessels (Fig.2.2). The coarser pottery contains a temper of either crushed shell, fine gravel, or quartz fragments, clearly visible on the surface. Whilst some of the coarse ware vessels are decorated with lines of finger-pinched impressions, most possess knobs or small protuberances just beneath the rim. Simple, horizontally-perforated lugs are found on all the categories of pottery. The fine-ware category seems to account for about two-thirds of the total number of vessels.

Fine ware can be equally divided into decorated and undecorated. Decoration involves incised lines and comb impressions, sometimes accentuated with a white incrustation. Whilst the two decoration techniques are often found on the same vessel, incised decoration on its own is very rare. There is considerable uniformity in comb type and size. The most frequently used combs have two or three teeth; four- or five-toothed combs are relatively uncommon. An impressed pattern was made by pivoting the comb across the damp surface of the clay; the comb was rarely lifted from the surface to make separate impressions. Decoration beneath the rim and on the neck of the pots includes various combinations of horizontal, comb-impressed bands and incised lines. The comb-impressed bands are sometimes interrupted. The main

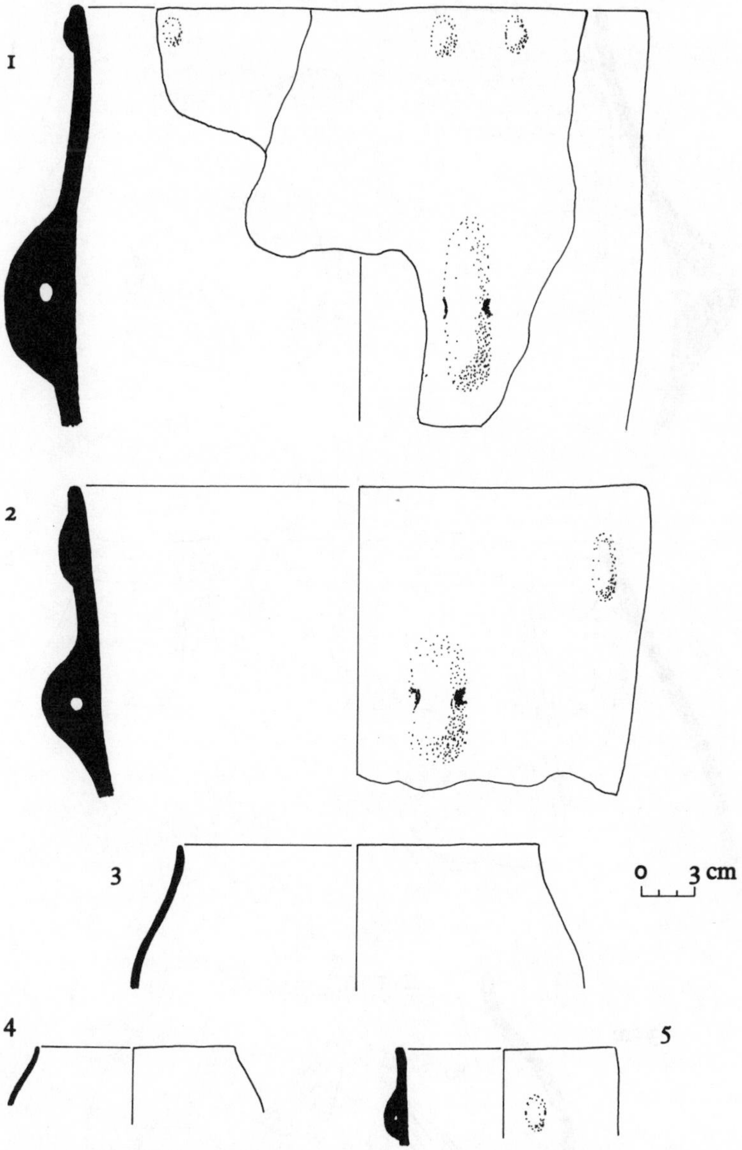

FIGURE 2.2. Late Bandkeramik pottery from Cuiry-lès-Chaudardes: 1, 2 coarse ware; 3-5 undecorated fine ware.

decoration on the body of the pot (Ilett and Plateaux, in press) is characteristically composed of either vertical bands of comb impressions, vertical bands combining comb impressions and incised lines, or oblique incised lines forming an inverted 'v' pattern (Fig.2.3). These motifs are repeated several times around the surface of the vessel. It is the high frequency of vertical band motifs, together with the occurrence of comb impressions on the over-

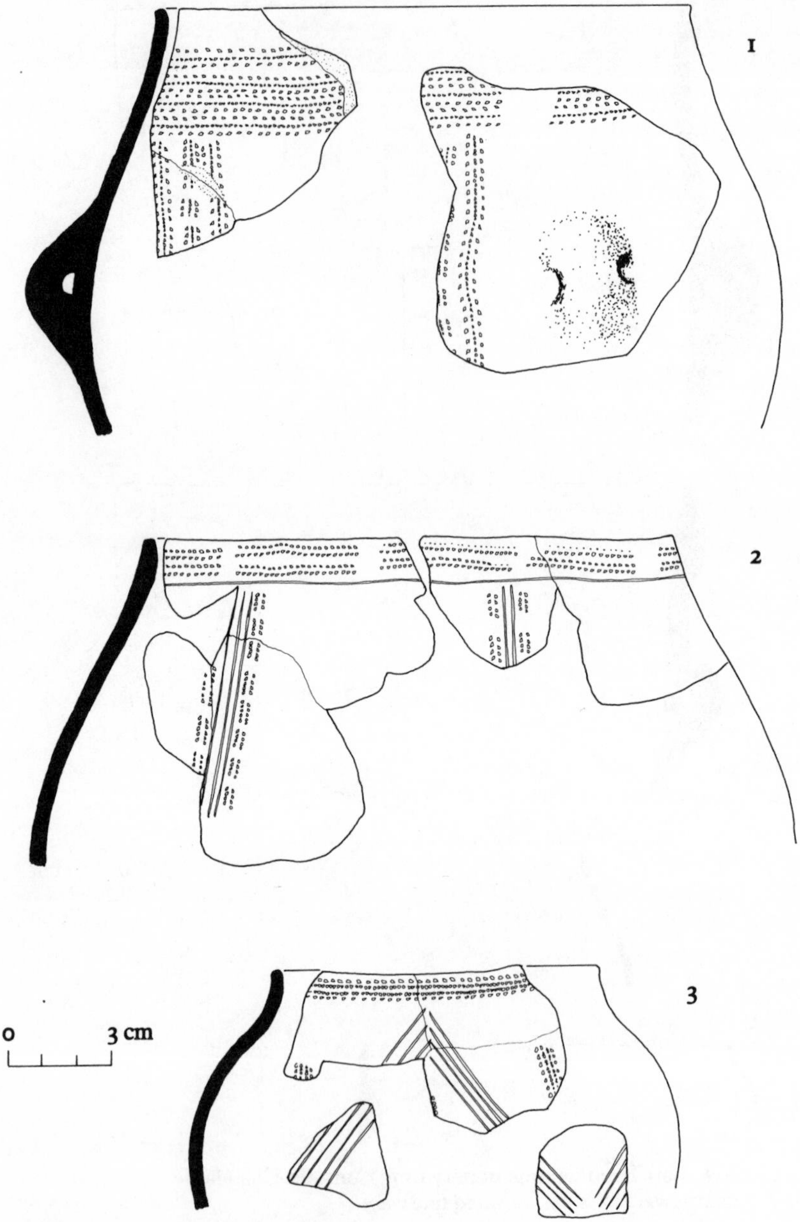

FIGURE 2.3. Decorated Late Bandkeramik fine ware from Cuiry-lès-Chaudardes. Decoration techniques: 1 three-toothed comb; 2 two-toothed comb and incisions; 3 incisions and four-toothed comb. (After Ilett and Plateaux, in press.)

whelming majority of the decorated vessels, that sharply distinguishes these assemblages from the Late Bandkeramik of Belgium, Holland, Germany, and Alsace. The Aisne valley material does include more 'typical' Bandkeramik motifs, such as incised bands filled with impressions or cross-hatched lines, but these are extremely rare.

Almost all the pits at Cuiry-lès-Chaudardes contain sherds of so-called Limburg pottery (Constantin *et al.*, 1981). With its crushed bone temper, grooved decoration, and open shapes with thickened rims, this pottery clearly stands out from the rest of the assemblage. Its social or functional significance has yet to be explained satisfactorily.

Lithics. A recent study of the lithics from Cuiry-lès-Chaudardes (Plateaux, 1982 and forthcoming) has shown that in both typology and technology the industry resembles that of Bandkeramik settlements elsewhere in western Europe (Schietzel, 1965; Löhr *et al.*, 1977). It is essentially blade-based; on average the blades are about 50mm long and just under 20mm wide. Retouched tools include scrapers, sickle blades (blades with silica gloss), asymmetric triangular arrowheads, borers, and burins (Fig.2.4). Some of the sickle blades are of an obliquely truncated or retouched type that otherwise occurs only in Rössen contexts in the Rhineland (Fiedler, 1979). Apart from the ubiquitous burins, which are rarely reported from Bandkeramik sites outside the Paris basin, an unusual feature of the assemblage is the relatively high proportion of arrowheads. Fragments of ground-stone adzes are very uncommon. Only three fragments have been found so far, and two of these fit together. The site has also produced three flaked flint axes, and broken querns and grindstones occur in most of the pits. A study has yet to be made of the raw materials used for the flint and stone implements.

Bone. Bone tools in varying states of fragmentation are a common occurrence amongst the domestic débris at Cuiry-lès-Chaudardes, and include the basic types described by Bailloud (1964, 25–6; 1971, 209). The most frequently occurring tools are points, or awls, made from split metapodials, and chisel-like implements of uncertain function (Fig.2.4). There are also several examples of a comparatively robust bone tool not dissimilar in shape to a stone adze. It is possible that these tools were used for woodworking, since suitable stone seems to have been in rare supply. This hypothesis will have to be tested by microwear analysis and experiment. In view of the evidence from a pit at Armeau (Yonne; m.r.29) (Poplin, 1975), it seems likely that the construction pits at Cuiry-lès-Chaudardes will eventually yield much information about how these bone tools were made.

How do the Late Bandkeramik assemblages from the Aisne valley compare with material from elsewhere in north-eastern France? As far as can be judged from the small samples available, the ceramics outlined above are representative of sites of similar date elsewhere in the Paris basin. Both the pivoted comb decoration technique and characteristic motifs are found on a wide range of sites from the Aisne-Oise confluence in the north (Blanchet *et al.*, 1980) to

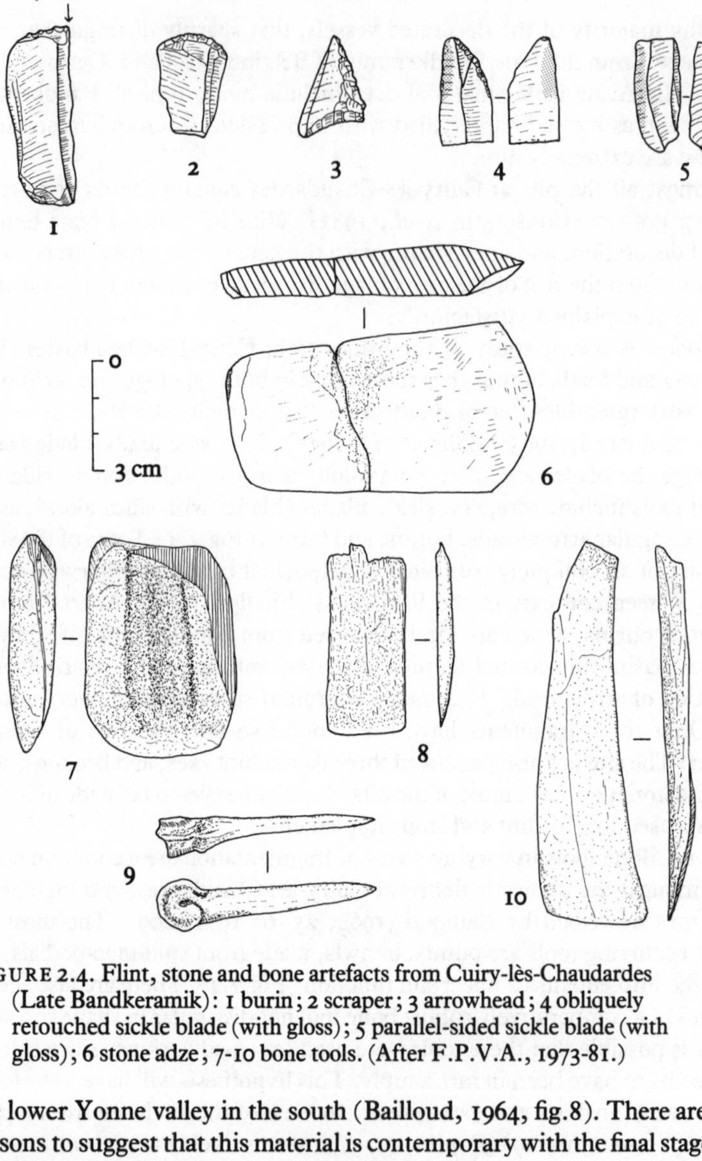

FIGURE 2.4. Flint, stone and bone artefacts from Cuiry-lès-Chaudardes (Late Bandkeramik): 1 burin; 2 scraper; 3 arrowhead; 4 obliquely retouched sickle blade (with gloss); 5 parallel-sided sickle blade (with gloss); 6 stone adze; 7-10 bone tools. (After F.P.V.A., 1973-81.)

the lower Yonne valley in the south (Bailloud, 1964, fig.8). There are several reasons to suggest that this material is contemporary with the final stages of the Bandkeramik sequence in the Rhineland. Comb decoration makes a late appearance in this sequence (Meier-Arendt, 1972; Dohrn-Ihmig, 1973, 1979). Furthermore, the presence of typologically-late sickle blades on the Paris basin sites has already been noted, and a late date is also implied by the trapezoidal nature of some of the houseplans (Coudart, 1982). An impressive cluster of radiocarbon dates from Cuiry-lès-Chaudardes supports these arguments. Nine out of twelve dates with acceptable standard deviations fall between 4050bc and 3850bc.

Whether or not this ceramic material represents the earliest Bandkeramik occupation of north-eastern France is another matter. The fact that the decorated assemblages are so different from Late Bandkeramik groups to the east hints at an earlier phase of colonisation. Evidence of such a phase has recently been discovered at Larzicourt (Marne; m.r.22). Here, a small assemblage (Chertier, 1980) is characterised by incised rectilinear and curvilinear motifs which have their closest parallels in the *Rubané Moyen* of Alsace (Schweitzer, 1980). Comb decoration is apparently absent, and this material sets the colonisation of the eastern Paris basin at a rather earlier date than was previously suspected.

As work progresses in the south-east of the Marne *département* and in Lorraine, where increasingly large numbers of Bandkeramik sites are being discovered along the Moselle and its tributaries (Decker and Guillaume, 1980), it may become possible to trace the chronological and geographical spread of colonisation more accurately. Nevertheless, it seems inherently unlikely that only one centre of Bandkeramik population contributed to the expansion into north-eastern France. With so many blanks on the distribution map, stretching from the Escaut basin down through the upper Meuse valley and Lorraine to the upper Saône, it is perhaps unrealistic to look for precise 'origins'. Adzes of Vosges quartzite (probably from a source just north of the Belfort Gap) on sites in the southern Paris basin, indicate contact between the two areas during the Late Bandkeramik (Petrequin, 1974, 525). Other adzes from north-eastern France remain unanalysed. Meier-Arendt (1966, 59–60; 1972, 118–20) has suggested that the idiosyncratic decoration technique and motifs of the Paris basin Late Bandkeramik could have resulted from early contact with west Mediterranean Impressed Ware groups.

Another intriguing indication of far-ranging interactions between Bandkeramik communities is the distribution of Limburg pottery. Sherds from these distinctive vessels are found in Bandkeramik pits right across the north-western fringe of the culture's distribution, from the lower Rhine basin to the Aisne valley (Modderman, 1981; Constantin, 1981). The Limburg sherds generally represent a very small proportion of the total ceramic assemblage, but rather larger quantities have been found on a site in Belgian Hainaut (Constantin and Demarez, 1981).

EPI-BANDKERAMIK. The principal group belonging to this period used to be the Cerny 'culture' (Bailloud, 1974, 61–73), which is described below. The recognition in recent years of an earlier *Villeneuve-Saint-Germain* group (Constantin and Demoule, 1982) has however considerably improved our understanding of the more important changes in material culture between the end of the Bandkeramik and the emergence of the Cerny group. The material from Villeneuve-Saint-Germain (m.r.11) differs from that of the Late Bandkeramik in the widespread use of bone temper, a new range of decoration styles, and the appearance for the first time of schist bracelets (FPVA, 1976). Associated with Bandkeramik-type houseplans, the finds from Villeneuve-Saint-Germain are of more than local significance, as it has become clear that related material is widely distributed over north-eastern France. Similarities

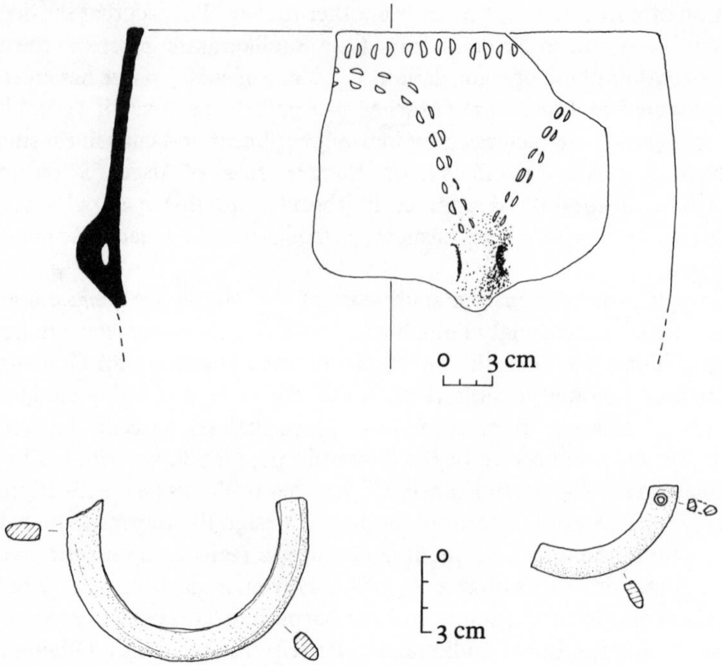

FIGURE 2.5. Pottery with finger-impressed decoration and schist bracelet fragments from Misy-sur-Yonne; Villeneuve-Saint-Germain group. (After Mordant and Mordant, 1977.)

with the recently-defined *Blicquy* group in Belgian Hainaut are particularly striking (Constantin *et al.*, 1978; Cahen and van Berg, 1979, 1980). However, none of the French settlements dating to this horizon has been extensively excavated, and knowledge of the structure of the assemblages and the manner in which they developed is consequently limited.

Pottery. Whilst bone temper is common in the pottery of the Villeneuve-Saint-Germain group, not all the vessels are tempered in this way and it appears that the frequency of bone tempered vessels falls off in a southerly direction across the Paris basin. Coarse ware includes large, straight-sided pots with flattened rims which are characteristically decorated with a row of finger or nail impressions. Further oblique lines of impressions form V motifs between lugs and rim (Fig.2.5). Applied cordon decoration is also found on the larger pots, often in similar V motifs. This type of decoration seems to be more common in the south of the Paris basin. Much of the material originally used to define the *Augy-Sainte-Pallaye* (m.r.32, 33) group in the Yonne valley (Bailloud, 1964, 125–36) can now be assigned to the Villeneuve-Saint-Germain horizon, as can related groups (e.g. *Marcilly*; m.r.34) in the Loire basin (Bailloud, 1971, 224–5).

Fine ware occurs in a simple range of shapes. Decoration includes incised and comb-impressed motifs, but the classic Late Bandkeramik styles are

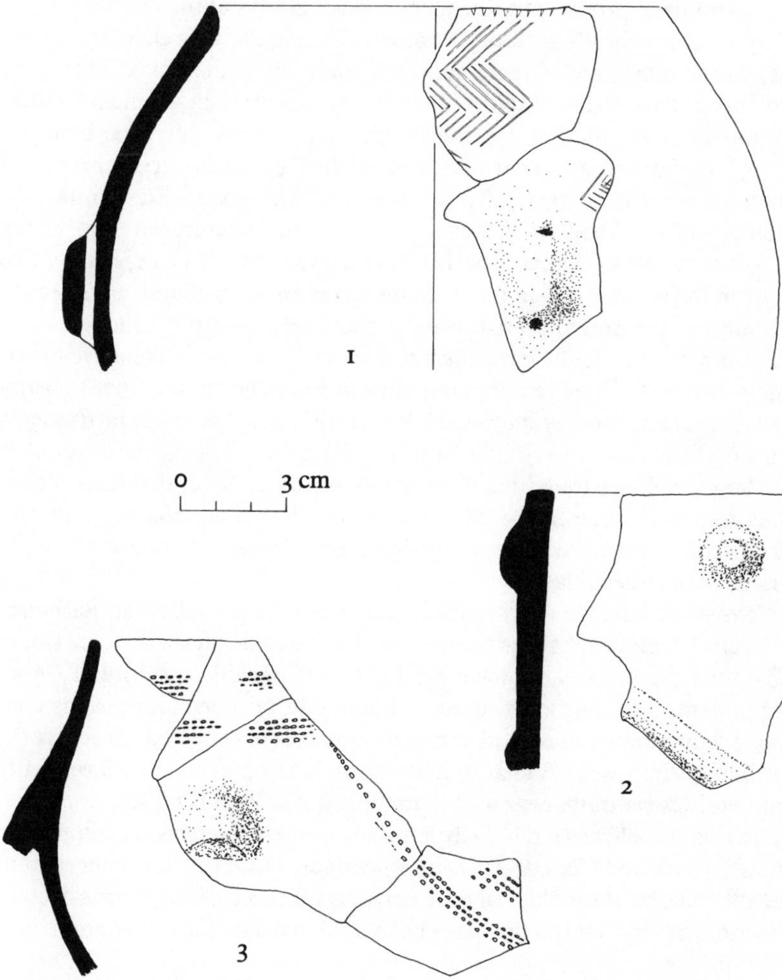

FIGURE 2.6. Villeneuve-Saint-Germain group pottery: 1 Villeneuve-Saint-Germain; 2 Pontpoint; 3 Champigny (comb-decorated). (After Constantin and Demoule, 1982.)

absent. Short, incised lines form herringbone patterns arranged in broad vertical bands (Fig.2.6). Comb-impressed motifs are often broken up into segments in curvilinear patterns centred on the lugs, or form concentric garlands. The decoration tends to cover a larger part of the vessel's surface than in the Late Bandkeramik, but the pivoted comb technique is still used. Notched or incised rims are common.

Lithics. Relatively little is known about the flint assemblages of the Villeneuve-Saint-Germain group, although much information is available from the Belgian Blicquy group excavations. These sites indicate an increased emphasis on flake production. Sickle blades are always of the obliquely truncated type. Arrowheads include asymmetric triangular as well as transverse forms. Stone adzes are absent, although there are some flaked flint axes. Fragments of flat-sectioned schist bracelets, in various stages of manufacture, are found in large numbers on the Belgian settlements. Identical bracelets (Fig.2.5) were distributed over wide areas of the Paris basin during this period (Blanchet and Fitte, 1978, fig.9; Mordant, C., 1980; Constantin and Demoule, 1982). There is evidence for their manufacture on sites in the extreme south-east of the Paris basin (Allain, 1974, 476–7), and possibly also at a site on the River Aisne in the Ardenne *département* (Bailloud, 1974, 405).

Many of the ceramic attributes of the Cerny group (Bailloud, 1971, 221–4; m.r.27) no doubt have their origins in the earlier Villeneuve-Saint-Germain material. Bone temper continues in use (Constantin, 1976). Cerny pottery is characterised by impressed decoration carried out with instruments which vary from combs to circular or triangular points. The combs have either rather large, well-separated teeth, or barely separated teeth that leave a continuous impressed line in the clay. Decoration forms horizontal bands and motifs are often organised around the lugs. The *bouton-au-repoussé* technique occurs in Cerny assemblages.

Pottery. A ditched enclosure in the wide Seine valley at Barbuise-Courtavent (Aude; m.r.23) is the only settlement, apart from the type site in the Essonne *département*, to have produced a reasonable quantity of Cerny pottery (Piette, 1973–4). Decoration commonly includes impressions containing a white incrustation and arranged in panels or broad bands across the upper half of the vessel. A characteristic form is an open bowl with vertically perforated lugs set quite near to the rim (Fig.2.7). The clay discs, or *plats-à-pain*, on this site suggest a relatively late date, as these artefacts are common in the Late Rössen and *Chasséo-Michelsberg* periods. However, it is important to underline that the chronological or regional significance of the various decoration techniques and motifs that have been used to define the Cerny group is at present obscure.

Lithics. The clear distinction between Late Bandkeramik and Cerny flint assemblages, noted by Bailloud (1964, 66), is now rather blurred by the chronologically intervening Villeneuve-Saint-Germain material. Cerny artefacts include flake scrapers, tranchet axes, and transverse arrowheads.

LATE RÖSSEN. The importance of this period has been underestimated in the past because of the minute quantity of material available, almost entirely derived from a single pit at Menneville (Aisne; m.r.15) (Bailloud, 1964, 123–6). Recent excavations at Berry-au-Bac (m.r.14), not far from Menneville, have produced a large quantity of Late Rössen data (FPVA, 1978, 1979–81; Dubouloz *et al.*, 1982).

Pottery. The ceramics from Berry-au-Bac are generally of superior quality to those of the earlier periods. Vessels are well-fired, temper is not usually visible on the surface, and despite considerable variation in vessel size, a fine/coarse ware division is not really applicable. The principal shapes are

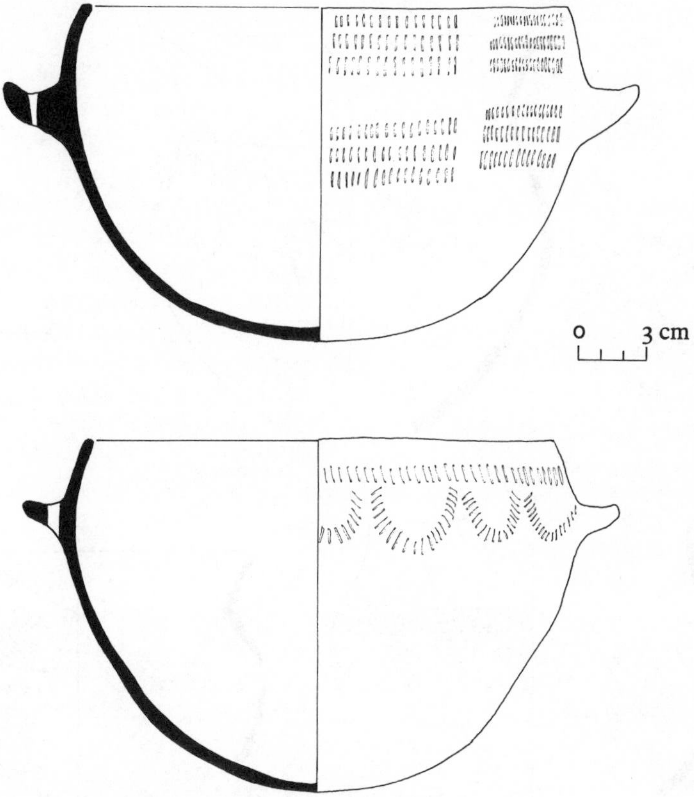

FIGURE 2.7. Cerny pottery from Barbuise-Courtavant.
(After Piette, 1973-74.)

S-profiled (or slightly shouldered) bowls, and wider forms with distinctive everted necks. There are also large storage jars and *plats-à-pain*. Decoration on the first bowl-category consists of horizontal band and hanging triangle motifs, and is largely restricted to the shoulder zone (Fig.2.8). There is no rim decoration. The motifs, composed of either stab-and-drag impressions or incised lines, both filled with white incrustation, are typical of Late Rössen over wide areas of western Europe (Lichardus, 1976, taf.82 and 102). In south-western Germany, this horizon is well-dated to around the middle of the 4th millennium bc (Lüning, 1981, 197–9). The bowls with everted necks are almost always decorated, where the neck joins the body of the pot, with a line of either quadrangular impressions, small *boutons*, or combinations of the two. Single lines of impressions, or stab-and-drag triangles, hang from this horizontal motif. Occasionally the *boutons* are of *repoussé* type, and these also occur on the inside of the everted necks, near the rim.

Lithics. The rich flint industry from Berry-au-Bac has yet to be studied in detail. A variety of retouched flake and blade tools are present; flake tools are

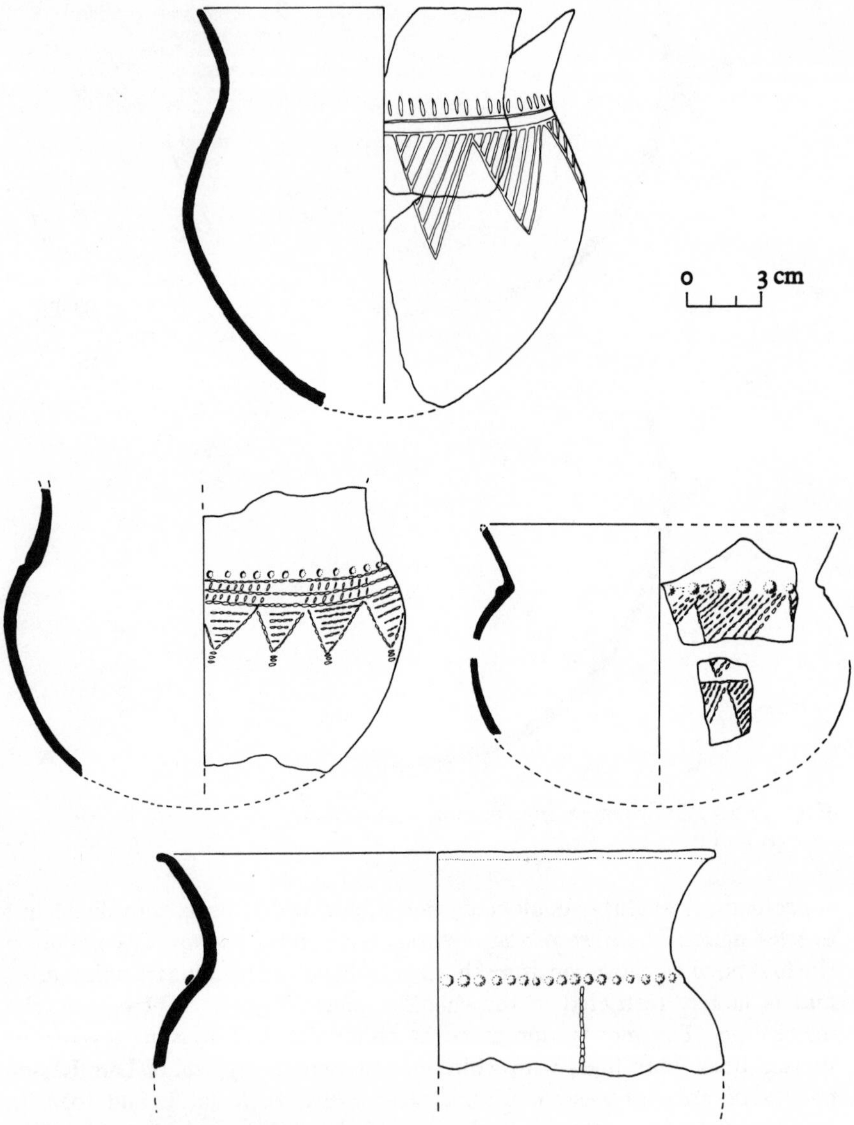

FIGURE 2.8. Decorated pottery from Berry-au-Bac.
(After Dubouloz *et al.*, 1982.)

in the majority. In addition to transverse arrowheads there are triangular types with extensive bifacial retouch (Fig.2.9). Fragments of polished flint and stone axes have also been found. Bone implements include a series of points made from metapodia. A group of small pits within the ditched enclosure yielded a number of perforated antler axes or picks (Fig.2.9). Another pit contained a perforated *Bos* scapula shovel. These tools can perhaps be related

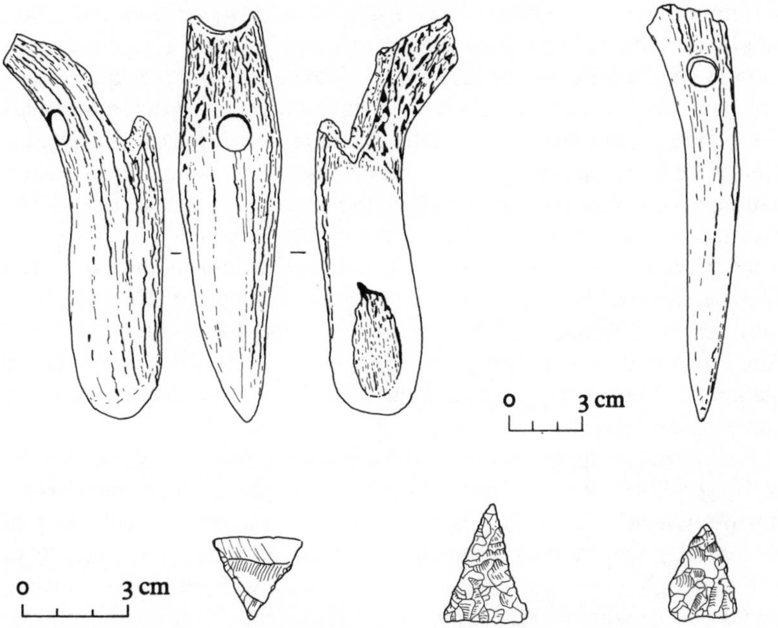

FIGURE 2.9. Antler axes or picks, and flint arrowheads from Berry-au-Bac. (After F.P.V.A., 1978; 1979-80.)

to the digging of the ditch and narrow palisade trench (see below).

Small quantities of comparable ceramics have recently been found at other sites in the Aisne valley, at Cannes-Ecluse (Seine-et-Marne; m.r.28) near the Seine-Yonne confluence (Mordant, D., 1980, fig.2), and, in a Chasséen context, at Joncquières (Oise; m.r.10) (Blanchet and Petit, 1972). Further north, the assemblage from Givry, just over the border in Belgian Hainaut (Michel and Tabary-Picavet, 1979), and possibly also Sailly-Labourse (Pas-de-Calais; m.r.3) (Piningre and Hurtrelle, 1979), belong to this period. Material of similar date has been found at Entzheim in Alsace (Schmitt, 1974, 1975).

BURIAL IN THE EARLIER NEOLITHIC

A fair number of inhumation burials of Late Bandkeramik or Epi-Bandkeramik date have been discovered in the Aisne, Marne, and Yonne valleys. Many are poorly recorded, however, and most of the more recent finds were made in active gravel pits at a stage when much of the evidence had been damaged or destroyed. At present it is unclear to what extent the variation displayed by these burials reflects chronological, regional, or social factors. Very little anthropological work has been carried out.

The shallow graves usually contain a single crouched skeleton. In contrast to Bandkeramik, Grossgartach and Rössen cemeteries elsewhere, the Paris basin graves very rarely include pottery, stone adzes, flint arrowheads and quern fragments as grave goods. The burials, often powdered with red ochre, are usually accompanied by shell ornaments, ranging from round-sectioned bracelets to small perforated beads of varying shape. In some cases the beads seem to have made up quite elaborate ornaments; over one thousand beads were found in a grave at Vert-la-Gravelle (Marne; n.r.19) (Joffroy, 1968, 340). Bracelets were also made of limestone, harder rocks, and bone. In the absence of decorated pottery, it is difficult to date the burials with any accuracy. The suggestion has recently been made, on the basis of typological comparisons with shell grave-goods from cemeteries in Alsace, that some of the Paris basin burials date to an early stage in the Bandkeramik sequence (Gallay, 1981). Two burials, at Frignicourt (Marne; m.r.20) and Léry (Eure; m.r.18), contained fragments of schist bracelets. The latter burial also included a group of bone points (Verron, 1975, 479). Some of the Yonne burials contained very few grave-goods indeed.

'Cemeteries' of up to twelve graves are known from the Yonne valley. Given the conditions under which excavation took place, rather more graves may formerly have existed. At Charmoy (Yonne; m.r.30), a small group of burials was only 30m from a Late or Epi-Bandkeramik longhouse (Joly, 1970, fig.24), although their chronological relationship was uncertain. Isolated burials also occur within settlements. Graves have been found within 10m of buildings at Cys-la-Commune (m.r.12) and Berry-au-Bac in the Aisne valley (Agache, 1968, fig.3; FPVA, 1981), and at Jablines (Seine-et-Marne; m.r.18) (Tarrête, 1981, 310). Three child burials have been discovered within the settlement at Cuiry-lès-Chaudardes. Two occurred in house construction pits; a third, rather older individual, was buried inside a house towards its east end. The Late or Epi-Bandkeramik ditch at Menneville (m.r.13) contained both an adult and a child burial, as well as an isolated skull (FPVA, 1977).

A small number of graves at Marolles (m.r.20) and Noyen (m.r.24) (both Seine-et-Marne) are associated with Cerny pottery and thus date to a late stage of the Epi-Bandkeramik. Two extended burials were placed in large rectangular pits (Mordant, D., 1980, fig. 1). Grave-goods included flint and bone tools.

At present no graves in north-eastern France can be securely dated to the Late Rössen period.

Settlement in the Early Neolithic

The first half of the fourth millennium bc witnesses a change from the mainly valley-based settlement system of the Late Bandkeramik to the occupation of wider parts of the landscape (Whittle, 1977, 183–7). The last section of this chapter examines the evidence for Late and Epi-Bandkeramik settlement distribution across the whole of north-eastern France, before assessing some of the new information about settlement structure and pattern from the Aisne valley.

Settlement at the Macro-Regional Level. At the beginning of this chapter the close relationship between archaeological discoveries and gravel-working in the major river valleys was stressed, a research bias which is important to remember in any analysis of the distribution of early neolithic settlement. As far as the Late Bandkeramik is concerned, however, the absence of sites from both the limestone plateaux of the central Paris basin and the dissected chalk plateaux of much of Picardy, despite extensive loess deposits, does seem to correspond to prehistoric reality. In the Aisne *département*, for example, large numbers of flint scatters are recorded on the plateaux, but none of these have produced diagnostic Bandkeramik artefacts, and the material is generally of much later date (Parent, 1971). One explanation for the Bandkeramik agriculturalists' avoidance of the plateaux probably lies in their dissected topography and lack of surface water, two factors that have been noted as important constraints on Bandkeramik settlement elsewhere (Bakels, 1978a, 128–40; Howell, this volume). The water-table is in fact quite low, and present-day agriculture can be seriously affected by drought. In these areas the most favourable ecological opportunities were offered by the low-lying gravel terrace locations.

The initial expansion of farming settlement onto the plateaux can now be dated as far back as the beginning of the Epi-Bandkeramik. Sites at Champigny and Villejuif (both Val de Marne; m.r.17, 16), which are not located on low gravel terraces, date to the Villeneuve-Saint-Germain horizon (Constantin and Demoule, 1982). While such sites indicate internal expansion into the zones between the major river valleys ('interfluves'), it also seems that the early Epi-Bandkeramik saw considerable external expansion of farming settlement. Late Bandkeramik occupation of the central Paris basin does not appear to have extended to the north or west of the Seine-Oise confluence. Decorated sherds and schist bracelet fragments recently reported from the Vexin plateaux, just to the north of the confluence (Letterle, 1976–7), are of Epi-Bandkeramik date, as are isolated finds of pottery from the Somme valley (Bailloud, 1964, fig.5; Agache, 1968, fig.36). Material from Léry (Verron, 1975, 476–82; m.r.8), a settlement on a terrace of the lower Seine some 60km from the estuary, belongs to the Villeneuve-Saint-Germain group. Pottery from Blangy-sur-Bresle (Seine-Maritime; m.r.7), only 25km from the coast, can also be attributed to this group (Constantin and Demoule, 1982).

Outside the plateaux of the central Paris basin and Picardy, the interpretation is less clear. In the flatter chalk landscape to the east, settlement may well have covered a relatively wide range of landscape from the very beginning. The Late Bandkeramik settlement at Ante (Marne; m.r.20) is located on a loess-covered terrace 25m above a small tributary of the Aisne near the river's source, and thus well away from the main valley (Chenet, 1926). The rich burial at Vert-la-Gravelle (m.r.19), though difficult to date precisely, is over 20km from a major river valley. In the south-east corner of the Marne *département*, the gravel terraces of the River Marne are very extensive. Here, vast areas of flat landscape, probably networked with small streams during the Neolithic, were available for settlement. The site at Larzicourt (m.r.22) is located about 2km from the River Marne, again suggesting that, given good opportunities elsewhere, a major watercourse was not a vital factor in the choice of settlement location.

North and east of the chalk plateaux of Picardy, in the Escaut basin, extremely little neolithic research has taken place. However, the recent discovery of Bandkeramik sites in Belgian Hainaut has dramatically stretched the known extent of colonisation in this region over 100km to the west (Cahen *et al.*, 1979; Constantin *et al.*, 1980). These sites, located on small tributaries of the River Dendre in a classic loess landscape, are not far from the French border and there is a distinct possibility that similar sites await discovery in adjacent areas of north-eastern France. The Lys and upper Escaut drainage basins in the Nord and Pas-de-Calais *départements* contain extensive loess deposits, and by examining topography, soils, and stream networks, it is possible to identify potential Bandkeramik settlement areas (Ilett, 1980). In the north, the loess extends as far as the edge of the marine sedimentation zone in the hinterland of Calais, within 10km of the modern coastline. There would seem to be no significant ecological barriers in the way of Bandkeramik expansion either towards the coast or further south into the Escaut basin. In a region that was peripheral to the main centres of population, settlement density may have been rather low, and this would perhaps explain the present lack of sites. Nevertheless, the example of Belgian Hainaut shows how a concentration of survey and excavation within a small region can radically change our understanding of its prehistoric occupation within the space of a few years, and there is no reason to doubt that the adjacent French loess zones hold similar surprises in store.

On present evidence, the appearance of farming in the Pas-de-Calais *département* dates back to c.3700bc, on the basis of two radiocarbon dates from the Cerny occupation at Etaples (m.r.1), near the Canche estuary (Hurtrelle and Piningre, 1978). Cerny pottery has also been found further north at the Montagne de Lumbres (Prévost, 1962; Piningre, 1980; m.r.2).

Summing up, there are substantial gaps in our knowledge of Bandkeramik and Epi-Bandkeramik settlement in both the eastern Paris basin and in the loess zones of the Nord and Pas-de-Calais *départements*. In the central Paris basin, however, Bandkeramik sites do seem to be restricted to the major river valleys to the south and east of the Seine-Oise confluence. The expansion of settlement, both internally onto the interfluves and externally into Normandy and the lower Seine basin, dates to the beginning of the Epi-Bandkeramik.

SETTLEMENT AT THE MICRO-REGIONAL LEVEL. The research and rescue project in the Aisne valley has provided a relatively complete picture of Late Bandkeramik settlement at a micro-regional level, as well as new information about the type of settlement that was emerging in the Late Rössen period.

At least nine Late Bandkeramik settlements have so far been found in the 80km stretch of the valley that has been intensively investigated over recent years (Boureux and Coudart, 1978; Ilett *et al.*, in press). On average these sites are about 7km apart. Allowing for the parts of the valley that have been

PLATE 2.2. Removal of topsoil by machine, Cuiry-lès-Chaudardes (1979). The post-holes and construction pits of a 19m Bandkeramik longhouse are visible as dark stains on the flood-loam subsoil. The west end of the house is in the foreground. (Photo: Unité de Recherche Archéologique No. 12, C.N.R.S.)

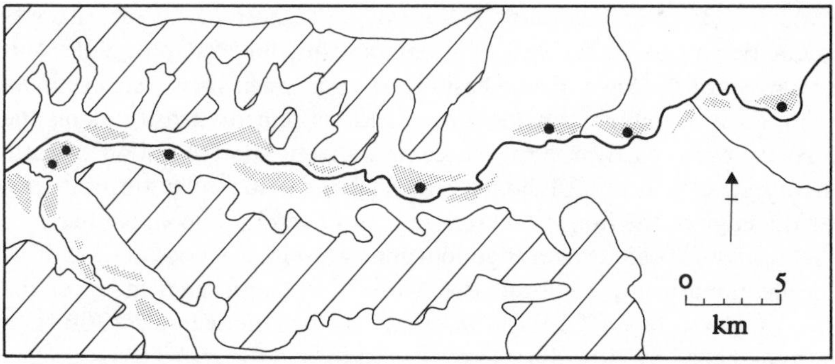

FIGURE 2.10. Distribution of Late Bandkeramik settlements in part of the Aisne valley; from west to east, Chassemy, Vailly, Cys-la-Commune, Cuiry-lès-Chaudardes, Pontavert, Berry-au-Bac, Menneville. Gravel terraces are shaded; oblique lines indicate limestone plateaux. The plateaux are on average about 100m above the valley floor. (After Boureux and Coudart, 1978; Ilett *et al.*, in press.)

PLATE 2.3. Post-holes and construction pits of a Bandkeramik longhouse showing up in wheat at Cuiry-lès-Chaudardes (Aisne), early June 1976. The diameter of the post-holes is about 1m. The same house can be seen under excavation in Plate 2.1. (Photo: Unité de Recherche Archéologique No. 12, C.N.R.S.)

destroyed by gravel extraction with little or no archaeological surveillance, settlement density is rather sparse in comparison, for example, with well-surveyed areas of the lower Rhine basin loess zone. Such areas were occupied throughout the Bandkeramik sequence, and settlement density along the River Aisne must partly reflect the comparatively short duration of Late Bandkeramik occupation. All the settlements in the Aisne valley are located on or near the edge of the first gravel terrace, out of reach of flooding (Fig.2.10 and Plate 2.2). These terrace-edge locations are characterised by bands of Pleistocene flood-loam, a subsoil that would have replicated many of the qualities of loess. In its Tertiary limestone sector, the valley constitutes a flat-bottomed corridor little more than 2km wide, and the gravel terraces form a linear series of discrete units, varying in size from well under 100ha to over 400ha. On present evidence, it seems that only the largest of these units contained more than one settlement. The settlement at Cuiry-lès-Chaudardes, centrally located on one of the better-surveyed terrace units, covers about 6ha. It is certain that we are here dealing with the site of a small village, rather than a dispersed occupation of extensive areas of the terrace edge. Rather different settlement configurations may well have existed, of course, along other rivers of the Paris basin where valley topography was less of a constraint. It is

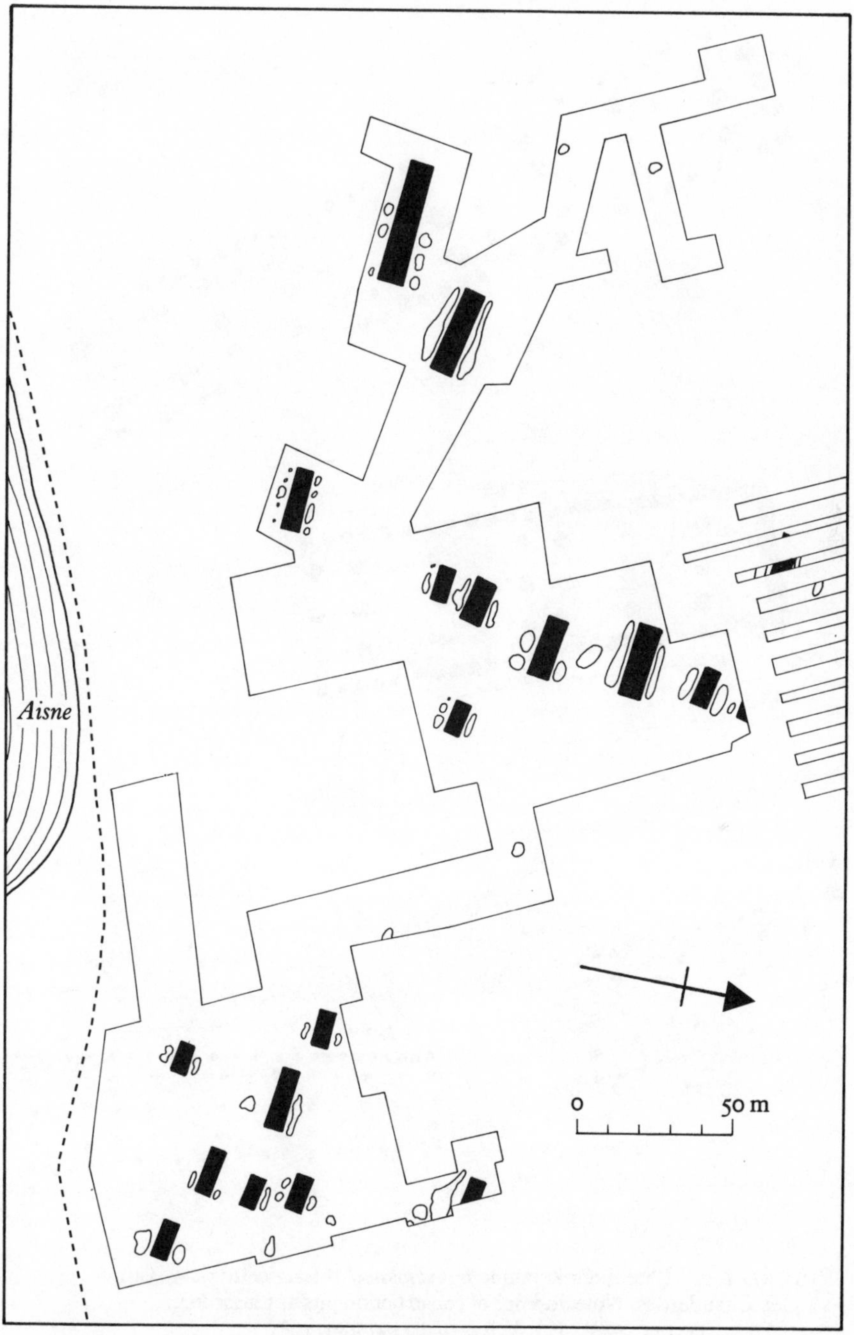

FIGURE 2.11. Schematic plan of Late Bandkeramik houses and pits at Cuiry-lès-Chaudardes (1972-81 excavations). The dotted line represents the edge of the first gravel terrace. (After F.P.V.A., 1981.)

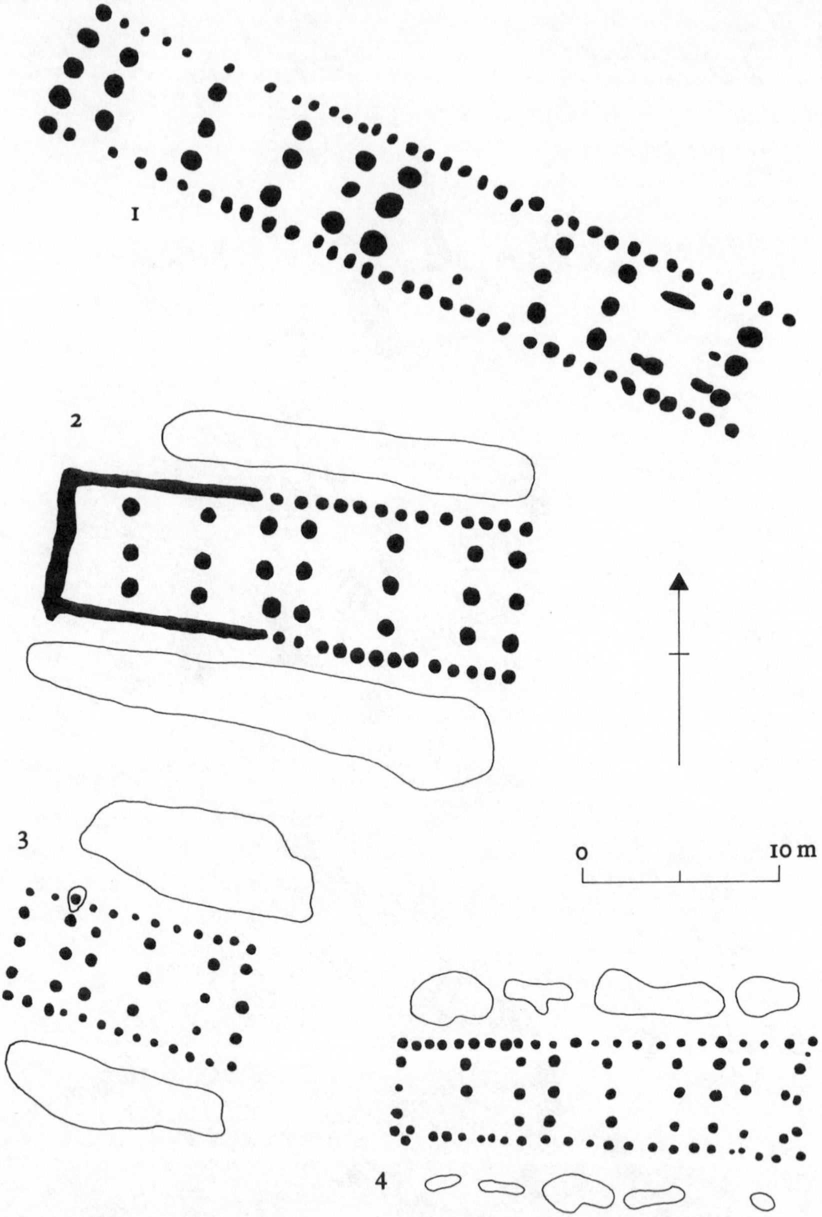

FIGURE 2.12. Late Bandkeramik houseplans: 1 Larzicourt; 2-4 Cuiry-lès-Chaudardes. Note absence of construction pits at Larzicourt. (After Chertier, 1980; F.P.V.A., 1978, 1979-80, 1981.)

reported, for example, that aerial survey at Larzicourt (m.r.22) has revealed buildings and pits over an area of 1×0.3km (Chertier, 1980, 51).

About half of the settlement at Cuiry-lès-Chaudardes has been excavated, and the density of features is quite low (Fig.2.11, Plates 2.1–3). Again, this must reflect the relatively short duration of occupation. Nineteen houses so far uncovered vary in length from 10 to 39m, and many of the groundplans are slightly trapezoidal (Fig.2.12). All the houses are flanked by construction pits, which were often dug right through the layer of flood-loam into the terrace gravel. Anticipating the results of future excavation and the seriation of ceramics associated with the various houseplans, it is likely that the settlement never consisted of more than five or six rather widely spaced buildings. There is also some evidence to suggest that each settlement 'phase' included a substantially larger house at the western edge of the village.

At present little is known about the subsistence economy of these villages; faunal and macrobotanical analyses are still in progress. Emmer, naked barley, hazel nut, and possibly pea have been identified at Menneville (Bakels, 1978b; m.r.15), but soil samples from the construction pits generally produce very few carbonised plant remains. All the datable storage pits at Cuiry-lès-Chaudardes belong to the *Michelsberg* occupation of the site (c.3000bc). The animal bones from the 1972–3 excavations at Cuiry-lès-Chaudardes (Desse, 1976), which represent less than 10 per cent of the bones now available, can be divided into 80.7 per cent domestic species, 13.7 per cent 'large wild' species, and 4.5 per cent 'small wild' species. Cattle bones predominate in the domestic category. Fish bones are also present. A changed emphasis in subsistence economy at the end of the Late Bandkeramik is perhaps indicated by the interrupted ditch enclosure at Menneville (FPVA, 1977, 1978). Covering an area of c.150×300m, this is at present the only enclosure of Late Bandkeramik date in the Aisne valley.

Defence. By c.3400bc, however, it is clear that major changes in settlement structure had taken place within the valley landscape. The enclosed Late Rössen settlement at Berry-au-Bac (m.r.14) provides the main evidence for these changes. Located at the edge of a gravel terrace that was also occupied during the Late Bandkeramik, the enclosure is defined by a ditch and internal palisade (Dubouloz *et al.*, 1982; Fig.2.13). The depth of the palisade trench varies between 0.7m and 1,7m; the ditch is comparatively shallow. The fill of the palisade trench (Plate 2.4) contains traces of posts at roughly 0.3m intervals. The firmly embedded palisade probably served to reinforce the outer side of an earth and gravel bank that has long since disappeared. At least half of the enclosure had been destroyed by a gravel pit before the site was discovered, but the 150m length of ditch and palisade that was excavated contained only one interruption, little more than 1m wide. This narrow 'entrance' reinforces the impression that protection was an important consideration in the design of the enclosure. The vast majority of refuse in the ditch was concentrated on either side of the interruption.

Assuming that the enclosure was roughly circular in shape, its original

PLATE 2.4. Section across Late Rössen palisade trench, showing trace of post, at Berry-au-Bac (Aisne). Scale is 1m. (Photo: Unité de Recherche Archéologique No. 12, C.N.R.S.)

surface area must have been between 2 and 3ha. Within the interior, a row of at least four timber buildings was set 10–15m back from the palisade trench. Orientated east-west, the groundplans are quite different from those of Bandkeramik longhouses. The largest structure, consisting of substantial, deep post-holes and foundation trenches, is about 10m wide and 20m long. The smaller structures are less well preserved, but include two quadrangular buildings. Like the Late Rössen houses from the Goldberg in south-west Germany (Bersu, 1936), the Berry-au-Bac structures were probably two-aisled. The lay-out of the settlement differs radically from that of Bandkeramik sites in the valley, and this must reflect change in social organisation. Large areas to the immediate west of the enclosure have been investigated, but have

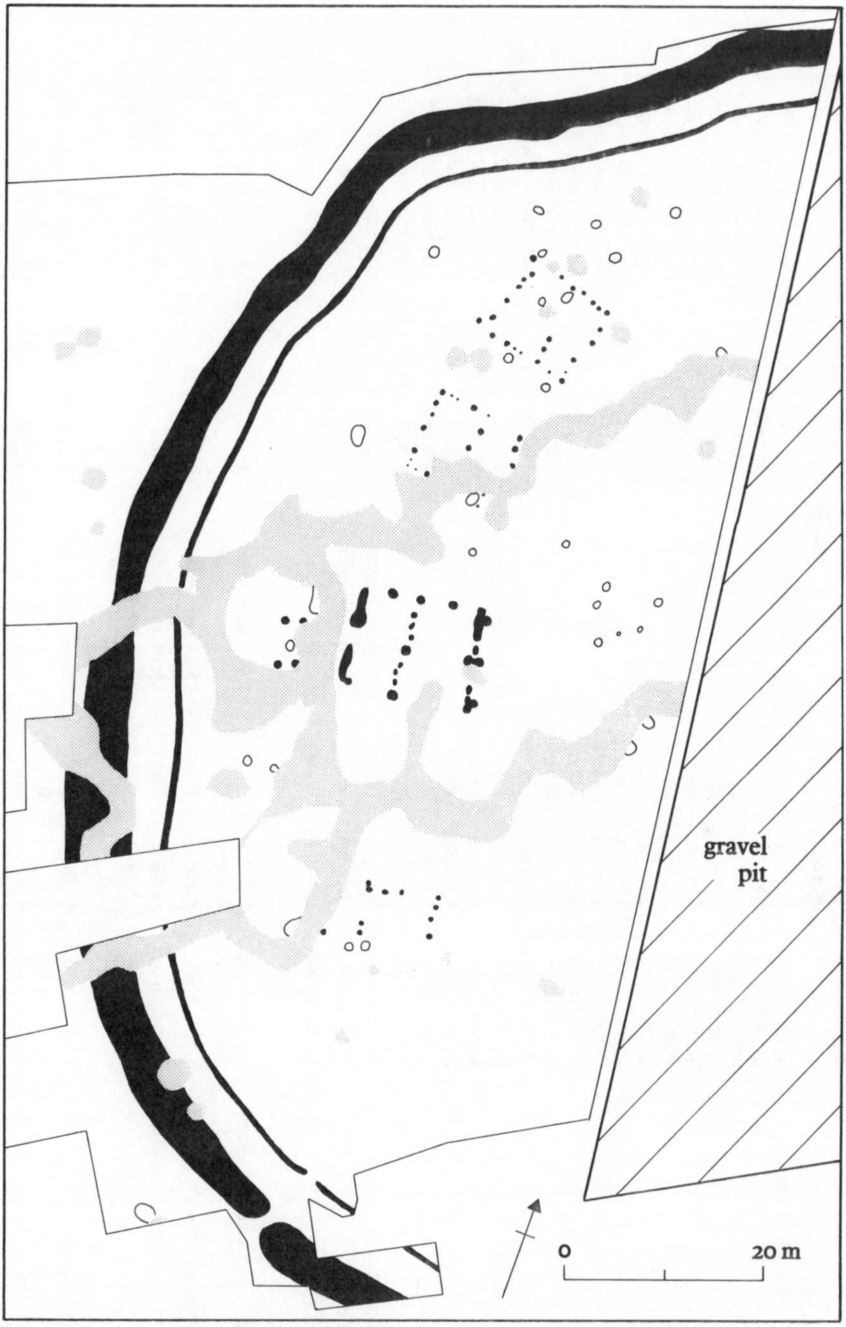

FIGURE 2.13. Late Rössen ditched enclosure, with pits and houseplans, at Berry-au-Bac; shading indicates First World War trenches and shell-holes. (After Dubouloz *et al.*, 1982.)

RADIOCARBON DATES

LATE BANDKERAMIK						
Cuiry-lès-Chaudardes (Aisne)	4500±160bc	Ly-1736	Bone	Open settlement	Pit 230	Delibrias *et al.*, 1982
	4270±230bc	Ly-1737	Bone		Pit 246	Delibrias *et al.*, 1982
	4050±120bc	Ly-2331	Bone		Pit 311	Delibrias *et al.*, 1982
	4030±110bc	Ly-2333	Bone		Pit 357	Delibrias *et al.*, 1982
	4010±170bc	Ly-2321	Bone		Pit 295	Delibrias *et al.*, 1982
	4010±150bc	Ly-2336	Bone		Pit 375	Delibrias *et al.*, 1982
	3980±190bc	Ly-1829	Bone		Pit 175	Delibrias *et al.*, 1982
	3960±130bc	Ly-2330	Bone		Pit 324	Delibrias *et al.*, 1982
	3920±170bc	Ly-2551	Bone		Pit 378	Delibrias *et al.*, 1982
	3890±140bc	Ly-2335	Bone		Pit 378	Delibrias *et al.*, 1982
	3850±170bc	Ly-2332	Bone		Pit 321	Delibrias *et al.*, 1982
	3780±170bc	Ly-2552	Bone		Pit 382	Delibrias *et al.*, 1982
Menneville (Aisne)	4250±190bc	Ly-1735	Bone	Open settlement	Ditch	Delibrias *et al.*, 1982
	4190±210bc	Ly-1734	Bone		Pit 1	Delibrias *et al.*, 1982
	4160±140bc	Ly-2324	Bone		Ditch	Delibrias *et al.*, 1982
	4080±130bc	Ly-2322	Bone		Pit 19	Delibrias *et al.*, 1982
	3910±190bc	Ly-2323	Bone		Pit 39	Delibrias *et al.*, 1982
Berry-au-Bac (Aisne)	4080±130bc	Ly-2327	Bone	Open settlement	Pit 124	Delibrias *et al.*, 1982
Armeau (Yonne)	4265±65bc	GrN-6781	Bone	Open settlement	Pit	Poplin, 1975
Chichery (Yonne)	3650±120bc	Gif-3354	Bone	Grave		Pellet *et al.*, 1978
EPI-BANDKERAMIK						
Villeneuve-Saint-Germain (Aisne)	4180±200bc	Ly-1824	Bone	Open settlement	Pit 70	Delibrias *et al.*, 1982
	4060±220bc	Ly-1825	Bone		Pit 114	Delibrias *et al.*, 1982
Jablines (Seine-et-Marne)	3560±140bc	Gif-5002	Bone	Open settlement	Pit	Tarrête, 1981
Etaples (Pas-de-Calais)	3740±120bc	Gif-4024	Charcoal	Open settlement	Pit	Hurtrelle and Piningre, 1978
	3710±120bc	Gif-3701	Charcoal			Hurtrelle and Piningre, 1978
LATE RÖSSEN						
Berry-au-Bac (Aisne)	3580±320bc	Ly-2326	Bone	Ditched settlement	Largest building	Delibrias *et al.*, 1982
	3390±130bc	Ly-2371	Bone		Pit	Delibrias *et al.*, 1982
	3380±130bc	Ly-2370	Bone		Ditch	Delibrias *et al.*, 1982
	3150±160bc	Ly-2329	Bone		Ditch	Delibrias *et al.*, 1982

produced very few contemporary features. It is clear that the main occupation was concentrated within the enclosure, and it is difficult to avoid the conclusion that this was a defended settlement.

Virtually nothing is known about the economy of the settlement, although a large faunal assemblage from the ditch is under analysis. The Late Rössen settlement pattern in the valley and also on the plateaux edges is at present poorly understood, and, faced with these gaps in the evidence, it is perhaps too early to speculate about the economic and social changes that had evidently taken place within five hundred years of the first appearance of farming settlement. One testable theory is that new patterns of animal exploitation may have emerged by the middle of the fourth millennium bc, as has recently been demonstrated in *Late Lengyel* contexts in lowland Poland (Grygiel and Bogucki, 1981, 26). Whether or not the defences at Berry-au-Bac were of a purely symbolic nature, their existence must in some way reflect demographic pressures and a growing competition for resources.

As far as the investigation of the latter processes is concerned, it would not be unfair to conclude that early neolithic research in north-eastern France has only just begun.

The Middle Neolithic of the Paris Basin and North-Eastern France

MARK BURKILL

The land o Burgundy/Franche-Comté o the Paris Basin o the *Chasséen* o MATERIAL CULTURE o chronology o *Néolithique Moyen Bourguignon* o *Civilisation Saône-Rhone* o settlements o Noyen-sur-Seine o the *éperon barré* type o defence o ECONOMY o fauna o La Vergentière o burials o pottery forms and decoration o *vases-supports* o tools and trade o INTERPRETATION o information exchange and social stress

THIS CHAPTER deals with the period from about 3500 to 2500bc in the large geographical area which lies to the north-east of a line running from Geneva to the mouth of the River Seine. Alsace and Lorraine have been excluded, for topographical and cultural factors distinguished them from the rest of the area at this particular time. Within so large an area the geography is diverse, but there is a basic distinction between the regions of the Paris basin and of Burgundy/Franche-Comté. These two regions broadly correspond to the material culture groups of the Middle Neolithic. We shall deal, first, with Burgundy/Franche-Comté, though sometimes it will be preferable to give priority to the Paris basin.

Burgundy/Franche-Comté. The Burgundy/Franche-Comté region consists of moderately high and broken terrain (Fig.3.1). The eastern part is dominated by the Jura range of mountains and is referred to by the historical name of the Franche-Comté. Most of the Burgundy/Franche-Comté region is above 200m, and the only part that is lower and relatively open is the plain where the rivers Loue, Doubs and Ognon flow into the Saône. However, few earlier neolithic sites have actually been found there. To the west of this plain lies the Morvan massif; to the east, the Jura, parts of which are over 1000m high; to the north lie the Vosges (which are however aligned north-south), and a high plateau. The Burgundy region is therefore surrounded and to a degree isolated by fairly high terrain. To the east, the only entrance is through the Belfort Gap, which lies between the Vosges and the Jura, and has featured prominently in French history. The gap is only c.20km wide and is itself quite high (over 300m).

The river formations of the Burgundy/Franche-Comté region do not bear much resemblance to those of the Paris basin, as described in the preceding

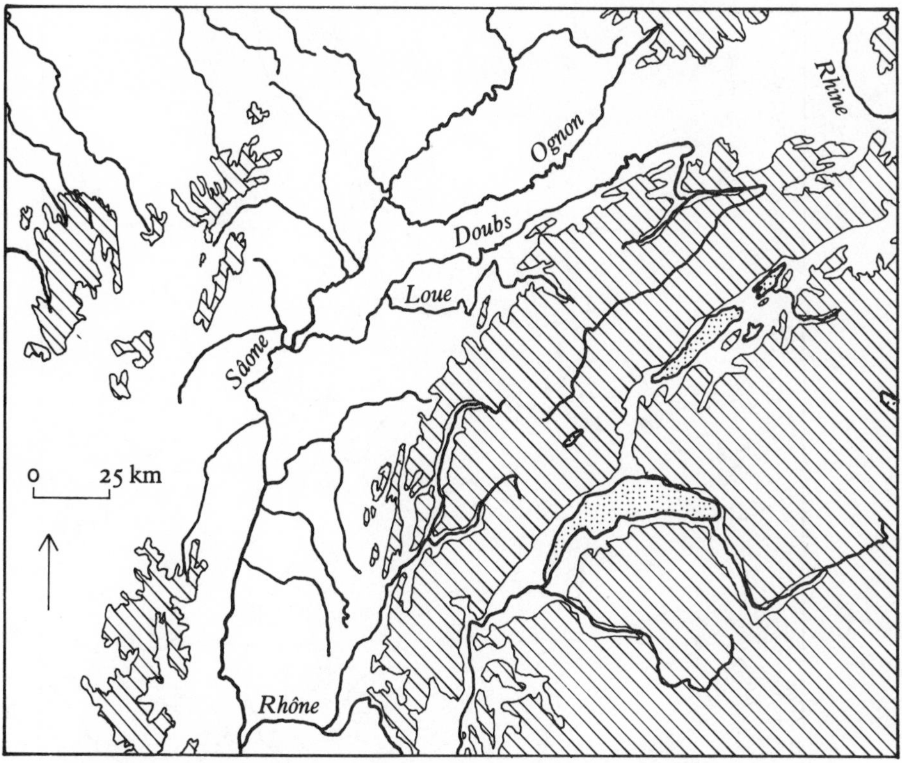

FIGURE 3.1. Map showing the principal physical features of the Burgundy/ Franche-Comté region. Land over 500m is shaded.

chapter, being more deeply incised, with some gorges (e.g. on the River Doubs between Besançon and Montbéliard). The northern parts of the Jura range which lie in the Doubs *département* consist mainly of plateaux, in contrast with the more broken nature of these mountains in Switzerland and to the south.

The nature of the Burgundy / Franche-Comté terrain means that a greater variety of settlement types may be found there, than in the Paris basin. In the Belfort Gap and along the north-western slopes and escarpments of the Jura mountains there are caves. In the mountains many small lakes offer possibilities for a type of settlement which is absent from most parts of France.

The Paris Basin. The geography of the Paris basin has been described in the previous chapter and little further comment is needed. It is essentially a low-lying area of plateaux and gravel terraces, cut through by a series of major rivers.

HISTORY OF RESEARCH. Any history of research on the Middle Neolithic of north-eastern France (Fig.3.2) must concern itself with the development of the concept of the Chasséen, and in particular with the site of

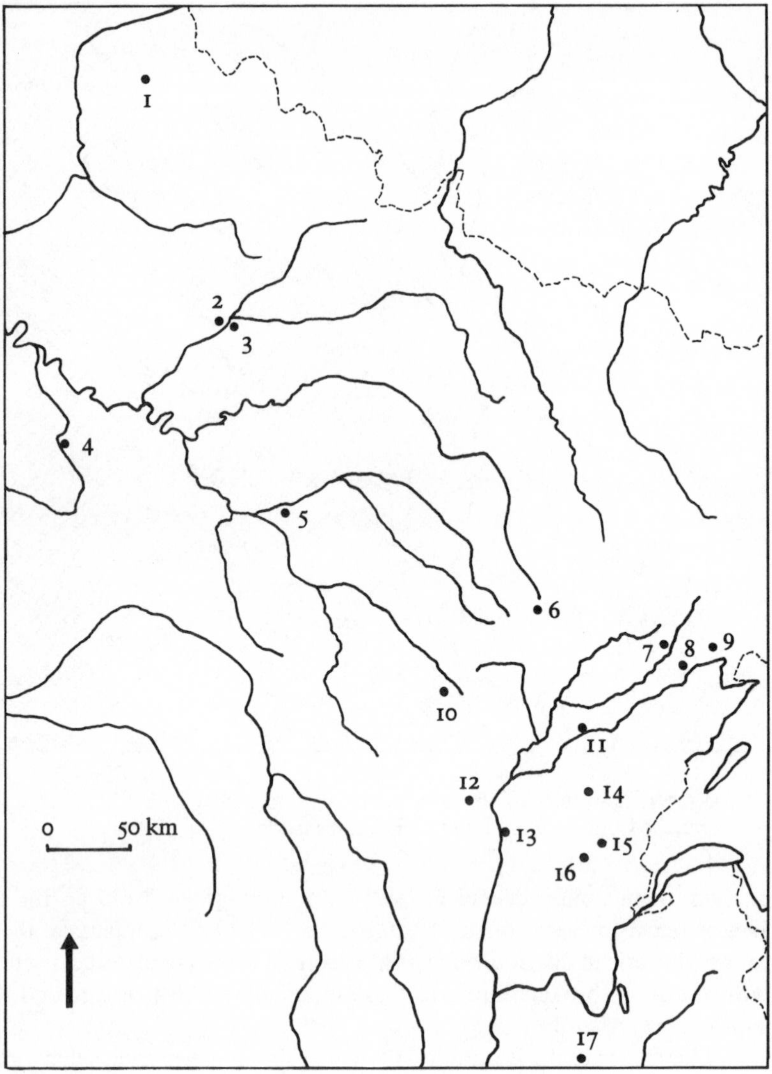

FIGURE 3.2. Map of north-eastern France, showing the location of some of the principal sites mentioned in the text.
1 Lumbres (Pas-de-Calais); 2 Jonquières (Oise); 3 Compiègne (Oise); 4 Fort Harrouard (Eure-et-Loir); 5 Noyen-sur-Seine (Seine-et-Marne); 6 La Vergentière, Cohons (Haute-Marne); 7 Aillevans (Haute-Saône); 8 Gondenans (Doubs); 9 Gonvillars (Haute-Saône); 10 Camp Myard, Vitteaux (Côte-d'Or); 11 Lavans-lès-Dole (Jura); 12 Chassey-le-Camp (Côte-d'Or); 13 Ouroux-sur-Saône (Saône-et-Loire); 14 Les Planches-près-Arbois (Jura); 15 Clairvaux-les-Lacs (Jura); 16 Gigny-sur-Suran (Jura); 17 Charavines (Isère).

Chassey-le-Camp (Côte-d'Or; m.r.12) itself. The Middle Neolithic of this whole region is essentially, yet not exclusively, the Chasséen. The importance of the site of Chassey may be gauged from the fact that it has been subject to numerous excavations from the mid-19th century onwards (Thommasset, 1927; Thévenot, 1969). The neolithic occupation was recognised here long before the Bandkeramik was discovered in the Paris basin. The importance of Chassey was noted by Déchelette in 1908; and in the 1930s by Childe and Hawkes in their attempts to understand the 'Western Neolithic' (Childe, 1931; Hawkes, 1934). The concept of a Chasséen culture, however, was first given precision by Arnal as recently as 1950. He identified an undecorated *Chasséen B*, which was later than a decorated *Chasséen A*. While the terms A and B have since dropped out of favour, because no stratigraphical excavations have shown such a division, it will be seen later that Chasséen pottery may indeed have had a tendency to become less decorated as time progressed.

Like Chassey, the lake-side site of Clairvaux-les-Lacs (Jura; m.r.15), and others similar, have been known since the 19th century, though these settlements have naturally tended to be considered alongside the lake-side sites of Switzerland.

For Burgundy and Franche-Comté, Gallay (1977, 29–35) offers a useful history of research within the region, as a background to his work on the Middle Neolithic. This work is fundamental to an understanding of the period, though (since it was originally presented in 1970) several important new features have come to light. Most notable is the reversal of the old typological succession of *Cortaillod ancien* and *Cortaillod récent*, by stratigraphical excavations. Another feature of the past decade has been the definition of a group called the *Néolithique Moyen Bourguignon* (NMB). As the name implies, this is a group which fits into the general Chassey-Cortaillod culture zone of the Middle Neolithic period, but it has certain regional features which enable it to be picked out as a Burgundian facies.

The developments in the Burgundy/Franche-Comté region are now much better understood thanks to excavations conducted by P. Petrequin at Gonvillars (Haute-Saône; m.r.9), Gondenans (Doubs; m.r.8), Lavans-lès-Dole (Jura; m.r.11), Clairvaux (Jura) and Les Planches-près-Arbois (Jura; m.r.14) (Petrequin, 1970a, 1970b, 1972). Further west, in Burgundy proper, recent excavations by J.P. Thévenot at the site of Chassey-le-Camp itself should provide well-documented stratigraphical sequences. He has conducted another important excavation, at the late neolithic site of Ouroux-sur-Saône (Saône-et-Loire; m.r.13) (Thévenot, 1973). Knowledge of the late neolithic period has also been greatly advanced by the excavations conducted by Bocquet at the site of Charavines (Isère) (Bocquet, 1974). Developments in the study of the late neolithic period in the Burgundy/Franche-Comté region are broadly reviewed in a symposium on the Saône-Rhône culture (Strahm and Thévenot, 1976). The Corded Ware and Beaker material of the region has been discussed by the Petrequins (1978).

The Chasséen of the Paris basin was defined by Bailloud in 1964; he has also studied this group within its wider context (Bailloud, 1974). The material available for study has been augmented by excavations at Noyen-sur-Seine (Seine-et-Marne; m.r.5) (Mordant and Mordant, 1972); Jonquières (Oise; m.r.2) (Blanchet and Petit, 1972); and Compiègne (Oise; m.r.3) (Toupet, 1980). In addition, the excavations carried out by the URA 12 team in the Aisne valley have given the Middle Neolithic of the Paris basin better definition, and clarified its relations with material to the east.

Material Culture

A brief comment on the types of evidence available and of their reliability is a necessary preliminary to an understanding of the chronological sequence. There are differences between the quality and quantity of the material found in the Paris basin and in the Burgundy/Franche-Comté region. Burials, for example, are rarely found in the Chasséen of the Paris basin (in contrast to the preceding and succeeding periods in that region), whereas in the Burgundy/Franche-Comté area they are more common. These latter are mostly megalithic in type, and were excavated many years ago, so the quality of their evidence is much reduced. Pottery *decoration* is virtually non-existent except on rare objects such as *vases-supports* and cannot therefore be used either as a chronological or a regional indicator. Pottery *shape*, however, is very variable and is therefore more suitable as a means for examining possible regional variability within north-eastern France at this time.

Excavated settlements provide the most important chronological information. This is especially the case in the Burgundy/Franche-Comté region, where caves and lake-side settlements provide sound stratigraphies, supported by radiocarbon dates. Many of these excavations, as well as several of those of camps in the Paris basin, have been conducted very recently, so the quality of their evidence is excellent. That of the distributional evidence is more difficult to assess. Present patterns of settlement distribution may to quite a large degree reflect recent archaeological activity rather than prehistoric reality. Many of these settlements have furnished sizeable faunal assemblages, but the detailed analyses of most of these have not yet been published. In a similar way the work on general environmental evidence is only just beginning, although the scope for this is immense, especially in the lake-side settlements. There are good assemblages of bone, antler and stone which show the tools used, but little systematic work has been done on them.

Chronology

Burgundy/Franche-Comté. During the period 3000–2400bc this region is broadly united by the Néolithique Moyen Bourguignon (NMB). This dating is supported, for example, by the series of dates from Camp Myard at Vitteaux (Côte-d'Or; m.r.10). Earlier dates of c.3300bc obtained from a NMB assemblage at the camp of La Vergentière at Cohons (Haute-Marne; m.r.6), are less useful owing to their large standard deviation. The period of the NMB is broadly comparable with that of the Chasséen of the Paris basin (see below), and the NMB can indeed be broadly characterised as a regional facies of the Chasséen.

The period preceding the NMB is, however, not so easily definable. The northern Jura follows a similar pattern to that of the Paris basin, as illustrated by the stratigraphical and radiocarbon sequences from the caves of Gonvillars and Gondenans. Here Bandkeramik-type material is known from as early as the late 5th millennium bc, yet by 3100bc (level X at Gonvillars) the first (non-decorated) pottery of NMB type has appeared alongside material marking the end of the *Rössen-Wauwil* style. In the southern Jura, sites such as Clairvaux and Les Planches-près-Arbois have middle neolithic occupations dating from the period preceding the NMB. Radiocarbon dates from the series of lake-side settlements at Clairvaux show this site to have been occupied from the early 4th millennium bc (the earliest date is 3940bc). Similarly, the cave site of Les Planches-près-Arbois was occupied in the middle of the 4th millennium bc. Its material has been termed *proto-Cortaillod* (see Barbier *et al.*, 1981) from its affinities with the Swiss material. By 3000bc however, NMB assemblages had appeared in the southern Jura (e.g. level V at La Motte-aux-Magnins, Clairvaux (Petrequin and Petrequin, 1980)).

In Burgundy the material of the 4th millennium bc is different yet again. Stratigraphical excavations at Chassey-le-Camp by Thévenot (1978) have shown that the NMB assemblage at this site is preceded by several levels which can be characterised as Chasséen, with affinities which are particularly southern in type. The earliest radiocarbon determinations for this material lie in the range c.3750–3250bc. Burgundy, therefore, like the northern and southern parts of the Jura, developed along independent lines during the period preceding the appearance of the NMB at about 3000bc.

The NMB can be traced down to c.2400bc. At this point in the Burgundy/Franche-Comté region the Late Neolithic begins, characterised by a material culture grouping termed the *Civilisation Saône-Rhône* (CSR). The concept of the CSR has emerged through the linking of material from lake-side settlements in the Jura with that from sites along the valley of the River Saône. A series of radiocarbon dates from various sites shows that the CSR seems to cover the period c.2400–1800bc. It is therefore contemporary with the SOM of the Paris basin. It has been suggested that many of the camps in the northern Franche-Comté are to be attributed to the CSR, but this remains uncertain, as they could be either of middle or late neolithic date. Corded Ware and, more frequently, Beaker material is sometimes found in association with later CSR assemblages.

The Paris Basin. The Middle Neolithic of the Paris basin is defined relatively easily by the distinctive character of the Bandkeramik-type material which precedes it, and of the *Seine-Oisne-Marne* (SOM) material which succeeds it. Radiocarbon dates define the period as c.3200–2700bc. This is confirmed by a date from Jonquières (3170bc), and by many SOM dates (see list at the end of Chapter 4). Dates from Montagne-de-Lumbres (Pas-de-Calais; m.r.1) (2620bc, 2420bc) and Fort Harrouard (Eure-et-Loir; m.r.4) (2450bc) indicate that there may have been some chronological overlap between the two types of material, though the discrepancies are no more than can be accounted for by the standard deviations.

The radiocarbon evidence does not allow the Middle Neolithic in the Paris basin to be subdivided, but tentative attempts to do this have been made on the basis of ditch stratigraphies and traditional typological methods (see Blanchet *et al.*, 1982). Thus the earlier Chasséen contains decorated sherds of late Rössen type (e.g. at Jonquières) and possesses decorated vases-supports. The later phase is marked by the progressive disappearance of carination, and of decoration on vases-supports. General comments by Louwe-Kooijmans (1980) tend to support this but the validity of such a division within the Paris basin remains to be tested.

Because of the chronological problems, the survey of the material culture evidence which follows will concentrate on the Chasséen of the Paris basin and its closely related contemporary, the NMB. However, where possible, the period c.400 (radiocarbon) years either side of the NMB in the Burgundy/Franche-Comté region will also be covered.

Settlement Types and Locations

The Paris Basin. Chasséen sites in the Paris basin occupy two basic types of location. Some are positioned in the bottoms and on the slopes of river valleys, such as Noyen-sur-Seine and L'Etoile (Plate 3.1). These reflect the long-established Bandkeramik type of location. Other sites, such as Fort Harrouard and Jonquières, are characteristically found on the edge of plateaux overlooking the river valleys. This also had been a preferred location type in the previous period, but had not such a long history as the valley-bottom location. There is no evidence that the central parts of the plateau-interfluves were occupied by settlements at this time (Fig.4.6), although it remains a possibility that this absence only reflects the concentration of archaeologists' activity along the river valleys.

A typical and important site for the Chasséen of the Paris basin is NOYEN-SUR-SEINE (see Mordant and Mordant, 1972, 1977). Figure 3.3 shows details of its location and features. Although the detailed depositional history of the site is not entirely clear, it seems likely that it was subject to frequent flooding by the River Seine. The most obvious conclusion to be drawn is that by this time defence was an important factor in a site's specific location. This is confirmed by the presence of a series of palisades which bar the meander in the river. It is interesting to note that this type of defensive system is entirely analogous to that at Jonquières, in which a ditch bars a high spur of land (the *éperon barré* type of location). At Noyen-sur-Seine a semi-circular enclosure with a ditch and palisade was later constructed within the area of the initial site. These two constructions need not have been widely separated in time, however, since both inside and outside the inner enclosure there are features remarkably similar in plan which appear to be huts. The Mordants' detailed analysis of an area excavation of the site showed the settlement to have had a certain degree of organisation. There were rubbish dumps, roughly paved

PLATE 3.1. Aerial view of the middle neolithic camp of L'Etoile (Somme). The ditch shows as a soil mark on this photograph taken early in the morning towards the end of winter. A slighter trace within the ditch marks the line of the palisade. Recent excavations at this site have recovered middle neolithic material. (Photo: Roger Agache, Direction des Antiquités Préhistoriques de Picardie.)

areas and spots where specific activities had been carried out (Mordant and Mordant, 1977). A site with interrupted ditch and palisade, similar to Noyen-sur-Seine, has recently been discovered at Charmoy (Yonne) (Plate 3.2).

Burgundy/Franche-Comté. The Chasséen and NMB sites of Burgundy and the Franche-Comté, unlike Noyen-sur-Seine, are not located in valley-bottoms. This probably reflects the different geography of this region, though the plain of the River Saône in the Châlon-Dijon-Dôle area might have been expected to provide some examples of sites in such a location. The number of sites in Burgundy and the Franche-Comté which are in high positions, analogous to sites in the Paris basin such as Fort Harrouard and Jonquières, is however very large. These camps vary in morphology (see Passard, 1980, for examples) but most are basically variations on the *éperon barré* type referred to above. They seem to be characteristic in this region of the entire Neolithic and not simply of the NMB. Chassey-le-Camp itself is a good example. Most of the camps have been very inadequately excavated if at all, or have been heavily disturbed by bronze age occupations, but recently excavations at sites such as Lavans-lès-Dôle (Jura; m.r.11), Roche d'Or near Besançon (Doubs), La Vergentière (Haute-Marne), and extensive excavations at Camp Myard, where occupation covers the entire NMB, have shown some of the details of this type of site. Camp Myard is a typical *éperon barré*, and for defence relied mainly on

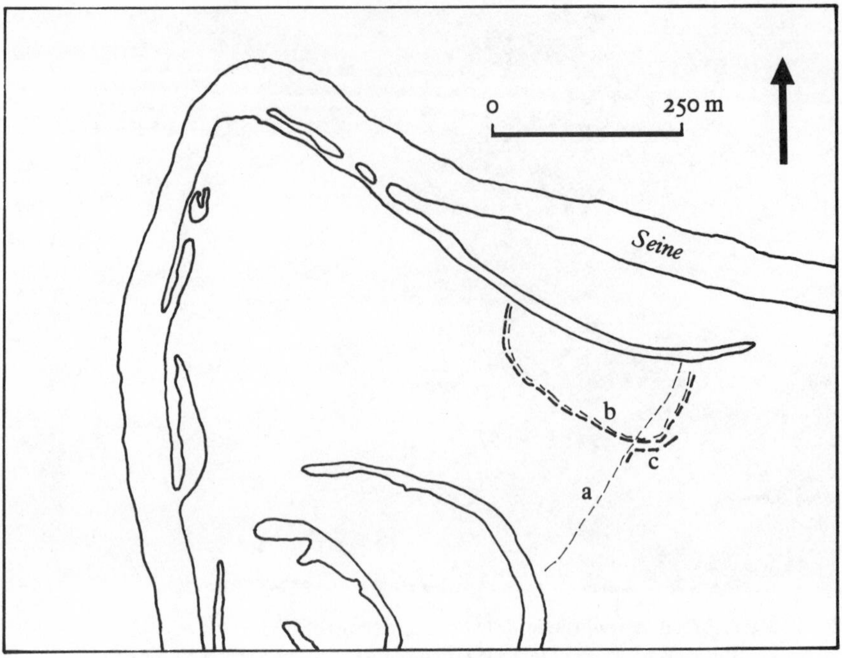

FIGURE 3.3. Map showing the location of the camp at Noyen-sur-Seine. (a) series of palisades barring old river meanders; (b) interrupted ditch and palisade system, stratigraphically later than a; (c) interrupted ditch, apparently associated with both a and b. (After Mordant and Mordant, 1978.)

a rampart made of stone blocks, rather than a ditch. The settlement itself appears to have consisted of huts aligned along the inside of the rampart, although no actual house-plans have been recovered. According to the excavator, Nicolardot (1974), there is even the possibility that these huts were elevated above a working area. If so, this would provide an interesting parallel with the constructional techniques of lake-side settlements.

The presence of occupation deposits at lake-side and cave sites in Burgundy and the Franche-Comté demonstrates a greater repertoire of middle neolithic settlement locations in this region than in the Paris basin. Some caves were used as temporary settlements throughout the 4th and 3rd millennia bc (e.g. Gondenans and Gonvillars), and the possibility of more permanent occupation is raised by the cave at Les Planches-près-Arbois (m.r. 14), dated to the middle of the 4th millennium bc. The excavations at this site show that the organisation of settlement within the cave may have included enclosures for animals, and Petrequin (in Barbier *et al.*, 1981) believes that huts may have been elevated above the floor to provide protection from a stream which ran through the cave. The site of Baume-sous-la-Roche at Gigny-sur-Suran (Jura; m.r. 16) (Barbier *et al.*, 1981) shows that such permanent settlement in caves may have continued later in the Middle Neolithic.

PLATE 3.2. Charmoy (Yonne): aerial view of the site showing the interrupted ditch and palisade. This site is similar in type to the recently excavated settlement of Noyen-sur-Seine. (Photo: Claude Pellet.)

The same concern with defence that is found in the camps can also be seen in the lake-side settlements. This has been most fully documented in the case of Clairvaux (Boisaubert *et al.*, 1974; Passard, 1980). Here there is a whole series of settlements along one sector of the lake-shore with a sequence of occupation spanning most of the 4th and 3rd millennia bc (Fig.3.4). The position of the settlements varied according to the water level in the lake. In some cases they were sited on small islands (e.g. Station 2bis), in others on peninsulas (e.g. Station 2). Once again defence seems to have been an important factor in location. In the case of Station 2 a palisade bars the peninsula upon which the settlement stands. House plans have been discerned for each of the settlements. These are generally rectangular: e.g. approximately 4–5m by 6–8m in the case of Station 2bis. In Station 2 the houses are positioned along the inside of the palisade in a manner similar to those at Camp Myard at Vitteaux. In Station 3 the houses appear to have been organised in rows in a manner somewhat akin to terraced housing.

The settlement types of the Late Neolithic in the Burgundy/Franche-Comté region may be illustrated by two sites. Ouroux-sur-Saône is situated on the bank of the river, in an area where no middle neolithic sites in valley-bottom locations have yet been found. The second type of site is the lake-side settlement, a form of habitation found in earlier periods. Charavines (m.r.17) is an important example. Here the village consisted of rectangular houses

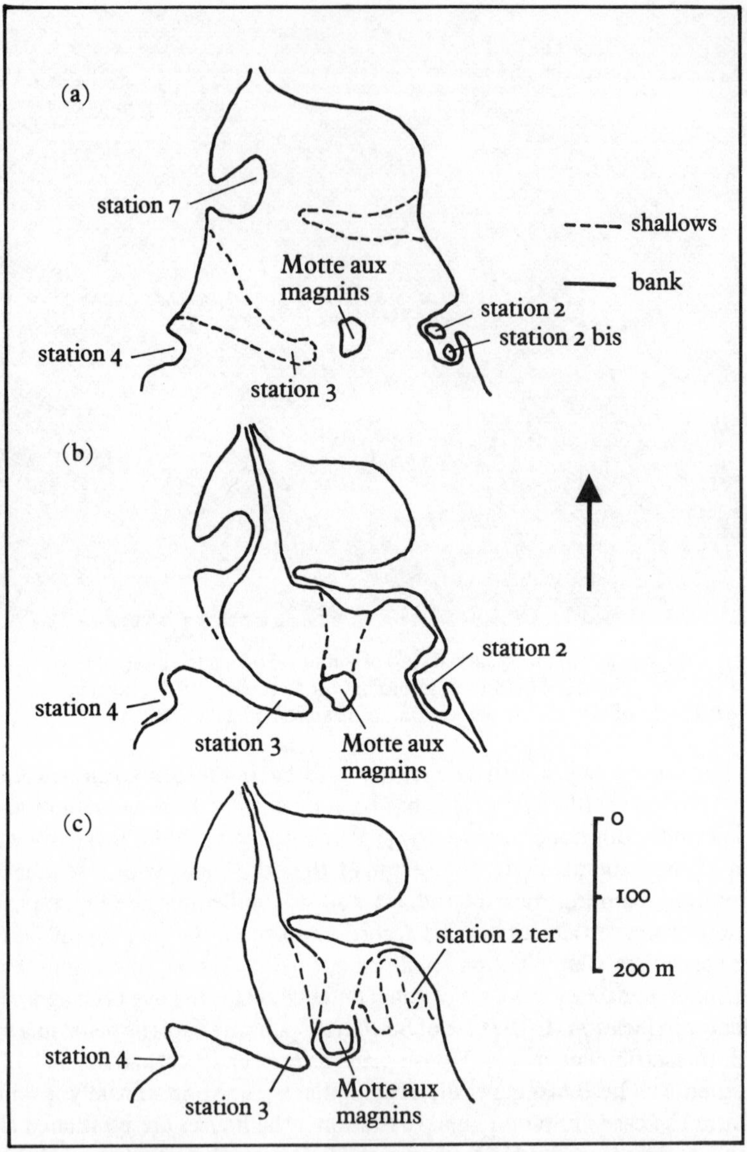

FIGURE 3.4. Clairvaux-les-Lacs. Development of the lake and location of settlements during (a) Middle Neolithic, (b) Late Neolithic, and (c) Late Neolithic/Early Bronze Age. (After Passard, 1980.)

organised in rows with small alleys between them. Like the earlier lake-side sites, Charavines also had a palisade on the landward side of the village, though Bocquet (1974) regards this as having served a non-defensive purpose.

Economy

It is not possible to describe in detail the economy of north-eastern France during the Middle Neolithic, because of the paucity of published information. Fortunately, this situation should soon be remedied since several recently-excavated sites have produced a considerable quantity of material. At present, however, there is a shortage of published faunal analyses. Many of those sites where faunal remains have been analysed yielded fewer than 100 species-determinable fragments, and cannot therefore be regarded as very reliable sources of economic information.

Faunal Remains. In the Paris basin, pits at Liévin (Pas-de-Calais) and Balloy (Seine-et-Marne) show a high percentage of domestic animals, with cattle and pig most important (Tuffreau, 1974; Mordant, 1967). In the larger assemblage from the site of Lumbres there were 838 species-determinable fragments, cattle accounting for 35 per cent, sheep/goat for 21 per cent, pig for 10 per cent, and deer for 14 per cent (domesticates 66 per cent) (Prévost, 1962). These percentages are calculated on the basis of the minimum number of animals of each species represented by the identified bones or fragments. The complete homogeneity of the sample may be doubtful because of the complex stratigraphy of the site, but it presents an interesting contrast with the earlier, Bandkeramik type of assemblage in which cattle overwhelmingly predominate and the proportion of wild animals is much smaller (e.g. Poplin, 1975).

Another site with a large faunal assemblage is Compiègne, and some preliminary notes on this have already been published (Toupet, 1980). In a sample of 355 species-determinable fragments, cattle comprised 68 per cent, pig 21 per cent and sheep/goat 9 per cent of the remains. Deer contributed only 1 per cent but no distinction was made between *Bos taurus* and *Bos primigenius* so the actual percentage of domesticated animals is unclear.

Within the Burgundy/Franche-Comté region the amount of information is even less. The camp at Marcilly-sur-Tille (Côte-d'Or; Planson, 1979) shows a similar proportion of domestic animals (67 per cent) to that at Lumbres, and the same relative importance of cattle over sheep/goat and pig is encountered. At Gonvillars, level Xb has 71 per cent of faunal remains belonging to domesticates, but among these over half belongs to pig. This site has to be treated with caution as far as its economic evidence is concerned, since the nature of the occupation within the cave appears to have been temporary and therefore can probably give only a partial picture of the economy of its inhabitants (Petrequin, 1970a).

Although the Burgundy/Franche-Comté region in general lacks good faunal evidence it is there that the site is to be found which has the best published information for the Neolithic of the whole of north-eastern France. This is the camp of La Vergentière at Cohons (Lepage *et al.*, 1980). A summary of the faunal information is given in Table 3.1. A total of over 1700 fragments from the middle neolithic layer were determinable as to species.

According to the number of individuals represented within the assemblage, 74 per cent were domesticates. This is in conformity with the material mentioned above from other middle neolithic sites, and 26 per cent represents a considerable increase in the proportion of wild animals over the Bandkeramik Early Neolithic. Perhaps the most surprising feature of the La Vergentière assemblage, however, is that pig represents the largest proportion of the faunal material, just ahead of cattle. This may indicate that diet varied quite widely from site to site during this period. Most of the deer remains were antlers, suggesting that it was specifically for this material that the animal was hunted.

Table 3.1. Middle neolithic faunal information from the Camp of La Vergentière at Cohons (Haute-Marne). (From Lepage *et al.*, 1980)

	No. individuals	% individuals
Pig	40	29.0
Cattle	38	27.5
Sheep	21	15.2
Goat	2	1.4
Dog	1	0.7
Total domesticates	102	73.8
Aurochs	10	7.2
Red deer	7	5.1
Boar	7	5.1
Roe deer	2	1.4
Horse	2	1.4
Beaver	2	1.4
Bird	2	1.4
Bison	1	0.7
Wolf	1	0.7
Fox	1	0.7
Hare	1	0.7
Total wild	36	25.8

The faunal evidence for north-eastern France during this period may be tentatively summarised as demonstrating a greater variety of diet as compared with the earlier Bandkeramik's heavy dependence on domesticates, and cattle in particular.

Many middle neolithic sites certainly demonstrate concern for protection. Yet they occupy such a variety of locations that it is reasonable to assume that choice of site reflects more than just a concern with defensive properties. It seems likely that this variety also relates to a greater variety in economic practices. The settlement system, which in the Bandkeramik period had had such a strong emphasis on valley-bottom locations, was transformed in the Chasséen period to allow a greater variety in the choice of settlement locations. The possible significance of this will be discussed later. The same is not however true of the Burgundy/Franche-Comté region where a wide variety of site locations is found already prior to the Néolithique Moyen Bourguignon.

Pollen evidence is confined to a diagram made from samples taken from Les Roches at Videlles (Essonne) (see Roux, 1967). Here layer E is dated to 2790bc and has a relatively high proportion of arboreal pollen (64 per cent). It appears that at this time clearances within the forests were neither widespread nor permanent since the percentage of arboreal pollen increases in the succeeding sterile layer and only falls markedly during the later SOM period. One problem with this site is that layer E produced Cerny type pottery which typologically therefore ought to belong to the period preceding the Chasséen, contrary to the evidence of the radiocarbon date (Bailloud and Coiffard, 1967).

The middle neolithic economic evidence may be summarised as indicating a greater variety of economic practices than in the Bandkeramik. The main evidence for this comes from the locations of the sites and the faunal assemblages. More detailed information is however required if this hypothesis is to be confirmed.

Burial Evidence. Chasséen burials are generally rare, and recent excavations in the Paris basin have begun to show that this may not be due to a lack of activity on the part of archaeologists. At Noyen-sur-Seine several complete inhumations were found in pits and ditches (Mordant and Mordant, 1978) but these are the exception rather than the rule. It is far more usual to discover merely portions of the human skeleton in articulation, as at Noyen-sur-Seine itself, at Jonquières and at Boury-en-Vexin (Oise) (Blanchet and Petit, 1972; Blanchet *et al.*, 1982). It is not clear, however, whether a deliberate disarticulation of human remains is represented here or whether the evidence is simply the outcome of the deposition of bodies on rubbish dumps. Whichever is the case, it represents a contrast with the flat graves of the Bandkeramik, although the site of Noyen may show a transition between the practices of the two periods. There are no chambered tombs of this period in the Paris basin, nor are there any collective graves.

Within the Franche-Comté, middle neolithic burials are known from Gondenans. These consist of extended inhumations within the cave (Petrequin, 1972). At the camp of La Vergentière at Cohons scattered fragments of human bones were found (Lepage *et al.*, 1980), which suggests analogies with the Paris basin sites mentioned above. However, the majority of the burial evidence from this region comes from megalithic tombs. Gallay (1977) tried to attribute some of these tombs to the Middle Neolithic but the excavations at Aillevans (Haute-Saône) (Fig.3.5) indicate that they most probably belong within the Late Neolithic. Petrequin and Piningre (1976) suggest that their origins must be sought in the SOM but that within the Late Neolithic a local evolution took place, simple dolmens with a perforated slab giving way to 'antennae' dolmens and finally to simple box-type megaliths.

Pottery forms are not often considered in a detailed way in descriptions of cultural assemblages, at least in comparison with the attention paid to decoration, but the Middle Neolithic of north-eastern France repays careful study in this respect. The way pottery shape varies provides several important clues to the basic nature of the Chasséen.

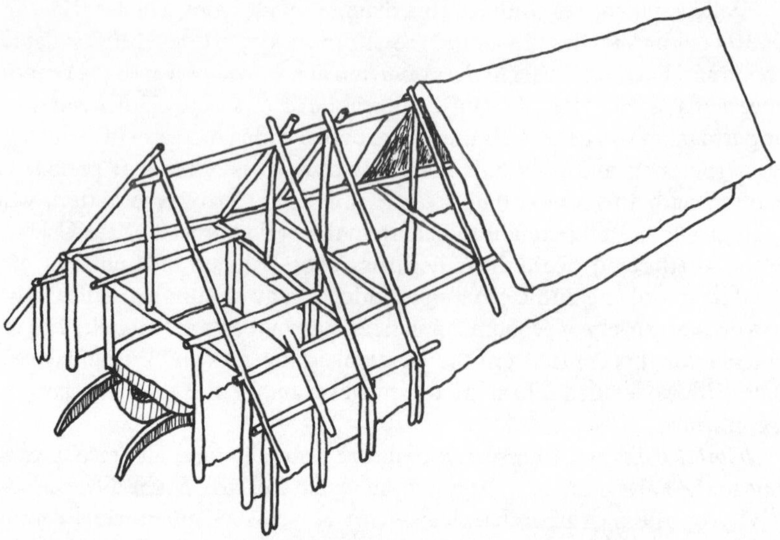

FIGURE 3.5. Possible reconstruction of dolmen no. 1 at Aillevans and its trapezoidal covering building. Overall length c.20m. (After Petrequin and Piningre, 1976.)

The basic repertoire of Chasséen pottery forms in the Paris basin is illustrated by Figure 3.6 (see also Bailloud, 1976, fig.21; Mordant and Mordant, 1972, figs 10–12). A great variety in shape is evident. There are large containers which appear to have been used for storage, and many sorts of bowls, some of which are open and some of which have carinations. Beyond this characteristic range of vessels there are also items such as spoons and vases-supports (Fig.3.7, 1–4; Blanchet and Petit, 1972; Bailloud, 1974). Flat, circular items of pottery are also encountered (Fig.3.7, 5 and 8). These are known as *plats-à-pain* and are very important for understanding the nature of the middle neolithic pottery assemblages, because they are characteristic of German and Belgian Michelsberg material. The presence of Michelsberg features in the Paris basin is further confirmed by examples of tulip-shaped pots (e.g. as far south as Balloy (Seine-et-Marne)). Bailloud (1976, 21) points out that, in the Aisne valley, Michelsberg characteristics far outnumber Chasséen. It is clear that to conceive of the Chasséen of the Paris basin in a similar way to the Chasséen du Midi is rather misleading. Louwe-Kooijman's (1980) conclusions support this view. It may be that a term such as Chasséo-Michelsberg would be better for the Middle Neolithic of the Paris basin.

The inappropriateness of terming the whole of the middle neolithic material Chasséen is even more obvious in the Burgundy/Franche-Comté region even though it is here that the type site is to be found. Thévenot (1969) shows clearly the immense variety of vessel forms which exist at Chassey-le-Camp (see particularly his fig.12). Most of these can be paralleled within the Chasséen of the Paris basin. As noted earlier it is only recently (since Théve-

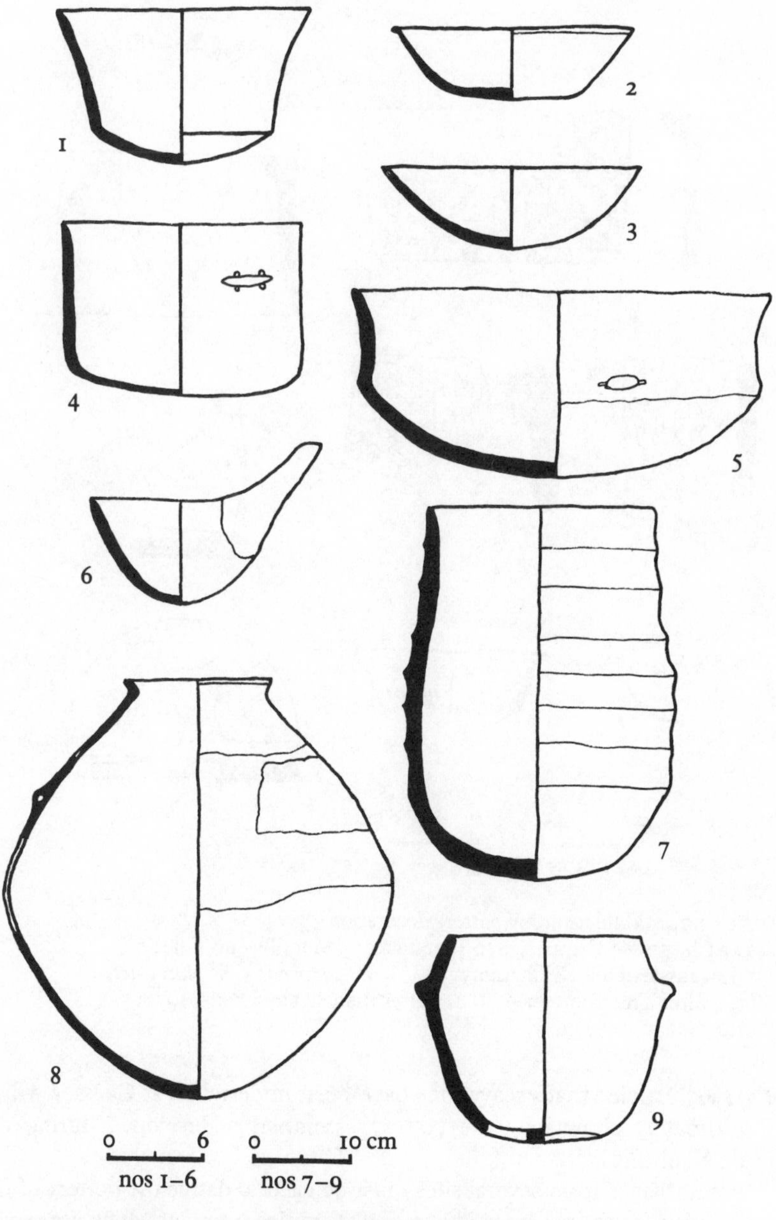

FIGURE 3.6. Middle and late neolithic pottery forms.
1-3 Lavans-lès-Dole; 4, 5 Jonquières; 6, 8 Noyen-sur-Seine; 7 Clairvaux-les-Lacs, Station III; 9 Charavines. (1-3 after Galley, 1977; 4, 5 after Blanchet and Petit, 1972; 6, 8 after Mordant and Mordant, 1972; 7 after Petrequin and Petrequin, 1980; 9 after Bocquet in Strahm and Thévenot, 1976.)

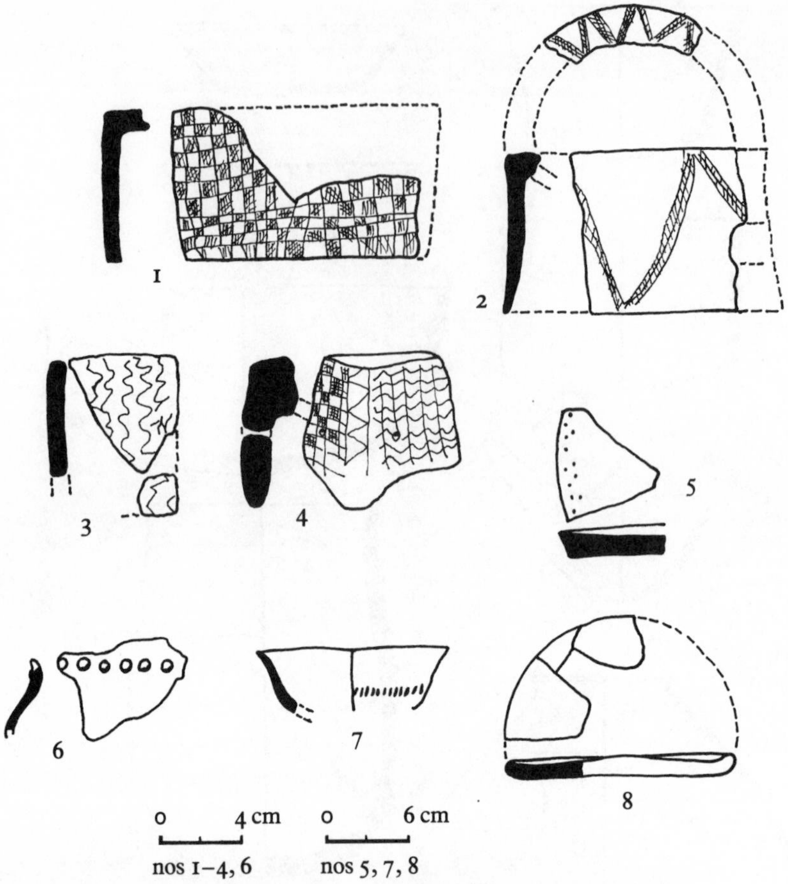

FIGURE 3.7. Middle neolithic pottery decoration.
1, 2 Chassey-le-Camp; 3, 4, 6 Jonquières; 5 Marcilly-sur-Tille; 7 Lavans-lès-Dole; 8 Charigny. (1-4: *vases-supports*; 5, 8: *plats-à-pain*.) (1, 2 after Thévenot, 1969; 3, 4, 6 after Blanchet and Petit, 1972; 5, 7, 8 after Gallay, 1977.)

not's 1969 article) that excavations have been undertaken at Chassey which will ultimately show how the pottery assemblages developed during the Middle Neolithic.

Assemblages from several sites must be used to define the pottery of the NMB. Gallay (1977) provides illustrative examples, some of which are reproduced in Figure 3.6. The assemblages from the camps of Lavans-lès-Dole (Gallay, 1977, pls 21–22; m.r.11) and Marcilly-sur-Tille (pls 22–23) are particularly noteworthy, and the lake-side site of Clairvaux also provides good examples (Petrequin and Petrequin, 1980, figs 1–3). Carinated vessels and other elements of these assemblages demonstrate that the NMB falls clearly within the Chasséen tradition. However, the bowls with flat bases found within the NMB are more characteristic of the contemporary Swiss Cortaillod. Michelsberg *plats-à-pain* are also very common. Michelsberg characteristics are especially widespread in the northern Jura area near the Belfort gap at sites such as Gondenans.

It has been argued (Carré and Thévenot, 1976, 408) that the range of vessel forms is smaller within the NMB than within the Chasséen. However, since the earlier Chasséen is represented principally at the site of Chassey itself it may be the absence of large assemblages of NMB material which is responsible for this impression. Some of the characteristics of NMB pottery, such as flat bases and Michelsberg-type shapes, are certainly new to this area, not being found here in the Early Neolithic. There seems in fact to be a far larger range of forms in the NMB than in the early neolithic assemblages of the region. Publication of the material from the stratigraphical excavations at Chassey should provide a clear answer to these questions. Overall, it can be concluded that the general range of vessel forms in the Middle Neolithic was greater than in the Bandkeramik, in which simple round-based spherical types predominated.

The Vases-Supports. It is rare to find middle neolithic vessels which bear any form of decoration. Such decoration as is found may usually be explained as merely a late manifestation of an earlier style. The decoration types (Fig.3.7) are usually found on sites which belong to the earlier part of the Middle Neolithic and on pots whose forms equally are characteristic of the previous period. Thus, in the Paris basin, the site of Jonquières possesses vessels which are decorated by rows of small pottery buttons applied round the neck of the pot. This style is known as *Menneville*, after an early neolithic site in the Aisne valley. Further to the south, at Noyen, one of the burials was accompanied by a pot with Cerny-type decoration (Mordant and Mordant, 1978, fig.13, no.5). On typological grounds this pot would probably be considered earlier than the rest of the material from the camp. There is however no stratigraphical or other evidence to suggest that it is other than contemporary. As at Jonquières, the presence of a decorated vessel here is probably to be understood as the persistence of an early neolithic trait into the middle neolithic period.

Moving now to the Burgundy / Franche-Comté region, it is noticeable that decorative features such as *flûte-de-pan* handles, present at Chassey, are absent on pots from NMB assemblages. In the northern Jura, at sites like Gonvillars, the Rössen-type decoration dies out in NMB layers.

There is one middle neolithic pottery type upon which decoration is persistent and widespread, and this is the *vase-support* (Figs 3.7 and 8). The study of Chasséen vases-supports has long been of great interest to French prehistorians. Thévenot (1969) gives a list of some of the previous discussions but many other authors have commented on them, usually with reference to a particular area (e.g. Bailloud, 1974; Guilaine *et al.*, 1976; Burnez, 1976). Much argument has centred on their name, and the following have been proposed: *brûle-parfum*, *coupe à socle*, and *vase-support*. Such discussion is

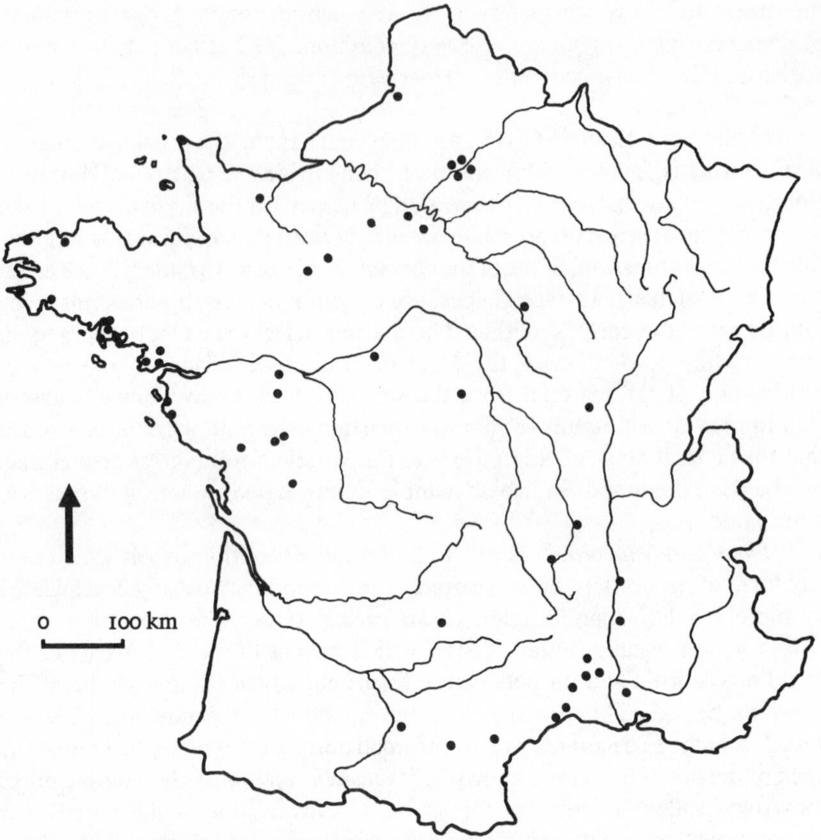

FIGURE 3.8. Map showing distribution of *vases-supports*. Based on information from Renouf and Urry, 1976, Guilaine *et al.*, 1976, and Giot, L'Helgouach and Monnier, 1979.

of course mainly with respect to their function, but in general the term *vase-support* seems to have stuck through popular usage. (Since this term will recur frequently in this book we shall hereafter cease to italicize it.) A particular problem of vases-supports is that of identifying them. In the past authors have far too frequently assigned to vases-supports certain sherds, which have no diagnostic form, on the basis of their decoration. This practice probably came about because of the eagerness to identify the presence of the Chasséen culture through this very diagnostic type.

The earliest examples appear to come from the Midi, where 15 sites with them are recorded by Guilaine *et al.* (1976). A vase-support from Font-Juvénal (Aude) is dated to 3400bc. However, the Midi cannot match the abundance of vases-supports found at sites in other parts of France. Giot, L'Helgouach and Monnier (1979) give a distribution map of vases-supports in Brittany and it is to be noted that one of these sites, Er Lannic, has perhaps 160 examples.

Another area with an important concentration of vases-supports is west-central France, where they are represented at about 15 sites. Within north-eastern France the most notable site is Chassey-le-Camp itself where many examples have been found. Sadly the state of the past excavations does not allow a date to be put on these. However, in west-central France there are two important dates: 2620bc from Les Sables-d'Olonne (Vendée) and 2840bc from Bougon F2 (Deux-Sèvres) (see Scarre, this volume). For Brittany there is a date of 2875±125bc from Kerleven (Finistère). In the Paris basin we have dates of 3170bc from Jonquières and 2450bc from Fort Harrouard.

The principal characteristics and contexts of vases-supports may next be considered. The most important morphological difference is between cubic and cylindrical examples. Whereas cylindrical vases-supports are found all over France the cubic ones are confined to the Paris basin, the site of Chassey in Burgundy, and the upper reaches of the Loire. Cubic vases-supports usually occur in association with cylindrical ones.

It is very rare to find vases-supports that are undecorated (for some from Chassey see Thévenot, 1969). Usually they are richly ornamented. Certain styles have been recognised which are generally regional in character, though not always so. In the west the Bougon and Er Lannic styles are found, whereas the more classic Chasséen style of decoration with squares, chevrons, etc., is most common in the east and south (although examples do occur frequently in the west). The decoration usually covers the entire exterior surface of the vases-supports except for the bowl part. Other features occasionally found include windows and small perforations in the side of the vessel. The windows seem to be a purely decorative feature, while Bailloud's conclusion that the small perforations must be for suspending the vessel (Bailloud, 1974, 96) seems the most likely explanation for the latter. Support for this is to be found in the fact that the small perforations frequently occur in pairs and when they occur on cubic examples they are located at a corner with one on each face. Some of the bowls of the vases-supports carry traces of burning.

The contexts in which the vases-supports are found are also illuminating. In the west, the overwhelming majority come from megalithic or funerary contexts (although Les Sables-d'Olonne appears to be an exception), and special note must be taken of the large number found inside the stone circle at Er Lannic, which is the centre of an area remarkable for the intensity of its megalithic and religious activities. In the Paris basin, vases-supports are generally found at high camps, and they occur in especially large numbers at Chassey, which is also a high site. In the south they are generally found in caves.

It is possible to draw certain conclusions from this information, about the function of vases-supports and their significance to the middle neolithic communities. It seems certain that they must have had some sort of ritual purpose. This much is indicated by their megalithic contexts in the west, especially at Er Lannic, though so few burials of this period are known in the Paris basin that we are unable to establish whether vases-supports played an important role in funerary ritual there as well. It is noteworthy too that they are highly decorated and frequently stand out by reason of this fact from the rest of the ceramic assemblage. The widespread distribution of the vases-supports is also remarkable and since in general they occur in no more than twos or threes it must be concluded that they were an item that was highly prized in various types of societies.

Their origin is unclear, despite the early dating in the Midi. Guilaine *et al.*'s (1976) attempt to show how they can be formed, by joining a stand onto the bowl-form well known in the Chasséen, still fails to account for the cubic examples which are found further north, unless these are regarded as later forms.

One seems bound to conclude that the way in which vases-supports were actually used was not to support vases. Far more likely, given the traces of burning that have been found, is their use as ritual vases, and the name *brûle-parfums* seems more appropriate. It would presumably not have been difficult for a powder to have been made to burn as incense, or for them to have been used as small lamps with floating wicks.

The hypothesis that vases-supports were used ritually is further reinforced by the discovery of figurines at some of the sites in the Paris basin where the former have been found. Several examples are known from each of the sites of Jonquières, Noyen-sur-Seine and Fort Harrouard. They are made of pottery but one example at Noyen may have had a wooden head which slotted into the clay body.

The association of these two objects, the vases-supports and the figurines, at sites in the Paris basin would appear to suggest the existence of a ritual assemblage in the Middle Neolithic. Added weight is given to this by the discovery at Jonquières of a small four-legged object identified as a miniature altar. However no traces of any ritual building have ever been found.

Tools and Trade. Lithic, bone and antler tools are relatively abundant in middle neolithic assemblages of north-eastern France but have been little studied by prehistorians. This may perhaps be because the variability they display is less than that of the pottery and is difficult to quantify. These materials are however more likely than the pottery to yield information about trade and general environmental management. A study by Billamboz (1977), for example, shows how the different parts of a deer's antler were utilised in the Franche-Comté during the neolithic period.

Hardly any petrographic studies have been conducted on material from this region, though it is known that aphanite was widely used in northern Franche-Comté during the Middle Neolithic (Piningre, 1974). The source of this rock lies in the Belfort Gap area and the distribution and concentration of material fit with this. Surface collections of waste material suggest that aphanite was worked at several of the high camps.

Aphanite is an example of the use made of relatively local materials at this period. The situation was similar in the Middle Neolithic of the Paris basin. At Chasséen sites such as Noyen-sur-Seine imported hard rocks seem to have been much less used than was common in the Early Neolithic. In general, local flints seem to have been preferred, though by the end of the Chasséen period the situation was changing. The large-scale exploitation of Belgian flint mines is well known, and ultimately northern France seems to have been affected by this development. In parallel with this was an increased use of harder Alpine rocks in Burgundy / Franche-Comté during the Late Neolithic.

In the Early Neolithic, shells such as *Spondylus* appear to have been traded over large distances. This practice does not however seem to have continued into later periods of the Neolithic in this part of France. The pattern may be distorted by the fact that the early neolithic *Spondylus* shells come from burials, of which middle neolithic examples are rare.

The earliest copper to appear in these regions takes the form of small beads in CSR assemblages. This must have been imported but so far no studies have shown where the metal might have come from.

INTERPRETATION

MIDDLE NEOLITHIC. The Middle Neolithic of north-eastern France shows a general uniformity of material culture, but diversities at sub-regional levels. This spatial patterning can be demonstrated in several ways.

The uniformity of the Middle Neolithic is recognised in the way it is usually referred to as Chasséen. Items such as vases-supports and carinated bowls, and traits such as incised ornamentation are found throughout the area and form the basis of this appellation. The distribution of such features is not however restricted to this part of France. Vases-supports are a feature of other regions also (Fig.3.8). Louwe-Kooijmans (1980) has pointed out links between Paris basin middle neolithic material and that of regions further east, and prefers to include the Paris basin material in a *Chasséo-Michelsberg,* which extends into Belgium and Holland. The *plats-à-pain* characteristic of the German Michelsberg are known in the Paris basin and the Franche-Comté. Defensive camps, such as those found in north-eastern France, appear to have been widespread in north-western Europe at this period.

Against features like these, which unify north-eastern France and adjacent territories in the Middle Neolithic, are other characteristics which suggest extensive variability at the more local level. We have noticed the distinction between the material culture of the Paris basin Chasséen and the NMB. Figurines are found in the Paris basin but are absent from Burgundy and the Franche-Comté. Valley-bottom locations appear to have been chosen for middle-neolithic settlements in the former region but not in the latter. Flat-based vessels are known from the Burgundy / Franche-Comté region but not from the Paris basin at this period.

Recent work has also considered local differences in material culture. Thus Blanchet *et al.* (1982) distinguish a Chasséen of the northern Paris basin, while Petrequin and Petrequin (1980) refer to the NMB in terms of specific site-varieties, e.g. NMB of Clairvaux V type.

It is not surprising that this spatial patterning has led to a bewildering complexity of nomenclature. The traditional method of dividing archaeological material into cultural blocks is not well-suited to describing this type of variability. Clarke's (1968) model of a series of entities at different levels is far more appropriate. The size of the entity depends on the trait used to define it. Thus at one level the whole of north-eastern France can be seen as a single entity, but other entities exist at the regional, sub-regional and site-specific levels. There may be an overlap in geographical distribution even between entities of the same size order. Such a hierarchy of entities may not be an appropriate model for all areas and periods of prehistory, but it provides a useful way of conceptualising the spatial patterning of the Middle Neolithic of north-eastern France.

How far do the middle neolithic assemblages relate to those of earlier phases of the Neolithic in this area? In Burgundy and the Franche-Comté, 4th millennium developments prior to the appearance of the NMB are unclear. Chassey is the key site and its stratigraphy seems to indicate that the NMB emerges from a Chasséen du Midi-type base. The details of this development await the results of excavations now in progress.

In the Paris basin, comparison of the Middle Neolithic with earlier (Bandkeramik) developments is easier. At Jonquières and Noyen there is some evidence for continuity; a small proportion of the vessels at Jonquières were decorated, while at Noyen inhumations were found similar in many respects to those of the earlier period. Such evidence of continuity needs to be balanced against the contrasts between the Early and Middle Neolithic of the Paris basin. Firstly, the majority of Chasséen vessels are undecorated. The vase-support, which is the only commonly decorated Chasséen vessel, is unknown from early neolithic contexts. The range of middle neolithic vessel shapes is rather wide, in contrast to the simple spherical-type shapes which are characteristic of the preceding period. Secondly, the treatment of human remains was very different in the Middle Neolithic from in the Early Neolithic. The careful early neolithic burial rite disappears, to be replaced by one apparently demanding complete disarticulation, since the human skeletal material of the middle neolithic period is found only in a fragmentary state, frequently mixed up with household rubbish. Thirdly, some features of the Paris basin Chasséen contrast with the earlier part of the preceding period (Ilett's Late and Epi-Bandkeramik) but can be paralleled in the later Early Neolithic (Ilett's Late Rössen). Such are for example the appearance of defended sites, a greater range of site locations and a greater variety in house plan. These features highlight the continuous nature of developments from the Bandkeramik colonisation of north-eastern France onwards.

The principal early neolithic/middle neolithic trend is towards a greater range of material culture. In comparison with the earliest Bandkeramik material, the Middle Neolithic of north-eastern France displays a greater range of pot-shapes and types of site-location, and a greater variety of house-forms. There is even some evidence that the type of economy practised in the later period made use of a greater range of resources. The considerable degree of subsistence uniformity found in the Early Neolithic can best be understood as a reflection not of external constraints, but of internal ones inspired by the nature of the society itself. The greater variety of middle neolithic subsistence practices indicates a relaxation of these internal social constraints.

During the Early and Middle Neolithic, defence emerges as an important consideration in the planning of settlements. Pottery decoration, on the other hand, virtually disappears, and in middle neolithic assemblages is found only on vases-supports, which may have formed part of a ritual complex along with the figurines which are known from the Paris basin at this period. The careful early neolithic burial rite involving inhumation, often with ochre, disappears at the same time, being replaced as mentioned earlier by the custom of depositing portions of the skeleton only in rubbish dumps and ditches.

LATE NEOLITHIC. It is difficult to follow these developments into the Late Neolithic in the Paris basin, because the emphasis in the archaeological evidence shifts from settlements to burials (see Howell, Chapter 4). Burgundy and the Franche-Comté, however, offer more scope. It is in the Late Neolithic that sites begin to appear for the first time along the river edges. Earlier types of settlement (high camps, caves, and lake-side sites) continue to be occupied. Although Bocquet regarded the palisade at Charavines (m.r.17) as non-defensive, there is little reason to doubt that defence continued to play an important part in settlement layout in this area, up to the end of the 3rd millennium. The palisade at Charavines is similar to the middle neolithic example at Clairvaux, and some of the high camps with ramparts are presumed to belong to the later 3rd millennium bc.

Most authors are agreed that pottery decoration continues to be rare in the Late Neolithic. Such decoration as exists tends to be simple and plastic in type. Vessels continue to take a wide range of forms, though some of the shapes have changed. It is only with the appearance of Beakers that pottery form becomes standardised once more and that profuse decoration reappears, but this material lies on the threshold of the Early Bronze Age.

In Burgundy and the Franche-Comté, therefore, the Late Neolithic shows much evidence of continuity with the NMB in the principal features of its material. There is every reason to suppose that the developmental processes outlined earlier continued to operate. The formerly widespread vases-supports and *plats-à-pain* are no longer found, however: evidence perhaps of a still greater regionalisation than in the Middle Neolithic, when these features had united large areas.

INFORMATION EXCHANGE. The Middle Neolithic in north-eastern France appears, therefore, to display greater variability in material culture than earlier periods, and the significance of this greater variability must now be considered.

Wobst (1977) has conducted a study which shows how items of material culture with stylistic behaviour patterns may be used to exchange information. Wobst believes that archaeologists in the past have not realised the full potential of the study of stylistic attributes, since they have used them only as a tool for the analysis of temporal and spatial distributions, whereas in fact the way in which style varies is itself an interesting field of study. Wobst defines stylistic behaviour as that aspect of artifact form and structure which can be related to processes of information exchange. Although this definition seems rather narrow, it does bring to the forefront the use of material culture items to exchange information. The greater variability in middle neolithic material culture in north-eastern France might be seen as an example of increased stylistic behaviour.

Wobst believes that an increase in stylistic behaviour represents an increase in the size of social networks. This latter term does not refer to the distance of the geographical movements which the people concerned were accustomed to make, but rather to the number of people involved in a network of dependent relationships. If one adopted Wobst's line of argument, therefore, the Middle Neolithic might in north-eastern France be a period when social networks increased in size relative to those of the previous periods. Unfortunately, the evidence of trade which might be used to test this hypothesis is lacking in the area studied here, but as more information becomes available it may be possible to investigate these ideas more closely.

This analysis suggests, then, that between the beginning of the Neolithic and the end of the Middle Neolithic the size of social networks in north-eastern France was increasing. What reason might be put forward to account for this? A study by Plog (1980) has certain parallels with the situation presented here. He studied the population increase that occurred in the Chevelon Canyon area of the American Southwest between AD 900 and AD 1300, and found that during that period areas which had previously been only sparsely inhabited and marginal for agriculture were colonised. Within the Bandkeramik tradition of central and western Europe the response to population pressure seems always to have been the occupation of new areas of fertile soil. In the Paris basin, however, this tradition reached its westernmost limit and the option of colonising new areas no longer existed. As a result, an increase in population density is likely to have occurred in the Paris basin, as in Plog's case-study.

Plog found that land which had been marginal agriculturally began to be colonised as a result of population pressures. A gradual increase in the area under cultivation can be documented in the Neolithic of the Paris basin also (see especially Howell, ch.4 below and Fig.4.6). Plog then suggests (1980, 130) that one effect of the increased population density would have been a reduction in mobility, with social groups not having free access to as many areas as they had previously had. Such a development might explain the greater regionalisation of middle neolithic pottery styles as compared with those of the Early Neolithic, which was noted earlier. Plog links this reduction in the size of the area which a group could exploit directly, with the development of larger social networks. An increase in the size of social networks would have provided a safeguard against the effects of seasonal environmental variability which would have been especially important now that the marginal areas were occupied.

Plog's study, together with Wobst's postulated link between larger social networks and increased stylistic variability, in this way provides a good explanation for many aspects of early and middle neolithic development in north-eastern France. One further element which fits Plog's model is to be found in this area, namely the increasing concern with defence shown by settlement sites, which are frequently in *éperon barré* locations and furnished with ramparts or palisades. This has often been presented as evidence of population increase and competition for resources.

The model outlined above is valuable, but fails to account for the decline in pottery decoration and for the changes in burial ritual which take place with the transition to the Middle Neolithic in the Paris basin. Hodder has recently pointed out that in the Dutch Bandkeramik there is greater differentiation in the organisation of decoration on the pottery as time progresses, and he suggests that this is a reflection of increasing social and economic stress (Hodder, 1982, 172). Nearer to the Paris basin, in Alsace, Schweitzer (1980) has outlined a sequence in the development of Bandkeramik (Rubané) pottery decoration similar to that which Hodder describes. The radiocarbon dates from Cuiry-lès-Chaudardes and Menneville (late 5th millennium bc) suggest that the Paris basin Bandkeramik sequence is contemporary with that of Alsace (date-list, p.60; Delibrias *et al.*, 1982, 191). In the Paris basin, however, strongly structured schemes of pottery decoration are found from the very outset, whereas in Alsace and Holland such schemes are characteristic only of developed stages of the Bandkeramik. If, as Hodder suggests, the structured pottery decoration is an indicator of social and economic stress, then one is led to conclude that such stress was felt by the Paris basin Bandkeramik communities from the very outset. Since the Paris basin marks the extreme western limit of Bandkeramik colonisation, such early manifestation of stress is not perhaps unexpected. The special treatment of certain burials is another early feature of the Paris basin Bandkeramik, and may reflect the development of social ranking in response to economic and social pressures.

The expression of stress in pottery and burial rites may have been the initial trigger which led eventually to the break-up of the Bandkeramik uniformity and ushered in the more varied material culture of the middle neolithic period. The economic stress which Bandkeramik communities seem to have experienced was relieved as time progressed by the use of an increasingly wide range of resources and habitats. Social networks appear to have become larger and more important as a result, and there was a corresponding decline in the use of pottery decoration as an indicator of small between-group differences. The relative homogeneity of middle neolithic pottery and the absence of decoration reflect this new situation of reduced economic stress coupled with greater interdependence between groups. Combined in this way, the models of Hodder and Plog are able to give us a new insight into the social and economic developments which lay behind the changes in material culture during the Early and Middle Neolithic of the Paris basin.

RADIOCARBON DATES

Paris Basin Middle Neolithic						
Fort Harrouard (Eure-et-Loir)	2450±125bc	Gsy-97	Charcoal	High camp	Level 1: Chasséen	Bailloud, 1974
Jonquières (Oise)	3170±130bc	Gif-2919	Bone	High camp	Sector 14: Chasséen	Blanchet, 1974
Lumbres (Pas-de-Calais)	2620±130bc	Gif	Charcoal	Settlement	Couche B: Chasséen	Prévost, 1962
	2420±130bc	Gif	Charcoal		Couche B: Chasséen	Prévost, 1962
Les Roches, Videlles (Essonne)	2790±140bc	Gif-720	Charcoal	Settlement	Couche E	Bailloud and Coiffard, 1967
Burgundy/Franche-Comté: Early, Middle and Late Neolithic						
Gondenans (Doubs)	4000±140bc	Gif-1561	Charcoal	Cave	Level IX: Bandkeramik	Petrequin, 1972
	3540±140bc	Ly-335	Charcoal		Level IXb: Bandkeramik	Petrequin, 1972
	2550±120bc	Gif-1388	Charcoal		Level VIII: Middle Neo.	Petrequin, 1972
	2050±120bc	Gif-1387	Charcoal		Level VII: Late Neo.	Petrequin, 1972
Gonvillars (Haute-Saône)	4300±300bc	Gif-469	Charcoal	Cave	Level XI: Early Neo.	Petrequin, 1970a
	3430±250bc	Gif-468	Charcoal		Level Xb: Rössen	Petrequin, 1970a
	3050±250bc	Gif-466	Charcoal		Level X: Rössen	Petrequin, 1970a
Les Planches-près-Arbois (Jura)	3570±130bc	Gif-3826		Cave	Level E: Early Neo.	Barbier *et al.*, 1981
Gigny-sur-Suran (Jura)	3190±140bc	Gif-4026	Charcoal	Cave	Pit: Early Neo.	Barbier *et al.*, 1981
La Vergentière, Cohons (Haute-Marne)	3400±270bc	Ly-1860	Charcoal	High camp	Sondage 1: NMB	Lepage *et al.*, 1980
	3280±300bc	Ly-1859	Bone		Sondage 1: NMB	Lepage *et al.*, 1980
Chassey-le-Camp (Côte-d'Or)	3750±150bc	Ly-1772	Charcoal	High camp	F50-56D: Chasséen	*Radiocarbon*, 25, 103
	3710±150bc	Ly-1768	Charcoal		F42-56TC: Chasséen	*Radiocarbon*, 25, 103
	3590±120bc	Ly-1769	Charcoal		F43-56A: Chasséen	*Radiocarbon*, 25, 103
	3430±140bc	Ly-1770	Charcoal		F42-55A: Chasséen	*Radiocarbon*, 25, 103
	3430±160bc	Ly-1771	Charcoal		F48-54F: Chasséen	*Radiocarbon*, 25, 103
	3270±140bc	Ly-1767	Charcoal		F43-56F: Chasséen	*Radiocarbon*, 25, 103
Camp Myard, Vitteaux (Côte-d'Or)	3225±135bc	Gif-2342	Charcoal	High camp	Wall: NMB	Nicolardot, 1973
	3040±130bc	Gif-3381	Charcoal		Occupation layer: NMB	Delattre and Nicolardot, 1976
	2930±135bc	Gif-2341	Charcoal		Wall: NMB	Nicolardot, 1973
	2820±140bc	Gif-3670	Charcoal		Occupation layer: NMB	Delattre and Nicolardot, 1976
	2750±135bc	Gif-2343	Charcoal		Hearth: NMB	Nicolardot, 1973

	2790±110bc	Gif-2298	Charcoal		Station II	Passard, 1980
	3100±200bc	Ly-801	Wood		Station II	Passard, 1980
	2500±150bc	Ly-802	Wood		Station III	Passard, 1980
	2670±130bc	Ly-1058	Charcoal		Station III	Passard, 1980
	2830±130bc	Ly-1059	Charcoal		Station III	Passard, 1980
	1930±110bc	Gif-2299	Wood		Station III: EBA	Passard, 1980
(La Motte aux Magnins)	2920±115bc	Gif-4370	Wood		Level VIb: silt	Petrequin and Petrequin, 1980
	2990±130bc	Ly-850	Charcoal		Level V: NMB	Petrequin and Petrequin, 1980
	3000±140bc	Ly-1154	Wood		Level V: NMB	Petrequin and Petrequin, 1980
	2410±110bc	Gif-4371	Wood		Level IV: silt	Petrequin and Petrequin, 1980
	2120±140bc	Ly-851	Wood		Layer II: CSR	Strahm and Thévenot, 1976
Charavines (Isère)	2590±120bc	Ly-908	Wood	Lake-side settlement	CSR	Strahm and Thévenot, 1976
	2490±230bc	Ly-793	Wood		CSR	Strahm and Thévenot, 1976
	2410±130bc	Ly-794	Charcoal		CSR	Strahm and Thévenot, 1976
	2280±130bc	Ly-907	Wood		CSR	Strahm and Thévenot, 1976
	2150±120bc	Ly-906	Charcoal		CSR	Strahm and Thévenot, 1976
Ouroux-sur-Saône (Saône-et-Loire)	1800±120bc	Gsy-1528	Bone	Settlement	Pit: CSR/EBA	Strahm and Thévenot, 1976

The Later Neolithic of the Paris Basin

JOHN HOWELL

The land ○ *Seine-Oise-Marne* ○ SOM tombs and ritual ○ MATERIAL CULTURE ○ Grand Pressigny flint and other artifacts ○ chronology of the SOM ○ SETTLEMENT ○ studies, patterns and process ○ the expanded village pattern ○ research in Aisne-Marne ○ in the Seine estuary ○ in the Loing valley ○ modelling ○ CONCLUSION.

THE LATE NEOLITHIC of northern France, covering approximately the period from 2700 to 1500bc, is known as the Seine-Oise-Marne culture (SOM) after the major rivers at the centre of its distribution; but the geographical definition does not do justice to the wide area over which this cultural phenomenon is spread (Fig.4.1a). De Laet (1974) has clearly shown that the Low Countries must be included within the distribution of the SOM; and arguments can be made for including the *Horgen* group of Switzerland. In addition, it is clear from pottery associations and tomb-types that something similar to the SOM occurs in Brittany and Normandy.

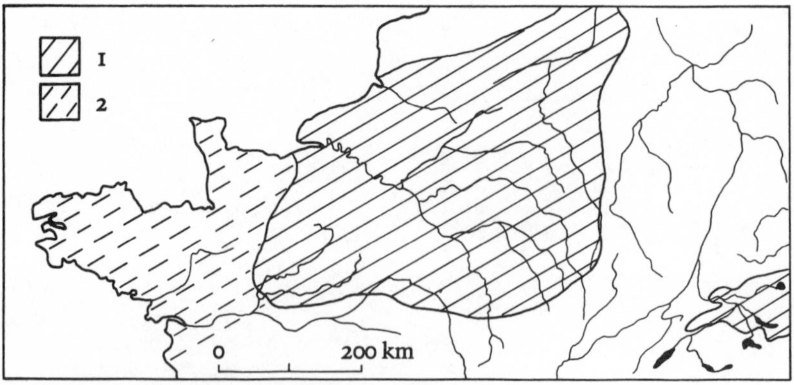

FIGURE 4.1. Distribution of material of SOM and Horgen type in northern France and Switzerland.
1 SOM and Horgen material; 2 material showing SOM influence.

In the Paris basin, the Seine-Oise-Marne culture is identified from three principal sources: tombs, artefact scatters and stray finds. There is an almost complete absence of 'settlements' in published accounts. The exception is the

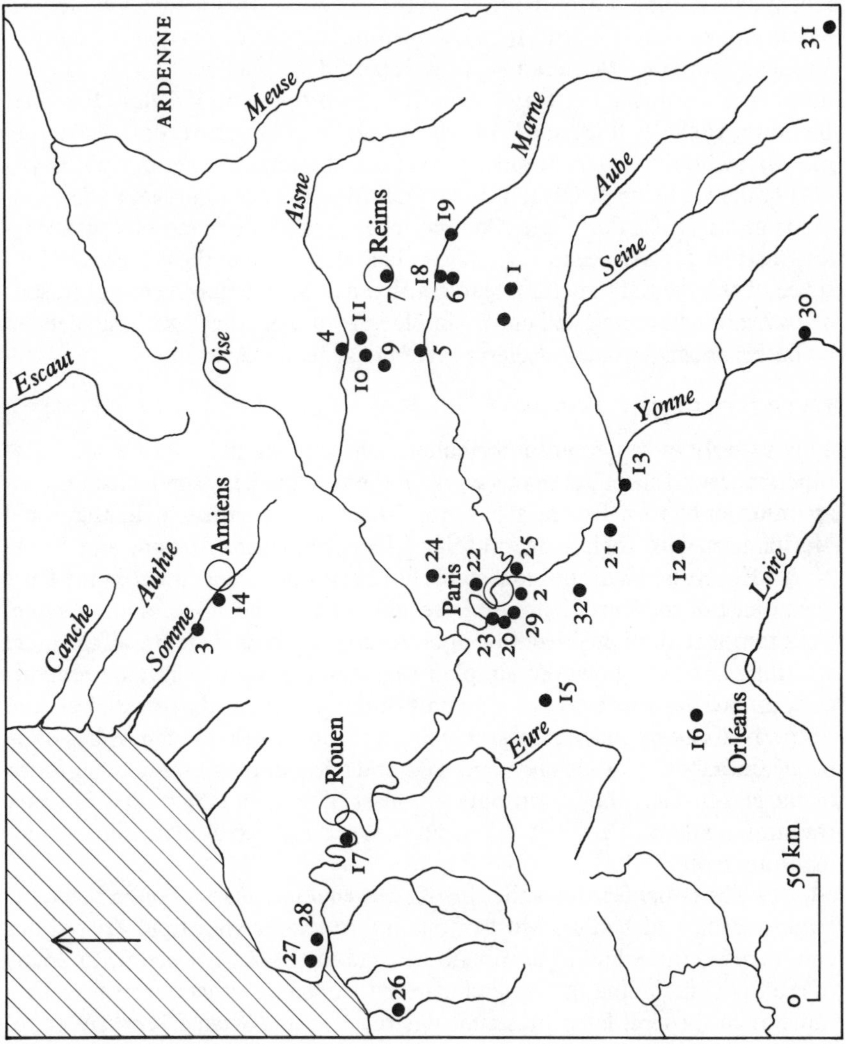

GENERAL MAP of sites.

1 Le Pré-à-Vaches; 2 Hautes-Bruyères; 3 La Portelette; 4 Cuiry-lès-Chaudardes; 5 Le Troncet, Nogent l'Artaud; 6 Les Mournouards; 7 Tinqueux; 8 Marais-Saint-Gond; 9 Vaux, Neuilly-Saint-Front; 10 Tannières; 11 Serches; 12 Girolles; 13 Marolles-sur-Seine; 14 La Chaussée-Tirancourt; 15 Fort-Harrouard; 16 Etauville; 17 Bardouville; 18 Chouilly; 19 Saint Martin-sur-le-Pré; 20 Le Parc-Saint-Cloud; 21 Noisy-sur-Ecole; 22 Guiry-en-Vexin; 23 Les Moulins-des-Fourneaux; 24 Trivaux; 25 Buisson Pouilleux; 26 La Hoguette; 27 Forêt de Montgeon; 28 La Grande Epauville; 29 Les Mureaux; 30 Augy; 31 Marcilly-sur-Tille; 32 Videlles.

recent excavations at Montivilliers, on the site of La Grande Epauville (Seine-Maritime; m.r.28) (Watté, 1976). An (unpublished) excavation at Le Pré-à-Vaches, Moraine (Marne; m.r.1) is reported by Bailloud (1974, 141). A number of insubstantial traces have also been found at Videlles (Essonne; Bailloud, 1958; Bailloud and Coiffard, 1967); Saint Martin-sur-le-Pré (Marne; m.r.19); Chouilly (Marne; m.r.18); Hautes-Bruyères (Seine; m.r.2); Buisson-Pouilleux (Seine-et-Oise; m.r.20); Les Moulins-des-Fourneaux (Seine-et-Oise; m.r.23); La Portelette (Somme; m.r.3); and, more recently, at Cuiry-lès-Chaudardes (Aisne; m.r.4). What characterises all of these sites is the absence of substantial structural features. Even at Montivilliers, several seasons of excavation have revealed only a simple hut not more than 12m long, defined by bands of small stones. (References are to general map of sites.)

Late Neolithic Tombs

This poverty of settlement information contrasts sharply with the wealth of funerary data. Indeed, previous work on the SOM has been conducted on what amounts only to a funerary culture. In marked contrast to Brittany and Normandy, with their long tradition of megalith construction, and to the North European plain, no stone-built funerary monuments occur in the Paris basin, east of the Eure, before this period. The sudden appearance of stone-built tombs in the Late Neolithic of Northern France is therefore all the more striking. They are, however, simple structures, generally built underground; and, unlike the impressive monuments of the Atlantic seaboard, they are not properly speaking monumental in character. Study of these tombs has often been conducted in diffusionist language and without reference to other forms of burial. In fact, they form only one part of a more varied SOM funerary tradition, and one is as likely to find an SOM grave of 200 or more inhumations in a simple pit.

The essential feature is the rite of *communal* inhumation, often involving large numbers of bodies. Most of our information comes from excavations conducted at these sites in the nineteenth and early twentieth centuries. Many of the finds, including the skeletal material, ended up either in private collections or in those ill-fated museums destroyed in the Second World War. In some cases 'excavation' was hurried. At Le Troncet (Nogent-L'Artaud, Marne), for example, Guillaume and Chevallier (1956) record how the tomb, discovered in the last century, was 'excavated' by dynamite before a hasty looting of its contents, amongst which was one of the rare finds of metal in a SOM context. In recent years this position has improved. Among the most spectacular of modern tomb excavations is Masset's work at La Chaussée-Tirancourt (Somme; m.r.14) (Masset, 1971), and other important tomb excavations have been conducted at Les Mournouards II (Marne; m.r.6) (Leroi Gourhan *et al.*, 1962), Tinqueux (Marne; m.r.7) (Bailloud and Brezillon, 1968), Etauville (Eure-et-Loir; m.r.16) (Nouel *et al.*, 1965), Bardouville (Seine-Maritime; m.r.17) (Caillaud *et al.*, 1971) and Noisy-sur-Ecole (Seine-et-Marne; m.r.21) (Brezillon *et al.*, 1973).

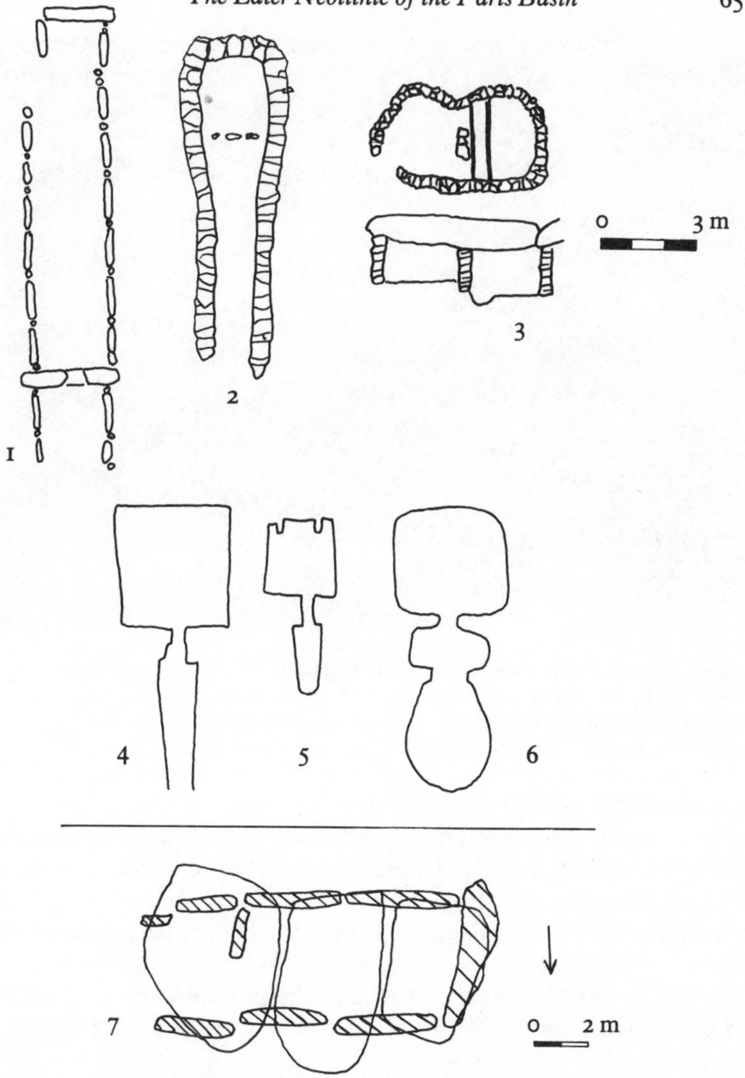

FIGURE 4.2. Late neolithic tomb-types of the Paris basin. 1, 2 and 7 *allées couvertes*; 3 *sépulture en fosse*; 4, 5, 6 *hypogées*.
1 La Pierre Plate, Presles (Seine-et-Oise); 2 Ermenonville (Oise); 3 Crécy-en-Brie (Seine-et-Marne); 4 Les Dimaines, Avize (Marne); 5 Razet 5, Coizard (Marne); 6 Les Ronces 22, Villevenard (Marne); 7 Saint-Antoine-du Rocher (Indre-et-Loire). (1-6 after Bailloud, 1974; 7 after Cordier, 1963.)

Tomb typology. The typology of the tombs is as follows (Fig.4.2): *Allées couvertes:* in the Paris basin these usually take the form of a stone-lined underground passage leading to a chamber with vestibule (Plate 4.1). The whole structure is built of dry-stone slabs. There is wide variation in the size of the tombs; they may be up to 2m deep and as much as 18m long. The most

PLATE 4.1. The *allée couverte* of La Pierre Turquaise (Seine-et-Oise), looking east-north-east towards the entry. In contrast to the *allées couvertes* of Brittany, which are upstanding, those of the Paris basin are commonly sunk into the ground up to the level of the capstones. (Photo: John Peek.)

elaborate occur in the Oise *département*.

Hypogées: the *hypogée* is also built underground but often the sides and walls are left unrevetted, hollowed out of solid chalk. The overall plan is rectangular with a trench leading away from the entrance. More elaborate examples have antechambers. In the Marne, access to the chamber is via a man-hole type of entrance.

Pits: this is a diverse category. Although the pits are often of simple construction, covered by a slab, they frequently contain among the highest numbers of bodies.

Simple dolmens: information on this class of monument is slight. Simple dolmens are likely to have been a frequent target for stone robbers.

Simple graves, rock-shelters and fissures: a diverse group of less formal areas of burial.

Little work has been carried out to ascertain whether these forms have a hierarchical relationship to each other, but there are geographical variations. The *hypogées,* for example, tend to be located on the Champagne while the megalithic tombs occur in the western part of the Paris basin. This may be explained by the varying geological character of these areas.

Ritual. With so few detailed excavations, evidence of ritual is restricted to a few tombs, of which the most informative is La Chaussée-Tirancourt (Plate 4.2). This *allée couverte* produced a minimum of 350 bodies, which had been

PLATE 4.2. The interior of the *allée couverte* of La Chaussée-Tirancourt (Somme) during excavation. Running across the photograph in the middle distance and background are transverse lines of stones dividing the chamber and its contents into sections. (Photo: Claude Masset.)

deposited in two main periods. In the first phase, about 50 bodies were arranged neatly across the floor of the tomb. A bone point and flint blade were found as gravegoods. In the second phase, the tomb was enlarged and rebuilt, and the earlier bones were jumbled up. During this phase 300 bodies were deposited, initially, at least, lying side-by-side with their feet towards the entrance. The whole structure was burnt down in an apparently deliberate act around the beginning of the 2nd millennium bc (Masset, 1971). At Les Mournouards (a *hypogée*), about 60 inhumations were recovered. Excluding the children, the average age of death was 37 years. The bodies appear to have been placed in the tomb in sacks (Leroi Gourhan *et al.*, 1962). In most cases, the SOM burial rite was inhumation, but there are indications that cremation was sometimes used as an alternative. A few examples are known from Les Ronces (Marne; m.r.8), where one cremation was found in a jar (Bailloud, 1974, 283), but the clearest example is a crematorium at La Hoguette, Fontenay-le-Marmion (Calvados; m.r.26). Here about 16 bodies appear to have been cremated in an elongated trench (Caillaud and Lagnel, 1972). SOM 'flower pot' vases and flints were associated as well as small, collared jars. At other tombs, traces of burnt bones and small patches of burning outside the structure have been noted but, as Bailloud (1974, 179) points out, the infrequency with which these patches occur does not suggest any elaborate and regular fire ritual.

There are a number of differences between the burial rite in the *hypogées* and in the *allées couvertes*. First, the *allées couvertes* generally contain more burials. The number can rise to over 150, as compared with a maximum of about 60 in the *hypogées*. Second, the bones in the *hypogées* tend to be found in better anatomical order. Third, it has been noted that *hypogées* occur in clusters and sometimes in cemeteries, although these are mostly restricted to a small area of the Champagne which is examined in detail below. Many of these distinctions stem from the geological constraints noted earlier, but the smaller size of the *hypogées* and perhaps a shorter period of use may suggest a less permanent settlement system on the rendzina expanses of the Champagne than in other parts of the Paris basin. A final aspect of ritual is that represented by the carvings sometimes found on the tombs. In the antechambers, the most frequent motif is the 'goddess motif' of face, neck, and breasts. Elsewhere, hafted axes, incised grilled-patterns and miscellaneous motifs either in bas-relief or daubed in charcoal also occur.

Material Culture

The original definition of the SOM culture was undertaken by Bosch-Gimpera and Serra Raffols in 1926, but in current research it is the check-list of type-fossils identified by Gordon Childe and Nancy Sandars in 1950 which principally shapes our impression of this culture-group. Recent accounts have tended to remain firmly centred on the material culture (Bailloud, 1974, 1976a, b; Verron, 1976). Itten dealt with some of the wider associations of the SOM in her monograph on the Swiss variant known as Horgen, but this was essentially background to a contorted periodisation, to derive Horgen by invasion from the Paris basin (Itten, 1970). The Childe-Sandars list of type-fossils is by far the most important basis for assigning sites other than tombs to the SOM.

Most areas of northern France have produced small scatters of late neolithic material. Stray finds are also frequent. Few of these scatters, save for those associated with flint-mining or -working, are extensive, and for this reason they have previously been omitted from any consideration of the settlement evidence. It is precisely here, however, that accurate periodisation can be of most use in analysing a wealth of settlement data collected by amateurs for over 100 years.

Bailloud's account of the Neolithic in the Paris basin (1974) contains an exhaustive description of the principal type-fossils. The major categories are as follows (Figs 4.3 and 4.4):

Pottery. One of the most striking features of SOM pottery is its homogeneity throughout the entire distribution of the culture. Its main characteristic is its poor quality, and, as has often been remarked, the word *grossier* (coarse) is perhaps the most suitable adjective used to describe it. With the exception of small collared jars, reminiscent of north European *Kragenflaschen*, in SOM-related assemblages towards the Atlantic coast, the form of the pots is generally restricted to what have been called 'flower-pot' vases. These are flat-based beakers with a slightly protruding foot. Below a small, raised neck of

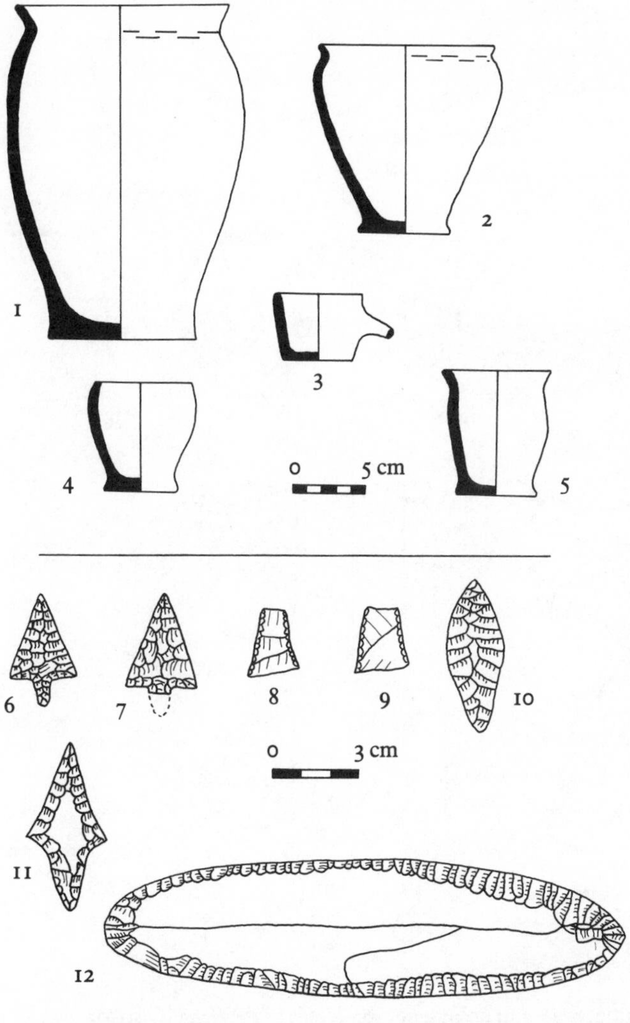

FIGURE 4.3. Pottery and flintwork of the Seine-Oise-Marne group.
1-5 Seine-Oise-Marne flat-based coarse pottery (all from funerary contexts): 1 Les Mureaux (Seine-et-Oise) (*allée couverte*); 2 Le Petit-Morin (Marne) (*hypogée*); 3 Tours-sur-Marne (Marne) (funerary pit); 4 Champignolles, Flavacourt (Oise) (*allée couverte*); 5 Vauréal (Seine-et-Oise) (*allée couverte*).
6 and 7 barbed-and-tanged arrowheads from the *allée couverte* of La Croix des Cosaques, Châlons-sur-Marne (Marne).
8 and 9 tranchet arrowheads from funerary contexts: 8 Montigny-Esbly, Lesches (Seine-et-Marne); 9 Coppières, Montreuil-sur-Epte (Seine-et-Marne).
10 leaf-shaped arrowhead from the *hypogée* of Le Petit-Morin (Marne);
11 tanged arrowhead from the *allée couverte* of Argenteuil 1 (Seine-et-Oise); 12 blade of Grand Pressigny flint from a *hypogée* at Les Ronces, Villevenard (Marne). (After Bailloud, 1974.)

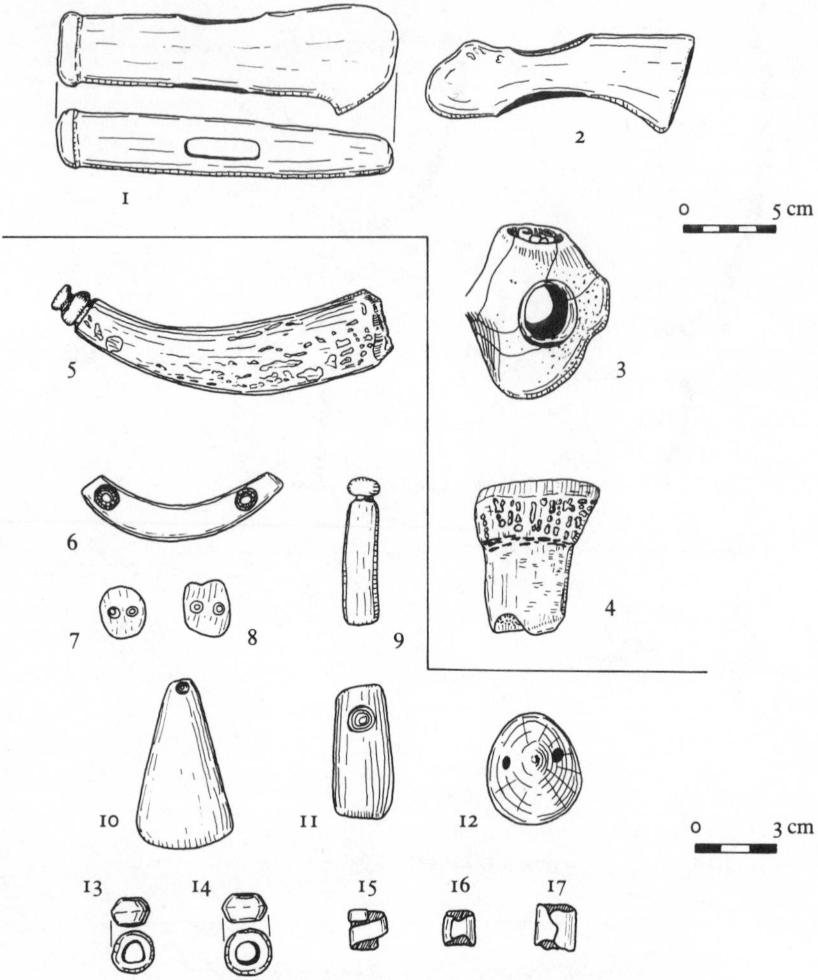

FIGURE 4.4. Antlerwork and ornament type-fossils of the Seine-Oise-Marne group. 1 antler battle-axe from the *allée couverte* of La Justice, Presles (Seine-et-Oise); 2 antler sleeve from tomb at Saint-Etienne-du-Vauvray (Eure); 3 antler mace-head from the *allée couverte* of La Pierre Plate, Presles (Seine-et-Oise); 4 antler sleeve from the settlement of Les Roches, Videlles (Essonne); 5 antler pendant (?) from the settlement of Les Roches; 6 *pendentif arciforme* of schist from a *hypogée* at Les Ronces, Villevenard (Marne); 7,8 perforated beads of nacre from (7) the tomb of Barbonne-Fayel (Marne) and (8) the *hypogée* of Cornembaux, Congy (Marne); 9 antler pendant from Congy (Marne); 10, 11 *haches pendeloques* from (10) the *allée couverte* of Argenteuil 1 (Seine-et-Oise) and (11) the *allée couverte* of Vauréal (Seine-et-Oise); 12 perforated *Patella* shell from the *allée couverte* of Les Mureaux (Seine-et-Oise); 13, 14 biconical bone beads from the *allée couverte* of La Justice; 15-17 copper beads from the *hypogées* at Courjeonnet (Marne). (After Bailloud, 1974.)

between 10 and 30mm the pot narrows briefly before swelling out to a wide belly, then contracting towards the base. These vessels are, on average, between 150 and 250mm tall. The main stylistic variations concern the height of the neck. Flat-based, handled 'soup-bowls' also occur. In general, however, lugs, handles and decoration are absent although a few sherds with simple impressions have been found. Parallels for this pottery have been seen by some to lie in the late Michelsberg and its successors in the Rhineland and Switzerland (Bailloud, 1974, 224).

Grand-Pressigny flint. A characteristic list of material recovered from an artefact scatter divides into that in which the community was locally self-sufficient and that which had to be imported. On SOM sites the latter predominantly takes the form of personal ornaments and objects which, at face value, are prime candidates for being identified as prestige goods. For the bulk of their requirements the SOM settlements were self-sufficient.

The honey-coloured iron-rich flint from the valleys of the Claise and Creuse at Le Grand-Pressigny (Indre-et-Loire) appears, however, in SOM contexts, as an exotic item. Despite earlier claims for a middle neolithic origin (Clark, 1952, 250), the main associations of this flint are of late neolithic date. At the maximum of its distribution it can be found as far north as the Netherlands, and here at least it appears to pre-date the appearance of metal artefacts (Lanting *et al.*, 1973). In northern France it was probably current for longer. The principal products are long daggers or lance-heads, which can be in excess of 100mm in length. Like the long blades which were also made in this flint they exhibit steep and elaborate pressure flaking along their edges. Sickle-elements have also been found in Grand-Pressigny flint. The large cores known from their shape as *livres de beurre* are occasionally present. All of these objects occur in artefact scatters, in graves, and as stray finds.

Arrowheads. The SOM has the widest range of arrowheads of any northern French neolithic group. Tranchet, leaf-shaped, triangular, lozenge and amygdaloid arrowheads are frequent finds. The diversity of types and their discovery as stray finds, often overlying former mesolithic hunting sites, suggests that hunting was an important element in the Late Neolithic. The most characteristic arrowhead is the barbed-and-tanged. Two chronologically successive forms have been recognised: rounded- and straight-edged. The latter are generally thought to be of early bronze age date. They measure between 30 and 50mm in length and are frequently finely worked.

Axes. Both flint and polished-stone axes are found in this region but they are difficult to assign to a chronological period. Their highly functional nature and short life-time seem to have produced few diagnostic eccentricities in their shapes. Most occur as stray finds. The long, narrow-edged polished-stone axes known as the Chevennes type appear to date to the Late Neolithic, however, as do the large axes with slight flattening of the edges often found in the Aisne. Some axes seem to imitate metal types and it is at this period that the number of jade axes in circulation appears to reach its maximum. Nevertheless, despite the great variety of rocks represented in SOM assemblages, hardstone artefacts are found less frequently than flint artefacts.

Ornaments. Another marked feature of the SOM is the increased number and variety of personal ornaments. These occur both in graves and on settlement sites. Nine major categories can be identified. One of the most frequent finds is the *hache pendeloque*. This is a small axe, 40–60mm long, with a perforation at the narrower end. *Haches pendeloques* are always made of hardstone rather than flint. Although many occur as stray finds they are also frequent in tombs, especially in the north-western part of the Paris basin. A second class of ornament consists of pendants in the form of between a third and a quarter of a circle (*pendentifs arciformes*). They are usually perforated at each end but examples with only a single perforation are known. They appear to have been made from fragments of schist bracelets or other broken ornaments. Amongst the antler ornaments are some curious pendants, 50–60mm in length. These are polished and rounded at one end, this end being separated from the main body of the object by a groove. Other objects of a more diverse shape occur in bone. Shells and teeth also appear to have been used as pendants and there are numerous finds of beads. A very few of these are of copper.

Antler. The antler hafts and antler-axes are among the most characteristic artefacts of this period. The most common type of haft is the sleeve with a transverse perforation. The axes also have transverse perforations and the butt is often carved into the shape of a button. Both types occur as stray finds and have frequently been found in dredging operations in the major rivers.

Other flint objects. The final characteristic type of artefact is the spokeshave-like piece known, after the pronounced notch at each end, as the *scie-à-encoche*. These are likely to have been used in composite sickle blades. Although the working of these artefacts and of many of the others examined is often of a fine quality, late neolithic flint-working frequently produces large, rough pieces. These are generally known by the terms *Campignien* or *Montmorencien*, depending on whether the artefact is made of flint or sandstone-chert (*grès*). There has been much confusion over the dating of such objects; it is now known that the flint manufacturing technique they represent is even associated with later Bandkeramik material (particularly in Normandy). Recent work has shown that the Campignien is not a cultural but a technological phenomenon. It was developed in many areas of Europe at different times and was associated with the exploitation of extensive flint deposits. In northern France, the Late Neolithic saw the widespread exploitation of local flint sources, often on a large scale.

Metal and Beakers. Towards the end of the 3rd millennium bc many areas of Europe began to produce elaborately decorated pottery (Corded Ware/Beakers). This was closely followed in most of those areas by the appearance of metal products and metallurgy. The Paris basin, however, did not participate in these developments, and the first metal objects here are rare finds of hammered copper beads probably imported from the Rhineland. More exceptional is the tanged dagger from the site of Les Mureaux (Seine-et-Oise; m.r.29) (Bailloud, 1974, 327–8), but the total number of sites producing metal at this period is only eleven. Similarly, remains of Beakers or associated grave-goods such as archers' wrist guards are rare in north-eastern France. Only one pure Beaker assemblage is known from this region: a single-grave inhumation at La Ferme de Champagne (Augy, Yonne; m.r.30). Here a young adult and child were found buried with three beakers and three barbed-and-tanged arrowheads (Kapps and Bailloud, 1960). Elements of the so-called 'Beaker package' of artefacts have occasionally been found in SOM tombs but do not form a consistent part of these assemblages.

CHRONOLOGY. The scarcity of excavated sites and the lack of long stratigraphical sequences mean that there is no basis for internal periodisation of the SOM. The periodisation used by Itten was derived from the site of Videlles (Itten, 1970, 60–2). Here there appeared to be a sequence based on typological changes in the antler-hafts. The lower levels had hafts with sleeves (*à talon*), and the upper levels had hafts with sockets (*à douille*). This periodisation must be treated with caution as it is based on very few artefacts. The radiocarbon dates (see list at end of chapter) present a number of problems. In dealing with collective tombs which have been subject to successive disturbances, it is rare to find a sample which dates the construction of the monument, rather than its use. Nevertheless, taken as a whole the dates available suggest a *floruit* from the last quarter of the 3rd to the second quarter of the 2nd millennium bc. There are, however, a number of dates which suggest that the beginning of SOM should be placed perhaps as early as the first quarter of the 3rd millennium bc. Traces of the culture can also be extended beyond the middle of the 2nd millennium and it has recently been suggested (Cahen and De Laet, 1980) that it continues into what elsewhere is already the Middle or even the Late Bronze Age.

Difficulties are also associated with the use of artefactual evidence for dating. The essential features of the Middle Neolithic (decorated pottery and ditched enclosures) have parallels in the later Bandkeramik tradition. Chasséen pottery, for example, seems to appear in the Paris basin as one among a range of pottery styles available to Epi-Rössen groups. Evidence for continuity from the Middle Neolithic to the SOM, on the other hand, has never been obvious. Recent work in the Oise (Blanchet and Decormeille, 1980) has suggested that middle neolithic decorated ware may relate to a relatively short phase at the beginning of the period, much as Arnal suggested in 1953. If this is so it can only sharpen the apparent dissimilarity between the Middle and the Late Neolithic. A later phase of the Middle Neolithic in the Oise, in which the pottery has less decoration and large necked jars appear, may reduce the starkness of this discontinuity. However, SOM material has not been found in great quantity above middle neolithic occupation layers and there is in general no late neolithic interest in the maintenance of the middle neolithic defended enclosures.

In contrast there is no secure artefactual evidence to define the end of the SOM. A 3rd millennium artefact scatter is almost completely indistinguishable from a 2nd millennium scatter. The stratified site of Fort-Harrouard (Eure-et-

Loire; m.r.15) is therefore of great interest. A second occupation, undated by radiocarbon but presumably 'Early Bronze Age', contains pots with sinuous profiles and frequent geometric decoration. These have traditionally been compared with the *Artenacien* of west-central France (Scarre, Chapter 8). SOM-type artefacts occur alongside with the pottery (Philippe, 1936, 1937). At Videlles, the post-SOM levels also show a wider variety of pottery forms, and the re-appearance of, for example, lugs (Bailloud, 1958). As already noted, the rare Beakers found in this region have come from 'native' SOM contexts.

SETTLEMENT

STUDIES, PATTERNS, AND PROCESS. One of the most influential studies of settlement change in neolithic Europe has been that of Janusz Kruk of the Polish Academy of Sciences, Krakow (1973; English edition 1980). His analysis of how settlement patterns changed on the loess uplands of southern Poland has become the classic model for the interpretation of this period elsewhere in Europe (e.g. Whittle, 1977). In essence, he showed how a pattern of settlement rooted in the Early Neolithic or Bandkeramik, based, at first, on naturally fertilised valley-bottom niches and only later on plateau-edges and promontories, was transformed in the Late Neolithic into an extensive, dispersed system based on the plateau soils themselves. The date of this change can be placed in the second quarter of the 3rd millennium bc. The same horizon can be distinguished in other areas of Europe. De Laet, for example, has demonstrated a similarly radical change in the Late Neolithic of the Low Countries (De Laet, 1974) and the results of recent work by Whittle (1977), Bradley (1978) and Burgess (1980) suggest that changes of a comparable magnitude were occurring in Britain as well. Andrew Sherratt has suggested that this horizon marks what has been called the *Secondary Products Revolution* (1981). This involved, first, the use of wheeled vehicles and the plough in extensive systems of agriculture; and second, the use of sheep for wool and cows for milk. The first of these changes seems to have been associated with the colonisation of the plateau and a possible shift from a cereal economy based on ground water to one based on rain water. For prehistoric Europe, the Late Neolithic marked a major change in economic development.

Following the work of Sielmann (1972), neolithic settlement patterns have been seen in terms of *Siedlungskammern* or settlement cells. These are most easily recognisable in the Bandkeramik period when they appear on the distribution map as tight clusters of settlement sites, but the middle neolithic pattern appears also to be based on these clusters. The common Bandkeramik tradition helps to explain the similarity of many aspects of middle neolithic material culture in different areas (Whittle, 1977). To the west of the Rhine, the *Siedlungskammer* is the arc of lowland plain which runs from the Dutch Limburn down to the Loire. In the Bandkeramik this is distinguished by the distribution of Limburg ware as far south as the Aisne valley and later by the distribution of the material of the Villeneuve-Blicquy group (Constantin and Demarez, 1981; see Ilett, this volume). Similarly, after a probably short

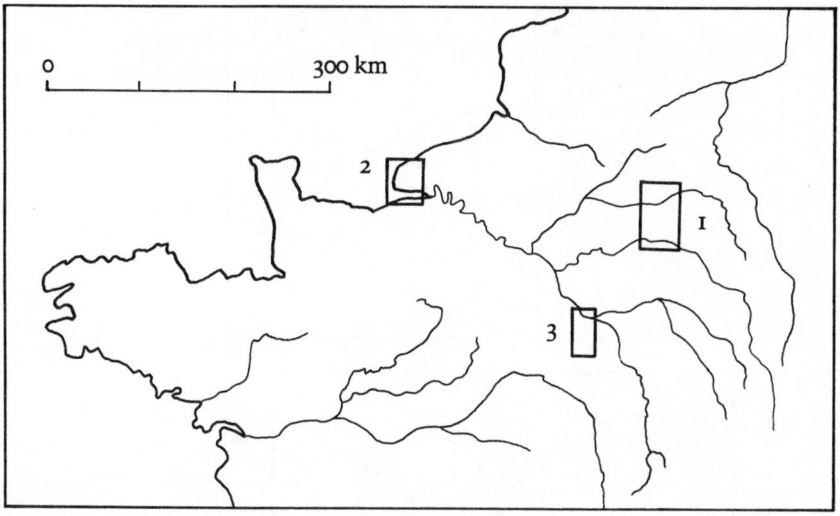

FIGURE 4.5. Northern France, showing the location of the three study-areas. 1 the Aisne-Marne area; 2 the Seine estuary; 3 the Loing valley.

period of Chasséen-type decoration, the principal links of the Paris basin Middle Neolithic are with the Michelsberg tradition to the east. The Belgian Michelsberg group, which extends into northern France, was one of the earliest regional groups within this tradition to be identified. It is not, perhaps, surprising to find that this arc of settlement maintained its common traditions into the Late Neolithic, in the form of the SOM culture.

Neat settlement cells are no longer readily discernible. Expansion onto, for example, the Champagne has occurred, but the broad underlying continuity is still apparent. Many authors have tried to carve off aspects of SOM material culture and to search for parallels for each one within the diverse repertoire of late neolithic western Europe, thus turning the SOM into a pot-pourri of late neolithic cultures. This has been most acute in regard to the tombs. Yet, as De Laet (1967) has shown, the essential features of this period can be traced back to a local middle neolithic ancestry.

Between 1978 and 1982, the present writer examined neolithic settlement patterns in three areas of northern France (Fig.4.5). These were (i) the area between the rivers Aisne and Marne to the east of Soissons; (ii) the Seine estuary at Le Havre and as far east as Lillebonne; and, (iii) the Loing valley. Examination of the flint scatters revealed a palimpsest of late neolithic sites in these areas. A site typology allowed the recognition of sites of different functions, and the particular location of these in different landscape zones or on particular soil-types, etc., showed the full extent of a complex SOM economy. From evidence around the upper headwaters of the Ourcq near Fère-en-Tardenois it appeared that the scatter sites could best be interpreted as individual family huts, loosely grouped around a common burial focus. This has been called the *Expanded Village Pattern* (Howell, 1983).

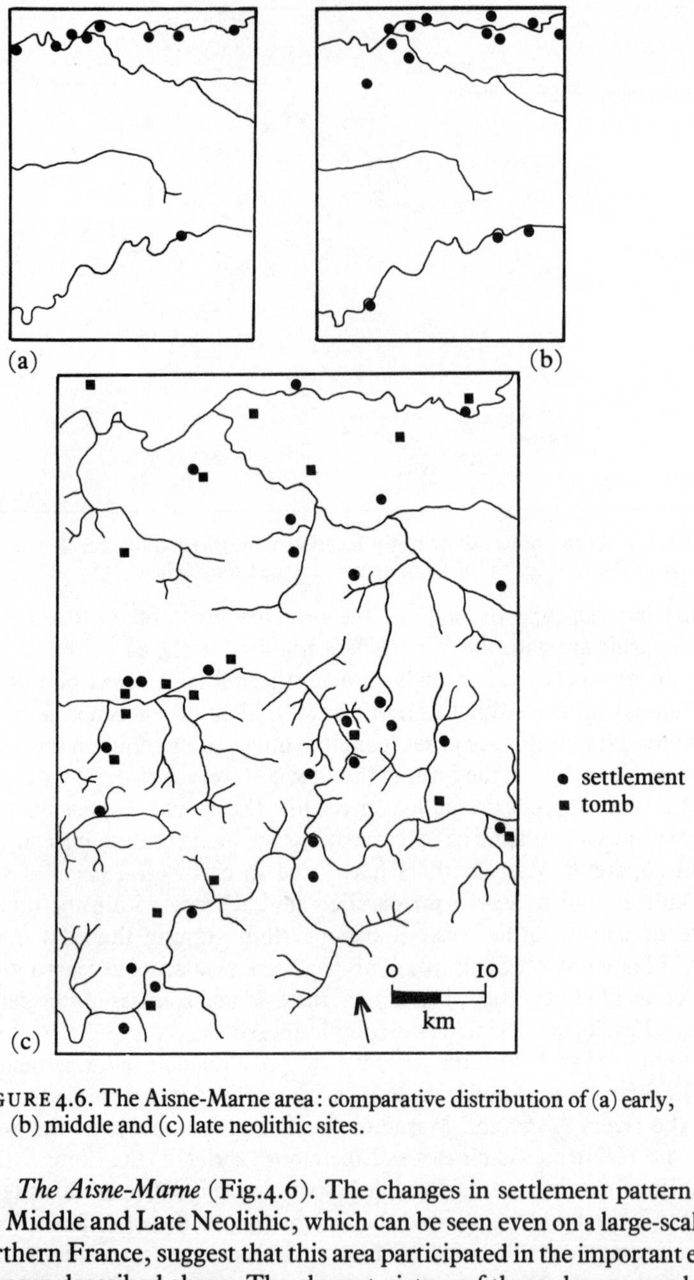

FIGURE 4.6. The Aisne-Marne area: comparative distribution of (a) early, (b) middle and (c) late neolithic sites.

The Aisne-Marne (Fig.4.6). The changes in settlement pattern between the Middle and Late Neolithic, which can be seen even on a large-scale map of northern France, suggest that this area participated in the important economic changes described above. The clearest picture of these changes can be seen in the region between the Aisne and the Marne (Parent, 1971). This lies just off the main arc of the Champagne and its dissected landscape is characteristic of much of the Paris basin. In Figure 4.6 the distributions of early, middle and late neolithic sites have been compared. The early neolithic Bandkeramik sites are restricted to islands of alluvium in the valley-bottoms, and this pattern continues into the Middle Neolithic, though information from other valleys in the Paris basin, particularly the Oise and the Seine, suggests that by the Middle Neolithic a bimodal pattern based both on the continued exploitation of valley-bottoms and the colonisation of promontories and plateau-edges was more usual. The economy of these periods has been reconstructed plausibly as fixed-plot horticulture of a naturally intensive kind. One of the features shared by the valley-bottom and plateau-edge locations is the presence of high ground water. In the case of the former this is provided by periodic floods and by hill-wash from the plateau behind. In the case of the latter it is provided by the sources of small streams which occur at the plateau-edge spring-line. Figure 4.6 shows how radical in these terms the late neolithic change in site distribution was. The late neolithic pattern can be broken down still further (Fig.4.7). A simple site-typology suggests that different types of site were located in different landscapes. The first type, settlement sites represented by large scatters of artefacts, show a preference for the plateau, while tombs, the second type, show a preference for valley slopes. This pattern is also reflected in the distribution of stray axes and stray arrowheads. The axes tend to be found on the plateau and often well away from its edges. An examination of the relationship of the sites to soil-types is instructive. Modern soils have been used in this analysis but only after a critical examination of the ways in which they are likely to have changed between the Neolithic and the present day (Howell, 1983). In the areas between the Rivers Aisne and Marne the following pattern was observed:

Table 4.1. Percentages of late neolithic sites by soil types in the Aisne-Marne area

	Settlements	Tombs	Arrowheads	Axes
Alluvium	8	10	0	5
Calcareous brown earth	0	0	3	5
Lessivated brown earth	69	30	58	75
Rendzina	20	60	29	10
Podzols	4	0	10	5

Statistical tests were conducted on these figures to see whether the patterns were random; that is, whether they were what one might have expected from the varying proportions of the different soils present. This appeared to be the case only with the axes. In the other cases, there was a heavy bias of sites towards the rendzina soils and the brown earths although the arrowheads also showed a bias towards podzolised soils. In fact, almost 30 per cent of stray arrowheads occurred on the sites of earlier mesolithic occupation. The large number of late mesolithic, Tardenoisien sites which occur on sandy formations, now podzolised, has frequently been commented on (Rozoy, 1978) and often described as the '*loi des sables*'. The finding of late neolithic arrowheads in

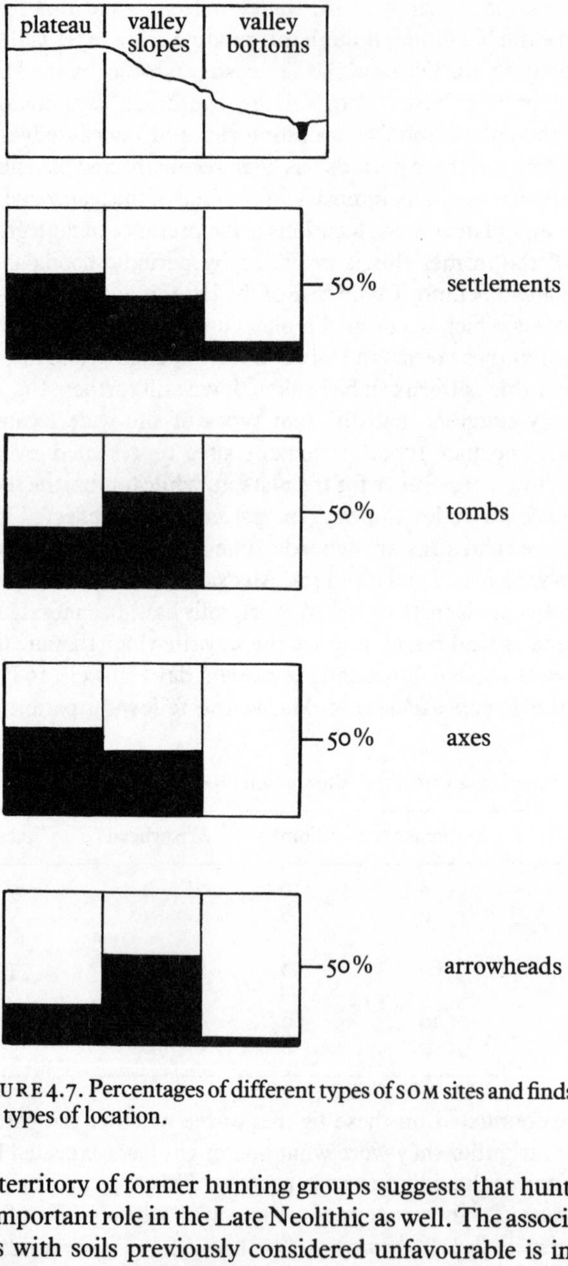

FIGURE 4.7. Percentages of different types of SOM sites and finds in different types of location.

the territory of former hunting groups suggests that hunting may have played an important role in the Late Neolithic as well. The association of late neolithic sites with soils previously considered unfavourable is interesting. However, rendzina soils have a rich A horizon, and where they are thick they are well able to support cereal production. The plateau is now the granary of northern France. In these latter areas the soils are heavily influenced by loess; in contrast to Dutch Limburg and the Rhineland, the loess formations of northern France are restricted to areas of plateau interior.

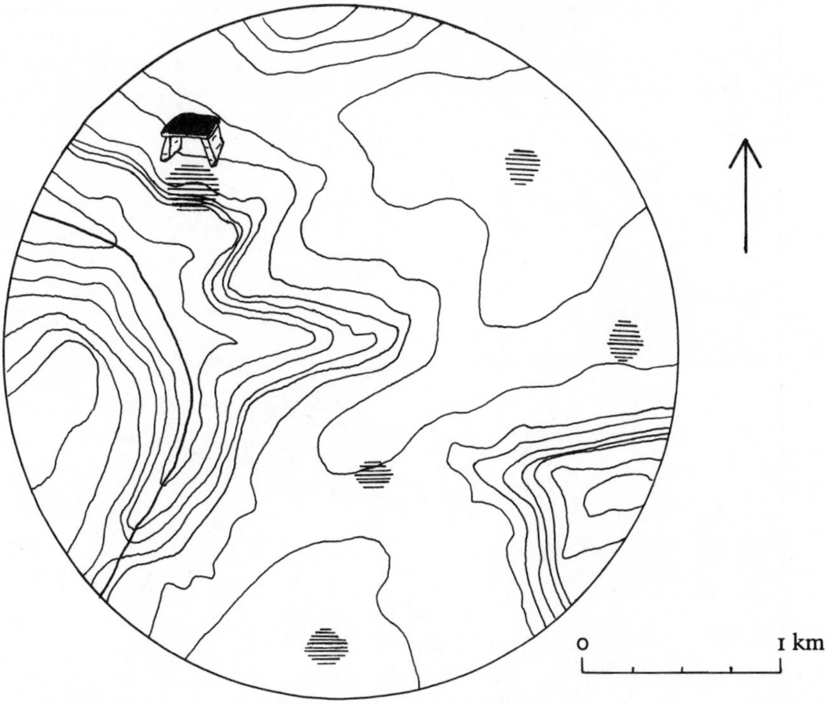

FIGURE 4.8. Distribution of SOM settlement sites (hatched) and tomb at Serches (Aisne).

A number of particular case-studies confirm the SOM interest in the plateau. At Tannières (Aisne; m.r.10) the finds occur in a line across the centre of the plateau. The area is dry, and the distance to the nearest current flowing water source is in some places as much as 1km. At Serches (Aisne; m.r.11) a number of small flint scatters occur across the plateau. These seem to be related to the tomb found on the western side of this distribution (Fig.4.8). In the region as a whole, however, by far the densest concentration of sites is found along the upper reaches of the Ourcq after its descent through the Tardenois. Forty-six per cent of all the late neolithic sites discovered between the Aisne and the Marne occur along the Ourcq, in what amounts to only 13 per cent of the land area. Here a classic example of an Expanded Village Pattern is to be found at Vaux (Neuilly-Saint-Front, Aisne; m.r.9) (Fig.4.9). The tomb is located on an area of flat ground at the head of a stream. The bowl-like structure opens only to the north. Scatters of late neolithic material occur around this tomb at distances of several kilometres, either on the plateau itself or on its edges.

The Seine estuary (Fig.4.10). Many recent settlement models have been developed in areas with strong contrast in relief and where no single economic constraint is obvious. Around the Seine estuary the amount of land available

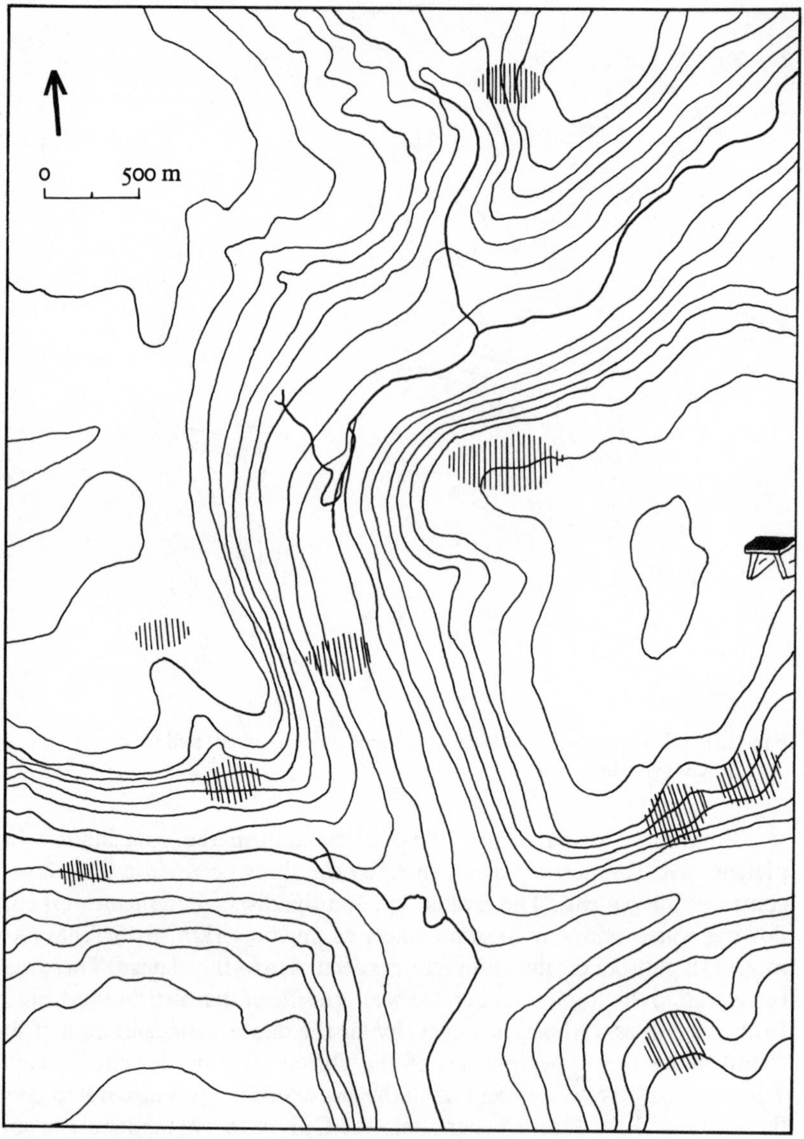

FIGURE 4.9. Distribution of SOM settlement sites (hatched) and tomb at Vaux (Aisne).

for settlement is restricted by the dryness of the central plateau of the Pays de Caux. To the west, sharp cliff formations provide a natural boundary and to the south the wide expanse of the estuary limits settlement. The marine resources of the estuary and their changing quality between periods of rising and falling sea-level acted as a focus for prehistoric interest. Briefly, periods of rising sea-level would have produced large areas of sand and mud on which salt-

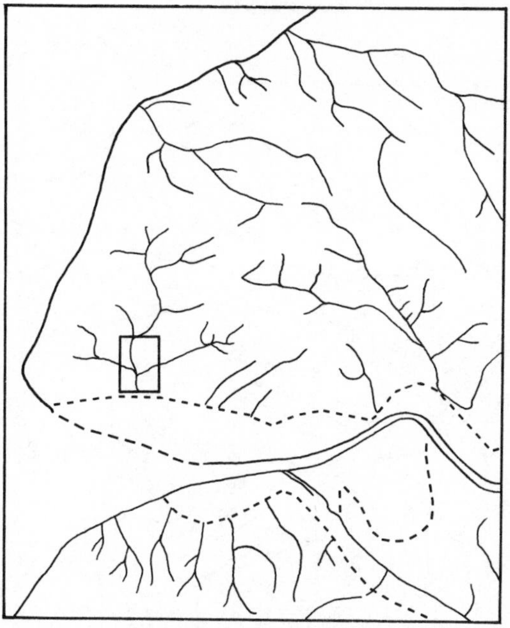

FIGURE 4.10. The Seine estuary. Tidal limits are indicated by broken lines. The box marks the location of Figure 4.11.

meadows and mud-flats could develop. Conversely, in periods of falling sea-level fresh-water bogs would have formed, separating areas of coastal fishing from dry land by large areas of marsh. Late neolithic material occurs either in the top of the early Sub-boreal peat or in the sandy deposits which cover it. This is the period of the deposition of the Upper Blue Sands in the Somme (Agache *et al.*, 1963).

In this area sites are found both on the shore and on the plateau behind. Many of the former are shell-middens, but the plateau sites of, for example, the Fôret de Montgeon (Seine-Maritime; m.r.27) take the form of the now familiar small scatters of artefacts. The organisation of these sites into a seasonal patern of exploitation may be inferred from the fish remains. On the coastal sites, species such as salmon and sturgeon suggest an occupation of the shore in spring-autumn. Low-lying areas here freeze over in winter even today. To the east, however, the pattern resembles more and more that discovered in the Aisne. At Montivilliers small scatters are spread across a variety of landscape zones (Fig.4.11). One of these, La Grande Epauville, has recently been excavated. Between 1977 and 1979 300m^2 were excavated. The excavator (Watté, 1976) has suggested that the bands of flint nodules recovered are the remains of a small trapezoidal structure measuring 12×9m. The site lies on the plateau about 250m from its edge. At Lillebonne, the sites show a clear preference for a plateau location. Funerary sites are rare in this area but there are indications in the survival of place-names such as *La Table du Mal Dîner*

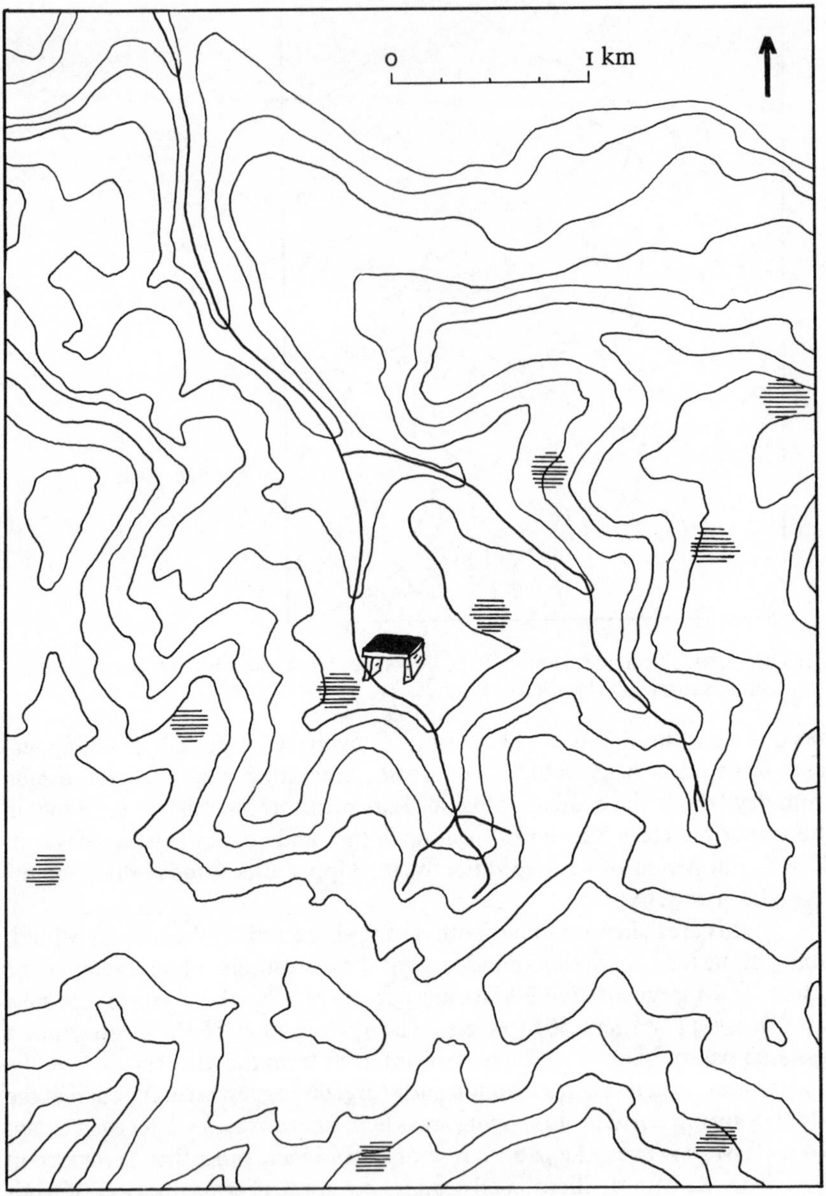

FIGURE 4.11. Distribution of SOM settlement sites (hatched) and tomb at Montivilliers (Seine-Maritime).

that their absence is a bias of agricultural activity and consequent destruction. The relationship of these sites to soil-types follows a pattern similar to the one examined in the Aisne. There is again a strong preference for rendzina soils. The distribution of stray axes confirms the general pattern of location of these

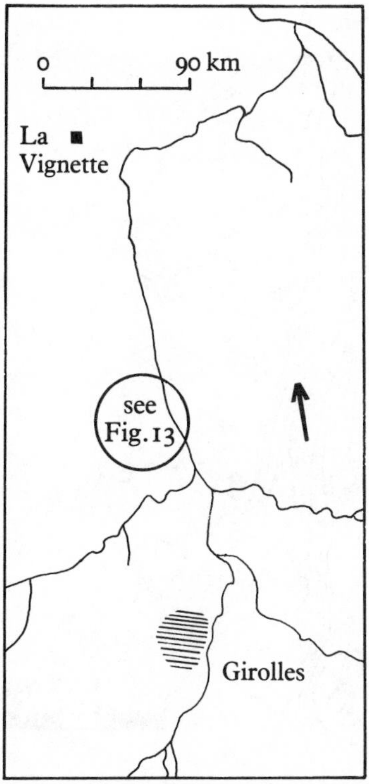

FIGURE 4.12. The Loing valley, showing the position of Figure 4.13.

artefacts. Compared with other areas of the Paris basin, the Seine estuary is poor in late neolithic evidence. Variations in the intensity and nature of fieldwork may be partly responsible. It should be noted, however, that this was not an area of intense early and middle neolithic settlement either; no Bandkeramik sites have been found here at all. The Seine estuary falls between two areas of more dense settlement: the *département* of Nord and the Plain of Caen. Without the foundation of early neolithic settlement the poverty of later neolithic settlement is more easily explicable. In the Aisne, the spread of late neolithic settlement represents the infilling of certain landscape zones in areas already long occupied. At the Seine estuary the evidence suggests the continued colonisation of new areas even into the 3rd millennium bc.

The Loing valley. In contrast to the two areas just discussed, the Loing valley (Fig.4.12) has produced evidence of a more industrial group of late neolithic sites based on the exploitation of flint outcrops at Les Portes Rouges, Girolles (Loiret; m.r.12). Where settlements can be identified, however, they follow the pattern of the other areas in being found well onto the plateau, away from its edges. Stray finds of axes extend the distribution into a variety of landscape zones. The exploitation of flint at Girolles appears to have begun in the late Neolithic. The site now covers many hectares, mostly as scatters of

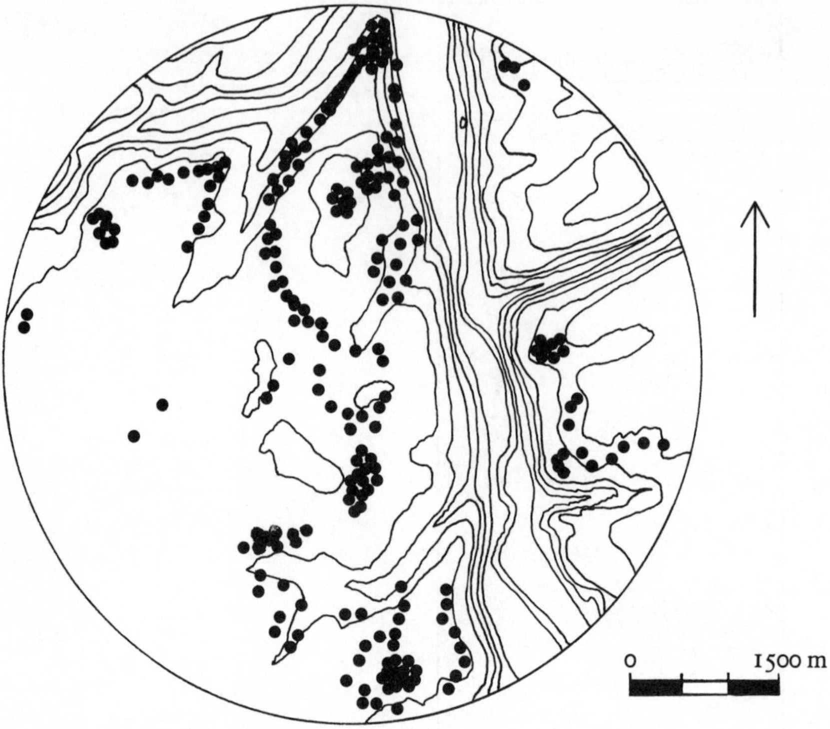

FIGURE 4.13. Distribution of SOM sites to the north of Girolles (Loiret). Dots show sites with 10-30 finds.

waste material. In recent years the tops of what are likely to have been three extraction pits have been found. The distribution of the flint is not wide. Although found in the Seine valley, it was being produced principally for local use in the Loing valley itself. To the north of the mining site a number of late neolithic scatters were recognised by Nougier (1950). Figure 4.13 shows how careful fieldwork has enabled these to be defined as discrete sites. Although the presence of querns and scrapers indicates that these sites were in part domestic (i.e. settlements), the workshop aspect of many of them was recognised as long ago as 1940 (Nouel, 1940). It is not, however, only Girolles flint which occurs on them. The site at La Vignette in the Fontainebleau forest is a Montmorencien site (Tarrête, 1977). The settlement of the valley should therefore be seen in terms of the exploitation both of flint and of sandstone-chert (*grès*).

MODELLING THE EXPANDED VILLAGE PATTERN. In assessing the amount of land required to support one settlement, an estimate has been made of a maximum of ten people per scatter of finds. Such a small size is borne out by the size of those sites that have been excavated. Earlier estimates of the land required to support an individual have averaged around 1–1½ha per group of six individuals, but Hassan (1981) has shown that swidden systems may support as many as 275–300 people per square kilometre. The example he quotes from a predynastic Egyptian context suggests a requirement of 164kg of wheat and barley per person per year. Such wide differences between figures are not surprising in view of the differences in environments and agricultural techniques. If the lower limit of 2½ha for ten people is applied to the settlement system around Vaux (Fig.4.9) the availability of land suggests that all the sites could have been contemporary. If the upper figure of 64ha is applied, between 5 and 7 of the 9 or so sites could have been contemporary. These figures take no account of other food sources and they represent opposing extremes. Even at its most extreme, however, the Expanded Village is unlikely to have consisted of more than 100 people. The occupation of each small site may be estimated to have lasted 50–55 years. A deposit of 200 inhumations, a figure not uncommon among the *allées couvertes* and pits, would, on the basis of the figures quoted above, indicate a life of 200–300 years for the village as a whole.

A form of extensive slash-and-burn is indicated at this period by the occurrence of layers of charcoal in late neolithic (not middle neolithic *pace* Howell, 1982) clearance phases in Brittany (Morzadec-Kerfourn, 1976). The organisation of this in a form of swiddening may be inferred from the small size and short duration of the flint scatters compared with the lengthy occupation of the tombs. Pollen diagrams associated with SOM tombs have suggested a figure of 30–75 per cent arboreal pollen. This figure is consistent with an expansive, colonising settlement system located on the forest edge. The distribution of axes further onto the plateau tends to confirm this. The forest-fringe environment is consistent with the evidence of an economy largely based on pig.

In a recent study, Poulain (1973) has tried to take a long-term view of the economic evidence to show that certain areas tended to specialise in particular domestic species for long periods of, if not throughout, later prehistory. In the Paris basin, the dominant neolithic domesticates are cattle and pig, and the change from the Middle to the Late Neolithic is marked by the rise in the importance of one element (pig) over the other. The type of site from which the bones come changes over time. In the Bandkeramik, the sources are domestic sites with longhouses; in the Middle Neolithic the bones come from the ditches of enclosures; but in the Late Neolithic, almost all the evidence comes from funerary monuments. Nevertheless, at Videlles and in the later rampart at Marcilly-sur-Tille (Côte-d'Or; m.r.31) an increase in the quantity of pig remains is attested at this period. Pig was also found at Etauville (Eure-et-Loir; m.r.16), Noisy-sur-Ecole (Seine-et-Marne; m.r.21) and Bardouville (Seine-Maritime; m.r.17) (Nouel *et al.*, 1965; Brezillon *et al.*, 1973; Caillard *et al.*, 1967). High percentages of wild animals and of dogs are also characteristic. Dogs have been seen (Bökönyi, 1974) as an important element of a pig-based economy. In regard to cereal cultivation, identifications of grains have been made at the following sites: Germigny l'Evêque (Seine-et-Marne), Marolles-sur-Seine (Seine-et-Marne; m.r.13), Guiry-en-Vexin (Val-d'Oise; m.r.22) and Etauville.

The overall picture of the SOM economy is one of diversity, but it can be

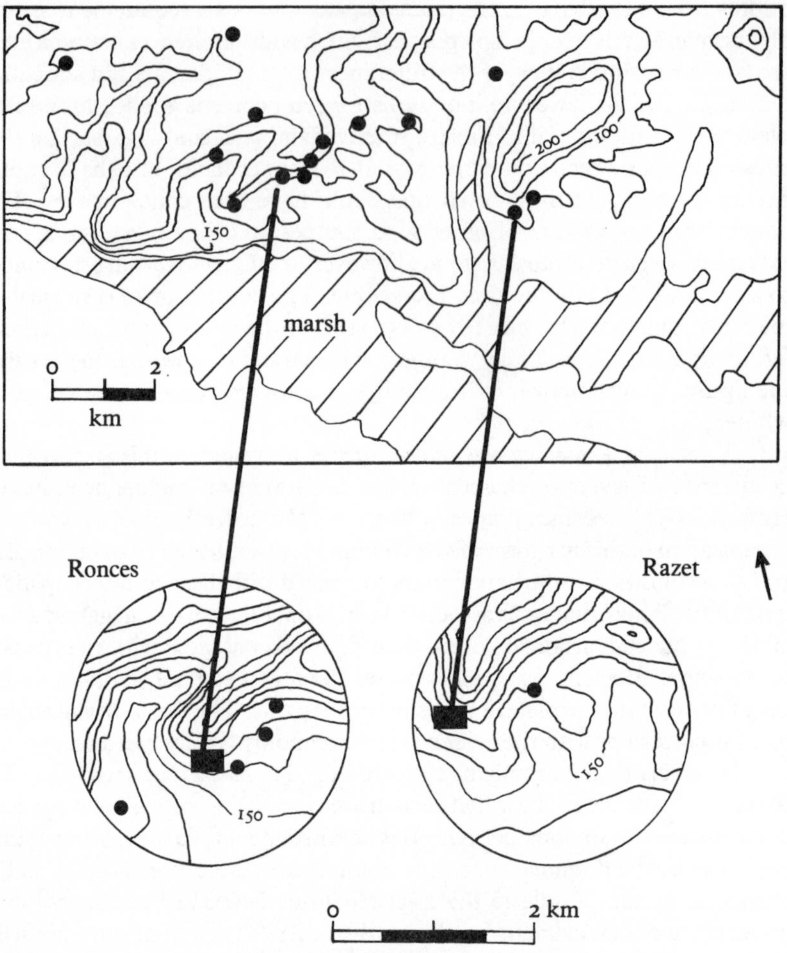

FIGURE 4.14. Late neolithic cemeteries (rectangles) and artefact scatters (dots) in the area of the Marais-Saint-Gond (Marne).

suggested that, like Horgen, SOM was a culture of swine-herders. This fact holds the key to the longevity of the SOM settlement system. As Lewthwaite has demonstrated, pigs are a more efficient converter of plant matter into protein than sheep, for example, and in south-west Iberia and Corsica they were managed in an extensive manner through what has been called an 'acorn-hog economy' (Lewthwaite, 1981).

John Peek has recently published a study of the megalithic monuments of the Paris basin (Peek, 1975). In using this information to see whether the patterns examined above have a wider application, a number of points should be borne in mind. First, megalithic monuments are not the only burial places with SOM material. Some SOM tombs are simple pits. Second, although the earliest megaliths in the Paris basin seem to date to the SOM period it is possible

British Museum Society

that a few in the west may be earlier. Third, SOM tombs have a locational bias towards the slopes and are not entirely representative of the settlement distribution. Nevertheless, statistical tests of Peek's tomb data against soils in the Paris basin produced an identical picture to that obtained from the Aisne and from the Seine estuary. The rendzinas and plateau-soils were again heavily favoured.

In contrast to the scattered pattern of tombs examined above, a dense concentration of SOM material occurs around the source of the Petit-Morin river at the Marais-Saint-Gond (Marne; m.r.8). Within about 275km^2 no fewer than 102 tombs occur. At Razet the tombs are grouped in a large cemetery arranged with uniform orientation in rows – an implication of some social cohesion at least. The concentration of tombs and this organisation suggests a monumental character comparable with centralised sites elsewhere in Europe at this period but totally absent in the rest of the Paris basin. The settlement sites, however, are still represented only by small flint scatters. The tombs tend to be located on the slopes of the plateau overlooking the marsh below, while the flint scatters are higher up on the plateau-edge. With such commanding views of the marsh, an economic emphasis on wild life should be expected and it is in the extent of this economic focus and its location in a constricted landscape at the junction of a major east-west route that the explanation may perhaps be found for this unusual density of sites.

Conclusions

The bimodal distribution of the later Bandkeramik, based on valley-bottoms and plateau-edges, persisted into the Middle Neolithic with few developments. The dispersal of sites across other landscape zones from the beginning of the SOM period is therefore all the more striking. The evidence for associating this move with the widespread use of the plough and the increased economic independence this would have afforded to individual family groups has been discussed elsewhere (Sherratt, 1981). It has been adopted here as the paradigm to explain the dispersed nature of SOM settlement patterns. A more important consequence of this change would however have been its impact on water budgeting and irrigation strategies. At no period of the Neolithic is there any evidence for man-made irrigation systems in this area, but the expansion from the earlier settlement pattern does mark a significant change in the availability of water for cultivation. The rich, meadow soils of the lower alluvial terrace are well watered both by the rise in the river level and subsequent flooding each spring and by run-off from the slopes behind. Water shortage is unlikely to have been a problem for cereal cultivation. Similarly, the most characteristic feature of the plateau-edge is the presence of a spring-line. In contrast, both the rendzinas and the plateau loess soils are dry. One of the clearer climatic features of northern France, however, is the increased amount of rainfall on the plateau as compared with the valley bottoms. On a yearly average this could mean an increase of 100mm, although nearer the coast the figure is much greater. Most of this rain falls in heavy showers in the autumn. The colonisation of these areas may therefore indicate a change from ground-water dependent cultivation to rain-water dependent cultivation. This conclusion is not new. Kruk's settlement evidence pointed in the same direction and Sherratt has recently reviewed the problem in a wider context (1979). In addition, the move onto the plateau could mark a change from spring-grown crops taking advantage of early floods, to winter-grown crops taking advantage of the autumnal rainfall maximum and pre-winter ploughing to break up the soil.

In summary, the SOM settlement pattern was open and expansive. With the exception of the Marais-Saint-Gond cluster, settlement takes the form of dispersed flint scatters. These did not exist in isolation but were centred on a communal, collective burial-place. While there is variety in site-size there is no real evidence for a developed site hierarchy. Without excavation it is difficult to tell whether these sites represent single- or multiple-period occupations and without an internal chronology the number of sites which are strictly contemporary cannot be ascertained. The same pattern can be distinguished around the Seine estuary, though there it was adapted to take account of the greater exploitation of coastal resources.

The diversity of the economy has already been indicated. An increase in hunting is reflected both in the faunal record and in the artefact assemblages. This diversity is indicative of the efficient exploitation of the new environments into which the SOM expanded. Clearance phases in pollen diagrams from Brittany show that the Late Neolithic saw renewed destruction of the forest associated with the use of fire. For a community on the edge of the forest, swine-herding is both efficient and an easy way of over-wintering stock.

The most striking feature of this pattern is its longevity. The radiocarbon chronology suggests that the SOM lasted from around 2700bc to beyond the middle of the 2nd millennium bc. This in itself contrasts with many of the adjacent areas of Europe. In Britain single-grave burials of the Early Bronze Age had already appeared by 1800bc; the same is true in Brittany. In Switzerland, Corded Ware had succeeded Horgen by the end of the 3rd millennium. The SOM pattern shows no move either towards the centralised sites and enclosures seen in late 3rd millennium Britain or towards the Corded Ware pattern. The absence of metallurgy has already been mentioned. The lack of an Early Bronze Age in the Paris basin has recently been confirmed by Gaucher (1976). Fewer than ten sites can be attributed to this period with any certainty. Even stray bronzes are not frequent. This pattern continues into the Middle Bronze Age when bronzes even then represent no more than the extension of external influences into the Paris basin.

Part of the contrast between the SOM and the Late Neolithic of other areas of Europe lies in the different conditions under which population expansion occurred. In Britain the growth associated with the henges did not involve large-scale expansion into new territory; causewayed camps and henges occur in the same areas, for instance in Wessex. The occurrence of central sites with large, labour-intensive monuments is indicative of *internal* reorganisation in relation to the resources of areas which had long been occupied. In northern

RADIOCARBON DATES

La Cave-aux-Fées, Breuil-en-Vexin (Val-d'Oise)	2220±130bc	Gif-3929	Bone	Tomb	Tarrête, 1978, 247
Champs-sur-Yonne (Yonne)	2200±180bc	Ly-1171	Bone	Tomb	*Radiocarbon*, 18, 73
La Chaussée-Tirancourt (Somme)	1700±120bc	Gif-1372	Charcoal	Tomb	*Radiocarbon*, 13, 222
	1700±120bc	Gif-1378	Charcoal		*Radiocarbon*, 13, 222
	1400±120bc	Gif-1289	Charcoal		*Radiocarbon*, 13, 222
La Côte de Bar (Meuse)	2220±70bc	Ly-285	Charcoal	Fint mine	*Radiocarbon*, 16, 122
	2110±50bc	MC-573	Charcoal		
	1820±230bc	Ly-1624	Charcoal		*Radiocarbon*, 21, 435
La Grande Paroisse, Pincevent (Seine-et-Marne)	1630±140bc	Ly-1171	Bone	Tomb	*Radiocarbon*, 20, 43
Etaples (Pas-de-Calais)	1470±100bc	Gif-2677	Charcoal	Settlement	Guilaine (ed.), 1976, 881
Germigny-l'Evêque (Seine-et-Marne)	2020±120bc	Gif-2723	Charcoal	Tomb	Baumann & Tarrête, 1979
Guiry-en-Vexin (Val-d'Oise)	1690±100bc	Gif-3329	Bone	Tomb	Guilaine (ed.), 1976, 881
La Hoguette, Fontenay-le-Marmion (Calvados)	2800±120bc	Gif-1347	Charcoal	Tomb	*Radiocarbon*, 14, 280
	2350±120bc	Gif-1346	Charcoal		*Radiocarbon*, 14, 280
	2770±120bc	Gif-1514	Charcoal		*Radiocarbon*, 14, 280
	2850±120bc	Gif-1513	Charcoal		*Radiocarbon*, 14, 280
Les Mournouards II (Marne)	1800±150bc	Gsy-114	Charcoal	Tomb	*Radiocarbon*, 8, 132
Noisy-sur-Ecole (Seine-et-Marne)	2530±110bc	Gif-2241	Charcoal	Tomb	Brezillon *et al.*, 1973
	2550±110bc	Gif-2242	Charcoal		Brezillon *et al.*, 1973
	2550±60bc	GrN-4675/6	Charcoal		Brezillon *et al.*, 1973
La Porte Joie, Beausoleil (Eure)	2090±180bc	Ly-703	Bone	Tomb	*Radiocarbon*, 17,18
	1310±190bc	Ly-705	Charcoal		*Radiocarbon*, 17, 18
	1090±280bc	Ly-704	Bone		*Radiocarbon*, 17, 18
Tinqueux (Marne)	1960±200bc	Gif-360	Charcoal	Tomb	*Radiocarbon*, 12, 429
Vers-sur-Selle (Somme)	2290±120bc	Gif-3700	Charcoal	Tomb	Piningre and Bréart, 1976
	2110±120bc	Gif-3699	Charcoal		Piningre and Bréart, 1976
	1120±110bc	Gif-3698	Charcoal		Piningre and Bréart, 1976
Les Roches, Videlles (Essonne)	2550±60bc	GrN-4675	Charcoal	Settlement: level D	*Radiocarbon*, 9, 133
	2550±50bc	GrN-4676	Charcoal	level D	*Radiocarbon*, 9, 133

France, the expansion was directed onto the plateaux whose only previous inhabitants had been small groups of late mesolithic hunters. Land was not in short supply and consequently the settlement system was open and expansive. The kinds of regional centres which emerged at this time in the British Isles were not needed. It is only in the constricted landscape of the Marais-Saint-Gond that anything approaching the British pattern can be observed.

The failure of the Paris basin SOM to develop more complex forms of social organisation may be linked to its economic structure. The change from pigs to sheep seen in the Swiss Late Neolithic with the appearance of Corded Ware has been linked by Sherratt (1981) and Sakellaridis (1979) to the breeding of these animals for wool. It seems more than coincidence that it is at this period that a decline in linen has been noted on the Swiss lake sites together with the keeping of sheep into adulthood. It was at this stage that metal production got under way. The association of a potential cash-crop (wool) with an exchange system including metal products did not occur in the rest of the SOM area. In the Paris basin, the pattern of simple expansion without pressure on resources persisted throughout the 3rd and early 2nd millennia bc, preserving a social and economic structure untouched by the innovations that had already carried other areas into the Bronze Age.

The Neolithic of Southern France

NIGEL MILLS

Environment and economy o geology o soil formation o agricultural potential o environmental change in the Holocene o vegetation o climate o soils o postglacial sea-level o history of research o MATERIAL CULTURE o *Early Neolithic* o pottery o lithics o settlement transition o *Middle Neolithic* o pottery o lithics o settlement o *Late Neolithic/Chalcolithic* o common elements o burial o settlement o regional cultures o *Vérazien* o *Ferrières* o *Fontbouisse* o *Gourgasien/Saint Ponien* o *Treilles* o *Couronnien* o current interpretative models o DISCUSSION AND CONCLUSIONS o the appearance of agriculture o the development of agricultural societies

THIS CHAPTER covers Provence and Languedoc, from the Italian border in the east to the River Aude in the west, and northwards into the *départements* of Aveyron, Lozère, Ardèche, Vaucluse, and Haute-Provence (Fig.5.1). Modern research objectives continue to follow a culture-historical approach, despite recent interest in palaeo-ecological and anthropological questions, and the data-base is heavily weighted by past research interests. My own research in the area has considered the development of neolithic societies from the standpoint of environment and subsistence, using the dynamics of the rural settlement/environment relationship during the historical period as a model for looking at prehistoric agricultural communities. Changes in material culture were considered in the context of changes in settlement and subsistence, and it is argued that this gives a better basis for looking at the development of neolithic societies than the culture-historical approach. In this chapter, the results of my environmental studies and field surveys are integrated with existing data, emphasising how these results contrast with, and demonstrate gaps in, current data samples. A general overview, based on these results, is given in the concluding section, and may be contrasted with the traditional interpretive models summarised earlier.

Apart from providing an introduction to neolithic societies in the area, the chapter has three main aims. The first is to emphasise how the current data are the product of past research designs, and contain consequent biases that must be appreciated before these data may be usefully analysed and interpreted in

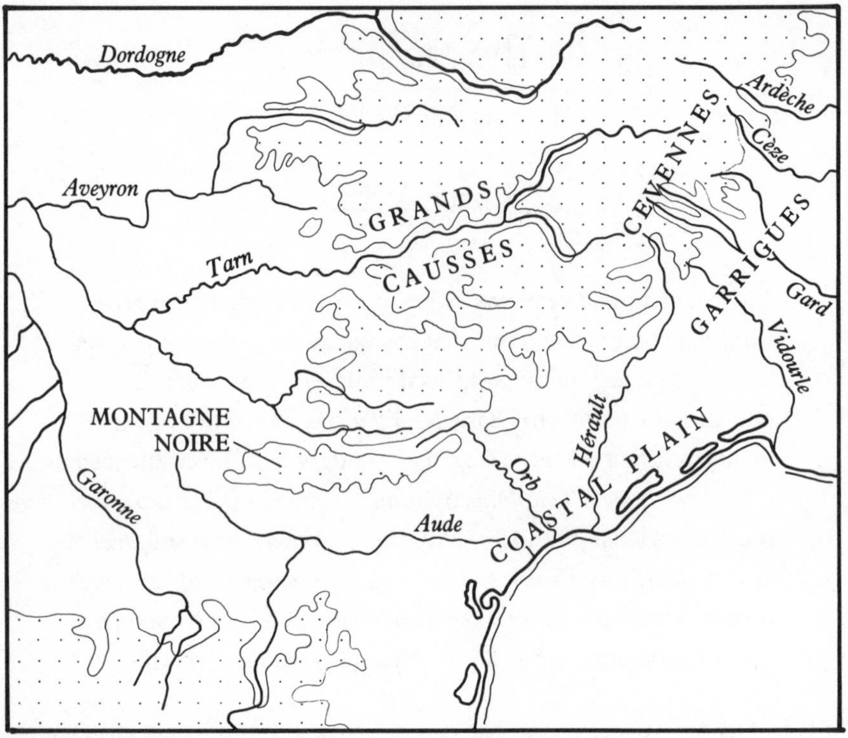

FIGURE 5.1a. Languedoc: relief and drainage (land over 500m stippled).

terms of processes of social and economic development. Present data samples are in many cases inadequate to answer the sorts of questions concerning social and economic processes in which archaeologists are currently interested, and future data collection should be carried out with respect to clearly defined and testable models of artefact variability and of settlement and societal change.

The second aim is to emphasise the crucial importance of understanding the environmental and economic context of neolithic societies in the area, using appropriate models of man-land relationships. Although only a first stage in research, an understanding of the long-term relationships between population, settlement, and subsistence resources is fundamental to any broader study of prehistoric communities.

The third aim is to produce a coherent overview of the data, based on this awareness of the long-term relationship between human populations and their natural environment. This overview has gaps, but outlines useful areas for future research.

Environmental Background

Geology. The relief of lower Provence is broken, and consists of ridges and basins interspersed with plateaux (Fig. 5.1) formed by limestone rocks, with

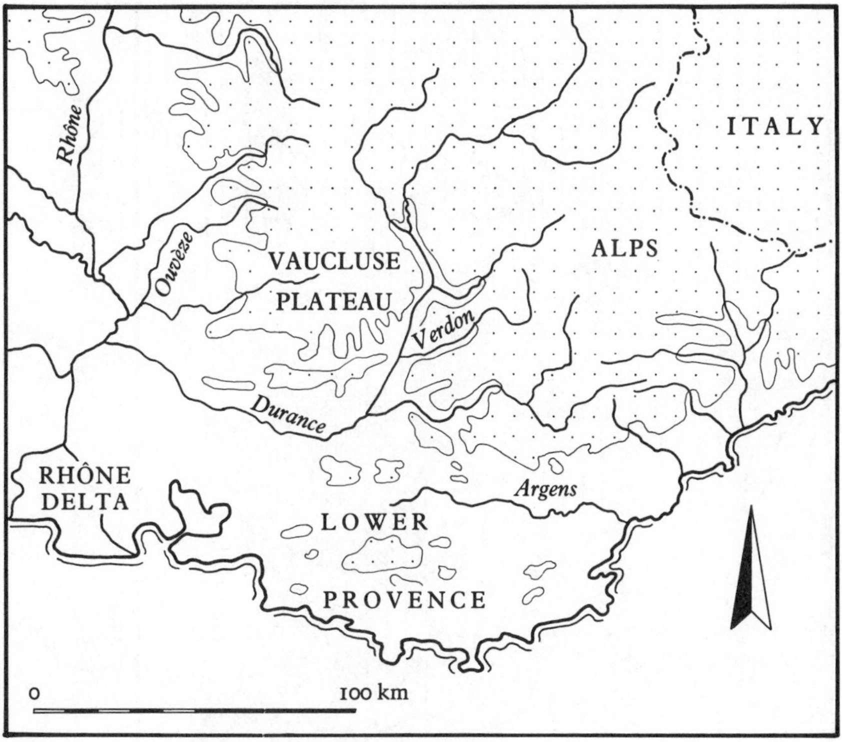

FIGURE 5.1b. Provence: relief and drainage (land over 500m stippled).

soft marl and clay-rich rocks occurring in the basins (Fig.5.2; Plate 5.1). The ridges are narrow, with an east-west trend, and rise sharply to heights of 500–800m near the coast, and over 1500m inland. This area of ridges and basins is backed by the high Vaucluse plateau of upper Provence, and by the Alps in the east.

Provence is separated from Languedoc by the alluvial trench of the Rhône valley, with its extensive deposits of silts and gravels. South of Arles, the Rhône has formed an extensive delta which presently covers some $1500km^2$.

West of the Rhône, the relief and geology of Languedoc is differentiated between eastern and western, and upper and lower areas. Eastern Languedoc is stepped from south-east to north-west, forming three major ecological zones: a coastal plain formed of soft marl and clay-rich rocks (Plate 5.2), covered in places by extensive gravel deposits and fringed by lagoons; the limestone plateaux of the Garrigues which lie at an average height of 200–250m (Plate 5.3); and the mountains and plateaux of upper Languedoc. The Cevennes mountains lie north of the Garrigues, while the high plateaux of the Grands Causses and the mountains of the Margeride, Aubrac, Rouergue, and Montagne Noire lie to the north-west. The Causses plateaux are limestone-based and range in height from 700m in the south to 1200m in the north (Plate

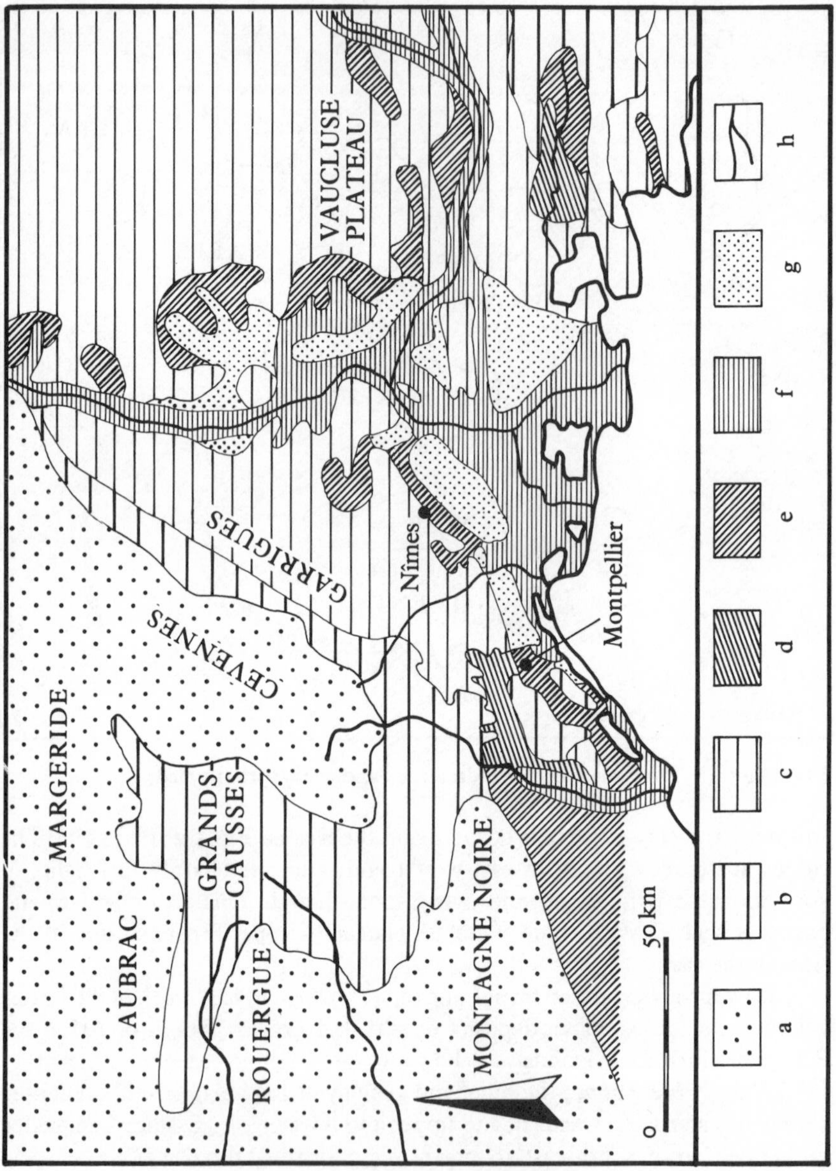

FIGURE 5.2. Provence and Languedoc: simplified geology.
(a) crystalline massifs; (b) hard limestones (Jurassic); (c) marly limestones (Cretaceous); (d) limestone, sands and clays (Eocene); (e) sands and clays (Pliocene); (f) fine alluvium (Holocene); (g) gravels (Pliocene and Quaternary); (h) rivers.

PLATE 5.1. Trets basin, Provence. Note arable soils overlying the soft rocks of the basin floor in the foreground and middle distance, and scrub on the limestone ridge beyond. (Photo: Nigel Mills.)

PLATE 5.2. Vaunage basin, Languedoc. Note arable soils in the foreground, and scrub on the Garrigues in the background. (Photo: Nigel Mills.)

PLATE 5.3. Montpellier Garrigues, Languedoc. Note poor arable soils round the village of Viols-le-Fort in the foreground, and scrub on the plateau in the background. (Photo: Nigel Mills.)

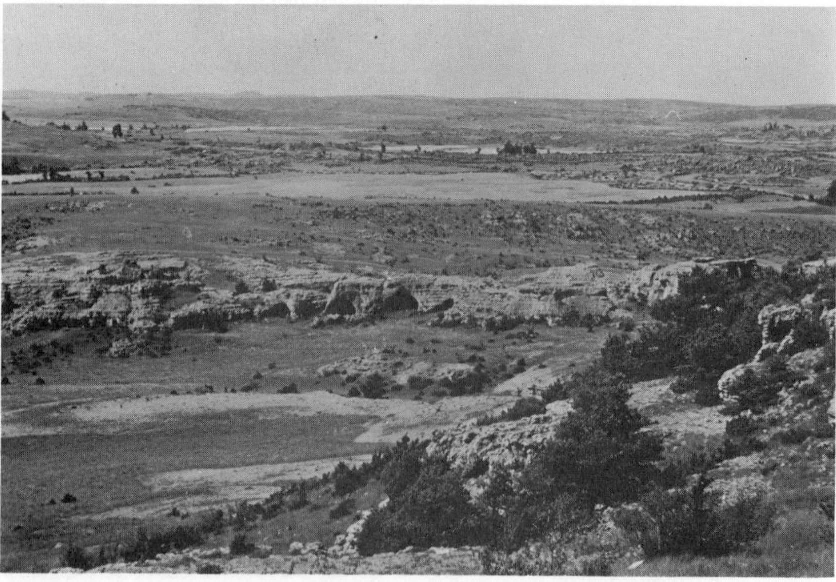

PLATE 5.4. Larzac plateau, Grands Causses. Note the extensive rough pasture, interspersed with higher quality pasture and arable soils in karst depressions, and the rock shelters in the foreground. A surface scatter of late neolithic/chalcolithic flints lies just in front of the shelter line, which was probably used as a transit site. (Photo: Nigel Mills.)

5.4). The plateaux are cut by narrow, steep-sided gorges in which marls are exposed below the limestones of the plateaux surfaces. Crystalline rocks form the Cevennes and other mountain massifs which rise to 1200–1500m, and have a heavily dissected relief with steep slopes and narrow valleys.

Western Languedoc is the area between the Hérault and Aude rivers. Most of this area consists of a narrow plain sandwiched between the sea and the Montagne Noire, formed of soft marl and clay-rich rocks, and extended westwards by the Aude valley. A variety of limestones and soft rocks outcrop in the valley.

Climate. Lower Provence and Languedoc have a Mediterranean climate with warm dry summers, tepid winters, and a markedly seasonal rainfall distribution with peaks in spring and autumn and a long dry period over the summer. The Grands Causses and the mountain massifs have a complex and changeable climatic régime with Mediterranean, Continental, and Temperate influences. There are harsh winters and warm summers, and rainfall is more equably distributed throughout the year than in the Mediterranean zone. Upper Provence has temperatures similar to those of the Mediterranean, but rainfall is more abundant and has a less markedly seasonal distribution.

Soil formation. Pedogenesis is slow under Mediterranean climatic conditions, since the marked dry season severely restricts biological activity. Most soils have undergone little leaching of minerals or fine particles, and bear a close relationship to their parent material. Exceptions to this rule are found in old soil profiles developed on Quaternary gravel terraces in Languedoc and in certain areas of Provence, and in relict soil profiles found in limestone fissures on the Montpellier Garrigues. Recent studies (H. Arnal *et al.*, 1973; Barrière *et al.*, 1966; Bouteyre, 1971) have shown that these and modern, poorly-developed soils in the Mediterranean climatic zone result from a continuous process of soil formation which began early in the Quaternary and continues today. While rates of pedogenesis have fluctuated between glacial and interglacial periods, there have been no major breaks in the sequence and direction of soil formation during the Quaternary and Holocene. This observation is of particular importance for the environmental history of the Garrigues. The rate of soil development is particularly slow on the limestone-based rocks due to their low content of insoluble residues. H. Arnal (1970) estimated that at least 12m of calcareous debris must have been weathered to produce a strongly leached 1.5m deep profile on early Quaternary calcareous gravels east of Montpellier.

Poorly-developed brown calcareous soils are most characteristic of the Mediterranean climatic zone, occurring on the soft marl and clay-rich rocks, and on colluvial deposits derived from these. These soils are usually deep, although the upper slopes of the stream interfluves are often heavily eroded and covered by thin lithosols. Thin, stony, rendzina-like soils are found on the marly limestones, while red, decalcified clays occur on hard limestones. These red clays form a thin soil cover on the Montpellier Garrigues, with remnant, heavily-leached red clay soils restricted to limestone fissures. Much of the surface of the Montpellier Garrigues is covered by gelifracted rock debris, or *lapiaz*. Upland limestone soils are little different from those of the Mediterranean zone. Other rocks tend to give more acid soils, the acidity of the crystalline rocks of the Cevennes and other mountainous areas being particularly marked.

Fine alluvial silts are extensive in the Rhône valley, in the lower courses of the main rivers, and along the northern margins of the coastal lagoons in Languedoc. Colluvial deposits are extensive over the soft rocks in the Provençal basins and on the Languedoc coastal plain where they occur in stream valleys. Colluvial deposits also occur in small depressions on the limestone plateaux.

Agricultural potential. The alluvial soils, and the colluvial and deeper *in situ* soils of the soft rocks and the depressions on the limestone plateaux, are today almost entirely under cultivation. Two main vegetation types exist elsewhere. Xerophitic scrub dominates in the Mediterranean zone, with oak (*Quercus ilex* and *Quercus coccifera*) associations on limestones. These scrubland associations are considered to have resulted from the degradation of climax evergreen oak forest through anthropogenic factors. The Aleppo pine (*Pinus halepensis*) is also extensive in the warmest and driest parts, while deciduous species, especially *Quercus pubescens*, are found on north-facing slopes in Provence, in the northern parts of the Garrigues, and on restricted areas of humid soils further south.

Deciduous vegetation is dominant under the more humid climatic conditions of the upland areas. Open herbaceous vegetation is widespread on the Grands Causses, but pine (*P. sylvestris*) is extensive on sandy soils overlying dolomitic limestones and oak (*Q. pubescens*) also occurs. Oak and chestnut dominate at mid-altitude in the Cevennes, with pines higher up, while oak is dominant on the high plateaux of the Vaucluse.

The various ecological zones provide sharp contrasts in agricultural potential which are of interest when considering prehistoric agricultural settlement. Areas presently suited to cereal cultivation comprise the fine alluvial soils in the main river valleys, the *in situ* and colluvial soils on the soft rocks, and the soils of the small depressions on the limestone plateaux. These arable soils are most extensive on the coastal plain of Languedoc and in the basins of Provence. They cover only 20 per cent of the Grands Causses, and both here and on the Garrigues, less than 10 per cent of the plateaux surfaces is suitable for cultivation.

The Quaternary alluvial deposits vary in their agricultural potential. Those lying immediately east and west of the Rhône delta are suitable only for arboriculture, particularly vines, and for pasture. The Quaternary alluvium of the Languedoc coastal plain is less stony and has been used for cereal cultivation in historical times, although vines are the main crop today. Arable land is extremely rare on the crystalline massifs where the soils are poor due to their high acidity, and where the relief is very broken.

The limestone areas and the crystalline massifs are marginal from the point of view of cereal agriculture, owing both to the poor quality and restricted extent of suitable soils. These areas have traditionally been used for sheep grazing, particularly the Causses, the Garrigues, and the Vaucluse plateaux, and have often been involved in transhumance since the southerly zones provide poor pasture during the summer because of the dry conditions, while the high plateaux provide poor pasture and harsh weather in winter.

ENVIRONMENTAL CHANGE IN THE HOLOCENE. The main geomorphic components of the landscape have not changed in the postglacial period, leaving climate, vegetation, soils, and sea-level rise as the main variables to be considered. Independent climatic data are scarce, and hypotheses concerning climatic change are based on inferences from data on vegetation development as shown by pollen diagrams and macro-botanical studies. Climatic change is therefore considered briefly, following the discussion of vegetation changes, and prior to the discussion of changes in soils and superficial sediments.

Vegetation. There are now over thirty pollen diagrams, as well as wood charcoal studies and several syntheses that are relevant to postglacial vegetation development in southern France. Planchais *et al.* (1977) and Vernet (1973, 1976) have proposed a regional scheme for the area, arguing that the wood charcoal and pollen data correlate, and that the wood charcoal results may be used to fill in the gaps in the pollen record for the Garrigues, inland Provence, and the Causses. The mountainous areas have a separate sequence with an independent series of pollen diagrams. However, Renault-Miskovsky (1976) and Triat (1978) consider that the pollen data reflect local situations, and are only strictly applicable to the lowlying coastal areas (i.e. not to the Garrigues, the Grands Causses, or the interior of Provence). Triat's scheme is followed here.

Triat emphasises that the pollen diagrams from the low-altitude coastal zone (Languedoc coastal plain and Provençal basins) mainly represent the local vegetation on the low-lying humid soils, and not that of the adjacent limestone hills. Wormwood (*Artemisia*) and horsetail (*Ephedra*) steppe and juniper scrub dominate during the late glacial period together with stands of pine (*P. sylvestris*). Local refuges of thermophilous vegetation (ilex, oak, Aleppo pine, olive, etc.) existed throughout the Quaternary on the now largely-submerged coastal plain, and on the southerly massifs of Provence, and provided an indigenous base for their expansion in the postglacial period (Bernard, 1972; Planchais *et al.*, 1977; Triat, 1978; Vernet, 1973, 1976). Pine (*P. sylvestris*) dominates in the Early Postglacial but then declines sharply with a slight but general increase in the 3rd millennium bc. The deciduous oak (*Q. pubescens*) takes over during the 7th millennium bc and is dominant until the 2nd millennium bc. Ilex initially developed on the rocky surfaces of the limestones, replacing the existing juniper scrub during the 6th to the 3rd millennia bc, dependent on latitude. Partly as a result of clearances by man, ilex spreads periodically onto the low-lying humid soils occupied by oak (*Q. pubescens*), but does not become dominant here until the 2nd/1st millennium bc, when arboreal pollen declines relative to herbaceous pollen. Subsequently ilex dominates and pine increases in modern times.

No pollen diagrams are currently available for the mid-altitude zone of the Languedoc Garrigues and the interior of lower Provence, so inferences about vegetation development are dependent on the wood charcoal studies and on comparisons between the ecologies of these areas and those of the coastal plain. The basin and ridge relief of interior Provence is similar to Triat's study area of the lower Rhône, although more broken and with more limestone. A similar vegetation sequence may therefore be suggested, with oak (*Q. pubescens*) dominating on the basin floors from the 7th millennium bc and ilex replacing juniper on the limestones between the 6th and 3rd millennia bc. The Languedoc Garrigues are mainly limestone plateaux. The traditional view of vegetation development here is that the present ilex scrubland and its associated thin soils results from the destruction by man of an original climax evergreen or mixed oak forest and brown forest soil through clearance for cultivation, lime kilns, boat building, fuel, and through overgrazing (Fig. 5.3). According to this model, the leached red clays found in the limestone fissures are relict Bt horizons of once extensive *terra rossa* soils which have been eroded and truncated following human action. These soils provided the parent material for the evergreen forest and brown forest soil development. The *terra rossa* were supposed to have developed under earlier, tropical climatic conditions, and consequently neither the forest nor the *terra rossa* can regenerate since present climatic conditions are unsuitable for the formation of the *terrra rossa*. Despite the almost universal acceptance of this model, there are no firm data to support its application to the Garrigues. There is also considerable confusion as to how early the vegetation was transformed into scrubland. Current data on human settlement show that the Garrigues were heavily exploited and densely settled during the 3rd millennium bc, so much of the deforestation may have taken place then. However, the palaeobotanical data in fact give no clear indication of vegetation development on the Garrigues.

Turning briefly to the upland zone, the pollen diagrams from the crystalline areas surrounding the Grands Causses show the dominance of pine (*P. sylvestris*) during the 6th and 5th millennia bc. Deciduous oaks expanded during the latter part of this period and beech (*Fagus*) increased during the 2nd and 1st millennia bc. Subsequently the arboreal pollen declined markedly in the historical period and herbaceous species came to dominate. No pollen diagrams are available for the Grands Causses, but wood charcoal from 19 sites is mainly of pine in the earlier Postglacial, with some oak (*Q. pubescens*). Oak became more frequent than pine during the 3rd millennium bc and remains of beech occur at several sites on the edges of the highest parts of the Causses dated to the 2nd/1st millennia bc, but not in the interior. There are no botanical data for upland Provence, although a similar vegetation sequence to that of the Grands Causses may be suggested.

Climate. The steppe vegetation indicates cold, dry conditions over most of the southerly zones in the Late Glacial, and the high altitude zone would also

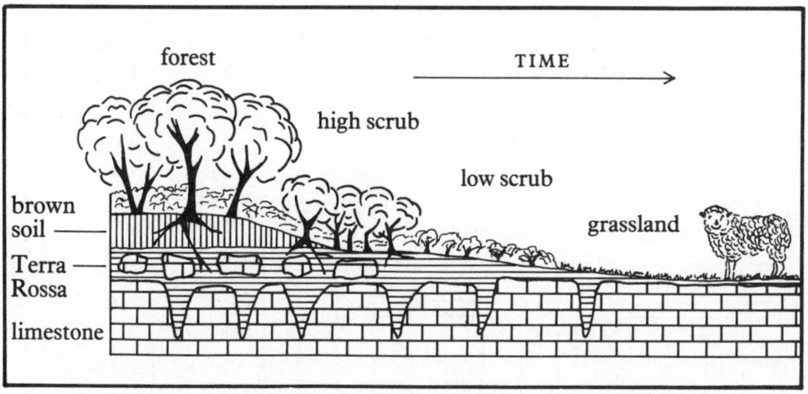

FIGURE 5.3. Schematic representation of the model of soil and vegetational degradation over the Garrigues due to human action, from climax forest associated with brown soils developed over Terra Rossa on the left, to scrub and grassland associated with thin soils and truncated Terra Rossa on the right.

have been cold at this period. In lower Provence and lower Languedoc the expansion of pine followed by deciduous, and later evergreen oaks, suggests a gradual warming in the Postglacial. Triat (1978, 261) argues that a climate with Mediterranean affinities was established during the 8th/7th millennia bc, allowing ilex to become established during the 6th millennium bc in the areas previously occupied by juniper. As Triat notes, a markedly arid climate would not have been necessary for this, particularly as the limestone areas are naturally dry due to the rapid rate at which water percolates through the rock.

At higher altitude also, the spread of deciduous oaks and related species suggests the climate was becoming warmer, tending towards present conditions. Temperatures may have become slightly cooler at lower altitude during the 3rd millennium bc (Triat, 1978, 262) and cooler and slightly more humid conditions are also indicated for the upland zone over the same period (Triat, 1978, 262; Vernet, 1976, 13).

Soil and geomorphology. Three questions apply here: first, has the agricultural quality of the soils declined through the removal of plant nutrients by erosion, particularly by the destruction of surface organic horizons; second, have there been gross regional changes in the distribution of arable soils, one zone being selectively impoverished or enriched relative to others; and third, has erosion significantly affected the preservation of archaeological sites either by destroying them, or by burying them beneath colluvial and/or alluvial deposits? If the various parts of the region have been affected differentially by these processes, our present samples of prehistoric settlement may be biased, and current land-use potential may not be an adequate guide to the prehistoric situation.

The current view is that anthropogenic degradation has occurred, and has been most extensive on the limestones, and particularly the Garrigues plateaux

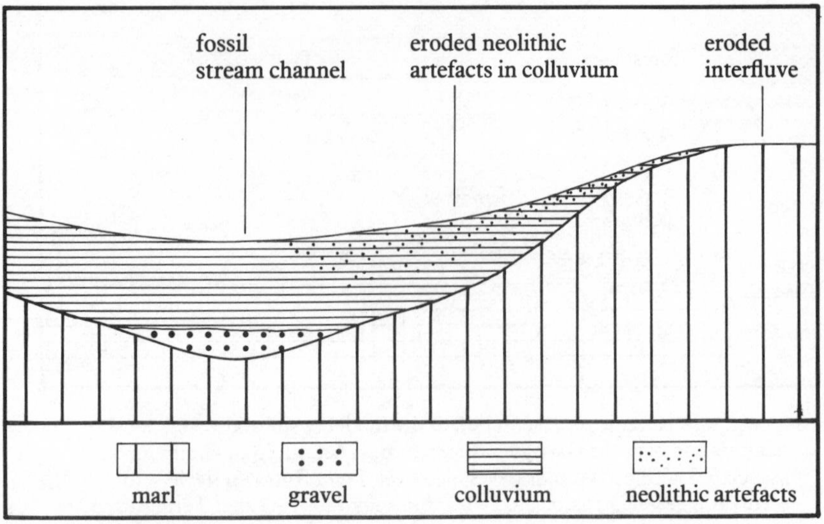

FIGURE 5.4. Schematic representation of soil erosion and deposition on the soft rocks of the Languedoc coastal plain and the Provençal basins, showing the destructive effects of this erosion on archaeological sites.

(Fig. 5.3). Extensive erosion and deposition has taken place on the soft rocks of the Languedoc coastal plain and the Provençal basins during historical times (D'Anna and Mills 1981; Mills 1980). These soil movements have resulted in local repositioning of arable soils by erosion of the interfluves and colluvial deposition in lower slope positions. In certain cases the erosion has led to widespread destruction of neolithic and other sites located on the interfluves, the remains of these sites being found mixed with the colluvial deposits in lower slope positions (Fig. 5.4). Similar evidence is available for Languedoc, although local topographic conditions have sometimes encouraged the preservation of archaeological sites beneath a thin layer of colluvium, as in the Vaunage basin near Nîmes (Gard).

The deposition of large quantities of fine alluvium in the lower courses of the rivers has significantly improved the agricultural potential of the lowland areas, but most of this alluvium would not have been available to neolithic agriculturalists since present data (J. Arnal *et al.*, 1974, 1977; Prades, 1972) suggest that it has accumulated since the Late Bronze Age. On the other hand, the alluvium has covered archaeological sites to depths of several metres in the main river valleys, which may be 2–3km wide in their lower courses. Delano-Smith (1979, 344–52) argues that the presently poorly-drained areas of the lagoonal fringes formed dry land in the Middle Neolithic-Chaleolithic, and carried soils suitable for cultivation during this period.

The model of environmental degradation would lead one to expect abundant evidence of recent erosion and deposition in the Garrigues. In fact, significant deposits of recent colluvium are only found where there are local outcrops of soft rocks, which, as we have seen on the coastal plain, have been susceptible to erosion during the historical period. Elsewhere the dry limestone valleys contain thin colluvial accumulations, while the intervening plateaux surfaces are covered by extensive areas of gelifracted rock debris. This debris accumulated during the last glacial period (Couteaux, 1974; Dugrand, 1964), indicating that the soil cover was not adequate to protect the rock from frost action. Since it requires many thousands of years for a deep *terra rossa* profile to develop over hard limestones, such a soil could not have formed in the relatively short interval between the end of the last glacial period and the advent of the Neolithic. The situation is different on marly limestones which contain 40–60 per cent of non-calcareous clay and silt residues which allow a 100–300mm rendzina-like soil to develop quite rapidly, over a period of 100 years or so. However, these soils remain thin and stony and would never have been particularly attractive to agriculturalists, although they have been used as marginal arable land and pasture during historical times. These thin soils could not have supported the development of climax forest (see also Couteaux, 1974) and it is likely therefore that scrub has been the natural vegetation of the area throughout the Holocene.

From the agricultural viewpoint there has probably been a general decline in soil quality due to the removal of plant nutrients by erosion and by thousands of years of cultivation. However, and contrary to the currently accepted model, there have *not* been major changes in the contrasts between land-use potential in different parts of the region, the relative richness of the coastal plain having merely been further enhanced by the addition of the fine alluvium. On the other hand, erosion and deposition have clearly had selective effects on the preservation of archaeological sites, those overlying the soft rocks having been particularly susceptible to destruction.

Postglacial sea-level rise. Recent studies of sediments in the Rhône delta (Bertrand and l'Homer, 1975) and in the Golfe du Lion (Aloisi *et al.*, 1975; Monaco *et al.*, 1972; De Lumley, 1976) show that sea-level was 60m lower than present in the late 9th millennium bc. A level of −30m to −20m was reached by about 6000 bc with coastlines at around −10m by 5000 bc. The submerged early neolithic site of Ile Corrège (Leucate, Hérault) is radiocarbon-dated to 4850 bc (see date-list at end of Chapter 7) and is located 6–7m below present sea-level. Present level seems to have been reached by about 2000 bc, although there have been slight fluctuations since then.

The steep, rocky coastline of Provence, and the gently sloping plain of the Golfe du Lion would have been differentially affected by sea-level rise, far greater land areas being drowned off the Languedoc coast. Some 20km of coastal plain were probably lost there between 8000bc and 4000bc, and although this area may seem relatively small, it should be emphasised that it represents the loss of a major part of an ecological zone, the coastal lowlands.

History of Archaeological Research

There have been three research phases, the first from the later nineteenth century to the late 1940s, the second lasting until the late 1960s. The third is continuing today.

Research in all three phases has concentrated on the limestone areas, and it is only over the last ten years that open air sites have been excavated on a regular and systematic basis. Excavations were not usually methodical in the early phase, the main excavating tool being the pick. Layers of different periods were often confused and the results poorly published, with the exception of a few useful regional syntheses (Cazalis de Fondouce, 1900; Cotte, 1924; Louis, 1931, 1932; Marignan, 1893). The artefacts were classified into Neolithic, Bronze, and Iron Ages, with a Chalcolithic being distinguished in eastern Languedoc. The Neolithic was poorly defined although a basic typological dichotomy was seen in the flint industries between those using a blade technique, and those using a flake technique (*pseudo-campignien*). The former were known particularly from sites in the Trets basin in Provence, and on the edges of the coastal lagoons in Languedoc, while the latter were known from the Languedoc Garrigues and the limestone hills of Provence.

Louis (1932, 1948) used this spatial and technical contrast in the flint industries to develop a culturo-economic model which has been fundamental to later research and interpretations of the Languedoc Neolithic. In 1948 he defined three cultures which he considered were contemporary, and had different subsistence bases: a *culture des sables* on the edge of the coastal lagoons with a blade-based lithic industry and a hunting and fishing economy; a *culture des plateaux* with a flake-based lithic industry, megalithic tombs, and a pastoral economy (*pasteurs des plateaux*); and a *culture des grottes* with polished-stone axes, fine pottery, and an agricultural economy.

The second phase of research saw the first major stratigraphic excavations by Escalon de Fonton (1956) at Abri des Pigeons, Châteauneuf-les-Martigues (Bouches-du-Rhône; m.r.7), and by J. Arnal (1956) at La Madeleine (Hérault; m.r.29). Both these sites are coastal caves. The different phases of the Neolithic were differentially represented in the two stratigraphies (Early Neolithic at Châteauneuf, Middle Neolithic at La Madeleine) but by cross-referring to the more complete stratigraphy at Arene Candide in Italy (Bernabo Brea, 1946, 1956) it was possible to define an Early Neolithic (Cardial) with a flake-based lithic industry, and pottery with simple forms and *Cardium* shell-impressed decoration; a Middle Neolithic (Chasséen) with a blade-based lithic industry and fine smooth pottery including carinated forms and rare incised decoration (Louis' *culture des sables*); and a Late Neolithic/Chalcolithic with a flake-based lithic industry, and a complex ceramic assemblage including a wide variety of vessel forms and decorative motifs (Louis' *culture des plateaux*).

Work in Languedoc then concentrated on the *culture des plateaux*, leading to the definition of the *Fontbouisse* chalcolithic culture (Louis *et al.*, 1947) and a *Ferrières* late neolithic culture (J. Arnal, 1954). Both these were concentrated on the Garrigues and characterised mainly by their ceramic assemblages. The *Rodezien* late neolithic/chalcolithic culture was identified on the Grands Causses by an arrowhead type (the 'crenellated' arrowhead) and the predominance of chert as a lithic raw material, and was considered part of the *pasteurs des plateaux* complex along with Ferrières and Fontbouisse.

J. Arnal (1963) and Audibert (1962), amongst others, made extensive surveys of the Languedoc Garrigues, finding and excavating numerous dolmens and a few open air sites. Louis' *culture des grottes* was shown to be a conflation of occupation levels from different periods, but the fundamental dichotomy between *pasteurs des plateaux* and the rest continued. Several local case studies of settlement in small valleys and basins were also carried out. Escalon de Fonton worked on the Mesolithic/Neolithic transition, excavating the inland site of Montclus (Ardèche: Escalon de Fonton, 1965, 1966, 1968, 1970a), and comparing its stratigraphy to that of Châteauneuf-les-Martigues. He also began excavating an important open air site at La Couronne (Bouches-du-Rhône).

The third research period has seen a proliferation of methodical stratigraphic excavations over the whole area of southern France (Fig. 5.7), aimed at closer definition of the neolithic material culture sequence and especially of the transition phases between the major culturo-chronological blocks. These excavations were initiated by Courtin (1967; Courtin and Pelouard, 1971; Escalon de Fonton, 1976a) in Provence, and followed in Languedoc by Guilaine at Montbolo (Pyrénées-Orientales: Guilaine, 1974a), Dourgne (Aude: Guilaine *et al.*, 1976a), Font-Juvénal (Aude; m.r.30: Guilaine *et al.*, 1976b), Gazel (Aude; m.r.39: Guilaine, 1970a), and Jean Cros (Aude; m.r.41: Guilaine, 1979); by Rodriguez at Camprafaud (Hérault; m.r.38: Rodriguez, 1970a, 1970b, 1976); by G. B. Arnal at Saint Etienne-de-Gourgas (Hérault; m.r.36: G. B. Arnal, 1972); by Costantini at Sargel (Aveyron; m.r.33: Costantini, 1970a, 1970b, 1978); and in Provence by Calvet at Saint Mitre (Basses-Alpes: Calvet, 1969). These excavations have led to a clearer understanding of the cultural sequence, but have also resulted in a proliferation of localised cultures, often based on a single type site and a limited number of type artefacts, and dated to the Mesolithic/Neolithic and Early Neolithic/Middle Neolithic transitions, and to the Late Neolithic/Chalcolithic.

An interest has also developed in settlement structures and the economy of cave and open air sites. Chalcolithic settlements are now fairly well known on the Languedoc Garrigues, but only one early neolithic, and about five middle neolithic open air sites have been systematically excavated or sounded.

This interest in settlement structures and economy is part of the recent concern with environmental, social, and economic questions reflected in the appearance of articles dealing specifically with economic and settlement evidence, as well as more general social and developmental problems. Good faunal and botanical reports remain scarce, however, and most current research is still carried out, implicitly or explicitly, within a normative culture-historical framework. This carries with it the fundamental assumption that artefact styles correlate directly with human groups, and it is further assumed that these groups express themselves most clearly in material culture remains through variability in ceramic form and decoration (G.B. Arnal, 1976; Guilaine, 1970b, 1976a, 1980, 1981; Gutherz, 1975; Vaquer, 1975). The main objective of research is to delimit these groups in time and space, and to study their mutation, formation, and evolution (Vaquer, 1975) through analysis of stylistic variation. Following the development of radiocarbon dating, the construction of independent chronologies, and the influence of Renfrew's publication (1973) concerning the effects of these on European cultural sequences, explanations of change involving population movements and diffusion have been treated sceptically. Change through time is now more often seen in terms of continuity, although an exception is made for the appearance of agriculture which is explained by acculturation or 'neolithisation'.

The present interest in palaeo-ecological and palaeo-anthropological problems has not radically altered research designs since the established 'cultures', and their spatial distribution, are used to define the human parameters of investigation. Thus one studies the adaptation of a particular culture to its environment, and settlement and economy are seen to be culture-dependent. As an extreme example of this view, Vaquer (1975) considers that environmental and economic data are irrelevant to the understanding of the development of the Chasséen culture through time.

Material Culture

The data for each period are presented in terms first, of material culture, and second, of settlement and economy.*

Early Neolithic

Pottery. The earliest pottery comes from coastal sites in Provence in levels dated to the earlier 6th millennium bc. Subsequently pottery appeared at inland sites over the whole of lower Provence and lower Languedoc during the 5th millennium bc, but with a variable local time lag. Early neolithic assemblages are rare in the Grands Causses, and date to the later 5th millennium bc. No early neolithic sites are known from the crystalline mountains or from upland Provence. The earliest ceramic assemblages at sites dated to the 6th and earlier 5th millennia bc include simple, rough-surfaced vessels, with decoration consisting predominantly of *Cardium* shell impressions. Subsequently the

* Further information, including illustrations of the artefact types, may be found in: G. B. Arnal (1976), J. Arnal (1963), Audibert (1962), Costantini (1978), Courtin (1974a, 1974b, 1977), Courtin and Erroux (1974), Delano-Smith (1972), Gasco (1976), Guilaine (1970b, 1976a, 1976b, 1977, 1980, 1981), Gutherz (1975), Mills (1976, 1980), Phillips (1975, 1982), and Vaquer (1975). For more information on the spatial distribution of sites at different periods see the figures in G.B. Arnal (1976), Courtin (1974a, 1974b), Delano-Smith (1972), and Gasco (1976). Radiocarbon dates, grouped according to areas and cultures, are given in a table at the end of this chapter. A selection of artefact types characteristic of the different phases of the Neolithic is illustrated in Figures 5.5 and 5.6.

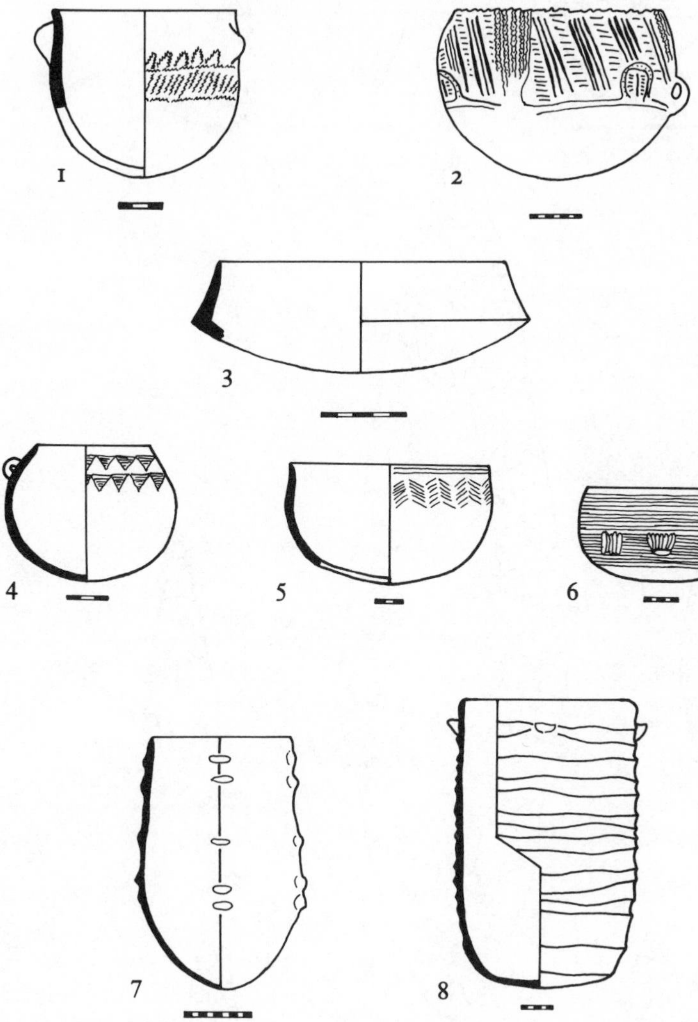

FIGURE 5.5. Pottery styles characteristic of the different phases of the south French Neolithic.
1 Early neolithic *Cardium*-impressed vessel from Provence; 2 Early neolithic vessel from Languedoc with incised and plastic decoration; 3 Middle neolithic carinated bowl; 4 Late neolithic vessel with hachured triangle decoration; 5 Late neolithic Ferrières vessel with incised chevron decoration; 6 Chalcolithic Fontbouisse vessel with channelled decoration; 7 Late neolithic Vérazien storage vessel with superposed lugs; 8 Late neolithic/chalcolithic storage vessel with horizontal cordons and lugs. (1 after Courtin, 1976; 3 after Courtin, 1974a; 2, 4-8 after Guilaine and Roudil, 1976.) Scales in centimetres.

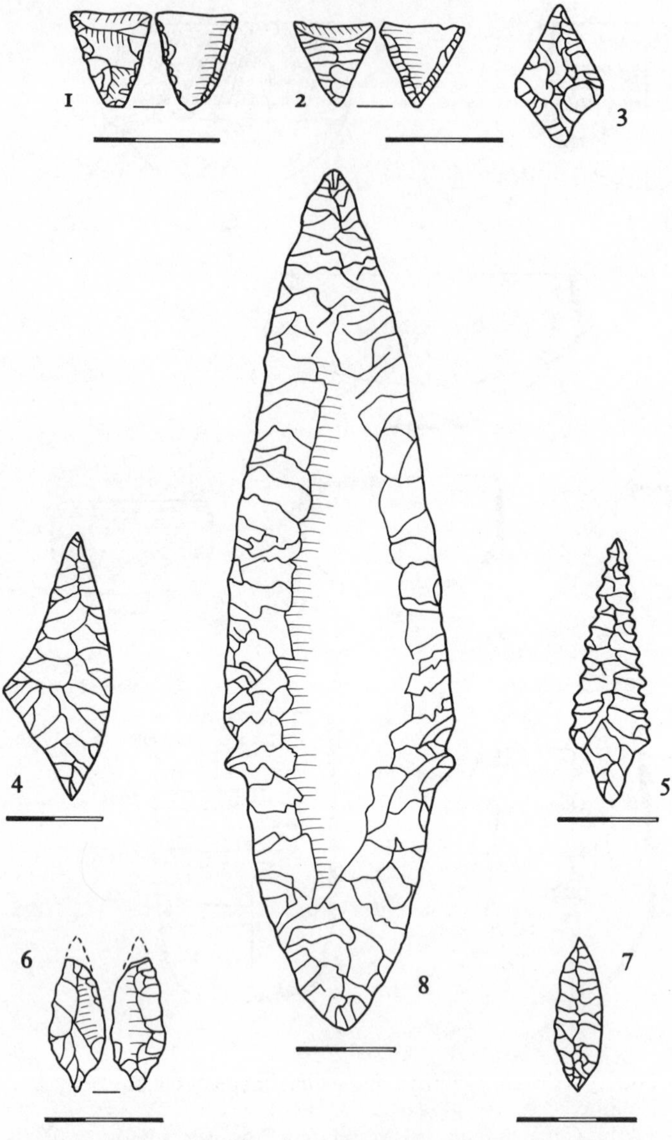

FIGURE 5.6. Flint types characteristic of the different phases of the south French Neolithic.
1 Early neolithic tranchet arrowhead with abrupt retouch; 2 Middle neolithic tranchet arrowhead with flat and semi-abrupt retouch; 3 Middle neolithic barbed-and-tanged arrowhead; 4 Late neolithic asymmetrical arrowhead with flat retouch; 5 Late neolithic/chalcolithic 'crenellated' arrowhead from the Grands Causses; 6 Late neolithic/chalcolithic tanged arrowhead with flat retouch; 7 Late neolithic/chalcolithic leaf-shaped arrowhead with flat retouch; 8 Late neolithic/chalcolithic dagger of Salinelles lacustrine flint. (1-3, 6-7 after Courtin, 1974a; 4, 5, 8 after G. B. Arnal, 1976.) Scales in centimetres.

decoration developed considerable local and regional variability with other types of impressed and incised motifs predominant in western Languedoc, channelled motifs in eastern Languedoc and the lower Rhône, and *Cardium* shell impressions continuing in Provence. This later pottery is classed as *Epicardial* in Languedoc and the Rhône valley. It dates broadly from the mid 5th to the early 4th millennia bc, though Epicardial wares continued in use on the edges of the Grands Causses into the mid and later 4th millennium bc, contemporary with the Middle Neolithic. At certain inland sites (e.g. Montclus; m.r.17: Escalon de Fonton, 1965, 1966, 1968, 1970a) these Epicardial wares are the first pottery to appear in stratigraphies which show continuous occupation during the 6th and/or 5th millennia bc, and in which, apart from the pottery, the assemblages show great continuity. The recent excavations at Peiro Signado (Hérault; m.r.37: Roudil and Grimal, 1978) show that there may have been even greater variety in the ceramics than this scheme anticipates, although in general terms the pottery from this site falls within the area of impressed and incised motifs of western Languedoc.

Lithics. The flint industries associated with these early ceramic assemblages are similar to those of the Mesolithic. The industries are usually flake-based, although some blades occur, and use local raw materials. These include a variety of flint types as well as chert, quartz, etc. Roudil and Grimal (1978) report that the flint industry from Peiro Signado is blade-based. There are slight changes in certain tool types with the appearance of pottery, notably among the arrowheads, but at several sites (Dourgne, Montclus) these changes take place independently of the pottery, while at others (Puechmargues II, Aveyron; m.r.30: Maury, 1967) there is hardly any change. The arrowheads are mainly regular trapezes, rectilinear in shape, with abrupt retouch. A few piercing arrowheads occur in the later Cardial sequence. Other tools include scrapers, awls, denticulates, and burins. The lithic assemblage also includes a few polished-stone axes, worked pebbles, 'chopping' tools, and grindstones.

Bone tools are fairly abundant, and include points, generally from caprovid metapodia, chisels, spatulae and spear points. Ornament is little different from that found in the Mesolithic, consisting of pierced marine shells (on inland and coastal sites) and a few stone bracelets. Few burials are known. They consist of individual inhumations, the body being placed in a contracted position with a few associated objects including pottery, marine shells, and stone bracelets.

Settlement. Settlement evidence is sparse. Some 80 to 100 early neolithic sites are known from Provence and Languedoc, including 24 open air sites, the rest being caves and shelters (G.B.Arnal, 1976; Courtin, 1974a, 1974b, 1976; Roudil and Grimal, 1978). The cave sites are concentrated in the Gardon and Verdon gorges, and along the Calavon and Ouvèze rivers, as well as in western coastal Provence. Only one open air site has been fully excavated, at Le Baratin (Vaucluse) in the lower Rhône (m.r.13: Courtin, 1974a, 51). Subcircular hut floors were found here, about 5m in diameter, made of river pebbles with post holes round the periphery and in the centre. Smaller pebble piles between 1m and 1.5m in diameter have been interpreted as hearths. The only sites known from upper Provence and upper Languedoc are found in the Grands Causses, and rare sites are also known on the Garrigues. The open air site of Ile Corrège, located 6–7m below sea-level off the Languedoc coast, shows that some early neolithic open air sites have been covered by the postglacial sea-level rise.

Quantitative economic data are scarce, particularly as several recently excavated sites have not yet been fully published, and there have been few detailed interim reports. Domestic sheep, goat, cattle and pig are present from the initial phases of the Early Neolithic, and most authors consider it likely that sheep and goat, and possibly also pig, were herded before the appearance of pottery. Domestic species dominate at the two open air sites with faunal samples, while at the caves, either the information is inadequate to assess proportions, or wild animals dominate (Courtin, 1977; Ducos, 1958, 1976, 1977; Guilaine, 1976a, 1977; Jourdan, 1976; Montjardin, 1979; Poulain, 1976).

Botanical data are even scarcer, but cereals including wheat and barley are present at several sites dated to the 5th millennium bc (Courtin and Erroux, 1974; Erroux, 1976) and Courtin has recently found carbonised cereals in the earliest levels with pottery at Châteauneuf-les-Martigues (m.r.7; Courtin, pers.comm.). Other plants exploited include vetch, chick pea, acorns, and juniper (Courtin and Erroux, 1974). The collection of marine foods and hunting seem to have been important at coastal sites in Provence, as in the Mesolithic (Escalon de Fonton, 1956), and freshwater fishing and the collection and processing of vetch appear to have been the main subsistence activities at Montclus throughout the sequence of occupation which begins in the early 6th millennium bc and ends in the late 5th millennium bc. There is increasing evidence (Escalon de Fonton, 1980; Roudil, 1981) that wild plant foods were exploited on a large scale during the Mesolithic, and that plant gathering and freshwater fishing were major components of subsistence strategies during this period.

Recent studies consider the development of the Neolithic in this region in terms of a process of 'neolithisation' in which indigenous local populations gradually took up stockraising, cereal cultivation, and the use of pottery (G.B.Arnal, 1976; Courtin, 1974a, 1976; Guilaine, 1976a, 1981, Phillips, 1975). The chronological variability in the appearance of pottery in different areas, as well as the variability of ceramic styles, is taken to indicate the localised nature of these developments. Mills (1976) has argued that cereal cultivation was of little importance during much of the Early Neolithic, most sites being similar to those of the Mesolithic (caves and shelters), with economies based on animal herding, fishing, plant gathering, and the exploitation of marine foods.

TRANSITION.

The assemblages of the Middle Neolithic contrast strongly with those of the Early Neolithic, and are marked by the appearance of great similarity over a vast area. These assemblages are characterised by, first, well-made, smooth-surfaced pottery, with a considerable range of forms including carinated vessels, and rare incised decoration; second, a flint industry overwhelmingly based on a blade and micro-blade technique; third, an abundant polished-stone industry.

Until the 1960s the Chasséen culture was considered to represent a sharp break with the Early Neolithic, resulting from outside influences. Cave excavations then revealed what were interpreted as transitional assemblages showing similarities with the Early Neolithic and/or the Middle Neolithic (Guilaine, 1970b). Subsequent studies have revealed a wide variety of late Cardial/early middle neolithic ceramics. Thus in western Languedoc, Guilaine (1970c) has defined a *Bizien* early Middle Neolithic with different pottery style and decoration to the Chasséen, while late Cardial pottery on the edges of the Causses is contemporary with early Chasséen pottery in lower Provence and lower Languedoc. A further early middle neolithic assemblage has been defined at Fontbrégoua in the Var (Escalon de Fonton, 1980). This variety of assemblages at the early/middle neolithic interface has complicated the picture of gradual transition, and no recent syntheses have emerged concerning this problem directly. The main emphasis has been on trying to define the different ceramic groups covering this transitional period.

Middle Neolithic. As noted above, the Middle Neolithic is characterised by a remarkable assemblage unity which extends over much of northern, western, and southern France. Vaquer (1975) and Phillips (1973) have noted some internal variability within the overall unity of the southern Chasséen (Chasséen du Midi), which is radiocarbon dated from the earlier 4th to the mid 3rd millennium bc. Chasséen assemblages do not appear in the Causses until the later 4th millennium bc.

Pottery. Chasséen pottery is characterised by its good quality and smooth finish. The vessel forms are often carinated and include shouldered and carinated bowls and plates, although hemispherical and simple bag shapes also occur. A few large storage vessels are known, usually globular in shape. Decoration is rare and consists predominantly of geometric motifs, particularly triangles, usually incised after firing, and which may have red or white encrustation. The handles are usually of suspension type, consisting of a wide range of perforated buttons and cordons, as well as unperforated lugs.

Lithics. The flint industry is blade-based, with blades and bladelets produced from pyramid or barrel-shaped cores. The raw material is usually of excellent quality and includes a high proportion of honey-coloured flint although other types are also well represented. This overriding selection of good quality flint is peculiar to the Middle Neolithic, and a large scale redistribution network must have been involved since the sources of this type of raw material lie in well-defined and restricted areas (Fig. 5.7). Good quality flint is used on the Grands Causses, for instance, where it does not occur locally. Phillips has initiated work on raw material characterisation, and early results show that the Rhône valley sources were extensively exploited during the Middle Neolithic. (Phillips 1982; Phillips *et al.*, 1977).

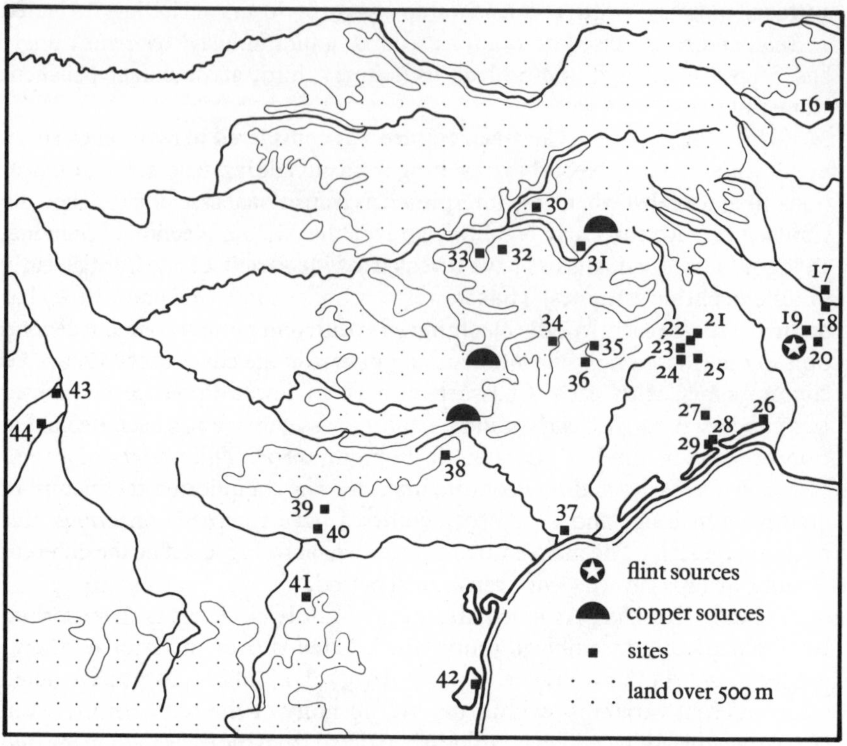

FIGURE 5.7a. Languedoc: important sites and flint and copper sources. 16 Peyroche II (Ardèche); 17 Montclus (Gard); 18 Gardon valley caves (Gard); 19 Fontbouisse (Gard); 20 Vaunage basin (Gard); 21 Ferrières-les-Verreries (Hérault); 22 La Conquette (Hérault); 23 Viols-le-Fort chalcolithic sites (Hérault); 24 Boussargues (Hérault); 25 Lébous (Hérault); 26 Lagoon-side neolithic sites (Hérault); 27 Montpellier neolithic sites (Hérault); 28 Mort des Anes (Hérault); 29 La Madeleine (Hérault); 30 Puechmargues II (Aveyron); 31 Pas de Julié (Aveyron); 32 Longues-Abrites (Aveyron); 33 Sargel (Aveyron); 34 Labeil (Hérault); 35 Saint-Pierre-de-la-Fage (Hérault); 36 Saint-Etienne-de-Gourgas (Hérault); 37 Peiro Signado (Hérault); 38 Camprafaud (Hérault); 39 Gazel (Aude); 40 Font-Juvénal (Aude); 41 Jean Cros (Aude); 42 Ile Corrège (Aude); 43 Saint-Michel-du-Touch (Haute-Garonne); 44 Villeneuve-Tolosane (Haute-Garonne).

The retouched flint tools include burins, points, round or carinated frontal scrapers, and transverse and leaf-shaped arrowheads. The largest flint assemblages occur at open air sites in the basins of Provence and beside the coastal lagoons in Languedoc where some sites have produced several thousand tools. Many of the blades and bladelets have sickle gloss, and have been interpreted as elements of composite sickles (Courtin, 1974a; Courtin and Erroux, 1974). Obsidian blades have been found on numerous sites and characterisation analysis has shown their source to have been Sardinia (Hallam *et al.*, 1976).

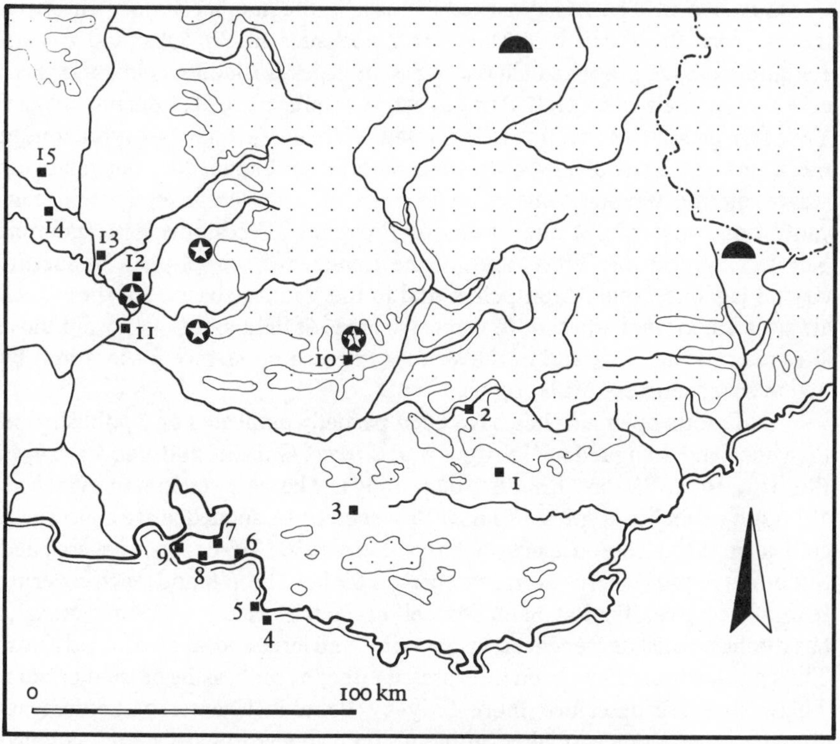

FIGURE 5.7b. Provence: important sites and flint and copper sources.
1 Fontbrégoua (Var); 2 Verdon valley caves (Var); 3 Trets basin (Var/Bouches-du-Rhône); 4 Ile Riou (Bouches-du-Rhône); 5 Ile Maire (Bouches-du-Rhône); 6 Cap Ragnon (Bouches-du-Rhône); 7 Châteauneuf-les-Martigues (Bouches-du-Rhône); 8 La Couronne (Bouches-du-Rhône); 9 Baume Longue (Bouches-du-Rhône); 10 Saint-Mitre (Haute-Provence); 11 La Balance (Vaucluse); 12 Roaix (Vaucluse); 13 Le Baratin (Bouches-du-Rhône); 14 Ouvèze valley sites (Ardèche); 15 Beaussement (Ardèche);

The lithic assemblage also includes numerous polished-stone implements. Small axes are the most frequent, but larger axes and 'hoes' occur. There are also 'chopping' tools and ground-stone mallets and picks, grindstones and rubbers. Raw material characterisation should help define the sources of the raw materials used, and the extent and scale of the redistribution systems (Ricq, 1980).

Bone tools are abundant but not diagnostic, and include points, chisels, polishers, and smoothers, usually made from cattle and caprovid metapodia. Antler is also used for hafts and shafts. Ornaments are rare and similar to those of the Early Neolithic. The principal raw materials are teeth, marine shells, bone and hard stone. These are worked to form bracelets, beads, and pendants. The few burials known are mostly individual, in pits or cists with poor funerary assemblages.

Settlements. There is a marked increase in the number of open air settlements from the Early Neolithic. Over 300 sites in Provence and eastern Languedoc have produced Chasséen assemblages, including about 180 caves and 130 open air sites (G.B. Arnal, 1976; Costantini, 1978; Courtin, 1974a). Very few sites are known from the crystalline areas. Cave sites are numerous in the limestone areas of lower Provence and lower Languedoc, but relatively scarce on the Grands Causses. The open air sites occur in specific concentrations in some of the basins of Provence (Forcalquier, Mormoiron, Salernes, Villecroze, Trets) and on the Languedoc coastal plain beside the coastal lagoons, round Montpellier and in the Vaunage basin. All these open air sites are located adjacent to extensive areas of light arable soils, and those sites near Montpellier and in the Vaunage show a preference for locations by major water sources (Mills, 1980).

Only four open air sites have been partially excavated and published in Provence and Languedoc (D'Anna *et al.*, 1977; Guilaine and Vaquer, 1973; Phillips, 1975, 88–90; Roudil, 1963, 1965). The best settlement evidence, although probably atypical as far as Provence and Languedoc are concerned, comes from the Toulouse area (Clottes *et al.*, 1980; Méroc, 1967; Méroc and Simonnet, 1970) where several extensive sites have been found, each covering several hectares. That at Saint-Michel-du-Touch (Haute Garonne; m.r.43) has ditches, palisade trenches, pits, hearths, and large and small cobbled areas. The cobbled areas have been interpreted either as pit hearths or as hut floors. These sites are described more fully by Bahn in Chapter 7. Settlements elsewhere seem much smaller, although they appear to have similar cobbled features, and pits and post holes have been found. However, no middle neolithic settlement in Provence or Languedoc has so far been adequately excavated, and references in the literature to clearly-defined hut floors (*fonds de cabane*) should be treated with suspicion.

Faunal data are poor but more abundant than for the Early Neolithic. Domestic sheep, goat, cattle, and pig have been present at all excavated sites, and make up the majority of the faunal samples where quantitative data are available (Courtin, 1977; Guilaine, 1977; Poulain, 1976). Sheep and goat are dominant in most of these samples (% number of bones) with cattle usually forming 20–30 per cent, and pig poorly represented. Cereals are known from several sites (Courtin and Erroux, 1974; Erroux, 1976).

The increase in the number of sites from the Early Neolithic is seen by most workers as the result of population growth associated with the successful development of an agricultural economy (Courtin, 1974a, 1976; Guilaine, 1976a; Phillips, 1975). Chasséen populations are considered to have consisted primarily of agricultural communities carrying out cereal and livestock farming, this conclusion being reached on the basis of the reduced percentage of wild animals in the faunal assemblages, the evidence of carbonised cereals, the abundance of bladelets with sickle gloss, the numerous grindstones, and the relatively numerous open air sites on arable soils.

Most workers think the Chasséen the result of local developments, particularly in view of the continuity evident in some of the cave stratigraphies. However, G. B. Arnal (1976) sees the contrast between the assemblage unity of the Middle Neolithic and the diversity of the Early Neolithic and the Late Neolithic/Chalcolithic in terms of the Chasséen being an intrusive culture, under which local traditions were subsumed for a period. The flint industries of the Trets basin of Provence have been regarded as a local variant of the Chasséen culture (Courtin, 1974a), but this argument has been criticised by D'Anna and Mills (1981). The unity of material culture in the Chasséen has provoked some discussion. Phillips (1975, 82) suggests that it reflects 'systemic change in the culture and economy' brought about by population expansion, while Vaquer (1975, 32) argues that the large scale redistribution system indicated by the flint assemblages was the key factor in the development and the unity of Chasséen material culture.

Late Neolithic/Chalcolithic

The 3rd millennium bc sees the break up of the assemblage unity of the Middle Neolithic, and numerous localised cultures have been defined, particularly in Languedoc. Most authors agree that there is continuity between middle and late neolithic assemblages, although G. B. Arnal takes a contrary view as noted above. The validity of the term Chalcolithic has also been questioned (Courtin, 1970) since copper artefacts are rare in Provence and western Languedoc. Copper objects are quite numerous in eastern Languedoc, appearing about 2500bc in the Grands Causses (Clottes and Costantini, 1976; Costantini, 1978, 48–54), and about 2200bc on the Garrigues (Gutherz, 1975). There is direct continuity between the Late Neolithic and the Chalcolithic in other aspects of the assemblages, and the flint industries are identical. The term Chalcolithic is used here as a cultural-chronological guide, although the shorthand 'Late Neolithic/Chalcolithic' is frequently necessary as the material cannot be attributed more precisely.

The local cultures of the Late Neolithic/Chalcolithic have mostly been defined on the basis of an extremely restricted range of type fossils. There are broad similarities between assemblages throughout the area and the common elements may be considered first, followed by a summary of the various local cultures. Current interpretative frameworks are considered in a third section.

Common elements: pottery. One of the most characteristic features of the ceramic assemblages is a thick-walled, round-bottomed cylindrical jar, up to 0.8m high, which is generally referred to as a storage vessel. In eastern lower Languedoc and the Grands Causses these vessels have a varying number of applied smooth cordons and lug handles, but in Provence they do not have smooth cordons, while in western Languedoc the *Vérazien* culture is defined by cylindrical vessels with superposed lugs and no cordons, although cordoned vessels also occur. Large vessels are less frequent at burial sites (Courtin, 1974a, 1970) but are abundant in small caves on the Grands Causses where they seem to have been used for water collection (Martin *et al.*, 1964). A range of globular and hemispherical pots is also common to most assemblages, with applied and *repoussé* pastil decoration. The pottery is generally smooth-surfaced and well-made, although not as finely finished as that of the Middle Neolithic.

Lithics. There is a sharp contrast between the blade-based industries of the Middle Neolithic and the flake-based flint industries of the Late Neolithic / Chalcolithic. Most of the late neolithic / chalcolithic industries use poor quality flint from local sources in the limestones; on the Causses, where there are no local flint sources, chert is used instead. A few blades occur, but most of the implements are awls, scrapers, and points on flakes. The arrowheads are bifacially retouched, and leaf-shaped or barbed-and-tanged. 'Crenellated' arrowheads are restricted to the Grands Causses where they have been used to define the Rodezien chalcolithic culture.

Good quality flint continues to be used for specific items in the late neolithic period although the raw material is different to that of the Middle Neolithic. The most numerous of these artefacts are long, fine blades, curved sickles, often with sickle gloss, and finely retouched daggers. Lacustrine flint is selectively used for these artefacts, and some of the sources have been identified. The flint mines at Salinelles (Gard) in eastern Languedoc have been excavated (Bordreuil, 1974), while Courtin (1974a, 187–8) suggests it was at this period that the flint extraction centres in upper Provence were exploited on a large scale. Well-made flint products are found in considerable numbers throughout the area on both settlement and burial sites. Polished-stone tools, and grindstones, rubbers, mallets and picks also occur.

Bone tools are numerous but not diagnostic, the types including points, chisels, and smoothers, and there are also antler hafts and shafts. The abundance of bone tools at cave sites on the edges of the Grands Causses has been used to define local late neolithic cultures there.

Ornaments are abundant and characteristic of the period. They are found mainly at burial sites, in caves and dolmens, and include a wide variety of beads and pendants in bone, teeth, steatite, calcite, hard rocks, shell, copper, and lead.

Copper. The earliest copper objects in this region are the beads found in late Chasséen levels at Sargel (m.r.33) on the Grands Causses (Costantini, 1970b, 1970c) dated to about 2500bc, and the use of copper is restricted to this area until about 2200bc (Gutherz, 1975). Subsequently flat axes, various types of dagger, and awls appear. They are mainly concentrated on the Grands Causses but some also occur in lower eastern Languedoc associated with the Fontbouisse culture. Courtin (1974a) argues that there is no real Chalcolithic in Provence since copper objects are scarce, and the same is also true of western Languedoc. Copper ores are found in the Grands Causses and to the east and west in the crystalline massifs, but are rare in Provence (Fig.5.7).

Burial. Collective burial in caves and megalithic tombs ('dolmens') is a general characteristic of the period. Inhumation, or simply placing the dead on the floor of a cave is the usual burial mode, although cremation is also known (Costantini, 1978). The numbers buried together vary. Courtin (1974a, 170) estimates between ten and sixty as the average in Provence, although in exceptional cases as at Roaix (Bouches-du-Rhône; m.r.12), several hundred have been found (Courtin, 1974a, 180–4). Similarly in Languedoc, remains of 300 individuals were found in the cave of Pas de Julié (Aveyron; m.r.31) in the Grands Causses (Costantini, 1978, 45), but a figure of ten to sixty seems reasonable for most dolmens. The burials include all ages and both sexes. Unfortunately, most of the dolmens were excavated in the 19th or earlier 20th centuries and there are consequently no detailed analyses of numbers, of age and sex distributions, of systematic differences in burial practices between different areas or types of site, or of social ranking or categorisation in the funerary assemblages.

The burial caves are often small, and difficult of access. They frequently produce homogeneous assemblages which suggest a short period of use, but the dolmens show evidence of prolonged utilisation throughout much of the Late Neolithic/Chalcolithic and into the Bronze and Iron Ages. Only the most recent burials are in anatomical connection, the earlier remains being scattered about although long bones and skulls may be carefully placed aside (Costantini, 1978, 45). Certain tombs appear associated with specific short-term events. Thus at Longues Abrites (Aveyron; m.r.32) on the Grands Causses there is a burned layer containing numerous carbonised bones and artefacts (Costantini, 1978, 44) while at Roaix in Provence, several hundred skeletons in the upper level were found in anatomical connection stacked on top of each other. Some of the skeletons at Roaix had arrowheads embedded in the bones, suggesting that the upper level of burials may have been a war grave (Courtin, 1974a, 180–4), and bones with arrowheads embedded in them are found quite frequently in Languedoc also (J. Arnal, 1963, 215; Costantini, 1978, 57). Several rock-cut tombs which probably belong to this period occur in the Arles-Fontvieille area at the head of the Rhône delta (Courtin, 1974a, 177–8).

The assemblages associated with the burials include numerous ornaments as well as flint tools, particularly arrowheads, and daggers and sickles in lacustrine flint, and metal objects in chalcolithic and bronze age contexts. Pottery is rare in the dolmens and this fact, together with the inadequacy of the excavations, has led to considerable dating problems as the ornaments do not give a firm relative chronology. It is now generally agreed that the first dolmens were constructed during the Late Neolithic, and that most of them date to the Late Neolithic/Chalcolithic though often continuing in use into the Middle Bronze Age, and into the Iron Age in some cases. Unfortunately it is not possible to date the sequence and relative frequency of dolmen construction in different areas and periods more accurately owing to the poor quality of the data.

Settlement. Several hundred late neolithic/chalcolithic cave and open air sites, and a few thousand dolmens are known, concentrated mainly in the limestone areas. Some 100–200 settlements with stone-built long houses occur on the Languedoc Garrigues, and open air sites are also numerous in the limestone areas of Provence, particularly inland Provence. There are a few open air sites in the Provençal basins, and recent field survey (Mills, 1980) shows that open air settlements are much more numerous than was previously thought on the coastal plain of Languedoc. The present scarcity of settlement evidence in these areas seems due to a combination of lack of research and the destruction of many sites by erosion. However, open air sites remain rare on the plateaux of the Grands Causses despite years of research by different workers. Dolmens are numerous on the Garrigues and the Grands Causses, but rare in Provence, while cave sites are abundant in all these areas. As with previous periods, there is little evidence of settlement in the crystalline massifs. The settlement evidence is on the whole far better than for preceding periods, however, since several open air sites have been or are being excavated. The data from the Languedoc Garrigues are particularly good, but important gaps exist in the coastal plain and in the Provençal basins.

Faunal and floral data continue to be rare in this period. Caprovids dominate the faunal assemblages on most sites, with cattle at 20–30 per cent and pig poorly represented (Courtin, 1977). Wild animals are dominant at a few sites in upper Languedoc, and this is considered a characteristic of the Saint Ponien and Gourgasien cultures. Cereals and a variety of legumes, fruits, and nuts occur at various sites (Costantini, 1978, 71; Courtin and Erroux, 1974; Gasco, 1976, 72).

REGIONAL CULTURES. The *Vérazien* occurs mainly in western Languedoc, west of the Hérault, and was identified by Guilaine and Rigaud (Guilaine and Rigaud, 1968; Guilaine, 1970d, 1976a, 1980; Guilaine and Roudil, 1976). The main distinctive artefact type is a round-bottomed cylindrical vessel with superposed lugs. The earliest levels with these vessels are dated to about 2600bc, and the pottery continues down to about 1700bc, spanning both the Late Neolithic and the Chalcolithic although no copper objects are known. Flint tools are rare but include blades, flakes, and fine items made of lacustrine flint. Settlement structures are also poorly known, pits filled with pottery and various other remains being the principal features to have been excavated apart from several cave sites. However, these pits have been found widely over the coastal plain of western Languedoc and along the Aude valley, and probably represent the remains of open air settlements. Gasco (1980a) has noted that Vérazien open air sites tend to be located on light arable soils, near water sources.

Ferrières. The principal late neolithic culture in eastern Languedoc is the *Ferrières*, which is also distinguished by its ceramic assemblage, particularly the decoration. This decoration is executed before firing, and consists of simple combinations of incised lines (continuous or broken) and chevrons, as well as incised garlands, various types of impressions, and some simple channelling (G.B.Arnal, 1976; J.Arnal, 1963; Guilaine, 1976a, 194–5; Guilaine and Roudil, 1976; Gutherz, 1975, 29; 1980; Montjardin, 1967, 1970). The pottery forms consist of simple rounded types.

The characteristic incised decoration was first recognised at the dolmen of Ferrières-les-Verreries (Hérault) on the Garrigues near Montpellier. Audibert (1958, 1962) criticised the definition of Ferrières on the grounds of an absence of stratigraphies and an inadequate assemblage, but subsequently Ferrières levels were found stratified at several sites and local variants distinguished in the Ardèche, the Gard and Hérault Garrigues, the Grands Causses, and the lower Rhône. However, the assemblage is still poorly known since only two sites, Peyroche II (m.r.16; Roudil and Saumade, 1968) and Beaussement (m.r.15; Montjardin, 1962, 1965, 1967) in the Ardèche have produced large, homogeneous ceramic groups. Radiocarbon dates suggest a period from about 2600–2200bc for the Ferrières culture.

Ferrières material is known mainly from caves. G.B. Arnal (1976) lists some 300 sites in the Hérault, Gard, and Aveyron, of which 60 per cent are caves and rock-shelters, 25 per cent open air sites, and 15 per cent dolmens and others. Most of these sites are located on the Garrigues, but they are also fairly numerous on the Grands Causses. The stone-built open air sites of the Garrigues are described below since most seem to belong to the Fontbouisse Chalcolithic. However, Ferrières pottery assemblages have been found at stone-built settlements on the southern edges of the Garrigues (see Mills, 1980, 125), and at several open air settlements consisting of pits and ditches on the coastal plain. Despite several excavations and test soundings, no open air settlements in the interior of the Garrigues have produced large Ferrières assemblages, although a few characteristic sherds were found at Cambous (Hérault) amongst abundant Fontbouisse material (Canet and Roudil, 1978).

Fontbouisse. The FONTBOUISSE culture has been the most studied and is the best defined of all the regional late neolithic/chalcolithic assemblages (J. Arnal, 1963; Gasco, 1976; Gutherz, 1975; Louis *et al.*, 1947; Montjardin, 1966a, 1970). The pottery provides the main characteristic attributes, but in contrast to Ferrières and other cultures is marked by the great variety and complexity of forms and decoration, and the good finish of the fine wares. The forms include a range of simple and complex carinated vessels, as well as rounded and cylindrical pots. The decoration occurs on the carinated and rounded forms, and is distinguished by the association of particular decorative themes (channelled, incised, and impressed garlands, checkboard patterns, chevrons, etc.) in complex motifs (Gutherz, 1975). Channelled checkboard decoration is especially characteristic and is used as a type fossil. The Fontbouisse culture is also defined by small numbers of copper artefacts, and the radiocarbon dates suggest a span of about 400 years for this culture, from 2200 to 1800bc.

Fontbouisse settlements. Sites with Fontbouisse assemblages are concentrated on the Languedoc Garrigues. This distribution is similar to that of the Ferrières culture although there are few traces of Fontbouisse assemblages on the Grands Causses. There is apparently, however, a radical change in the nature of the evidence since Fontbouisse sites include a high proportion of open air settlements. Gutherz (1975) records 104 cave and 100 open air sites in the Hérault, Gard, and Ardèche Garrigues, and suggests that as an estimate of the real number of open air sites this is conservative. These settlements are best known in the Montpellier Garrigues where several have been excavated and

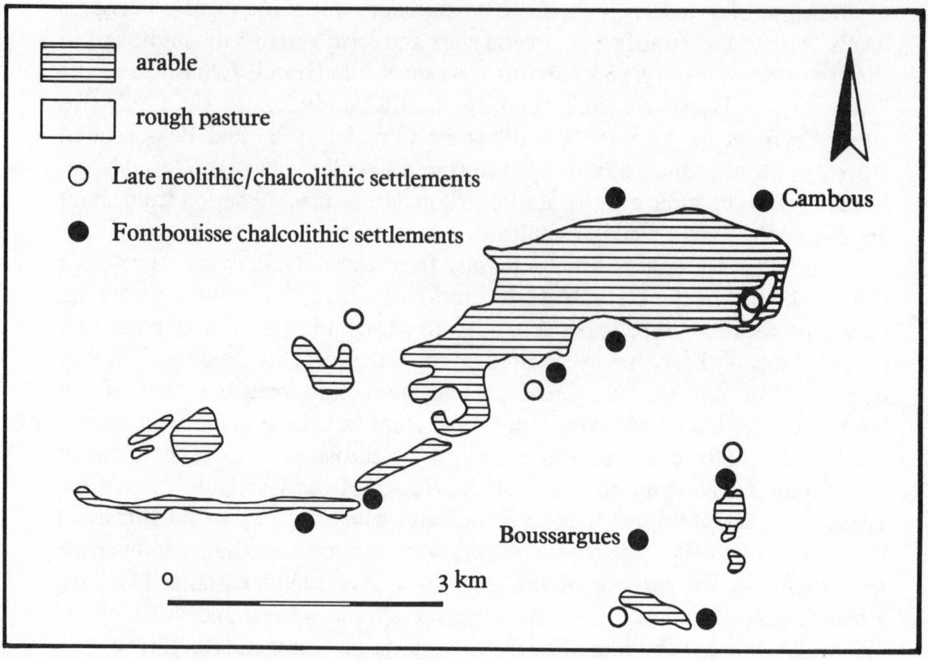

FIGURE 5.8. Distribution of the chalcolithic settlements in the Viols-le-Fort area.

found to consist of groups of dry-stone walled long houses. The settlements are distributed over the whole surface of the Garrigues, located preferentially adjacent to small areas of cultivable soils found in depressions in the plateaux. In the Viols-le-Fort area (Fig.5.8), north of Montpellier, 13 settlements are known, positioned round a series of small depressions which provide a maximum of about 600 hectares of arable soil. Nine of these settlements have been excavated or sounded, and all these have produced Fontbouisse assemblages.

The settlements consist of groups of long houses or huts, with rubble-filled dry-stone walls (Plate 5.5). The groups tend to be closely knit, with adjoining but not shared walls. There is no rigorous planning in the grouping or orientation of the huts, either in relationship to streets or squares or to each other. Some huts are positioned in rows, but others may be joined to these at varying angles. The standard hut type is sub-rectangular in plan, with one apsidal and one straight end, although there are examples with two rounded ends. In the former case the entrance is at the apsidal end. The internal dimensions of the huts vary from about 1.5–3.5m wide by 7–15m long, with an average floor area of 20–30m^2. This standard hut type occurs in groups of 3–5 to 30–50, the average being between 5 and 15, although single isolated huts are known and Cambous (Canet and Roudil, 1978) has over 50 huts.

Excavation of a group of these huts at La Conquette (Bailloud, 1973)

PLATE 5.5. Cambous (Hérault): long hut with rubble-filled dry-stone walls of the late neolithic/chalcolithic Fontbouisse group. (Photo: Nigel Mills.)

suggested that in most cases each hut represents a discrete habitation unit with a series of well-defined activity areas (Fig. 5.9). Bailloud found a recurrent pattern, with a hearth located at the opposite end to the entrance, and the majority of the artefacts clustered round it. Large storage vessels were aligned against the rear wall, with smaller vessels round the hearth, all broken *in situ*. Stone and flint tools and some *débitage* were found in the same general area, artefacts being rare over the rest of the hut floor. Similar spatial patterning, particularly as to the alignment of large storage vessels against the end walls of the huts, has been found at Gravas (Hérault: J. Arnal *et al.*, 1967), Lébous (Hérault: J. Arnal, 1973a, 1973b) and Boussargues (Hérault; m.r.24: Colomer *et al.*, 1980). Larger huts with a floor area of up to $130m^2$ also occur, as do small huts which may be circular, rectangular, or irregular in shape. Present data are inadequate to show whether these two hut types are functionally distinct, or are merely smaller and larger variations of the standard unit. Some of the larger huts are probably discrete habitation units as they are the dominant type at several sites, but at Cambous they are associated with smaller huts in a multiple unit with interconnecting doorways (Canet and Roudil, 1978). The large huts have also been interpreted as communal meeting houses and/or stalls (Gasco, 1976, 36).

Enclosure walls have been identified at Boussargues (Fig. 5.10; Colomer *et al.*, 1980) and Lébous (m.r.25; J. Arnal, 1973a, 1973b). These walls have circular constructions of 2m diameter built into them at intervals (Plate 5.6). Arnal interpreted Lébous as a fortified site, but Gutherz (pers.comm.) con-

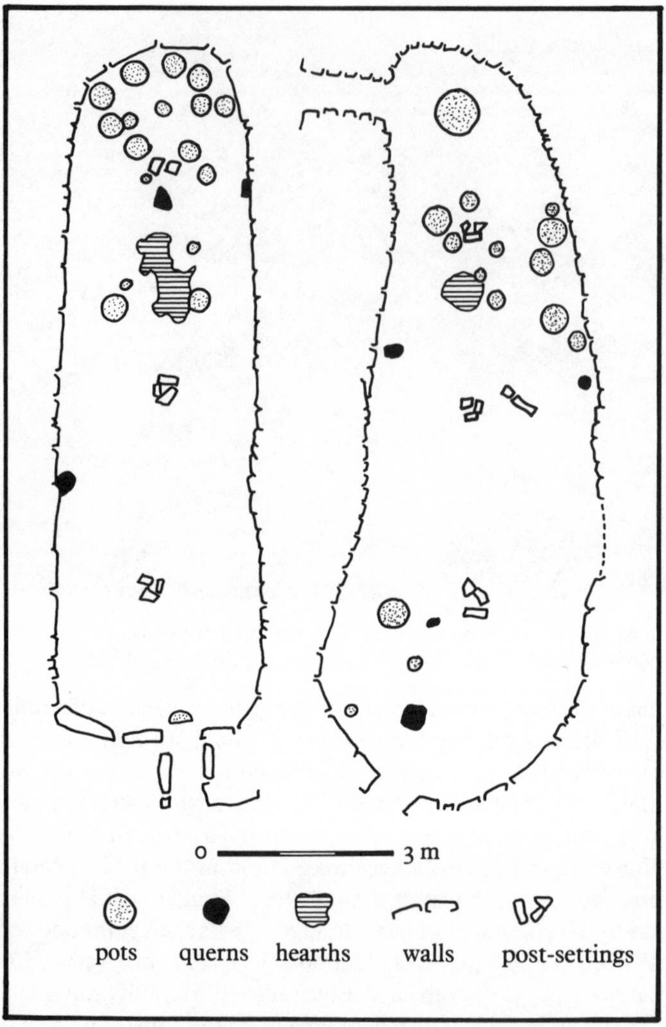

FIGURE 5.9. Internal plan and artefact distributions of the chalcolithic (Fontbouisse) huts at La Conquette. (After Bailloud, 1973.)

siders the circular 'towers' and the walls too insubstantial for this. He interprets the walls as stock enclosures, and makes an analogy between the circular constructions and shepherds' huts or *borries* of historical times. Huts are found inside the perimeter wall at both sites and they also occur outside and against it at Boussargues. The two sites are located in prominent positions relative to local topography, in contrast to most other sites which are lowlying, adjacent to the small arable depressions. Neither site has produced a particularly rich or otherwise distinctive assemblage.

These settlements with stone-built huts are best known from the Mont-

PLATE 5.6. Boussargues (Hérault): circular dry-stone structure attached to the enclosure wall (see also Figure 5.10). (Photo: Nigel Mills.)

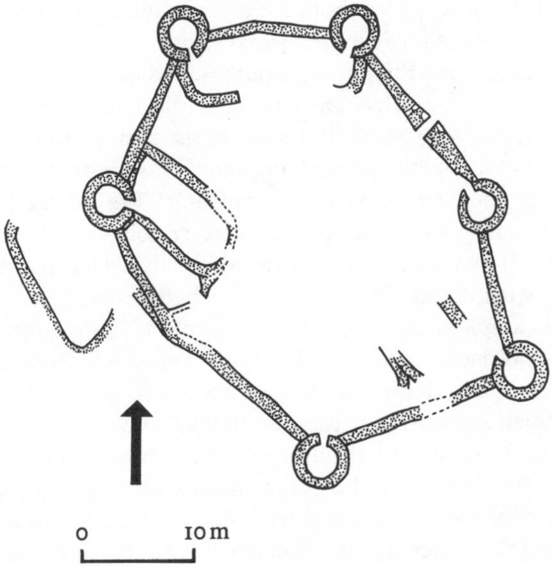

FIGURE 5.10. The chalcolithic enclosure of Boussargues (Hérault). (After Colomer *et al.*, 1980.)

pellier Garrigues, but they also occur on the Nîmes Garrigues, although the construction is slightly different (Gasco, 1976), probably due to a difference in building material, the soft limestones of the Nîmes area breaking up differently to the hard limestones of the Montpellier area. Several settlements with stone-built huts are also known from the coastal plain including three in the Vaunage basin near Nîmes (see Mills, 1980). The walls are less substantial than at settlements on the plateaux, perhaps because stone is less easily available here than on the Garrigues, and more wood was used in their construction. Other settlements on the coastal plain, further from the Garrigues, have pits, ditches and hearths, but no evidence of dry-stone construction (Gasco, 1976; Prades, 1972). Recent survey work in the Vaunage (Mills, 1980) shows that Fontbouisse settlements are far more numerous in the coastal plain than has previously been thought, with a likely density of at least one late neolithic/chalcolithic site per square kilometre. The pottery preserves badly so that most of these sites are defined by flint scatters. However, of the fifteen probable open air settlements in the Vaunage basin, eight have produced clearly defined assemblages as a result of excavations or soundings, and all eight have produced Fontbouisse material.

Gourgasien/Saint Ponien. Two late neolithic cultures have been defined at cave sites in upper Languedoc, on the south-western border of the Grands Causses. G. B. Arnal (1970, 1972, 1976) defined the *Gourgasien* culture from the type site of Saint-Etienne-de-Gourgas (m.r.36). The assemblage is characterised by pottery with hachured, incised triangles, or with sinuous cordons, and flat-based vessels with reinforced, overhanging rims; asymmetrical arrowheads; polished haematite; an abundant bone industry including much antler; and a high proportion of wild animals in the faunal samples. These attributes are found in levels 14–18 at Saint-Etienne-de-Gourgas, and radiocarbon dated to between 2600 and 2400bc. G. B. Arnal considers the Gourgasien to be distributed south and west of the Causse du Larzac in the area round Lodève.

Rodriguez (1968, 1970a, 1970b) defined the *Saint Ponien* culture from the stratigraphies at Camprafaud (m.r.38) and Resplandy. The characteristic attributes are pottery, undecorated except for some vessels with a smooth cordon just below the rim; asymmetrical arrowheads; polished haematite; an abundant bone industry including much antler; and a high proportion of wild animals in the faunal samples. The Saint Ponien levels at Camprafaud are bracketed by radiocarbon-dated middle neolithic and chalcolithic levels, indicating a mid 3rd millennium bc date as for the Gourgasien. Sites considered to belong to the Saint Ponien are centred to the west of the Gourgasien.

Treilles. The Late Neolithic/Chalcolithic of the Grands Causses was initially termed *Rodezien*, characterised by crenellated arrowheads (J. Arnal, 1953). A *Treilles* late neolithic culture was later defined, distinct from the Rodezien chalcolithic (the latter being associated with the arrowheads: J. Arnal *et al.*, 1960). However, at the Sargel cave, Costantini (1967, 1970a, 1970b) found levels containing pottery with hachured triangle decoration below levels with Treilles assemblages, and above middle neolithic levels.

Costantini noted continuity throughout the sequence at Sargel, and prefers to group all the late neolithic/chalcolithic material of the Causses as the Treilles culture (Costantini, 1978), with chronological stages: the first, 2600–2300bc characterised by pottery with hachured triangle decoration; the second, 2300–2000bc associated with winged bead ornaments; the third, 2000–1700bc defined by crenellated arrowheads. Lorblanchet (1965, 1970) takes a similar view, but prefers to term the culture Rodezien rather than Treilles. G. B. Arnal suggests a different classification. He considers the use of the term Treilles anomalous since most of the assemblage is common to the whole of the Languedoc Late Neolithic/Chalcolithic, except for the tendency for more numerous cordons on the large cylindrical vessels. Incised chevron decoration is fairly common on the Causses and G. B. Arnal classifies the Late Neolithic as part of Ferrières, distinguishing the crenellated arrowheads and hachured triangle decoration as artefact horizons specific to the area which give it cultural identity but which do not distinguish it as a separate unit.

Similar problems of definition exist with the Saint Ponien and Gourgasien cultures. G.B.Arnal (1976) subsumes the Saint Ponien of Rodriguez within his own Gourgasien, while Guilaine (1976a; Guilaine and Roudil, 1976) notes that the two are very similar, and Costantini (1978; Clottes and Costantini, 1976) groups them together as Saint Pono-Gourgasien. Bailloud (1970) considered the ways in which the cultures had been defined and observed that the researchers could be divided into lumpers and splitters, depending on whether similarities or differences were stressed. Quantitative analysis would be a useful means of assessing the degree of difference or similarity between the assemblages, but has not yet been attempted.

In the opinion of the present writer there is a basic homogeneity in the late neolithic assemblages of the Causses and lower eastern Languedoc, and the type fossils are useful for cross-dating but have varying and overlapping spatial and chronological contexts and do not define distinct regional groups. Thus the hachured triangle decoration characteristic of the early phase of the Treilles culture also occurs in the middle phase and is associated with Gourgasien sinuous cordon decoration at the type sites of both cultures. Ferrières ceramic decoration is associated with hachured triangles at Labeil (Hérault: Bousquet *et al.*, 1966, 1970) and at Font-Juvénal (Guilaine *et al.*, 1974, 1976b) and is actually more widespread over the Causses than the latter, which, however, were used by Costantini to characterise the early Late Neolithic of the Grands Causses. Costantini also used winged bead ornaments to define the middle phase of the Treilles culture, but these are widespread in lower Languedoc as well (J. Arnal, 1963). The same point applies to the asymmetrical arrowheads of the Saint Ponien and Gourgasien, which are found widely in western Languedoc throughout much of the 3rd millennium bc (Aubert, 1979). However, important regional differences exist between upper and lower eastern Languedoc in the Chalcolithic (late Treilles or Rodezien culture on the Grands Causses). Fontbouisse ceramic decoration has a limited, largely southern distribution (Costantini, 1978) and carinated forms are rare. In contrast, the crenellated arrowhead which is the type fossil of the Causses Chalcolithic is only rarely found in lower Languedoc (J. Arnal, 1963; Costantini, 1978) but is abundant on the Causses. These arrowheads appear late in the Chalcolithic, and continue into the Early Bronze Age, and are therefore contemporary with later Fontbouisse.

The Causses Final Neolithic/Chalcolithic is known almost exclusively from dolmens and cave sites. Despite many years of research, sometimes specifically orientated towards finding open air settlements (Durand-Tullou, 1956), few surface sites are known. Apart from a few probable settlements located adjacent to the larger areas of cultivable soils, the open air sites on the plateaux consist of flint scatters in thin soils in exposed positions, often associated with nearby rock shelters. These sites seem more akin to temporary camps than permanent settlements. Very few open air sites are known from the more extensive areas of cultivable soils in the narrow valleys.

The general distribution and specific locations of dolmens on the Causse du Larzac show three main features (Mills, 1980), similar patterning being noted by Combarnous (1960) for the southern Larzac, and by Lorblanchet (1965) for the Causses Noir, Bégon, and Méjean. First, the dolmens are distributed on the pure limestones and avoid the dolomitic limestones. Lorblanchet (1965, 277) observed this and noted that some dolmens are made from dolomitic blocks so that this selective distribution is unlikely to be due to differences in the construction quality of the rock itself. An important agricultural difference between the limestones is that the soils on the hard limestones support better quality pasture than the dolomites (Saussol, 1971).

Second, the dolmens are located adjacent to, or dominating, the karst depressions where deeper soils occur. Where the monuments are located adjacent to the depressions the association is obvious, but in perched positions also, the dolmens are sited on false crests or on small eminences on the slopes so that they are visible from the depressions and not from the other sides of the raised ground.

Third, the monuments tend to occur in small groups of two or three, either together or strung out at intervals along the edges of a depression or series of depressions. In some cases the dolmens seem consciously sited so that each dolmen is intervisible with one or more of the others in its group.

Couronnien. The COURONNIEN is the only localised late neolithic/chalcolithic culture identified in Provence, and this is defined by the absence of pottery decoration and the abundance of large storage vessels (Courtin, 1974a, 1976; Escalon de Fonton, 1947, 1970b). The forms are almost exclusively rounded and the culture is known principally from the open air site of La Couronne (Bouches-du-Rhône) where excavations have revealed several timber and dry-stone walled long houses located on a limestone plateau adjacent to a small area of arable land (Escalon de Fonton, 1976b). The Couronnien is dated to 2200–2000bc.

The left bank of the Rhône is closely associated with eastern Languedoc, and Ferrières and Fontbouisse decorative motifs have been found at several sites (Courtin, 1974a, 1976; Montjardin, 1966a, 1966b, 1967). Courtin notes that the Ferrières and Fontbouisse material is often mixed, while Montjardin suggests that Ferrières decoration persists much later in the lower Rhône than in Languedoc.

Courtin (1970, 1974a, 1976) considers the rest of Provence to have had a generalised late neolithic/chalcolithic culture. Cordons applied in a chevron style seem specific to Provence while the bands of smooth cordons characteristic of Languedoc are absent. The pottery known is mainly from burials and Courtin (1974a, 197–201) distinguishes between funerary and settlement assemblages. The former have small, fine vessels, while coarse, large domestic wares dominate on the few open sites that have been excavated. The open sites usually consist of flint scatters, with no evidence of dry-stone wall construction, and are numerous on the limestone plateaux of inland Provence. Late neolithic/chalcolithic flint assemblages also occur in the basins of Provence, but are much rarer there than blade-based industries. In the Trets basin, for instance (Courtin, 1974a; D'Anna and Mills, 1981; Mills, 1980), flake-based industries and typical late neolithic/chalcolithic flint implements occur, but blades and bladelets are predominant at all the sites currently known. This situation contrasts with the Vaunage basin in eastern Languedoc where the flint industries are almost exclusively flake-based, apart from a few clearly-defined scatters of blades and bladelets associated with middle neolithic pottery.

Beaker assemblages occur widely in Provence and Languedoc. International combed and corded wares occur in local chalcolithic assemblages in Provence and western Languedoc, but are rare in eastern Languedoc (Courtin, 1976; Guilaine and Roudil, 1976). Beakers with regional decorative motifs are more numerous (incised and stamped decoration in Provence and the lower Rhône, incised, stamped, and combed decoration in western Languedoc) and a few cave and open sites have produced homogeneous regional Beaker assemblages including domestic wares. The lithic industry is poorly known, but a few ornaments (archer's wristguards, arc-shaped pendants, various button types) characteristic of Beaker assemblages have been found. The International combed and corded types are seen as intrusive, whereas regional groups are considered to represent local Beaker cultures existing contemporaneously with other chalcolithic cultures (Courtin, 1976; Guilaine and Roudil, 1976).

Current Interpretative Models

All authors contrast the assemblage unity of the Middle Neolithic with the diversity of the Late Neolithic/Chalcolithic and two explanations are given for this change: first, a resurgence of local traditions following the intrusion of the Chasséen culture (G.B. Arnal, 1976); second, population growth following improved adaptation to local ecological conditions (Guilaine, 1976a; Hodder, 1979, 451–2; Phillips, 1975). Hodder and Phillips consider that the stylistic variety reflects changes in social structure brought about by stress induced by a high density of population, and this argument is developed by Mills (1980). Other writers see the variety as the social manifestation of the adaptation of particular human groups to particular ecological zones; thus the Gourgasien and Saint Ponien cultures in the mountainous areas on the edges of the Grands Causses (G.B.Arnal, 1976; Guilaine, 1976a) and the Ferrières and Fontbouisse cultures on the Garrigues (Delano-Smith, 1972; Gasco, 1976; Guilaine, 1976a; Gutherz, 1975).

The latter model of a culture being adapted to a particular ecological zone fits the Ferrières and Fontbouisse cultures best, and is in this case derived from Louis' (1948) model. The abundant remains of these cultures on the Garrigues, and their scarcity in the coastal plain, are taken to show that both were specifically adapted to life on the limestone plateaux, hence their distinctive assemblages, settlements, and burial monuments. Ferrières 'people' practised a pastoral economy since few settlements are known (Guilaine, 1976a) while Fontbouisse 'people' practised a mixed farming economy, the importance of cereal cultivation being shown by selective site location adjacent to cultivable depressions (Delano-Smith, 1972; Gasco, 1976; Guilaine, 1976a; Guilaine and Roudil, 1976; Gutherz, 1975). The selection of the Garrigues as a preferred area of settlement by Ferrières and Fontbouisse is assumed either to result from cultural choice, or to be due to changes in environmental conditions since the Chalcolithic (Delano-Smith, 1972), following the model of environmental degradation discussed earlier in this chapter. Delano-Smith suggests the plateau soils would have been light and easily tilled prior to erosion, in contrast to the heavy, forested soils of the plain. Middle neolithic settlements concentrated by the coast and on the edges of the Garrigues, but population growth in the Chalcolithic led to settlement expansion into the interior of the Garrigues while the major part of the plain was avoided.

Mills (1980) has argued against this view of environmental degradation, pointing out the bias against the coastal plain in present data samples, and arguing that the available botanical and pedological data show that the Garrigues would not have offered opportunities for settlement and land-use that were radically different from today. Data from the Vaunage survey show a high density of late neolithic/chalcolithic settlements, spaced a few hundred metres apart over the arable soils of the basin (Fig.5.11). There is an apparent increase in settlement density in the Late Neolithic, but the greatest number of sites belongs to the Fontbouisse Chalcolithic. This high population level is seen to coincide with the evidence of Fontbouisse settlement on the Garrigues, indicating a major growth of population and consequent expansion into marginal areas. The main centre of Ferrières and Fontbouisse settlement would have been the coastal plain, the construction of dolmens on the Garrigues during the Late Neolithic showing that these plateaux formed part of the annual territories exploited by the plain-based populations, probably for pastoral purposes.

The Treilles culture has also been seen as adapted to the Causses plateaux, with an economy based on small-scale transhumance from the valleys to the plateaux, and some cereal cultivation. In Provence, Courtin (1974a) suggests that a mixed agricultural economy was practised.

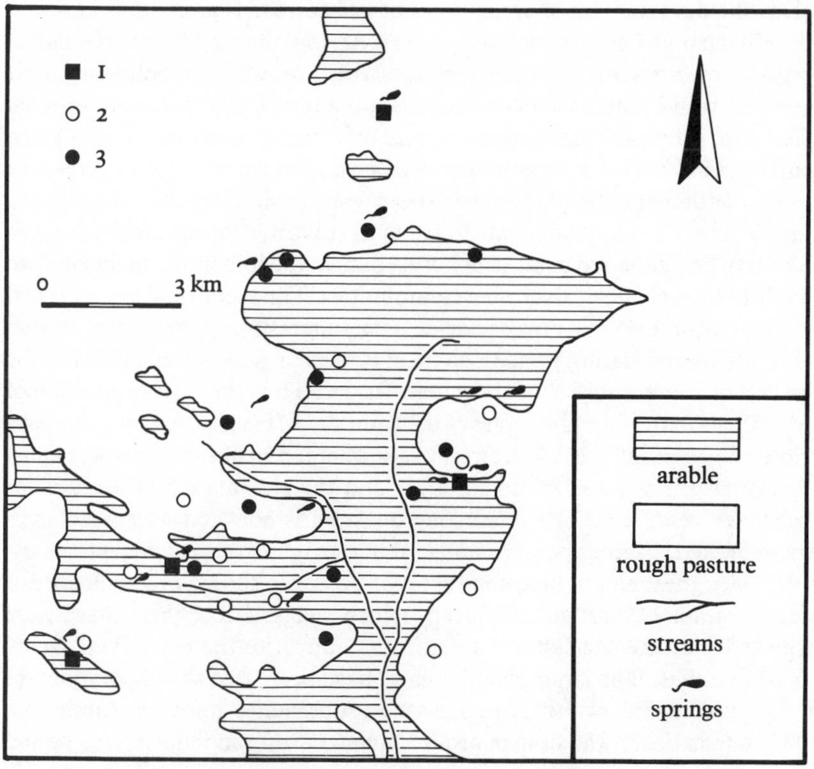

FIGURE 5.11. Distribution of neolithic settlements in the Vaunage. Six of the eight settlements located on arable soils in the south-west part of the Vaunage basin were found by field survey in 1978.
1 Middle neolithic settlements; 2 Late neolithic/chalcolithic settlements; 3 Fontbouisse chalcolithic settlements.

Discussion and Conclusion

Present data provide an important and detailed chronological framework for assessing the development of the Neolithic in southern France. Unfortunately, much of the data is otherwise inadequate to answer the sorts of questions concerning social and economic processes which are now considered as key areas of archaeological investigation. Nor will this situation change unless future data collection is designed to provide information relevant to these questions. Much of the data has been collected in response to questions posed by the culture-historical paradigm, the most recent example being the selection of cave sites for excavation on the grounds that their deep stratigraphies would provide detailed chronological sequences, thereby providing the key to understanding cultural evolution. The first, chronological objective has been partly achieved, but the cave data give only a partial and biased view of human social and economic development, and make it difficult to address questions such as the development of agriculture, of village-based agricultural societies, and/or exchange and production systems. As Guilaine and others (Guilaine, 1979), following work by American and British researchers, point out, most cave sites would only have been occupied on a temporary, probably seasonal basis, and offer an incomplete picture of human activities for a given group or period. This is especially true of agricultural communities for whom the main settlements are likely to have been open air sites located on or adjacent to arable land. In a modern context, using the cave assemblages as the basis of study may be likened to using shepherds' huts in the hills as the main guide to the way of life of historical farming communities. The shepherds' activities and material cultural remains may provide some interesting perspectives on that way of life, accentuating perhaps some of its eccentricities, but can hardly be regarded as representative of the whole system. Thus the high proportion of wild animals in the faunal samples of the Saint Pono/Gourgasien cave sites, at a period when agriculture is well attested elsewhere, probably reflects occasional or seasonal use of these mountain areas and the exploitation of local, wild, subsistence resources. The interesting question is how and why these areas were exploited. Contemporary faunal samples from cave sites in the Causses, on the Garrigues, and in limestone areas of Provence show a predominance of domestic animals, particularly sheep, which suggests that these areas were integrated into the agricultural system, in contrast to the Saint Pono-Gourgasien cave sites. The latter may therefore have been used as temporary bases for the exploitation of other, perhaps non-subsistence resources (antler for hafts?, haematite?), the human groups 'living off the land' during the period of their stay.

At a regional scale, and although there have been some attempts to redress the situation, the data are heavily biased towards the limestone areas, and towards cave and burial sites. The recent geomorphological studies show that this biasing effect is further complicated by widespread destruction of archaeological sites over the soft rocks of the coastal plain and the Provençal basins. The Vaunage survey (Mills, 1980) increased the number of late neolithic/chalcolithic sites in the area of the basin covered by intensive field survey (4.3km^2) from one to seven, demonstrating the extent of the biasing effect induced by lack of research and site destruction.

Our interests as archaeologists lie ultimately in the area of social and economic relations of and between human groups, and recent work in southern France has begun to address these problems by looking at production and exchange systems (Phillips, 1982; Phillips *et al.*, 1977; Hallam *et al.*, 1976; Ricq, 1980), and the detailed internal organisation of occupation sites (Bailloud, 1973; Guilaine, 1979; Colomer *et al.*, 1980). However, these human relations exist within an economic and settlement framework that is limited to a greater or lesser extent by the distribution and quality of subsistence and other resources in the landscape, and by the needs and extractive capabilities of the human groups involved. Over the long term, the natural environment imposes constraints which partly limit and condition human activities, and which may result in recurring behavioural patterns. Some idea of the nature of these constraints, and of the responses to them by human groups, is essential before we can go on to design research concerned with more complex aspects of past human behaviour in the region.

In the following discussion I shall try to show how such an approach helps our understanding of the development of neolithic society in southern France, and provides guidelines for future research. It should also become clear that present views which see material culture as a direct indicator of human groups, and economy as entirely culture-dependent, are not helpful. This is a point which has been made frequently over the last ten years or so, but unfortunately requires emphasising again in the present context. The variability in material culture is a function of socio-economic and natural (depositional and post-depositional) processes which may vary through time and space. The nature of these processes has to be identified before we can assess the relationship of the artefacts to particular human groups, and that relationship should not be simplistically assumed as it so often is at present.

The regional distribution and dynamics of agricultural settlement and land-use during the historical period provide a framework or model against which to assess the prehistoric evidence. Neither the botanical nor the pedological evidence support the model of long-term degradation of the Garrigues environment by man. The pedological evidence suggests that the area has been broadly similar to today throughout the Holocene, dominated by scrub vegetation associated with thin soils. Elsewhere, although localised redistribution of arable soils from the interfluves to the stream valleys has occurred in areas of soft rocks, and fertile alluvium has been deposited in the lower courses of the main river valleys, the essential regional contrasts in agricultural potential have remained the same.

Agricultural settlement has been concentrated in the Languedoc coastal plain and the Provençal basins from the Roman period onwards. In eastern Languedoc, the Garrigues have formed a well-defined area of marginal agricultural land and rough pasture which has been extensively settled only during phases of high population on the coastal plain when additional land was needed to provide food (Leroy Ladurie, 1966). This simple dichotomy between preferred and marginal agricultural land is complicated in Provence by the broken and more varied relief, but localised areas of limestone plateaux with small, dispersed patches of arable land were used in a similar way. The limestone areas of upper Provence and upper Languedoc form a third major unit providing a contrasting set of subsistence and other resources. Thus the high plateaux of the Vaucluse and the Grands Causses have been used as summer pasture for transhumant flocks at various periods during historical times (Arbos, 1922; Saussol, 1970; Sclafert, 1959). These transhumance systems have normally operated in the context of modern commercial economics, but have also occurred as part of subsistence economies when arable resources have been scarce and sheep and goat have provided an alternative means of food production or procurement through exchange. Small numbers of sheep and goat may be kept permanently in the lowland zones but transhumance is necessary where large flocks are involved, owing to the summer drought. The upland areas also contain important sources of raw materials, flint and copper being of particular interest here (Fig. 5.7).

The Cevennes and other crystalline massifs form a fourth zone, of less obvious interest to early agriculturalists. Like the Grands Causses, they have been used to provide summer pasture, but arable land is even more restricted, and of poorer quality, than on the limestone areas. In historical times, one of the principal subsistence activities in the Cevennes was the cultivation of chestnuts.

Using this picture of historical land-use, we might expect that following the establishment of arable agriculture as the basis of the subsistence economy, settlements would have been preferentially located on the arable soils of the Languedoc coastal plain and the Provençal basins. The use of transit sites such as caves in other areas might indicate the integration of these areas into the economic system, while the expansion of permanent settlement onto agriculturally marginal land should reflect a scarcity of arable resources in the preferred settlement areas and the consequent need to exploit new land. Depending on the nature of the evidence, occupation and exploitation of the upland areas might indicate the use of raw material sources, the development of transhumance systems, the local establishment of large populations, or other processes. The important point is that the different parts of the area would have been linked, and the development of settlement in one part cannot be considered in isolation.

The Appearance of Agriculture

Present data suggest continuity between the Mesolithic and the Early Neolithic in many aspects of material culture and economy. At first sight, pottery, domestic animals, and cereals all seem to behave independently, as if the taking up of each was conditioned by different factors, and they did not develop as an agricultural 'package'. Thus the earliest pottery appears at the coastal shell midden and fishing sites of Ile Maire (m.r.5), Ile Riou (m.r.4) (Bouches-du-Rhône: Courtin, 1974a, 48) and Cap Ragnon (Courtin *et al.*, 1972), which have direct Mesolithic antecedents at Châteauneuf-les-Martigues and the Baume Longue (m.r.9; Bouches-du-Rhône: Escalon de Fonton, 1956). The stratigraphic evidence at Châteauneuf-les-Martigues is becoming increasingly suspect, but there is much corroborative information to show that caprovids were present well before the appearance of pottery in different areas, and there is some support for the view that these animals are indigenous to the area. Pig is also present in pre-pottery levels at Dourgne in the Pyrenees and at Gazel in the earlier 5th millennium bc (Bahn, p. 196). However, and although cereals are present in the earliest levels with pottery at Châteauneuf-les-Martigues (Courtin, pers.comm., following re-excavation of the site). The dominance of wild animals at most sites, and the evidence from the early neolithic levels at Montclus of fishing and wild plant food collection similar to that from mesolithic levels at this site, at the Grotte de l'Abeurador (Hérault: Roudil, 1981) and at Fontbrégoua (Escalon de Fonton, 1980), suggest that hunting and gathering activities continued to provide the main subsistence base, with cereals perhaps being grown on a small scale.

Such an overview, however, takes little account of the nature of the evidence or of the biases it contains. In fact, in most cases we have the wrong kinds of evidence to answer our questions concerning the appearance of agriculture. The cave sites would have operated as components of a subsistence system, whether that system were agriculturally or hunter-gatherer based. Unless we have some idea of the total system, and the rôle different sites played in it, we cannot compare them since we do not know whether the comparison is valid. Thus if agriculture did develop rapidly as the subsistence base, we would expect the major settlements to have been open air sites on the better agricultural land, and it is precisely this type of site that is most lacking in our current samples. As Montjardin (1979) points out, domestic animals form a far larger proportion of the fauna at the only two open air sites that have been studied, Ile Corrège (m.r.42) and Le Baratin (m.r.13), than at the cave sites. No cereals have been found at Le Baratin, but the pollen samples from the area (Triat, 1978, 87–92) include cereal pollen and reveal clearances contemporary with the occupation at the site. There are no faunal or floral remains from the open air site of Peiro Signado, but the fact that this site has produced an apparently atypical ceramic and flint assemblage when compared with the cave sites is perhaps further evidence that we are dealing with a heavily biased sample. The site of Ile Corrège is of particular interest since it demonstrates the obvious – that early neolithic settlements have been submerged by the post-glacial rise in sea level. The process of agricultural adaptation may therefore have begun where we might have expected it, on the arable soils of the coastal plain, the earliest evidence now lying beneath the sea. If this were the case, the cave settlements which provide the majority of the current data might be the truncated ends of the annual site territories, and the variability in the faunal, floral, and artefactual assemblages might merely reflect the different function of each site in the annual exploitation system rather than serving as a direct guide to the chronology and process of agricultural development. Several possible models exist, of which two may be considered here.

First, pottery may have appeared in coastal areas as a prestige exchange item amongst hunting and gathering populations, as has also been suggested by Lewthwaite (1981). The different elements of the agricultural subsistence system may later have been gradually adopted into pre-existing and pre-adapted subsistence strategies in response to environmental and demographic pressures brought about by the submergence of the coastal plain, with resultant truncation of annual territories, and the northwards advance of Mediterranean climate and vegetation (see also Clarke, 1976a). While domestic animals were rapidly integrated into the existing economy, cereals were at first grown only on a small scale, providing a dependable, but not yet essential source of food in the face of the decreasing availability of subsistence resources at critical periods of the year. No radical changes in the organisation of subsistence strategies occurred, and hence preferred hunter-gatherer sites such as Châteauneuf-les-Martigues, Montclus, and Gazel continued to be occupied. During the later 5th millennium bc cereals started to be grown on a larger scale, as shown by the clearances at open sites such as Le Baratin. However, even here, the clearances were localised and short-lived, and it was only during the 4th millennium bc that cereal agriculture became the main subsistence base, with correlated radical changes in artefact assemblages and site distributions (see below).

A second possibility is that we have lost the major early neolithic open air agricultural sites on the submerged areas of the Languedoc coastal plain, while sites on extant arable areas are only poorly known due to destruction and lack of systematic research. The sites of Ile Corrège, Le Baratin, and Peiro Signado demonstrate that such settlements existed, but it is difficult to assess their relative importance. The early dates for pottery in south-western Provence are in keeping with this model since the sites from which they come are located on a rocky coastline that would have been little affected by sea-level rise. At the same time, they are not representative of the Languedoc coastal plain since their economies relate to the local coastal ecology. While agriculture was rapidly established as the subsistence base on the plain, inland communities would have continued the hunting and gathering way of life, becoming increasingly networked with the agricultural communities further south, the date of appearance of domestic animals, cereals, or pottery depending on local circumstances. As in the first case, the spread outwards from the coastal plain would have been affected by the submergence of the coastal lowlands and changing climatic and vegetational régimes.

The Development of Agricultural Societies

Some variant of the first model seems likely since this would also help to explain the radical changes that occur in material culture, and apparently in settlement distribution, at the Early Neolithic/Middle Neolithic transition. All the elements of an agricultural economy were present by the 5th millennium bc, but the evidence of settlement distribution, subsistence economy and material culture suggests that it was not until the Middle Neolithic and the 4th millennium bc that agriculture became firmly established as the subsistence base. Middle neolithic open air settlements are concentrated in the historically preferred arable areas of the Provençal basins and the Languedoc coastal plain. This is certainly the case in Provence where unfortunately many of the settlements have now been destroyed as is the case in the Trets basin. In Languedoc, the distribution of middle neolithic open air sites reflects the work of particular archaeologists round Montpellier, along the coastal strip, and in the Vaunage (Fig. 5.12). These sites are located on light arable soils, and positions adjacent to major water sources are preferred. The economic evidence is scarce, but most excavated sites have produced evidence of cereals and domestic animals, and domestic species dominate the faunal samples.

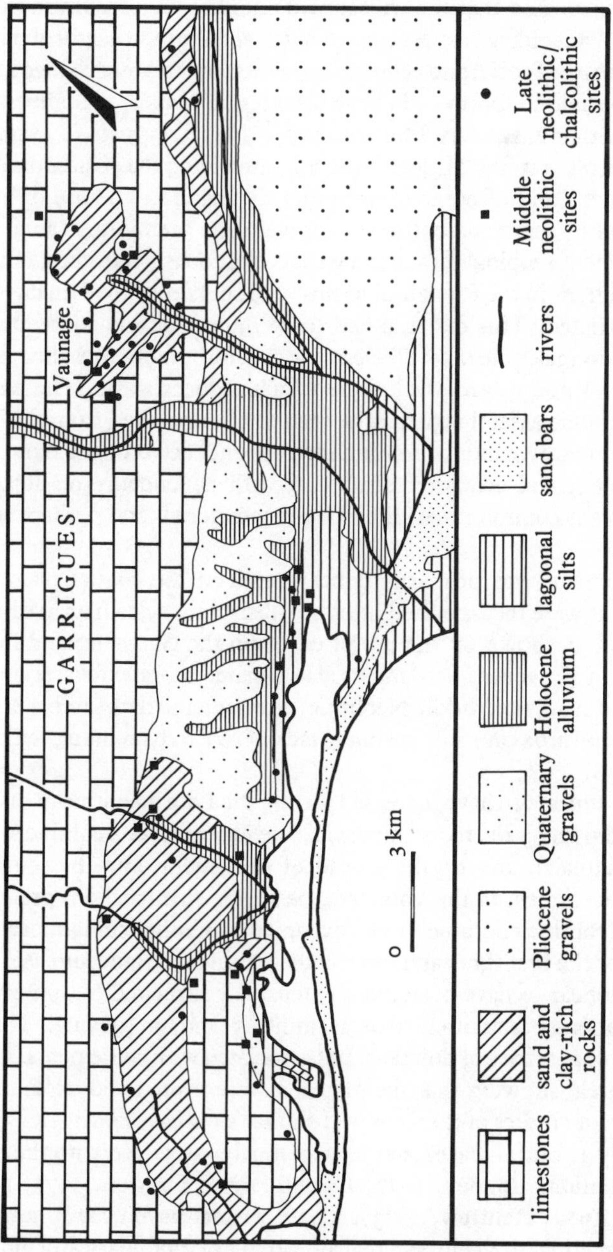

FIGURE 5.12. Eastern Languedoc: simplified geology and distribution of neolithic and chalcolithic open-air settlements on the coastal plain. Sites on the garrigues are not marked. Note the high density of settlement in the Vaunage revealed by recent field survey, compared with other parts of the coastal plain.

It might be expected that the widespread adoption of agriculture would have led to significant changes in aspects of material culture, brought about by changes in the nature of social and economic interaction, and by a change in the tool kits since specialised tools would have been required in large numbers for harvesting and other tasks. As Phillips (1975, 1982) suggests, a systemic change does take place in the Middle Neolithic, involving the standardisation of the flint industry and of ceramic form and decoration. The use of high-quality flint suggests that good cutting edges were at a premium, as might be expected for efficient reaping. At the same time, flint does not occur naturally in the coastal plain, or in the Provençal basins, and sources of good quality raw material are restricted. This material had to be imported, and consequently there was a need to make the most efficient use possible of the cores, hence the use of a blade and micro-blade technique which reduces waste. The homogeneity of the ceramic assemblage may be seen to have resulted from the high degree of non-competitive interaction and interdependence brought about by a common settlement and economic structure, with dependence on adjacent and/or more distant communities for certain raw materials and perhaps some subsistence needs.

While settlement was primarily concentrated in the coastal plain and basins, other areas were incorporated into the subsistence system on a seasonal or periodic basis, as shown by the use of caves on the Garrigues and in the limestone areas of Provence. Settlement also became more extensive on the Grands Causses during the Middle Neolithic, although the data sample here is probably biased towards cave sites owing to lack of research on the agricultural soils of the valleys.

Population appears to have increased during the Late Neolithic in eastern Languedoc, as shown by the more numerous late neolithic/chalcolithic settlements in the Vaunage, and by the spread of settlement onto the southern margins of the Garrigues. In the Vaunage, the spring-side locations preferred in the Middle Neolithic continued to be occupied, but other similar locations were taken up for the first time, and intermediate positions came into use. The Garrigues also appear to have been more extensively exploited but purely for seasonal or temporary activities such as hunting and/or grazing. This is indicated by the appearance of dolmens, not associated with settlements, in the interior of the area, showing that the plateaux were visited and exploited at this period. Recent studies of dolmens and similar sites have considered them neither primarily as burial places, nor as necessarily associated with the main centres of population (Bonney, 1977; Darvill, 1979; Drewett, 1975, 1977; Fleming, 1971, 1973; Renfrew, 1973). These writers have usually seen the tombs as demarcating the centres (real or ritual) or boundaries of human territories, but Fleming (1973) has suggested they may have been used also to establish rights of use over particular types of land. Many of the Garrigues dolmens are located well away from cultivable areas, on the tops of low ridges now covered by scrub. The presence of dolmens suggests that these ridges were cleared at the time, and the dolmens may have served as territorial demarcators, establishing animal grazing rights over different parts of the Garrigues. In western Languedoc, Vérazien open air sites are concentrated on the light arable soils of the coastal plain, in keeping with an economy based on cereal agriculture (Gasco, 1980a).

Changes in material culture appear to tie in with these changes in settlement and population. These include a renewed emphasis on local flint sources and increasing diversity within the ceramic assemblage, although high quality items continued to be exchanged over long distances. The reasons for these changes may lie in the increased stress between local groups produced by population growth and pressure on the available subsistence resources. Recently, several writers have been concerned with the concepts of stress, symbolism, and group identity and their possible expression in the archaeological record as stylistic traits in artefact assemblages (Hodder, 1977; Pierpoint, 1980). In ethnographic situations Hodder has suggested that 'the material cultural differences between tribes can only be understood if material culture is seen as a language, expressing within-group cohesion in competition over scarce resources', and that 'much of the recent temporal variation in material cultural patterning, in addition to the spatial variation . . . could be related to changes in the degree of conflict and competition over resources and resulting need to stress overtly clear, unambiguous identities' (Hodder, 1979, 447). Hodder used the ceramic variability of the south French Late Neolithic as an archaeological example of this process, developing a similar view expressed by Phillips (1975).

The greatest ceramic variability occurs in eastern Languedoc in the Chalcolithic, when evidence from the Vaunage shows that the highest density of settlement is achieved. This population maximum on the coastal plain coincided with the extension of settlement over the Garrigues plateaux, a process which seems parallel to the cycles of population expansion observed during the historical period in response to changes in the pressure of population on agricultural resources in the lowland area. Stress and conflict are also indicated in a more tangible form in the 'war grave' at Roaix, and by other instances of arrowheads found implanted in human skeletons.

The changes in the flint industry may reflect these and other processes. First, the changes appear to show a complete transformation of the redistribution networks, perhaps brought about by the breakdown of the earlier system in response to stress. The continued trade in high quality items might reflect the restriction of the networks to prestige exchange, or to crucial tools and weapons that could not be made from local raw materials. However, it should be remembered that late neolithic/chalcolithic sites are known mainly from the limestone areas in which poor quality flint occurs in abundance. Flint does not occur locally in the coastal plain and must have been imported as in the Middle Neolithic. Flint tools are rare on Vérazien plain sites in western Languedoc (Guilaine, 1980), while very few sites with flake-based industries are known from the Provençal basins. At Trets, for instance, the industries are almost exclusively blade-based despite definite evidence of late neolithic/chalcolithic occupation. Similarly, blades dominate at the early neolithic coastal site of Peiro Signado, and at the similarly located late neolithic/chalcolithic site of Mort des Anes (Gasco, 1980b). Blade-based industries may therefore have started early and continued later in areas where flint is scarce and needed to be imported, and the present assumption that Middle Neolithic equals blade-based and Late Neolithic/Chalcolithic equals flake-based may obscure many of the processes affecting lithic variability, the accessibility of and the need for particular types of raw material having been the major underlying factors through time.

Other changes occurred which can be placed in the context of the observed demographic and economic changes of the 3rd millennium bc, and which, again, are best illustrated in eastern Languedoc. The numerous dolmens on the Grands Causses show that these areas were extensively exploited in some way, but years of research have failed to produce much evidence of permanent settlement. Such surface sites as exist consist mainly of scatters of flint on thin soils in exposed positions, often associated with caves and shelters. It is likely that permanent settlements were located in the valleys, which have not been adequately surveyed, but the numbers of dolmens (several thousand) seem out of all proportion to the number of permanent settlements which could have existed on the restricted arable soils here. As suggested for the Garrigues, the dolmens may have been used primarily as territorial demarcators rather than as burial places. The dolmens are positioned by or dominating areas of better quality pasture on the pure limestones, and particularly beside the depressions where the best pasture occurs. This distribution, the numbers of dolmens involved, and the labour invested in their construction, suggest that these pasture areas were of special importance, and consequently that herding of sheep and goat occurred on a large scale. Large flocks cannot be kept on the Causses over winter without stalling, which would have involved permanent settlement, so that transhumance systems must have operated. This would tie in with the very high density of population on the Garrigues and the evidence of pasture use there, since the restricted arable soils would have been heavily exploited. Herding of sheep and goat on a large scale would have provided a means of supplementing cereal production either directly or through exchange, but would have necessitated transhumance since the Garrigues pastures cannot support large flocks over the summer.

Other aspects of material culture show interesting trends which may be associated with these suggested transhumance links. On the one hand, a marked dichotomy appears between upper and lower Languedoc in the Chalcolithic, seen in the use of markedly different arrowhead types. However, it is also evident that contacts between the two areas continued, perhaps on a greater scale than previously. Copper artefacts found at Fontbouisse sites in lower Languedoc were most likely made from ores originating in the Causses since there is no evidence that the Cevennes were exploited at this time. The absence of copper artefacts from contemporary late 3rd millennium bc sites in Provence and western Languedoc suggests particularly close contacts between lower eastern Languedoc and the Causses at this period. Conversely, the good quality flint items found in the Grands Causses must have come from lower Languedoc either as blanks or as finished products. These apparently contradictory data may be the result partly of stress between the two areas induced by competition for pasture resources between transhumant and local flocks, a familiar pattern from historical times (Sclafert, 1959), and partly of the increased exchange of prestige and other goods between the two areas.

There is no clear evidence that these processes led to major changes in social organisation. The burial data are too poor for us to assess whether particular individuals were attributed high status through rich grave goods, especially since the high quality flint artefacts are found at both burial and settlement sites. It has been suggested that sites such as Lébous and Boussargues (Fig. 10) might have represented central places of some sort, but here also the evidence is ambiguous. The walls and towers are too insubstantial as defensive systems, while the assemblages are no different to those found at other Fontbouisse sites. The huts at Boussargues may have been constructed after the enclosure wall, in which case the latter would fit better as a livestock corral, subsequently re-used for a settlement. Two probable corrals have been excavated recently in Provence (Escalon de Fonton, 1980). They are located in isolated positions, in both cases on sites which are still used as sheep camping grounds because of their sheltered micro-environments (D'Anna, pers. comm.).

Conclusions

The above discussion illustrates how current research designs and the data base are inadequate for a clear understanding of social and economic development during the Neolithic in southern France. There is a need for problem-orientated data collection, using explicit models which may be tested in the field. The most basic need is to obtain representative samples both of the distribution of different types of settlement across the various ecological zones contained within the region, and of the range of chronological and spatial variability in material culture independent of accepted notions of cultural groups. It is also vital to carry out this data collection in close association with geomorphological studies aimed at assessing the extent of soil erosion and deposition in different areas, and the effect of this on the preservation of archaeological sites and on changes in agricultural potential at a regional scale through time. The diachronic environmental/economic approach used above provides a basis for such research, by pointing out the gaps and strengths of current data, and giving a framework for research design. For instance, the well preserved sites on the Garrigues provide an excellent field laboratory for studying assemblage variability amongst probably contemporaneous settlements located within a short distance of each other, where it would also be possible to assess the size and nature of the human groups involved. At the same time, these sites would have to be understood in terms of regional development and interaction through time, as outlined here.

RADIOCARBON DATES

EARLY NEOLITHIC						
(a) Coastal Provence						
Cap Ragnon	6020±150bc	MC-500A	Shell	Cave	Cardial	*Radiocarbon*, 15, 329
(Bouches-du-Rhône)	5700±150bc	MC-500B	Shell		Cardial	*Radiocarbon*, 15, 329
Ile Riou (Bouches-du-Rhône)	5650±150bc	MC-440	Shell	Open settlement	Cardial	*Radiocarbon*, 15, 329
	5420±150bc	MC-441	Shell		Cardial	*Radiocarbon*, 15, 329
Châteauneuf-les-Martigues	4480±140bc	Ly-446	Charcoal	Cave	Level C6: Cardial	*Radiocarbon*, 15, 527
(Bouches-du-Rhône)	4830±100bc	MC-531L	Shell		Level C5: Cardial	Delibrias *et al.*, 1976, 881
	4810±100bc	MC-531T	Shell		Level C5: Cardial	Delibrias *et al.*, 1976, 881
	4120±490bc	Ly-623	Charcoal		Level F5: Cardial	*Radiocarbon*, 15, 527
	3960±290bc	Ly-622	Charcoal		Level F1: Cardial	*Radiocarbon*, 15, 527
(b) Inland Provence						
Le Baratin (Vaucluse)	4650±140bc	Gif-1855	Charcoal	Open settlement	Cardial	*Radiocarbon*, 16, 32
Fontbrégoua (Var)	4750±100bc	Gif-2990	Charcoal	Cave	Level C47: Cardial	Delibrias *et al.*, 1976, 883
	4230±120bc	Gif-2989	Charcoal		Level C45: Cardial	Delibrias *et al.*, 1976, 883
	3850±150bc	Gif-2988	Charcoal		Level C43: Cardial	Delibrias *et al.*, 1976, 883
	3740±190bc	Gif-2757	Charcoal		Level C42: Cardial	Delibrias *et al.*, 1976, 883
	3740±190bc	Gif-2756	Charcoal		Level C40: Cardial	Delibrias *et al.*, 1976, 883
Saint-Mitre III	6000±150bc	MC-266	Charcoal	Cave	?	Delibrias *et al.*, 1976, 883
(Haute-Provence)	4150±180bc	MC-265	Charcoal		Level Y11: Cardial	*Radiocarbon*, 15, 336
	4750±130bc	MC-264	Charcoal		Level 3 28/9: Cardial	*Radiocarbon*, 15, 335
	4450±130bc	MC-263	Charcoal		Level 3 Y10: Cardial	*Radiocarbon*, 15, 335
Saint-Mitre II (Hte-Prov)	4000±200bc	MC-202	Charcoal	Cave	Level 12/2: Cardial	*Radiocarbon*, 11, 123
Abri-du-Capitaine (Hte-Prov)	4100±150bc	Gif-1111	Charcoal	Cave	Level C18: Cardial	*Radiocarbon*, 16, 32
(c) Lower Eastern Languedoc						
Montclus (Gard)	4220±150bc	MC-694	Charcoal	Cave	Level C4:Epicardial	Delibrias *et al.*, 1976, 881
	4190±140bc	Ly-304	Bone		Level C4: Epicardial	*Radiocarbon*, 13, 62
	4350±140bc	Ly-303	Charcoal		Level C4: Epicardial	*Radiocarbon*, 13, 62
Aigle (Gard)	4250±100bc	MC-563	Charcoal	Cave	Epicardial	Delibrias *et al.*, 1976, 881
Bourbon (Gard)	4230±100bc	Ly-538	Charcoal	Cave	Level C5: Epicardial	*Radiocarbon*, 15, 526
	4130±100bc	MC-794	Charcoal	Cave	Epicardial	Delibrias *et al.*, 1976, 881
(d) Upper Eastern Languedoc						
Saint Pierre (Hérault)	3750±150bc	Gif-2180	Charcoal	Cave	Level 4A: Epicardial	*Radiocarbon*, 16, 30
	3250±400bc	Gif-1922	Charcoal		Level 2A: Epicardial	*Radiocarbon*, 16, 30

	4350±140bc	Gif-1491	Charcoal		Level C19: Cardial	*Radiocarbon*, 14, 285
	3850±140bc	Gif-1490	Charcoal		Level C18: Epicardial	*Radiocarbon*, 14, 285
	3950±140bc	Gif-1489	Charcoal		Level C17: Epicardial	*Radiocarbon*, 14, 285
	3950±130bc	Gif-1488	Charcoal		Level C16: Epicardial	*Radiocarbon*, 14, 285
Combe Obscure (Ardèche)	4450±160bc	Ly-423	Charcoal	Cave	Level C5: Cardial	*Radiocarbon*, 15, 145
Chazelle (Ardèche)	3710±100bc	Ly-395	Charcoal	Cave	Level C7: Cardial	*Radiocarbon*, 12, 555
Puechmargues (Aveyron)	4470±180bc	Gsy-446		Cave	?	Delibrias *et al.*, 1976
Poujade (Aveyron)	6060±130bc	MC-1239		Cave	Level 8B: ?	Clottes, 1979, 663
MIDDLE NEOLITHIC						
(*a*) *Inland Provence*						
Grotte de l'Eglise (Var)	3810±140bc	Gif-1334	Charcoal	Cave	Level C8b: Middle Neolithic	*Radiocarbon*, 14, 287
	3550±140bc	Gif-1333	Charcoal		Level C8a: Middle Neolithic	*Radiocarbon*, 14, 287
	2875±130bc	Gif-112B	Charcoal		Level C9: Middle Neolithic	*Radiocarbon*, 8, 129
Fontbrégoua (Var)	3660±130bc	Gif-2754	Charcoal	Cave	Level C33: Middle Neolithic	Delibrias *et al.*, 1976, 883
	3710±130bc	Gif-2755	Charcoal		Level C31: Middle Neolithic	Delibrias *et al.*, 1976, 883
	3600±120bc	Gif-2436	Charcoal		Level C28: Middle Neolithic	Delibrias *et al.*, 1976, 883
(*b*) *Lower Eastern Languedoc*						
Tournié (Hérault)	3950±100bc	MC-797	Charcoal	Cave	Level C4 C19: Middle Neolithic	Delibrias *et al.*, 1976, 879
(*c*) *Upper Eastern Languedoc*						
Camprafaud (Hérault)	3350±130bc	Gif-1487	Charcoal	Cave	Level C15: Middle Neolithic	*Radiocarbon*, 14, 285
	3500±130bc	Gif-1486	Charcoal		Level C14: Middle Neolithic	*Radiocarbon*, 14, 285
Sargel (Aveyron)	2700±150bc	Gif-3007	Charcoal	Cave	Level C13: Middle Neolithic	*Radiocarbon*, 14, 285
(*d*) *Coastal Provence*						
Escanin (Bouches-du-Rhône)	3210±120bc	Gif-1995	Charcoal	Cave	Chasséen	*Radiocarbon*, 16, 31
	3050±250bc	Gif-450	Charcoal		Chasséen	*Radiocarbon*, 12, 426
Miouvin (Bouches-du-Rhône)	3430±110bc	MC-1224	Charcoal	Open settlement	Level C3: Chasséen	Camps-Fabrer and D'Anna, 1980, 167
	2620±200bc	MC-1365	Charcoal		Level C2: Chasséen	Camps-Fabrer and D'Anna, 1980, 167
	2075±165bc	MC-1223	Charcoal		Level C2: Chasséen	Camps-Fabrer and D'Anna, 1980, 167
Trets, Tr 25 (Bouches-du-Rhône)	2750±300bc	MC-2023	Charcoal	Open site	Hearth	D'Anna and Mills, 1981, 12
	2950±100bc	MC-2022	Charcoal		Hearth	D'Anna and Mills, 1981, 12

(e) Inland Provence						
La Bertaude (Vaucluse)	3450±170bc	MC-765	Charcoal	Open settlement	Chasséen	Delibrias *et al.*, 1976, 881
Grotte de l'Eglise (Var)	2550±130bc	Gif-1331	Charcoal	Cave	Level C3: Chasséen	*Radiocarbon*, 14, 287
	2250±130bc	Gif-1332	Charcoal		Level C5: Chasséen	*Radiocarbon*, 14, 287
	2560±125bc	Gif-112A	Charcoal		Level C5: Chasséen	*Radiocarbon*, 8, 129
Baudinard C (Var)	2850±140bc	Gif-1621	Charcoal	Cave	Chasséen	*Radiocarbon*, 14, 287
Fontbrégoua (Var)	3570±120bc	Gif-2437	Charcoal	Cave	Level C27: Chasséen	Delibrias *et al.*, 1976, 883
	3190±120bc	Gif-2434	Charcoal		Level C18: Chasséen	Delibrias *et al.*, 1976, 883
	2930±110bc	Gif-2433	Charcoal		Level C12: Chasséen	*Radiocarbon*, 16, 32
	3100±120bc	Gif-2101	Charcoal		Level C11: Chasséen	*Radiocarbon*, 16, 32
	3150±110bc	Gif-2432	Charcoal		Level C9: Chasséen	Delibrias *et al.*, 1976, 883
	1720±110bc	Gif-2435	Charcoal		Level C8: Chasséen	Delibrias *et al.*, 1976, 883
Saint-Mitre III (Hte-Prov)	3200±200bc	MC-203	Charcoal	Cave	Level F12/1: Chasséen	*Radiocarbon*, 11, 123
Saint-Mitre II (Hte-Prov)	2400±150bc	MC-201	Charcoal	Cave	Level F12/2: Chasséen	*Radiocarbon*, 11, 123
Perthuis II (Haute-Provence)	2500±230bc	MC-10	Charcoal	Cave	Chasséen	*Radiocarbon*, 6, 196
Grotte Murée (Hte-Prov)	2790±130bc	Gif-867	Charcoal	Cave	Level C10: Chasséen	*Radicarbon*, 13, 219
Grotte d'Unang (Vaucluse)	4000±130bc	Gif-1796	Charcoal	Cave	Level F: Chasséen	*Radiocarbon*, 16, 32
	3820±130bc	Gif-1795	Charcoal		Level C3: Chasséen	*Radiocarbon*, 16, 32
	4050±130bc	Gif-1794	Charcoal		Level C6: Chasséen	*Radiocarbon*, 16, 32
	3990±130bc	Gif-1793	Charcoal		Level C3: Chasséen	*Radiocarbon*, 16, 32
(f) Lower Eastern Languedoc						
La Madeleine (Hérault)	3150±250bc	MC-7	Charcoal	Cave	Level C7: Chasséen	*Radiocarbon*, 6, 195
	3270±230bc	MC-8	Charcoal		Level C10: Chasséen	*Radiocarbon*, 6, 195
Maquis (Ardèche)	3610±170bc	Ly-491	Charcoal	Cave	Chasséen	*Radiocarbon*, 15, 144
(g) Upper Eastern Languedoc						
Soulatget (Hérault)	2830±140bc	Gif-1918	Charcoal	Cave	Level 2A: Chasséen	*Radiocarbon*, 16, 30
St Etienne-de-Gourgas (Hér)	2620±300bc	Gif-154i	Charcoal	Cave	Level F22: Chasséen	*Radiocarbon*, 8, 84
Claux (Hérault)	3770±170bc	KN-315	Charcoal		Chasséen	Delibrias *et al.*, 1976, 879
Camprafaud (Hérault)	3150±130bc	Gif-1485	Charcoal	Cave	Level C13: Chasséen	*Radiocarbon*, 14, 285
	2950±130bc	Gif-1484	Charcoal		Level C12: Chasséen	*Radiocarbon*, 14, 285
Sargel (Aveyron)	2620±150bc	Gif-445	Charcoal	Cave	Level C10: Chasséen	*Radiocarbon*, 12, 423
	2700±150bc	Gif-3007	Charcoal		Level C13: Chasséen	Delibrias *et al.*, 1976, 877

La Couronne (Bouches-du-Rhône)	2110±220bc	Ly-301	Charcoal	Open settlement	Level 3D: Late Neo./Chalc.	*Radiocarbon*, 13, 61
	2020±130bc	Ly-302	Bone		Level 3D: Late Neo./Chalc.	*Radiocarbon*, 13, 61
	2360±100bc	MC-714A	Shell		Level 3D: Late Neo./Chalc.	Delibrias *et al.*, 1976, 883
	2290±100bc	MC-714B	Shell		Level 3D: Late Neo./Chalc.	Delibrias *et al.*, 1976, 883
Saint-Marc (B-du-Rhône)	2000±140bc	Gif-1613	Bone	Chambered tomb	Late Neo./Chalc.	Delibrias *et al.*, 1976, 893
La Balance (Vaucluse)	2150±120bc	Gif-705	Charcoal	Open settlement	Level C3: Late Neo./Chalc.	*Radiocarbon*, 12, 427
La Fontaine (Vaucluse)	1800±110bc	Gif-2758	Charcoal	Open settlement	Late Neo./Chalc.	Delibrias *et al.*, 1976, 881
Roaix (Vaucluse)	2090±140bc	Gif-857	Charcoal	Chambered tomb	Level C2: Late Neo./Chalc.	*Radiocarbon*, 13, 219
	2150±140bc	Gif-1620	Charcoal		Level C5: Late Neo./Chalc.	*Radiocarbon*, 13, 219
Roque d'Aille (Var)	1760±90bc	MC-720	Bone	Chambered tomb	Late Neo./Chalc.	Delibrias *et al.*, 1976, 893
Bouissière (Var)	2025±130bc	Gsy-57	Charcoal	Chambered tomb	Late Neo./Chalc.	*Radiocarbon*, 8, 129
Abri-du-Capitaine (Hte-Prov)	2150±140bc	Gif-704	Charcoal	Cave	Level C2A: Late Neo./Chalc.	*Radiocarbon*, 12, 427
Grotte Murée (Hte Provence)	2010±175bc	Gif-116		Cave	Level C6: Late Neo./Chalc.	*Radiocarbon*, 8, 129
Berthuis (Haute-Provence)	2130±250bc	MC-11		Cave	Level CB6: Late Neo./Chalc.	*Radiocarbon*, 6, 196
Carluc (Haute-Provence)	1790±100bc	MC-364		Cave	Late Neo./Chalc.	Delibrias *et al.*, 1976, 893
(b) Lower Eastern Languedoc						
Pins (Gard)	2400±130bc	Gif-1360		Cave	Ferrières	*Radiocarbon*, 14, 285
Sartanette (Gard)	2320bc			Cave	Ferrières	Guilaine *et al.*, 1974
Traves (Gard)	2310±140bc	Gif-1909		Cave	Level C2: Ferrières	*Radiocarbon*, 16, 31
Beaussement (Ardèche)	2220±250bc	Gif-246		Open settlement	Level C4: Ferrières	*Radiocarbon*, 8, 83
	2150±250bc	Gif-245			Level C4/6: Ferrières	*Radiocarbon*, 8, 83

(c) Upper Eastern Languedoc

Roc-du-Midi (Gard)	2430±120bc	MC-764	Charcoal	Cave	Level C2: Ferrières	Delibrias *et al.*, 1976, 879
Tournié (Hérault)	2250±100bc	MC-906	Charcoal	Cave	Level F5 CE22: Saint Pon./Gourg.	Delibrias *et al.*, 1976, 879
	2350±100bc	MC-905	Charcoal		Level F5 CE22: Saint Pon./Gourg.	Delibrias *et al.*, 1976, 879
	2220±90bc	MC-795	Charcoal		Level F2: Saint Pon./Gourg.	Delibrias *et al.*, 1976, 879
	2275±100bc	MC-716	Charcoal		Level C3 D19: Saint Pon./Gourg.	Delibrias *et al.*, 1976, 879
	2825±90bc	MC-796	Charcoal		Level C4 C19: Saint Pon./Gourg.	Delibrias *et al.*, 1976, 879
Serpents (Hérault)	2690±140bc	Gif-1923	Charcoal	Cave	Level C2A: Saint Pon./Gourg.	*Radiocarbon*, 16, 29
	2350±140bc	Gif-1924	Charcoal		Level C3A: Saint Pon./Gourg.	*Radiocarbon*, 16, 29
	2550±140bc	Gif-1925	Charcoal		Level C4A: Saint Pon./Gourg.	*Radiocarbon*, 16, 29
Saint Etienne-de-Gourgas (Hérault)	2660±120bc	KN-160	Charcoal	Cave	Level F19: Saint Pon./Gourg.	Delibrias *et al.*, 1976, 879
	2340±120bc	KN-159	Charcoal		Level F13: Saint Pon./Gourg.	Delibrias *et al.*, 1976, 879
	1780±250bc	Gif-154f	Charcoal		Level F18: Saint Pon./Gourg.	*Radiocarbon*, 8, 84
	1930±250bc	Gif-154a	Charcoal		Level F14: Saint Pon./Gourg.	*Radiocarbon*, 8, 84
Resplandy (Hérault)	2100±140bc	Gif-1090	Charcoal	Cave	Level F: Saint Pon./Gourg.	*Radiocarbon*, 14, 285
Camprafaud (Hérault)	2400±140bc	Gif-1157	Charcoal	Cave	Level C19: Saint Pon./Gourg.	*Radiocarbon*, 14, 285
	2350±140bc	Gif-1156	Charcoal		Level C9: Saint Pon./Gourg.	*Radiocarbon*, 14, 285
Pas de Julié (Gard)	2290±110bc	Gif-4358	Charcoal	Cave	Treilles	
Gendarme (Aveyron)	1940±150bc	Gsy-38	Charcoal	Cave	Treilles	*Radiocarbon*, 8, 30
Treilles (Aveyron)	2650±130bc	Gif-1517	Charcoal	Cave	Level C4: Treilles	*Radiocarbon*, 16, 25
	2650±130bc	Gif-1516	Charcoal		Level C3: Treilles	*Radiocarbon*, 16, 25
	2700±130bc	Gif-1515	Charcoal		Level C2: Treilles	*Radiocarbon*, 16, 25
Sargel (Aveyron)	2550±150bc	Gif-444	Charcoal	Cave	Level C6: Treilles	*Radiocarbon*, 12, 423
	1850±130bc	Gif-3005	Charcoal		Level C5: Treilles	Delibrias *et al.*, 1976, 877
	1760±180bc	Gif-328	Charcoal		Treilles	*Radiocarbon*, 12, 423
Cascades (Aveyron)	1320±150bc	Gif-442	Charcoal	Cave	Level C6: Treilles	*Radiocarbon*, 12, 423
Camprafaud (Hérault)	2110±100bc	Gif-3074	Charcoal	Cave	Level C3: Véraza	Delibrias *et al.*, 1976, 879

(e) Lower Eastern Languedoc						
Boucoiran (Gard)	2190±120bc	Ly-554	Charcoal	Cave	Fontbouisse	*Radiocarbon*, 13, 62
Bois Sacré (Gard)	1940±140bc	Ly-422	Charcoal	Open settlement	Fontbouisse	*Radiocarbon*, 15, 144
Prével (Gard)	1930±180bc	Gif-191	Charcoal	Cave	Fontbouisse	*Radiocarbon*, 8, 84
Lébous (Hérault)	1930±120bc	Gif-156	Charcoal	Open settlement	Fontbouisse	*Radiocarbon*, 8, 83
Beaussement (Ardèche)	2025±220bc	Gif-451	Charcoal	Open settlement	Level C3: Fontbouisse	*Radiocarbon*, 12, 426
(f) Upper Eastern Languedoc						
Corneilles (Lozère)	2680±110bc	Ly-462	Charcoal	Cave	Level F: Fontbouisse	*Radiocarbon*, 14, 285
	2060±120bc	Gif-3322	Charcoal		Fontbouisse	Delibrias *et al.*, 1976, 879

The Neolithic of Corsica

JAMES LEWTHWAITE

The land o neolithic environment o history of research o MATERIAL CULTURE o *preneolithic* settlement o *Early Neolithic* o *Curasien* o *Middle Neolithic* o *Late Neolithic* o punch decoration o Basi o Monte Lazzo o Monte Grosso o Terrina o the megalithic dimension o *Chalcolithic* o *Torréen* o ECONOMY AND SETTLEMENT o early neolithic settlement and subsistence o late neolithic settlement and subsistence o long term settlement and subsistence patterns o CONCLUSIONS.

THE CORSICAN environment is the product of four factors: insularity, position, elevation and geological composition (Simi, 1981). Corsica is approximately the same size (8,722km²) as Crete and Cyprus, and lies 12km from Sardinia, 50km from Elba, 82km from the Italian (Tuscan) coast, and 160km from the nearest point on the French mainland.

Because of the location and relief (Fig.6.1c), precipitation is unusually heavy for a Mediterranean region (Fig.6.1b). The mean annual rainfall per unit area is higher than that of the Paris basin or the Massif Central, but because of the concentration and intensity of the downpours and the largely impermeable subsoil, this runs off or evaporates rapidly and is lost to agriculture. The distribution of rainfall is Mediterranean (autumn and spring maxima, summer minimum). The summer drought lessens in intensity with altitude but there is a corresponding decrease in winter temperature: snowfall in the alpine zone (above 1200m) lasts for some months and blocks the central passes between the west and the east.

Vegetation varies as climate changes with altitude: Mediterranean (to c.600m), montane (to 1200m), subalpine (to the treeline at 1700–1800m), and alpine. In the Mediterranean zone, the former evergreen oak forest survives only where human activities have been insignificant, elsewhere being degraded to form 'high macchia' (scented thickets of lentisk, myrtle, tree-heath and strawberry tree) or 'low macchia' (spiny bushes of rock-roses, lavender and rosemary). Some Mediterranean species survive in the montane zone alongside more temperate associations: deciduous oak, chestnuts planted by historical communities to provide their subsistence, and northern species such as elm, ash, alder and poplar along watercourses. Corsican pine, beech and fir

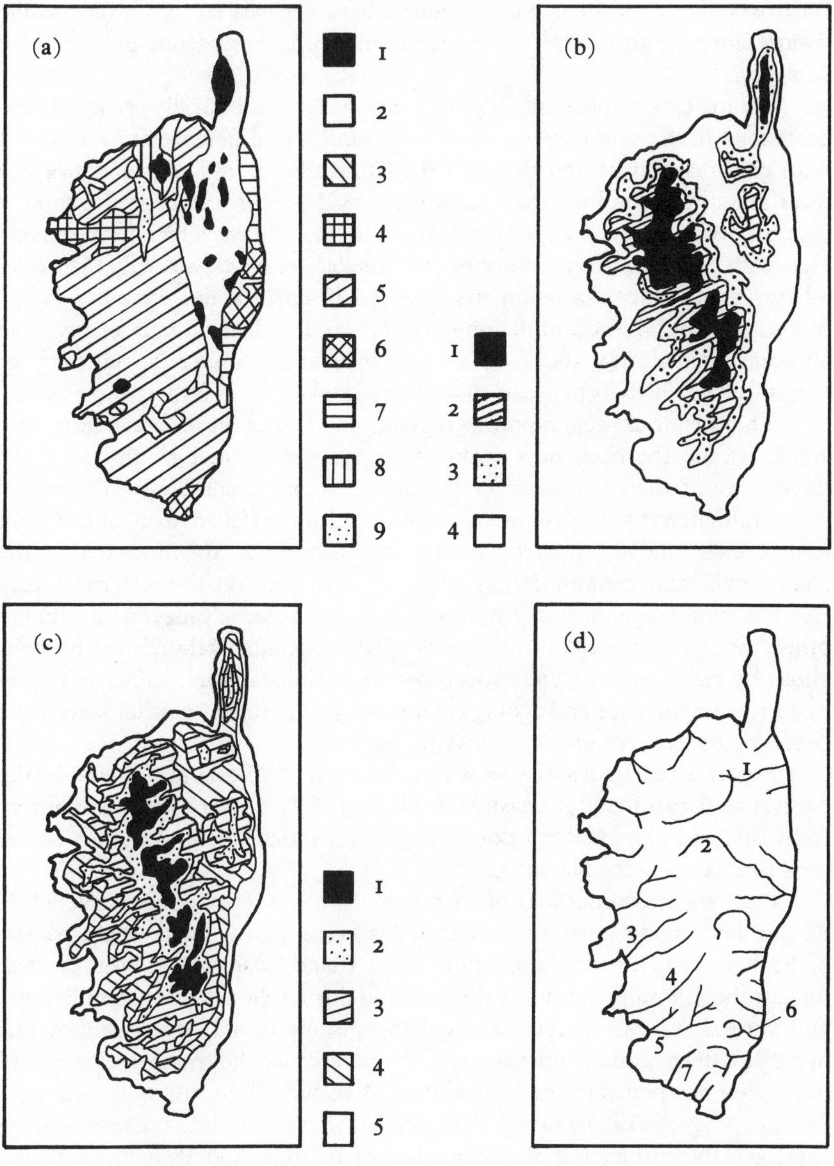

FIGURE 6.1. Corsica, showing the two massifs of unequal size and distinct geological composition of which the island is composed, and the variations in rainfall and drainage that they cause.

(a) *Geology:* 1 ophyolites; 2 schists; 3 rhyolites; 4 granites; 5 Miocene sediments; 6 Quaternary sediments; 7 Eocene sediments; 8 gneiss; 9 diorites.

(b) *Rainfall:* 1 > 1500mm; 2 1250-1500mm; 3 1000-1250mm; 4 < 1000mm.

(c) *Relief:* 1 > 1600m; 2 1000-1600m; 3 600-1000m; 4 200-600m; 5 0-200m.

(d) *Drainage,* showing principal rivers: 1 Golo; 2 Tavignano; 3 Gravone; 4 Taravo; 5 Rizzanese; 6 Oso; 7 Ortolo.

form woodlands in the subalpine zone where not cleared for pasture, while dwarf alder scrub occupies the transition to the herbaceous or bare rock summits.

Geological composition (Fig.6.1a) retouches this basically vertical differentiation: in the south-west a variety of granites of different hardness mixed with gabbros, diorite and rhyolite (the latter used in lithic manufacture as a local substitute for imported Sardinian obsidian); in the central furrow a diversity of sedimentary rocks; schists in the north-east, which form mountains with more rounded contours and thicker, more clayey soils than elsewhere. Quaternary glaciation has resulted in cirques and moraines in the mountains, and the accumulation in the lowlands of half a dozen recognisable superimposed alluvial glacis – mixtures of clay and pebbles relatively poor for agriculture – which form the so-called 'eastern plain' from Bastia to Solenzara.

The historical-geographical regions of Corsica have been extremely stable, as has the basic opposition between a conservative south-west – the 'land beyond the mountains' (Oltremonte) – and a north-east (Cismonte) more influenced by the progressive civilisation of the Italian mainland. Within each region, the morphology of the landscape is so fragmented that the traditional rural community, the 'pieve', has been on the one hand very isolated from neighbouring groups even within the same valley, while, on the other, being able to exploit the finer detail of environmental variation brought about by relief, geology and aspect so as to permit local self-sufficiency. The historical importance and ecological necessity of pastoral transhumance have been greatly exaggerated (Lewthwaite, 1981).

PREHISTORIC ENVIRONMENT. The environment encountered by the earliest settlers differed in coastal morphology, forest cover and faunal content from that of today, and considerable changes independent of human action took place during the Neolithic.

Only the broad outlines of coastal development can be reconstructed. If de Lumley's model is correct for Corsica as well as for the Mediterranean coast of France (1976), then the flooding of coastlands would have been greatest during the 7th millennium bc, diminishing during the 6th and 5th millennia, and very slow since 4000bc. Coastal topography would have modified this overall pattern so that, for example, the severity of the transgression would have been postponed in the Gulf of Porto-Vecchio till the 5th millennium bc. The deep lagoons of Diana and Urbino would have come into existence during the Early Neolithic, but the formation of Biguglia and Palo, through the growth of longshore sandy cordons, may have been at a much later date.

The postglacial vegetation dynamics are better understood, though only from the limited perspective of upland pollen profiles, as a result of the researches of Reille (1976, 1977). The palynological reconstruction of the Atlantic environment (c.5500–c.2700bc) differs considerably from that hypothesised by phytosociologists: the expansion of evergreen species of oak was not a primary postglacial development, but a late prehistoric and medieval phenomenon.

The Atlantic climax at middle altitudes consisted of temperate zone species – deciduous oaks such as *Quercus petraea* and *Q. pubescens*, even ash and elm. The vegetation of the lower zone consisted formerly of a macchia-forest of tree heath (*Erica arborea*), while Corsican pine almost alone peopled the montane woodlands in the Early Holocene, the expansion of fir and beech beginning in the Sub-boreal. Reconstruction of the exact vegetational environment of early settlement is little advanced since neither the deciduous oak nor the tree-heath communities can be readily found in a pristine state on the island today.

The faunal environment of the early postglacial settlers would have been extremely impoverished: the attrition of species during the Late Pleistocene due to climatic deterioration had not been offset by the immigration of rapidly evolving continental faunas (Thaler, 1973). The only endemic species definitely known to have survived into the Holocene, indeed until the eighteenth century, is the so-called 'lapin-rat' or 'rat-rabbit' *Prolagus sardus* (Gauthier and Thibault, 1979) which was undoubtedly consumed by prehistoric populations, although the individual meat value would have been negligible (Ferton, 1898, 1899; Lanfranchi and Weiss, 1979; Vigne *et al.*, 1981). The only large species which might have coexisted with the earliest settlers was the extinct endemic deer *Megaceros (Nesoleipoceros) cazioti*, referred to in the older literature as *Cervus cazioti* (Depéret, 1897; Gauthier and Thibault, 1979). The palaeontologically-competent observer Ferton claimed the association of *Cervus cazioti* with artefacts in several shelters around Bonifacio, the identification of the remains from the Santa Manza road being checked by Depéret (Ferton, 1898, 351–5, 358–9; 1899, 141–2). However, no cases of such associations have been discovered since (Vigne, pers.comm., 1982). Since there is no independent palaeontological evidence of the presence of the small Corsican red deer *Cervus elaphus corsicanus* before the eighth century bc, it is likely that the earliest settlers encountered no potential prey larger than *Prolagus sardus* (Vigne and Lanfranchi, 1981).

There is equally no palaeontological evidence for any ancestral populations of sheep, goat, cattle, pig or dog from the Quaternary of Corsica, nor of Sardinia. The recent 'wild' flocks of mouflon, which might appear to be plausible sources of the domestic species because of the common chromosome number, are more likely to be feral populations descended from neolithic introductions (Poplin, 1979). A similar explanation has been proposed for the feral pigs, which are cytogenetically similar to domesticates rather than to the European wild boar (Popescu *et al.*, 1980).

HISTORY OF RESEARCH. The history of archaeological research in Corsica falls naturally into two cycles, separated by forty years of neglect between 1914 and 1954. The arrival of Roger Grosjean as a CNRS researcher in the latter year initiated the modern era of discovery. The first cycle spans just over a century, beginning in 1810 with the description of two 'Celtic' monuments (dolmens) by an army captain with geology as his hobby. Army officers and palaeontologists such as Caziot, Ferton, Depéret and Forsyth Major pursued the archaeological approach which now seems the least dated: they carried out stratigraphic excavations and recorded the domestic and endemic species encountered, interesting themselves in the date of the earliest settlement, the environment and the subsistence of neolithic Corsicans. Caziot introduced the three-age system to the island (Caziot, 1897; Ferton, 1898, 1899). A second approach favoured multi-disciplinary syntheses, drawing on classical accounts, physical anthropology, comparative ethnology, linguistics and archaeology *sensu stricto,* to construct models of racial strata produced by a series of immigrations (Bloch, 1902). Professional archaeology, however, favoured the cataloguing of 'megaliths', notable advances being made by the writer Prosper Mérimée (1976 (1840)), by A. de Mortillet (1892) and by the various scholars who attended the 30th session of the *Association Française pour l'Avancement des Sciences,* held at Ajaccio in 1901. Between 1901 and 1914 collaboration between the Corsican Tomasi and the mainland Frenchman Giraux resulted in a series of papers which combine the topographic and megalithic approaches, and deal with the monuments of the area south-west of Sartène (Giraux, 1914).

When Grosjean began his researches in 1954, the Neolithic was formally indistinguishable from any other period of material culture prior to the Classical contacts, the prehistoric inventory consisting largely of megaliths without datable associations. Most of Grosjean's efforts were devoted to the definition of a megalithic artistic tradition and of the *Torréen* civilisation of the Bronze Age. His major contribution to the Neolithic was the recognition of the existence of a local facies of the pan-Mediterranean CARDIAL culture group (Grosjean, 1971a). Grosjean's pupils and early associates, Lanfranchi and Weiss, began the scientific study of the Neolithic in the late 1960s with a series of stratigraphic excavations in the rock shelters of Curacchiaghiu (Levie; m.r.2 – all map references are to the general map on p. 180) (Lanfranchi, 1967) and Araguina-Sennola (Bonifacio; m.r.1), (Lanfranchi and Weiss, 1977), and at the open site of Monte Lazzo (Tiuccia; m.r.7) (Weiss and Desneiges, 1971, 1974).

Lanfranchi and Weiss also suggested for the first time the existence of parallel cultural traditions within the Neolithic, in their pioneering synthesis (1973; see also Weiss and Lanfranchi, 1976). The *18th Congrès Préhistorique de France,* held at Ajaccio in 1966, encouraged the interest of mainland French scholars such as Bailloud, who excavated the important site of Basi (Serra-di-Ferro; m.r.3) (Bailloud, 1969), and Sardinians such as Lilliu (1966) and Atzeni (1966, 1975). While the appreciation of the 'vertical' axis of prehistory is evident from the many stratigraphic excavations of cave, shelter and open sites which are in progress, the complementary spatial dimension, principally at the level of the regional survey, is only beginning to be documented (Acquaviva, 1976; Pasquet, 1979; Camps, 1979).

Material Culture

The Corsican Neolithic suffers from excessive reliance on a few sites which through the accident of discovery were the first to be excavated during the formative period of the late 1960s and early 1970s. All of the three major stratified sites – Araguina-Sennola (Bonifacio), Curacchiaghiu (Levie) and Basi (Serra-di-Ferro) lie in the south; only very recently has a shelter with a similar depth of accumulation begun to be excavated in the north, at Scaffa Piana (Saint Florent) (Jehasse, 1978, 731–4). Each of the three key sites can now be seen to have occupation hiatuses (Fig.6.2). Araguina alone appears free from the mixing of levels, while at Curacchiaghiu the small size of the shelter and the extent of the mixing, indicated by the dispersion of matching sherds (Lanfranchi, 1974a) raise serious doubts about the utility of the sample: unfortunately this site has been assigned a crucial status in the dual-culture model (Lanfranchi and Weiss, 1973; Weiss and Lanfranchi, 1976). In fact, of all the stratified sites currently published, it is clearly Basi which has the fullest and most reliable sample, although even here a hiatus in the 5th and 4th millennia bc must be recognised (Fig.6.2).

The traditional view of the Early Neolithic of the Mediterranean regarded the settlement of the previously uninhabited islands of both the eastern and western basins as part of the process of the maritime diffusion of neolithic culture (food production, ceramic technology, polished-stone tools). Navigation was developed, on this view, by Levantine populations whose diaspora as far as Iberia was delineated by their characteristic impressed ceramics (Bernabò Brea, 1950).

Excavation at the Curacchiaghiu shelter has produced the earliest evidence of preneolithic voyaging anywhere in the west Mediterranean (Cherry, 1981). The artefactual material, consisting of stone tools made of local quartz and rhyolite (Lanfranchi, 1967) was undiagnostic in itself, but associated with 7th millennium bc radiocarbon dates, and in a clear stratigraphic relationship to early neolithic ceramics with plausible 6th millennium bc dates. Some initial doubt was caused by the presence of four pieces of Sardinian obsidian and eight sherds below the layer of granite plaques which seemed to separate the preceramic and early ceramic levels. The excavator now holds that the fires of the first pottery-using occupants caused the detachment of the plaques from the granite masses, sealing their debris in with the earlier material (Camps, 1978, 19).

Subsequent excavations at the more deeply-stratified shelter of Araguina-Sennola (Plate 6.1) have eliminated remaining doubts about the preneolithic occupation of Corsica (Lanfranchi and Weiss, 1977). Although the artefacts themselves are culturally undiagnostic, they were associated with a burial and with a radiocarbon date consistent with those from Curacchiaghiu, while the separation of the preneolithic (XVIII) and early neolithic (XVII) levels is much less ambiguous. The preneolithic burial rite itself differs in a number of respects from that of the early neolithic burials in the same shelter: the

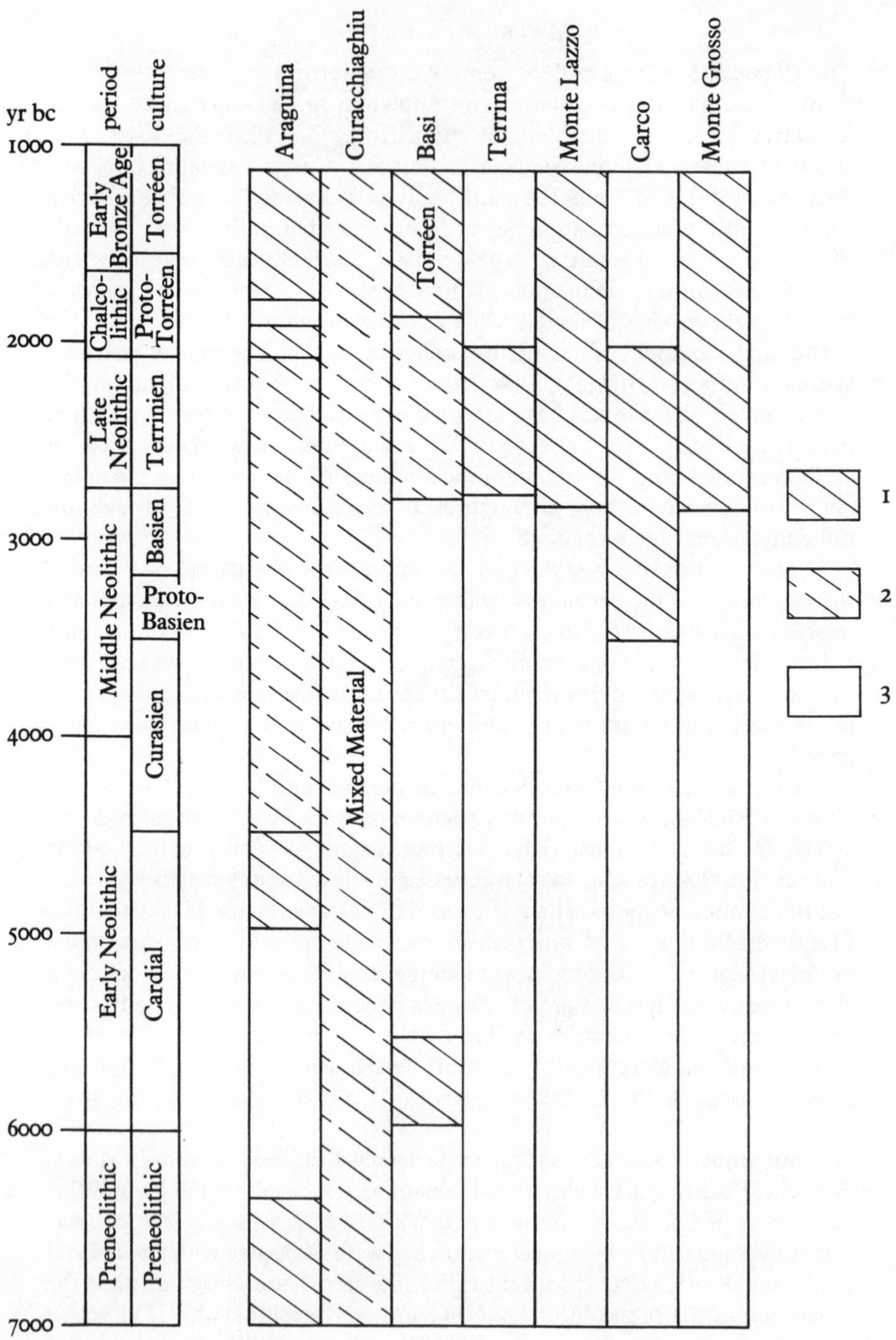
yr bc
1000
2000
3000
4000
5000
6000
7000
period
culture
Early Bronze Age
Torréen
Chalcolithic
Proto-Torréen
Late Neolithic
Terrinien
Middle Neolithic
Basien
Proto-Basien
Curasien
Early Neolithic
Cardial
Preneolithic
Preneolithic
Araguina
Curacchiaghiu
Basi
Terrina
Monte Lazzo
Carco
Monte Grosso
Mixed Material
Torréen
1
2
3

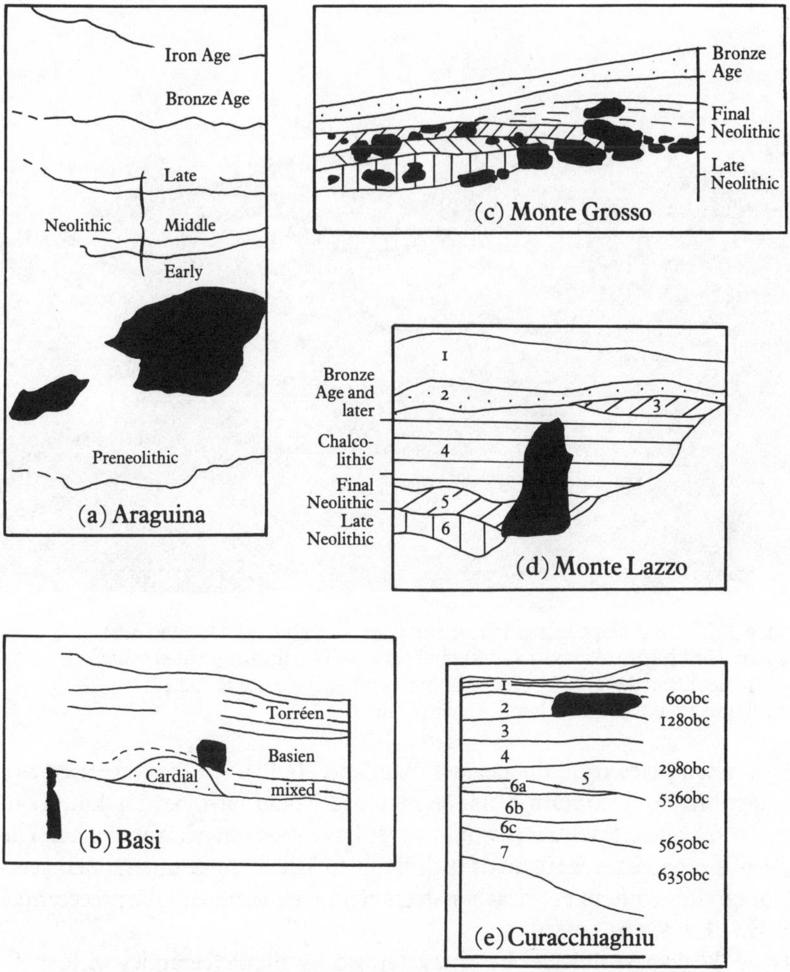

FIGURE 6.2. Chronological chart of the Corsican Neolithic, and the five principal stratigraphic sequences upon which it is based.
Key to chronological chart: 1 undisturbed material of secure date; 2 sparse occupation or mixed material; 3 no evidence of occupation.
Black areas on section drawings represent rocks. Section drawings after: Lanfranchi and Weiss, 1973 (a and e); Bailloud, 1969 (b); Magdeleine, 1979 (c); Weiss and Desneiges, 1971 (d).

skeleton was deposited, extended, in a depression marked by limestone blocks and covered with layers of reddish powder and then sand.

The discovery of Melian obsidian, first in the 7th, and more recently in the 10th millennium bc deposits at the Franchthi cave in the Argolid (Greece) confirms the preneolithic development of navigation within the Mediterranean as a whole (Cherry, 1981). The settlement of Corsica in the 7th millennium bc, when the sea levels were over 20m lower than at present, is generally assumed

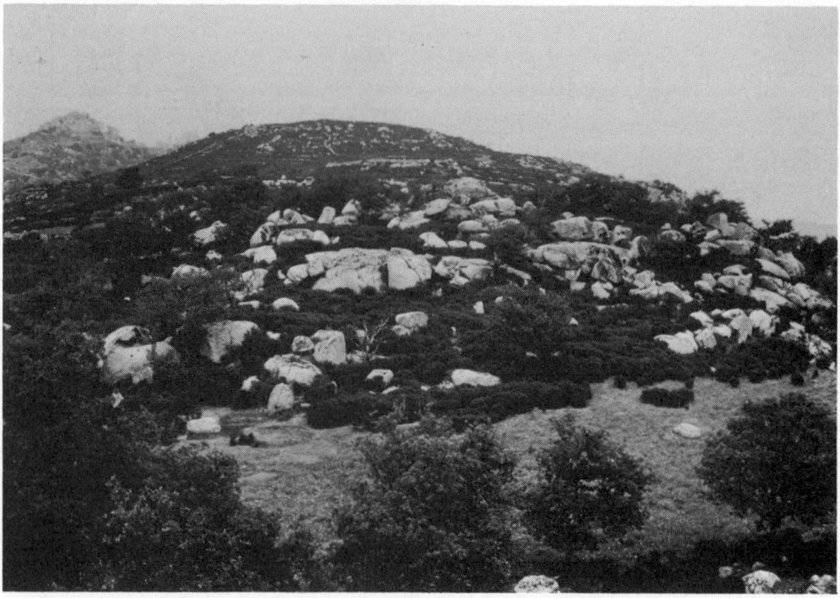

PLATE 6.1. The hill-slope settlement site of Carco, strategically located next to a col linking the Algajola and Regino valleys. The site has yielded some early neolithic material but its principal occupation dates to the 4th millennium bc. (Photo: James Lewthwaite.)

to have taken place from the nearest mainland (Italy). If Elba were used as a transit point the maximum distance involved would have been 45km (Conchon, 1976), and the voyagers would never have been out of sight of land. The extent of preneolithic settlement is difficult to assess, since unstratified aceramic open sites without radiocarbon dates cannot be assumed to be preceramic.

THE EARLY NEOLITHIC

Early neolithic assemblages are characterised by simple ceramics with shell-edge impressions or punched decoration and a lithic inventory of obsidian, flint and local rocks in which the predominant forms are obliquely-truncated blades and tranchet arrowheads (Weiss and Lanfranchi, 1976, 433–5). The known sites (Fig.6.3) fall clearly into two altitudinal groups: a lowland coastal series in basins and lower valleys at less than 400m within 5km of the coast (Bailloud, 1969; Lanfranchi, 1976a; Lanfranchi and Weiss, 1973, 1977; Jehasse, 1974, 1976, 1980; Camps, 1978, 1979; Pasquet, 1979); and an upland series at over 800m on plateaux and in upper valleys some 30 or 40km from the nearest shore (Passemard, 1925; Southwell Colucci, 1930; Lanfranchi, 1967, 1974a; Weiss, 1976).

The lowland series consists of a number of 'clusters', the internal spatial and chronological relationships of which are not clearly understood.

The heterogeneity of the early neolithic assemblages from Curacchiaghiu and Basi was early recognised. While the ceramics of the latter, with their

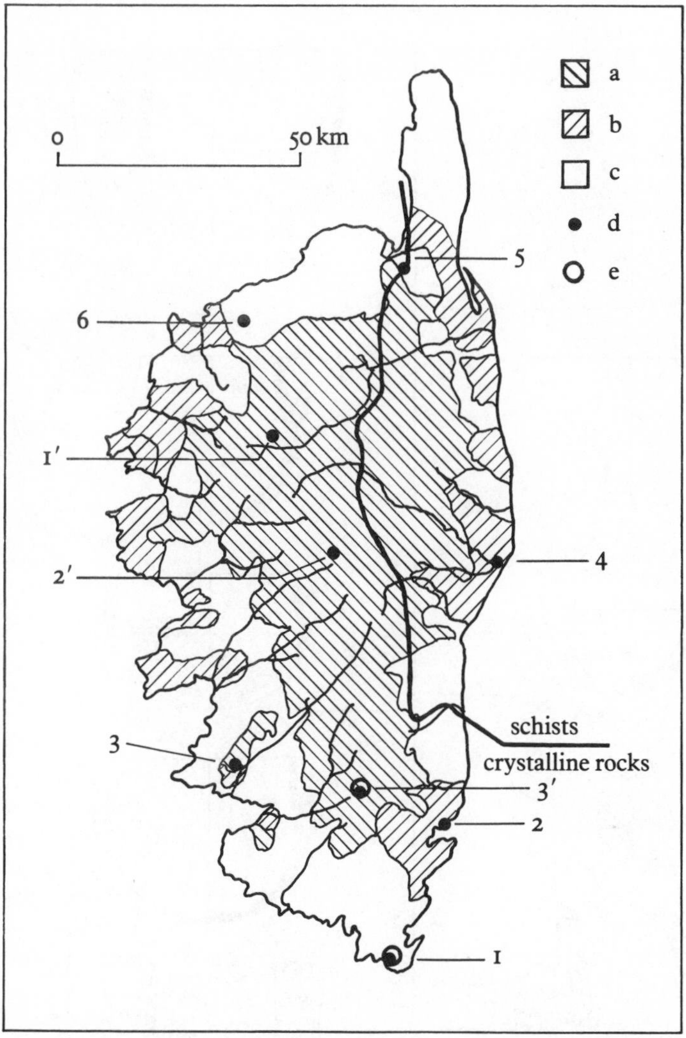

FIGURE 6.3. Preneolithic and early neolithic sites.
(a) mountains; (b) hills; (c) littoral; (d) early neolithic site; (e) pre-neolithic site.
Upland sites: 1′ Abri Albertini; 2′ Grotte Southwell; 3′ Curacchiaghiu.
Lowland sites: 1 Araguina-Sennola; 2 San Cipriano; 3 Basi and Filitosa D′; 4 Aléria; 5 Grotta Scritta; 6 Carco.

abundant shell-edge impressions, were easily assimilable to the general definition of the Cardial culture (with particularly strong resemblances to the material from Pienza in Tuscany (Camps, 1978, 1979)), the forms, fabric and decoration of the former were held to be distinctly different. Since radiocarbon dates for the respective levels were approximately synchronous (6th millennium bc), Lanfranchi and Weiss postulated the existence of parallel and

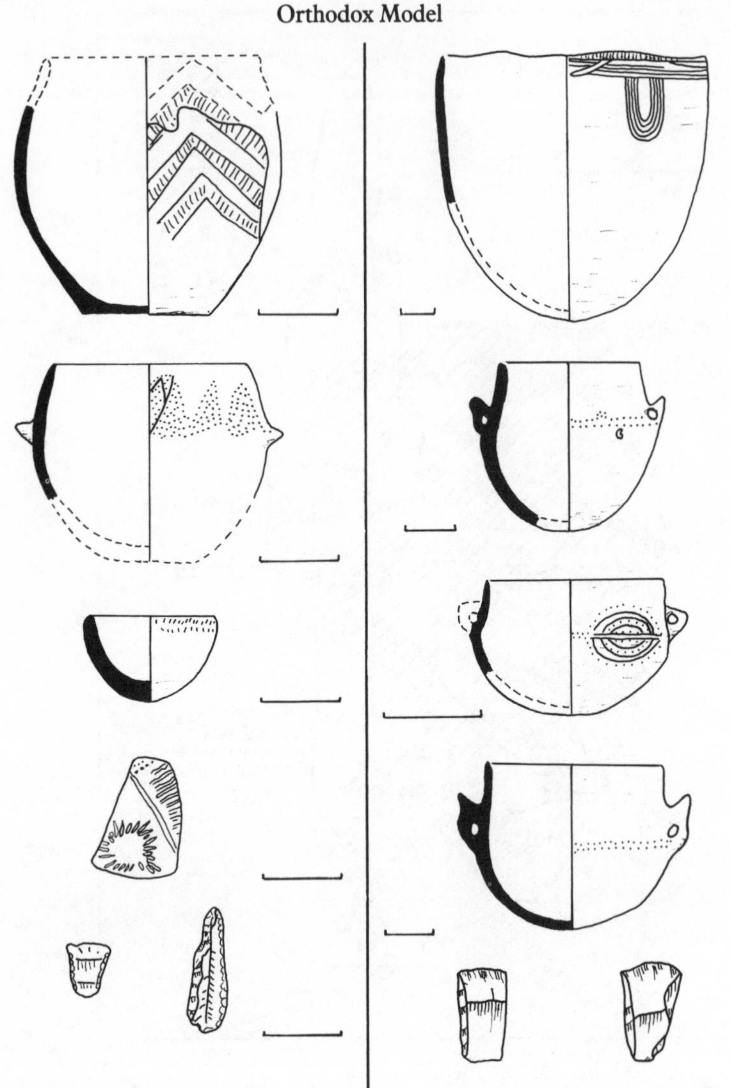

FIGURE 6.4. Early neolithic material culture.
Orthodox model: Parallel traditions. A Material of Cardial tradition from Basi (after Weiss and Lanfranchi, 1976); B Material of Curasien or Punch-decorated tradition from Curacchiaghiu (after Weiss and Lanfranchi, 1976).
Alternative model: Cardial-Curasien development. 1 Cardial decorated sherd from Basi; 2 Cardial decorated sherd from Barbaggiu; 3 bowl with impressed decoration from Araguina-Sennola; 4 bowl with incised decoration from Filitosa D′; 5-7 Curasien or Punch-decorated material from Curacchiaghiu. (1, 3-5 after Weiss and Lanfranchi, 1976; 2 after Jehasse, 1980; 6, 7 after Lanfranchi and Weiss, 1973.) All scales are 5cm.

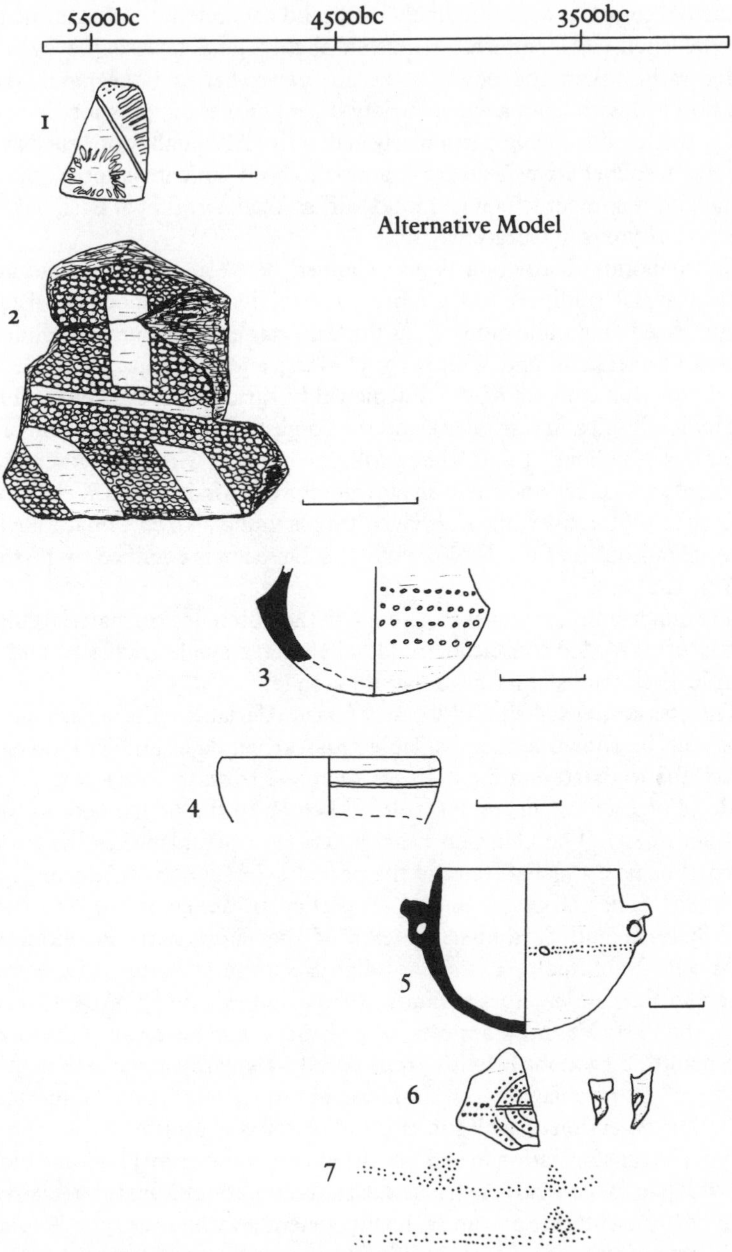

distinct cultural traditions in the Early Neolithic, a model accepted by other prehistorians (Camps, 1978).

The material culture attributes of the two groups – the Cardial facies of Basi and the *Curasien* or 'Punched' facies of Curacchiaghiu – are usually held to be quite distinct (Fig.6.4).

Cardial ceramics are more finely made and decorated, the diagnostic trait being the shell-edge patterns. Curasien shapes tend toward the ovoid or cylinder rather than the bowl, bases are never flat and the modicum of decoration is drawn from a wider variety of techniques (impression, incision, plastic), the handles being particularly elaborate. Although forms such as the transverse tranchet arrowhead are common to both lithic inventories, the raw material and manufacturing techniques differ: blades of flint at Basi, flakes of obsidian or rhyolite at Curacchiaghiu.

An economic distinction is also claimed between an innovative, agro-pastoral Cardial tradition and a more conservative, indigenous subsistence tradition based on mobile hunting, fishing and gathering at Curacchiaghiu and Araguina (Lanfranchi and Weiss, 1973; Weiss and Lanfranchi, 1976). The evidence for this consists of the few plausibly agricultural artefacts (a blade with 'sickle-gloss', and a grinder), and the domestic status of 98 per cent of the fauna at Basi (Bailloud, 1969; Vigne, 1982), compared with the predominance of *Prolagus sardus*, fish and shellfish at Araguina (Lanfranchi and Weiss, 1979; Vigne, 1982). Moreover, the Cardial culture is found all over Corsica, including the inland basin of the Niolo, while the Curasien is confined to the south (Fig.6.3, 1, 2, 3, 3′).

It is much simpler, however, to explain the differences in material culture in terms of pan-Mediterranean trends affecting a single tradition, and the economic distinctions in terms of the site sample.

The classic Cardial sites of Corsica (Basi, Alèria, Bonifacio harbour and Strette) can be shown by the available radiocarbon dates and by typological comparisons to dated continental sites such as Pienza in Tuscany and Peiro Signado (Portiragnes) in the Hérault, to belong to the period 6000–4500bc (Guilaine, 1980). The Curasien bears a generic resemblance to the various Epicardial or post-Cardial facies of the period 4500–4000bc (Guilaine, 1976, 1979, 1980). The elaborate handles, in particular, are comparable to Portuguese, Spanish and Sardinian contexts of the latest Early Neolithic and even Middle Neolithic (e.g. the Sardinian *Bonu Ighinu* culture of c.3700bc) (Asquerino Fernandez, 1977; Tanda, 1980). Indeed, much of the Curasien facies of the Early Neolithic appears to be no more than the result of the mixing of late neolithic (3000bc) sherds from later levels with earlier carbon at the type-site of Curacchiaghiu, on Lanfranchi's own admission (Lanfranchi, 1974a). The detection of such sub-cultural patterns as lithic exchange spheres and stylistic transformation in ceramic design are the essential building blocks out of which more general constructs such as polythetic cultures or networks of general cultural interaction can be finally generated when the sample is large enough. At present, the sample of information on the period 7000–4000bc in Corsica is so small and biased that the culture-historical terminology should be as open-ended as possible, to incorporate the maximum of future 'surprises' without the necessity of constant revision. Similarly, the contrasts in lithic material appear to be the logical result of developments in the radius of exchange systems over the 6th and 5th millennia bc. The Basi flint on the one hand might have been derived from northern Sardinia, for instance the Concas (Perfugas) source in the Anglona (Moravetti and Lo Schiavo, 1979, 340); significantly, Cardial sherds occur in proximity. From the later 5th millennium bc onward, obsidian from Monte Arci, Sardinia, appears to have been transported not only to Curacchiaghiu and other Corsican sites, but to mainland France (Lanfranchi, 1976b); polished serpentine bracelets from the Porto-Vecchio area of Corsica also appear to have featured in an interaction sphere involving Sardinia (Pasquet, 1979).

THE MIDDLE NEOLITHIC

The period 4000–3200bc is the most poorly documented of all in the Corsican Neolithic. The level which produced a radiocarbon date of 3700±150bc at Tappa yielded no material (Gagnière, 1972, 565); the scanty artefacts from Araguina XV lack absolute dates (Lanfranchi and Weiss, 1977); the typologically '*Proto-Basien*' material from San Vincente (Sartène) remains unpublished (Bailloud, 1969; Lanfranchi and Weiss, 1973; Weiss and Lanfranchi, 1976) although fresh excavations have begun. The claim for middle neolithic occupation in the lowest levels of the site of Carco (Catteri; m.r.5) remains unverified, since the site itself appears very disturbed (Lanfranchi and Weiss, 1973; Weiss and Lanfranchi, 1976; Jehasse, 1976, 1978). Only at Scaffa Piana (Saint Florent) in the Nebbio has middle neolithic material, including basketry, been found in a clear stratigraphic context; unfortunately the radiocarbon samples were not yet available at the time of writing (Jehasse, 1978, 734; Magdeleine, pers.comm.).

THE LATE NEOLITHIC

The criteria for the identification of a late neolithic site – the presence of dark-faced burnished ceramics with incised or plastic decoration, piercing arrowheads alongside tranchets and great quantities of fixed and mobile grinding equipment – are readily recognisable. The number of open sites discovered even during non-systematic field surveys has risen to a figure far exceeding that of the Early Neolithic; however, the proportion of known sites to have been excavated is much smaller. To a far greater extent than in the previous period, the chronological and culture-history subdivision of the Later Neolithic (4th and early 3rd millennia bc) depends on extrapolation from a relatively precarious sample – the stratigraphies of a few key sites. The later neolithic sites occur in clusters in natural and historical regions (Fig.6.5).* The eastern

* (a) The hinterland of Bonifacio (Ferton, 1898, 1899; Passemard, 1925; Gagnière *et al.*, 1969); (b) the Figari-Porto Vecchio depression (Lanfranchi and Weiss, 1973; Pasquet, 1979); (c) the Sartenais; (d) the Alta Rocca (Lanfranchi, 1967, 1974b, 1976, 1979); (e) the lower Taravo valley (Atzeni, 1966; Bailloud, 1969; Césari and Jehasse, 1978); and (f) the Gulf of Ajaccio (Doazan, 1967) in the well researched south of the island. The north is much less investigated but each of the major regions has yielded at least one later neolithic site: (g) the Cinarca (Weiss, 1973; Weiss and Desneiges, 1971, 1974); (h) the Niolo (Acquaviva, 1976); (i) the Filosorma (Gagnière, 1968; Weiss, 1966); (j) the Balagne (Lanfranchi, 1972a; Jehasse, 1976, 1978, 1980); (k) the Nebbio (Jehasse, 1978), and (m) the Marana (Magdeleine, 1979). The defensive enclosure of Tesoro (Erbalunga), datable to the end of the Chalcolithic at the earliest, testifies to the lateness of the settlement of Cap Corse (l) and the schistous zone generally.

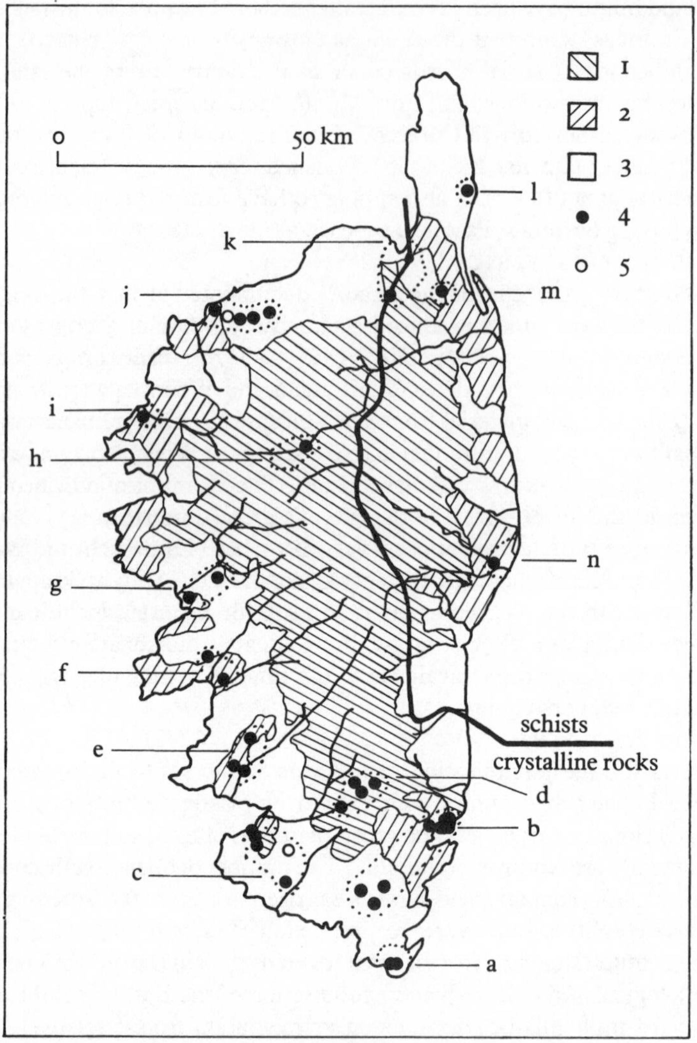

FIGURE 6.5. Later neolithic and chalcolithic sites.
1 mountains; 2 hills; 3 littoral; 4 late neolithic and chalcolithic sites; 5 middle neolithic sites.

Site groups: (a) Araguina-Sennola; (b) Figari-Porto Vecchio; (c) San Vincente-Capo di Logu-Cuncutu; (d) Curacchiaghiu-Sapara Alta-Compolaggia; (e)Basi-Filitosa-Castellucciu; (f) Tralavetto-San Simeone; (g) Monte Lazzo-Castaldu; (h) Castellu di Marze; (i) Galeria; (j) Carco-Mutola-Monte d'Ortu; (k) Scaffa Piana; (l) Tesoro; (m) Monte Grosso; (n) Aléria-Terrina IV.

region around Aléria, which has been intensively researched in recent years (n) (Jehasse, 1974, 1976, 1978, 1980; Camps, 1979) has incidentally produced evidence of copper-working at 2700bc, i.e. in a 'late neolithic' rather than a 'chalcolithic' context.

Lanfranchi and Weiss (Lanfranchi and Weiss, 1973; Weiss and Lanfranchi, 1976) recognise a multiplicity of later neolithic cultures (Fig.6.6), only one of which, the Punch-decorated tradition of Araguina and Curacchiaghiu, they regard as entirely indigenous. At the same time, all but the Punch-decorated are regarded as agricultural in economy. Both material cultural and economic innovation are thus ascribed to extra-Corsican developments.

The Punch-decorated tradition. Three stages of development are recognised: a 'Middle Neolithic' at Araguina (XV) in which carinated ceramics and piercing arrowheads appear; a 'Later Neolithic' with a coastal (Araguina XIII) and a montane facies (Curacchiaghiu 5 and 4), distinguished from the Middle Neolithic by additional ceramic forms and fabrics, by the use of incisions to border the punch-decorated motifs, and by the association of piercing and semi-lunate arrowheads; and a Chalcolithic at Araguina (XI–VIj) with a further expansion in ceramic forms and fabrics, and the first appearance of true handles. Radiocarbon dates provide fixed points of c.3000 bc (Curacchiaghiu level 5) and 2000bc (Araguina level VIj), the latter a *terminus ante quem* for the sequence.

The Basien group. Ceramics found by Bailloud in level 5 at Basi were sufficiently distinctive within the western Mediterranean to be identified as the *Basien* group or culture (Bailloud, 1969, 369). Although sharing certain general features with the contemporary Chasséen (lustrous black finish, carination, perforations for string suspension) the ceramic is distinguished by plastic decoration (rectilinear and curvilinear cordons) and bases (flat, open with ring-feet). The lithics, while based on blade and bladelet forms, as in the Chasséen, are made of Sardinian obsidian as the predominant raw material, rather than flint. Confusingly, Weiss and Lanfranchi both suggest an extra-Corsican origin, and at the same time envisage a proto-Basien, middle neolithic facies in the lower level (4) at Carco (Catteri), and at San Vincente (Sartène) (1976, 435; Jehasse, 1976, 612).

If there is in the orthodox model a certain ambiguity over derivation, there is none over the contrast between the Punched and Basien traditions in material culture, economy and distribution (the Punched tradition in the Alta Rocca and the Causse of Bonifacio (Fig.6.5: a,b,d), the Basien sites in lower valleys of the south-west in an arc from the Gravone to the Ortolo (Fig.6.5: c, e, f)). Weiss and Lanfranchi (1976) regard the contrast as impossible to explain in terms of temporal variation, since the radiocarbon dates for Curacchiaghiu and Basi are so similar and the links with the contemporary Sardinian Ozieri culture equally marked in both traditions.

The Monte Lazzo group. In 1973, Lanfranchi and Weiss suggested that the ceramics from Monte Lazzo (Tiuccia) indicated the existence of a third late

A

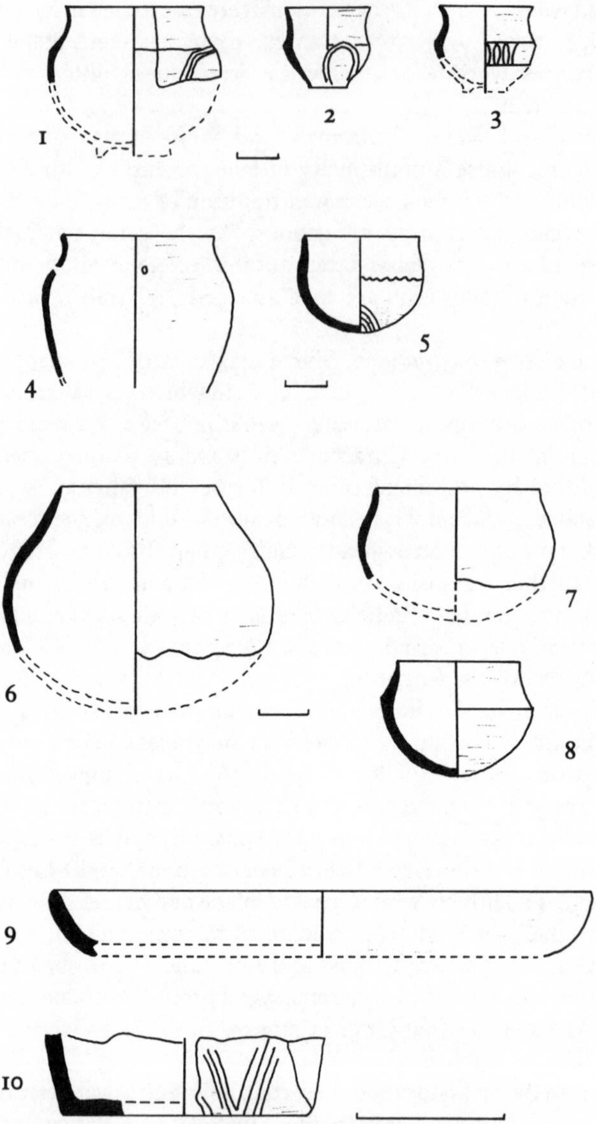

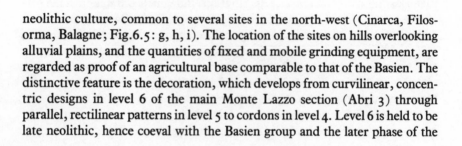

neolithic culture, common to several sites in the north-west (Cinarca, Filosorma, Balagne; Fig.6.5: g, h, i). The location of the sites on hills overlooking alluvial plains, and the quantities of fixed and mobile grinding equipment, are regarded as proof of an agricultural base comparable to that of the Basien. The distinctive feature is the decoration, which develops from curvilinear, concentric designs in level 6 of the main Monte Lazzo section (Abri 3) through parallel, rectilinear patterns in level 5 to cordons in level 4. Level 6 is held to be late neolithic, hence coeval with the Basien group and the later phase of the

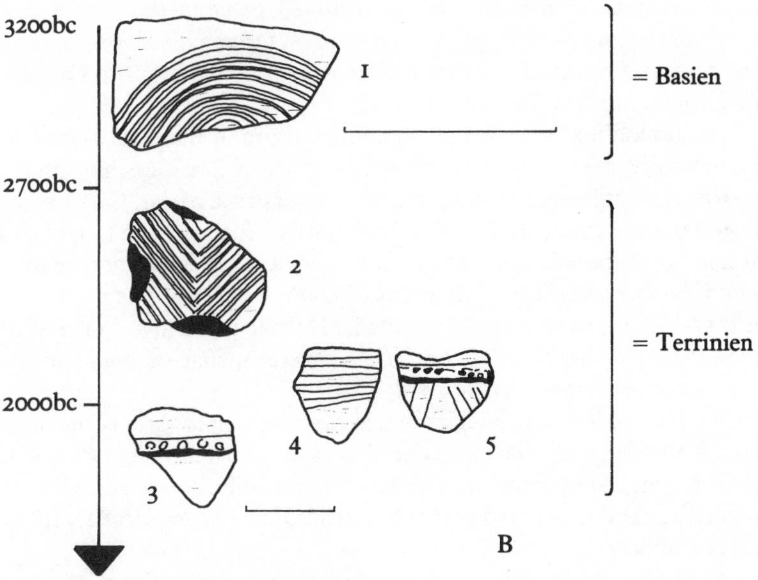

FIGURE 6.6. Later neolithic material culture.
A *Cultural divisions:* 1-3 Basien material from Basi; 4-5 Later Curasien material from Curacchiaghiu; 6-8 Late neolithic material from Monte Grosso; 9-10 Terrinien material from Terrina. (1-8 after Weiss and Lanfranchi, 1976; 9, 10 after Camps, 1979.)
B *Chronological relationships:* 1 Basien-related material from Monte Grosso; 2-5 material related to and contemporary with the Terrinien from (2) Monte Grosso and (3-5) Monte Lazzo. (1, 2 after Magdeleine, 1979; 3-5 after Weiss and Lanfranchi, 1976.) All scales are 5cm.

punch-decorated tradition, while level 5 is regarded as chalcolithic, therefore parallel to Araguina VIj (Weiss and Lanfranchi, 1976).

The Monte Grosso group. The progress of excavations at Monte Grosso I (Biguglia; m.r.6) led to the separation of this site from the Basien group, in which it had been placed in 1973 (Lanfranchi and Weiss, 1973, 109), as a distinct facies (Weiss and Lanfranchi, 1976, 440–1) but on unspecified grounds. Magdeleine (1979, 36) notes resemblances to both the Basien and Monte Lazzo facies which he explains in terms of cultural diversity occasioned by geographical factors.

The Terrinien. Recent excavations at Terrina IV (Aléria; m.r.4) by Camps (1979) brought to light an assemblage of basically Monte Lazzo level 5 type (parallel rectilinear incisions or fine channels) with a particular prevalence of perforations under the rim, which for the first time could be securely dated by a dozen radiocarbon dates to the later 3rd millennium bc, i.e. late neolithic rather than chalcolithic (1979, 18). Such a dating raised the possibility that the contrast between the Monte Lazzo and Basien cultures might be temporal rather than spatio-cultural, and this was confirmed by the recognition of the same assemblage at Basi in level 4, stratified between the Basien and the Torréen of the 2nd millennium bc. This facies, termed the *Terrinien,* has been recognised at Terrina III (Aléria), Carco-Modria (Catteri) and Castellucciu (Pila-Canale; m.r.11) (Camps, 1979, 12).

The undoubted diversity of material culture of the Late Neolithic has conventionally been explained in terms of extra-Corsican innovation and intra-Corsican cultural cantonment. The significance of pan-Corsican trends has been underestimated. This is at least partly because of the lack of clearly-stratified multi-period open sites. Chronological differentiation within the Monte Grosso assemblage is extremely difficult, since only 0.55 per cent of the sherds are decorated (Jehasse, 1978, 726). Despite much investment of effort, Carco (Plate 6.1) has failed to produce a coherent, consistent and absolutely dated sequence (Jehasse, 1976, 1978).

One particularly crucial horizon feature common to various late neolithic groups is the motif of concentric curvilinear impressions (Fig.6.6) which has been frequently compared to Ozieri decoration of the classical period (recently shown to be datable to c.3300–2700bc) in Sardinia (Trump, 1982). Its occurrence is as follows:

(a) At *Basi,* within level 5, alongside classic Basien cordon decoration, on a polished stone vessel (Gagnière, 1972, 563. (b) At *Curacchiaghiu,* on the base of a vessel of uncertain date; fragments lay in both early and late neolithic levels, probably derived from level 4, i.e. from a little after 3000bc according to the level 5 radiocarbon date (Lanfranchi, 1976, 14–15, fig.14(1)). (c) At *Monte Lazzo,* both in the surface deposits (Weiss and Desneiges, 1971, fig.4(7)) and stratified in Shelter 3, level 6, below the 'Terrinien' level of rectilinear parallel incisions (1971, 425). (d) At *Monte Grosso,* in the lowest level, V, along with other Basien attributes (Jehasse, 1978, 726 and fig.6, 727).

The plausibility of this trait as a horizon-marker is increased by the frequency with which other Ozieri features such as 'tunnel-handles' are associated and the obvious correlation with the peak period of importation of Sardinian obsidian from Monte Arci (Lanfranchi, 1976b). The final problem is that of the integration of the 'punched' motifs of Araguina and Curacchiaghiu into the seriation. In fact, the patterns of punched decoration bounded by incisions in Araguina level III (Lanfranchi and Weiss, 1977, fig.34(15)) and Curacchiaghiu levels 4 and 5 (Lanfranchi, 1976b, 14–15, 18, and fig.14(2, 4)) can be found at Basi in the classic Basien level 5 (Bailloud, 1969, fig.11(15–18)). This strongly suggests that the variability of the two assemblages may be due to sampling, in that the shelter sites lack the finer grade of ceramics with the most distinctly 'Basien' features.

This seriation model of late neolithic material culture (Fig.6.6) cannot be regarded as firmly established, until confirmed by many more radiocarbon dates and reliably stratified contexts. In particular, the relationship between the early neolithic Curasien and the proto-Basien Middle Neolithic is still unclear, although the recognition of 'Bonu Ighinu' features (datable to c.3700

PLATE 6.2. The great dolmen of Fontanaccia, which forms part of the complex of megalithic monuments on the Cauria plateau. The Riniau and I Stantari alignments lie only a few hundred metres away. (Photo: James Lewthwaite.)

bc in Sardinia) within the Curasien suggests that the transition lay between 3700bc and 3300bc. Similarly, at the end of the 3rd millennium, the lower limit of the 'Terrinien' is not securely related to the latest undisturbed levels at Monte Lazzo (level 4 of Abri 3, level 2 of Sondage A) and the chalcolithic level (VIj) of Araguina. Above all, most of the known late neolithic sites remain undatable even in relative terms.

The Megalithic Dimension. Paradoxically this, the oldest tradition of research in Corsican archaeology, has advanced the least beyond cataloguing and morphological analysis.

Morphology clearly divides burial monuments from standing stones. The former are subdivided into various classes both in native tradition (bancali, stazzone) and by archaeologists (cists, coffers, dolmens) (Giglioli, 1932). The best-preserved example is the dolmen of Fontanaccia (Sartène; m.r.11) in the Cauria area (Plate 6.2). The latter (menhirs, stantari) vary in their approximation to the human outline and in their inclusion of anatomical or artefactual detail, some being clearly of 2nd millennium bc date, judging by the representation of bronze age weaponry. The general model seriating the periods of construction of various monument classes deduced by Grosjean (1966a, 1967) is inherently difficult to test. The excavation of various burial monuments has produced disappointingly little information of chronological or cultural value: the typical co-occurrence of tranchet and semi-lunate arrowheads, beads, and

PLATE 6.3. The alignments of Palaggiu, which consist of 258 monoliths and are the largest in the western Mediterranean. The site lies in a basin, with bronze age Torri on the surrounding hills. (Photo: James Lewthwaite.)

undiagnostic ceramics within a single small assemblage would on a settlement point to the accumulation of material between 4000bc and 2000bc; in a tomb the same logic need not apply (Grosjean, 1964; Grosjean and Liégeois, 1964; Lanfranchi, 1972b; Lanfranchi and Weiss, 1973, 130–43; Jehasse, 1976, 615; 1980, 557–9).

Insofar as chronological and cultural comparisons can be made beyond Corsica, the most striking characteristic of the Corsican Late Neolithic is the scarcity of mortuary ceremonial sites comparable to the thousand rock-cut tombs of contemporary Sardinia (Lilliu, 1973, 105–25). Only a handful of small *hypogées-sous-taffoni* are known, in the Sartenais (Grosjean *et al.*, 1976) where they contain early 2nd millennium bc ceramics, and at Tappa (Porto-Vecchio) (Gagnière, 1972, 565). The Sartenais has been known since the time of de Mortillet (1892) to have the densest concentration of megaliths, both burial chambers and standing stones, within Corsica (Fig.6.7), and the great alignments of Palaggiu (m.r.8; Plate 6.3) and the Cauria (m.r.9) plateau are comparable in size with those of Brittany (Grosjean, 1966b). The only other aspect of megalithic architecture which can at present be investigated is that of the spatial patterning. In view of the poor chronological resolution, the correlation between the locations of megaliths and of settlements cannot be pursued beyond the gross observation that a southern concentration of sites is common to both classes. Certain locational associations with natural features such as cols suggest a variety of possible functional explanations, e.g. the roles

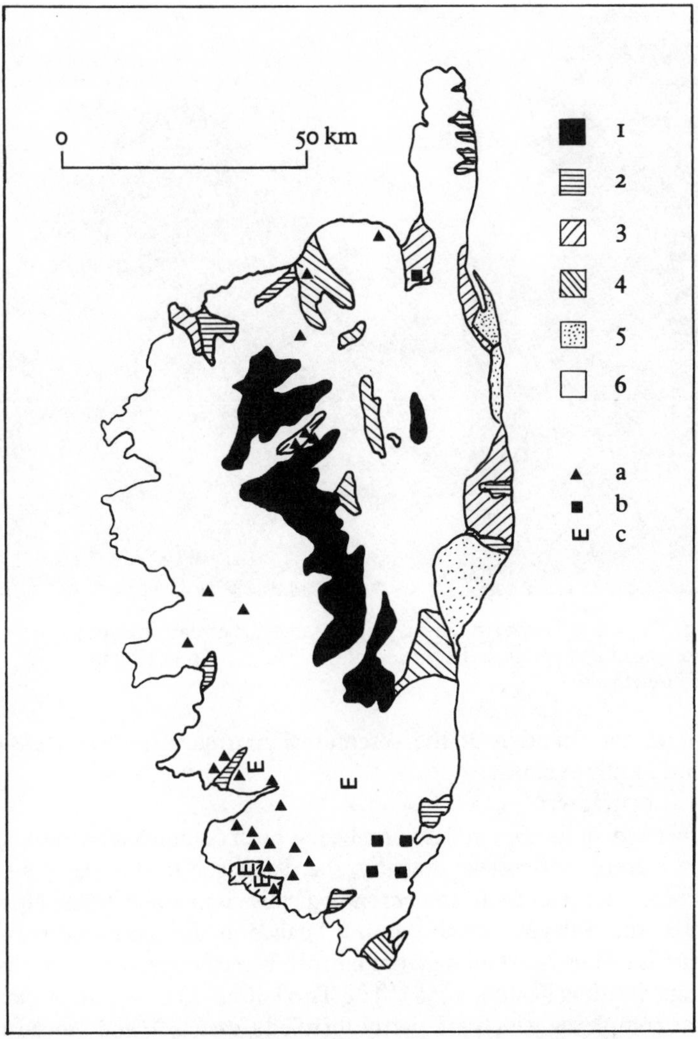

FIGURE 6.7. Distribution of Corsican megaliths in relation to soil types.
Soils: 1 rankers; 2 riverine alluvium; 3 Mediterranean brown earths; 4 rendzinas and lithosols; 5 marine sediments; 6 acid brown soils.
Megalith types: a dolmen; b coffer/cist; c alignment.

of territorial demarcation, ritual connected with nodal points or a connection with peripheral subsistence activities, for instance pastoral stock movements.

Very little can therefore be said positively of the social archaeology of late neolithic Corsica from the megaliths, although their apparent variability in density both within Corsica (correlation with settlement density in the south) and in comparison with Sardinia suggests that the levels of population concentration and social complexity which required the integrative ritual usually

PLATE 6.4. The site of Tappa, which has yielded radiocarbon dates of around 2000bc, placing it amongst the earliest of the Corsican Torri. (Photo: James Lewthwaite.)

envisaged as the function of the ceremonial mortuary features were only weakly and locally extant.

THE CHALCOLITHIC

The archaeology of the 2nd millennium bc has been dominated by the concept of a *Torréen* culture (Grosjean, 1971b), the diagnostic feature being a stone tower (Torre) architecturally and chronologically comparable to the Nuraghi of Sardinia, the Talayots of the Balearic Islands or the recently discovered Motillas of La Mancha. The material culture is particularly close to that of Bronze Age Sardinia (Lilliu, 1966). The Torri often occur within or close to settlement complexes which are partly fortified ('castelli'), and indeed Lanfranchi has suggested (1978, 1982) that the term 'Castelli culture' be substituted for 'Torréen' as a more accurate description of the Middle Bronze Age of Corsica. The *terminus post quem* for this culture is set at 1600bc by the majority of Torréen radiocarbon dates (Lanfranchi, 1978, 254–74).

Since the *terminus ante quem* for the Terrinien phase of the Late Neolithic can be set at around 2200bc by the series of dates from Terrina IV (Aléria), a period of some 600 radiocarbon years, corresponding to the Chalcolithic and the Earlier Bronze Age on the mainland, remains without precise cultural definition. The two radiocarbon dates from the Torre of Tappa (Porto-Vecchio; m.r. 10) (Plate 6.4; Grosjean, 1962; Virili and Grosjean, 1979, 128), and that from the western, non-Torréen structure at the Castello d'Alo (Bilia) (Grosjean, 1967, 711) cannot be related to material assemblages, nor

PLATE 6.5. The rocky citadel of Castaldu, a late 3rd millennium site in an inaccessible, easily defensible location dominating the upper reaches of the Liamone river valley. (Photo: James Lewthwaite.)

are they reliable indications for the antedating of the Torréen.

The only assemblages which can confidently be assigned on typological grounds to this period are the grave goods of the Palaggiu (Sartène) cist (Peretti, 1966), the *hypogées-sous-taffoni* of the Sartenais (Grosjean *et al.*, 1976); and the San Simeone (Ajaccio) burial cave (Doazan, 1967) although the latter is clearly mixed with later material. The Palaggiu artefacts are comparable to Beaker assemblages found throughout the west Mediterranean, although no actual Beaker has ever been found in Corsica (Camps, 1978), and also to the Bonnanaro culture of Sardinia, suggesting a date of around 1800bc; the pedestalled cups of the other sites resemble Sicilian, Sardinian and Provençal assemblages of the Early Bronze Age (Ferrarese Ceruti, 1972–4; Courtin, 1978). Unfortunately these assemblages cannot be related to any domestic material from settlement sites.

Significant changes in settlement morphology and location do occur within this grey period, of which the most noticeable is the growing defensibility of sites. Many late neolithic sites such as Monte Lazzo or Monte Grosso had been located on hillslopes and summits during the Terrinien period (equivalent to Monte Lazzo level 5), terracing being used to increase the habitable surface. However, during the subsequent period represented by the assemblages of Monte Lazzo level 4 new sites began to be founded in which internal habitable space and accessible arable land were minimal, while the natural inaccessibility of some existing settlements was supplemented by

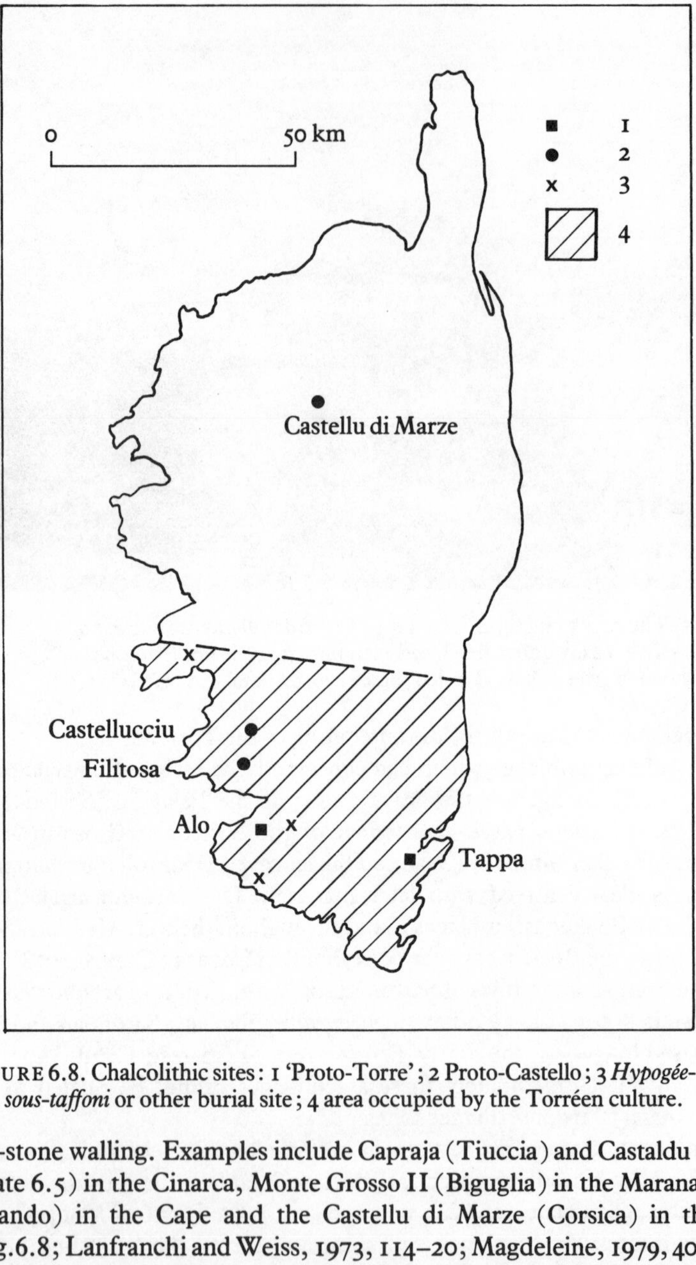

FIGURE 6.8. Chalcolithic sites: 1 'Proto-Torre'; 2 Proto-Castello; 3 *Hypogée-sous-taffoni* or other burial site; 4 area occupied by the Torréen culture.

dry-stone walling. Examples include Capraja (Tiuccia) and Castaldu (Arbori) (Plate 6.5) in the Cinarca, Monte Grosso II (Biguglia) in the Marana, Tesoro (Brando) in the Cape and the Castellu di Marze (Corsica) in the Niolo (Fig.6.8; Lanfranchi and Weiss, 1973, 114–20; Magdeleine, 1979, 40; Acquaviva, 1979), some of which enjoy an additional regional strategic significance in controlling a pass. This pre-Torréen phase of defensive enclosures and eyries is broadly paralleled by chalcolithic developments in Languedoc and Provence (Courtin and Onoratini, 1976; Courtin, 1978; Gutherz, 1982), Sardinia (Moravetti and Lo Schiavo, 1979) and the Baleares (Lewthwaite, 1982a), some of which are connected with the Beaker cultural phenomenon, although certain authors (e.g. Mills, ch.5 above) are unhappy to ascribe a defensive function to the south French enclosures.

The fact that assemblages of artefacts with precisely such extra-Corsican associations are found solely in the hinterland of the Gulfs of Ajaccio and Valinco is unlikely to be only coincidentally related to the antiquity, density and importance of later Torréen settlements in these regions, such as the major sites of Castellucciu (Pila-Canale) (Césari and Jehasse, 1978), Filitosa (Sollacaro) (Grosjean, 1961) and those of the Sartenais (Liégeois and Peretti, 1976). Research bias and preservation factors alone cannot explain away this correlation, which appears to indicate a genuine cultural centre of gravity and of innovative interaction in the south-west. Most authors, apart from Grosjean, have linked this proto-Torréen development with the elaboration of the armed stature-menhirs (Paladini) which are confined to precisely the same part of Corsica (Gorsjean, 1967; Camps, 1978). The north, on the other hand, appears extremely sparsely populated during the Bronze Age (Magdeleine, 1979, 40). The evidence of the links between Torréen ceramics and the Bonnanaro facies of northern Sardinia and between Torri and Nuraghi themselves (Lilliu, 1966) suggests that southern Corsica may be regarded as culturally within the orbit of Sardinia during the earlier 2nd millennium bc, the influence of the Italian mainland in the form of the Appennine culture becoming significant only after 1400bc (Camps, 1979, 19–20).

Economy and Settlement

Preneolithic Settlement and Subsistence

Of the two known sites with preneolithic occupation, only Araguina-Sennola has, thanks to its calcareous environment, preserved bone and shell debris (Vigne, 1982). Nearly all the bones (99.7%) were of *Prolagus sardus*, the remainder of monk seal (*Monachus monachus*) and sea birds. Lanfranchi and Weiss (1979) mention also red mullet and molluscs. The vegetal contribution to the subsistence of the preneolithic inhabitants cannot be determined. Such a sample conforms with the artefactual and occupational evidence of temporary use by a small group.

The key questions to be considered are, first, the extent to which the Araguina sample can be considered 'typical' of the preneolithic settlement and subsistence pattern of Corsica, and secondly, what a comparison with contemporary continental material can reveal concerning the process of colonisation.

The concentration on small game and aquatic resources is entirely logical in view of the palaeontological evidence, and as a result, it is improbable that groups of more than band size or permanent base camps would have been possible. The existence of an upland site such as Curacchiaghiu is hardly proof that groups moved between upland and lowland, since the only terrestrial 'complementarity' to be exploited would have been the differences in the vegetal resources of the lowland tree-heath macchia and the developing upland deciduous mixed-oak forest. Stochastic movement between different sites within a weakly differentiated landscape appears far more probable.

Contemporary mesolithic populations in mainland France and Italy exploited red deer, boar, ibex and hazelnuts (Phillips, 1975), none of which were available to the early settlers of Corsica. The increasing exploitation of less attractive resources such as rabbits, terrestrial and aquatic molluscs and small-seeded legumes (Guilaine, 1980) appears to bear out Clarke's suggestion (1976) that population pressure on resources was approaching critical limits during the 7th millennium bc, though his theory of the progressive replacement of deciduous by evergreen forest at this period appears mistaken (Lewthwaite, 1982b). The settlement of Corsica, given the paucity of resources, can hardly have acted as a major demographic safety valve for populations of the adjacent mainland despite the island's size, its accessibility and its proximity to Sardinia. Since voyaging is now attested between mainland Greece and Melos in the 10th millennium bc (Cherry, 1981), the absence of watercraft alone is less likely to have delayed mesolithic settlement than the lack of resources. It was probably, therefore, the essential poverty of Corsica's resources which was responsible for the island's relatively late human colonisation.

Early Neolithic Settlement and Subsistence

Although the increase in site numbers between the Preneolithic and the Early Neolithic is of an order of magnitude, only two of the latter sites have produced worthwhile bone samples, and none plant remains, while locational (catchment) information is difficult to interpret because of the poor chronological control.

The Cardial levels at Basi were associated with an overwhelmingly (98 per cent) domestic fauna, dominated by sheep (72 per cent), with a complement of pigs (27 per cent) and goat (1 per cent). The sheep population was morphologically domesticated, the age and sex patterns indicating husbandry, while the pigs were uniformly larger than the recent Corsican boar (Vigne, 1982).

The Araguina-Sennola early neolithic occupations were associated with a completely different faunal spectrum: 96.2 per cent *Prolagus sardus* supplemented by red mullet, sea bream (*Chrysophyrys aurata*) birds and shells. Of the few domestic animals identified, twice as many bones belonged to sheep as to pigs (Lanfranchi and Weiss, 1979; Vigne, 1982).

The presence of domestic sheep in the early neolithic levels at Basi may be explained in two ways: as the more visible component of a fully-developed mixed-farming system, or as a purely pastoral 'bow-wave' preceding the much slower diffusion of cereal cultivation as argued by Guilaine (1976) and Uerpmann (1979). The key question is: what benefits did the sheep confer which offset the cost of their importation, in the case of Corsica across 45km of open sea, looked at in the context of the Early Neolithic of the Mediterranean as a whole, from Anatolia to Iberia? Dairy and wool pastoralism can be excluded, as these characteristics were not developed in the early neolithic sheep (Ryder, 1981). Although large territories are required to support even band-sized groups on meat-pastoralism alone (Halstead, 1981), the circumstances of the initial colonisation of islands may have proved suitable for such a strategy.

Space would hardly have been a scarce resource, and importation the only means of stocking the hinterland with animals of worthwhile size. The sheep would have been the smallest and most docile species available and in its mouflon form capable of subsisting on much coarser feed (Lewthwaite, 1981).

The other areas of colonisation might seem to support this model. In the case of aceramic neolithic Cyprus the extent of the reliance on imported Syrian fallow deer can hardly be explained by dairying (Stanley Price, 1977a). On Mallorca, an endemic species, *Myotragus balearicus,* the size of a small antelope, survived into the postglacial and was exploited by colonists during the early settlement period (Waldren, 1979). Since Mallorca lies 167km from the nearest mainland (Cherry, 1981), the costs of importing domesticates may have exceeded the 'benefits' threshold, and the endemic species, despite its deficiencies, may have been pressed into service as a substitute. These attempts at local domestication may therefore provide an insight into contemporary pastoral techniques (Lewthwaite, 1982c). However, cereal cultivation is in fact well-attested in the Aceramic Neolithic of Cyprus (Stanley Price, 1977a), while the earlier colonists of Mallorca cannot have subsisted on *Myotragus balearicus* alone, and it is likely that the size of the site sample is responsible for exaggerating the importance of this species as a resource.

Sampling error is likely to have affected the evidence for horticulture still more severely than that for pastoralism; palaeoethnobotanical remains are sparse and artefacts of limited diagnostic value. Horticultural base camps located near the coast, on low river terraces or in the centre of plains would have suffered more severely from the postglacial sea-level rise and later alluviation than pastoral outstations in adjacent rugged terrain, as the examples of the Ile Corrège (Leucate) (Freises *et al.*, 1976) and the Abri Jean Cros (Labastide-en-Val) (Guilaine, 1979) suggest. Indeed, the greater survival of hortopastoral base camps or permanent settlements on islands (Khirokitia, Cyprus; Knossos, Crete) may simply indicate areas of relatively stable coastline morphology and minimal riverine aggradation.

The location of Basi on a low hill roughly 5km from the (stable) coastline is remarkably similar not only to Knossos (Roberts, 1979) and to Mari-Tenta (Kalavasos) on Cyprus (Todd, 1978) but also to the position of the Ile Corrège site prior to the formation of the Leucate lagoon (Freises *et al.*, 1976).

How to interpret the small numbers of ovicaprines at Araguina-Sennola and Curacchiaghiu (Lanfranchi and Weiss, 1973, 44) is more of a problem. There are three possible explanations. Transhumant pastoralism as part of a seasonal cycle of broad-spectrum exploitation in the developing forest milieu is one; the prevalence of pines and herbaceous species in the Curacchiaghiu pollen sample (Lanfranchi and Weiss, 1973, 44) contrasts markedly with Reille's zonal patterns (1976, 1977) and may reflect the use of fire to clear primary forest for cereals, pasture or preferred tree species. Second, such sites could equally well be interpreted as the seasonal outstations of hortopastoral camps (such as Basi). Depending on the availability of springs and the complementary resources of the forest and the sea, shepherds might have moved to the coast rather than to the mountains in summer, as in sectors of the Argolid, Cyprus and Sardinia (P. Halstead and A. Griffiths, pers.comm.). Third, and finally, the 'domesticates' might simply be ferals from domestic flocks at base camps such as Basi, exploited in the hinterland as game.

The occurrence of pigs of a morphologically robust variety alongside the sheep at both Basi and Araguina is equally ambiguous. The pig would have been able to exploit the primary forest better than the sheep, produce larger litters and hence produce meat more efficiently. Unless used as a 'plough' (Rowley-Conwy, 1981), its direct utility to a horticultural plot would be less, though its role as a diversifying and stabilising factor in the total economy would be a definite advantage. Pigs can transhume as well as sheep; a robust morphology might have been a desirable trait to retain. At the same time, the contrast between the fully domesticated sheep and robust pig populations may reflect two distinct patterns of animal husbandry appropriate respectively to the field and the forest.

In conclusion, the importation to Corsica of ovicaprines and pigs alone may explain the increase in site numbers and the appearance of open sites such as Basi during the 6th and 5th millennia bc, but the alternative model of fixed-plot horticulture in the most favourable locations and perhaps even, though less probably, of fire-clearance farming in marginal areas would explain still better the rapidity and impact of the dispersion of these domestic species within the west Mediterranean basin.

Late Neolithic Settlement and Subsistence

Lanfranchi and Weiss (1973, 73–5) characterise the Late Neolithic as the period in which the transition to food production effectively occurs, largely as a result of the arrival of agricultural groups from outside the island. The direct evidence for agriculture is admittedly weak: no more than two sherds with cereal impressions from Monte Lazzo (Lanfranchi and Weiss, 1973, 85). Considerable weight is however placed on artefactual evidence. Sickle gloss admittedly was found on only 1 out of 150 bladelets at Monte Lazzo (Weiss and Desneiges, 1974, 56) but the same site yielded 131 upper and 261 lower parts of grinding implements (Weiss and Desneiges, 1974, 49; Lanfranchi and Weiss, 1973, 85). Not all of these were suited to the processing of cereals. The 'cupules', in particular, would have been better employed for the crushing of nuts and acorns, or of minerals for industrial purposes. Such processing equipment has been found on all major sites – Mutola (Ville-di-Paraso: Lanfranchi, 1972a), around Grossa (Lanfranchi, 1972a), Punta Campana (Sotta: Lanfranchi and Milleliri, 1972) and Basi (Bailloud, 1969, 382), although it usually takes the form of mobile querns rather than clusters of depressions as in the living rock of Monte Lazzo. The major argument for agriculture is however that of the density and location of settlements, as compared with the Early Neolithic, the typical late neolithic site occurring on a hill with a view over and adjacent to a coastal plain (Lanfranchi, 1972a).

The evidence for pastoralism is still more restricted than that for arable farming owing to the largely acid conditions, in which animal bones do not survive. The only systematic study is that of the anomalously well-preserved deposits of level 4b at the site of Terrina IV (Aléria), uncovered by the 1976–8 campaigns. According to Poulain-Josien, this assemblage consists of 25 per cent domestic pig, 7.5 per cent wild boar, 32 per cent cattle, and 22 per cent sheep, plus goats and dog (Jehasse, 1980, 553).

The excavations at Terrina IV have also uncovered the only direct evidence of supplementary activities such as fishing (Jehasse, 1980, 553) and, more significantly, perforated ceramics which Camps has suggested can be interpreted on ethnographic analogies as vessels for leaching acorn flour of tannic acid (Camps, 1979, 13). The occupation of the upland basin of the Niolo in the Late Neolithic has been interpreted by both Grosjean (1956, 22–3) and Acquaviva (1976, 58–60) as impossible without transhumant pastoralism, Grosjean arguing that settlement would only have taken place at all under duress, i.e. by lowland groups seeking a refuge during a period of strife. Transhumant pastoralism, however, is a relatively recent specialisation of a formerly agropastoral subsistence in the Niolo (Lewthwaite, 1981). Settlement of this area may have occurred through population growth alone.

The key question concerns the nature of the developments attested by the growth in site numbers during the Late Neolithic or, more precisely, the 3rd millennium bc. The evidence assembled by Lanfranchi and Weiss, in support of qualitative and directional as opposed to quantitative and cumulative change, is questionable. On most of the criteria advanced, there appears to have been little structural change between the patterns of subsistence and settlement associated with the Cardial occupation at Basi and those associated with the sites of the 3rd millennium bc. The farming economy appears to have been present for many millennia prior to the expansion in site numbers, and there may even have been a regression during the poorly known Curasien of the later 5th and early 4th millennia bc, such as occurred on contemporary Cyprus (Stanley Price, 1977b).

Insofar as comparison on the basis of single samples is valid, the economy of the Terrinien period at Aléria appears to have been 'devolved' and significantly more dependent on forest resources than that of the Cardial levels at Basi. The frequency of occurrence of acorn-processing equipment during the Terrinien phase (2300–2200bc) suggests the rapid adoption of a toolkit facilitating the exploitation of forest resources, perhaps as supplements or substitutes for cereals during a period of population growth. This phenomenon can be observed throughout the western Mediterranean, both directly in the form of finds of charred acorns in chalcolithic contexts, and through the expansion of evergreen oaks, quicker to adapt to fire, at the expense of the former deciduous oak climax. The chalcolithic intensification of forest exploitation, a 'tertiary products' revolution as it were (Cherry, pers.comm.), may have been as critical a development as that of ard agriculture or specialised pastoralism in permitting the colonisation of marginal Mediterranean areas (Lewthwaite, 1982d).

The most significant aspect of later neolithic settlement may have been

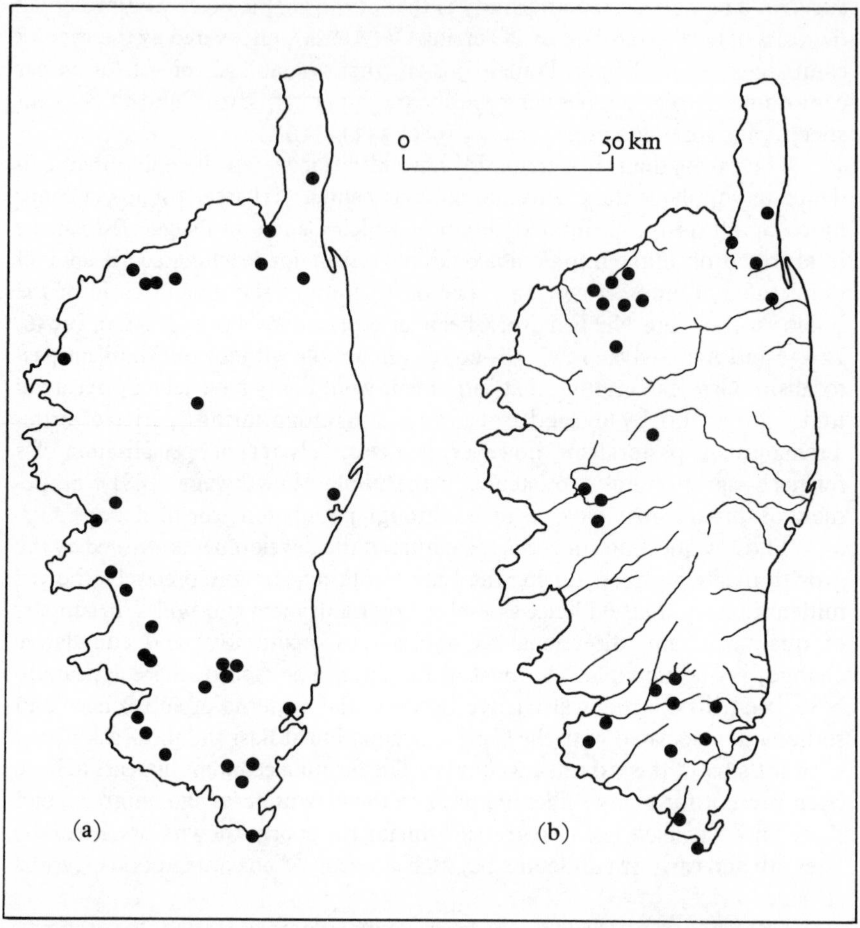

FIGURE 6.9. Distribution of (a) late neolithic settlement sites, and (b) stray finds of neolithic stone axes. Note the concentration of both in the granitic and calcareous regions at the expense of the schist massif and the schist-derived eastern plain.

overlooked since first noted by Ascari (1939, 165–6). This is the density of settlement within the granite region of the south and west (Fig.6.9), with its light sandy soils more tractable for simple farming implements than the heavier clay soils of the schist region, densely settled in the historic period (Fig.6.10). Not only are the inland areas of the schist and sedimentary regions distributional blanks, but many of the coastal plains between the eastern Balagna and Solenzara lack the sites predicted by Lanfranchi and Weiss' model. It is important to remember that the older, Würmian alluvium of these plains is intractable, deficient in minerals and prone to drought (Simi, 1981, 24), while much of the younger, finer material may be post-Roman in date; such younger fill has been observed stratified above classical sites in the

Marana (Conchon, 1977). The distribution of stray polished-stone axe finds (Fig.6.9; Lanfranchi, 1972a, fig.4) confirms the importance of the granite zone. Sites such as Monte Grosso or Terrina enjoy significant zonal advantages from their location, in the former case at the hill-plain interface, and in the latter adjacent to major estuaries and lagoons. The location of sites on hills at the margins of plains, such as those of the river Regino in the Balagne or the Figari/Porto-Vecchio lowlands, suggests that the lighter colluvial and brown forest soils of the piedmont rather than the heavier alluvium were chosen for arable exploitation. The provision of manure could have become a critical variable for permanent agriculture on these soils, necessitating the maintenance of a larger pastoral sector in the immediate vicinity (*saltus*). Fire may have been used on an increasing scale to create and maintain pasture, favouring pyrophytes such as evergreen oaks and macchia. The resulting mosaic of vegetation types would have benefited both loose-herded domesticates (especially swine) and ferals treated as game, besides increasing the areal production of spontaneous vegetable resources. Thus the unexpected 'regressive' traits of late neolithic sites which suggest the substitution of sylvan or pastoral resources for cereals may only result from sampling the more visible components of a more diversified and productive subsistence system.

Long-term Settlement and Subsistence Patterns

Sufficient data is now available from the six radiocarbon millennia of preclassical occupation to attempt to review the role of geographic factors on Corsican patterns of prehistoric settlement and subsistence. A Mediterranean context, and insularity, appear generally to have been positive attributes in prehistory. Although late pleistocene isolation had clearly reduced the terrestrial resources available to the earliest settlers, the similarity of climate to and relative accessibility by sea from the west Asiatic centre of domestication and economic innovation permitted an unusually rapid implantation of the food-producing economy, although at a reduced scale: Basi is clearly not comparable to contemporary Karanovo. The subsequent stagnation of the island between the 6th and later 3rd millennia bc cannot be ascribed to either factor, since Sardinian and Maltese cultures made notable progress, only the Baleares within the western basin being less dynamic than Corsica during the Later Neolithic (Lewthwaite, 1982a).

The relief and geological composition of Corsica appear to be the significant negative variables which explain the delayed clearance of the climactic deciduous forest (which seems to have been the most extensive landscape unit) for cultivation and pasture. The substitution of an extensive subsistence base, exploiting forest resources both directly and indirectly (cattle pasture, swine pannage), appears to have a considerably greater antiquity not only in the middle altitude plateaux and basins where the chestnut orchards proliferated in the medieval and recent periods (Lewthwaite, 1981, 1982d) but in locations as historically favourable for more intensive exploitation as Terrina, close to the classical settlement of Aléria.

The prehistoric (late neolithic) and historic settlement patterns are almost

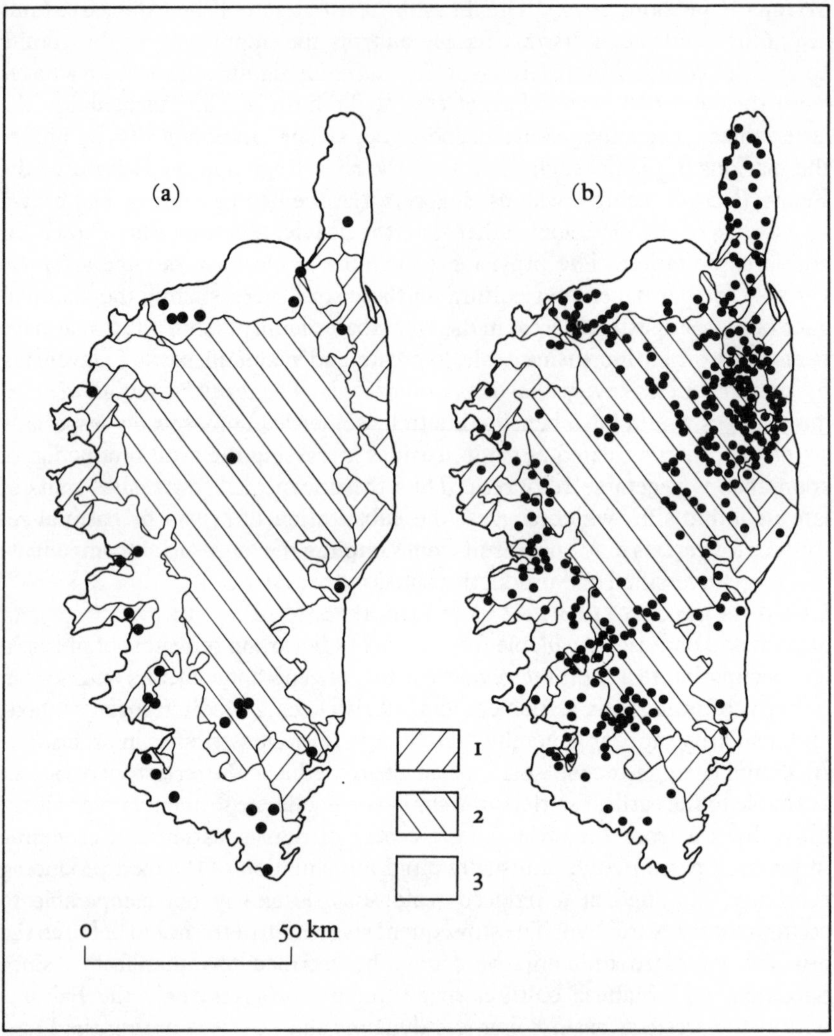

FIGURE 6.10. Distribution of (a) late neolithic settlement sites, and (b) modern communes: complete contrast due to the historic withdrawal from the coastal plains to the mountains and to the development of subsistence strategies based on the chestnut, well-suited to the humid schist massif of the north-east.
Key: 1 hills; 2 mountains; 3 littoral.

mirror images (Fig. 6.10). The recent predominance of the north-east is explicable partly in terms of the strength of the political and economic dependence on Tuscany and Liguria, partly on the success of the exploitation of the sweet chestnut for subsistence and industrial products, for which the humid schists of the Castagniccia region provide ideal growing conditions (Blanchard, 1914; Fel, 1975). The obviously greater extent of the interaction with Sardinia in prehistory is unlikely to have modified the settlement pattern to the same degree; this must have been determined by the carrying capacity of the local environment given the technology of the 3rd millennium bc.

Mills (forthcoming) has suggested that certain regions of Languedoc are intrinsically marginal for agricultural populations over the long term, and therefore that periodic episodes of colonisation indicate phases of population growth or technical development. Corsica might be expected *a priori* to reveal a similar distinction between agriculturally nuclear and marginal areas. Such marginality cannot be assigned on the basis of geological composition, since the change in preference from light granite-derived soils to clays and older alluvium appears to have been correlated with improvements in agricultural technology and with instances of the positive selection of unpopulated or refuge areas, such as the medieval monastic penetration of the Castagniccia or the later flight thither in the Genoese period (Lücke, 1976). Nor can altitudinal zonation be regarded as a significant factor, for settlement in the Niolo since the Late Neolithic has been both more continuous and more successful than that of lowland 'deserts' such as the Filosorma (or 'Balagne déserte') and the Agriates (Simi, 1981, 106), while the recent concentration of population in the mid-altitude upper valley segments, formerly occupied by deciduous forest, was not a cycle of population growth in Mills' sense but a net displacement from the lowlands caused by war, piracy and malaria (Blanchard, 1914).

The undoubted demographic cycle during the nineteenth century between the French conquest and the collapse of the traditional subsistence economy did not lead to marginal colonising activity as much as to local intensification (Pernet and Lenclud, 1977). Historical Corsican subsistence-settlement problems reveal unusual stability coupled with an ability to respond rapidly to changed circumstances such as the opportunities for lowland settlement under the *Pax Gallica*. This appears to be due to two factors which have enhanced ecological adaptation. First, the maintenance of an unusually high level of familial independence within the typically Mediterranean pattern of concentrated settlement, typified by the dispersed layout of the Corsican 'villages', often mere names for groups of hamlets sharing certain resources (Simi, 1981, 114). The tendency towards fission and centrifugal expansion is therefore latent. An example of the success of the Corsican pattern of dispersal in marginal regions is the adjacent Sardinian region of the Gallura, settled by southern Corsican families since the seventeenth century AD (Lewthwaite, 1982c). Secondly, subsistence has been based on a wider range of plants than the classic Mediterranean triad of wheat, vines and olives or, in the case of livestock, than the zonal preference for ovicaprines. Agro-sylvo-pastoral polyculture has been practised even down to the level of the nuclear family. Individual families have exploited resources from seasonal, ecologically complementary zones rather than depending on specialisation and exchange (Bigot, 1971 (1887); Fel, 1975). It is striking how Corsican prehistoric cultures differed from other Mediterranean regions in precisely the same respects: dispersed and frequently displaced settlements, broad spectrum subsistence,

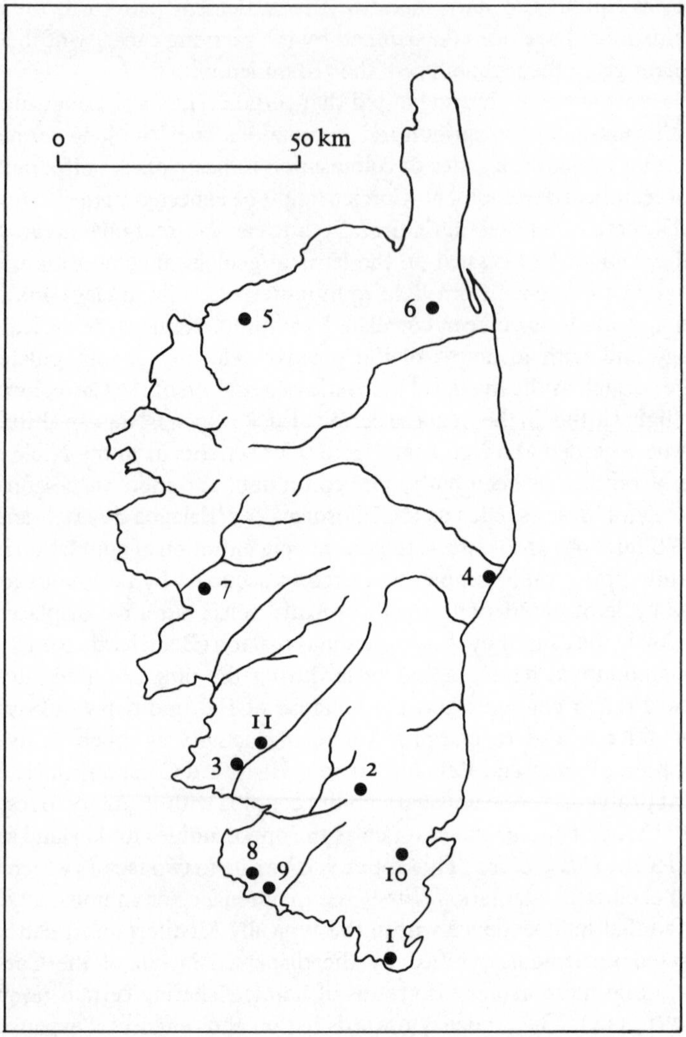

GENERAL MAP of the Neolithic of Corsica.
1 Araguina-Sennola (Bonifacio); 2 Curacchiaghiu (Levie); 3 Basi (Serra-di-Ferro); 4 Terrina-Casabianda (Aléria); 5 Carco (Catteri); 6 Monte Grosso (Biguglia); 7 Monte Lazzo (Tiuccia); 8 Palaggiu (Sartène); 9 Cauria (Sartène); 10 Tappa (Porto Vecchio); 11 Castellucciu (Pila-Canale).

the insignificance of intra- and extra-Corsican exchange systems.

CONCLUSIONS

The Neolithic of Corsica presents a curious combination: on the one hand, a surprising precocity – as in the dates of first settlement, ceramic and food production or copper-using; on the other, a structural tendency towards conservatism – as in the tardiness of the widespread adoption of food production and in the persistence of extensive subsistence strategies into the historic period. Conventional explanations have resolved this paradox by postulating the arrival of successive groups of innovative aliens (Cardial shepherd-potter-seamen; Basien agriculturalists; Torréen sea-raiders) impinging on a conservative local tradition. In fact, the evidence suggests that the phenomena treated as if parallel are in fact successive (Cardial-Curasien, Basien-Terrinien), the real pattern being a step-like progression consisting of periods of innovation and interaction (e.g. c.57/5500–47/4500bc, c.3300–2700bc and c.2200–1800bc) and intervals of apparent stagnation, disunity and isolation. The striking conclusion which emerges is that the horizons of culture change and the periods of innovation and stagnation are synchronous with those of Mediterranean France, Iberia and Italy.

The decisive factor in the long-term pattern of subsistence and settlement in Corsica has been the relative inability of the west Asiatic cultural landscape based on the cereal-ovicaprine food production system to replace more than a fraction of the formerly extensive deciduous mixed-oak forest of the mid-altitude slopes.

From at least the 3rd millennium bc until the fourteenth century AD there is evidence for the extensive utilisation of this natural landscape through the harvesting first of acorns and later the substitution of the still more efficient chestnut. The triumph of the cereal-ovicaprine system occurred only in the early modern period at a time of unusually rapid population growth, which equally rapidly collapsed through emigration. This pattern differs distinctly from that of the adjacent Mediterranean islands of Sardinia and the Baleares, strongly suggesting that the relief and geological composition of Corsica have played an important role.

RADIOCARBON DATES

PRENEOLITHIC						
Curacchiaghiu	6610±170bc	Gif-795	Charcoal	Rock-shelter	Old level 6=new 7: Preneolithic	*Radiocarbon*, 13, 221
	6350±180bc	Gif-1963	Charcoal		Level 7: Preneolithic	*Radiocarbon*, 16, 34
Araguina-Sennola	6570±150bc	Gif-2705	Charcoal	Rock-shelter	Level XVIIIa: Preneolithic	Camps, 1978, 19
EARLY NEOLITHIC						
Basi	5750±150bc	Gif-1851	Charcoal	Open settlement	Level 7: Cardial	*Radiocarbon*, 16, 34
Curacchiaghiu	5650±180bc	Gif-1962	Charcoal	Rock-shelter	Level 6c: Curasien facies of Punch-impressed culture	*Radiocarbon*, 16, 34
	5360±170bc	Gif-1961	Charcoal		Level 6: Curasien facies of Punch-impressed culture	*Radiocarbon*, 16, 34
	5350±160bc	Gif-796	Charcoal		Old level 5=new 6: Curasien facies of Punch-impressed culture	*Radiocarbon*, 13, 221
Casabianda residence	4720±150bc	MC-2243	Charcoal	Surface scatter	Cardial	Camps, 1979, 6
Araguina-Sennola	4700±140bc	Gif-2324	Charcoal	Rock-shelter	Level XVII: Araguina group of Punch-impressed culture	Camps, 1978, 15
	4480±140bc	Gif-2325	Charcoal		Level XVII: Araguina group of Punch-impressed culture	Camps, 1978, 15
MIDDLE NEOLITHIC						
Tappa shelter EA1	3700±150bc	Gif-2104	Charcoal	Rock-shelter	Level VI	*Radiocarbon*, 16, 34
Basi	3300±120bc	Gif-1849	Charcoal	Open settlement	Level 5c6: Basien	*Radiocarbon*, 16, 33
	3250±120bc	Gif-1848	Charcoal		Level 5b1: Basien	*Radiocarbon*, 16, 33
	3250±120bc	Gif-1850	Charcoal		Level 5b8: Basien	*Radiocarbon*, 16, 33
Terrina IV	3000±90bc	MC-2077	Charcoal	Open settlement	Level 4aC1, C-1: Terrinien	Camps, 1979, 18
Curacchiaghiu	2980±140bc	Gif-1960	Charcoal	Rock-shelter	Level 5: Curasien Late Neolithic	*Radiocarbon*, 16, 34
LATE NEOLITHIC						
Terrina IV	2770±300bc	MC-2079	Charcoal	Open settlement	Level 4aG: Terrinien	Camps, 1979, 18
	2700±100bc	MC-2235	Charcoal		Level 4bG: Terrinien	Camps, 1979, 18
	2580±90bc	MC-2078	Charcoal		Level 4aG: Terrinien	Camps, 1979, 18
	2540±90bc	MC-2075	Charcoal		Level 1B1: Terrinien	Camps, 1979, 18
	2500±120bc	MC-2076	Charcoal		Level 2C1, C-1: Terrinien	Camps, 1979, 18
	2480±140bc	MC-2237	Charcoal		Level 4cC1: Terrinien	Camps, 1979, 18
	2480±160bc	Mc-2232	Charcoal		Level 2-3A1: Terrinien	Camps, 1979, 18
	2470±100bc	MC-1403	Charcoal		Level 4aC1: Terrinien	Camps, 1979, 18
	2430±80bc	MC-2231	Charcoal		Level 2A1: Terrinien	Camps, 1979, 18
	2320±100bc	MC-2236	Charcoal		Level 4bC1: Terrinien	Camps, 1979, 18
	2260±160bc	MC-2234	Charcoal		Level 4bC1: Terrinien	Camps, 1979, 18

	1915±125bc	Gsy-94B*	Charcoal		Niche B, hearth	*Radiocarbon*, 8, 130
	1907±100bc	Gif-94A*	Charcoal		Niche B, hearth	Grosjean, 1962, 214
Castellucciu	1970±200bc	Gif-5117	Charcoal	'Proto-Torre'	Monument central	Delibrias *et al.*, 1982
Araguina-Sennola	2030±140bc	Gif-779	Charcoal	Rock-shelter	Araguina group of Terminal Neolithic	*Radiocarbon*, 13, 220
Castello d'Alo	1870±200bc	Gif-480	Charcoal	Torre	Main hearth, western monument	*Radiocarbon*, 12, 424

* The Gsy-94B and Gif-94A dates from Tappa are the same determination, which is quoted differently in *Radiocarbon* and in Grosjean, 1962.

The Neolithic of the French Pyrenees

PAUL BAHN

Previous research o MATERIAL CULTURE o the Western Pyrenees o the Central and Eastern Pyrenees o plant resources o animal resources o SETTLEMENT o Early Neolithic o Couladère o Las Morts o Dourgne II o Abri Jean Cros o Grotte Gazel o Ile Corrège o Middle Neolithic o Montbolo o the Languedoc Chasséen o Villeneuve-Tolosane o Saint-Michel-du-Touch o Late Neolithic and Chalcolithic o Beakers o burials o megaliths o lake settlements o CONCLUSION.

THE MOUNTAIN CHAIN of the Pyrenees stretches from Atlantic to Mediterranean across one of the land 'exits' leading south from the main body of Europe (Fig.7.1). Its structure comprises an axial zone of crystalline massifs and, to the north, long parallel folds of secondary limestones. The apparent structural unity disguises an enormous variety of rocks and soils caused by phases of weathering and superimposed folding, faulting, and other disturbances since the mountains arose in early Tertiary times.

The chain, some 400km in length and with an average height of just under 2000m, descends gently in the west; the Mediterranean extremity, higher and wider than the Atlantic, descends relatively steeply from its high plateaux to the coastal plain. Between the two ends lie the massive Central Pyrenees with their deep, steep valleys which descend in a series of steps to the lowlands with their fertile Eocene soils.

The western end of the chain is almost constantly bathed in wet winds, while at the Mediterranean end, with the winter rain and summer drought of its eponymous climate, annual rainfall is low even in the mountains. The Atlantic extremity has very mild winters and later summers; the Mediterranean has equally mild winters and much warmer summers.

It is known from historical and classical accounts that until the 16th century AD forests covered not only most of the mountains but also the plains which today are heaths and moors (Bahn, 1979). Today, however, 'garrigue' scrub with evergreen oaks dominates in the foothills of the Mediterranean area, while the humid western uplands have a quasi-Breton appearance, with stands of deciduous trees.

In short the region contains a series of climatic and vegetational zones, from the Atlantic to the Mediterranean, together with an environment that changes rapidly in the abrupt descent from high mountain to foothills. This pattern obviously affected the distribution and seasonality of human occupation in prehistoric and historic times: each extremity seems to have undergone different influences, while the central area tended to be rather conservative. Lateral communication was almost impossible between many of the parallel valleys, a fact which enhanced the individuality and self-reliance of their occupants.

For the purposes of this chapter, the Pyrenean region will be extended northward to include, in the centre, the Toulouse area, and, in the east, the uplands of the Corbières and the Montagne Noire (Fig.7.1).

Work on the Pyrenean Neolithic was begun in the 19th century by pioneers such as Noulet, Piette and especially Garrigou. However, the methods involved were crude – Garrigou, when aged 39, claimed to have dug 275 caves – and the Neolithic, or rather *Age de la Pierre Polie,* comprised all material sandwiched between the final palaeolithic industries and the first metal objects, with no attempt at further division. Moreover, to 19th-century scholars this period was epitomised by the lake-settlements of Switzerland, and all material was assessed in relation to that of the Swiss 'norm'. Many polished-stone axes, bone tools and potsherds were recovered and summarily described (e.g. see Garrigou and Filhol, 1866), but few illustrations were provided and little cultural or economic information can be gleaned from these early reports.

Subsequent work added little to knowledge of the Neolithic, although studies of megalithic monuments and burial caves gradually built up a picture of the 'Pyrenean Culture' of the Chalcolithic. However, excavations about forty years ago by Durand in the cave of Las-Morts (Ariège) and by Robert in that of Bédeilhac (Ariège) provided the first good stratigraphies. This was followed by the pioneering work of Méroc at the Chasséen sites of Villeneuve-Tolosane (Haute-Garonne; m.r.6) and Saint-Michel-du-Touch (Haute-Garonne; m.r.7); and the last twenty-five years have seen a remarkable series of excavations and studies by Guilaine and his associates which have provided a typological, chronological and economic framework for the Neolithic of the Pyrénées-Orientales and Aude.

All but the most recent of these studies of the Pyrenean Neolithic rested on the traditional view that the period was radically different to what went before: that preneolithic man led a parasitic, predatory existence, whereas the neolithic way of life was a sedentism made secure by producing a surplus of food. However, in southern France, as in many other parts of Europe, the archaeological and environmental evidence shows no clear distinction between mesolithic and early neolithic communities: lithic industries, for example, display remarkable continuity, and no skeletal distinction can be made between mesolithic and neolithic populations in France (Duday, 1977).

In many Pyrenean 'neolithic' sites, moreover, no traces of animal or plant domesticates are to be found. In these cases, artefacts such as polished-stone axes, pots, grinders and sickles have been taken as proof of agriculture, under

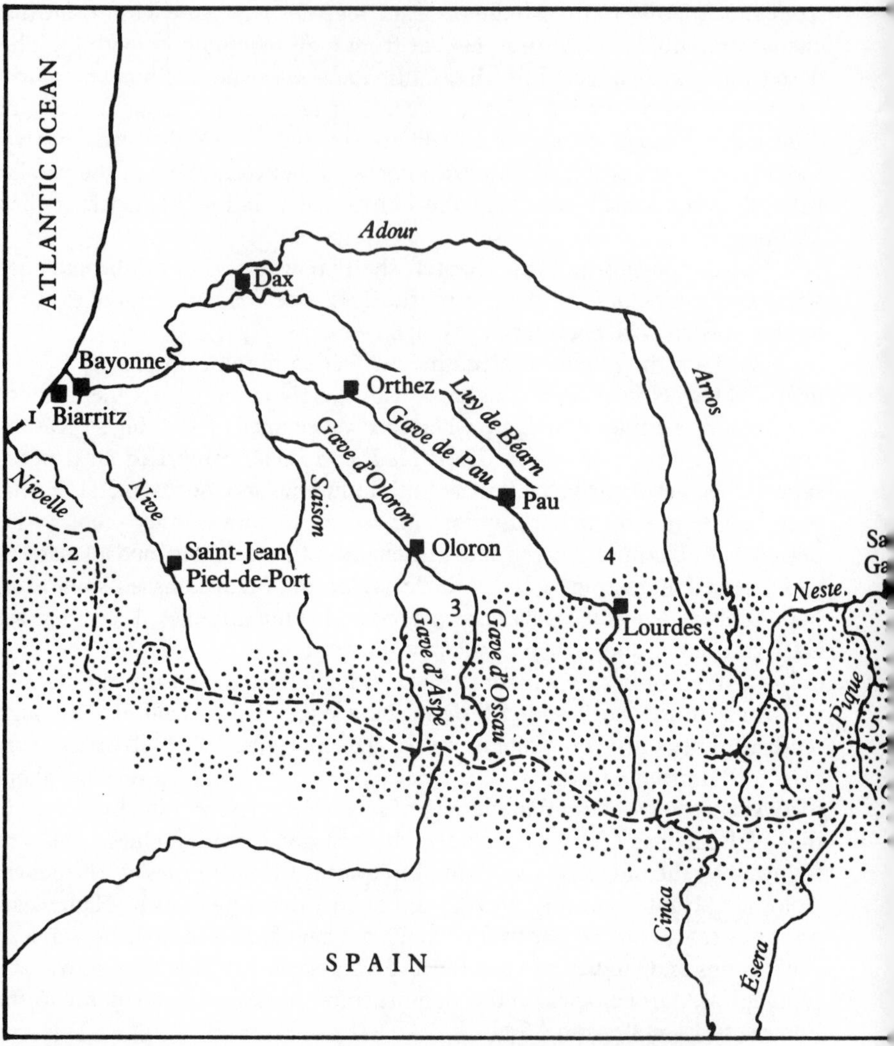

FIGURE 7.1. Relief, drainage and major towns of the French Pyrenees (land over 400m shaded). Important neolithic sites mentioned in the text are also shown.

1 Mouligna and Ilbarritz (Pyr-Atl); 2 Berroberría (Navarra); 3 Poeymaü (Pyr-Atl) and other Arudy sites; 4 Monuments of Pouey-Mayou and La Halliade (Htes-Pyr); 5 Saint Mamet (Hte-Gar); 6 Villeneuve-Tolosane (Hte-Gar); 7 Saint-Michel-du-Touch (Hte-Gar); 8 Le Mas d'Azil (Ariège); 9 Bédeilhac (Ariège); 10 Niaux (Ariège); 11 Balma Margineda (Andorra); 12 Las-Morts (Ariège); 13 Dourgne (Aude) – just to the south is the grotte d'Usson; 14 Montou (Pyr-Or); 15 Montbolo (Pyr-Or) – just to the south is Can Pey; 16 Ile Corrège (Aude); 17 Grotte des Bruixes (Pyr-Or) and, to the east, Cova de l'Espérit (Pyr-Or); 18 Véraza (Aude); 19 Auriac (Aude); 20 Jean Cros (Aude); 21 Font-Juvénal (Aude); 22 Grotte Gazel (Aude) and, nearby, the Grotte des Cazals; 23 Bize (Aude).

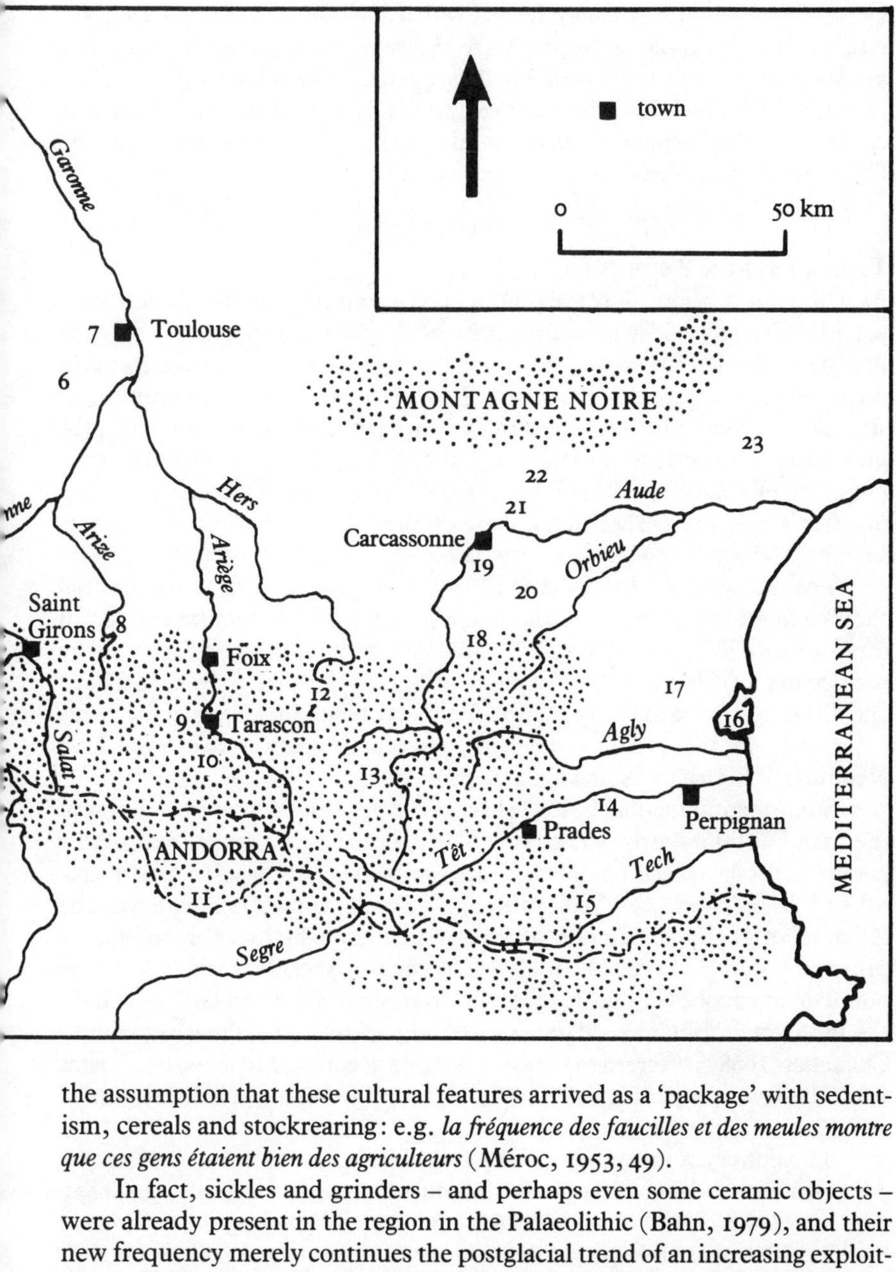

the assumption that these cultural features arrived as a 'package' with sedentism, cereals and stockrearing: e.g. *la fréquence des faucilles et des meules montre que ces gens étaient bien des agriculteurs* (Méroc, 1953, 49).

In fact, sickles and grinders – and perhaps even some ceramic objects – were already present in the region in the Palaeolithic (Bahn, 1979), and their new frequency merely continues the postglacial trend of an increasing exploitation of plant resources. Kraybill (1977, 485) has shown that the presence of pottery, mortars and querns is in no way definitive of settled agricultural life; and Garrigou (1883, 30) pointed out that the Pyrenean neolithic 'meules' were very similar to those still in use in the 19th century for grinding salt.

Cereal crops in Mediterranean and temperate Europe are demanding and vulnerable throughout their cycle, and with a neolithic technology the areas of fertile soil which could be worked were highly restricted in the Pyrenees. In a marginal area of this type, with a well-forested environment, a full 'neolithic' economy is unlikely to arise very early, and it is probable that the arable component of the economy will reach full development considerably later than the pastoral component.

Material Culture

The Western Pyrenees

As will be seen below, only the central and eastern parts of the region have as yet produced any evidence of agriculture in this period. Even today in the Pays Basque, excessive humidity prohibits the cultivation of wheat above 300m. In the west, therefore, it is no surprise to find a continuity of material culture, of site location and of economic strategy through postglacial times into the protohistoric period: for example, the site of Berroberría (Spanish Navarre, but on the French side of the Pyrenees; m.r.2) has a layer labelled 'neolithic' because it contains potsherds, but these are the only neolithic element present, so that Maluquer (1965, 139) was compelled to call it 'atypical', a 'vida neolítica con una clara economía de recolectores'. Certainly the faunal material shows a 'mesolithic' economy based on red deer and boar. Similarly, layers at the Grotte du Bignalats, Arudy (Pyrénées-Atlantiques; m.r.3) and the nearby rockshelter of Houn de Laa contain potsherds as their only neolithic or eneolithic feature amidst mesolithic flints and bones of cervids and caprids (Marsan, 1972); the only trace of a domestic animal is a dog in the Late Neolithic of Bignalats (Marsan, 1979, 67).

Some mention should be made here of the problematic *asturien* industry of the area. Within a strip 500m wide along the Atlantic littoral, macrolithic pebble picks have been found which are sometimes in association with microliths, polished-stone axes and potsherds. Through comparison with the true *Asturian* of Iberia, this material was at first thought to be mesolithic or protoneolithic. However, the presence of potsherds together with a radiocarbon date of 3200bc (Oldfield, 1960, 62) from some wood in a level just above the industry at Mouligna (Pyrénées-Atlantiques; m.r.1) led to a rethinking: Chauchat (1968) preferred to see everything as neolithic, and indeed new dates from the layer containing the relevant industry at Mouligna indicate 3810bc and 3600bc (Chauchat, 1974).

The pottery is rare, crude, badly fired and 'ne peut être attribué jusqu'à présent à aucune des civilisations néolithiques connues' (Chauchat, 1968, 129). The material is clearly much later than, and very different to, the Asturian of Spain or Portugal; the 'pick', whatever its function – and it is an unlikely mollusc-gathering tool – is not a useful type-fossil. Nevertheless it is important to note occupation of the coastal area at this time – perhaps on a seasonal basis, in view of the climatic advantages of the Biarritz region in winter.

Little economic information has been found, though hazelnuts and acorns were associated with flints at Ilbarritz (Pyrénées-Atlantiques) (Daguin, 1936):

oak and hazel feature in the pollen of this phase at Mouligna (Oldfield, 1960) and it is probable that these plantfoods made some contribution to the diet, particularly in the colder months. The pollen from the layer dated to 3600bc shows continuously high frequencies of *Pteridium* (bracken), together with low values for pine and hazel. This may indicate deforestation, especially as charcoal is also present in the layer: bracken is greatly favoured by clearance through burning; other features of the pollen sample point to the same explanation, and while Chauchat (1968) suggests the cause may have been an accidental or natural fire, it seems more probable that intentional clearance was involved (Roux and Leroi-Gourhan, 1964), carried out – in the absence of cereal pollen – for the purpose of animal husbandry.

It is difficult to give an outline of the development of material culture in the western Pyrenees at this time (Bahn, 1982a). As mentioned above, a good deal of material was dubbed neolithic simply because it consisted of or was associated with potsherds and polished stone. A more recent trend has been to assign most finds of this kind to the Chalcolithic on the basis of ceramic typology or because the stone axes resemble metal types (Fabre, 1943). A great lack of stratified sites and of absolute dates adds to the problems: the extent of the difficulties is shown by recent work at the Grotte du Phare (Biarritz, Pyrénées-Atlantiques) whose material was originally assigned to the Late Neolithic (Chauchat, 1968, 103) but which proved to belong to the Late Bronze Age (Mariezkurrena, 1979, 249). Marsan (1972) attempted to make some sense of the region's neolithic material, but the potsherds are too fragmentary and undiagnostic to be of much help, and the stone tools merely show continuity from the Mesolithic.

Unfortunately there is as yet no economic information which can indicate when and how the modern domesticates became established. One site which may provide some answers is the cave of Poeymaü at Arudy (Pyrénées-Atlantiques; m.r.3). The original excavations here (Laplace, 1953), at the front of the site, had a sauveterroid layer, dated to 6350bc, followed by a chalcolithic layer dated to 2020bc (Evin, 1979). Thus, over 4000 years separated these two levels despite their contact, and it appeared that the cave – and indeed the region – had been abandoned during the later Mesolithic and Neolithic. A similar hiatus is found elsewhere: e.g. the rock-shelter of Duruthy (Landes) has no evidence of use between the *Azilien* and the Chalcolithic, and it is thought that much of the western region was inaccessible and/or uninhabitable due to the postglacial humidity and vegetation (Arambourou, 1981). Some areas may well have been abandoned at this time; but new excavations by Laplace in the late 1970s, further inside Poeymaü, produced a stratigraphic sequence (Rigaud, 1980, 416) which fills the hiatus and proves occupation in the Neolithic, with dates from 3880 to 2730bc. No details are yet available; but the Chalcolithic (*couche de transition*) is known to contain polished stone, barbed-and-tanged arrowheads, and a fragment of Beaker (Laplace, 1953, 204). No metal is present. The layer represents an eneolithisation of the local mountain facies of the Mesolithic, itself derived from the local Palaeolithic.

The fauna still features red deer and boar, but these are now joined by a bovid and a goat: future analysis of the site's material may answer many questions about their status.

Neolithic material – in the broad sense – has been reported from many sites in the western Pyrenees (Bahn, 1979), but few details were ever given. One should mention the hoard of 30 expertly-made barbed-and-tanged arrowheads found by Roseville des Grottes (1911) at the cave of Espalungue at Arudy (Pyrénées-Atlantiques). In the absence of dating or of anything more diagnostic than sherds and flints, it is hard to assign the material to a specific phase, and this problem is especially acute in the numerous burial caves where, often, sherds are the only 'modern' feature, and the sites have been reused over a long period. There are many in and around Arudy, and Marsan (1972) has shown that their lithic assemblages are all part of one industrial complex. Omnès (1980) supplies a catalogue of the 40 known in the *département* of Hautes-Pyrénées: they vary in altitude (380–1170m) and in funerary practices, and three have been dated to the early 2nd millennium bc, while the final neolithic burial deposit of the Grotte du Castillet at Lourdes (Hautes-Pyrénées) has been dated to 2430bc (Omnès, 1981).

The Central and Eastern Pyrenees

It is in the centre and more especially in the east of the region that a fuller cultural and economic picture can be gained from some outstanding excavations of the last few decades. Previously, the region faced the same problems as the west: e.g. Durand (1968, 10) pointed out that, owing to Pyrenean conservatism, only a stratified position could give a date for the later prehistoric material of the *département* of Ariège. Such a stratigraphy was first explored in the 19th century by Piette, at the cave of the Mas d'Azil (Ariège; m.r.8), whose left bank had an uninterrupted transition from the (mesolithic) *Arisien* to the 'Neolithic' and later periods. The 'neolithic' layer H was characterised by an abundance of sherds and bonework (Piette, 1895, 280) and the presence of polished-stone axes. The upper part of the layer saw the appearance of bronze, with no visible effect on the stone and bone industry. Similar transitions existed at other, smaller sites in the region, but are poorly documented. One important feature to note is the recurrence, both in this period – at the Mas d'Azil and elsewhere – and in later periods up to medieval times, of crude macrolithic pebble tools associated with the fine microlithic implements and polished stone.

Plant resources. Many sites in the *département* of Ariège, as in the west, have potsherds as their only 'modern' feature; notable examples are burial caves, such as that of Quérénas (Vézian and Vallois, 1927) which contained human remains associated with red deer, a few sherds and a microlithic stone industry which, according to Guilaine (1971, 105) is allied to the 5th millennium bc material of the Abri Jean Cros (Aude; m.r.20). Human teeth from Quérénas were very worn, as were those from Espérit (Pyrénées-Orientales; m.r.17) (Abelanet, 1953) and Lombrives (Ariège): at the latter, wear was even advanced on a child's teeth and was attributed to bread made of badly-ground grains (Garrigou, 1865). It is most likely that acorn bread was involved, since even in Strabo's time this was of great importance in the Pyrenean diet. As already noted, it is often assumed that the numerous 'meules' and 'broyeurs' of the area were for grain (e.g. see Durand, 1968, 174), but Octobon (1937) was probably nearer the truth in equating them with the constant use of seeds and nuts: certainly these are the only plant remains in evidence in the Neolithic of all but the easternmost Pyrenees; the Mas d'Azil yielded a few walnuts (Piette, 1896); the 'Petite Caougno' of Niaux (Ariège; m.r.10) had nutshells and a few cherry-stones (Garrigou and Filhol, 1866, 30); while two dolmens near the Mas d'Azil contained abundant fruitstones (Pouech, 1872). Even in the east, the Early Neolithic of the Abri Jean Cros yielded only burnt hazelnuts and acorns (Gasco, 1979); the Middle Neolithic of the Abri de Font-Juvénal (Aude) also contained roasted acorns (Guilaine, 1976a, 62). According to Clark (1952, 59–60) acorns are a very important substitute for cereal flour, once the indigestible tannin has been boiled out.

Palynology (Jalut, 1977) suggests that present-day vegetation was becoming established in the region by early postglacial times; it is thought that oak forests were formerly far more widespread in the area than at present (Gaussen, 1926, 45) and this helps to explain the prominence of acorns in archaeological sites. However, there is evidence of cereal consumption in the Neolithic of the eastern Pyrenees: wheat and legumes have been found in the *Montbolo*-group cave of En-Gorner (Pyrénées-Orientales); abundant cereal grains and legumes are known from the Chasséen levels (3400bc) of Font-Juvénal to the north (Guilaine *et al.*, 1976; Roudil, 1978, 663); and there is evidence of lowland clearance and cultivation in two pollen samples (containing 15.38 and 14.14 per cent cereals) from the Chasséen site of Saint Michel-du-Touch (Haute-Garonne; m.r.7) (Guilaine, 1978, 90), though no grains or even grain-impressions have yet been reported from this site, but many grains have been recovered by wet-sieving in recent excavations at the nearby Chasséen site of Villeneuve-Tolosane (Haute-Garonne; m.r.6), including several thousand (mostly wheat) in a deep well (Clottes, 1981, 557).

Jalut's palynological work has produced interesting results: the bog of the Ruisseau de Fournas at 1510m in the eastern Pyrenees has evidence in the Atlantic phase for forest-clearance – i.e. a proliferation of herbaceous heliophiles and a reduction of arboreal pollen – accompanied by cereal pollen in an irregular fashion. This phase begins before a point dated to 4250bc and ends c.3560bc (Jalut, 1976a, 181; 1976b, 316; 1977) when the clearings were apparently abandoned to the forest. At the bog of La Borde (1660m) in the high valley of the River Têt, wheat (*Triticum*) pollen appears just before a point dated to 3450bc, but traces of deforestation are unclear.

Interpretation of these samples from lakes and bogs, in upland areas open to pollen from the lowlands and subject to strong winds from a number of directions, is somewhat delicate, especially as cereal pollen is extremely rare (less than 0.5 per cent of the total). The Atlantic phase at areas in close proximity shows no trace of agriculture whatsoever (Jalut, 1976a). On the other hand, as Coles (1976) has pointed out, by the time clearance becomes visible in a pollen diagram it is probably already at an advanced stage of joining up small cleared areas. One can conclude from Jalut's evidence and the grains at a few sites that cereal cultivation was under way in some parts of the region in the 5th and 4th millennia bc, but it is difficult to estimate the economic importance of cereals at this time.

Animal resources. Doubt has been expressed, most recently by Poplin, about the validity of claims for sheep in European palaeolithic sites. Many such claims rest on only one or two bones from early excavations, and in view of the difficulties and the dubious criteria involved in the differentiation of the bones of *Ovis* from those of other small artiodactyls, there is certainly room for doubt. However, it is possible that, in the past, many undiagnostic bones have been assigned to other species precisely because palaeolithic sheep were thought to be non-existent. The paucity of evidence for wild sheep in the Pleistocene may also be a consequence of their elusive nature and preferred habitat. It should be borne in mind that there have been quite a few claims – from the 1860s to modern excavations – for palaeolithic sheep (and dogs) in the Pyrenees (see Bahn, 1979).

Recent work on faunal remains from mesolithic and neolithic sites of the eastern Pyrenees has led Geddes (1980a) to the conclusion that the sheep were introduced to the region from the east, albeit rather earlier than one might expect. For example, Balma Margineda (m.r.11), a small rock-shelter at c.1000m altitude in Andorra, contains neolithic material including Cardial pottery, and was interpreted as a temporary habitation and a burial place for mobile pastoralists (Maluquer and Fusté, 1962). Recent excavations by Guilaine have revealed a series of sauveterroid layers below the Cardial Neolithic; the mesolithic fauna is heavily dominated by ibex (73 to 94 per cent of bone fragments – Geddes, pers.comm.), supported by boar, red deer, etc. A transitional, final mesolithic layer sees a minor appearance of sheep (*Ovis aries*), and the neolithic levels are dominated by domestic ovicaprids. The site, clearly occupied in warm seasons, will perhaps prove as important to the study of the rise of pastoralism as those further east.

One such is the small (10m^2) cave of Dourgne II (Aude; m.r.13) in the upper Aude valley. This site's fauna is very fragmented, and only a few bones are identifiable. Whereas Balma Margineda shows a fairly abrupt switch from the ibex/boar/deer economy of the Mesolithic to one based on ovicaprids, the stratigraphy at Dourgne allows one to see the transition in more detail. Postglacial reforestation seems to have caused a sudden fall of ibex numbers, while suids and aurochs also began a decline. The most important feature is the appearance in layer 8 (mid-6th millennium bc) of apparently domestic ovicaprids in an aceramic evolved Mesolithic (Geddes, 1980a,b, 1981), as at Balma Margineda and in Grotte Gazel (Aude; m.r.22) at the start of the 6th millennium bc; pottery does not appear until c.5000bc.

At the end of Dourgne's Mesolithic, the ovicaprids represent 30–40 per cent of the fauna, though species exploited earlier persist, and indeed last well into the Neolithic. Guilaine (1975, 13; 1977) has claimed an *élevage* of the ovicaprids, and a 'new economic stage': certainly his suggestion of an *élevage en semi-liberté* of Pyrenean type may be justified, since this still exists in the region for bovids and sheep (Durand, 1968, 15).

A small bovid and suid – apparently domestic – coincide with the first pottery at Dourgne (Geddes, 1980b), but seem to have little effect on the overall faunal picture, since aurochs and boar equal them in abundance, and the other 'mesolithic' species are still present. Similarly, a small bovid appears with the first pottery at Gazel (c.4900bc) and a domestic pig at c.4600bc, but seem to have little impact. One intriguing phenomenon at Dourgne in the Early Neolithic is an abrupt increase and abrupt decline in small carnivores such as polecats and lynx, which may denote a specialised exploitation for pelts.

The evidence from these three sites clearly suggests that the characteristic features of the Neolithic did not arrive abruptly *en masse,* but instead were adopted piecemeal. The available data show a successful and long-lasting ibex/boar/cervid economy in the Mesolithic which was slowly transformed into an ovicaprid/cattle/pig economy, eventually to be integrated with arable agriculture.

SETTLEMENT

THE EARLY NEOLITHIC

The start of the Neolithic is generally taken in France to coincide with the first potsherds, and in the eastern Pyrenees and Aude the earliest phase is characterised by simple pottery bowls and jars bearing decoration made with *Cardium* shells or with grooves or jabs (Fig.7.2), although usually few of the sherds are decorated. Guilaine (1976b) provides a list of Pyrenean sites which have yielded this kind of ware; the westernmost are the open-site at Couladère (Haute-Garonne: Méroc, 1963, 200; 1970), and the caves of Quérénas and Las-Morts (Ariège; m.r.12); the highest is the Balma Margineda in Andorra (m.r.11), where the sherds were associated with bone awls and with short, unretouched blades – a poor cultural industry derived from the Ariège Mesolithic. This picture is repeated at other sites, for this phase is constituted by a number of disparate groups which evolved *in situ* and which have Cardial pottery as their principal common denominator. We shall briefly review the following: Couladère; Las Morts (m.r.12); Dourgne II (m.r.13); Abri Jean Cros (m.r.20); Grotte Gazel (m.r.22); Cova de l'Espérit (m.r.17); Ile Corrège (m.r.16); and Trou des Fées.

The *Couladère* site is the only early neolithic site so far explored in the mid-Garonne valley. There are other finds (Méroc, 1970) but they are impossible to differentiate from Chasséen material on the surface, and so until more sites are excavated the density, origin and development of early neolithic occupation in this area remains unknown.

Las-Morts. The Early Neolithic sees the first occupation of Las-Morts, a tunnel-cave, 160m long, at almost 700m altitude. The crude pottery, mostly

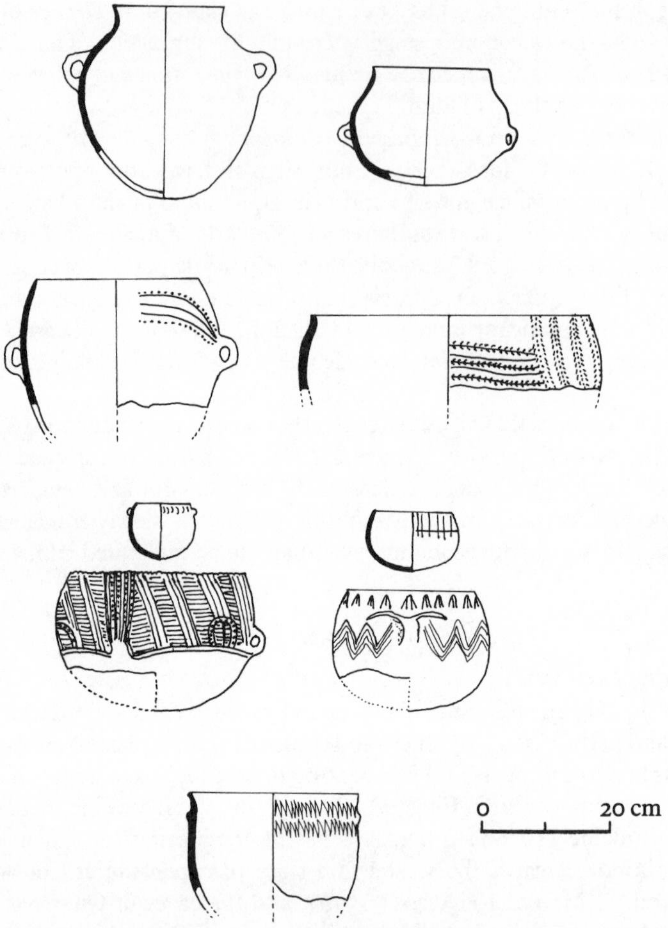

FIGURE 7.2. The development of pottery forms and decorative motifs in the Early Neolithic of Grotte Gazel (Aude). The four phases, from bottom to top, correspond to those outlined in the text. (After Guilaine, 1970a.)

bowls and globular forms, is derived from Cardial types (Durand, 1968, 141), but has no decoration: this may reflect its distance inland, but may also equate it with the epicardial phase at other sites (see below). The stone tools are also crude and archaic, and the bone tools, including awls and 'sagaies', are clearly of palaeolithic descent (Durand, 1958). Some grinders carry depictions of animals, including a duck-head (Durand, 1968, 117). There is no evidence, other than grindstones, for plant-use. The site's fauna (Bahn, 1979) is not very informative, but shows the continuing importance of red deer and ibex alongside sheep and cattle.

Dourgne II. Occupation at Dourgne II lasts from at least the Late Mesolithic to the Middle Neolithic. The continuity in stone tools can be seen in the retouched transverse arrowheads which occur in this phase, and which are

PLATE 7.1. Abri Jean Cros (Labastide-en-Val, Aude). Early neolithic rock-shelter excavated by Guilaine. (Photo: Jean Guilaine.)

clearly derived from the triangles, points and trapezoid flints of the site's Late Mesolithic and Protoneolithic (Guilaine, 1975, 14–15). Dourgne is located in the precipitous gorges of the Aude, which are extremely narrow; the land which could be exploited from the site is heavily restricted, with poor soil, and crops endangered by frosts. The cave's location and altitude thus make it an unlikely base for an agricultural economy, but it is well suited to the exploitation of herds and small game in the surrounding rocks and forests, and this is precisely what its contents suggest: there is no evidence for agriculture except for the Fournas pollen mentioned above, though Guilaine (1978, 87) has suggested that the high percentage of boxwood charcoal in the late 5th millennium bc at Dourgne may indicate human interference with vegetation. It was most likely a transitory, warm-season camp for a group exploiting animal herds.

The *Abri Jean Cros*, at 500m in the Corbières, was excavated in the 1960s and has recently been published very thoroughly (Guilaine, 1979). The shelter (Plate 7.1), about 20m long and 7m deep, has a single occupation level, up to 15cm thick, and dating to the mid-5th millennium bc. The site can be divided into a bright, sheltered habitation zone where artefacts were made and food was prepared and consumed; a low, inner zone where pots may have collected water dripping from the roof; and a southern zone, separated by a small drystone wall, where more hearths and more 'combustion pits' containing wood-charcoal were found. Guilaine and his team believe that the restrictions of the site's habitable area mean that only a small group of 5–10 people could have used it.

The stone industry has few worked pieces, and the only common tool-type is a small, transverse arrowhead (Fig.7.3). Polished stone exists; pottery is rare, simple and atypical, mostly undecorated. Bonework features awls and other tools, as well as decorative objects made of boar-tusks and shells. As at the other sites mentioned earlier, the occupants had domestic ovicaprids, but 'mesolithic' species such as red and roe deer and boar were still of importance. As in other Pyrenean postglacial sites (Bahn, 1979, 1982b), the terrestrial snail *Helix nemoralis* was consumed as a minor complementary resource. Despite the presence of grindstones, the only clues to plant-use were the nuts and acorns. Evidence from both flora and fauna points to an occupation of the site primarily in the spring and autumn. The shelter of Jean Cros displays a rather idiosyncratic assemblage clearly derived from a local mesolithic substratum.

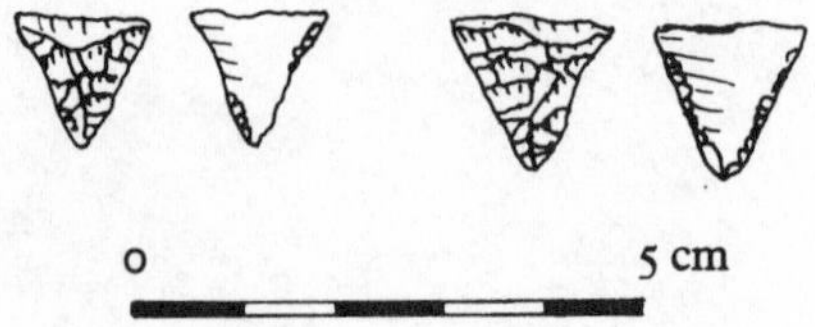

FIGURE 7.3. Tranchet arrowheads from the Early Neolithic of the Abri Jean Cros (Aude). (After Guilaine, 1976b.)

Grotte Gazel. A somewhat different and much fuller picture of the period is found at the Grotte Gazel (Aude), just north of Carcassonne, on the southern flank of the Montagne Noire. Human occupation varies in different sectors of this large cave, but an integrated view shows a Mesolithic, rich in *Helix nemoralis* and dating to 5880bc, that is covered by a transitional Protoneolithic in which, as in other sites mentioned earlier, pottery is absent but sheep – and *perhaps* domestic pig and a small bovid – are present; traditional 'wild' species are still of great importance (Geddes, 1980a, b). Backed triangles are frequent in the lithic industry. This phase dates to the mid-6th millennium bc. Cardial pottery appears at a time when modern domestic animals are becoming better established (sheep, pig, goat, bovid) – the dog is also present, as at Jean Cros. This phase, dating to the early 5th millennium bc, is followed by an Epicardial which persists to the end of the millennium.

The Early Neolithic of Gazel spans up to 1.8m in the cave's stratigraphy, and Guilaine (1970e) has therefore been able to trace the evolution of its pottery in some detail (Fig.7.2). The lowest level has the *Cardium* decorative technique, and some comb-decoration. This dates to 4830bc. In the 'middle horizon' (4590bc) Cardial decoration has already become extremely rare, to be replaced by a profusion of striations, incisions and grooves of various forms; the vessel shapes, however, remain simple and globular. The 'recent horizon' (4195bc) has no shell-decoration at all, and only crude grooves lined by impressions are found. The 'final horizon' (4000–3700bc) has vessels retaining the original Cardial shapes but almost entirely without decoration. However, the lithic industry has meanwhile remained much the same, showing a basic unchanging cultural substratum.

Sites of the Early Neolithic also occur on the coastal lowlands: an important example is the *Cova de l'Espérit* (Pyrénées-Orientales) in the Corbières, where a few sherds (one Cardial) and a microlithic industry showed continuity from earlier material at the site (Abelanet and Charles, 1964), while the sparse fauna showed a persisting abundance and importance of 'wild' species as well as the appearance of *Bos taurus* and *Capra hircus*. There is again no evidence whatsoever for agriculture or even for use of plants, unless some microliths were used in composite tools other than missiles. The cave is small ($35m^2$) – Phillips (1973, 532) estimated a population of 8 – and located at the mouth of the wild gorges of Roboul, a barren, rocky area with poor soils unsuited to cultivation.

Ile Corrège. The most important coastal site, the Ile Corrège (Aude), is submerged, and was found in 1972 in the course of dredging in the Etang de Leucate-Barcarès (Freises *et al.*, 1976; Freises and Montjardin, 1982); thus the material dredged out has no stratigraphic context, and it is difficult to estimate the size of the original settlement. The site is extremely rich in Cardial pottery with a wide variety of decorative types and motifs; the material also includes polished-stone axes, grindstones, and bone awls; the site has been dated to 4850bc (Guilaine, 1975, 14).

An earlier concentration along the coast may follow an earlier (seasonal?) mesolithic presence here – now drowned – and in any case is hardly surprising in view of the rising sea-level (only −20m at 6000bp (4050bc), according to Monaco *et al.*, 1972) which brought the rich marine resources ever nearer. It is probable that the economy of such major lowland Cardial sites was largely turned to the sea, and there is evidence from Espérit to support this in the form of a variety of Mediterranean molluscs (including numerous mussels) and an abundance of vertebrae and jaws of large dorado fish (Abelanet and Charles, 1964; Abelanet, 1979). Various marine fish, including dorados, are also known from Ile Corrège in this period, and most notably two fragments of a sword-fish blade which seems to denote open-sea fishing (Poplin, 1975) and considerable skill, since the Mediterranean species can be over 5m in length. In addition, many bone tools from the site seem to be points of fish-gigs (Guilaine, 1980a, 36), and some probable net-weights have been found. The fauna (Geddes, 1980a, b) includes both domestic cattle and aurochs, but domesticated sheep account for 50 per cent of the bones.

Finally, the *Trou des Fées* (Aude), not far to the north, was occupied towards the end of the Early Neolithic (Guilaine, 1971) and features typical pottery with cordons, grooves, comb-motifs and, more exceptionally, some possible stylised people. Grindstones and net-weights also exist in the cave. Farther north, the uplands which encircle the Narbonne plain contain a series of sites with Cardial pottery: e.g. La Crouzade (Aude) and Bize (Aude), which eventually join those of eastern Languedoc (Freises *et al.*, 1974, 292). There is therefore a marked geographic continuity in the distribution of Cardial sites in this region, both in the coastal area and the uplands of the interior.

The Middle Neolithic

In the *département* of Pyrénées-Orientales, and eastern Ariège, the transition into a Middle Neolithic is characterised by the *Montbolo* group (m.r.15), named after a small cave in the Pyrénées-Orientales excavated by Guilaine, although a date of 4500bc from the site makes it contemporaneous with the Early Neolithic of Jean Cros and Gazel (Guilaine *et al.*, 1974). Nevertheless, the cultural succession envisaged in the area (i.e. Cardial to Montbolo to Chasséen) is repeated in Spanish Catalonia; certainly typology shows that Montbolo material is in no way intrusive, having its prototypes in the Cardial, and occupying the same areas and often the same sites. There seems little need to equate new ceramic developments with new peoples, especially as Montbolo, like the Cardial, seems to represent a cluster of local facies (Roudil, 1980, 470). Baills, in the Grotte de la Chance at Ria (Pyrénées-Orientales), has uncovered a fine stratigraphy for these periods from an Early Neolithic with undecorated pottery through an Epicardial, a Montbolo facies, and into an early and then classic Chasséen (Roudil, 1978, 694; 1980, 469).

Montbolo. Montbolo pottery, like that of Las-Morts, consists largely of simple undecorated globular forms, but it is of excellent quality, smooth and well-fired, and characterised by prominent handles and vertically-pierced lugs (Fig.7.4). The lithic industry is poorly known, but bonework is abundant and comprises numerous awls and polishers. At Montbolo and other sites, there are a few grinders but no trace of agriculture – not a single grain impression on the abundant pottery which may, on the contrary, have been used for dairying activities. Certainly the modern animal domesticates seem of great importance, with sheep representing over half of the herbivores present (Guilaine *et al.*, 1974b). The faunal sample is small, but bovids, sheep and pigs all include a high percentage of 'very young' and 'young' animals; it is known that the exploitation of young sheep and young/subadult boars was practised in the Mesolithic of the region, and lasted well into the Neolithic (Geddes, 1980a, b).

The Montbolo fauna also shows a persisting importance of small game, which is unsurprising in view of the surroundings: the cave is located halfway up a rock-face in a ridge high above the Tech, and is somewhat difficult to reach. A settlement based on cultivation would more sensibly have been founded on the first slopes of a wider part of the Tech valley; the steep mountains around Montbolo gave it an inevitable pastoral bias, supplemented by hunting or trapping, and its abundance of pottery may indicate a function as a storehouse.

The cave of Montou (Pyrénées-Orientales; m.r.14) was dug some years ago and proved to have a stratigraphy of major importance for the region, including a homogeneous ensemble of Montbolo material, purposely sealed into a gallery (Treinen-Claustre *et al.*, 1981, 214). Unfortunately it has never been published, but new excavations begun recently by Treinen-Claustre should provide some information in the near future.

Elsewhere in the region a different kind of transition is seen, particularly

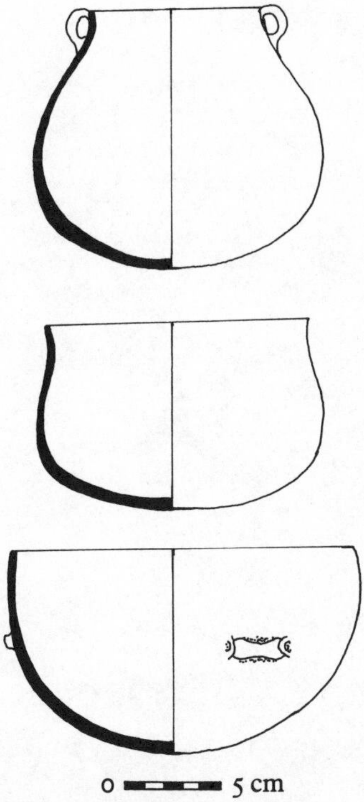

FIGURE 7.4. Typical Montbolo-type pots, showing prominent handles. Early to Middle Neolithic transition. From the Balma de Montbolo (Pyr-Or). (After Guilaine *et al.*, 1974.)

in the great stratigraphy of the Abri de Font-Juvénal (Aude; m.r.21), north of Carcassonne between the plain and the southern flank of the Montagne Noire. The shelter, c.20m long and up to 5m deep, has been excavated since 1970 by Guilaine and his team, and up to 7m of layers have been uncovered so far (Guilaine *et al.*, 1976), including 5m of neolithic levels (Plate 7.2). The site may well prove to contain early neolithic material below. However, the excavations have so far investigated the layers above an epicardial occupation, and have revealed a complete picture of the Middle and Late Neolithic of western Languedoc. The occupants of the early 4th millennium bc made smooth, undecorated pottery similar to the epicardial ware at Gazel. They are succeeded from 3500 to 2700bc by the Chasséens. The site has been thoroughly radiocarbon-dated, and spans at least 5800 years. The excavations are notable for the attention paid to the distribution and function of features such as structures, hearths and 'combustion-pits' (Gasco, 1980c). Moreover, as mentioned earlier, abundant carbonised remains of barley and of two varieties of wheat have been found in the Chasséen levels (Guilaine *et al.*, 1980), together with acorns and hazelnuts. Stockrearing was also of great importance throughout these levels. The material culture includes thick retouched flint points,

PLATE 7.2. Abri de Font-Juvénal (Conques, Aude). View of the northern 'section témoin' spanning much of the Neolithic (see text). Excavations by Jean Guilaine. (Photo: Jean Guilaine.)

bone awls and spatulae, and pottery basins and bowls with horizontally-perforated lugs, or with decoration such as engraved triangles (Guilaine *et al.*, 1976).

The Languedoc Chasséen also occurs at Grotte Gazel, above the epicardial layer. Hearths, pots and lithic implements have been uncovered. According to Jane Renfrew (quoted by Phillips, 1975, 86) a Chasséen sherd from this site bears an impression of an Emmer wheat grain, which fits the far-more-abundant data at nearby Font-Juvénal.

The sites in western Languedoc included under the blanket term of Chasséen seem to represent a number of local facies; one can trace differences in lithic industries and ceramic styles in both space and time. One group which has been differentiated, that of Bize (Aude; m.r.23), is centred in the Aude plain and part of the Corbières (Guilaine, 1970b). It is characterised by pottery which, while similar to normal Chasséen wares and of equal quality, bears exuberant decorative motifs such as undulating lines, chevrons and even sometimes has a daubing of red or pink paint.

Some open-air sites of the period have recently been found on light, sandy, easily-worked soils along the rivers and by the former lagoons of the plain of Roussillon (see Treinen-Claustre *et al.*, 1981, 218). They are hard to locate since they are covered by alluvium, and the erosion or ploughing which exposes them also brings destruction. Their contents are usually restricted to a few sherds and crude macrolithic tools. Very fine, classic Chasséen material, both ceramic and lithic, has however been found in an open-air site at Les Escaldes (Pyrénées-Orientales) in the high plateau of Cerdagne (Vaquer, 1976), a site which also yielded a Cardial sherd (Guilaine and Martzluff, 1976).

The most spectacular Chasséen sites of the region are located on loams in the Garonne valley around Toulouse. The first major site of this type to be found, Villeneuve-Tolosane (Haute-Garonne; m.r.6), was originally investigated by Méroc (1962), but rescue excavation has recently been undertaken here by Clottes, Vaquer *et al.* The site is located on well-watered loam, and, as mentioned earlier, thousands of cereal grains have been found. Potsherds are abundant, and the stone industry ranges from finely made arrowheads to crude quartzite implements, polished-stone axes, and weights for nets or looms. The site is a vast (30ha) Chasséen agglomeration: Méroc first detected c.220 structures which he called *fonds de cabanes*; these are circular areas consisting of a 0.2m layer of burnt cobbles, with wood charcoal underneath (Méroc and Simonnet, 1970, 38). He believed the site to comprise a series of hamlets, 50–100m apart, with habitations scattered haphazardly. Cultural material was very abundant on the surface, but very scarce in the cobbled areas themselves, except for typical undecorated Chasséen sherds. Bones were absent from the 'village', but were found in a burial which will be studied in a later section.

The most recent excavations (Clottes *et al.*, 1979, 1981) have exposed over $3000m^2$ and have brought the number of known structures – both circular and subrectangular – to over 700 (Fig.7.5; Plate 7.3). The former are up to 2.4m in diameter, the latter up to 11m long and 1.9m wide. The long structures tend to

PLATE 7.3. Villeneuve-Tolosane (Haute-Garonne). Some of the cobbled areas uncovered in the 1978 excavations by Clottes, Giraud, Rouzaud and Vaquer. (Photo: Jean Clottes.)

be arranged in parallel and linear fashion, whereas the circular seem to be placed haphazardly, as Méroc thought, though they cluster at one end of the site. Where there is overlap, the circular tend to overlie the long.

The construction method has now become clear: fire was lit in pits, 0.3m deep, and cobbles placed in them – all the pebbles are burnt – but whereas the long pits have baked sides and charred remains of great logs below the cobbles (see Simonnet, 1980a), the circular have few remains of charcoal. On the other hand, grindstone fragments are frequent in the circular, but almost absent from the long.

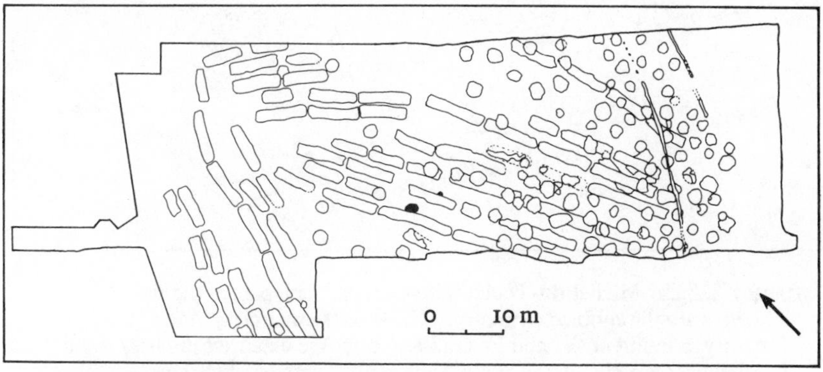

FIGURE 7.5. Villeneuve-Tolosane (Hte-Gar). General plan of area excavated in 1978 by Clottes, Giraud, Rouzaud and Vaquer, showing the lines of long cobbled areas and the clustering of round structures (see also Plate 7.3). (After Clottes *et al.*, 1981.)

A water well, 1.5m in diameter and 7.5m deep, has been found at the site, some distance from the cobbled structures (Vaquer, 1980a; Clottes, 1981). As well as the thousands of cereal grains it contained a rich assemblage of stone and bone tools, potsherds and animal bones: mostly bovids, with suids in second place; ovicaprids are rare, red deer and dog are present. Similar material has been found in a number of storage pits at the site (see Clottes, *op.cit.*). One remarkable pit contained well over 50,000 snailshells, mostly *Helix/Cepaea nemoralis*; the first open-air 'escargotière' to be found in France (Bonzom *et al.*, 1981) it has not yet been assigned to a precise date, but it certainly testifies to the continuing importance of this gasteropod as a supplementary resource, an importance seen most clearly in the postglacial occupation of Poeymaü in the western Pyrenees (Bahn, 1979, 1982b).

The recent excavations have revealed that the site was one of the biggest neolithic camps known, and was surrounded by at least two vast quadrangles, c.250m by 500m, made up of interrupted ditches. These were 3–4m wide, 1.5m deep, and were placed end to end; one excavated stretch, 30m long, showed traces of a palisade of wooden stakes, 0.2m in diameter and placed every 0.5m in the ditch (Bonzom *et al.*, 1981). However, some of the ditches are isolated, some are rich in archaeological material, and indeed seem to have

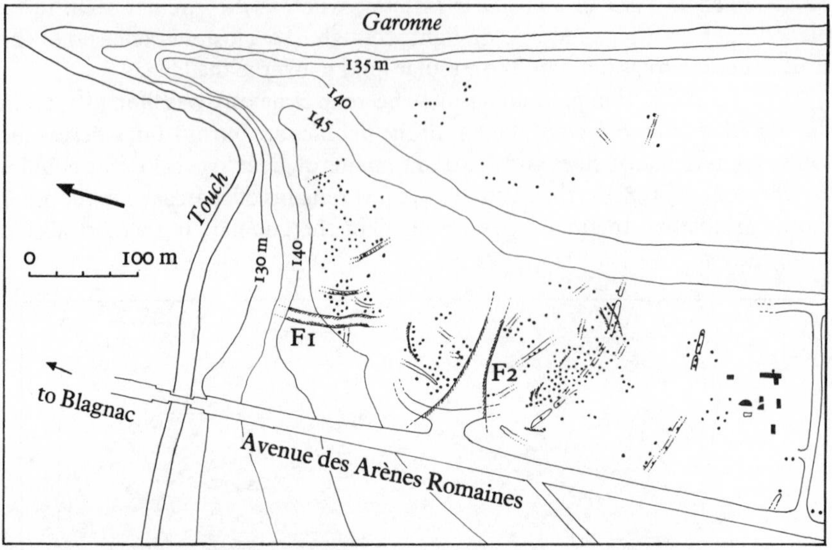

FIGURE 7.6. Saint-Michel-du-Touch (Hte-Gar). General plan of the site. The dots are the cobbled structures. The black semicircle is 'A185', the funerary monument. F1 and F2 are later, Iron Age defensive ditches. Parallel lines are big ditches; parallel lines filled with hatching are defensive palisades; single lines with hatching are the light palisades. Excavations by Méroc and Simonnet. (After Méroc and Simonnet, 1979.)

been purposely filled with debris. Thus it appears unlikely that their purpose was defensive.

It is clear that the enclosures, palisade, well and multitude of cobbled structures indicate a high degree of sophistication and an organised communal effort by a large number of people. This part of the Garonne valley contains numerous sites of similar type (e.g. see Simonnet, 1980a, 145; Clottes *et al.*, 1977; Giraud and Vaquer, 1981; Phillips, 1982, 10), some known only from surface finds or one or two *fonds de cabanes*; they range from 4ha to huge sites such as the 30ha Villeneuve-Tolosane (Haute-Garonne). Most are located at a confluence with the Garonne. The economic basis must have been remarkably sound to support so dense a network of major settlements; and good evidence for agriculture and stockrearing has also been found at the other major site to have been extensively excavated, that of Saint-Michel-du-Touch (Haute-Garonne; m.r.7), in the suburbs of Toulouse itself.

This site, located on a promontory above 30m cliffs at the confluence of the Touch and the Garonne (Fig.7.6), was excavated by Méroc and Simonnet (1970; Simonnet, 1976). It featured two strong defensive palisades, made of tree trunks standing in 2m ditches, protecting the northern end of the site; seven sections of lighter palisades, possibly for corrals; a series of ditches, up to 4m wide and a metre deep, arranged end to end in arcs crossing the site;

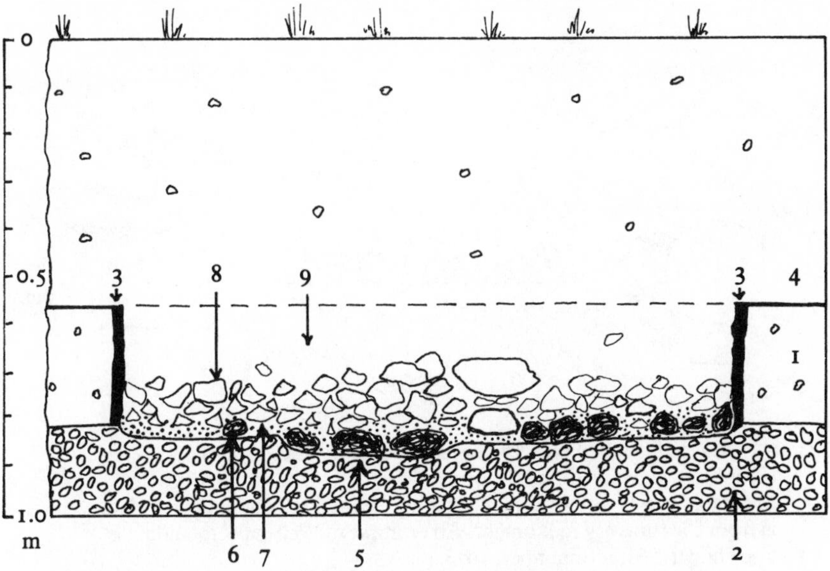

FIGURE 7.7. Saint-Michel-du-Touch (Hte-Gar). Transverse section of a long cobbled structure: 1-2 soil and gravel; 3 baked sides of the pit; 4 neolithic land surface; 5 heap of carbonised logs, burnt *in situ*; 6 large isolated lump of charcoal; 7 layer of earth mixed with charcoal; 8 cobbles; 9 covering of earth. Excavations by Méroc and Simonnet. Scale 1:21. This structure was dated to 3180±100bc. (After Simonnet, 1976.)

funerary monuments, which will be studied in a later section; and over 300 of the characteristic cobbled areas. The existence of shallow 'interrupted ditches' and the fact that almost all of the artefacts and refuse were found in them, invites comparison with the 'causewayed camps' of southern Britain; and just as some of the latter seem to have a heavy pastoral emphasis (Barker and Webley, 1978), the fauna of Saint-Michel shows a great development of stockherding, with bovids representing half the bone fragments and a third of individuals (Simonnet, 1976) though 'wild' species, especially boar, were still making a notable contribution to the diet. Nevertheless, as mentioned earlier, the site also has evidence for clearance, and cereals in two pollen samples.

Saint-Michel is very well dated and spans over a millennium, from 4100bc to 2550bc, so that it is difficult to estimate how many structures were in use at any one time: Phillips' estimate (1975, 94) of a population of 2000 people can thus be no more than a guess, especially as more structures have been exposed outside the zone originally dug (Giraud and Vaquer, 1981). As at Villeneuve-Tolosane, the cobbled areas seem to be grouped in 'hamlets' about 50m apart, consist of both long and circular types, and have a disorderly distribution. The same methods were employed in their construction (Fig.7.7).

The cultural material again represented a typical Chasséen: pottery vessels and plates, with a variety of handles including the 'Pan-pipe' motif, and

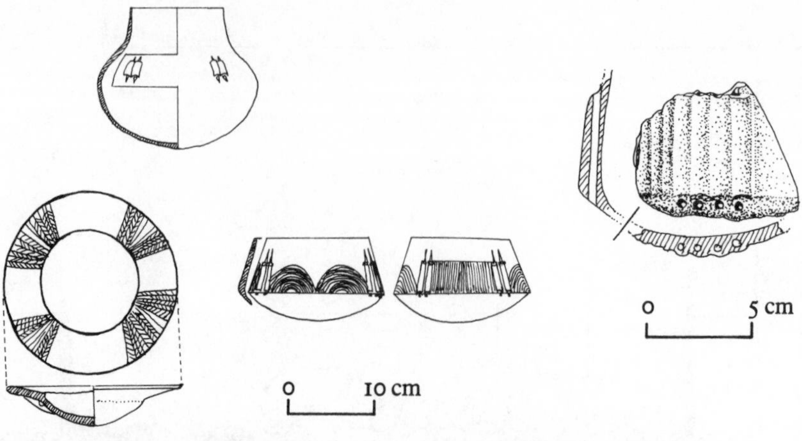

FIGURE 7.8. Selection of pottery vessels from Saint-Michel-du-Touch (Hte-Gar), showing different forms of decorative motifs. The heavily decorated bowl was found in one of the great ditches. The engraved plate is from the funerary monument. An example of 'Pan-pipe' moulding is also shown. (After Simonnet, 1976.)

rare decoration, including engraved bands and chevrons (Fig.7.8). Grindstones and sickles are abundant, as are net/loom weights, polished-stone axes and transverse arrowheads. As at Villeneuve, no hearths or bones were found in the cobbled areas, and cultural material was rare; at both sites, the bulk of objects and bones occur in pits and ditches: the Saint-Michel ditches contain the site's only hearths, a huge amount of pottery, very abundant animal bones, and a few stone and bone tools (Simonnet, 1976; Méroc and Simonnet, 1981).

One should note that sites of this type are not limited to the Garonne valley: for example, a similar Chasséen 'village' has been excavated at Auriac (Aude; m.r.19); it has a typical promontory/confluence location, cobbled areas, and an abundance of net/loom weights (Guilaine and Vaquer, 1973). Like Saint-Michel-du-Touch, Auriac has a predominance of domestic bovids, with sheep in second place; but its only evidence for agriculture is one grinder and a 'heavy stone industry'. It is probable that sites like these had a mobile-cum-sedentary economy, sending their animals to the fine upland pastures nearby in the warm season.

Finally, there remains the problem of the cobbled areas: what are they? A lot of attention has been paid to this question in recent years, but results are still inconclusive. Méroc, the first person to excavate one, was convinced that they were *fonds de cabanes*, i.e. hut-bases, despite the fact that there was no trace of walls or posts, nor indeed of hearths or living-refuse – 'Manifestement, les occupants vivaient ailleurs durant la journée' (Méroc and Simonnet, 1970, 43). His view has been upheld recently by Simonnet (1980b) who has published several of the Saint Michel examples in detail; he believes that the great masses of charcoal were used to absorb humidity, and thus to drain the hut floors and keep them dry. He also notes (*op.cit.*, 473) that the question of a superstructure is still unsolved: a few postholes have turned up, but it has never been possible to gain any idea of the construction. Earthen walls are a possibility, since the local clay is well suited to the task; but evidence is totally lacking. Simonnet, then, feels that the long structures are best described as huts, and the round as possible storehouses.

The recent excavators of Villeneuve-Tolosane (Clottes, Giraud, Rouzaud and Vaquer (1979, 1981)) have also tackled the question, and have divided opinions. Clottes and Rouzaud, on the one hand, support the *fonds de cabanes* theory, although they point out that some of the round structures were too small for habitation; that some of the long structures seem uncomfortably narrow; and that firing new hut floors would have endangered nearby huts; and humidity could have been controlled by far less complex and laborious methods. Giraud and Vaquer (1981), on the other hand, propose a different hypothesis, in which the cobbled structures were 'activity areas', and notably 'combustion structures' used at periodic/seasonal gatherings for the cooking of great feasts or the mass drying/smoking of meat or fish. Simonnet (1980b, 474) disagrees since, once again, the pits and cobbles seem to be an unnecessarily complex way to perform a task which could have been carried out on the surface; moreover, the round structures appear to have been used only once, with minor fires; and why were so many areas accumulated instead of a few being reused? And if these thousands of structures *are* all simply activity areas, where did their users live? Vaquer (1980a, 1981) has made a fairly convincing case for his view, but one is forced to conclude that the Chasséen cobbled structures remain an enigma for the present.

The Late Neolithic and Chalcolithic

The Neolithic of the 3rd millennium bc sees a further fragmentation of culture groups developing *in situ* from the Chasséen. The eastern Pyrenees and Aude constitute the centre of the *Véraza* group, named after a site in the western Corbières (Aude; m.r.18); it is known, albeit poorly, from both caves and open-air sites, and stretches south into Catalonia, and westward as far as the Garonne, like earlier cultures. Its industry includes a flake assemblage, polished-stone axes and bone tools, but the real distinguishing feature of this phase is its pottery which features bowls and jars – often quite tall and voluminous – bearing prominent nipples and lugs (Fig.7.9) or cordons; another novel feature is the frequent application of vegetation to the wet paste, at times even as a decorative motif: one example of a cereal-grain impression, probably of barley, from the site of Valentines (Aude) has recently been published by Vaquer (1980b).

The Véraza group has been studied from various angles in a recent publication (Guilaine, 1980); in radiocarbon dates it stretches from 2620bc to at least 1800bc, and thus through the Chalcolithic, alongside Beakers, although it certainly predates the latter at some sites such as Font-Juvénal; however, it also has a final facies *after* the Beakers at this site (Guilaine *et al.*, 1976, 1980). Some sherds of Ferrières type (see above, Chapter 5) also appear – but also disappear – before the Beaker complex at Font-Juvénal

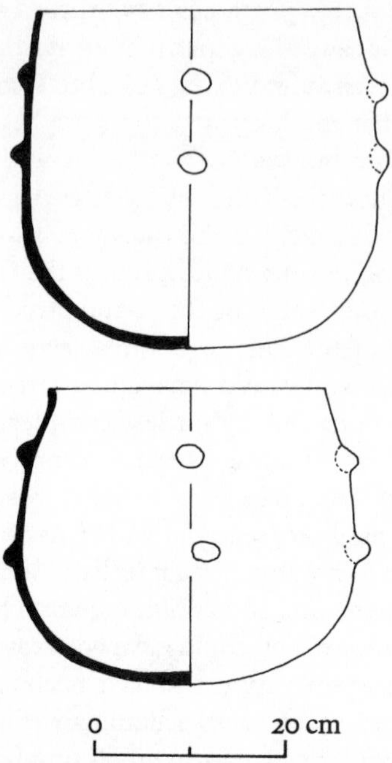

FIGURE 7.9. Examples of the large pottery storage-vessels of the Véraza group (Late Neolithic), showing the prominent nipples. The upper example is from the open-site of Grépiac (Hte-Gar), studied by Méroc; the lower is from the Grotte Gazel (Aude), excavated by Guilaine. (After Guilaine, 1970c.)

(m.r.21). The important stratigraphy of this site suggests that the Véraza-type material evolved *in situ*, and was contemporaneous for a while with Beaker material which appears relatively suddenly.

Vaquer (1980c) has divided the Véraza-group cultural material into three phases: early (2600–2300bc), classic (2300–2000bc) and recent (2000–1900 bc at least). Gasco (1980d) has undertaken a study of the habitation- and combustion-structures of Font-Juvénal in this phase, suggesting different cooking methods for which the latter might have been designed; these problems, however, are very difficult to solve since ovens and hearths can have a wide variety of purposes.

The principal late neolithic sites of the Pyrenees include the unpublished Grotte de Montou (m.r.14), and the Grotte des Bruixes at Tautavel (Pyrénées-Orientales): this site was too small and uncomfortable to be a habitation, and seems to have served as a storehouse (Abelanet, 1979; 1980, 55) since it is rich in pottery and little else. The large undecorated vessels – some of which hold over 20 litres – can be classed as 'vases à provisions'; some of them have repair-holes, which makes it likely that solids were stored in them, although there is no proof of grain-storage. The bone and stone material is very poor.

An open-air site of this phase at Moli Cremat, near Perpignan (Pyrénées-

Orientales) was probably also a storage point, since it had no cultural material or features other than some grindstones and over 23kg of potsherds, some of which bore impressions of straw or grass (Abelanet, 1980); while an open-air site at Lesquerde by the River Agly (Pyrénées-Orientales) gave a cheese-drainer and potsherds including some from a vessel so similar in paste, technique and decoration to one in the Grotte des Bruixes as to suggest the same potter (*ibid.*, 57).

Pollen from the burial cave of Can-Pey, in Vallespir (Pyrénées-Orientales; m.r.15), shows an increasingly humid and temperate climate in this phase (Pi and Baills, 1980), and one sample included rye. The presence of weeds and meadow plants such as *Plantago* is thought to denote agriculture, though this does not necessarily follow (Dennell, quoted in Phillips, 1975, 53). However, the Grotte des Cazals (Aude; m.r.22), near Gazel, has yielded carbonised wheat grains from this period (Barrié, 1980). Little faunal information, however, is at present available from Véraza-group sites.

Further west, in Ariège, a rather different cultural development can be seen in the caves of Las-Morts (m.r.12) and Bédeilhac (m.r.9), whose stratigraphies span the later Neolithic and Chalcolithic. The Las-Morts material is presented in full by Durand (1968): the late neolithic pottery is still undecorated; in the Late Chalcolithic appears the polypod bowl, a characteristic of this period – though more especially of the Bronze Age – in the Pyrenees (see Nougier, 1954; Guilaine, 1972).

The second, later neolithic layer of Las-Morts corresponds roughly to the earliest neolithic level at Bédeilhac, which Nougier called the *Néolithique II Pyrénéen*. Restricted excavation in this huge cave by Robert exposed a series of six layers spanning a period from the end of the Neolithic to a point far into the Bronze Age. Pottery is extremely abundant at the site and, oddly, it is the lowest level (VI), mentioned above, which contains the finest and best-fired wares (Assaillit, 1953, 56), alongside cruder forms. It has been claimed (Nougier and Robert, 1953) that the fine ware may have been imported, and Nougier (1952) stressed the close similarities of the material from Bédeilhac and other sites of the region to that of the Swiss Neolithic and allied cultures; however, it is clear from sites like the Mas d'Azil and especially the stratigraphy of Las-Morts that the Ariège Neolithic is of indigenous origin and in no way derived from the Cortaillod or elsewhere.

Bédeilhac's pottery (Nougier and Robert, *op.cit.*,) in layer VI has a fine, smooth glossy paste, well-fired, and comprises globular forms. The chalcolithic layers yielded hundreds of sherds, of inferior quality, and including two decorated with fine, white-encrusted incisions which almost hark back to Chasséen decoration. The site is also rich in bonework, though poor in stone tools (Nougier and Robert, 1956), and its material is representative of the many sites around Tarascon-sur-Ariège, where Garrigou did a lot of his 19th century 'sondages' (Garrigou and Filhol, 1866). The stone implements are made of granular rocks such as quartzite, schist and ophite, and include axes, crude scrapers and chisels. Grindstones are especially abundant in the Chalcolithic. Bone tools include awls and polishers, and some large tools made of bovid ribs which have been linked with butchering and hide-preparation (Nougier and Robert, 1956, 768). Of particular interest are a series of hafts and handles in red deer antler (Nougier and Robert, *ibid.*), and a fine hook in the same raw material. These objects, too, are represented in other sites around Bédeilhac, and were compared by Nougier (1952) with finds in the Swiss lake sites.

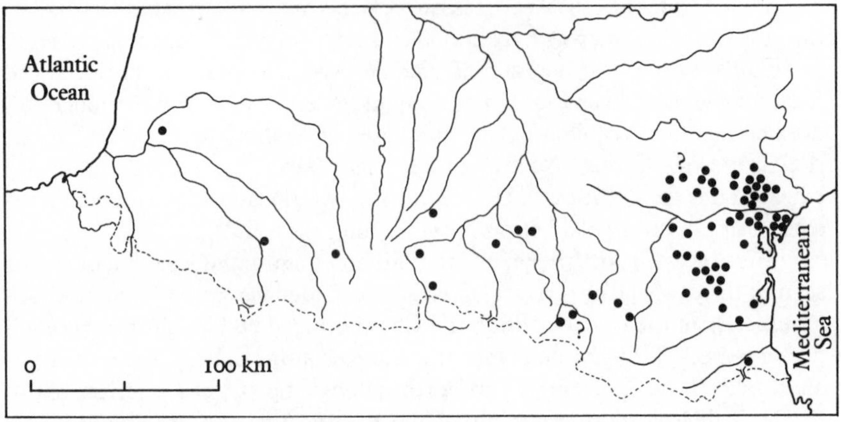

FIGURE 7.10. Distribution of Beakers in the French Pyrenees. The western-most dot is a tumulus in the Landes; the second from the left is Poeymaü (Pyr-Atl). The third is the tomb of La Halliade (see Figures 7.11-12). The doubtful sites to the east are Ussat (Ariège) and Gaougnas-Cabrespine (Aude). (After Guilaine, 1967.)

Finally, it should be noted that dating of torch debris from Niaux (Ariège) shows that the remote depths of this huge decorated cave were visited in neolithic times (3700bc, 2640bc) (Delibrias *et al.*, 1976, 877).

Unfortunately little is known of the Late Neolithic of the middle Garonne valley: an open-site at Grépiac (Haute-Garonne), 15km south of Toulouse, and three 'pit-structures' with traces of combustion and some burnt cobbles. The abundant potsherds included a few of Chasséen type, but most are attributable to the Véraza group and later periods (Méroc, 1961; Vaquer, 1980d). It could be argued that this represents some sort of transition *in situ* from the enigmatic Chasséen sites of the area; further support for this idea is found in recent excavations at Muret (Haute-Garonne) near Toulouse (Clottes, 1979, 631–2; 1981, 560) where structures of burnt cobbles – not in pits but on the old land surface – are associated with Véraza-group pottery and Beaker sherds, the only *Epicampaniforme* site in the whole region; sporadic chalcolithic occupation also occurred at Villeneuve-Tolosane (Bonzom *et al.*, 1981; Clottes, 1981, 558), and a new 'village' was established there in the Middle Bronze Age. Future work may reveal more information concerning developments in this area after the Chasséen 'expansion'.

Beakers. The eastern Pyrenees are one of the richest areas in Europe for

PLATE 7.4. Beaker pottery from the Dolmen de Saint-Eugène (Laure-Minervois, Aude). (a) Pyrenean-style Beaker, height 105mm; (b) Pyrenean-style 'bowl-beaker', height 118mm, diameter 200mm. The stamped and incised decoration is typical of the eastern Pyrenees. Musée de la Société d'Etudes Scientifiques de l'Aude, Carcassonne. (Photo: Jean Guilaine.)

Beakers (Fig.7.10). Beakers in the Pyrenean region as a whole have been studied by Guilaine (1967, 1976c), but the west and centre of the chain only provide a few examples. The vessels have been divided into three major

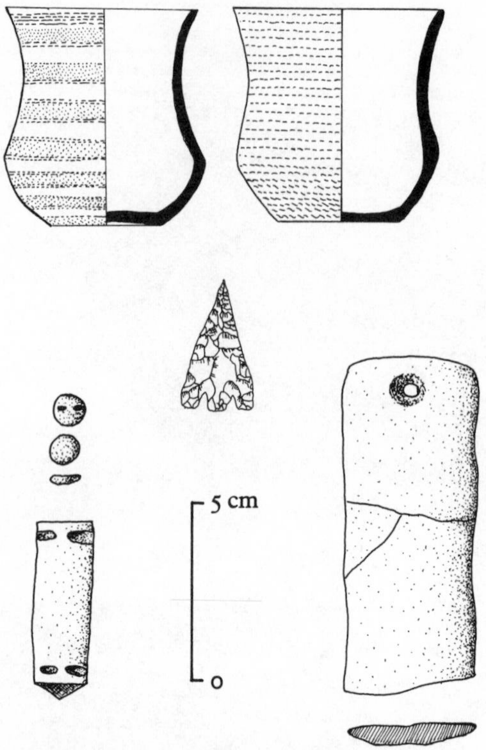

FIGURE 7.11. Typical assemblage of the Chalcolithic of the French Pyrenees: two Beakers from the tomb of La Halliade (Htes-Pyr): that on the left has 'International-style' decoration. The barbed-and-tanged arrowhead and the small V-perforated bone button are from the nécropole de la Clape (Aude); the large V-perforated bone button is from the Grotte d'Usson (Ariège); the archer's wristguard is from the Grotte d'Estagel (Pyr-Or). (After Guilaine, 1976b.)

groups: those with 'international style' decoration, which are found throughout the chain, from the tomb of La Halliade (Hautes-Pyrénées; studied below; m.r.4) to dolmens in Aude; those with 'corded decoration' which often accompany the first group; and the 'Pyrenean type' proper (Plate 7.4) which feature a variety of decorative motifs and methods and which, though present in the west, are heavily concentrated in the east. The Beakers are usually associated with a range of objects (Fig. 7.11) such as barbed-and-tanged arrowheads, wristguards, and especially V-perforated bone buttons (Guilaine, 1963, 1967), of which about 500 were found in the Grotte d'Usson (Ariège; m.r.13). It is this assemblage of material, largely from burial caves and megalithic monuments, which came to epitomise the *cultura pirenaica* of Bosch-Gimpera and Pericot (e.g. see Pericot, 1950), but the term should be restricted to the eastern region (Guilaine, 1967, 131).

In recent years some Beaker habitation sites in the region have proved that the material is not restricted to funerary contexts: layer 2b at Font-Juvénal is a notable example, and is dated to 2240bc; other dates from this phase (Guilaine *et al.*, 1974b) include one from a late utilisation of Montbolo (2170bc). It should be noted that Clarke (1970) originally saw the Gulf of Lions as a possible point of origin for Beakers, though he later dropped the idea.

The question of the origins of metallurgy in the region is still to be resolved, but in view of the Pyrenees' great wealth of minerals, it is unsurprising that sporadic finds of pre-Beaker goldwork and copper daggers are being discovered (Guilaine, 1976b; Guilaine and Vaquer, 1979). The Beaker phase itself has copper daggers, and decorative objects in copper, gold and lead.

Burials

Burials in caves are extremely abundant in the Pyrenees, and are often almost impossible to date accurately. Some early neolithic examples have been noted (Quérénas, Cova de l'Espérit), and comprise inhumations in habitation sites. The Grotte Gazel also had a flexed burial of the epicardial phase (Duday and Guilaine, 1980): it was an adult, whose hand rested on the skull of a young suid.

In the Middle Neolithic the Aude region has a number of open-air cist burials (Duday and Guilaine, 1975) containing usually two or more flexed inhumations, and often occurring in groups. They are usually accompanied by polished-stone axes, transverse arrowheads, decorative objects and pots, but not animal bones. Related to this group is the cist of Arca de Calahons (Pyrénées-Orientales), excavated by Abelanet (1970a); unlike the others it featured a small cairn. Its structure and its transverse arrowheads linked it closely to the *sepulcros de fosa* culture of Spanish Catalonia.

Flexed burials under small cairns were also found grouped at Mailhac (Aude), but lay in pits without cists, and were accompanied by pots and animal bones (Duday and Guilaine, *op.cit.*). At Villeneuve-Tolosane, flexed burials occur without cists or cairns: one was excavated in 1961 (Méroc and Simonnet, 1970, 39) – a woman, lying on her left side, wearing a necklace comprising beads and a baby's vertebra, and accompanied by (ritually broken?) pottery vessels and stone and bone implements; a second burial dug by Méroc, however, was on its *right* side (Méroc and Simonnet, 1979, 381). The recent excavations in the site (Clottes, 1981, 557) uncovered the skeleton of a small, arthritic old lady, buried on her left side in a shallow pit in one of the interrupted-ditches; she was accompanied by a pot and two boar-tusk pendants. Another burial, of two people, in a subrectangular ditch was destroyed at the site by building work; and, most recently, the burial of a young child was found in another interrupted-ditch (Bonzom *et al.*, 1981).

This group constitutes a fairly uniform type of Chasséen burial, and one of those found at Saint-Michel-du-Touch was of this type: i.e. a teenager, on his left side, accompanied by a small, crude Chasséen vessel containing a pot, a bone awl and four hedgehog jaws. Hedgehog jaws have also turned up in food debris at the site, and the species may thus have been a delicacy. The other burial at Saint-Michel, however, is radically different (Méroc and Simonnet, 1970, 1979): a large pit, 7.4m by 4m, 0.8m deep, contained remains of two adults together with 12 pottery vessels of various types, grindstones, beads, polished sandstone plaquettes, other objects, some animal bones and even dog excrement! Above, 25m^3 of unburnt cobbles had collapsed onto them. It is thought the tomb originally featured a wooden sepulchral chamber covered by the cobbles so as to form a low cairn. Such elaboration led Méroc and Simonnet (1970, 44) to call it a *tombe royale*. These seem to be secondary burials, since the skeletons were 'sketched' with just a few bones. In a full study of this remarkable monument, now called simply 'A185' (Méroc and Simonnet, 1979) it has been revealed that about 10 similar structures were detected at Saint-Michel: at least one of these was certainly a tomb; others were simply enigmatic pits full of cobbles mixed with stone implements, sherds and animal bones; while 6 had to remain unexplored. Simonnet (Méroc and Simonnet, *op.cit.*) therefore seems inclined to drop the 'royal tomb' theory – there are too few of them for a 1000-year timespan – and instead to envisage a general 'cult of the dead', a ritual reburial of symbolic significance. At any rate, all of these structures, like the 'normal' cobbled areas of the site, certainly point to considerable collective efforts. The great funerary monument has been dated to 3490bc.

The principal characteristic of the 3rd millennium bc cultures is collective inhumation, both in natural caves/shelters and in the artificial shelters known as megalithic monuments; in view of the latter, it is clear that collective effort was utilised far more widely, rather than limited to a few special monuments. Unfortunately the constant re-use of these burial caves and monuments usually disturbed the original burials, and removed a great deal of archaeological information: for example the Grotte de Can-Pey (Pyrénées-Orientales; m.r. 15) contained the remains of at least 58 people (Baills, 1980). The richness and abundance of grave goods varies greatly, and finds in caves and dolmens are closely similar. Some examples of burial caves have been presented in previous sections, though special mention should be made here of the chalcolithic ossuaries of Pyrénées-Orientales, studied by Abelanet (1960): that of Portichol, for example, is arranged rather like a dolmen. It should also be noted that areas rich in cavities suitable for ossuaries are poor in dolmens, and vice versa.

MEGALITHS. The French Pyrenees have a great abundance of megalithic monuments: over 100 dolmens known in the Pays Basque (de Barandiarán, 1953; Blot, 1974), and about 100 in Pyrénées-Orientales (Abelanet, 1970b, 1975) though considerably fewer in between (see Bahn, 1979). The uplands of the *département* of Aude are also rich in monuments: e.g. the necropolis of 8 tombs at La Clape (Guilaine *et al.*, 1972).

Unfortunately there is a complete lack of absolute dates, since the great majority were disturbed in historical times, or proved to contain no grave goods or even bones. The commonest form is the simple, small, rectangular dolmen (Plate 7.5), often covered by a tumulus; since these man-made caves could be erected in particular desired locations, it is not surprising that their distribution is by no means random: e.g. in the Pays Basque they occur at

PLATE 7.5. Dolmen de Tignac (Ariège) in winter. A small rectangular structure, typical of those in the Pyrenees, facing SSE and without a trace of a tumulus. Roof slab 2.1m by 1.9m. Back wall partly collapsed. Located at 1070m, it underlines the seasonal utilisation of these uplands by prehistoric man. (Photo: Paul Bahn.)

medium altitude (150–600m - though up to 1100m across the frontier) along tracks, ridges, watersheds, crests; in pastures and in flat spaces on mountain sides. One consistent factor is that the site has a vast view, especially to the east: if a col is not open to the east, it is most unlikely to have a monument. Areas with great concentrations of monuments are always excellent for pastoralism: as de Barandiarán (1953, 150) stressed, 'la casi totalidad de los dólmenes vascos . . . se hallan en pasturajes y en puertos y collados que dan acceso a ellos'. The monuments of Pyrénées-Orientales and the central region occupy identical locations. Some are *dolmens à couloir*: i.e. a little longer than the simple type.

Typologically, the French Basque megaliths form part of a large group which stretches through Alava to the Ebro, and is connected to the Atlantic group west of the Meseta (Maluquer, 1974) while, to the north, the group occupies most of Aquitaine, although rare in the littoral zones. It is thought that the concept spread to south-western France from the Atlantic coast of Portugal; Maluquer (*op.cit.*) believes that the building of megaliths at the Mediterranean end of the Pyrenees (the Catalan and Roussillon group) began later than in the Basque area, judging by the tombs and their contents, and had therefore received the idea from the west.

A tumulus near Arudy (Pyrénées-Atlantiques; m.r.3) has recently been found to contain material which may date it to the Middle or Late Neolithic (Rigaud, 1980, 413). In the lowlands of Hautes-Pyrénées, the plateaux contain a wide variety of monuments under tumuli (e.g. see Pothier, 1900; Fabre, 1952), but their dating is often imprecise. Two large tumuli, excavated by Piette (1881), were found to contain major, idiosyncratic and markedly different monuments; that of Pouey-Mayou, at Bartrès (Hautes-Pyrénées; m.r.4), is the finest *dolmen sous tumulus* of the Central Pyrenees. The great oval mound contained a rectangular chamber, with two skeletons, a flint knife, a gold bead and some crude, undecorated sherds. Thought to date to the Chalcolithic, it may already foreshadow Hallstatt funerary rites (Coquerel, 1971, 194).

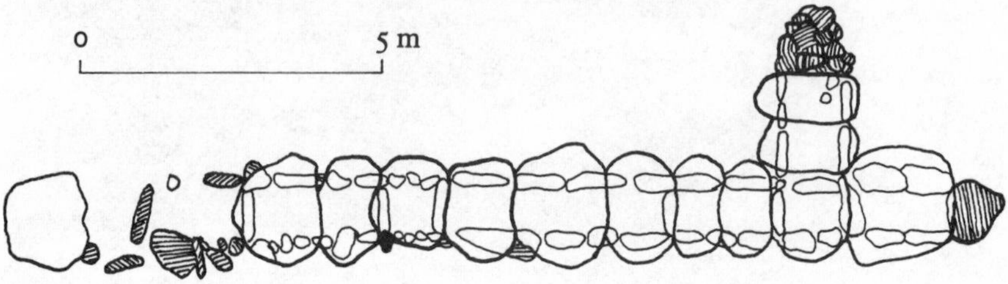

FIGURE 7.12. Plan of the tomb of La Halliade (Htes-Pyr). (After Piette, 1881.)

The other tumulus nearby, that of La Halliade – recently destroyed maliciously (Clottes, 1975, 619) – was 24m in diameter and 2m high, and contained a bizarre structure, over 14m long, comprising eight cists joined together in a line, with another joined on at one side (Fig.7.12; see also Daniel, 1960, pl.2). The first three segments were empty; in the fourth Piette found 14 pots, 8 in the fifth, 8 in the sixth, and nothing in the others. The lateral chamber had a polished-stone axe; other finds included flint knives, a necklace of callais beads, and a rectangular gold plaque. The 30 pots include 3 Beakers (Fig.7.11) and also large polypod bowls, some of which contained cremated remains. Coquerel (*ibid.*) again sees this as a Hallstatt funerary rite with objects of eneolithic tradition, and it is certainly a complex and enigmatic mixture of chalcolithic, bronze age and early iron age objects and features (see Mohen, 1978).

Lake Settlements

As was noted in the Introduction, the 19th century view of the Neolithic was heavily influenced by the Swiss lake-settlements, and it therefore seemed logical for scholars of this period to expect and search for similar sites in other areas. It is a little known fact that much evidence turned up in the Pyrenean region, principally, though not exclusively, in the lowland heaths. It was already known that there were local legends of such settlements existing in the past: e.g. there was said to be a submerged village in the Lac de Lourdes; Strabo and Justin talk of the draining of the 'Toulouse lakes' (Garrigou, 1871a,

219); and there is evidence in names and legends for the previous existence of water/lakes in various places, especially near Tarascon-sur-Ariège, one of the major concentrations of late prehistoric habitation (Garrigou, 1872a, 356), and in many of the high plateaux around the source of the Têt and the Aude (Moulis, 1936).

Armed with such knowledge, Garrigou explored a number of areas and found an apparent proliferation of lake- or marsh-sites (1871a; 1872b); they are particularly numerous in the Landes and the lowlands which stretch from Bayonne to Salies and beyond. Most of this area is now dried out, and the remains of wooden stakes and platforms were found in the peatbeds. Little detail was ever given, though Garrigou believed that the sites dated from the Neolithic to the Iron Age and onward. This has been confirmed to some extent by Fabre (1943) who stressed the great mixture of artefacts in these areas and drew close comparisons between the pottery and that from the Swiss lake villages. There is some evidence that these marsh settlements originated in the Palaeolithic (see Bahn, 1979).

The Luchon area is extremely rich in prehistoric monuments (Bahn, *op.cit.*) and also features several habitation sites nearby, most notably the Abri de Saint Mamet; this rock-shelter, formed in the postglacial period, produced a quantity of quartzite flakes, arrowheads, polished-stone axes and pots of neolithic, Beaker and bronze age types (de Chasteigner, 1874; Cartailhac, 1889, 148). Scholars agree that the Luchon basin is the former bed of a postglacial lake, c.9 by 10km, and Garrigou reaped his usual harvest of wooden stakes there (Sacaze, 1887). Numerous deeply-sunk stakes were found beneath Luchon itself in the 19th century (Astre, 1935, 310). Thus the rock-shelter was on the lake-shore at the time of its occupation.

Garrigou (1871b, 1222) claimed to have detected prehistoric lake-sites in Haute-Garonne and Ariège, and to have found stakes and planks at many points, including at upland lakes which are frozen in the winter (1871a, 219-20; 1872a, 357–9). He also claimed abundant evidence of lake-settlements in Aude and the eastern Pyrenees (1871b, 1222). It is known (Galy, 1966) that much of the eastern littoral used to be very marshy, and it was natural for Vidal to postulate (1922, 19) the existence of prehistoric shore- and lake-settlements here. Ile Corrège is vindication of these views, and is no doubt only the first of many such sites in the Pyrenees to be discovered. Waterlogged sites with good preservation of organic materials will be of immense importance to the study of the region's Neolithic.

Conclusion: Economic and Social Questions

It will have emerged from the foregoing that the Pyrenees have numerous and varied neolithic sites and monuments, but that little information is as yet available on the period. The systematic and painstaking excavations of recent years are beginning to remedy this position, but a great deal remains to be done.

Little importance should be attached to the distribution map which accompanies this chapter: it merely pinpoints some major sites. Even more detailed maps are of limited worth; much evidence of neolithic occupation is restricted to surface finds of sherds or polished-stone axes; not only are these very difficult to date, but their very location may mislead the archaeologist: for example, it is known that Languedoc shepherds used to put prehistoric stone axes in a bag around the neck of the leading ram to protect the flock (Sire, 1938, 80) or carried them themselves as amulets (Vidal, 1922, 15–17). Basque shepherds had similar customs.

Despite these problems, however, some points can be made about site-distribution in the Pyrenees; first, as has been mentioned, there are very close links between megalithic monuments and pastoralism: the links are particularly clear between megaliths and known pastoral tracks; monuments are strung out along the tracks, cluster at crossroads and abound in the pastures to which they lead. This is, in fact, the norm in upland areas of southern France and elsewhere. In the eastern Pyrenees, for example, the monuments and tracks follow lines north-south, on axes where the distance between winter and summer pastures is shortest (Galy, 1966). The upland monuments are noticeably smaller and simpler than those of the lowland, and their lack of grave-goods reflects the occupants' status as poor, mobile pastoralists with few material possessions. I have argued (1979) that in many cases the upland dolmens may have been built originally as permanent shelters for shepherds in areas where there were no suitable caves, and became tombs later when someone died who was associated with or in proximity to them. Thus the very frequent orientation of their entrances to the east may reflect not simply a sun-worship but also a desire to face away from the prevailing wet, westerly winds and to catch the first rays of the sun.

Visits by pastoralists to the high uplands were necessarily seasonal, and although it is not possible to prove that their movements were transhumant (i.e. undertaken by a few people, leaving the rest of the group in a home-base elsewhere) rather than nomadic (i.e. undertaken by the whole group) (see Bahn, 1979), it seems probable that by the Neolithic, and certainly by the Chalcolithic, transhumance was the norm: e.g. Roubet (1979) has proved the existence of seasonal, altitudinal transhumance in the Neolithic of eastern Algeria. In the Pyrenees, flocks were undoubtedly taken to the high pastures in the summer: Méroc (1953, 50) pointed out evidence for neolithic transhumance in the Caougno (1700m) near Las-Morts, and the Grotte de Riusec (Ariège) (1230m). The toolkit in these sites is light and portable, mostly of bone; shepherds left little trace of their presence. A polished-stone axe was found at the Port d'Orle, Ariège (2363m), though my earlier *caveat* about such finds applies here. Moreover, some dolmens in the western Pyrenees are the highest (1600–1650m) in France (Méroc, 1969).

However, despite the use of high pastures, traces of habitation are scarce. It will be recalled that some caves seem to contain very little occupation debris other than large storage vessels or pots of the big-bellied type commonly associated with dairying activities. According to 19th-century travellers,

Pyrenean shepherds made a light wattling of willow boughs, thatched with straw, and carried this about with them for shade and shelter, resorting to caves only occasionally or in adverse weather.

The neolithic sites and artefacts of the Pyrenees do not point clearly to any form of hierarchy: unfortunately the evidence from the monuments is either non-existent, poor or confused due to early excavation. Major collective or 'cumulative' monuments like Pouey-Mayou or La Halliade *may* represent important personages or groups, but one cannot be more precise. Similarly, the 'royal tomb' of Saint-Michel-du-Touch is not as unique as was first thought, and, as we have seen, is open to other interpretations. Collective work seems to become well established in the Chasséen, and spreads in the Late Neolithic.

Other trends can be discerned during the course of the period. The Early Neolithic seems to be characterised by small cave-sites and Cardial impressed pottery, but it has been shown that major open-sites, and sites with different types of pottery also exist. The Chasséen certainly sees an expansion of occupation in the Garonne and Aude lowlands, based on a successful mixed-farming economy with a rise in importance of the modern domestic animals. However, reasons have been given for being wary of using the size of sites like Saint-Michel-du-Touch as evidence for population increase and thus for pressure on resources. Sites of this type grew over many centuries, and we simply do not yet understand what they are. It is therefore too early to produce hypotheses concerning their development and decline; but, as noted earlier, recent excavations are beginning to cast light on these problems.

The Cardial and Chasséen phases, as has been stressed, are blanket-terms for widely-differing sites and artefacts, and this diversity persists and perhaps even increases in the 3rd millennium bc. Major developments of the Late Neolithic include the spread of collective burial, and the rise of megalithism. Attempts are being made to link this trend towards cultural fragmentation in the French Neolithic with an increase in 'local within-group dependence as strains and pressures on the environments increased' (Hodder, 1979, 451), but such a view is rather premature, at least as far as the Pyrenees are concerned; evidence for population increase, let alone economic stress, is extremely sparse; and to view megalithic tombs merely as symbolic of local competing groups, and thus of economic stress, is simply not possible in the Pyrenees – their locations tend to deny this theory, as does their complementarity to burial caves and their growth, in the east, from small cists! Far more information of the type sought by Phillips *et al.* (1977), concerning the raw materials used in each phase and the type/extent of exchange, is required before these social and economic problems are clarified.

The Early Neolithic shows very strong continuity from the local Mesolithic, and evolved *in situ,* with 'neolithic' artefacts and species appearing at different times rather than abruptly or all at once. Conversely, the 'mesolithic' species and artefacts persisted for millennia, a reflection of the successful economic adaptations of the postglacial Pyrenean communities. This weakens

RADIOCARBON DATES

Mouligna (Pyrénées-Atlantiques)	3810±150bc	Ly-882	Peat/charcoal	Settlement	Asturien: top of layer	Chauchat, 1974
	3600±150bc	Ly-883	Peat/charcoal		Asturien: base of layer	Chauchat, 1974
Poeymaü (Pyrénées-Atlantiques)	3880±330bc	Ly-1840	Charcoal	Rock-shelter	bca: Neolithic	Rigaud, 1980
	3220±330bc	Ly-1842	Charcoal		gca: Neolithic	Rigaud, 1980
	2730±300bc	Ly-1841	Charcoal		alsn: Neolithic	Rigaud, 1980
	2020±270bc	Ly-1383	Charcoal		als2: Chalcolithic	Rigaud, 1980
Grotte-du-Castillet (Hautes-Pyrénées)	2430±140bc	Ly-1903	Bone	Burial cave		Omnès, 1981
Réseau Clastres, Niaux (Ariège)	3700±200bc	Gif-1938	Charcoal	Cave	Floor of gallery	Delibrias *et al.*, 1976
	2640±280bc	Ly-621	Charcoal		Gallery	Delibrias *et al.*, 1976
Dourgne (Aude)	3600±80bc	MC-1105	Charcoal	Rock-shelter	Layer 6: Early Neolithic	Delibrias *et al.*, 1982
	3150±00bc	MC-1103	Charcoal		Layer 6: Early Neolithic	Delibrias *et al.*, 1982
	2910±75bc	MC-1100	Charcoal		Layer 5: Early Neolithic	Delibrias *et al.*, 1982
Ile Corrège (Aude)	4850±90bc	MC-788	Wood	Settlement	Dredgings: Cardial	Guilaine, 1975
Montbolo (Pyrénées-Orientales)	4500±170bc	Gif-1709	Charcoal	Cave	Montbolo group	Guilaine, *et al.*, 1974
	2170±90bc	MC-592	Charcoal		Burial deposit	Guilaine, *et al.*, 1974
	2150±140bc	Gif-1710	Charcoal		Burial deposit	Guilaine, *et al.*, 1974
Can Pey (Pyrénées-Orientales)	2470±120bc	Gif-3282	Bone	Cave	N2: burial deposit	Guilaine, 1980b
	2110±200bc	Gif-4045	Charcoal		N3F3: burial deposit	Guilaine, 1980b
Grotte-des-Cazals (Aude)	2125±40bc	GrN-8077		Cave	Verazien	Guilaine, 1980b
Abri Jean Cros (Aude)	5210±130bc	Gif-3576	*Helix* shell	Rock-shelter	Layer 2a/b/c: Early Neolithic	Guilaine, 1979
	4650±130bc	Gif-3575	Charcoal		Layer 2b/c: Early Neolithic	Guilaine, 1979
	4590±300bc	Gif-218	Charcoal		Layer 2: Early Neolithic	Guilaine, 1979
	4450±300bc	Gif-218	Charcoal		Layer 2: Early Neolithic	Guilaine, 1979
Grotte Gazel (Aude)	4900±90bc	GrN-6702	Charcoal	Cave	Porch, C4: Cardial	Guilaine, 1974
	4860±130bc		Charcoal		Cardial	Guilaine, 1974
	4830±200bc	Kn.s.m.	Charcoal		Salle centrale N., F4: Cardial	Guilaine, 1974
	4590±200bc	Kn.s.m.	Charcoal		s.c.N., F1: 'Epicardial'	Guilaine, 1974
	4355±55bc	GrN-6707	Charcoal		s.c.S., 2f: 'Epicardial'	Guilaine, 1974
	4145±65bc	GrN-6706	Charcoal		s.c.S., 2d: 'Epicardial'	Guilaine, 1974

	3400±100bc	MC-497	Charcoal		Layer 10: Chasséen classique	Delibrias *et al.*, 1976
	2850±150bc	MC-496	Charcoal		Layer 8: Chasséen évolué	Delibrias *et al.*, 1976
	2910±90bc	MC-495	Charcoal		Layer 7: Chasséen évolué	Delibrias *et al.*, 1976
	2620±90bc	MC-494	Charcoal		Layer 6: Late Neolithic	Delibrias *et al.*, 1976
	2540±80bc	MC-493	Charcoal		Layer 5: Late Neolithic	Delibrias *et al.*, 1976
	2580±90bc	MC-569	Charcoal		Layer 4: Late Neo: Véraz. facies	Delibrias *et al.*, 1976
	2250±90bc	MC-491	Charcoal		Layer 3: Late Neo: Véraz. facies	Delibrias *et al.*, 1976
	2240±90bc	MC-567	Charcoal		Layer 2b inf.: Beaker	Delibrias *et al.*, 1976
	2210±90bc	MC-568	Charcoal		Layer 2b inf.: Beaker	Delibrias *et al.*, 1976
Villeneuve-Tolosane (Haute-Garonne)	3350±100bc	MC-948	Charcoal	Settlement	Chasséen: structure VT 215	Simonnet, 1980a
	3250±80bc	Gif-4848	Charcoal		Structure 9	Delibrias *et al.*, 1982
	3130±80bc	Gif-4849	Charcoal		Structure 30	Delibrias *et al.*, 1982
	2830±80bc	Gif-4850	Charcoal		Structure 113	Delibrias *et al.*, 1982
Saint-Michel-du-Touch (Hte-Garonne)	4100±150bc	MC-2090	Charcoal	Settlement	Chasséen: palisade A62 P	Méroc and Simonnet, 1979
	3650±90bc	MC-847	Charcoal		Chasséen: grande fosse A150	Méroc and Simonnet, 1979
	3570±100bc	MC-2092	Charcoal		Chasséen: structure A96 C	Méroc and Simonnet, 1979
	3510±90bc	MC-843	Charcoal		Chasséen: grande fosse A18	Méroc and Simonnet, 1979
	3490±90bc	MC-848	Charcoal		Chasséen: palisade A100 P	Méroc and Simonnet, 1979
	3490±130bc	MC-2089	Charcoal		Chasséen: funerary mon. A185	Méroc and Simonnet, 1979
	3430±200bc	MC-109	Charcoal		Chasséen: structure A61 A	Méroc and Simonnet, 1979
	3400±90bc	MC-844	Charcoal		Chasséen: grande fosse A21	Méroc and Simonnet, 1979
	3380±100bc	MC-2091	Charcoal		Chasséen: structure A96 A	Méroc and Simonnet, 1979
	3320±140bc	MC-2216	Charcoal		Chasséen: structure A168 H	Méroc and Simonnet, 1979
	3310±200bc	MC-104	Charcoal		Chasséen: structure A34	Méroc and Simonnet, 1979
	3300±150bc	MC-2215	Charcoal		Chasséen: structure A122	Méroc and Simonnet, 1979
	3240±90bc	MC-845	Charcoal		Chasséen: grande fosse A168	Méroc and Simonnet, 1979
	3180±100bc	MC-846	Charcoal		Chasséen: structure A58 A	Méroc and Simonnet, 1979
	3180±100bc	MC-2217	Charcoal		Chasséen: structure A223	Méroc and Simonnet, 1979
	2950±190bc	MC-105	Charcoal		Chasséen: structure A34	Méroc and Simonnet, 1979
	2950±130bc	MC-106	Charcoal		Chasséen: structure A38	Méroc and Simonnet, 1979
	2630±120bc	MC-103	Charcoal		Chasséen: structure A18 W	Méroc and Simonnet, 1979
	2550±200bc	MC-102	Charcoal		Chasséen: cavity crossing a structure	Méroc and Simonnet, 1979

the traditional emphasis on the Neolithic as a new era. Indeed, the 'Neolithic Revolution' could be said to occur in the Bronze Age in much of the region. Moreover, it is pastoralism which characterised and dominated the Pyrenees in both prehistoric and historic times, by nature of the terrain. Only the eastern sites and those around Toulouse have any direct evidence of neolithic agriculture. Poor preservation of evidence may have led to a minimal view of Pyrenean neolithic agriculture in this chapter; but low quality and insufficient quantity of cereal-growing persisted in the region throughout history and still exist; so that it would be a surprise if the prehistoric evidence showed a different picture. The French Pyrenees are an archetypal pastoral stronghold, and a number of the recently excavated sites at the eastern extremity of the chain are starting to reveal how and when modern pastoral practices arose in the area.

The Neolithic of West-Central France

CHRIS SCARRE

The land ○ history of research ○ MATERIAL CULTURE ○ Early Neolithic ○ Impressed ware ○ *Roucadourien* ○ Middle Neolithic ○ chambered tombs ○ pottery ○ vases supports ○ Late Neolithic ○ the Coastal zone ○ *Matignons* ○ *Peu-Richardien* ○ fortified settlements ○ burial deposits ○ other settlement sites ○ the Inland zone ○ Vienne-Charente ○ Dordogne and Quercy ○ Chalcolithic ○ *Artenacien* ○ Beaker material ○ beginnings of metallurgy ○ late neolithic and chalcolithic trade ○ LATE NEOLITHIC FORTIFIED SITES ○ the Royan area ○ the Saintes area ○ the Cognac area ○ neolithic settlement in West-Central France.

WEST-CENTRAL FRANCE (Fig. 8.1) borders the Atlantic Ocean, and is bounded by the Loire to the north, the Gironde and the Dordogne to the south, and the edge of the Massif Central to the east. Its core is a saucer-shaped depression of sedimentary rocks (limestones and chalks) with relatively gentle relief and fertile soils. The coastline is punctuated by a series of marshlands, some of considerable extent (e.g. the Marais poitevin: 91000ha). The depression is crossed by rivers, the most important being the Charente, whose basin dominates its southern half. The limestone and chalk fall into two zones. The first is nearer the coast, where the soils are thin and dry and settlements tend to cluster along the edges of the wetter valleys and marshlands. Further inland the limestone soils have more clay and are more water-retentive, and the prehistoric settlement of this zone was less closely tied to the valleys.

To the north and east of the depression are the crystalline massifs of Armorica and the Massif Central. These are less fertile than the limestone and chalk areas, and their neolithic occupation appears different in character, with few major settlement sites. Southwards, the limestones and chalks merge gradually with the sands which are the outliers of the 'Landes' of Aquitaine. To the south-east are the limestone landscapes of the Dordogne and Quercy, which we include in this account, though properly speaking they lie outside the limits of west-central France.

HISTORY OF RESEARCH. The neolithic material of this part of France was first recognised and discussed in the middle decades of the 19th century.

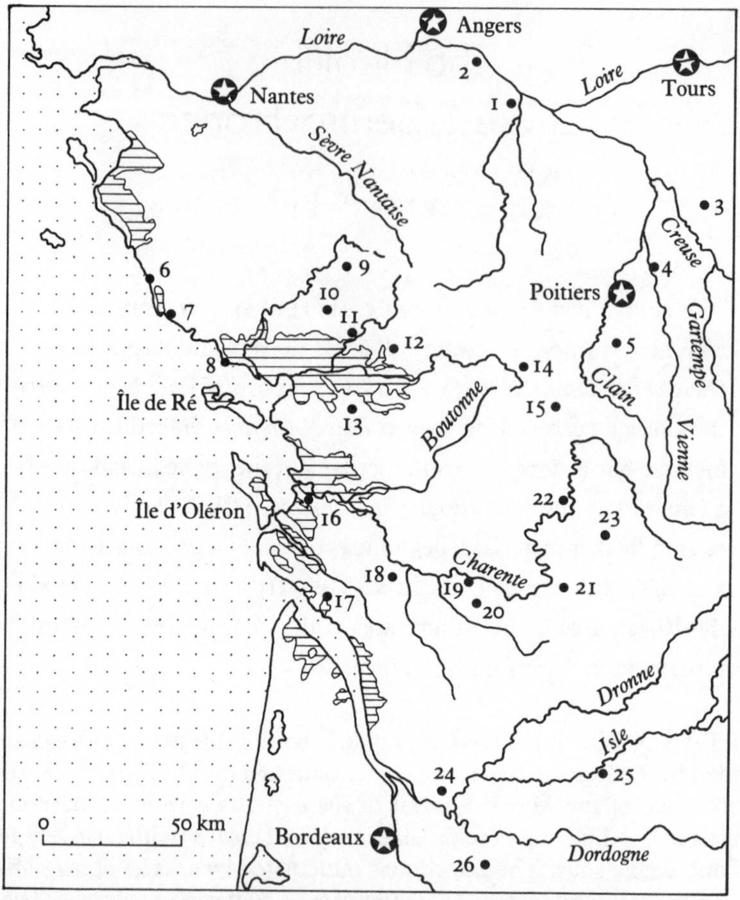

FIGURE 8.1. West-central France, showing the locations of some of the sites mentioned in the text. Major towns and rivers are marked. Coastal marshlands shaded.
1 Bagneux (Maine-et-Loire); 2 La Bajoulière, Saint Rémy-la-Varenne (Maine-et-Loire); 3 Le Grand Pressigny (Indre-et-Loire); 4 Bellefonds (Vienne); 5 Camp Allaric, Aslonnes (Vienne); 6 Brétignolles-sur-Mer (Vendée); 7 Les Sables-d'Olonne (Vendée); 8 La Tranche-sur-Mer (Vendée); 9 La Ciste des Cous, Bazoges-en-Pareds (Vendée); 10 La Pierre-Folle, Thiré (Vendée); 11 Les Châtelliers-du-Vieil-Auzay (Vendée); 12 Champ Durand, Nieul-sur-l'Autize (Vendée); 13 Les Moindreaux, Saint Jean-de-Liversay (Charente-Maritime); 14 Bougon (Deux-Sèvres); 15 Le Montiou, Sainte-Soline (Deux-Sèvres); 16 La Sauzaie, Soubise (Charente-Maritime); 17 Chez-Reine, Semussac (Charente-Maritime); 18 Peu-Richard, Thénac (Charente-Maritime); 19 Soubérac, Gensac-la-Pallue (Charente); 20 Les Matignons, Juillac-le-Coq (Charente); 21 Recoux, Soyaux (Charente); 22 Chenon (Charente); 23 Artenac, Saint-Mary (Charente); 24 Roanne, Villegouge (Gironde); 25 La Fontaine de la Demoiselle, Saint Léon-sur-l'Isle (Dordogne); 26 Roquefort, Lugasson (Gironde).

Burial mounds in Vienne, Deux-Sèvres and Charente attracted the curiosity of local antiquarians and several were the subject of cursory investigation, often without adequate recording or publication. Among the earliest were the excavations carried out by Arnauld, Baugier and Sauzé at the Bougon cemetery (Deux-Sèvres; m.r.14) in the 1840s (Sauzé, 1845). The megalithic tombs of Vienne suffered similarly (e.g. Brouillet, 1862; Gennes *et al.*, 1863). Towards the end of the century, however, attention was diverted by the discovery of the fortified settlement of Peu-Richard (Charente-Maritime; m.r.18) with its flamboyantly decorated pottery and impressive circuits of defences (Eschasseriaux, 1882). Several other sites of this kind were discovered in the Saintes area in the years leading up to the outbreak of the First World War.

The inter-war years were by comparison relatively uneventful. The 1950s, however, saw a revival of interest in the Neolithic of the region, particularly as a result of Burnez' work in the Cognac area. His field survey led to the discovery of a dozen or so new Peu-Richardien sites, several of which he excavated, either alone or in collaboration. The results of this research were incorporated in a valuable synthesis which presented for the first time all the neolithic and chalcolithic material from the region, arranged according to a chronological scheme (text completed 1962; published as Burnez, 1976). This work has been the point of departure for all subsequent research on the Neolithic of west-central France.

Several important advances have been made since the 1950s. First, parts of the region which received relatively little attention from Burnez have been the subject of more intensive research, notably the Vendée (Joussaume, 1981), whose place in the prehistory of west-central France can now be more clearly discerned. One result of this has been the discovery of a group of early neolithic Impressed Ware sites on the Vendéen coast with 5th millennium radiocarbon dates. A second advance has come with the introduction of aerial survey and photography which, though known and used to a limited extent by Burnez in the 1950s, has really proved its value only in the last decade. A considerable number of late neolithic fortified sites has been discovered in this way, and their overall distribution has been extended so that it now takes in the northern side of the Marais poitevin (Fig.8.8; Dassié, 1978; Marsac and Scarre, 1979). Third, the last decade has seen the organisation of more rigorous, longer term and larger scale excavation projects. Among the most notable are the excavations by Mohen at Chez-Reine (Semussac; m.r.17) in Charente-Maritime (1965–71) and, together with the writer, at Bougon in Deux-Sèvres (begun in 1972 and continuing) and by Joussaume at Champ Durand in the Vendée (m.r.12) (begun in 1975 and continuing). Interdisciplinary work involving the examination of soils and pollen has been or is to be carried out in connection with these excavations and should extend the range of information and allow new types of questions to be investigated. The Neolithic of Quercy has become known principally through work carried out since 1945 (e.g. Niederlender *et al.*, 1966; Galan, 1967; Clottes, 1977a).

Although rich overall, the known neolithic material of west-central

France is defective in various respects. A major shortcoming is the scarcity of reliable stratigraphies. The only long stratigraphic sequence is at the settlement of Les Châtelliers-du-Vieil-Auzay (Vendée; m.r.11), where middle and late neolithic and chalcolithic levels are superimposed. This has been investigated only recently (Birocheau and Large, 1982). Earlier writers such as Riquet (1953) and Burnez (1976) had to rely largely on parallels with material from other regions when devising a culture sequence and chronology, though an increasing number of radiocarbon dates has now allowed these to be placed on a firmer footing.

A second shortcoming is the uneven distribution of the material in time and space. A broad band of territory from the southern flank of the Armorican Massif round to the Dordogne, taking in Vienne and the eastern part of the Charente basin, is virtually devoid of neolithic settlement sites. In contrast, the part of the region nearer the coast is rich in settlement sites of the late neolithic period but has almost no contemporary burial sites. These variations in the completeness of the evidence restrict the reliability of the inferences which may be drawn. It is sometimes unclear, for instance, whether the absence of settlement evidence of a certain period is due to a lack of adequate fieldwork or whether it indicates that the pattern at that period was one of small and dispersed settlements which have left only insubstantial traces. The early and middle neolithic settlement evidence is particularly difficult to interpret and it is only in the late neolithic and chalcolithic periods that the material available becomes of a quality to support much social or economic interpretation.

As for most of France, the neolithic material of this region has traditionally been interpreted in terms of a series of cultures. Much effort has gone into the definition of these, and they form the essential spatial and chronological units for any analysis. As a vehicle for interpretation, however, the culture framework leaves much to be desired. Most of them are defined principally on the basis of pottery, and some may be little more than fine-ware traditions. In this account, therefore, an attempt has been made to interpret the neolithic record in terms rather of changing settlement patterns and social development.

Material Culture

The Early Neolithic (5th millennium bc)

Recent fieldwork has led to the discovery of Impressed Ware, broadly comparable with that from Mediterranean France, at several sites on the coast of west-central France. This may be added to the similar material which was excavated from the Bellefonds cave, inland, some years ago (Fig.8.2; m.r.4). One of the Impressed Ware sherds from Longeville (Vendée) and several of those from the Bellefonds cave (Vienne) bear the characteristic rocker pattern motif, though this is not executed with the edge of a *Cardium* shell as is normal in the Impressed Ware of Mediterranean France (Joussaume *et al.*, 1979; Patte, 1971). The impressions on a sherd from Les Gouillauds (Charente-Maritime) are, however, thought to have been made with a *Cardium* shell (Pautreau and Robert, 1980); if so, this is the only true Cardial decoration yet

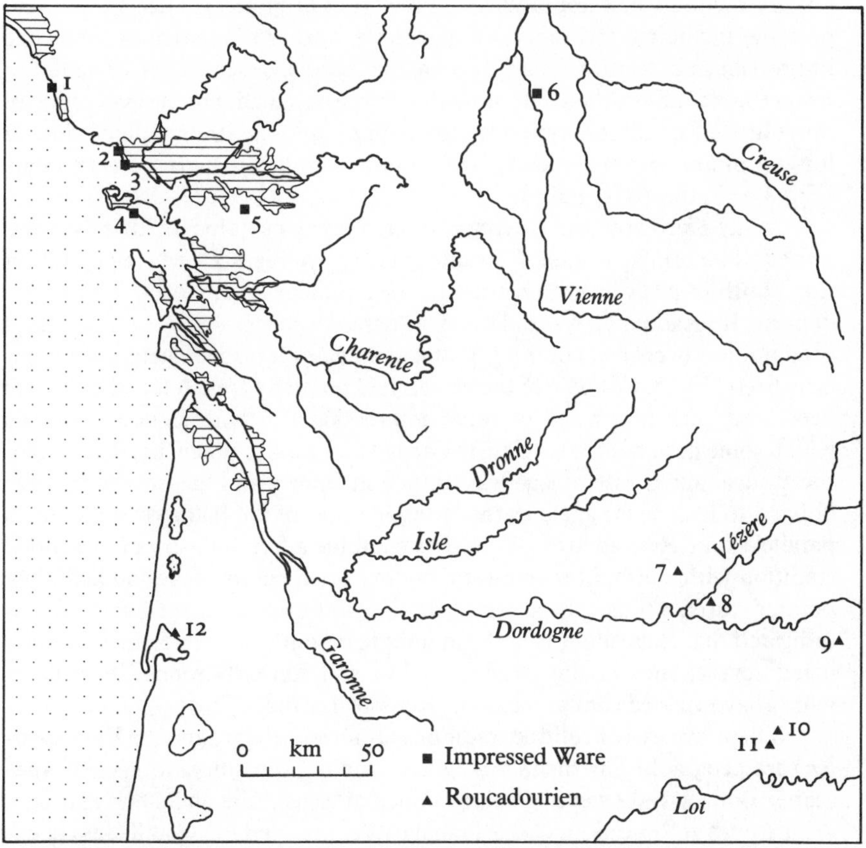

FIGURE 8.2. The two early neolithic traditions of western France:
(a) *Impressed Ware:* 1 Brétignolles-sur-Mer (Vendée); 2 Longeville-Plage (Vendée); 3 La Tranche-sur-Mer (Vendée); 4 Les Gouillauds, Ile de Ré (Charente-Maritime); 5 Benon (Charente-Maritime); 6 Bellefonds cave (Vienne).
(b) *Roucadourien:* 7 Rouffignac (Dordogne); 8 Abri Pageyral, Les Eyzies (Dordogne); 9 Roucadour, Thémines (Lot); 10 La Borie del Rey, Blanquefort-sur-Briolance (Lot-et-Garonne); 11 Le Martinet, Sauveterre-la-Lémance (Lot-et-Garonne); 12 Le Bétey, Andernos (Gironde). (After Joussaume *et al.*, 1979; Roussot-Larroque, 1977.)

known from west-central France, and further evidence for contact with the Mediterranean world at this time. The attribution of this material to the Early Neolithic is supported by a series of 5th millennium bc radiocarbon dates.

Only one site, the Bellefonds cave in the valley of the River Vienne, has been properly excavated. The deposits were divided into three units, the uppermost being a chalcolithic funerary deposit which need not concern us here. All the layers below this contained microliths and were of considerably earlier date. They were divided by the excavator into two, at the point where pottery made its first appearance. Three types of impressed decoration were present, including decoration by a roulette wheel in imitation of shell-edge impressions (a feature found also in the Cardial assemblages of southern France). No radiocarbon determinations were obtained, but the association of microliths of mesolithic type with the pottery, and the stratigraphic evidence for continuity with the underlying aceramic mesolithic, suggest an early date (Fig.8.3; Patte, 1971, 146–74).

In the Dordogne and Quercy a different early neolithic tradition is represented. The principal site is Roucadour (Lot; see Fig.8.2), where deposits at the mouth of a cave were excavated (Niederlender *et al.*, 1966). The lowest deposit, Roucadour C, was radiocarbon-dated to 3980bc and yielded sherds of predominantly coarse, coil-built pottery, much of it inadequately and irregularly fired (Fig.8.3). Some of the vessels had pointed bases. A few sherds were decorated with finger-nail or other impressions, or with sinuous incisions which some have wished to relate to Cardial decoration. When first discovered, the Roucadour C assemblage was unique in France and the excavators were obliged to look as far afield as the Ertebølle sites of the Baltic coasts to find a parallel. Like Roucadour C these sites combine a flint industry of mesolithic tradition with coil-built coarse-ware pottery often poorly made and including pointed-based vessels. In a recent article, however, Roussot-Larroque has indicated that Roucadour is far from unique in south-western France, and has listed several sites in the Dordogne, Lot and Lot-et-Garonne *départements* which have yielded similar material (Roussot-Larroque, 1977).

These two early neolithic traditions (Impressed Ware and the *Roucadourien*) are geographically distinct (Fig.8.2) and occupy different types of landscape. Both have however given evidence of agriculture and stock-rearing – grindstones at Roucadour C, La Tranche (Vendée) and Les Gouillauds; bones of domestic cattle and sheep at Rouffignac level 2 (Dordogne) and, accompanied by domestic pig, at La Tranche; cereal grains at Roucadour C. In both cases it is the pottery and domesticates that are the principal new elements; the flintwork is developed from earlier mesolithic types and some of the sites had long been in occupation before the new features appeared. The gradual adoption of neolithic traits by interlinked mesolithic communities is the most likely explanation for the origin of both these early neolithic groups.

Impressed Ware is the characteristic early neolithic pottery of Mediterranean France, where the earliest is dated to the late 7th millennium or early 6th millennium bc, a millennium and a half before the earliest currently-available dates for such material from west-central France. The earliest Impressed Ware sites in southern France are on the coast, and it is probable that the pottery and early domesticates were spread around the shores of the west Mediterranean by sea traffic. At a somewhat later date the use of Impressed Ware spread to sites further inland, and it is possible that it reached west-central France as a result of this expansion inland. Joussaume has noted (1981) that there are strong similarities between the forms of the mesolithic arrowheads in use in southern and in west-central France, which suggest contact between these regions in the

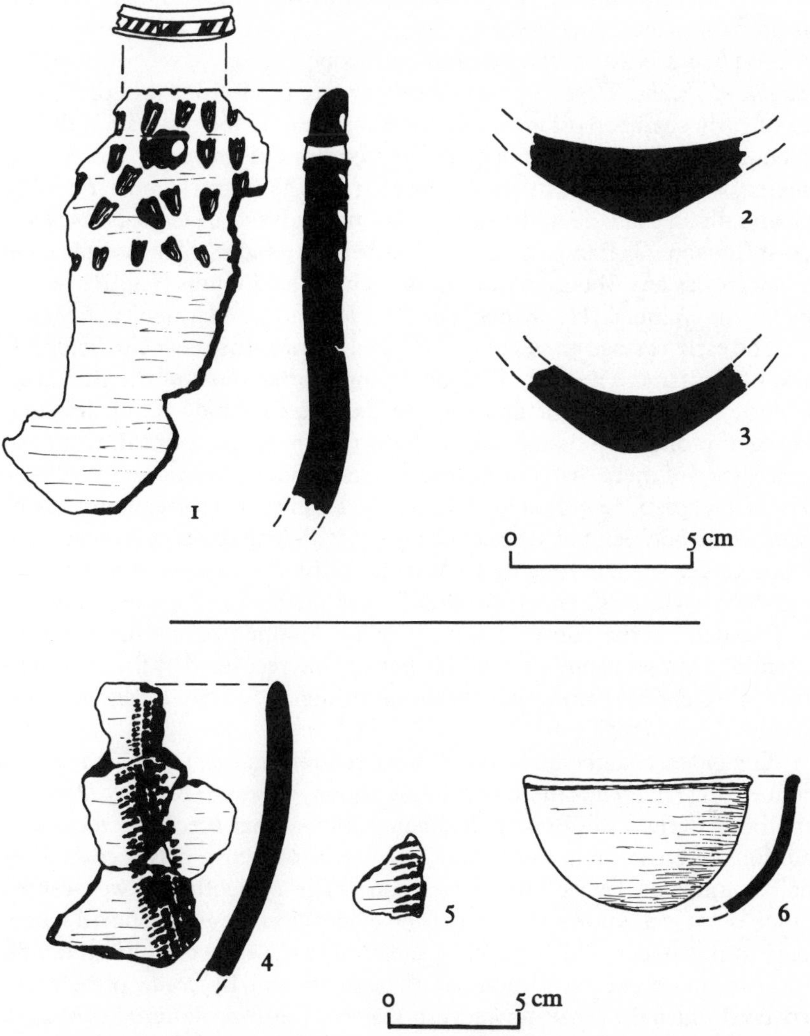

FIGURE 8.3. Early neolithic pottery from western France.
1-3 Pottery from Roucadour (Lot), showing (1) the coil construction of one of the vessels and (2 and 3) the pointed bases which are characteristic of this group. 4-6 Impressed Ware from the Bellefonds cave (Vienne). (1-3 after Niederlender *et al.*, 1966; 4-6 after Patte, 1971.)

preneolithic period, and the spread of the Impressed Ware may therefore represent merely the 'ceramicisation' of a network of exchange or cultural contract which was already in existence. The case is not clear-cut, however, since Joussaume *et al.* (1979) see the closest typological parallels for the Impressed Ware of west-central France in that of Portugal (whence it may have spread northwards along the western seaways) rather than in southern

France. The Roucadourien has no obvious ancestry in any adjacent area and was probably a local development.

THE MIDDLE NEOLITHIC (c.4000–c.2800bc)

Chambered Tombs. West-central France may be considered part of the Breton area of early chambered tombs. Radiocarbon dates in the first half of the 4th millennium bc have been obtained for two passage graves in the Bougon cemetery (Deux-Sèvres; m.r.14) (chamber E1: 3850bc; chamber F0: 3880 bc), and for an example of the supposedly more advanced *dolmen angoumoisin* type at Chenon (Charente; m.r.22) (chamber B1: 3590bc). The Bougon dates are as early as any obtained from Breton chambered tombs (e.g. Barnenez: 3800bc; Ile Guinnoc III: 3850bc (Giot, L'Helgouach and Monnier, 1979)).

The early passage graves of west-central France are similar also in form to those of Brittany. The early Bougon examples, like those of the Breton Ile Guennoc III and most of those in the Barnenez mound, are of dry-stone construction and have chambers of roughly oval or circular plan. In both areas the presence of more than one chamber side by side in the same mound is an early characteristic (e.g. Bougon E: Fig.8.4, 1). There is a particularly striking resemblance between the series of chambers with long passages arranged side by side under a single roughly rectangular cairn at Le Montiou in southern Deux-Sèvres (m.r.15) and such early Breton mounds as Barnenez (Fig.9.3, 2). The date of the construction of the Le Montiou tombs has not been determined but some middle neolithic pottery was recovered by the excavators (Fig.8.5, 3 and 4), alongside the usual evidence for late neolithic re-use (Germond *et al.*, 1978).

The oldest chambered tombs of west-central France are situated, as one might expect, in the northern part of the region, closest to Brittany. A recent hypothesis derives the Breton chambered tombs from preceding mesolithic traditions of burial, represented notably by the collective graves covered by small mounds at Teviec (Renfrew, 1976). The Mesolithic of west-central France is not well known and there is no evidence of mesolithic burial monuments in this region which could be ancestral to the early chambered tombs. However, in recent excavations at Bougon mound B, crude pottery was recovered which the excavator suggests may be of early neolithic date (Mohen, unpublished interim report (1980)), and a similar date has been suggested for simple burial cists with collective inhumations at Saint-Martin-la-Rivière (Vienne) (Patte, 1971, 234–9; early neolithic date suggested by Pautreau and Robert, 1980, and Joussaume, 1982).

It is very difficult to date the construction of passage graves in west-central France since so many appear to have been re-used in the late neolithic and chalcolithic periods. Middle neolithic material which might be closer in time to the construction of many of the monuments is only occasionally encountered, and in most cases the burial deposit must be considered as providing no more than a *terminus ante quem* for the construction of the tomb. As well as passage graves, the region also has a substantial number of so-called *dolmens simples*. These consist of a passage-less chamber, normally of rectangular plan, covered

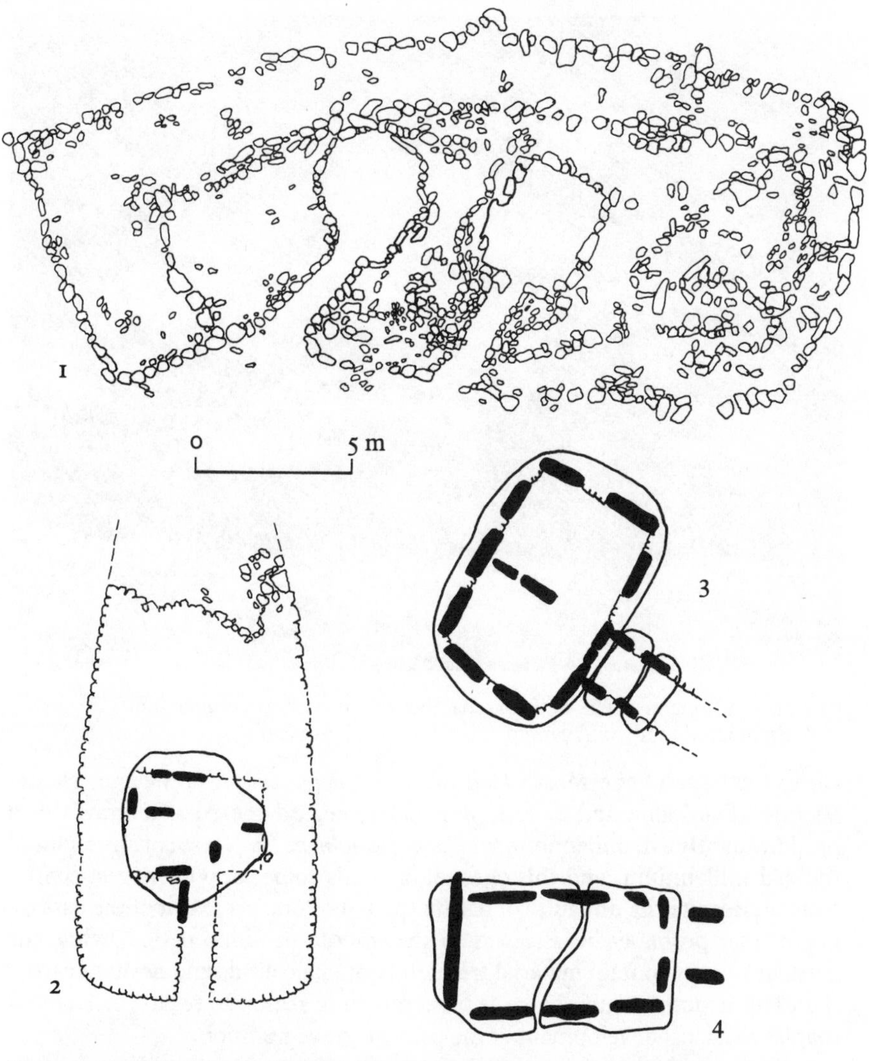

FIGURE 8.4. Chambered tombs of west-central France.
1 The early 4th millennium cairn of Bougon E (Deux-Sèvres), with chambers of 'Atlantic' type. 2 La Pierre-Levée, Nieul-sur-l'Autize (Vendée), a long mound with chamber of *dolmen angoumoisin* type. 3 The *dolmen angoumoisin* of Bougon A (Deux-Sèvres), perhaps the most impressive of this type. 4 The *dolmen angevin* of La Frébouchère at Le Bernard (Vendée), with elongated chamber and entrance porch at one end. (1 after Mohen, 1977; 2 after Joussaume, 1976b; 3, 4 after Burnez, 1976.)

by a small oval or circular mound. They have a more southerly distribution within France than the passage graves, and are well represented in the Mediterranean zone. In west-central France *dolmens simples* are found principally

PLATE 8.1. Bougon (Deux-Sèvres): chamber Fo, an early 4th millennium chambered tomb of 'Atlantic' type. (Photo: Chris Scarre.)

along the edge of the Massif Central in the *départements* of Vienne, Haute-Vienne, Dordogne and Lot. It is usual to regard the passage graves as a predominantly 4th millennium type and the *dolmens simples* as constructions of the 3rd millennium, and this chronology finds some support in west-central France, despite the difficulty of dating these monuments. Most of the passage graves can probably be assigned to the middle neolithic period, while the *dolmens simples* contain material frequently of chalcolithic and never of earlier than late neolithic date. There is no compelling reason to regard the *dolmens simples* as a local development of the passage grave tradition.

The principal types of passage grave found in west-central France are as follows (Burnez, 1976, 21–56, 69–87; Joussaume, 1981, 182-206):

(1) Passage graves of *Atlantic* type, consisting of a circular or polygonal chamber with entrance passage. They are usually of dry-stone construction with a corbel-vault, but occasional megalithic examples are known. The early 4th millennium dates from Bougon and the Breton sites are for chambers of Atlantic type (Fig.8.4, 1; Plate 8.1).

(2) The *dolmen angoumoisin* is of megalithic construction with a rect-angular chamber and an entrance passage, the latter often off-centre and leading into one of the long sides so as to give rise to 'p', 'q' and 'T' varieties (Fig.8.4, 2 and 3). As the name suggests, this type of monument is particularly well represented in the Angoumois (around Angoulême). A *dolmen angou-*

PLATE 8.2. The *dolmen angevin* of La Bajoulière at Saint Rémy-la-Varenne (Maine-et-Loire). (Photo: Chris Scarre.)

moisin at Chenon (Charente; m.r.22) has a mid-4th millennium bc radiocarbon date, showing that the earliest examples of this type may not be much later than the Atlantic passage graves.

(3) The *dolmen angevin* consists of an elongated rectangular chamber with the entrance and sometimes a trilithon porch at one end (Fig.8.4, 4). The best examples are in the Loire valley, to the north of west-central France proper, where the *dolmens angevins* of Bagneaux and La Bajoulière (Maine-et-Loire) are among the finest megalithic tombs of France (Plate 8.2; Gruet, 1967; Gruet and Passini, 1982). The careful tooling of the huge slabs of which they are constructed gives an impression of sophistication suggestive of a relatively late date in the tomb sequence, but there is as yet no firm evidence for this.

Pottery. The middle neolithic period in this part of France is defined principally on the basis of the pottery, most of which falls within the generalised family characterised by the undecorated carinated round-based bowl which is sometimes referred to as Chasséen. Material of this type has been found in contexts dated to the early 3rd millennium bc. An earlier phase with simpler vessel forms has been dated to the first half of the 4th millennium at Bougon and (mixed with early neolithic sherds) at Les Gouillauds (Mohen, 1977; Pautreau and Robert, 1980). The Chasséen tradition may have begun in this region around 3500bc. It is difficult to give a firm terminal date, since in inland parts of west-central France middle neolithic pottery seems to have developed without interruption to give rise to the late neolithic or chalcolithic *Artenacien* group at about 2300bc (see below). In more coastal areas the late neolithic Matignons and proto-Peu-Richardien groups succeed the middle

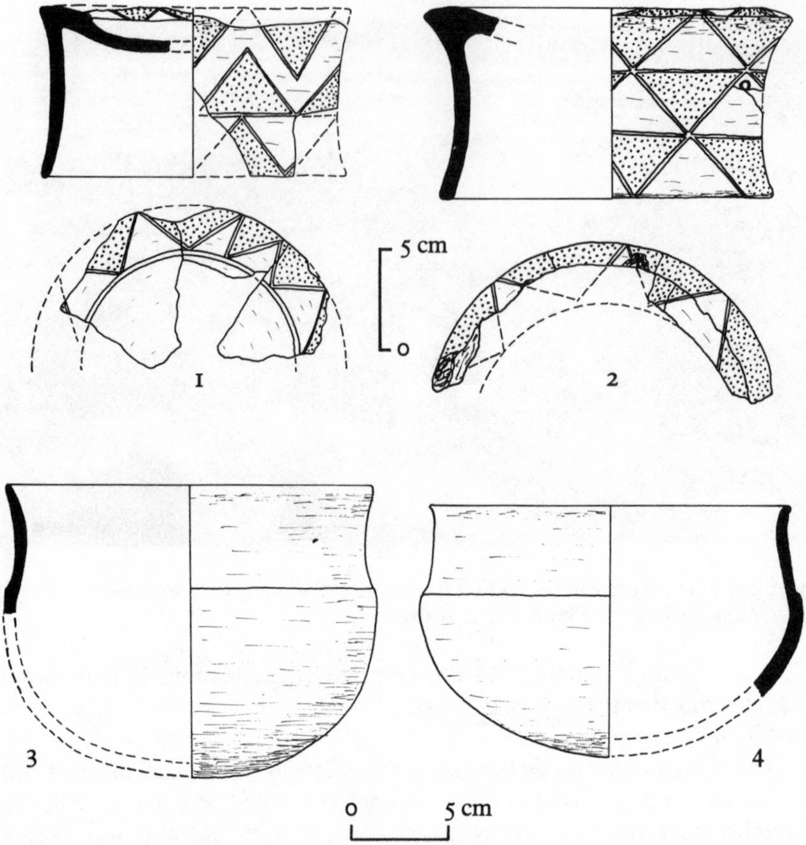

FIGURE 8.5. Middle neolithic *vases-supports* and carinated bowls. *Vases-supports* from (1) Bougon A (Deux-Sèvres) and (2) La Villedieu-de-Comblé (Deux-Sèvres); 3-4 Carinated bowls from the burial mound of Le Montiou at Sainte-Soline (Deux-Sèvres). (1, 2 after Pautreau and Gendron, 1981; 3, 4 after Germond *et al.*, 1978.)

neolithic traditions at about 2800bc.

Figure 8.5 illustrates some examples of middle neolithic pottery. The same range of types is found in all parts of west-central France, though recent work has enabled two separate styles to be distinguished in the northern part of the region (Cous and Chasséen: Joussaume, 1978), and one (the Groupe de Roquefort: Roussot-Larroque, 1976) to the south in the *département* of Gironde. These groups are distinguished from one another principally by the presence or absence of vases-supports (of which more below), and by small differences in the form of the round-based bowls. Further south, the Middle Neolithic of Quercy is part of a separate tradition with links via the Toulouse region to the Chasséen du Midi of southern France (Clottes and Costantini, 1976).

Most of the middle neolithic pottery found in west-central France has come from passage graves of the types discussed earlier. The discovery of material of this kind in association with a group of flat graves at the site of Les Châtelliers-du-Vieil-Auzy (m.r.11) (Joussaume, 1972) is unique. Very few settlement sites are known which can be dated to this period and this seriously hinders our understanding of the middle neolithic social and economic organisation of the region. Special mention should perhaps be made of the middle neolithic settlements of Roquefort (Gironde; m.r.26) and Les Châtelliers-du-Vieil-Auzay (Vendée), since they occupy good naturally defensible locations which were later fortified. There is however no evidence of middle neolithic defensive works at either of these sites. It is unlikely that the lack of substantial settlements is simply the result of inadequate fieldwork, since the intensity of research to which some parts of the region have been subjected would have been expected to lead to the discovery of such sites had they existed. The explanation may be that the settlement sites of the period were small in size and dispersed in distribution, perhaps hamlets or individual farmsteads rather than villages. Such settlements may have left only insubstantial traces which would have been further reduced by the destructive effects of later agricultural operations. Scatters of material which may represent the remains of small settlements have been found, and some can be shown to date from the middle neolithic period.

Discussion. Passage graves and pottery of middle neolithic type have been found throughout virtually the whole of west-central France. This marks a considerable increase in the scale and area of settlement over that represented by early neolithic finds. The soils of the central chalk and limestone basin which forms the heart of the region are very fertile, and it is reasonable to suppose that agriculture was well established there by the middle of the 4th millennium bc. Hence the widespread distribution of middle neolithic material may represent the agricultural colonisation of most of west-central France. In the light of this, the number of passage graves and the lack of substantial settlement sites which can be associated with them take on a new significance. In many parts of France such a situation seems to characterise a phase of colonisation or settlement expansion in which the monumentality of the tombs counterbalanced the insubstantiality of the settlements. A chambered tomb may have served in such circumstances as a group focus and a territorial marker. This may well have been the case during the middle neolithic period in west-central France as agricultural settlement spread inland along the river valleys. Though the settlement sites of the period are only poorly known, this hypothesis suggests that the passage graves should provide a rough indication of their location. In the drier coastal half of the region the distribution of the tombs follows the major river valleys. This distribution is relatively easy to understand, since the valleys provide the main areas of wetter land in this rather dry part of the region. Further east, around the upper valley of the Charente and in Deux-Sèvres, for instance, the passage graves are not so closely tied to the river valleys. The limestone soils of this area have a higher

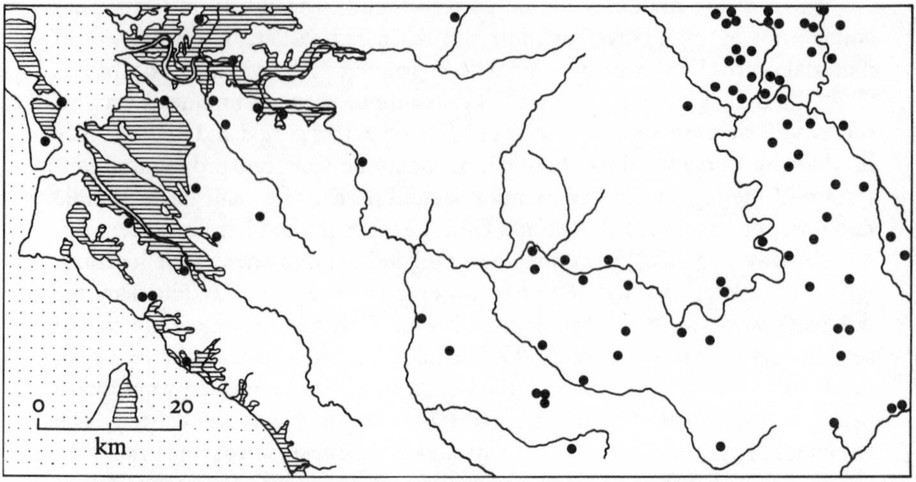

FIGURE 8.6. Distribution of chambered tombs in the Charente basin. The shaded areas represent the coastal marshlands. In the western and central parts of the basin the tombs lie predominantly along the edges of the coastal marshlands and the major valleys but in the east, where the soils are more moisture-retentive and the dryness of the landscape is a less severe constraint, their distribution is more even and they are commonly found on the interfluves.

clay content and are more water-retentive than those of the more western parts, and this seems to have allowed a more evenly spread occupation (Fig.8.6). The effect of the landscape on site distributions is the subject of the third and final parts of this chapter.

The middle neolithic material of Quercy is rather different from that of west-central France proper and has not been included in this discussion. In that region there are no chambered tombs datable to this period and very few burials in other contexts. Several settlement sites have however been investigated, notably La Perte du Cros (Galan, 1967) and Capdenac-le-Haut (Clottes, 1977b) (Lot), though none is of great size.

Vases-supports. As a footnote to this discussion of middle neolithic material something further should be said of the vases-supports which have played a prominent rôle in the identification of Chasséen-type assemblages in west-central France. These highly decorated objects are especially remarkable in that they are usually the only decorated item in an otherwise plain ceramic assemblage (Fig.8.5, 1 and 2). They have been variously interpreted as supports for round-based vessels and as ritual incense-burners; the latter hypothesis derives some strength from their highly-decorated nature and the fact that they are found predominantly in a ritual context in tombs. The case for associating vases-supports exclusively with the Middle Neolithic is not conclusive, however, and in west-central France they occur in several assemblages which seem rather to be of late neolithic or chalcolithic date. The characteristic vase-support decoration of incised dot-filled triangles and lozenges reappears towards the end of the 3rd millennium bc on Artenacien pottery (see Fig.8.9), and there are dates for vases-supports from the Vendéen coast of around the middle of the 3rd millennium, suggesting that they continued in use into the second half of the millennium. They may indeed have formed part of the earliest Artenacien assemblages (see below). Vases-supports cannot therefore be regarded as the sure mark of a middle neolithic assemblage.

THE LATE NEOLITHIC (c.2800–c.2300/2100bc)

The Late Neolithic of west-central France must be considered in two parts, since there are important differences between developments in the coastal and inland zones. The contrast is between major innovations and evidence of an emerging social hierarchy in coastal west-central France, and relative conservatism in the inland part of the region.

THE COASTAL ZONE. Two features of this area are particularly worthy of remark. First, fortified settlement sites, often with elaborate systems of ditches and ramparts, appear at the beginning of this period, making a sharp contrast with the dearth of middle neolithic settlement evidence. The second feature is the flamboyantly decorated Peu-Richardien pottery, which again contrasts with the middle neolithic period when the pottery was predominantly undecorated. Much of the known Peu-Richardien decorated ware has been found at the fortified sites (Table 8.1), and there is clearly a strong association between the two, though some of the fortified sites seem already to have been in existence before this type of pottery came into use.

Table 8.1. Occurrence of Peu-Richardien decorated ware at different types of site.

Burial monuments	14
Fortified sites	23
Other substantial settlements	13
Small and indeterminate sites	12
Total	62

Pottery. In pottery terms, however, the Late Neolithic of coastal west-central France begins not with the Peu-Richardien but with the *Matignons* style (Burnez, 1976, 127–49), named after one of the ditched enclosures at Les Matignons (m.r.20) in Charente where it was first recognised (Burnez and Case, 1966). The principal distinguishing marks are the decoration which consists of vertical and horizontal applied relief lines, and the basketry impressions on the flat bases of some vessels. The latter are presumably the result of the manner in which the vessels were made, the pot being placed on a mat to facilitate turning during manufacture. Curiously enough, such basketry impressions seem to be restricted in the Neolithic of this region to the Matignons pottery. Matignons ceramic assemblages are the first in west-central France to include coarse utility wares, principally large, flat-based vessels. Their appear-

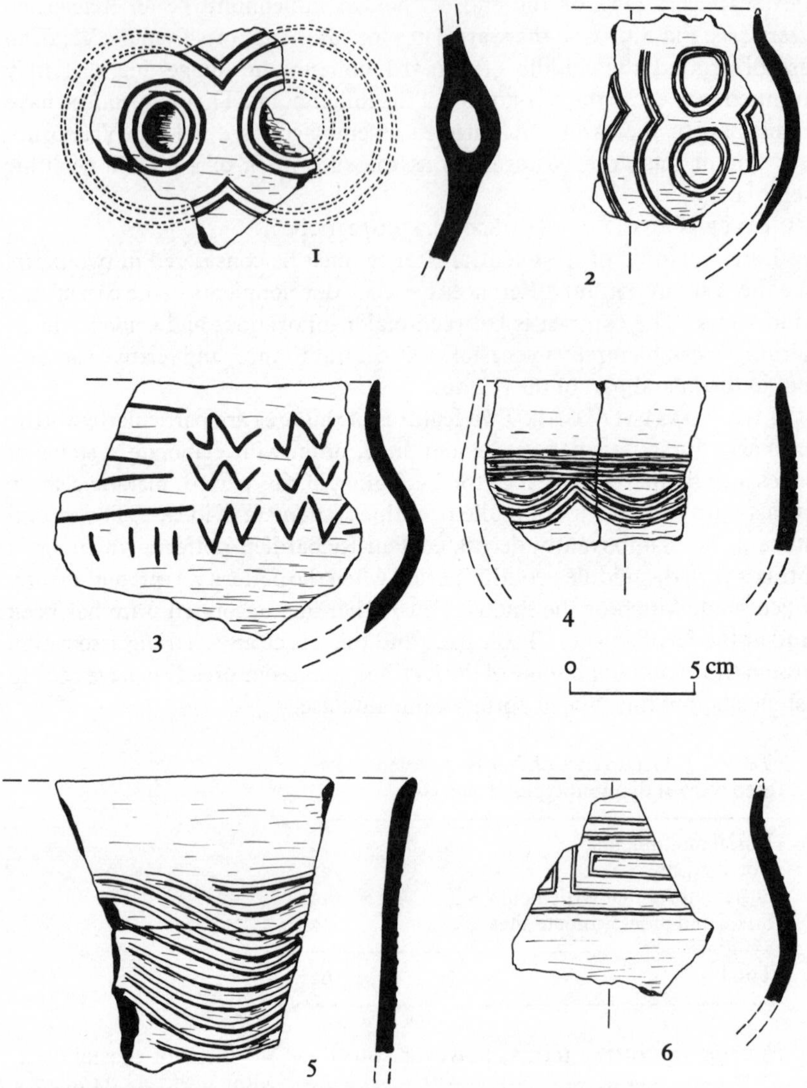

FIGURE 8.7. Late neolithic Peu-Richardien decorated pottery. 1-4 Incised and/or channelled decoration: Poitou variety (1, 3) and Saintonge variety, early phase (2, 4). (1 *Anse tunnelée* from Champ Durand, Vendée; 2, 4 Ors, Charente-Maritime; 3 Availles-sur-Chizé, Deux-Sèvres); 5 Roanne variety: relief decoration (Roanne, Gironde); 6 Saintonge variety, later phase: relief and pseudo-relief decoration (Ors, Charente-Maritime). (1 after Joussaume, 1980; 2, 4, 6 now in Musée Fleuriau, La Rochelle; 3 in Musée du Pilori, Niort; 5 in Musée de Libourne.)

ance may reflect an important change in domestic arrangements, though whether they were for storage, cooking or other food processing we are unable to say. However, unlike the later Peu-Richardien, Matignons pottery also has features which indicate continuity with middle neolithic traditions, such as the undecorated carinated bowl. It is therefore possible to regard it as intermediate between the Middle and the Late Neolithic. Radiocarbon dates indicate a range c.2800–2600bc. Matignons pottery is the earliest evidence of occupation at some of the fortified sites, but it is as yet unknown from burial contexts.

Peu-Richardien. The Peu-Richardien group (c.2600–2100bc) follows the Matignons pottery in coastal west-central France and is characterised by flamboyantly decorated pottery (Fig.8.7; Burnez, 1976, 151–217). Four regional sub-styles may be distinguished, the principal division being between the relief-decorated ware of the *Moulin-de-Vent* and *Roanne* groups in the east and south respectively, and the incised and channelled decoration of the *Saintonge* and *Poitou* groups in the west and north (Fig.8.8). Pot forms and decorative motifs are generally similar in all the groups, though the characteristic *anse tunnelée* or tunnel handle is restricted to the Saintonge and Poitou groups. Reliable stratigraphic information is scarce, and only in the Saintonge and Poitou groups can any internal development be recognised. The coarse ware is essentially the same as that found with Matignons pottery. Characteristic of both are the flat-based straight-walled 'flower-pot' shapes, sometimes with a horizontal cordon a little way below the rim, perhaps to assist with lifting or the tying-on of a lid.

Matignons and Peu-Richardien are essentially successive fine pottery traditions, rather than cultures in the usual sense of the word. The late neolithic flintwork which is found with them is unremarkable, consisting principally of such ubiquitous neolithic types as points and scrapers. The tranchet arrowheads are somewhat more characteristic. They are of trapezoidal form and are thus distinguished from the triangular tranchet arrowheads of the Middle Neolithic on the one hand, and from the barbed-and-tanged arrowheads of the Chalcolithic on the other. The *Moulin-de-Vent perçoir* which Burnez (1976, 186–9) saw as an integral element of some Peu-Richardien assemblages is now thought to be of chalcolithic or early bronze age date (Morris and Scarre, forthcoming). The bonework in these late neolithic assemblages takes the form of spatulae or knives and points. Basketry is attested by the impressions on the bases of some of the Matignons pots. Polished-stone axes are a fairly common feature at these sites.

The striking character of the Peu-Richardien decorated pottery, and the appearance of fortified settlements at about the same time, led earlier writers to suggest that they reached the shores of Saintonge together, as the result of a foreign invasion. Riquet found support for this theory in the strongly coastal distribution of the Peu-Richardien material then known and the apparent absence of links with the preceding middle neolithic assemblages of the region (Riquet, 1953). Burnez explained the differences between the coastal Saintonge Peu-Richardien and the more inland Moulin-de-Vent group as the result

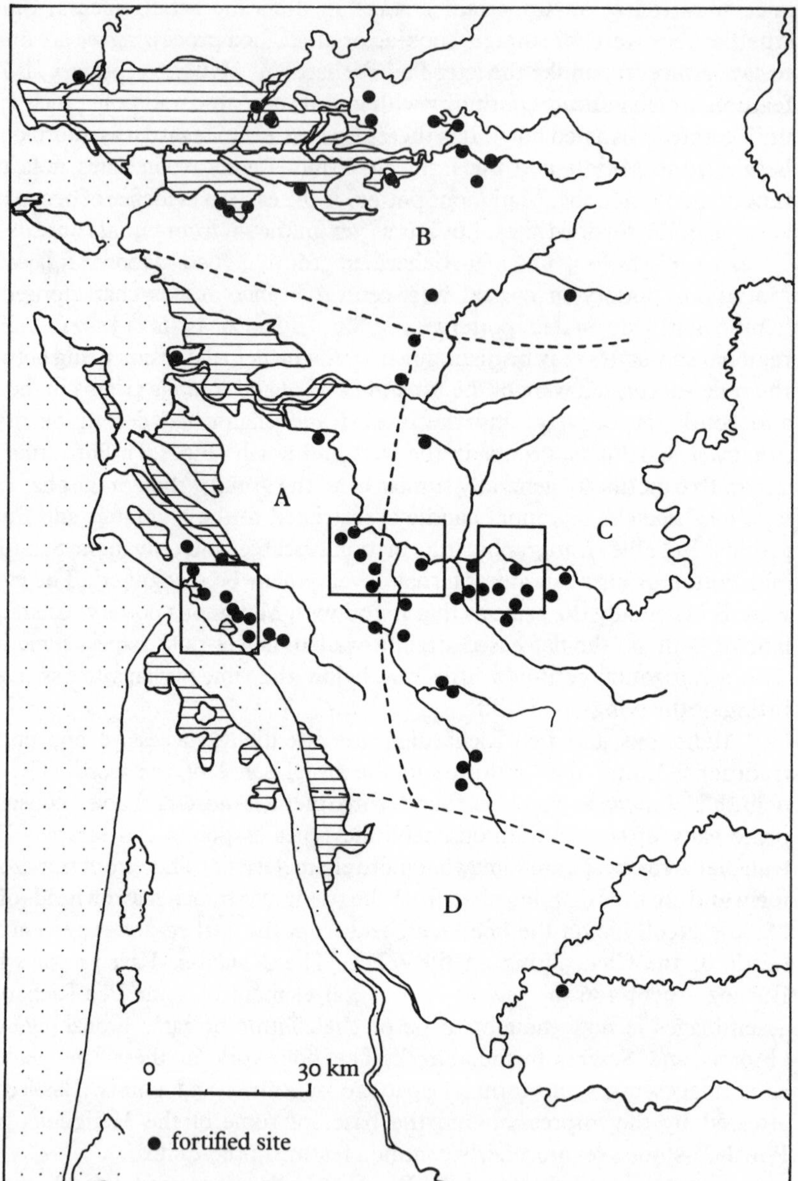

FIGURE 8.8. Distribution of late neolithic fortified sites and Peu-Richardien decorated pottery varieties in west-central France. Broken lines demarcate the areas of the four Peu-Richardien decorated pottery varieties: A Saintonge variety; B Poitou variety; C Moulin-de-Vent variety; D Roanne variety. The boxes indicate the positions of Figures 8.12, 13 and 14.

of the increasing admixture of indigenous Matignons elements (e.g. relief-decoration) as the invaders pushed their way inland. The oculi motifs of the Saintonge Peu-Richardien made that breeding-ground of neolithic invaders, the Iberian peninsula, a favoured place of origin (Burnez, 1976, 217).

Recent discoveries and a reassessment of the available evidence suggest that the Peu-Richardien was not a foreign introduction but originated locally. Recent excavations at La Sauzaie (Charente-Maritime; m.r.16) have discovered levels with simply decorated pottery which can be regarded as proto-Peu-Richardien stratified below levels with classic Saintonge Peu-Richardien (Pautreau *et al.*, 1974). The Moulin-de-Vent variety of the Cognac area may well have developed from the preceding Matignons group which has roots in the Middle Neolithic of the region. However, while abandoning the theory of a foreign origin for the Peu-Richardien, it is important to remember that it is the northernmost in a whole family of late neolithic and chalcolithic decorated pottery traditions centred on the west Mediterranean basin. Notable amongst these are the *Ferrières* and *Fontbouisse* groups of southern France and the *Ozieri* of Sardinia, to which the *Millaran* of Almerian Spain may perhaps be added (Phillips, 1975). These are characterised by elaborate incised and/or impressed decoration, and in a few cases are like the Peu-Richardien associated with enclosed settlement sites. In seeking to explain the origin of the Peu-Richardien, these parallel developments in adjacent areas should be borne in mind.

The appearance of the fortified sites provides a clue to the interpretation of the Peu-Richardien pottery. It is likely that both reflect a situation of increasing tension. The scale of the defensive works suggests the existence of an authority capable of organising and directing their construction, and the appearance of such an authority may have been a direct response to inter-community stress and competition. The tension can be explained in terms of population pressure and the necessity to control critical but limited resources; this is discussed at greater length in the third part of this chapter. The flamboyantly decorated Peu-Richardien pottery would no doubt have been costly to produce and may have served in this context as a prestige ware, closely associated with the emerging social élite.

Support for this interpretation of the Peu-Richardien pottery is to be found by considering the types of site at which it occurs. These are (see Table 8.1):

Fortified settlements (Figs 8.8, 8.10). Twenty-three of the sixty known sites have yielded Peu-Richardien pottery, and only in two cases have investigations failed to recover it where it might reasonably have been expected to be found had it been present. In several other cases Matignons sherds or undecorated late neolithic pottery have been found (Table 8.2). The fortified sites were probably centres of population and power, though their precise functions and their relationship to other classes of settlement are unclear. They do not appear to have items of an obvious prestige or exotic nature which are absent from other late neolithic sites, save perhaps for the decorated pottery, which is not always abundant. In certain areas, the spacing and location of the fortified sites suggests that each may have been the principal settlement in a territory of a social, political or economic nature. They were also strategically located in relation to critical areas of lowland wet pasture, control of which seems to have been essential for their survival and was probably the principal reason for the provision of elaborate defences.

Table 8.2. Fortified sites in west-central France.

With excavated late neolithic material	19
Late neolithic material found on surface	10
Known only from aerial survey	31
Total	60

Burial deposits. Three types of burial deposit have yielded Peu-Richardien decorated sherds. In some fourteen instances this pottery has been found in a megalithic tomb. Most if not all of these are cases of the re-use of an existing monument. The small number of such burials suggests that this was not the customary funerary mode associated with the users of Peu-Richardien decorated ware and it seems that megalithic chambers were no longer being constructed in the coastal zone at this period. Peu-Richardien decorated ware has also been found associated with the skeletal remains of two individuals in a section of ditch at Champ Durand. This appears to have been an intentional funerary deposit, with grave goods, rather than a chance association (Bresson and Gadé, 1980). Peu-Richardien pottery, of fine quality though undecorated, has recently been discovered in association with a double burial in a shallow stone-lined grave under a low mound at Les Châtelliers-du-Vieil-Auzay (Joussaume, 1981, 365-8). Multiple burial seems thus to have been a common feature of graves with pottery of Peu-Richardien type.

Other settlement sites. Most of the *unenclosed* sites at which Peu-Richardien decorated ware has been found have been shown to be substantial settlements (e.g. La Garenne, Charente-Maritime: Gabet and Massaud, 1965; La Sauzaie (m.r.16), Charente-Maritime: Pautreau *et al.*, 1974). The material recovered from them is closely similar to that from the fortified sites, and it is only the absence of defensive works which sets them apart. Future work may show that they too were once enclosed, whether by rampart and ditch or, as at Soubérac (Charente; m.r.19; Burnez, 1965), by rampart alone. If this were so, it would mean that excepting a few megalithic tombs virtually all the known Peu-Richardien decorated pottery is in fact from fortified settlement sites. There must have been smaller late neolithic settlements, and surface scatters of pottery and flint have been found which may be their remains, but they do not appear to have had Peu-Richardien decorated ware, which was perhaps restricted to the major sites.

This evidence suggests that the late neolithic period saw the development in coastal west-central France of a settlement hierarchy and perhaps a social

PLATE 8.3. The sole surviving 'long tumulus' of the Les Moindreaux group at Saint Jean-de-Liversay (Charente-Maritime). The mound, which may be of middle neolithic date although no chambers, cists, or associated finds are known, is some 80m in length and 10 to 15m wide. (Photo: Chris Scarre.)

hierarchy also. The association of flamboyantly decorated Peu-Richardien pottery with substantial fortified settlements strongly suggests that these developments were linked.

This discussion of social and settlement organisation will have made it clear that the middle neolithic evidence from coastal west-central France is very different to that of the Late Neolithic. For the earlier period there is little settlement data and for distributional information we are forced to rely on the monumental chambered tombs, while in the late neolithic period the principal class of site is the fortified settlement. This reflects a change in the organisation of society such as has already been suggested. The scarcity of burial sites which can be assigned to this period is particularly striking. Passage graves seem no longer to have been built, and relatively few of those in the coastal zone show evidence of continued use or re-use in the Late Neolithic. The monumental tombs seem largely to have lost their importance as territorial markers or group foci in this part of the region in the changed economic and social circumstances. What new forms of burial may have replaced them it is difficult to say. Skeletal material has been found in the ditches of several of the fortified sites, in some cases if not all as the result of intentional burial. Remains of five individuals were recovered from the ditches of Champ Durand (Vendée; m.r.12; Jousssaume, 1981), including the two mentioned earlier, and other examples are reported from Les Matignons (Charente; m.r.20; Burnez and Case, 1966) and Mourez-de-Berneuil and Peu-Richard (Charente-Maritime: Burnez and

Morel, 1965; Eschasseriaux, 1884). A further class of burial site which may belong to this period is the *long tumulus,* several examples of which, surviving only as crop marks, have been found by aerial survey in the Marais poitevin area. They occur both singly, and in groups of four or five. Excavation at one of these sites demonstrated that there had formerly been a tumulus (the sites have all been ploughed flat) but recovered no evidence of date or even of funerary function (Marsac and Joussaume, 1973). The principal argument for assigning them to the Late Neolithic is their similarity in distribution to the fortified settlements of the same area. They may, however, be related to the upstanding long mounds of known funerary function which are a feature of the coastal zone of west-central France, most of which are probably of middle neolithic date though some have yielded Peu-Richardien pottery (Plate 8.3; Joussaume, 1978; Marsac, Riley and Scarre, 1982).

THE INLAND ZONE. The period 2600–2100bc is represented in inland west-central France by two groups of material. The first of these will be discussed here and is known as the *Vienne-Charente,* characterised by coarse ware pottery and certain ornament types. The second is the *Artenacien* group, which belongs in part to the chalcolithic period and will be dealt with in a later section, though there are radiocarbon dates as early as c.2300bc from Artenacien sites in this part of west-central France.

The Vienne-Charente group was first defined by Riquet in 1953. Its principal feature is the flat-based, straight-walled *flower-pot* vessel, though Riquet included coarse-ware round-based vessels as well (Plate 8.4). Such pottery is not however exclusive to the Vienne-Charente group but occurs also alongside decorated pottery at the contemporary Matignons and Peu-Richardien settlements of the coastal zone of west-central France. Two feature distinguish Vienne-Charente assemblages from these. First, fine or decorated pottery is virtually absent from Vienne-Charente assemblages, and secondly, almost all Vienne-Charente material comes from funerary contexts. Very few Vienne-Charente settlement sites are known, and none of them is substantial. Some authorities regard certain non-ceramic features as characteristic of the Vienne-Charente, in addition to the ceramic material. Principal among these are the arc-shaped stone pendant known as the *pendentif arciforme*; the miniature polished-stone axe perforated for suspension (the *hache* or *hachette pendeloque*); and a certain type of flint dagger which seems to make its first appearance in these assemblages (Burnez, 1976, 252–5). None of these can be held to be truly characteristic of or exclusive to the Vienne-Charente. The other features of these assemblages are much as in the Peu-Richardien and other late neolithic groups – scrapers and tranchet arrowheads of flint, bone needles, points and knives.

Most of the funerary contexts from which Vienne-Charente material has come have been megalithic tombs, either re-used or newly constructed at this period. The difficulty of establishing the date of construction of a megalithic tomb was discussed earlier and makes it impossible to distinguish with confidence between these options, though it is likely that some at least of the

PLATE 8.4. Late neolithic pottery recovered by the 19th-century excavations in the chamber of Tumulus A at Bougon (Deux-Sèvres). The flat-based vessels (above) are a type characteristic of the 'Vienne-Charente' group, though the round-based vessels (below) carry a small amount of decoration and some have preferred to regard them as late Peu-Richardien. Material now in the Musée du Pilori, Niort. (Photo: Chris Scarre.)

dolmens simples were built in this period. Some megalithic chambers have yielded a considerable quantity of human remains in association with Vienne-Charente material (e.g. 200 individuals arranged in three layers separated by stone slabs at Bougon A: Mohen, 1973b), and it seems there was a change at this period from successive inhumation, where older burials were pushed aside to make space for new arrivals, to a practice where the bodies were laid out side by side, new burials not disturbing old. Another feature of Vienne-Charente burial was the placing with the dead of coarse ware vessels only; it would be interesting to know what these contained.

The material placed with the dead in these late neolithic tombs is likely to have been only a selection of that in everyday use, and it is reasonable to suppose that, when they are discovered, assemblages from contemporary settlement sites will prove to contain fine and perhaps decorated pottery also.

Joussaume has suggested (1981, 356-8) that material from the edge of the Peu-Richardien area which has previously been considered Vienne-Charente, notably the assemblage from Bougon A, is in fact a late peripheral variety of Peu-Richardien in which decoration has become rare and simple (e.g. a single horizontal incised line). Further inland, Artenacien fine ware has dates as early as 2310bc (Camp Allaric, Vienne (m.r.5) and Grotte du Quéroy, Charente). Both Pautreau (1979) and Gomez (1980) regard the Vienne-Charente as an early phase of the Artenacien, and the close resemblance between Artenacien coarse ware and the Vienne-Charente coarse pottery strongly suggests that the latter will ultimately be shown to have been the coarse ware of an early Artenacien or proto-Artenacien group, the fine pottery of which has not yet been identified. If that proves to be the case the most striking feature will be the exclusion of the fine ware from the late neolithic burial assemblages in inland west-central France. Only further work can verify these hypotheses.

Riquet (1953) presented the Vienne-Charente group as a local manifestation of the Paris basin SOM, while Burnez (1976, 267) saw it as the result of a westward expansion of the SOM, halted at the boundary of the Peu-Richardien. Like the Vienne-Charente, the SOM is characterised by coarse ware flower-pot vessels and is known principally from burial sites. However, better parallels for the Vienne-Charente pottery are to be found in the Matignons and Peu-Richardien groups to the west, while such Paris-basin features as *allées couvertes* and *hypogées* are, respectively, rare and absent in west-central France. A local origin seems more likely. There is nevertheless evidence of contact between the SOM and Vienne-Charente groups. *Haches pendeloques*, *pendentifs arciformes* and flint daggers are common to both groups, but unknown in Matignons and Peu-Richardien contexts. SOM assemblages contain elements indicating contact with this and other regions of western France, notably flint from the mines of Le Grand Pressigny (which is also found occasionally in Vienne-Charente contexts) and igneous stone from Brittany. The principal similarity between the two groups, however, the selection of coarse ware flower-pot vessels for placement with the dead, may be seen either as the result of parallel development or as the spread of a fashion or ritual.

The evidence provided by the Vienne-Charente group resembles that of the middle neolithic period in its emphasis on burial sites and the virtual absence of settlements. It is likely that the Late Neolithic of inland west-central France is a continuation of the Middle Neolithic in these respects. The absence of substantial settlement sites and the emphasis placed on monumental tombs may be taken as evidence that the late neolithic pattern was one of small, dispersed settlements, as suggested above for the middle neolithic period. The resemblance to the Paris basin SOM group both in terms of the material (pottery, ornament types) and the sites at which it is found (chambered tombs) would be in accord with this view. Howell (this volume) has interpreted the SOM evidence in terms of small scattered settlements and monumental tombs. The Vienne-Charente and SOM groups are the principal members in a family of coarse-pottery traditions which dominates most of northern

France at this period and stands in strong contrast to the decorated pottery traditions of the south and south-west of which the Peu-Richardien is a notable example (Fig. 10.3). The decorated wares may have been associated with the development of stratified societies and the establishment of ruling élites; such an interpretation is supported by the evidence of fortified settlements and long-distance trade in exotics. The SOM and Vienne-Charente groups, in contrast, may correspond to areas of comparative social conservatism; they give little indication of social stratification. In the Paris basin the situation appears to have remained unchanged well into the Bronze Age, but in inland west-central France the period of social conservatism was relatively short and gave way at about 2300bc to a new phase of development marked by the appearance of Artenacien fine ware and promontory forts, and a little later by copper metallurgy and Beaker-related prestige objects.

The reason why for much of the 3rd millennium inland west-central France seems retarded when compared with the development of the coastal zone is not clear. The appearance of the Peu-Richardien decorated pottery and the establishment of the fortified settlement sites may however have been stimulated by favourable changes in the landscape, consequent on a fall in sea-level which did not extend to the inland zone. These changes and their effects will be discussed in detail in a later part of this chapter.

THE DORDOGNE AND QUERCY. The distribution of undecorated coarse ware broadly of the Vienne-Charente type extends southwards into the Dordogne and Quercy. In the former area it has been labelled *Isle-Dordogne*, and, as in the Vienne-Charente area, the find contexts are funerary sites, though in this case burial caves rather than megalithic tombs as further north. Anchor-shaped pendants are a characteristic feature of this group, but decorated pottery is unknown (Roussot-Larroque, 1976). In Quercy, undecorated coarse ware is represented in level A1 at Roucadour, but a small group of sites including La Perte du Cros has yielded late neolithic sherds with incised decoration which are assigned to the *Crosien* (Clottes and Costantini, 1976). The Crosien has been compared with the Fontbouisse group of southern France but though it may be a member of the same west Mediterranean incised pottery family the specific parallel is not convincing. Later developments in this southern area are similar to those in inland west-central France, with the first Artenacien assemblages appearing at c.2300bc, one of the earliest being at La Fontaine de la Demoiselle (Dordogne) (Roussot-Larroque, 1973).

THE CHALCOLITHIC (c.2300/2100bc–c.1800bc)

The Artenacien group. This is widely represented in western France, from Quercy in the south (where it appears at the Grotte du Noyer and the Grotte de Marsa: Clottes, 1977a) to the edge of the Loire valley in the north, replacing the Peu-Richardien, Vienne-Charente, Isle-Dordogne and Crosien traditions of the late neolithic period. It is distinguished principally by its fine pottery, especially the decorated ware which is often very well made, thin-walled and crisp (Fig. 8.9). Sharply carinated forms occur which are similar to those of the Middle Neolithic. The decoration also includes middle neolithic features such

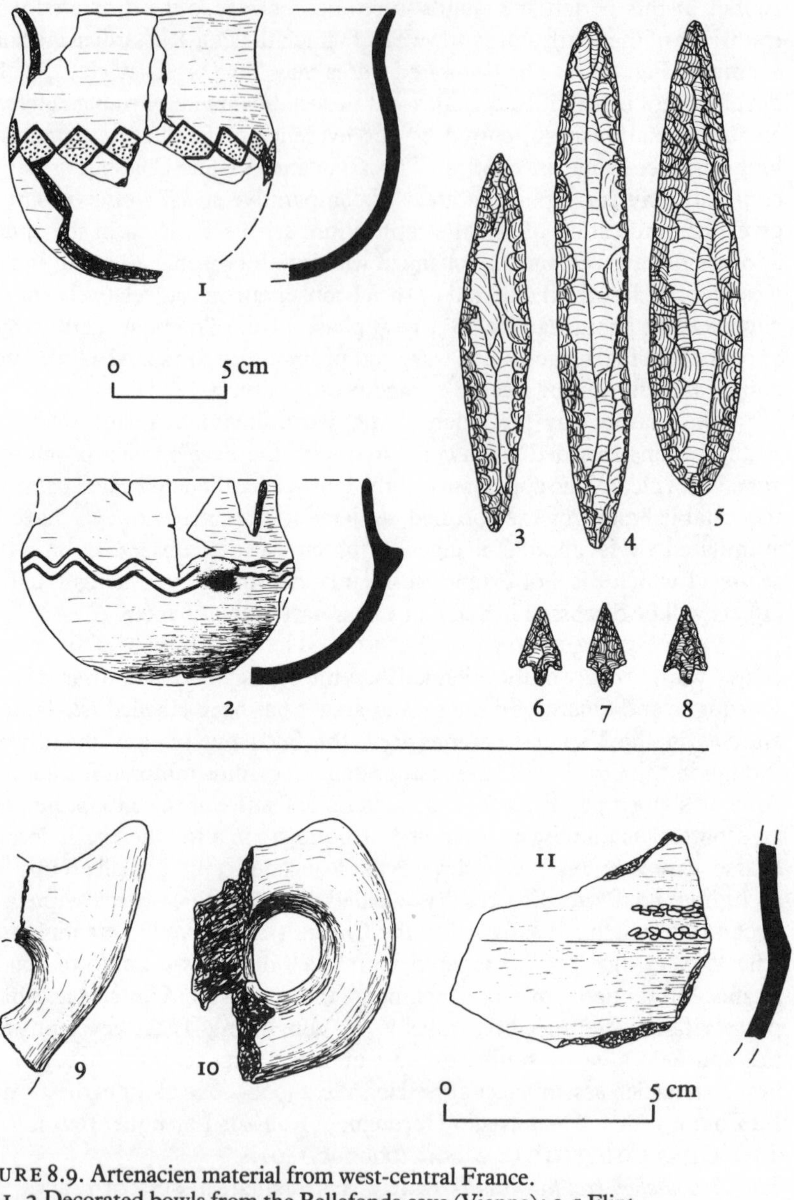

FIGURE 8.9. Artenacien material from west-central France.
1, 2 Decorated bowls from the Bellefonds cave (Vienne); 3-5 Flint daggers, and (6-8) barbed-and-tanged arrowheads from the megalithic tomb of La Motte de la Garde (Charente); 9, 10 'Anses nasiformes' from the promontory settlement of Recoux (Charente); 11 Carinated vessel fragment from the Artenac cave (Charente). (1, 2 after Patte, 1971; 3-8 after Burnez, 1976; 9, 10 now in the Musée de la Faculté des Sciences, Poitiers; 11 in the Musée des Antiquités Nationales, Saint Germain-en-Laye.)

as hatched and cross-hatched triangles, usually incised before firing and similar to the decoration of the vases-supports. There is every reason to suppose that the Artenacien pottery developed directly from that of the Middle Neolithic, and vases-supports may have been an integral part of the earliest Artenacien assemblages. Artenacien fine ware also includes forms of decoration not known from middle neolithic contexts, for instance a row of bosses or horizontal *braided* lines around the belly of the pot, and there is a distinctive type of horned handle known as the *anse nasiforme*. The incised decoration on some vessels still bears traces of its original white paste infilling. The coarse ware is similar to that found in Vienne-Charente contexts, and many of the flint daggers have close Vienne-Charente parallels though there is also a new type, the *barre de chocolat* form. Small metal objects occur in Artenacien contexts, the commonest finds being copper beads in burial assemblages (Burnez, 1976, 285–308).

Bailloud and Burnez (1962) originally defined the Artenacien as a chalcolithic group on account of the copper beads at the Grotte d'Artenac (Charente) itself. Recent discoveries have shown, however, that Artenacien material can be dated as early as 2300bc in inland west-central France (Camp Allaric (m.r.5), Grotte du Quéroy) and in the Dordogne (La Fontaine de la Demoiselle); and at Camp Allaric Pautreau (1976) was able to distinguish two Artenacien levels, the lower with tranchet arrowheads and probably late neolithic, the upper with the barbed-and-tanged variety and chalcolithic. In most areas it continued without a break into the full Early Bronze Age.

In its early phase the Artenacien group was restricted to inland parts of west-central France, but after the demise of the Peu-Richardien group towards the end of the 3rd millennium bc it spread throughout the coastal zone also, with dates of 2040bc at La Sauzaie (Charente-Maritime; m.r.16) and 2090 bc at La Pierre-Virante, Xanton-Chassenon (Vendée). Artenacien material occurs as surface finds at some of the Peu-Richardien fortified settlements, but never in such a way as to suggest a substantial post-Peu-Richardien occupation of these sites. At Champ Durand, Artenacien and Beaker sherds were found together in the upper fill of one of the enclosure ditches, above the material of the collapsed rampart (Joussaume, 1980). Thus here the Artenacien pottery belongs to the period when the defences had gone out of use, and this may have been the general case. There is nothing to suggest that the spread of Artenacien material into the coastal part of west-central France was heralded by the violent destruction of the Peu-Richardien settlements. Their abandonment was probably due to other, perhaps natural, causes, and the Artenacien material merely filled the void that was left.

In inland parts of western France Artenacien material is found most often in burial contexts, like the Vienne-Charente and Isle-Dordogne material which preceded it in these areas. Both burial caves and megalithic tombs were used, the former well represented by the upper layer in the Bellefonds cave and by the Grotte d'Artenac itself (Patte, 1971, 146–74; Bailloud and Burnez, *op. cit.*). Many of the middle neolithic passage graves were re-used, and some of the *dolmens simples* which are found on the western fringe of the Massif Central contained Artenacien deposits. This type of tomb consists of a simple passageless chamber under a small circular or oval covering mound, and many if not all of these are thought to have been built at this period (Burnez, 1976, 221–36). Those on the higher plateaux may have been connected with summer pastoral activities, representing perhaps the first regular use of these upland areas.

Artenacien material is also well represented at settlement sites, frequently promontory forts where only a short length of ditch or rampart was needed to complete the site's natural defences. In many cases (e.g. Recoux, Charente (m.r.21)) the visible defensive works are of later date and the chalcolithic arrangements are unclear. At the Camp de Pierre-Dure (Charente), however, the rampart and the shallow scoop in front of it were shown to be associated with a late 3rd millennium occupation (Gomez, 1975). Recent work has established that the core of the rampart at the Fort des Anglais (Charente) is also of chalcolithic date (Gomez, 1983). Despite the presence of these larger sites, it is clear that most of the population must have continued to live in smaller settlements, of which very little is known.

In inland west-central France the Artenacien group is a direct development of what had gone before, continuity with the Vienne-Charente being shown by the coarse pottery, the flint daggers, and the use of similar burial contexts. Its appearance at c.2300bc, however, probably marks the end of the period of relative social conservatism referred to earlier, and the defended promontory settlements suggest that a more complex social order and settlement system developed. This hypothesis is confirmed in part by the association of Beaker and Artenacien material at many sites; the Beaker pottery and related objects may have been symbols of social prestige.

In the coastal zone, the pattern of development at the end of the 3rd millennium is very different. The Artenacien material spread into this area from the east, but is much less suggestive of a stratified society than the preceding Peu-Richardien pottery and the fortified late neolithic settlement sites. The abandonment of the fortified settlements and the demise of the Peu-Richardien pottery style appear to have been relatively sudden and roughly simultaneous events, and may well have been associated with some kind of social and economic decline, a possibility which will be discussed in more detail below. The scale of the decline may however have been less than it appears, since occasional chalcolithic metal objects have been found in this area and there are a few Beaker burial assemblages which seem to testify to the survival of a ranked society. Large chalcolithic settlement sites are virtually unknown from the coastal part of west-central France, however, and a pattern of small hamlets and farmsteads should perhaps be envisaged.

Beaker material. The Beaker material of west-central France is approximately contemporary with that of the Artenacien group and the two are often found in association. It should be noted that Beaker material is never associated with Peu-Richardien pottery, despite their apparent chronological overlap.

Beaker pottery is particularly well-represented in the northern part of west-central France, where there is a whole series of small Beaker settlements on the Vendéen coast and a group of especially rich Beaker burial deposits inland (Joussaume, 1981). This may be regarded as part of the Breton Beaker concentration. Both Iberian and Dutch types of Beaker are present in the region. Maritime Beakers are particularly well represented at the sites on the Vendéen coast, one of which (Le Petit Rocher) has an early radiocarbon date of 2340bc. The Maritime Beakers go together with the Palmela points as indicators of Iberian influence. Beaker pottery appears to have continued in use in west-central France for approximately half a millennium; the latest radiocarbon date currently available is 1900bc from the site of Anse de le Republique (Vendée).

Apart from the pottery, other commonly Beaker-associated objects have been found in this region, including archer's wristguards, V-perforated bone tortoise and disc buttons, copper knives and daggers and the distinctive Palmela points.

The early dates show that the Beaker pottery of this part of France is among the earliest in western Europe, though there is no question of local development since all the elements of the Beaker assemblage are new to the region. The Beaker material commonly occurs alongside coarse wares of local tradition, however, or in earlier burial monuments. Perhaps the most noteworthy feature is the richness of some of the Beaker burial deposits – for instance at La Pierre-Folle, Thiré (Vendée; m.r.10), where there were some 17 decorated and 3 undecorated Beakers, 4 V-perforated buttons, an engraved bone tube, 6 gold beads, 7 gold plaques, a copper awl and a copper spiral ring (Joussaume, 1976a). It is not clear with how many interments this material was associated, but it is of a richness unknown in neolithic burial deposits and is the type of evidence which some have used to argue for the rise at this time of an aristocracy based on wealth. Thus here as in many parts of western Europe the Beaker material seems to be connected with heightened social stratification at the dawn of the Bronze Age, with the decorated Beakers, the metal objects and the archer's wristguards serving perhaps as insignia of rank.

The beginnings of metallurgy. With the Artenacien and Beaker groups, the first metal objects make their appearance (Pautreau, 1979; Gomez, 1980). Copper beads have been found in several Artenacien contexts, including the Grotte d'Artenac itself. Beaker pottery occurs in burial deposits associated with copper daggers and awls, copper and gold beads, and gold plaques and spirals. It is customary to regard copper daggers and Palmela points as Beaker-related, even when they occur outside sealed contexts. There is no evidence of pre-Beaker metallurgy in this region, and the strong Beaker associations of the earliest metal types suggest that the currents which brought Beaker pottery to this part of France brought metal objects and metalworking as well. The Palmela point from Sainte-Gemme (Charente-Maritime) has been claimed to be in mint condition and of local manufacture (Gachina, 1979); this would be the earliest evidence of metalworking in west-central France.

The single most common early metal type in ths region is the copper flat axe. Some 59 of these are known from the *département* of the Vendée alone (Baudouin, 1911, with additions in Pautreau, 1979, 45–6). The flat axes are difficult to date since they so rarely occur in association with datable material in a sealed context. The hoard from Trentemoult near Nantes (Loire-Atlantique) consisted of nine flat axes of arsenical copper and a Palmela point (Giot, Briard and Pape, 1979, 38–9), and at both La Chapelle-Achard (Vendée) and Saint-Père-en-Retz (Loire-Atlantique) flat axes were associated with metal types thought by some to be Beaker-related (Joussaume, 1981, 512). The appearance of low-flanged axes of bronze marks the end of the period being dealt with here and the beginning of the full Early Bronze Age.

Late Neolithic and Chalcolithic Trade

The limestone and chalk basin in which the Peu-Richardien settlements are situated has flint deposits but no sources of hard igneous stone suitable for the manufacture of polished-stone axes. This deficiency appears to have been remedied by trade, principally with Brittany. Axes of type A dolerite, probably from the Plussulien mines, have been found at the Peu-Richardien settlements of La Sauzaie and Champ Durand, while the former site has also yielded an axe of type C hornblendite, the source of which is thought to have been Kerlevot in southern Finistère (Gachina *et al.*, 1975; Joussaume, 1980). Trade would have been encouraged and facilitated by the proximity of most of the major Peu-Richardien settlements to navigable waterways. Dug-out canoes have been found, and one (recently discovered) has been dated to 2590bc (Gomez, 1982). Isolated finds of dolerite, hornblendite and jadeite axes have been particularly common in the Vendée; the jadeite may derive from the Alpine region rather than Brittany (Jauneau, 1974, 1976). Igneous stone from the Massif Central was also employed.

Local flint sources are fairly numerous, and often several types are represented at individual sites. The best known late-neolithic variety is banded flint from Douhet-Taillebourg in Charente-Maritime, where large areas of chipping debris have been found, though no flint mines as such (Burnez, 1976, 15). The chalcolithic period sees the *floruit* of the flint mines at Le Grand Pressigny (Indre-et-Loire). Grand Pressigny flint was traded within west-central France and far beyond its frontiers, appearing for instance in Beaker graves in the Low Countries (Lanting and Van der Waals, 1976).

The most striking feature of chalcolithic trade is the wide geographical extent of the contacts represented by the copper, Grand Pressigny flint, and Beaker-related elements. Many of the Beaker-related elements must have been imported, including the raw materials for metallurgy. Copper may have come from Brittany along trade networks which had been developed for the distribution of hard stone axes; the part of west-central France richest in copper axes, the Vendée, is also the richest in Breton dolerite and hornblendite. Briard, however, considers that Breton copper deposits were probably not exploited before the Late Bronze Age (Giot, Briard and Pape, 1979, 30–1), so

Brittany may have been only a staging post in this trade. Small sources of copper exist in the western part of the Massif Central and in the Pyrenees, but it may have been Irish or Iberian copper which was used in west-central France at this period.

The geographical expansion of the trade in which the late neolithic and chalcolithic communities of west-central France participated may have been related to the development of more highly stratified societies suggested from other evidence. Emerging social élites may have sought to demonstrate their exclusiveness by the possession of traded objects or materials not in common circulation. Much of the widespread 'Beaker phenomenon' could be explained in such a way; the decorated pottery and associated objects may have become internationally recognised symbols of rank, available only to a few, and may have acted as catalysts in the rise of the Bronze Age aristocracies of western Europe.

Late Neolithic Fortified Sites

Nature, Distribution and Location

The evidence for a study of settlement patterns and site locations in coastal west-central France during the late neolithic period consists principally of the impressive fortified sites of which some sixty examples are now known, and though they were only one element of the settlement hierarchy we are forced to rely on them for an indication of the settlement pattern and land-use strategies. The fortified sites were briefly described earlier in this chapter, but it may be helpful to give a fuller account here before proceeding to consider their distribution and location. The first to be found was Peu-Richard (Charente-Maritime), just over a century ago (Eschasseriaux, 1882). Further sites of this type were discovered in the years leading up to the outbreak of the First World War, and later in the 1950s. However, two-thirds of the current total have been discovered only in the last decade or so as a result of aerial survey and photography (Plate 8.5; Dassié, 1978; Marsac and Scarre, 1979). Pottery and radiocarbon dates place them in the period 2800–2100bc. Many have yielded Peu-Richardien decorated ware, and in some cases Matignons pottery has also been recovered, generally from the lower ditch fill. Not all the fortified sites need have been in occupation at the same time, though radiocarbon determinations have demonstrated half a millennium of use in some cases.

The sites may be divided into two groups on the basis of differences in the form of their defences (Fig.8.10). This is a useful classification particularly since it can be applied to sites known only from aerial photographs, where excavation or other types of ground-based survey have not been attempted. The *first* group consists of those sites which have one or more circuits of ditch with simple entrance-gaps; examples are Champ Durand in the Vendée (Fig. 8.10, 4; m.r.12) and Pont-d'Husson in Charente-Maritime, with frequent interruptions, or Les Matignons in Charente (Fig.8.10, 1; m.r.20), where the entrances are fewer and more widely spaced. The *second* group is the more numerous and consists of enclosures with entrances of the *pince de crabe* or

PLATE 8.5. Aerial view of the late neolithic fortified site of L'Angle at Longèves (Charente-Maritime). Note the two sets of *pince de crabe* entrance-works. The upper set appear to have been blocked at some stage. Between the arms of the lower set the traces of a series of pairs of post-holes which may once have held gate-timbers can be made out. (Photo: Maurice Marsac.)

crab's pincers type, where the gateway is protected by a small outwork. These can be qute elaborate, as at Chez-Reine, Semussac (Charente-Maritime; Fig. 8.10, 3; m.r.17). There is some evidence that the simple entrance-gaps are earlier than the *pince de crabe* entrance-works.

Excavations have shown that the defensive works, even at their simplest, were of substantial proportions. Indeed, these seem to be the most heavily fortified of all the groups of neolithic enclosed sites of France. At Champ Durand the inner ditch was rock-cut, 5m across at the lip and 2.5m deep. The entrances were simple interruptions in the ditch, but investigations at one of these revealed the presence of post-holes designed to take substantial gate-timbers, and the base of a solid dry-stone flanking tower (Joussaume, 1981).

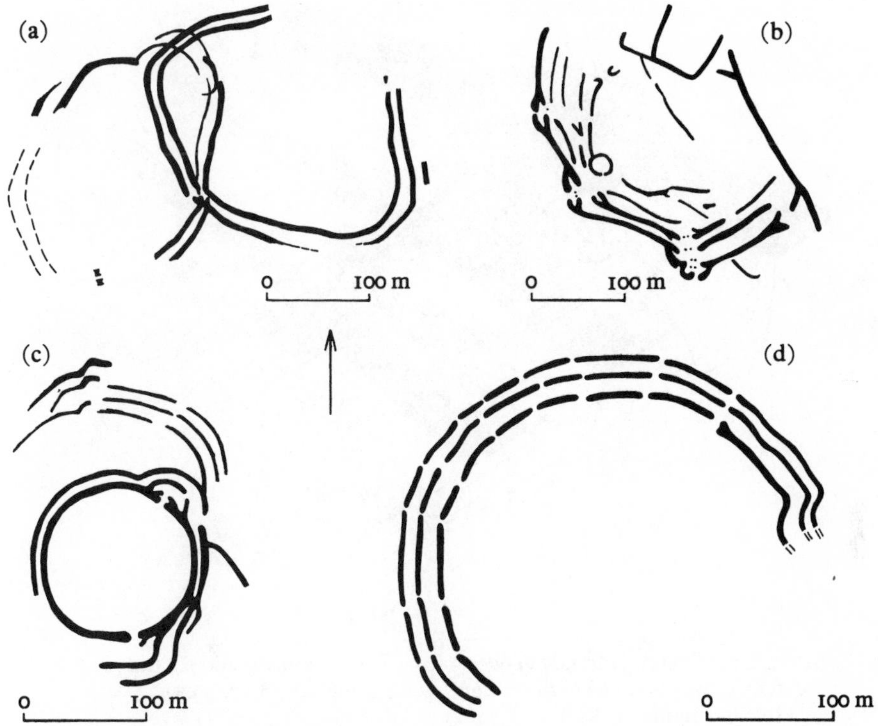

FIGURE 8.10. Late neolithic fortified sites.
1 Les Matignons (Charente); 2 Le Moulin de la Coterelle (Charente-Maritime); 3 Chez-Reine, Semussac (Charente-Maritime); 4 Champ Durand (Vendée). (1 after Burnez and Case, 1966; 2 after Dassié, 1978; 3 after Mohen, 1973a; 4 after Joussaume, 1980.)

The inner, middle and outer ditches were of successively shallower depth, and the excavator envisages a concentric system of defences involving three circuits, of successively greater proportions towards the interior of the site (Fig.8.11). This would have enabled defenders stationed on the inner rampart to fire over the heads of those on the two outer ramparts, in the manner of certain medieval castles (Joussaume, 1980).

It is unfortunate that most of the fortified sites are on plateaux with thin but fertile soils which have been subjected to repeated ploughing, so that little evidence has survived within the defences and it is difficult to determine the nature of the occupation in other than its defensive aspect. Recent area excavations in the interior of Champ Durand (Joussaume, 1981) have recovered quantities of animal bones, hearths, quernstones, potsherds, flint tools and other evidence of domestic activity, though little of it was *in situ* and there were no traces of buildings or other structures. Similar material is found in the ditch fills of these enclosures, and allows us to suggest they may have been fortified villages. The sites vary in size from one hectare or smaller to 8 or

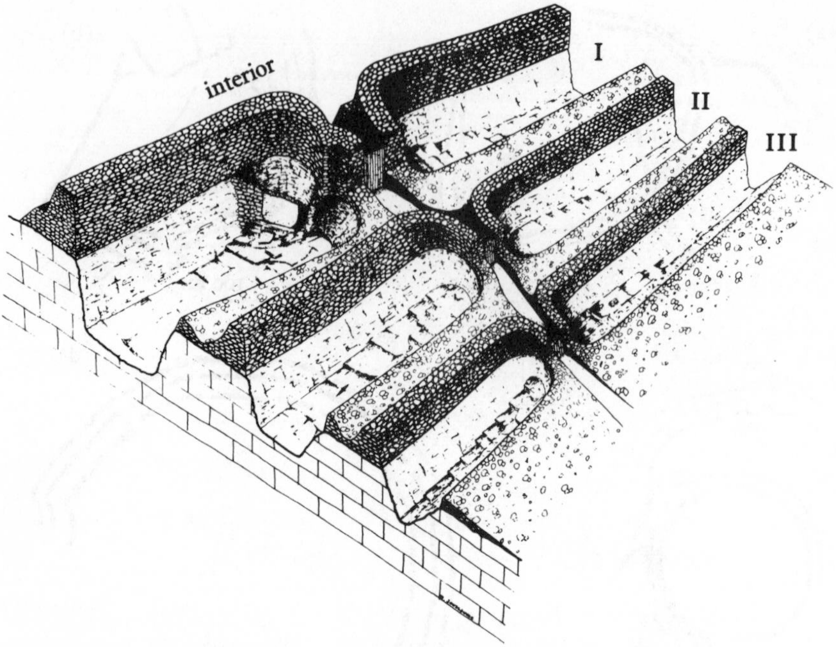

FIGURE 8.11. Champ Durand (Vendée). Excavator's reconstruction of the defensive works at one of the entrances (see also Figure 8.10, no.4). (After Joussaume, 1980.)

9 hectares, and the larger examples may have had considerable populations. It is unlikely that all the space within the defences was occupied by dwellings, and workshops and animal pens may also be envisaged. If, however, for argument's sake it is assumed that dwellings occupied on average 25 per cent of the total site area, then, using Naroll's formula (Naroll, 1962), we obtain a figure of over 2000 inhabitants for some of the larger sites such as Moulin-de-Vent (Charente-Maritime).

The recent campaigns of aerial survey and photography have given us a fairly good idea of the distribution of the fortified sites and the types of location chosen for them. The picture is no doubt incomplete, but is probably reasonably representative of the late neolithic pattern. The principal feature to emerge is the considerable degree of regularity in location. Almost all are on the edge of a wet lowland area, either a marshland or a river valley. This is particularly striking in the case of the Marais poitevin settlements, and here a study of landscape development in the 4th and 3rd millennia suggested that land-use strategies lay behind the choice of such locations (Scarre, 1982). Patterns of land-use are, however, unlikely to have been the only consideration, and there is evidence that the needs of defence were also taken into account. It is also possible that factors such as proximity to trade routes exerted some influence, and if each settlement was associated with a territory, as some indications suggest, this too would have had an effect on the spacing of sites. It is not possible to investigate all these factors here, not least because the available evidence is inadequate, but an attempt will be made to identify those considerations which seem to have been most consistently influential in the choice of location. In order to do this, it has been necessary to study the 3rd millennium landscape and the effect of changes in sea-level which occurred at about that time. Three areas have been selected for detailed consideration (Fig.8.8): first, an area around the coastal marshlands of the Gironde, where site locations are comparable to those in the Marais poitevin area and a similar explanation, in terms of prehistoric land-use strategies, is suggested; second, in the middle valley of the River Charente near Saintes, where wide and marshy valley floors seem to have been important to late neolithic settlement; and third, in the chalkland south of Cognac, where the mix of factors affecting site location was apparently rather different.

The Royan area (Fig.8.12). This gently undulating chalkland is fringed by a series of coastal marshlands and backed by a limestone plain. The fortified sites are located on the chalk, mostly (e.g. Barzan, Château-de-Didonne) on low hills overlooking the marshlands, though at least one is actually on the marsh edge (Les Brandes). All lie within 2km of one of the coastal marshlands, and most are less than 1km away. This pattern strongly suggests that the fortified settlements were sited in order to be able to control and exploit the marshland areas. The importance of defence is borne out by the scale of the fortifications revealed at excavated examples such as Chez-Reine (Semussac), and is probably also the reason for the common choice of a location not on the marsh edge but on a hilltop nearby.

The chalkland seems to have changed little since the late neolithic period, but the marshlands have undergone considerable development. Unfortunately there is little geomorphological evidence from the Gironde marshlands themselves, and for the reconstruction of their development it is necessary to rely on information collected from marshlands further north. The coastal marshlands of west-central France were marine bays or inlets in the middle of the post-glacial period. As sea-level continued to rise increasing quantities of marine sediment were deposited in them. The pattern of sea-level change (Scarre, 1982, fig.3) is of a gradual rise reaching a peak at about 3000bc, followed by a fall and a period of low sea-level during the 3rd millennium, and then by a slow rise to the present level during the 2nd and 1st millennia bc. The effect of the fall in sea-level in the marine bays was probably to expose areas of the sediment which had accumulated around their edges during the preceding millennia, and to allow them to dry out and become stable. These areas may have undergone change from a saltwater to a freshwater régime. The marine sediment consists of clay with seashell inclusions, and recent evidence has shown that it can be very ferrtile when properly drained, supporting rich grassland or even fields of cereals.

It can be no coincidence that the late neolithic fortified sites appear around the edges of the coastal marshlands at just the time when grassland may have been developing on the marine sediment. The chalkland would have been

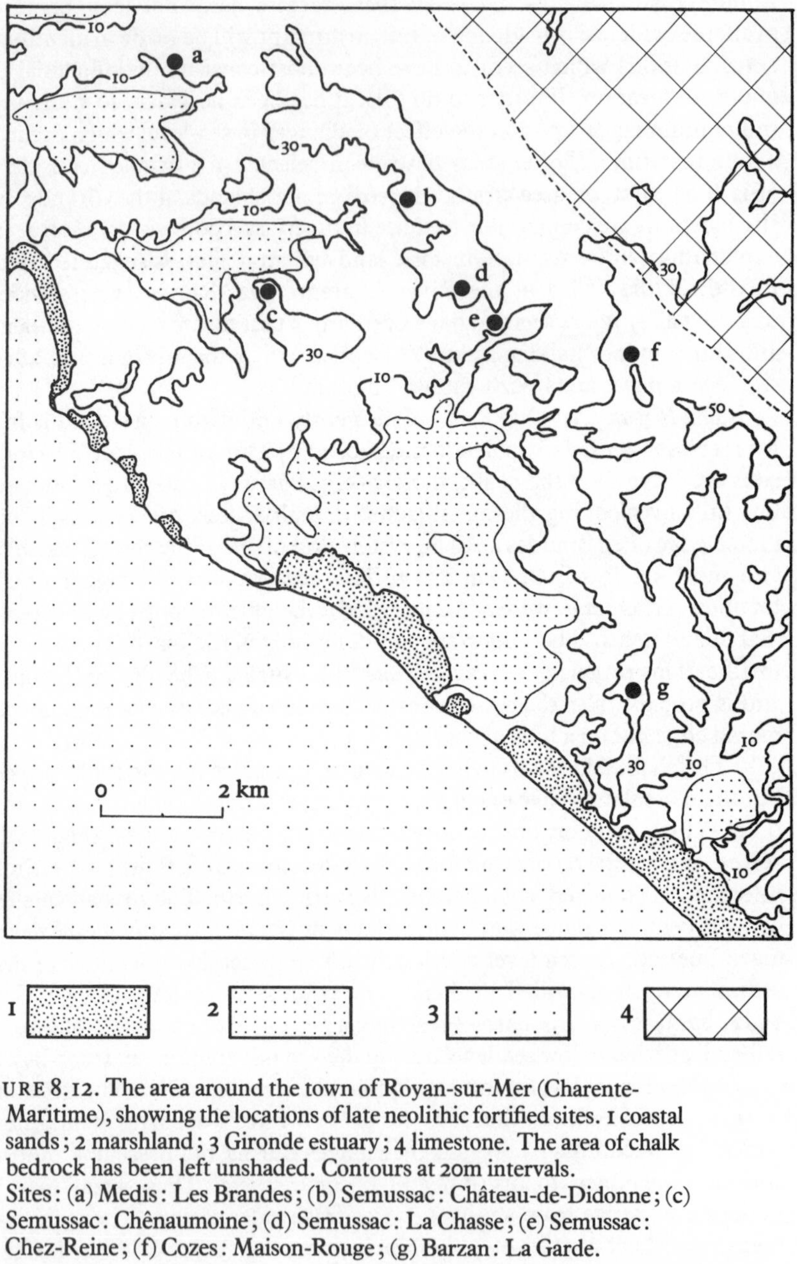

FIGURE 8.12. The area around the town of Royan-sur-Mer (Charente-Maritime), showing the locations of late neolithic fortified sites. 1 coastal sands; 2 marshland; 3 Gironde estuary; 4 limestone. The area of chalk bedrock has been left unshaded. Contours at 20m intervals. Sites: (a) Medis: Les Brandes; (b) Semussac: Château-de-Didonne; (c) Semussac: Chênaumoine; (d) Semussac: La Chasse; (e) Semussac: Chez-Reine; (f) Cozes: Maison-Rouge; (g) Barzan: La Garde.

limited in the range of resources it provided, suitable for cereals and perhaps for sheep and goat, but too dry for cattle or for moisture-demanding legumes and root-crops. It is natural, therefore, that the appearance of new wet pasture should have had a substantial effect on settlement location and density, and this is probably the principal factor behind the development of the fortified sites. The areas of wet pasture were limited in extent, and it may have been competition for their control which prompted the construction and elaboration of the defensive works around the settlements.

One of the late neolithic settlements of this area, Chez-Reine at Semussac ('e' on Fig.8.12), was excavated between 1965 and 1971 and an analysis of the faunal material recovered from one of the trenches has been published (Table 8.3; Poulain-Josien, 1967). This throws some light on the use which was being made of the chalkland and grassland elements of the landscape. Cattle were the dominant domesticate, followed by sheep and goat and then by pig. Other species (dog, wild boar and red deer) were present only in relatively insignificant quantities. Cattle are the dominant domestic animal in most of the faunal assemblages from settlements with Peu-Richardien decorated ware, and this could indicate a cultural preference. The chalkland may have provided grazing for sheep and goat, but for cattle pasture the inhabitants of Chez-Reine would have had to rely on the wetter pastures of the valley floors and present-day marshlands. The site lies on a hillslope immediately above a small valley which would have furnished some wet pasture but whose main importance was probably as a routeway leading to the more extensive pastures of the coastal marshland a little over a kilometre away. The critical importance of the lowlands to the economy of the site was probably the main reason for its location and for the elaborate defences with which it was surrounded (Fig. 8.10, 3).

The Saintes area (Fig.8.13). In the middle valley of the River Charente at its confluence with the River Seugne is a series of marshy areas which appear to have attracted late neolithic settlement. The mouth of the River Seugne where it joins the Charente is partially blocked by a bank of clay, and the area behind this is and has long been marshy and subject to seasonal flooding. In addition, seasonal flooding originating in the lower reaches of the River Charente is transmitted far upstream owing to the relative narrowness of the valley, and affects the middle valley of the Charente (Callot, 1971, 150). Hence at the present day the valley floors are used as wet pastures, on which cattle and other livestock are raised.

It is difficult to determine the condition of the valleys in the 4th and 3rd millennia bc. Soundings have been made in the floor of the Charente valley and these have shown its present surface to consist of a layer of riverine alluvium 1–2m thick. This is presumably material deposited by the seasonal floods. Beneath are layers of peat and marine clay, the latter indicating that at some time in the Postglacial even a part of the valley so far inland as this must have been invaded by the sea (Enjalbert, 1960, 168–9). The pattern of sea-level change suggests that this may have been the situation up to the end of the 4th millennium. The subsequent fall in sea-level and the progressive infilling of the valley floor, coupled with the lowering of the water-table, may in the 3rd millennium have led to the drying of these deposits and the change from a saltwater to a freshwater régime. This means that the marshy areas in the

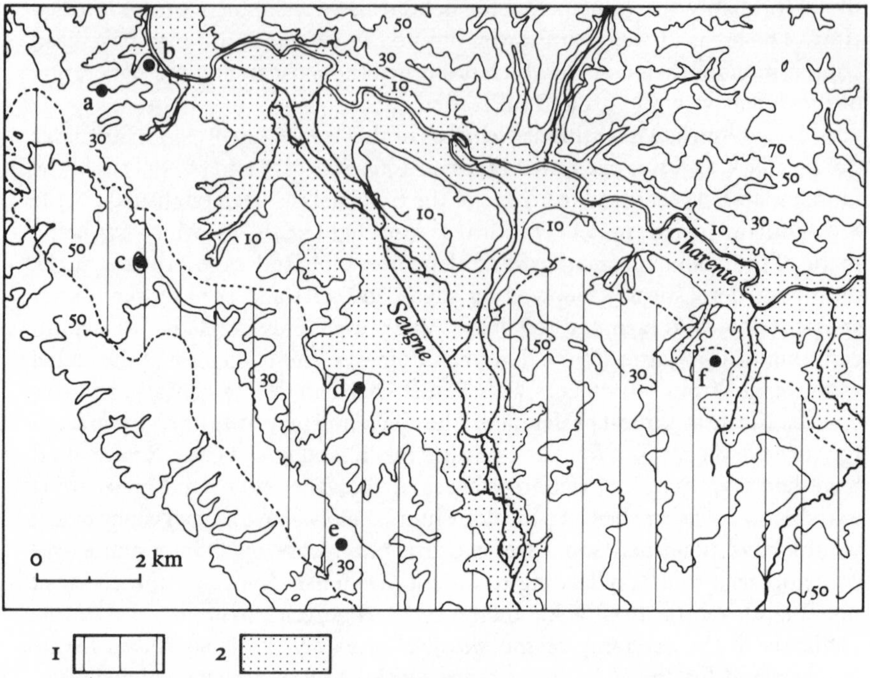

FIGURE 8.13. The area around the town of Saintes (Charente-Maritime), showing the locations of late neolithic fortified sites. 1 chalk; 2 valley floor and marshy areas. Contours at 20m intervals.
Sites: (a) Saintes: Le Petit Chadignac; (b) Saintes: Diconche; (c) Thénac: Peu-Richard; (d) La Jard: Le Chaillot; (e) Berneuil: Le Mourez; (f) Montils: Moulin-de-Vent.

middle Charente and lower Seugne valleys were very probably grasslands in the 3rd millennium, as at the present day. If so, they would have been important agriculturally as valuable areas of wet grazing in an otherwise rather dry chalk and limestone landscape.

The late neolithic fortified sites of this area are not located at the valley edge but, as in the Royan area, seek more defensible positions on low hills 0.5–2km distant. The settlements overlook the valley floors and may have been sited so as to control and exploit them. It is unfortunate that despite the 19th century excavations at four of these sites and the recent re-excavation of three of them there are no published faunal analyses to throw light on prehistoric patterns of land-use. The principal feature common to all the locations is their proximity to the lowland/chalkland interface, and the sites would have been well-placed to make use of these complementary resource areas. The requirements of defence seem also to have influenced site location strategies, not only in the choice of hilltop positions but also in the general avoidance of the hard limestone zone (Fig.8.13). Most of the ditched enclosures are on the softer chalk, where ditch-cutting would have been relatively easy. The exceptions are Diconche and Le Petit Chadignac at Saintes ('a' and 'b' on Fig.8.13), which appear to be on the hard limestone, and Moulin-de-Vent ('f') which is on a small knoll of gravel, the remnant of a former river terrace. In the Cognac area it was found that unditched late neolithic settlements were present on the hard limestone, but that the ditched sites were confined to the chalk areas (see below); no unditched late neolithic sites are yet known from the area around the Charente-Seugne confluence.

The principal factor guiding the location of late neolithic sites in the Saintes area appears from this discussion to have been the same as in the Royan area, that is to say, proximity to both wet lowland and chalkland or limestone plateau. The second most important consideration was the need for a reasonably defensible location, usually met by a low hill. These seem to have been supplemented by the attraction of the softer chalk for the cutting of ditches. It is however in the Cognac area that the differing hardness of the chalk and limestone zones seems to have had the greatest impact on the location of the late neolithic ditched sites.

The Cognac area (Fig.8.14). This was the area in which Burnez carried out his relatively intensive search for neolithic sites in the 1950s, so that although there has been no systematic aerial survey here the distribution of the known enclosed sites probably gives a fairly accurate indication of the prehistoric pattern. Unditched late neolithic settlements are also known in this area. All these sites lie to the south of the River Charente; to the north the absence of neolithic settlements (with the exception of a possible late neolithic enclosure at Ebéon, Charente: Dassié, 1978) may be due to the unsuitability for agriculture of the heavy clay soils of the *Pays-Bas de Matha* and the clay-with-flints of *Les Borderies*.

This part of the Charente valley lay beyond the reach of marine influences, which penetrated only a short distance upstream of the Seugne confluence. The postglacial changes in sea-level may nonetheless have had an impact on the level of the water-table in this area. There is little direct environmental information for the later prehistoric period. A peat deposit at Garde-Epée near Cognac yielded pollen which was tentatively dated to the Atlantic period (Guillien, 1979). Alder was the predominant tree throughout the 1.1m sequence, indicating damp conditions. In the upper part an increase in the frequency of *Sphagnum* spores suggests increased waterlogging and bog formation. If the peat is of Atlantic age as claimed (i.e. c.7800–5700bp: Morzadec-Kerfourn, 1974, 180), it must pre-date the early 3rd millennium fall in sea-level. That fall may by lowering the water-table have made the floor of the Charente valley drier and possibly suitable for use as pasture, as at the present day. Other areas which may have provided lowland pasture in the 3rd millennium are the marshlands of *Grand Marais* and *Gâte-Bourse le Marais* which open off the southern and northern sides respectively of the Charente valley a little to the east of Cognac (Fig.8.14).

There are eight ditched Peu-Richardien settlements in the Cognac district, and four of these fall within the area being considered here (Fig.8.14).

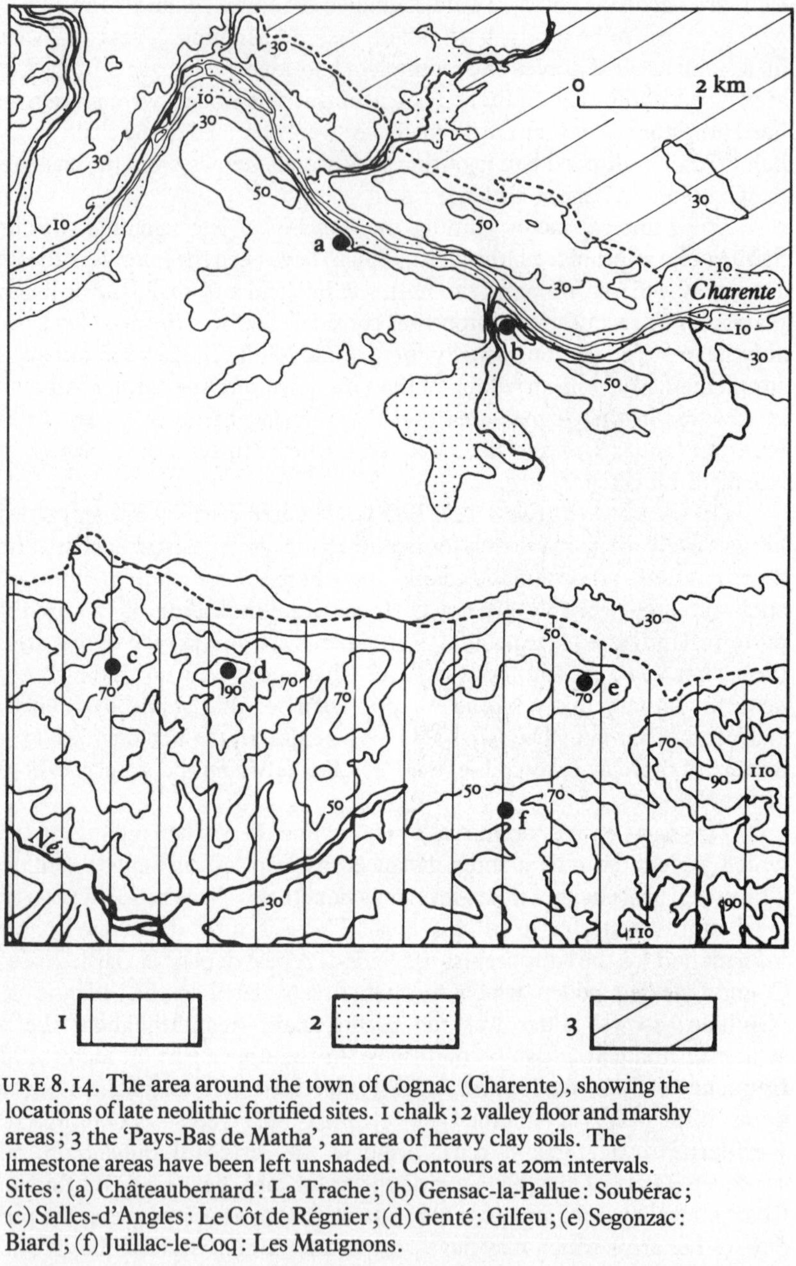

FIGURE 8.14. The area around the town of Cognac (Charente), showing the locations of late neolithic fortified sites. 1 chalk; 2 valley floor and marshy areas; 3 the 'Pays-Bas de Matha', an area of heavy clay soils. The limestone areas have been left unshaded. Contours at 20m intervals. Sites: (a) Châteaubernard: La Trache; (b) Gensac-la-Pallue: Soubérac; (c) Salles-d'Angles: Le Côt de Régnier; (d) Genté: Gilfeu; (e) Segonzac: Biard; (f) Juillac-le-Coq: Les Matignons.

Like the sites of the Royan and Saintes areas they are situated on low hills in rolling chalkland, and in at least one case the hill is substantial and an excellent position for a fortified site (Biard: Plate 8.6 and 'e' on Fig. 8.14). It is however difficult to reconcile the location of these sites with the model of land-use

PLATE 8.6. The area around the town of Cognac (Charente). View looking north over some of the vineyards for which the region is famous towards the late neolithic site of Biard, which occupies the prominent hill in the distance (see Figure 8.14). (Photo: Chris Scarre.)

strategy put forward for the late neolithic settlements of the Royan and Saintes areas discussed above, or for those around the Marais poitevin (Scarre, 1982), on account of their distance from any of the lowland areas. The nearest site is over 5km from the southern edge of the Charente valley. In the hollows between the chalk hills on which the sites stand there are occasional patches of wetter land, but the free-draining nature of the bedrock means that these are few, small and in some cases only seasonal. The landscape is otherwise very dry and water sources are not abundant. In the other areas considered the late neolithic settlements take care to avoid this kind of landscape setting with its limited range of resources and tendency to summer drought.

The explanation for the location of these sites may lie in the suitability of the bedrock for the cutting of ditches. We have suggested that in the Saintes area the hardness of the limestone was a partial deterrent to the late neolithic enclosure-builders. In the Cognac area the problem was compounded by the fact that the soft chalk does not extend to within a reasonable proximity of the Charente valley. A hard limestone plain 5km wide intervenes (Fig.8.14). Under these circumstances the ditched settlements had to be located some distance away. This demonstrates that though locations close to marsh and valley edges were favoured by the late neolithic settlers, considerations other than land-use, and particularly the needs of defence, sometimes led them to found substantial settlements elsewhere.

The hardness of the limestone did not prevent the establishment of unditched settlements on the edge of the Charente valley. The best known of these is at Soubérac ('b' on Fig.8.14), where excavation revealed the base of a well-constructed dry-stone rampart, but apparently no ditch (Burnez, 1965). A similar solution may have been adopted at the promontory site of La Trache ('a') a little way to the west, though here later fortifications have obscured the late neolithic arrangements. Both these sites take advantage of the river cliff as a natural defence, but each is located beside one of the rare defiles which provide an easy means of access from the plateau land to the valley floor. Thus it would have been possible for the inhabitants of Soubérac and La Trache to take cattle down from the settlement to valley floor pastures. In addition, Soubérac stands next to the peaty area known as the Grand Marais referred to earlier, while opposite La Trache on the northern side of the Charente valley is the similar area of Gâte-Bourse le Marais. Finally, both sites would have had access to the Pays-Bas de Matha, which may have provided habitats for hunted forest or woodland species. There is a possible late neolithic enclosure at Ebéon, referred to earlier, but apart from this the earliest artefacts from the Pays-Bas de Matha date from the Late Bronze Age and take the form of a palstave and three socketed axes, perhaps indicating forest clearance at this period.

The variety in the types of landscape accessible from the valley-edge settlements contrasts with the limited possibilities of the chalkland where the ditched sites are located. It is with all the more interest, therefore, that we compare the faunal reports from valley-edge Soubérac and chalkland Les Matignons. The two assemblages are, in fact, broadly similar in terms of the relative frequencies of the different species represented (Table 8.3).

Table 8.3. Faunal assemblages from late neolithic fortified sites in west-central France.

	Chez-Reine	Soubérac	Les Matignons
Cattle	641	713	1746
Pig	140	238	475
Sheep/Goat	231	316	795
Dog	4	15	364
Wild boar	5	36	162
Red deer	1	66	161
Total identifiable	1025	1438	3923

Figures are for numbers of bone fragments. Information from Poulain-Josien, 1965 (Soubérac), 1966 (Les Matignons) and 1967 (Chez-Reine).

How are we to explain the similarity between the faunal assemblages for these two sites which are in such different landscape settings? Cattle were the predominant species not only in the Soubérac and Les Matignons faunal assemblages but also at Chez-Reine (discussed above) and other Peu-Richardien sites, suggesting a cultural preference for beef or cattle products. At both

Soubérac and Chez-Reine wet pasture on which cattle could have been raised may have been available near the settlement in the 3rd millennium bc. At Les Matignons, however ('f' on Fig.8.14), not only is it unlikely that there was suitable pastureland nearby, but the provision even of sufficient drinking water for the human and animal populations must have posed something of a problem, because of the dryness of the chalkland. It is possible that the animals whose bones were found at Les Matignons had been raised elsewhere, perhaps at a valley or marsh-edge site such as Soubérac or Chez-Reine, and were only moved to the site immediately prior to consumption. (Since most parts of the skeleton were represented, the livestock would have to have been moved to Les Matignons 'on the hoof' rather than in the form of meat joints.) Even if this were so, however, the lack of adequate natural water sources at the chalkland settlements would have made an artificial supply essential. It is conceivable that rainwater was stored in artificial ponds or even in the ditches which enclosed the sites. In view of the permeable nature of the chalk bedrock, it would have been necessary to line such excavations with clay if they were to retain water. Proudfoot's analysis of the ditch sediments at Les Matignons (in Burnez and Case, 1966) led him to conclude that the ditches had held water at least periodically, though no traces of a clay lining were detected. The structure reported by the 19th century excavators at the centre of Peu-Richard, approximately circular, 6m deep, and approached by a sloping ramp, may have been a well or cistern, though conclusive evidence of a prehistoric date was not presented and there was no mention of a lining (Eschasseriaux, 1882). It is to be hoped more effort will in future be devoted to the investigation of water storage facilities at these sites.

Conclusion

The palaeoenvironmental evidence which has been presented suggests that the fall in sea-level which occurred in the early 3rd millennium bc had repercussions far inland. In the Charente valley the resulting fall in the water-table may have allowed the hitherto marshy valley floors to be used as wet pasture; while, near the coast, areas of pastureland appeared around the edges of the former marine bays. The importance of the new wet pasture resources is shown by the speed with which a whole series of fortified sites was established overlooking the lowlands. The scale of the defensive works suggests there was competition for control of the limited lowland pastures and a need to protect livestock. The theory put forward here to account for the enclosed settlements of the late neolithic period is therefore one of *geographical opportunism*, advantage being taken of peculiarly favourable environmental circumstances to establish substantial settlements. The favourable circumstances seem only to have been transient, however, and when sea-level began to rise again towards the end of the 3rd millennium the water-table will have risen and there may have been a return to conditions of waterlogging in the lowlands. This may have been one reason for the abandonment of the fortified sites at about this time; there is nothing to indicate that they were violently overthrown. By the end of the millennium the fortified settlements and the Peu-Richardien decorated pottery were already things of the past.

While the late neolithic fortified settlements may as a group have owed their existence to environmental circumstances in the lowlands, this discussion has shown that other factors must be taken into consideration when interpreting the precise locations of individual sites. It is only rarely that the settlements are actually on the marsh or valley edge, and for reasons of defence a position on a hilltop a little distance away is more usual. This is well seen in the Saintes and Royan areas. In the Cognac area, the hardness of the bedrock led to the sites being founded in chalkland well away from any wet lowland area. This is a vivid illustration of the importance which defensive needs could assume in site location strategies. It also suggests that these sites depended for their survival not on the resources of their immediate surroundings only, but also on their interrelationship with similar sites in different types of landscape setting. Whether these links took the form of seasonal cycles of occupation involving two or more sites, or simply of the exchange of products between settlements, it is difficult for us now to say. However, it may be in terms of such networks that the different style-zones of Peu-Richardien pottery referred to earlier (Fig.8.8) should be interpreted. This interdependence between sites may have united them into a single system, relying for its survival on the availability of wet pasture in the region as a whole. The most extensive pastures were probably those of the coastal marshlands, and whatever the local importance of the river valleys it was on the former that the prosperity and continued existence of the late neolithic fortified sites essentially depended. Hence even if the sea-level rise of the late 3rd millennium bc did not seriously affect the middle reaches of the major valleys, the increased waterlogging and salinity which must have resulted in the coastal marshlands may have been sufficient by itself to cause the collapse of the whole settlement system. The marshland edges were not abandoned in the centuries which followed but there seems to have been a return to a pattern of smaller, dispersed settlements, comparable perhaps to that of the period before the favourable 3rd millennium episode. The changes in social organisation with which the abandonment of the fortified sites and the demise of the Peu-Richardien pottery style may have been associated were discussed in an earlier part of this chapter.

Neolithic Settlement in West-Central France

The study of the location of late neolithic fortified sites in west-central France has identified some of the principal factors affecting settlement distribution. It is also important to bear in mind the distinction referred to earlier between the coastal and inland parts of the region. In the coastal zone, the dry limestone plateaux and chalk hills contrast with the wetter river valleys and marshlands while in the inland zone this contrast is less marked because the river valleys are much narrower and the limestone soils of the interfluves have a greater clay content and are more water-retentive than those of the coastal zone. Naturally, this has led to differences in the development of settlement patterns in the two areas. The pattern of chambered tomb distribution shows that the distinction was important in the middle neolithic period, when agricultural settlement seems first to have spread across the landscape. The contrast between late neolithic developments in inland and coastal west-central France may be explained in similar terms, and the distinction between the two zones continued to be of relevance in the Bronze Age.

The development of neolithic settlement in west-central France is still only imperfectly understood and much further research is needed. The evidence which has been presented here, however, allows the following broad outline to be discerned. Only a handful of sites are known which may be dated to the early neolithic period, and most of these are on the coast. The evidence suggests that even the earliest of the known pottery-using sites had an agricultural base, and the spread of settlement around the edges of the dry but fertile plateau-lands of the coastal zone may have begun during this period. The middle neolithic evidence is principally in the form of monumental chambered tombs and no substantial settlement sites are known. It was argued earlier that this could indicate a pattern of settlement consisting of small, dispersed hamlets or farmsteads. Middle neolithic material has been found in most parts of west-central France, in contrast to the predominantly coastal distribution of the earliest agricultural sites, which suggests that this was a period of major settlement expansion and colonisation. The chambered tombs are concentrated in the inland part of the region where the soils are less dry, but they are also found along the edges of the valleys and marshlands in the coastal zone. They may have been foci of dispersed settlement clusters, and their distribution and location may therefore give a broad indication of the distribution pattern of the contemporary settlements.

A major change takes place in the middle and later 3rd millennium bc, first in the coastal zone and later inland. In the coastal zone a whole series of substantial and elaborately fortified settlements appears at c.2800bc, associated with late neolithic Peu-Richardien pottery. These sites are generally on or not far from the edges of coastal marshlands or major river valleys. Their appearance and location can be related to favourable changes in these lowland areas consequent upon a fall in sea-level in the earlier 3rd millennium bc. It was argued above that the fortified sites depended for their support on the availability of the lowland pastures which came into existence as a result of the sea-level fall. Some of the fortified sites were not close to marshland or valley floors, but they were part of the same settlement system and probably still relied indirectly on the resources of the lowlands. Towards the end of the 3rd millennium changes in sea-level and water-table upset the fragile ecological balance in the lowlands and the abandonment of the fortified sites may have been a result of this. The concentrations of population which these settlements appear to have represented were dispersed across the landscape once more.

In inland west-central France the middle neolithic pattern of insubstantial, dispersed settlements and monumental tombs continued down to c.2300 bc, when larger settlement sites made their appearance. These did not become

RADIOCARBON DATES

Early Neolithic						
Les Gouillauds (Charente-Maritime)	4000±120bc	Gif-4878	Charcoal	Open settlement	Impressed Ware	Pautreau and Robert, 1980
Roucadour (Lot)	3980±150bc	Gsy-36A	Charred grain	Settlement	Level C: Roucadourien	*Radiocarbon*, 8, 128
La Tranche (Vendée)	4530±150bc	Gif-5034		Open settlement	Impressed Ware	Joussaume, 1981, 111
	4500±150bc	Gif-5042			Impressed Ware	Joussaume, 1981, 111
	4350±160bc	Gif-4372	Charcoal		Impressed Ware	Joussaume, 1981, 111
Middle Neolithic						
Bougon (Deux-Sèvres)	3880±140bc	Ly-1700	Human bone	Tomb	Tumulus F0	*Radiocarbon*, 21, 438
	3850±230bc	Ly-966	Human bone	Tomb	Tumulus E1	*Radiocarbon*, 18, 75
	3530±170bc	Ly-1699	Human bone	Tomb	Tumulus F0	*Radiocarbon*, 21, 438
	2840±220bc	Ly-967	Human bone	Tomb	Tumulus F2	*Radiocarbon*, 18, 75
	2750±140bc	Ly-1195	Human bone	Tomb	Tumulus E2	*Radiocarbon*, 20, 41
Capdenac-le-Haut (Lot)	3190±120bc	Gif-3715	Charcoal	Open settlement	Level XX: Chasséen	Clottes, 1977b, 540
	3240±120bc	Gif-3714	Charcoal		Level XVI: Chasséen	Clottes, 1977b, 540
	2920±110bc	Gif-3713	Charcoal		Level IX: Chasséen	Clottes, 1977b, 540
	3150±140bc	Gif-2632	Charcoal		Levels IV-V: Chasséen	Clottes, 1977b, 540
Chenon (Charente)	3590±140bc	Ly-1105	Human bone	Tomb	Tumulus B1, chamber T	*Radiocarbon*, 20, 41
La Ciste des Cous (Vendée)	2730±130bc	Gif-3676	Carbonised wood	Tomb		Joussaume, 1978
La Perte du Cros (Lot)	3260bc	H		Settlement	Level III: Chasséen	Clottes, 1977a, 32
	2850±130bc	Gsy-36B	Charred grain		Hearth III: Chasséen	*Radiocarbon*, 8, 128
	2700bc	H			Level II: Chasséen	Clottes, 1977a, 32
Roquefort (Gironde)	3050±140	Gif-1732	Charcoal	Open settlement	Level C2	*Radiocarbon*, 16, 28
	2850±140bc	Gif-1731	Charcoal		Level C1: Roquefort group	*Radiocarbon*, 16, 28
Roucadour (Lot)	3230±140bc	Gsy-36B	Charred grain	Settlement	Level B1: Chasséen	*Radiocarbon*, 8, 129
Les Sables-d'Olonne (Vendée)	2620±110bc	Gif-4880	Animal bone		'Vase-support'	Joussaume and Robin, 1980
Late Neolithic						
Biard (Charente)	2391±137bc	Gsy		Ditched settle.	Moulin-de-Vent group	Coursaget *et al.*, 1961
Bougon (Deux-Sèvres)	2520±230bc	Ly-968	Human bone	Tomb	Tumulus F2: Vienne-Charente	*Radiocarbon*, 18, 74
Champ Durand (Vendée)	2160±130bc	Gif-3675	Charcoal	Ditched settle.	Peu-Richardien	Joussaume, 1977

Le Montiou (Deux-Sèvres)	2580±110bc	Gif-4373	Human bone	Tomb	Vienne-Charente	Germond *et al.*, 1978
Ors (Charente-Maritime)	2130±120bc	Gif-1330	Charcoal	Open settlement	Peu-Richardien II	*Radiocarbon*, 14, 283
	2120±120bc	Gif-1329	Charcoal		Peu-Richardien II	*Radiocarbon*, 14, 283
La Sauzaie (Charente-Maritime)	2550±140bc	Gif-1557	Shell	Open settlement	Peu-Richardien I	*Radiocarbon*, 16, 24
	2460±120bc	Gif-2608			Peu-Richardien II	Burnez, 1976, 373
	2410±120bc	Gif-2610			Peu-Richardien II	Burnez, 1976, 373
Semussac (Charente-Maritime)	2770±110bc	Gif-1718	Shell	Ditched settle.	IX, level 2: Matignons	*Radiocarbon*, 16, 24
	2740±250bc	Gif-474	Shell		IX, level 2: Matignons	*Radiocarbon*, 12, 435
	2450±135bc	Gif-1717	Shell		IX, level 3: Peu-R. II	*Radiocarbon*, 16, 24
	2300±250bc	Gif-475	Shell		IX, level 3: Peu-R. II	*Radiocarbon*, 12, 435
	2120±110bc	Gif-1719	Shell		X: Peu-Richardien II?	*Radiocarbon*, 16, 24
LATE NEOLITHIC/CHALCOLITHIC						
Camp Allaric (Vienne)	2310±140bc	Gif-3009	Charcoal	Promontory fort	Trench VI: Artenacien	Pautreau, 1976, 407
	2270±140bc	Gif-3010	Charcoal		Trench VI: Artenacien	Pautreau, 1976, 407
Anse de la République (Vendée)	1900±130bc	Gif-3828	Charcoal	Open settlement	Beaker	Joussaume, 1977
Grotte d'Eybral (Dordogne)	2190±135bc	Gif-2384	Charcoal	Burial cave	Isle-Dordogne	Roussot-Larroque, 1973
La Fontaine de la Demoiselle (Dordogne)	2300±140bc	Gif-1733	Charcoal	Open settlement	Levels B1/B2: Late Neo.	*Radiocarbon*, 16, 25
	2300±140bc	Gif-2617	Charcoal		Level A2: Artenacien	Roussot-Larroque, 1973
	2280±140bc	Gif-2618	Charcoal		Ditch FW: Artenacien	Roussot-Larroque, 1973
	2260±140bc	Gif-1734	Charcoal		Levels B1/B2: Late Neo.	*Radiocarbon*, 16, 25
La Pierre-Levée, Nieul-sur-l'Autize (Vendée)	2090±130bc	Gif-3417	Human bone	Tomb	Beaker	Joussaume, 1976b
Le Petit Rocher (Vendée)	2340±130bc	Gif-3761	Charcoal	Open settlement	Beaker	L'Helgouach, 1977
Camp de Pierre-Dure (Vienne)	2200±130bc	Gif-2743	Charcoal	Promontory fort	Rampart: Artenacien	Gomez, 1975
Grotte du Quéroy (Charente)	2310±110bc	Gif-3285	Charcoal	Burial cave	Level 7: Artenacien	Gomez, 1978
La Sauzaie (Charente-Maritime)	2040±110bc	Gif-2245	Shell	Open settlement	Level 2: Beaker/Artenacien	*Radiocarbon*, 16, 24
La Pierre-Virante, Xanton-Chassenon (Vendée)	2090±130bc	Gif-3762	Bone	Tomb	Beaker/Artenacien	Joussaume, 1977

as numerous as those of the coastal zone and a considerable part of the population must have continued to live in small, insubstantial settlements as in the preceding period. The larger late neolithic settlements of inland west-central France continued in occupation well into the Bronze Age, however, long after the more numerous Peu-Richardien fortified sites had been abandoned.

The Neolithic of Brittany and Normandy

JAMES HIBBS

The land o coastal changes o vegetational history o history of research o MATERIAL CULTURE o settlement and sites o *Carn* o RITUAL MONUMENTS o chambered tombs o early passage graves o earthen long mounds o passage grave development o lateral entry passage graves o angled passage graves o V-shaped passage graves o *allées couvertes* o *dolmens simples* o menhirs and alignments o megalithic art o PRODUCTION CENTRES and exchange networks o flint o dolerite o hornblendite o neolithic pottery o *Castellic* o *Souc'h* o *Conguel* o *Kerugou* and others o lithic artefacts o ornaments o mortuary ritual o ROLE OF RITUAL MONUMENTS.

THROUGH THE RICHNESS of its archaeological record, north-western France is one of the areas of Europe best known to prehistorians. Large numbers of megalithic tombs and menhirs testify impressively to the activity of neolithic communities, and these early attracted the interest of antiquarians. A long tradition of research increased our knowledge of the neolithic ritual monuments of the region, but much less is known about prehistoric settlement sites and economies than in many adjacent parts of France.

For the purposes of this survey Brittany is defined as the *départements* of Morbihan, Finistère, Côtes-du-Nord, Ille-et-Vilaine, and Loire-Atlantique north of the Loire. Western Normandy forms part of the Armorican Massif and will also be dealt with here. It covers the *départements* of Manche and Orne, together with western Calvados and northern Mayenne. Only the accident of history has divided the Channel Islands from the adjacent mainland with which they belong both culturally and geographically, and they also will be included in this survey as an integral part of north-western France (Fig.9.1).

These areas together constitute the Armorican Massif, a relatively unified geographical, topographical and climatic region, distinct from neighbouring regions. The massif is based on ancient Precambrian formations, covered to some extent by sedimentary slates, sandstones and shales with locally small areas of Tertiary sands and clays. The principal upland elements are resistant granites, faulted ENE/WSW. The eastern and southern limits of the massif are defined by the junction with Jurassic and Cretaceous sedimentary formations –

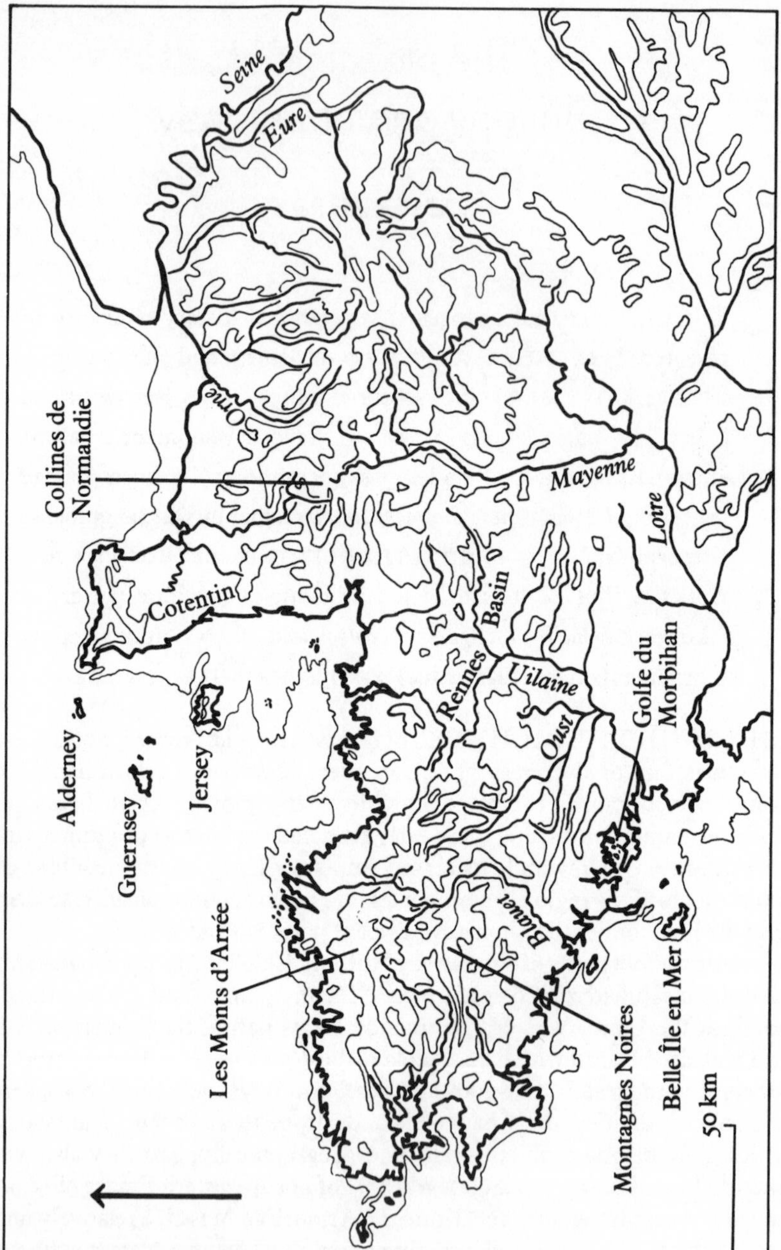

FIGURE 9.1. General topography of Brittany and Normandy. Contours at intervals of 100m; submarine contour at −25m.

to the east, those of the Paris basin; to the south, the limestone Vendéen plain and the Jurassic formations of Poitou. The boundary to the east is not sharp, since the limestones and chalks east of Caen are sealed by clays which give rise to patterns of land-use similar to those of the Armorican Massif (Naval Intelligence Division, 1942; Cogné, 1974).

The *Breton peninsula* is traditionally divided into two areas – internal upland (Breton: Argoat) and lower, coastal areas (Breton: Arvor). The eastern Argoat is characterised by the quartzitic formations of the Monts d'Arrée in the north and the Montagnes Noires in the south, which are aligned east-west and reach heights of 384m and 326m. The Landes de Lanvaux, in Morbihan, are chiefly granitic and belong to a separate system. Lower down, there is an upland gneiss and schist-based plateau, on average 250m above sea-level. This plateau descends to the Arvor areas which are characterised by resistant granites and schists, forming the headlands and promontories of an indented coastline. Besides this differentiation, other major lowland areas are present, in particular the Rennes basin in the east and the smaller Châteaulin basin in the west. The northern coast generally takes the form of a cliff, up to 65m in height, but in the south the Arvor area is both wider and lower and coastal features are less dramatic, with few cliffs over 20m in height.

Western Normandy is separated from the Argoat by the Rennes basin, the reclaimed Marais de Dol and by lowlands around La Baie du Saint-Michel (Cogné, 1974). To the east of these plains the Bocage normand rises sharply, with two major granite ridges running east-west and reaching heights of 361m and 416m. North of these ridges lie the lowlands of the Carentan basin and the west Norman coastal plain (Bender, 1967). The Channel Islands to the west of the Cotentin peninsula consist of granite outcrops and repeat many of the principal features of the mainland in miniature (Elhäi, 1963).

The soil cover of north-western France is varied, but on the whole poor and thin. Podzols are common, especially in upland areas and the northern Arvor. The soils of the Bocage areas are mainly clays, but in sandstone and some granitic areas high proportions of sand are found. Clays predominate again in the Carentan basin of Normandy, though around Caen there are better, limestone-based soils. Loess deposits occur in places, notably along the coast of Côtes-du-Nord and northern Finistère, in central Ille-et-Vilaine, and in parts of Calvados, the central Cotentin and the Channel Islands. As in central Europe, the loess seems to have attracted early agriculturalists, and early settlement is found particularly in those parts of north-western France where loess is a major soil component (Kinnes, 1982; Caillaud and Lagnel, 1972).

Predominance of acid soils in this region has considerably affected the survival of organic material. A high survival rate of bone and antler in the Calvados group of megalithic tombs, where the soils are alkaline and based on chalks and limestones, graphically illustrates the destructive effect of soil acidity in the west of the region (Verron, 1973; Caillaud and Lagnel, 1972). In the Channel Islands, the effect of soil acidity was offset to some extent by the prehistoric practice of placing shellfish remains in the mortuary deposit; bone was preserved in 25 of 65 excavated sites on the Channel Islands because of this (Kendrick, 1928; Lukis, F.C., 1845). Similarly, shell midden material at the sites of Téviec and Hoëdic (Morbihan) contributed to good bone preservation (Péquart *et al.*, 1937; Péquart and Péquart, 1954).

Soil cover in the interior and upland areas of Brittany is often shallow. This has hindered the build-up of stratigraphic sequences, and archaeological deposits are not protected by depth of soil from the harmful effects of ploughing. Unstratified scatters of material are common. In addition, owing to the hardness of the bedrock, ditches in which sequences of archaeological deposits could have collected are rare.

Coastal Changes. Local sequences of postglacial sea-level change have been established for Normandy, northern Brittany and the Channel Islands. While there has been a general rise in sea-level during this period, on the local scale there have been considerable variations (Elhäi, 1963; Morzadec-Kerfourn, 1973, 1974; Jones and Keen, in prep.).

The evidence of peats and other organic deposits in the intertidal zone or on the sea-bed, and of submerged archaeological sites, shows that significant areas of land have been lost to the sea during the last few millennia. Between 6000bc and 4000bc sea-level rose by approximately 16m. By the end of the Atlantic period, around 3800bc, the rapid postglacial sea-level rise had passed its peak and present-day low-tide levels had been reached. Major oscillations continued throughout the later prehistoric period. A post-neolithic rise in sea-level caused the submergence of the menhir of Men Ozac'h, the *allée couverte* of Kernic (Finistère) and many other sites, and resulted in the deposition of marine silts at the Gasworks megalithic site on Jersey (Morzadec-Kerfourn, 1969; Wedgewood and Mourant, 1954). The submergence of these sites is almost certainly to be dated to after 2000bc. Comb-decorated Maritime Beaker and Beaker-derived pottery has been found in peat deposits sealed by marine clay at Halkett Place, Jersey; and at Cherbourg (Manche) bronze axes were found at a depth of 1.50m in a peat level sealing sand in which lay a neolithic arrowhead (Hawkes, 1939; Bender, 1967). These finds suggest a major rise in sea-level between the neolithic and middle bronze age periods.

Changes in sea-level will have had three effects on the archaeological record. First, many coastal areas will have been drowned, leading to the loss both of individual sites and of their economic exploitation ranges. The sites of Téviec (m.r.1) and Hoëdic (m.r.2), for instance, which are now on islands, represent the remains of a settlement and activity pattern in a littoral zone which it is now impossible to reconstruct. The high density of neolithic sites around the coasts of the Channel Islands and the Golfe du Morbihan occurs in areas where large amounts of land have been lost, and suggest that those areas which have been most affected by sea-level change were the ones preferred by neolithic communities.

Sea-level rise will also have affected the archaeological record through the formation of coastal dunes. The areas of sand cover involved are large enough to distort distribution patterns, making the detection of archaeological sites very difficult (Oliver, 1870; L'Helgouach, 1970; Kinnes, 1982). The agriculturally unattractive nature of dune areas does however lead to the preservation of prehistoric sites in the long term.

The third effect of sea-level change concerns the interpretation of prehistoric behaviour. Rising sea-level would have had a substantially dislocating impact on human communities which were wholly or partly dependent for their livelihood on marine or littoral resources. Even relatively small-scale changes may have had important consequences in this respect.

Vegetational History. The correlation between the postglacial development of the vegetation of England and of northern France is in general terms very close. The sequence in north-western France begins with a developing Boreal mixed oak woodland, where pine (*Pinus*) and hazel (*Corylus*) were gradually declining and lime (*Tilia*) and alder (*Alnus*) increasing (Bender, 1967). The end of the Atlantic period is marked by a major change, with an increase in alder pollen (up to 90 per cent of the total arboreal pollen at Tréompan, Finistère: Morzadec-Kerfourn, 1969), and a corresponding decline in most other species, including elm (*Ulmus*) and lime. The elm decline is particularly well represented at Saint Michel-de-Brasparts (Finistère), where it is associated with a slight increase in ribwort plantain (*Plantago lanceolata*) and bracken (*Pteridium*). This horizon is dated 3450bc. The evidence from this site may be held to indicate human clearance, with the bracken reflecting the subsequent abandonment of the cleared land, though the low levels of ribwort plantain prior to 3450bc might indicate its survival as a relict species in certain Atlantic coastal habitats throughout the Last Glacial, a point Van Zeist admits (M. Jones, pers.comm.; Van Zeist, 1964). Nevertheless, palynological information from the pre-mound surface at Dissignac (Loire-Atlantique), which is dated to between 4300bc and 3830bc, indicates an open, already cleared landscape. Oak and hazel pollen were present but there were high levels of ribwort plantain, sorrel (*Rumex*), mugwort (*Artemisia*) and *Compositae tubuliflorae*. There was also cereal pollen, the association of which with ruderals suggests some form of agricultural clearance in the 5th millennium bc (L'Helgouach, 1977a; Visset, 1974).

Clearance of Atlantic forests seems to have taken place prior to the construction of the monuments of Dissignac (m.r.4), Ile Carn (m.r.10) and Les Fouaillages (m.r.7), but this cannot be seen as evidence of large-scale agricultural clearance, until more data are available. The indications are, however, that sporadic forest clearance for pastoral and arable activities was undertaken by late mesolithic groups, prior to the introduction of full neolithic economies and the construction of ritual monuments.

The elm decline is also represented in a pollen core from the Bellengreville marsh (Calvados) in western Normandy. Here again, plantain increases in abundance just below the Atlantic/SubBoreal boundary. It is associated at this site with peaks of grasses (*Gramineae*) and hazel. The evidence suggests that clearance took place on various occasions prior to and at the Atlantic/Sub-

Boreal transition (Elhäi, 1963). The Bellengreville marsh is close to several megalithic tombs and the relationship between early clearance and the construction of ritual monuments could here be tested. Without the benefit of radiocarbon dates, however, the value of the Bellengreville evidence for the interpretation of late Atlantic clearance is limited. It suggests nonetheless that in Normandy as in Brittany permanent clearings were being made prior to the construction of ritual monuments.

In Brittany, forest clearance appears to have intensified during the middle and later 3rd millennium bc. This may have been related to the uptake of new land in central Brittany, changes in social and economic relationships and the adoption of the allée couverte. At La Plage de Porsguen (Finistère) an increase in pollen of bracken and plantain was associated with burnt wood and flint artefacts suggestive of human activity. The base of the deposit was dated to 2170bc, which compares well with the date of 2285bc for a similar deposit at Correjou (Finistère). At the latter site there is a burnt horizon, above which plantain and bracken increase, sorrel and nettle (*Urtica*) appear, while oak declines and ash (*Fraxinus*) disappears. Some cereal pollen was present, but the primary land-use seems to have been pastoral rather than arable (Morzadec-Kerfourn, 1969, 1974).

By the end of the neolithic period, clearance specifically for arable purposes was taking place, even in the central uplands of Brittany. At Spézet (Finistère) a clearance horizon dated to 1990bc shows elm, lime and ash pollen decreasing and a corresponding increase in ribwort plantain, sorrel and bracken, while wheat (*Triticum*) appears for the first time. A similar clearance horizon at Saint Michel-de-Brasparts is dated to 1820bc (Van Zeist, 1964).

HISTORY OF RESEARCH. The dominance of ritual monuments in the archaeological record of Brittany and western Normandy has conditioned the development of research and interpretation. The impression which the ritual monuments, immediately visible both to local communities and to antiquarians, made on historical communities is demonstrated by the association of many of them with supernatural place names and legends (De Guérin, 1921). This association has helped the preservation of some sites through the fear of supernatural sanction if they were disturbed. Christianisation of tombs and menhirs is another reflection of this attitude. The fear of supernatural sanction was not, however, enough to protect all or even a majority of these sites. Written evidence from Jersey suggests that at least 45 monuments were destroyed by agricultural operations between 1682 and 1785, leaving now only 14, all discovered since 1785 (Poingdestre, 1682; Hibbs, forthcoming). Place-name evidence from Guernsey suggests a total of 68 tombs and 39 menhirs in the 14th century, of which only 12 and 5 respectively survive today (De Guérin, 1921; Kinnes, forthcoming).

In mainland France, 19th century agricultural intensification and uptake of marginal land are well documented (Sutton, 1977). Figures for the amount of wasteland in Brittany in 1733 indicate that nearly half the total land area was uncultivated, and that significant amounts of wasteland could be found in all parts of the region, though especially in Finistère and Morbihan. This suggests that there may have been a high rate of site survival up to the 18th and 19th centuries. The pattern may have been similar to that documented in Mecklenburg (East Germany), where many sites survived into the 19th century, with increased destruction of monuments within the last 150 years (Sprockhoff, 1938, 48–52; Schuldt, 1972, 14–18).

The attraction of the prominent ritual monuments of Brittany and western Normandy for antiquarians unfortunately led to the growth of a rather narrow outlook on the neolithic remains of the region. Sites tended to be seen in terms of their architecture and as containers for artefacts, and while these attitudes have fostered the development of comprehensive typologies and comparative collections, they have obscured many of the deeper issues and have limited the type of information recorded from early excavations.

The earliest references to Breton neolithic monuments illustrate the way in which the eye was drawn towards these features. The mounds of Locmariaquer (Morbihan), for instance, were used as fixed points in the sailing instructions of Pierre Garcie dit Ferrande as early as 1483/4 (Giot *et al.*, 1979, 16). This early reference is typical of accounts prior to 1800, in that the sites are mentioned not for their own interest, but in connection with other concerns.

By 1820, antiquarian interest in the ritual monuments of north-western France had become well-established, and surveys and excavations were taking place (e.g. Mahé, 1825; see also Daniel, 1960). Individual investigators tended to confine their activities to a local level, and this restricted the kinds of conclusion which could be drawn. Mahé's survey of 1825, for example, was concerned only with the Morbihan. The work of the Lukis family, however, forms an exception to this pattern. They were based on the Channel Islands, where most of their activities were located, but they also investigated monuments in different parts of Brittany and Normandy, and their interests reached as far afield as India (Atkinson, 1976; Lukis, F.C., 1865; Lukis, W.C., 1868).

Although the antiquarians preserved much information which has since been destroyed by agricultural and industrial development, their techniques of investigation and excavation were relatively crude and many types of evidence went unrecognised. By the end of the 19th century the situation was improving, and it was at this time that a series of major regional accounts became available, covering Ille-et-Vilaine (Bézier, 1883), Côtes-du-Nord (De la Chénelière, 1880, 1883), and Finistère (Du Châtellier, 1907). Between 1894 and 1929 the megalithic monuments of Normandy were studied by Coutil (1894, 1895a, b, 1907; Bender, 1967), and in 1897 Du Châtellier published a comprehensive survey of Breton prehistoric pottery. With these developments, the basic work of documenting existing sites and artefacts reached the point where new information could be provided with a context (Giot *et al.*, 1979, 20–1).

The foundation of the Société Préhistorique Française in 1904 marked the beginning of the period of controlled investigation of the prehistoric monuments of north-western France, and provided a national organisation and a more critical context for research. The period after 1918 is dominated in Brittany by the work of Zacharie Le Rouzic and the Sub-Commission for Prehistoric Monuments. Le Rouzic inherited the mantle of doyen of Breton prehistory from James Miln, the founder of the Carnac Museum. From 1909 to 1939 his publications provided a wealth of information about his enthusiastic, some would say over-enthusiastic, excavations and restorations (L'Helgouach, 1965). The period between the wars also saw notable work carried out by Marsille in the Morbihan, by Devoir in Finistère, by Colline in Ille-et-Vilaine, and by S-J. and M. Péquart in southern Britanny. The Péquarts' excavations of mesolithic and neolithic sites, including the famous Téviec and Hoëdic, marked a major advance in the excavation techniques in use in the region (Giot *et al.*, 1979, 21–2).

The interpretation of archaeological evidence is always largely conditioned by the accepted methodological and intellectual approaches, and in north-western France the difficulties of organising and ordering the large amounts of material which are available have led to the predominance of classification in most published work. Le Rouzic (1933), Forde (1930, 1932) and Daniel (1939, 1941) have all followed W. C. Lukis (1868) in producing important works of classification and interpretation. Since the war, the classificatory approach has been continued by the work of Giot and L'Helgouach; the published work of these scholars provides much of the documentation for this study. To cite it in detail would punctuate every other sentence with a cross-reference, so due acknowledgment is made here (see Bibliography at end of book). Interpretations have however changed, as new types of information have become available and as new types of data collection have been employed. These have led to a gradual move away from the traditional concentration on ritual monuments and to the realisation of the breadth of the archaeological record. Absolute dating methods have provided information crucial to the understanding of the development of the various types of ritual monument and their interrelationships, and this in itself has stimulated new analytical approaches and interpretative hypotheses (Giot, 1971; Renfrew, 1976). The problem of the predominance of ritual monuments in the prehistoric record of Armorica remains important, however, and is only gradually being corrected by work at other types of site.

Material Culture

(References to sources have as far as possible been grouped at the end of paragraphs)

The neolithic material culture of north-western France consists principally of megalithic and other ritual monuments and the artefacts associated with them. The ritual nature of most sites makes it difficult to decide whether the objects deposited at or in them are a sample of the entire range of material in use, or whether they were specially selected for ritually-related activities. Other sources of information include a handful of settlement sites and a few lithic artefact production centres. Characterisation of lithic artefacts has provided some information about social and economic exchange in this region during the neolithic period (Le Rouzic, 1934; Godfray and Burdo, 1949, 1950; Le Roux, 1971; Verron, 1981).

The typology of the chambered tombs provides a chronological framework to which other artefacts can be related and suggests that the Neolithic may be broadly divided into two periods. The first of these lies between c.4000bc and 2500bc, and can be subdivided into an earlier phase (4000bc–3000bc) characterised by early passage grave types, and a later (3000bc–2500bc) when *evolved* passage graves were common. The second period, c.2500–1900bc, is characterised by the *allée couverte* and *dolmen simple* types of chambered tomb. There is an underlying trend during the Neolithic towards increasing diversification and regionalisation in most aspects of material culture. This is well illustrated by the regionally- and locally-specific pottery and tomb types which became common towards the end of Period 1 and in Period 2. It will be argued later, however, that despite the spatial variability of material culture, the building and use of large-scale ritual monuments served to maintain and articulate relationships between communities in different parts of north-western France throughout the Neolithic. Only with the introduction of new stimuli, including Beakers and metal technology, in the 3rd millennium, did a major social and economic realignment take place.

SETTLEMENT AND SETTLEMENT SITES. Few early neolithic settlement sites are known from Brittany and western Normandy, though their number is increasing as a result of recent work (Verron, 1976; Kinnes, 1982). The earliest evidence for sedentary groups belongs to the middle and late 5th millennium, and takes the form of land-clearance indications together with a small group of excavated settlements including Téviec and Hoëdic (Morbihan) and Beg an Dorchenn (Finistère; m.r.3). Téviec and Hoëdic appear to have been mesolithic midden settlements similar to those known from the Hebrides and Denmark (Albrethsen and Brinch Petersen, 1976). Hoëdic has yielded a radiocarbon date of 4625bc. The economy of these sites was based on the exploitation of coastal and marine resources, shellfish in particular, with elements of hinterland hunting and gathering, a type of economy thought sometimes to represent an intermediate stage between hunting and gathering and settled agriculture. The presence of domesticates (dog and sheep or goat at Téviec, cattle at Hoëdic and Beg an Dorchenn) suggests there was a pastoral element in the economy of these mesolithic groups (Péquart *et al.*, 1937; Péquart and Péquart, 1954; L'Helgouach, 1971).

Sedentary and semi-sedentary groups such as these, concentrated in littoral areas and practising some clearance of the forest for pastoral activities, seem to have provided the context in which the first neolithic communities appeared. It is likely that the earlier social organisations and economic strategies did not disappear but continued to exist alongside the new.

Development of the Proto- and Primary Neolithic is clearer in Brittany than in Normandy, where there is little evidence either of mesolithic activity or of mesolithic-neolithic acculturation (Verron, 1976). The earliest Neolithic in this part of France is represented by some groups using material ultimately of Bandkeramik derivation and by others using material of indigenous type (L'Helgouach, 1971; Godfray and Burdo, 1949; Ilett, this volume). The origins of the indigenous material are obscure. The material of Bandkeramik tradition belongs to a phase in the early 4th millennium bc when increasing regionalisation of pottery styles was taking place. This was associated with the expansion of settlement onto types of land not previously occupied, and with an increasing variety of economic strategies. The occupation at this period of defensible sites, often promontories or hill-spurs, such as La Brèche-au-Diable (Mont Joly) (Calvados; m.r.5), Mont Orgueil (Jersey) and L'Erée (Guernsey) has been noted as a feature also of early and middle neolithic settlement in north-eastern France (Chapters 2–4 above). The early occupation at La Brèche-au-Diable, which is associated with material of Bandkeramik tradition and which underlies middle neolithic levels, has yielded a radiocarbon date of 3830bc, which compares closely with the dates of 3640bc and 3560bc for similar material from the site of Les Fouaillages (m.r.7). These dates agree well with the early neolithic sequence in the Paris basin (Constantin, pers. comm.). The suspect date for material of Bandkeramik tradition at Le Pinacle, 3070bc, can now be seen to be too young.

Material similar to the fine wares from Le Pinacle (Fig.9.2, 2; m.r.6) has come from the long mounds of Mané Ty Ec and Mané Pochat er Ieu in the Morbihan, suggesting that Bandkeramik influences extended into western Brittany. In the south-eastern corner of the region, a settlement of the Bandkeramik-derived *Augy-Sainte-Pallaye* group has recently been discovered at La Bajoulière, near Angers (Maine-et-Loire: Gruet and Passini, 1982).

Material of Bandkeramik tradition is also known from ritual monuments such as Les Fouaillages, but does not appear to have been associated with the use of chambered tombs. Bandkeramik-related sherds at La Hoguette (Calvados; m.r.14) were stratified below the passage grave, although the date of 3610bc from chamber IV suggests there can have been no great difference in time (Fig.9.2, 1; Caillaud and Lagnel, 1972). The presence of material of Bandkeramik tradition in passage graves, such as for example La Varde (Guernsey), is almost certainly the result of processes of redeposition.

Evidence of primary neolithic settlement sites in Brittany itself is very limited. Potsherds were found in pre-passage grave levels at Dissignac (Loire-Atlantique; m.r.4). These are of a type which is only known from this one site, and is distinct from the *Carn* ware associated with the early passage graves. Carn pottery (Fig.9.2, 3–6) comes principally from chambered tombs, and with the possible exceptions of Prat ar C'hastel (Finistère) and La Butte-aux-Pierres (Loire-Atlantique) is not represented at settlement sites (Giot *et al.*, 1979; Bellancourt, 1966).

Middle neolithic settlement sites are also rare. Many of those known appear to have been new foundations, for example Curnic (Finistère; m.r.8) and Herquemoulin (Manche). There are radiocarbon dates from Curnic but

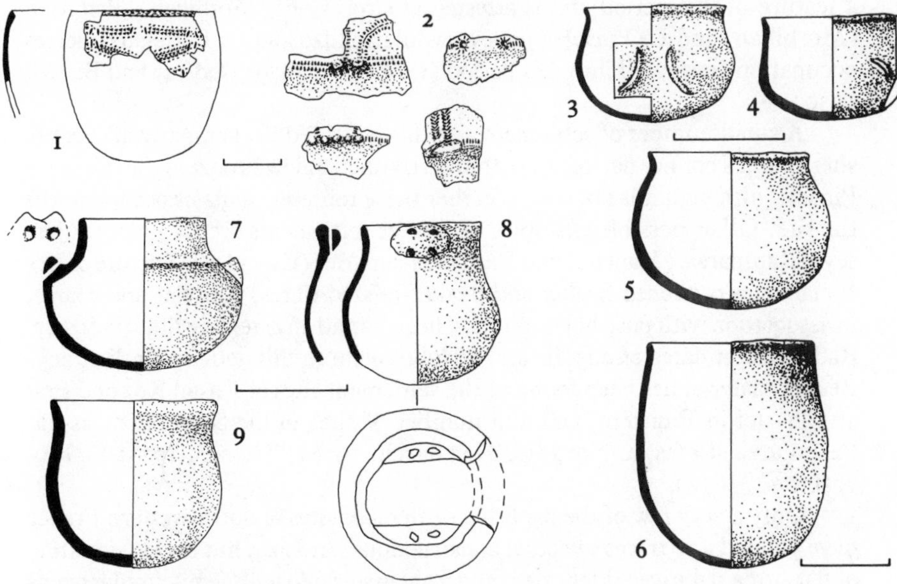

FIGURE 9.2. Primary neolithic pottery.
1, 2 pottery of Bandkeramik tradition from (1) La Hoguette (Calvados) and (2) Le Pinacle (Jersey).
3-6 Carn ware: Round-based bowls with applied 'crescent' motifs from (3) central chamber of Ile Carn (Finistère) and (4) Kervadel (Finistère). Undecorated round-based bowls from (5) Ile Carn and (6) Larcuste 1 (Morbihan).
7-9 Normandy primary neolithic/middle neolithic round-based vessels: 7 bowl with bi-perforated lugs from Metreville (Eure); 8 bowl with bi-perforated internal lugs from Vierville (Manche); 9 round-based bowl from La Hoguette.
(1, 9 after Caillaud and Lagnel, 1972; 3, 4 after Giot, L'Helgouach and Monnier, 1979; 5 after L'Helgouach, 1965; 6 after L'Helgouach and Lecornec, 1976; 7, 8 after Verron, 1976; 2 after material now in the Museum of the Société Jersiaise.) All scales 10cm.

these are not entirely reliable and range between 4030bc and 2650bc. Axes of Plussulien dolerite found at the site link the occupation to the exploitation of the Plussulien quarries, dated to between 3320bc and 2100bc. Middle neolithic settlements are also attested at La Butte-aux-Pïerres (Bellancourt, 1966), Er Lannic (Morbihan; m.r.9: Le Rouzic, 1930), La Motte (Jersey: Hawkes, 1939) and at the 3ha fortified site of Lizo (Morbihan: Le Rouzic, 1933), among others. Most of these are on coasts or islands, and it is clear that the coastal areas continued to be important during this period.

Major developments took place at the end of the 3rd millennium, associated with the introduction of new traditions. The uptake of new land in the central areas of Brittany occurred at about this time, and this expansion of settlement may indicate a realignment of economic strategies. Direct evidence of settlement sites is still, however, limited. Reoccupation of earlier sites was a feature of this period and is attested at Croh Collé (Morbihan), Pen Men (Morbihan) and Le Pinacle (Jersey), while at Lizo and La Butte-aux-Pierres occupation continued into this period (Giot *et al.*, 1979; Godfray and Burdo, 1950).

A small number of settlement sites have yielded Beaker material. Beaker sherds and a copper flat axe were found stratified below bronze age levels at Le Pinacle, although it is not clear whether these represent a major occupation of the site. Other possible examples of Beaker settlements are La Pulente (Jersey), Raumarais (Manche) and Bernières-sur-Mer (Calvados). The site of Les Fouaillages produced Beaker and Beaker-related wares, both fine and coarse, in association with post-holes, pits and hearths and an extensive lithic industry. Radiocarbon dates of 2050bc and 1880bc relate to this activity. In Brittany, Beaker material has been found at the settlement sites of Kastel Koz and Prat ar C'hastel in Finistère, and at a number of sites in the Saint Nicholas-du-Pelem area (Côtes-du-Nord) (L'Helgouach, 1976a; Treinen, 1970; Le Provost *et al.*, 1972).

Only a very few of the neolithic settlement sites of north-western France have yielded any traces of actual constructions. At Lizo, hut floors consisting of flat stone slabs were identified, and were associated with semi-circular ovens set into the defensive banks. The structures measured up to 3m×4.5m in size (Le Rouzic, 1933). Hut floors of large slabs were also found at Er Yoh. More common are stone-built hearths, which have been reported from Lizo, Er Yoh, Curnic, Er Lannic and Le Pinacle (Giot *et al.*, 1979, 343–6; Godfray and Burdo, 1949, 1950). A single pot, filled with limpets and set on a hearth, was found beneath a layer of blown sand at Les Blanches Banques (Jersey: Hawkes, 1939).

The poverty of settlement site evidence from Brittany and western Normandy is disappointing, particularly in view of the richness of this part of France in burial and other ritual monuments. The virtual absence of a whole class of site places severe constraints on the interpretation of the neolithic record of the area. As survey and excavation techniques improve, however, more settlement sites are being reported, and it is hoped that a fuller picture will soon emerge.

Ritual Monuments

Chambered Tombs. The ritual monuments of north-western France have been well described both by antiquarians and more recently by prehistorians, from Blair, Rowlands, and Lukis in the 19th century to L'Helgouach and Verron in the postwar period. The complexity of the ritual landscape which these monuments represent, however, has yet to be fully recognised and understood.

Megalithic tombs form the dominant class of ritual monument (Figs 9.3–6). They display a clear range of architectural and functional variations. The basic form is found at the earliest sites – a chamber with internal divisions set within a mound or cairn and reached by a passage. This early form underwent a series of transformations during the course of the neolithic

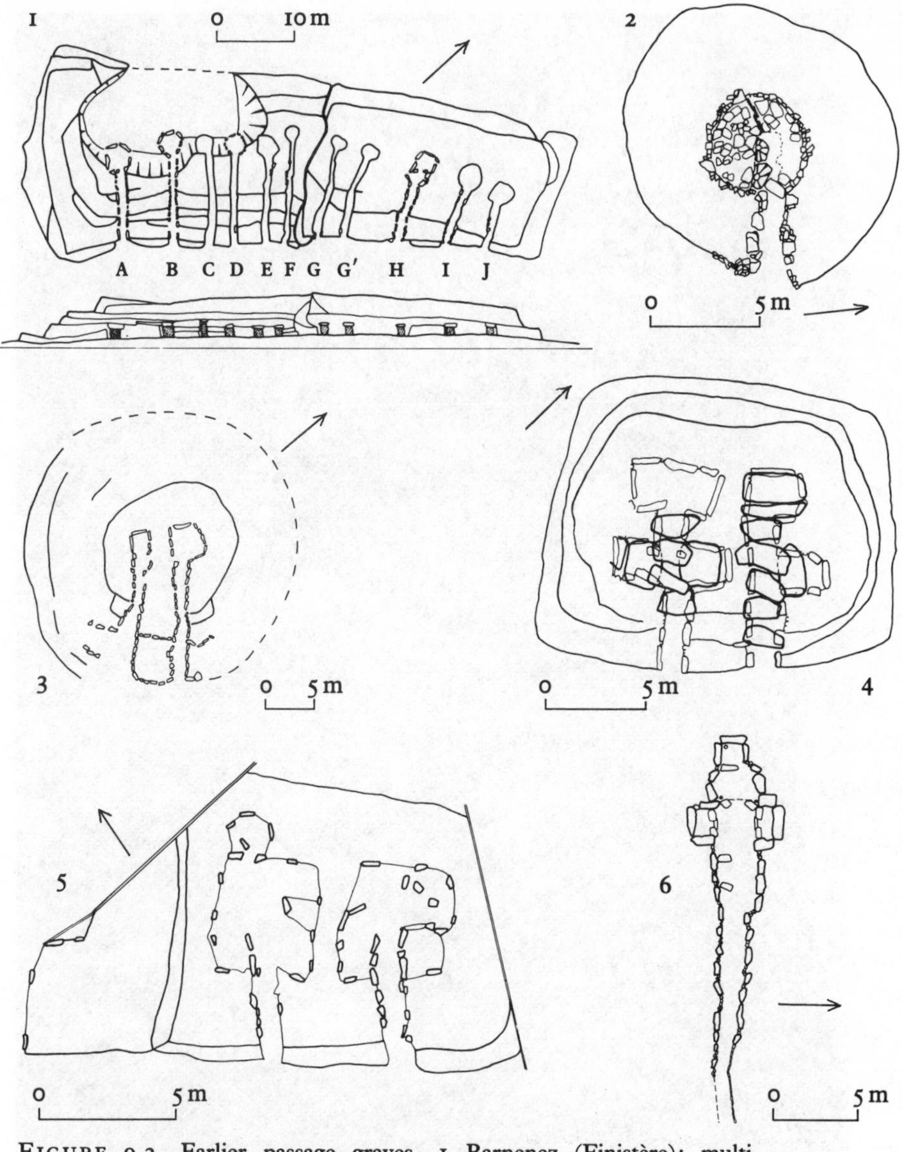

FIGURE 9.3. Earlier passage graves. 1 Barnenez (Finistère): multi-chambered long cairn with simple passage graves; 2 Vierville (Manche): simple passage grave in round mound; 3 Dissignac (Loire-Atlantique): pair of simple passage graves in round mound with multiple revetments; 4 Les Mousseaux (Loire-Atlantique): pair of transepted passage graves in sub-rectangular mound; 5 Kerleven (Finistère): two quadrangular chambers with complex internal divisions, one with terminal cell, in sub-rectangular mound; 6 La Hougue Bie (Jersey): cruciform passage grave with lateral and terminal chambers and internal subdivisions. (1 after Giot, 1970; 2 after Verron, 1975; 3 after L'Helgouach, 1976b; 4 after L'Helgouach, 1977b; 5 after Le Roux and L'Helgouach, 1967.)

PLATE 9.1. The multi-chambered long cairn of Barnenez (Finistère), showing the corbelled roofing of chambers C and D, as revealed by quarrying. The combination of dry-stone walling and orthostatic construction is characteristic of the early passage graves. (Photo: A. F. Harding.)

period, but the principal components and their interrelationships remained broadly the same and can easily be identified even in the later series of tombs.

Early Passage Graves. Radiocarbon dating suggests that the construction of early passage graves began at the beginning of the 4th millennium bc and continued down to the middle of the millennium. The graves are of generally similar design, though some variation is present even at the earliest sites; for instance, between the chambers G, G′, H, I and J of Barnenez phase I (Finistère; m.r.11: Fig.9.3, 1; Giot, 1970). The chambers of Barnenez illustrate the combination of dry-stone corbelling and orthostatic construction which was used in this series (Plate 9.1). The central chamber is of orthostatic construction with capstones, though corbelled vaulting was used at its southern end. The other chambers at Barnenez have passages constructed of orthostats and capstones but corbelled roofing in the chamber proper. This combined use of orthostats and dry-stone walling continued throughout the passage grave series, with increasing emphasis on the orthostatic technique as designs became more elaborate and monuments larger and larger. The early passage graves were set in a mound or cairn of circular (Kercado, Morbihan), trapezoidal (Ile Guennoc, and Barnenez, Finistère), or sub-circular (Larcuste 1, Morbihan) plan. The form of the cairn could be extremely complex, and was frequently stepped (e.g. Dissignac, Loire-Atlantique: Fig.9.3, 3). Orthostatic revetments are a common feature. The cairns were often enlarged during the course of the Neolithic, as for example as Dissignac, and at Le Noterio (Morbihan), figure 9.4 (L'Helgouach, 1965, 1976b, 1979). The early passage graves are found in Brittany principally near the coast, but some inland sites are known, such as Larcuste (Morbihan) and Ty Floc'h (Finistère; m.r.12: Fig.9.4A). They are concentrated in Morbihan and along the northern coasts of Finistère and Côtes-du-Nord. Although most are in the west and south of the region, examples are also known from Jersey (La Sergenté, Nicolle, 1924) and in Normandy, where the distribution is riverine (for example La Hogue (m.r.13) and La Hoguette at Fontenay-le-Marmion (Calvados), Vierville (Manche; m.r.15: Fig.9.3, 2).

Earthen long mounds. Evidence is accumulating that earthen long mounds were among the earliest ritual monuments of north-western France, alongside the early passage graves. This is reflected in the range of the available radiocarbon dates (Tumulus de Saint-Michel: 3770bc; La Grée de Coujoux (m.r. 17): 3710 bc and 3600bc; Les Fouaillages: 3640bc and 3560bc) (Le Rouzic *et al.*, 1923; Le Rouzic, 1932; Bender, 1967; Le Roux, 1981; Kinnes, 1982 and forthcoming b). Pottery broadly of Bandkeramik type has been found at certain of these sites and suggests an early neolithic date, though activity appears to have continued into the middle neolithic. Although these sites show as much diversity as the passage graves and though, like them, they were in use for a long period, the hearths, cists and standing stones beneath the mounds or cairns, perhaps at first free-standing and only later covered over, demonstrate a certain consistency of design.

Passage grave development. The advent of southern and eastern influences

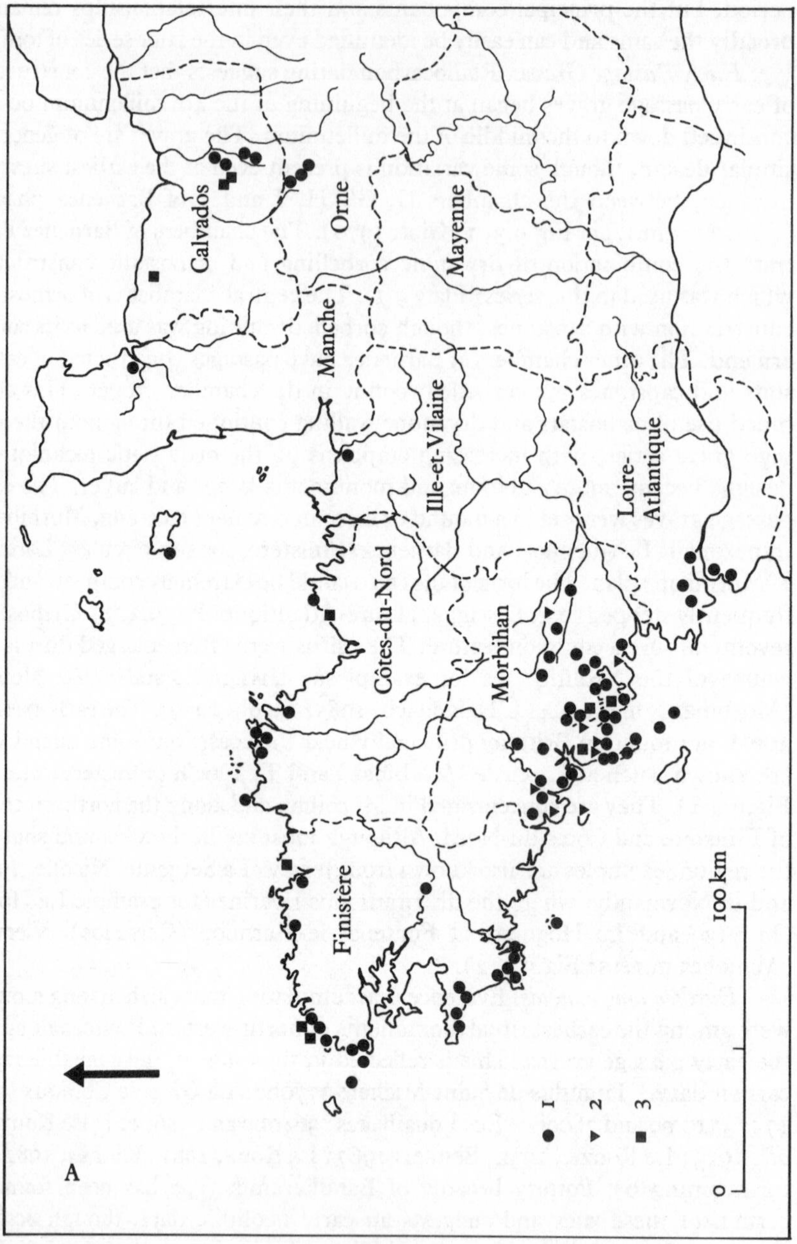

FIGURE 9.4. Distribution of earlier passage graves.
A Simple passage graves: 1 single chambers; 2 multi-chambered round cairns; 3 multi-chambered long cairns.
B Passage graves with lateral cells and internal compartments: 1 with lateral cells; 2 with internal compartments. (After L'Helgouach, 1965, and Verron, 1976.)

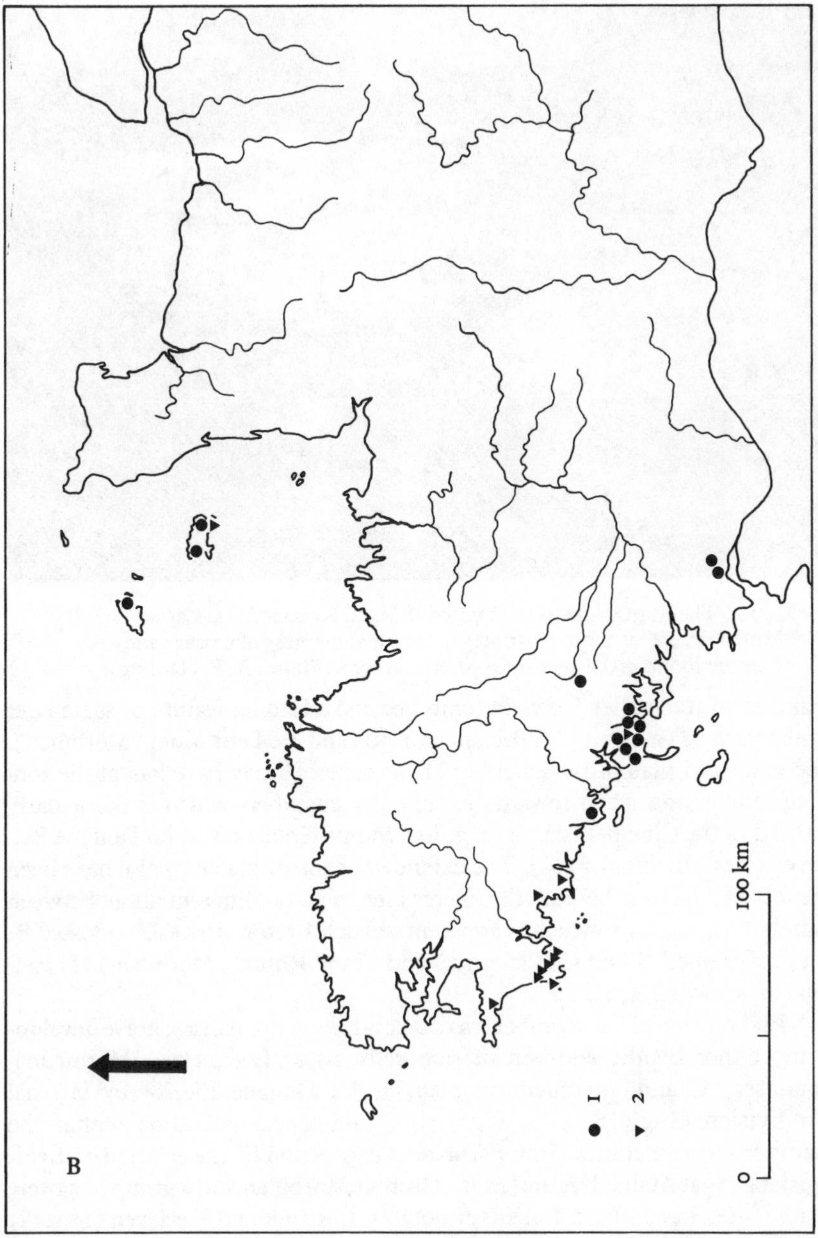

related to the middle neolithic Chasséen tradition appears to have coincided with a period of increasing regionalisation in the design of megalithic tombs. The regionalisation consisted in emphasising some of the characteristics of the early tombs at the expense of others. For example, the angularity of the

PLATE 9.2. The trapezoidal passage grave of Mané Kerioned C at Carnac (Morbihan). This tomb illustrates the gradual merging of passage and chamber found in the developed passage graves. (Photo: A. F. Harding.)

chamber of the earlier Kercado tomb became a leading feature of some later tombs such as Gavrinis (Morbihan; m.r.30) and Le Petit Mont (Morbihan). The extended plan of the chamber of Barnenez H may have lain at the root of the increasing trend towards rectangular chambers which is particularly marked in the Channel Islands (e.g. Les Monts Grantez, and La Hougue Bie, Jersey (m.r.16; Fig.9.3, 6)). The extended chamber plan may also have been one of the factors behind the increasing lack of differentiation between chamber and passage which is apparent at such Breton sites as Rondossec B, Mané Kerioned B and C (Plate 9.2) and Mané Rutual (Morbihan) (L'Helgouach, 1965, fig.5, 1).

Elaboration of the chamber was a second feature of passage grave development, either by the addition of side cells, as at Locqueltas (Morbihan), Rondossec C and, in cruciform plan, at La Hougue Bie, or by internal sub-division (Fig.9.3, 4–6; Fig.9.4B). Compartmentalisation within the chamber was sometimes given permanent expression by the erection of dividing slabs, as at Mané Bras and Mané Groh in Morbihan and a group of closely related sites in southern Finistère, notably Lesconil and Kerleven (m.r.18; Fig.9.3, 5) (L'Helgouach, 1965, figs 52, 53, 55; Le Roux and Helgouach, 1967). Non-structural division, however, is the norm in the Channel Island sites and is also found on the French mainland in sites such as Ty Floc'h. The Kerleven tomb has been dated to 2875bc and a date of 2720bc has been recovered from Ty Floc'h. These are similar to dates from the transepted sites of southern Morbihan and Loire-Atlantique; activity within the chamber of

PLATE 9.3. Passage grave of the lateral entry type at Kergüntuil (Côtes-du-Nord). This view illustrates the strong similarity between the lateral entry graves and the *allées couvertes*, both of which consist of parallel-sided chambers composed of orthostats of uniform height. (Photo: A. F. Harding.)

Larcuste 2 (Morbihan) is dated between 2660bc and 2110bc, while the site of Les Mousseaux (Loire-Atlantique; m.r.19: Fig.9.3, 4) has yielded a range of dates between 2827bc and 2453bc. These sites have elaborate side chambers and their very limited distribution (Fig.9.5A) illustrates the process of regionalisation of monument design.

The increasing lack of differentiation between chamber and passage and the multiplication of ritual foci which are apparent in the transepted designs dominate the later neolithic tomb types. Processes of regionalisation and design elaboration give rise to the development of several distinct types, notably the lateral entry, angled and V-shaped varieties. Alongside the construction of new tombs, however, the use of existing monuments continued, as shown for example by the late neolithic material from Kercado and many other sites (L'Helgouach, 1965 figs 110–13, 1967, 1973).

Lateral entry passage graves (Plate 9.3). This type shows clearly the decline in importance of the passage and the increased emphasis placed on the chamber. At Crec'h Quillé (Côtes-du-Nord; m.r.20: Fig.9.6, 3) for example, the passage is short relative to the chamber, and the latter is the principal element of the tomb. This group of tombs takes its name from the manner in which the passage is set to one side of the chamber. In some examples, however, such as Kerlescan (Morbihan) the passage disappears altogether and the lateral entrance consists only of a break in the surrounding kerb and a 'porthole' in the

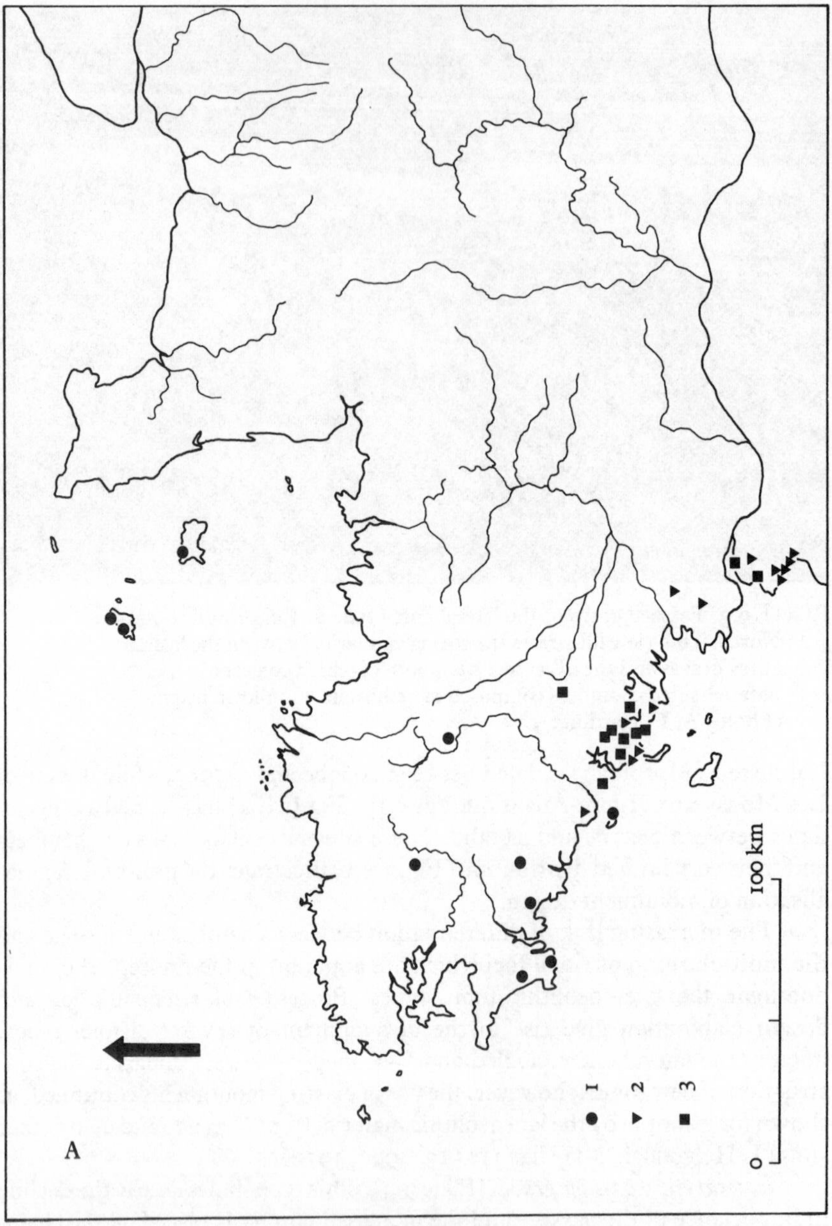

FIGURE 9.5. Distribution of developed passage graves and *allées couvertes*.
A Developed passage graves: 1 V-shaped passage graves; 2 transepted passage graves; 3 angled passage graves.
B Lateral entry graves and *allées couvertes*: 1 lateral entry graves; 2 *allées couvertes*; 3 *allées couvertes arc-boutées*. (After L'Helgouach, 1965, and Verron, 1976.)

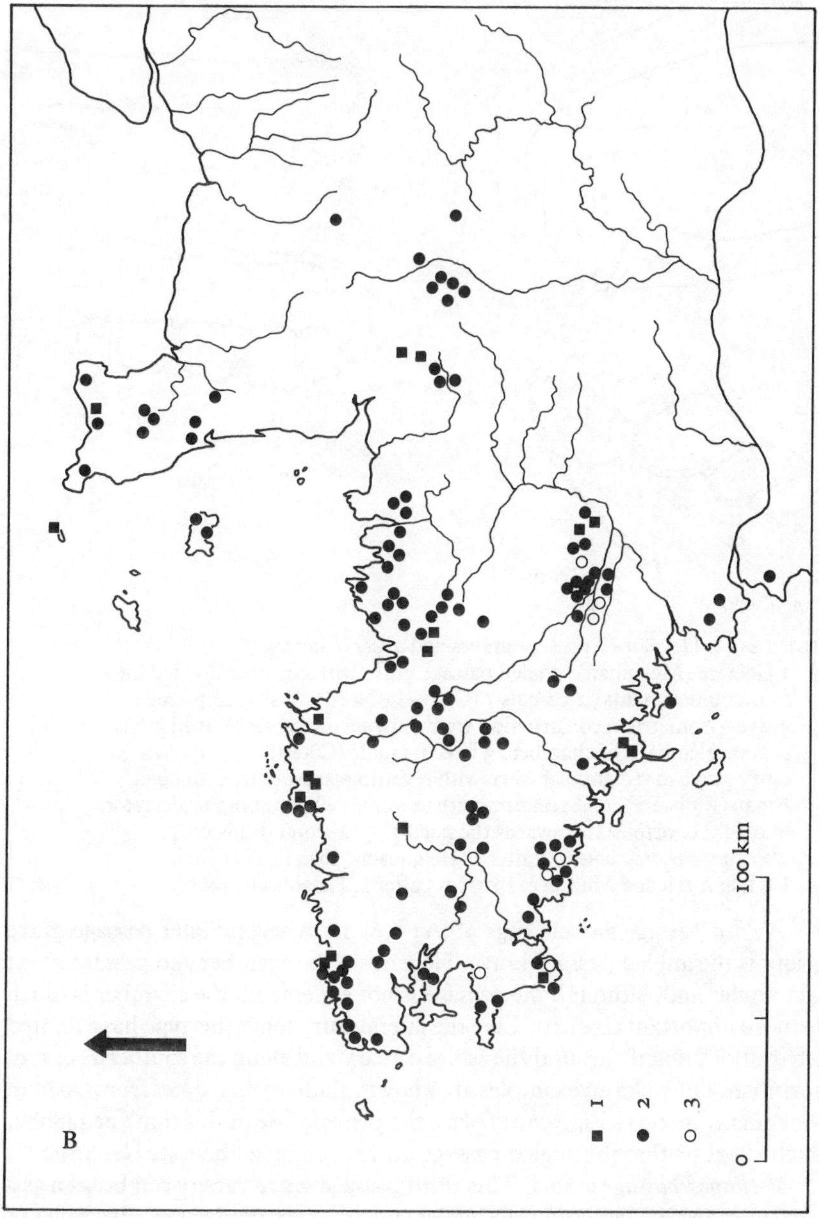

wall of the chamber. Lateral entry monuments are concentrated along the northern coast of Brittany, although examples are known from Morbihan in the south and there is another group in Manche which includes Breteville-en-Saire and Les Cartésières (Fig.9.5A) (L'Helgouach, 1965, 1967; Bender, 1967).

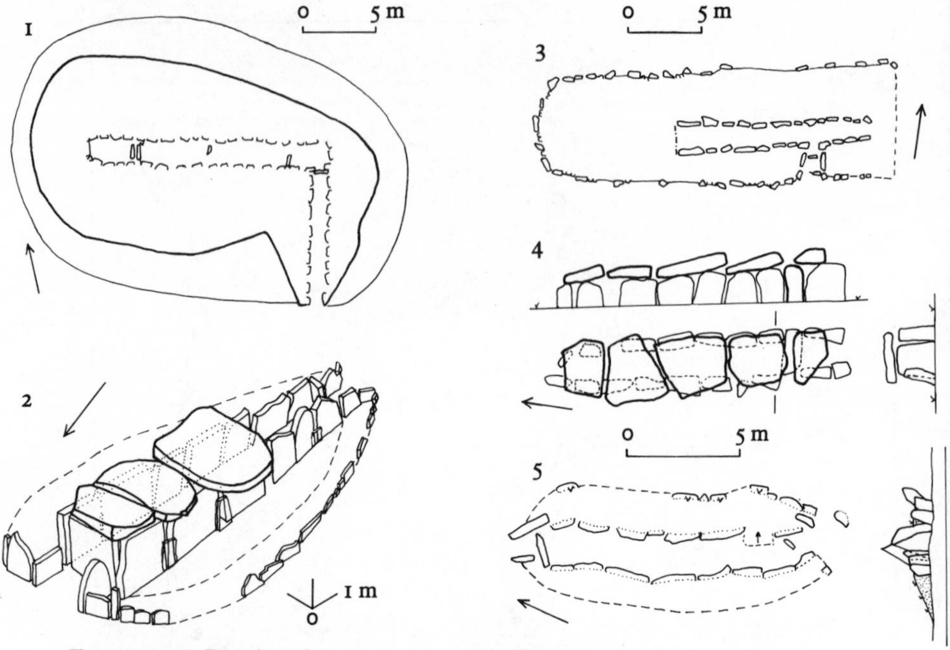

FIGURE 9.6. Developed passage graves and *allées couvertes*.
1 Goërem (Morbihan): angled passage grave with chamber divided into four compartments; 2 Liscuis 1 (Côtes-du-Nord): V-shaped passage grave – isometric reconstruction view showing oval peristalith and 'false entrance' at back of chamber; 3 Crec'h Quillé (Côtes-du-Nord): lateral entry grave in rectangular cairn with revetting peristalith; 4 Mougau Bihan (Finistère): *allées couverte* with terminal cell (note gradual decrease in height of orthostats towards the north); 5 Lesconil (Finistère): *allée couverte arc-boutée*. (1 after L'Helgouach, 1970; 2 after Giot, L'Helgouach and Monnier, 1979; 3-5 after L'Helgouach, 1965.)

Angled passage graves (Figs 9.5A; 9.6, 1). A second later passage grave variety is the angled passage grave. Here again the chamber and passage are at right angles and, although the passage is not ephemeral, the chamber is much the more important element. Like the lateral entry tomb this type has a limited distribution, mainly around the Loire estuary and along the southern coast of Morbihan. Only eleven examples are known. Radiocarbon dates from Goërem (Morbihan; m.r.21: Fig.9.6, 1) place the primary use of this tomb at 2480bc, which suggests that the angled passage graves belong to the Late Neolithic.

V-shaped passage graves. This third passage grave variety can be seen as a form intermediate between trapezoidal and *allée couverte* designs. Examples of this type have a limited distribution in Finistère (e.g. the site of Liscuis 1, (m.r.22; Fig.9.6, 2) dated 3190bc: Le Roux, 1976) in south-western Côtes-du-Nord and in western Morbihan (Fig.9.5A). In the Channel Islands, the tombs of Le Creux ès Faïes (Guernsey), Le Trépied (Guernsey) and possibly Les Pourciaux 1 (Alderney) reflect the first steps towards a similar design (L'Helgouach, 1965; Kendrick, 1928).

Allées couvertes (Fig.9.5B; 9.6, 4–5). It has been suggested that the *allées couvertes* of Brittany were the result of the local development of existing types of tomb such as the V-shaped and lateral entry varieties, and not the result of outside inspiration (L'Helgouach, 1973). While the design is clearly derived in part from existing traditions, however, the similarity in general morphology to the Paris basin *allées couvertes* and the parallel use of certain artistic motifs mean that influence from north-eastern France cannot be ruled out. A realignment of social and economic networks and the introduction of new artefact types seem to have taken place at approximately the same time as the adoption of the *allée couverte* (later 3rd millennium bc) and suggest that influences from outside the region were important. The Breton series of *allées couvertes* constitutes a distinctive group, however, and the nine known from the Cotentin and the two outliers on Jersey belong to the Breton rather than to the Paris basin series (Bender, 1967).

The basic design of these monuments (parallel-sided with internal divisions) reflects the same set of spatial relationships as is found in the passage graves. Usually the chamber is closed at one end, the orthostats are all of the same height, and the structure is set into an oval or rectangular mound with, in many cases, an orthostatic peristalith. Transverse orthostats were used to divide the chamber internally into sections of unequal size and to create terminal cells (well seen at Prajou Menhir, Côtes-du-Nord; m.r.23). A short porch, divided from the chamber by orthostats and sometimes with a worked 'porthole' entrance slab, is a common feature, encountered at sites such as Liscuis 2 (Plate 9.4) and 3 (Côtes-du-Nord) and La Bertinière (Orne) (Giot *et al.*, 1979; L'Helgouach, 1967).

A variant of the *allée couverte* is the *arc-bouté* type, where the orthostats of the side walls slope inwards and the roof was formed without capstones. It is probable that sites of this type were not completely covered by a mound (e.g. Lesconil, Finistère, m.r.26: L'Helgouach, 1965, fig.108).

Radiocarbon dates from Breton *allées couvertes* are limited to those from the Liscuis group (Liscuis 2: 2500bc and 2220bc; Liscuis 3: 2250bc). The date of 3380bc from Prajou Menhir is thought to be anomalous. Artefact associations suggest that in Brittany as in the Paris basin the *allée couverte* is a late 3rd millennium tomb type.

Dolmens simples. A common element of the neolithic ritual landscape were the small megalithic structures referred to as dolmens or *dolmens simples*. Much controversy surrounds their date and function, caused chiefly by the extremely degraded state of the majority of examples and the lack of clear associations or stratigraphy. Many dolmens are probably of middle neolithic date, but the small, simple chamber, often totally enclosed in a mound with peristalith, appears to be related to a common later neolithic preference for smaller structures and simple chambers. The dolmens may derive certain of their features from the closed chambers under mounds of the *Grands Tumulus* series, such as Tumiac (m.r.27) and the Tumulus de Saint-Michel (Morbihan) and La Hougue Böete (Jersey) (Giot *et al.*, 1979, 218–22; Hawkes, 1939). Evi-

PLATE 9.4. The *allée couverte* of Liscuis 2 (Côtes-du-Nord), with vestibule at the entrance which may reproduce in vestigial form the passage of the earlier passage graves. The remains of the encircling kerb or peristalith and of the rubble mound which it revetted can be seen. (Photo: A. F. Harding.)

dence from the islands of Guernsey and Herm suggest that simple megalithic chambered tombs, such as La Platte Mare and L'Islet on Guernsey, and the Herm series, belong late in the Neolithic (Kinnes, 1982; Kendrick, 1928). The dating evidence is not absolute, but the artefactual associations of SOM pottery types from L'Islet, and Beaker material from La Platte Mare and the Herm sites suggest a date in the late 3rd millennium bc, and the association of a dolmen with the *allée couverte* of Ville ès Nouaux (Jersey: Hawkes, 1939) provides some support for this. The evidence from the Channel Island examples can be extended to those of the mainland, Normandy in particular, but more research is needed to define their interrelationships more precisely (Bender, 1967).

MENHIRS AND ALIGNMENTS. Brittany is extremely rich in the remains of menhirs and alignments. Dating evidence is limited, but where foundation deposits at the foot of the stones are present they suggest dates lying between the Middle Neolithic and the Early and Middle Bronze Age. Between 1100 and 1200 menhirs are known in Brittany, suggesting an original total of perhaps 3000–5000. In Normandy there are 86, including seven groups of two or three menhirs together (Verron, 1977a). The principal concentrations are in the three western *départements* of Brittany, in the north of the Cotentin to the west of Caen, and on Jersey and Guernsey. Groups of two or three menhirs together are not uncommon (e.g. Pergat, Côtes-du-Nord, and Peumerit and

Kerscaven, Finistère) although it is difficult to distinguish between deliberate small groupings and the remains of alignments.

The menhirs vary in their dimensions, almost all lying between 1.5m and 10m, and most between 6m and 8m, though larger examples are known, the most famous being the Grand Menhir Brisé of Locmariaquer (Morbihan; m.r.29), which would have stood 20–30m high and whose remains are estimated to weigh 350 tonnes. Groups of menhirs of different heights are known; at Pergat, a menhir 7.5m high is associated with one only 2m high.

Menhirs frequently display traces of deliberate shaping, notable instances being visible on the Grand Menhir Brisé (Morbihan) and the menhir of Kerloas (Finistère). The Broken Menhir at Saint Brelade on Jersey and the menhir at Les Fouaillages, Guernsey, appear to have been roughly carved into an anthropomorphic shape (Hawkes, 1939; Kinnes, 1982). Other decoration is rare, and limited to nine sites. Two semi-circular designs and seven definite and two possible 'shepherd's crooks' in relief are known from Kermarquer (Morbihan). The menhir of Saint-Denec (Finistère) bears two hafted axes carved in relief. The axe motif is in fact the commonest found on menhirs in north-western France, where a total of four examples is known, including one on the Grand Menhir Brisé (Shee Twohig, 1981). The shepherd's crooks carved on the menhir of Kermarquer belong to Shee Twohig's first phase, but all the other decorative motifs found on these menhirs are of her second phase. These include a Mané Rutual-type axe carved on the Grand Menhir Brisé and a buckler of Prajou Menhir type on the menhir of Tremblais (Côtes-du-Nord). The motifs suggest a late 4th or early 3rd millennium bc date for those menhirs which are decorated except perhaps for the Tremblais menhir, which might by its association with the Prajou Menhir buckler design be considered later (Shee Twohig, 1981).

The function of the menhirs is obscure. Their erection seems to have been associated with ritual deposition, however, and it is likely that they served as foci for subsequent ritual activities. Middle neolithic pottery was found at the foot of the Kerlay menhir (Finistère), and there was a cist of burnt wood in a similar position at Picaigne (Côtes-du-Nord). Perforated polished-stone pick-axes were found in association with menhirs on Guernsey, while a cache of limpet shells in a stone surround lay at the foot of the Dame Blanche menhir on Jersey. Bronze age deposits associated with menhirs include five stop-ridge axes and a spear-head found in the foundation deposit at the base of the menhir of La Sergenté at Saint Brelade, Jersey (Kendrick, 1929; Hawkes, 1939).

Isolated menhirs and groups of menhirs are closely related to the alignments of standing stones which are a notable feature of some parts of Brittany. Unfortunately, too much speculation has surrounded the interpretation of alignments, and their logical place in the spectrum of neolithic ritual sites has all too often been obscured (e.g. Thom and Thom, 1978). Some alignments are of complex design, others fairly simple. The alignment of Le Cordon des Druides (Ille-et-Vilaine) consists of a single line of small quartz blocks, 1–2m high, and this need not be part of any more complex alignment. At Poul ar

PLATE 9.5. The Le Menec alignments at Carnac (Morbihan). These consist of 1099 stones arranged in 11 lines and are the largest alignments in Brittany. (Photo: A. F. Harding.)

Varquez (Côtes-du-Nord) an alignment of three menhirs is set within a banked enclosure (Giot *et al.*, 1979, 414), and the stones of the Er Lannic circles are set into an earthen and stone bank (Le Rouzic, 1930).

Simple alignments are very common in Finistère. The offshore islands, notably L'Ile Béniguet and L'Ile Molène, have dense concentrations of sites of this type. More complex alignments are also fairly widespread and abundant; the famous examples of Le Menec (Plate 9.5), Kermario, Kerlescan and Le Petit Menec in the Carnac area of Morbihan (m.r.28), though perhaps the most impressive, are not isolated examples. Complex alignments are found in Ille-et-Vilaine (e.g. Les Demoiselles de la Lande du Moulin: 37 stones in two lines; Saint-Just: 30 stones in two lines), in Côtes-du-Nord (Le Champ des Roches: 65 stones in five lines), in Finistère (La Madeleine: originally 500/600 stones; Lagatjar: 65 stones in three lines), and in Loire-Atlantique (Arbourg: 57 stones in seven lines). Alignments are however rare in Normandy, where only two sites are known (Giot *et al.*, 1979; Verron, 1979).

The alignment of Le Moulin at Saint-Just (Ille-et-Vilaine) was excavated recently. It was found that timber uprights had taken the place of some stones in some of the lines, and that timber structures, possibly roofed, and a hearth had been integrated into the design. The possibility that timber components were incorporated into alignments has not generally been considered, but they may have been quite common. In the case of Le Moulin the three lines of the alignment are roughly orientated so as to focus the eye on a range of hills to the west. There are several notches and hilltops which could have been used as markers for the setting of the equinoctial sun, and it has been suggested that the alignment had some astronomical function in addition to its social role. Dating evidence suggests the first stones at Le Moulin were erected in the 3rd millennium bc on the site of an existing long mound, with subsequent use extending into the Beaker period and the Early Bronze Age. The final occupation has been dated to 1990bc (Le Roux, 1979b, 1981).

Alignments are frequently associated with stone 'circles', but the relationship of the two types of site is poorly understood. There is a stone 'circle' at each end of the Le Menec alignment, and two at Kerlescan, and single 'circles' are associated with the Cojou menhirs (Ille-et-Vilaine) and the Crozon alignment (Finistère). Long mounds seem also to be associated with some alignments, though it is difficult in many cases to determine which of the monuments was the earlier. The mound of Le Manio, however, clearly lies below the lines of the Kermario alignments (Giot *et al.*, 1979).

Isolated 'circles' of standing stones are widely distributed and take quadrilateral, oval, circular and semi-circular forms. There are some double 'circles', at Er Lannic (Morbihan: Le Rouzic, 1930), Tossen Keler (Côtes-du-Nord), Kermorvan (Finistère) and Crucuno (Morbihan). A triangular example is known from Crozon (Finistère) which seems to be associated with alignments (Giot *et al.*, 1979, 417). Er Lannic consists of a double oval of standing stones, averaging 2.3m in height, set within an encircling bank. Hearths covered by small corbelled cists were found both inside and outside the bank. It has been suggested that these cists formed a ritual monument similar to Le Manio, on which the stone enclosures were superimposed (Giot *et al.*, 1979, 412–3). The excavations did not clarify this point. Barbed-and-tanged arrowheads, polished-stone axes of type A dolerite, querns and animal bones were found both in the cists and, probably as foundation deposits, at the base of the stones. It is clear that much of this material is domestic debris collected from a settlement site. The presence in large numbers of Chasséen vases-supports suggests a middle neolithic date for the initial activity, while pottery of upper Conguel type and barbed-and-tanged arrowheads indicate late neolithic presence, probably associated with the erection of the circles (Le Rouzic, 1930).

Megalithic Art

A distinctive but scarcely understood feature of ritual monuments in north-western France is the use of a variety of techniques and motifs to decorate the stones. In Brittany, decoration has been found at 29 passage graves, 6 angled passage graves, 7 allées couvertes, 5 other megalithic monuments, 9 menhirs, and 15 other stones from eight sites (Shee Twohig, 1981). The art found in the earlier passage graves is distinct from that in the angled passage graves and in the allées couvertes. The decoration of the passage graves can itself be divided into two phases on the basis of the motifs used, those of the second phase showing more developed technique and being more elaborate, with a tendency to combine motifs into extensive abstract designs, often covering the whole surface of a stone (e.g. at Gavrinis; Plate 9.6). The principal motifs are radial

PLATE 9.6. Decorated orthostat in the simple passage grave of Gavrinis (Morbihan). (Photo: Hervé Champollion.)

and wavy lines, so-called *axe* and *buckler* shapes, and cup marks. No examples of painted decoration are known (Shee Twohig, 1981).

The angled passage graves are the class of site richest in megalithic art – six sites with a total of 39 decorated stones. The buckler motif, which may be a stylised human form, predominates, though there are also cup marks and 'shepherd's crooks' at some sites.

An anthropomorphic element is the dominating feature of *allée couverte* art. A total of 24 decorated stones is known from seven sites, and the motifs used include hooks, daggers, axes and pairs of breasts or breasts and necklace. The breasts and necklace motif is the most common.

Anthropomorphic designs are also found on some of the menhirs. These are statue-menhirs, with breasts, arms and necklace carved in relief. The stone is roughly shaped to give the outline of head and shoulders. Good examples are the Kerméné menhir (Morbihan) and that at Laniscar (Finistère). Individual motifs similar to those of the megalithic tombs are occasionally found carved on menhirs which are not of the 'statue menhir' type (Giot, 1960; Kinnes, 1980).

The discovery of similar motifs at both menhirs and chambered tombs demonstrates the link between the two types of site and the essential unity of the Breton ritual monument complex. It is impossible now to interpret the symbolic meaning of the art, though decorated stones may have served as markers at some monuments, especially in the *allées couvertes* and some of the passage graves where the chamber was relatively long and there was no internal structural subdivision of the space. The limited distribution of the art shows that it cannot have been crucial to all the communities which engaged in ritual monument construction, but that it was a local development.

Production Centres and Exchange Networks

Flint. The Armorican Massif does not have natural deposits of flint, and this difficulty was bypassed in two ways. First, in the western part of the region, polished hardstone axes were employed as the principal macrolithic type, and supplemented by flint from secondary sources, such as beach pebbles. The hardstone was derived from extensively exploited quarries, the most important being that at Sélédin, Plussulien (Côtes-du-Nord; m.r.31: Le Roux, 1971, 1979a). The second expedient involved the importation of flint from the flint-rich areas bordering the Armorican Massif. Flint mines are known at Soignelles, Les Carrières (Soument-Saint-Quentin), Potignay and La Fordelle in the *département* of Calvados (Edeine, 1960, 1962; Verron, 1981). In the same *département* there are also working areas around flint outcrops, such as those of La Burette and Olendon; the traces of the latter cover 5 hectares. At Olendon the working areas were supplemented by several undated pits which were probably also designed for flint exploitation, and which may be neolithic although the range of activity represented at the site extends from the Palaeolithic to the Chalcolithic. The flint mines of Les Carrières are not far way (Bender, 1967; Doranlo, 1951).

A good example of a Normandy flint mine is the recently excavated site of La Fordelle near Breteville-le-Rabet (Calvados; m.r.32). A bell-shaped pit was first dug, 2.6m deep, and gradually extended in order to exploit two seams of flint 1.5m and 2.5m below the surface. Once the principal chamber had been exhausted, a gallery 3m long was dug to the north so as to exploit both seams simultaneously. When this gallery had been exhausted it was filled with debris and a second gallery was opened to the east of the main chamber. In the backfilling of the mine were found thirty flint picks, mostly broken, together with antler and wooden tools. This site would seem to have been fairly typical in size, and is similar to those known at Poignay and Les Carrières (Verron, 1981; Edeine, 1962). Mining on the scale of Grimes Graves or Cissbury was apparently unknown.

Flint axes account for only 2 per cent of the total in Finistère and 5 per cent in the rest of Brittany. While there is a clear fall in quantity from east to west, with increasing distance from the Normandy sources, it appears that the competition from hardstone axes was too strong to allow flint a major role in Brittany, even in areas close to the sources; and production and distribution cannot have been so highly organised as those of the hardstone axes (Le Roux, 1979a).

Dolerite. In the west of the region several sources of igneous and metamorphic rocks are known which were used during the neolithic period for the production of axes. The dolerite A source at Sélédin, Plussulien, is the largest and accounts for 50 per cent of all the known axes in Brittany. Exploitation began at this site around 3200bc (see list of radiocarbon dates at end of chapter). In the first phase, outcrops of dolerite which had been crushed by faulting were the principal focus of activity, but soon pits similar to those found at the flint mine sites were sunk for the extraction of blocks of material, and in the course of time larger and larger outcrops were attacked. Some very large blocks were removed for use as working benches on which the roughing-out of axe blanks was carried out. In the third phase of activity, the use of fire for quarrying was introduced. Techniques of axe-production changed little, however, and the industrial debris of the third phase differs from that of the earlier phases only in the abundance of charcoal and ashes, which have provided a reliable series of radiocarbon dates (Le Roux, 1971; Delibrias and Le Roux, 1975).

The production and distribution of stone axes postulates organised economic and social activity. This would have been particularly the case with the axes of type A dolerite, which are not only the most common type in Brittany but are also found widely outside the Armorican region (Fig.9.7). One of the principal concentrations, comprising 20–40 per cent of all the axes of this type which are known, is situated in the Loire valley, and there are smaller concentrations in the Seine valley and eastern France, and individual finds in southern France, Alsace, Jersey and southern Britain (Le Roux, 1979a). This distribution suggests that coastal and river transport were important in the spread of these axes. Even within Brittany, however, there are substantial variations at the local level, particularly near the sources of fibrolite in north-western Finistère and epidiorite in Morbihan and south-eastern Finistère. Neither the epidiorite nor the fibrolite production was on the same scale as the diorite; fewer than 5 per cent of all known fibrolite axes have been found outside Finistère and Morbihan (Le Roux, 1979a).

The wide distribution of dolerite A axes is reflected in the scale of operations at Sélédin. The main factory site covers about 10,000m² with peri-

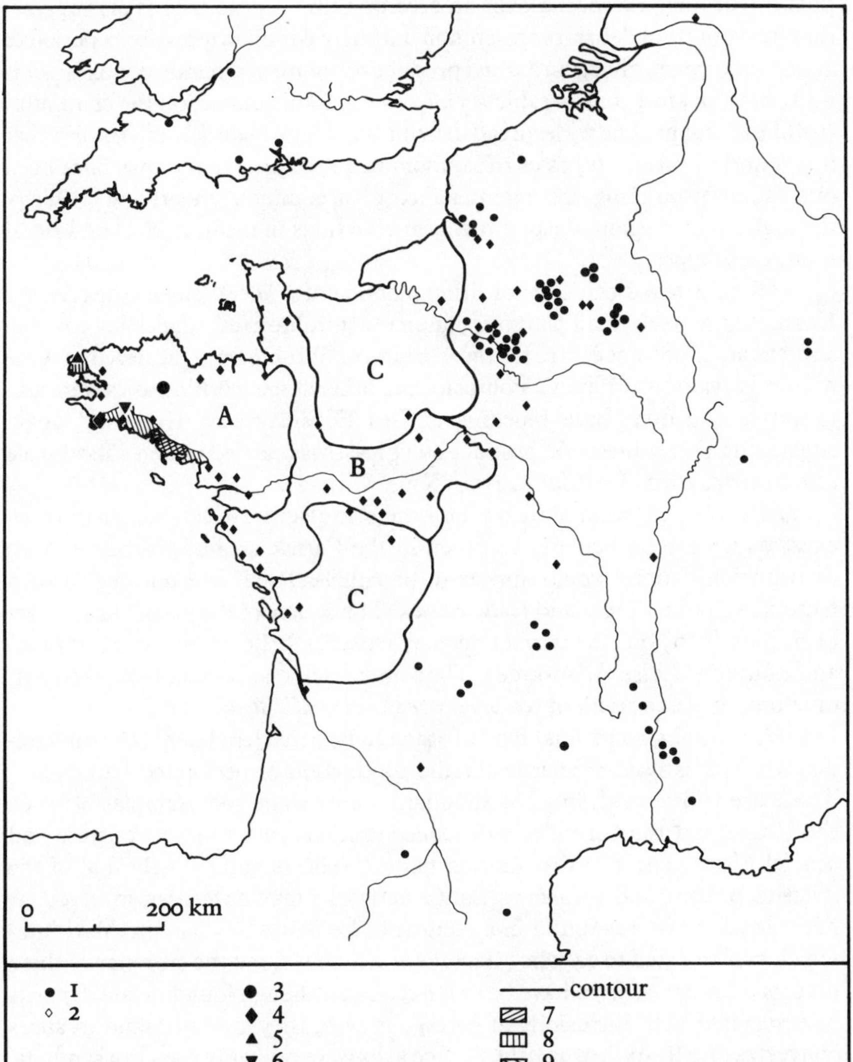

FIGURE 9.7. Distribution of Breton hardstone implements in France and neighbouring areas. 1 finds of type A dolerite; 2 finds of type C hornblendite; 3 Sélédin (Plussulien) axe factory; 4 hornblendite source; 5 fibrolite source; 6 epidiorite source; 7 principal concentration of hornblendite artefacts; 8 principal concentration of fibrolite artefacts; 9 principal concentration of epidiorite artefacts. Contours mark percentages of hardstone implements which are of type A dolerite: A over 40%; B 20-40%; C 10-20%. (After Le Roux, 1979a.)

pheral workings extending over an area of 1km². Le Roux (1979a) suggests that the volume of debris represents an output of 6 million tools over a period of about 1200 years, giving an annual production figure of around 5000 axes. This must have made a considerable social and economic impact on the communities of the region. The widespread distribution of the material, and the fact that it is found in various types of ritual monument, suggest that it may have been one factor promoting the maintenance of a common underlying ideology throughout the region, despite the local variations in many artefact and ritual monument types.

There is some evidence of lithic manufacture at settlement sites. At Er Lannic there were small *polissoirs* and many fibrolite axes, suggesting that the site was an important centre for the working of fibrolite from the nearby source of Port Navalo (Morbihan). Polissoirs and other stone-working tools were also found in the first-phase blocking at Les Fouaillages on Guernsey, again suggesting that some lithic production at least was carried out on a local scale (Le Rouzic, 1930; Le Roux, 1979a; Kinnes, 1982).

Fibrolite and *jadeite* were used for the manufacture of ceremonial or ritual axes, which are particularly common in the Carnac area of Morbihan. This distribution pattern would appear to be ritual-related, and not due to such factors as market forces and trade routes. The source of the jadeite has not yet been identified, but the correct geology exists at L'Ile de Groix (Morbihan) and Bouvron (Loire-Atlantique). The source itself may have been worked out, or submerged as a result of sea-level rise (Giot *et al.*, 1979, 357).

Hornblendite. The final type of stone to be considered here is hornblendite, which was used primarily for the production of perforated battle axes. These are widespread, but not abundant – only some 100 examples between the Rhine and the Gironde, with concentrations in southern Finistère and coastal Morbihan. The distribution pattern reflects quite closely that of the dolerite A axes, and similar exchange networks may have been involved. A hornblendite axe was found in a context at La Sauzaie (Charente-Maritime) which can be dated to 2450bc (Gachina *et al.*, 1975), but the currency of these objects does not seem to have been long, since although found in late deposits or associated with intrusions in passage graves, they are not found in allées couvertes (Le Roux, 1979a). These fine axes were probably used in a symbolic or status-related manner.

In the late 3rd millennium bc Brittany fell within the area of distribution of the honey-coloured Grand Pressigny flint. Daggers are one of the commonest types of artefact made from this distinctive material, and have been found in north-western France at allées couvertes such as Kergus (Morbihan) and Tressé (Ille-et-Vilaine). At the settlement site of Le Pinacle on Jersey two knives and 18 barbed-and-tanged arrowheads of Grand Pressigny flint were found within an area of 10m², and of eight paired barbed-and-tanged arrowheads found at Les Fouaillages on Guernsey, four were of this material (Kinnes, pers.comm.). One of the latter had had a barb broken during manufacture and could never have been used. The Grand Pressigny flint was probably traded principally as unretouched blades or finished tools. Two hoards have been found in Normandy, each consisting of 100 Grand Pressigny blades. Cores, however, are also known (e.g. one from Saint-Saens, Seine-Maritime, with seven blades removed from one side: Bender, 1967).

NEOLITHIC POTTERY

Most of the portable neolithic artefacts from north-western France have come from deposits in chambered tombs. Early excavations often confused primary and secondary deposits and neglected some artefact types in favour of the more spectacular categories of finds. It is nonetheless possible, using the results of these early investigations and of more recent work, to establish a comprehensive picture of the pottery types in use in this part of France during the Neolithic.

The best preserved deposit from an early megalithic site is that from the tomb of Ile Carn (Finistère: Giot and L'Helgouach, 1955). The pottery characteristic of this deposit, which was clearly sealed, is of a type labelled *Carn* ware, and consists principally of thin-walled, round-bottomed, short-necked bowls. Decoration is limited to applied *croissants,* a motif which is found only on this type of pottery (Fig.9.2, 3–6). The distribution of Carn ware is wide, and covers Finistère, Morbihan and Loire-Atlantique. The early radiocarbon dates from the simple passage graves where this pottery has been found support the view that it represents the earliest Breton pottery type, although the sherds from the pre-monument land surface at Dissignac are of different form and fabric and must belong to a separate early type (L'Helgouach, 1965, 1979).

In western Normandy and the Channel Islands some of the earliest pottery is clearly related to the Bandkeramik tradition (e.g. beneath the monument of La Hoguette: Fig.9.2, 1; and at Le Pinacle on Jersey: Fig.9.2, 2). Much of the pottery is however undecorated and is similar to the Breton Carn style, though in this area the round-bottomed bowls are less well made and have higher necks. Examples from Vierville (Manche) and La Hoguette (Calvados) have internal multi-perforated lugs for suspension (Fig.9.2, 7 and 8; Verron, 1975; Caillaud and Lagnel, 1972). Decoration is very rare on these vessels.

Middle neolithic pottery of Brittany and western Normandy shows clearly the influence of the broadly-defined Chasséen ceramic tradition. Shouldered and carinated designs are the principal types, with S-profile round-bottomed vessels and flattish dishes also important though less common (Figs 9.2, 9; 9.8, 4). The addition of lugs for suspension is a leading feature of the pottery of this period; vertically-perforated, horizontally-perforated and trumpet varieties are all found. Decoration is present but is not common, and is restricted to a limited repertoire of geometric motifs, chiefly triangles, lozenges and squares, often arranged in a chequerboard pattern. The fabric and manufacture of these vessels are usually of fine quality (L'Helgouach, 1965, 1971; Giot *et al.*, 1979, 199–205).

A common middle neolithic pottery type in Brittany is the vase-support (Fig.9.9, 1–3), which some have regarded as a Chasséen type-fossil. The

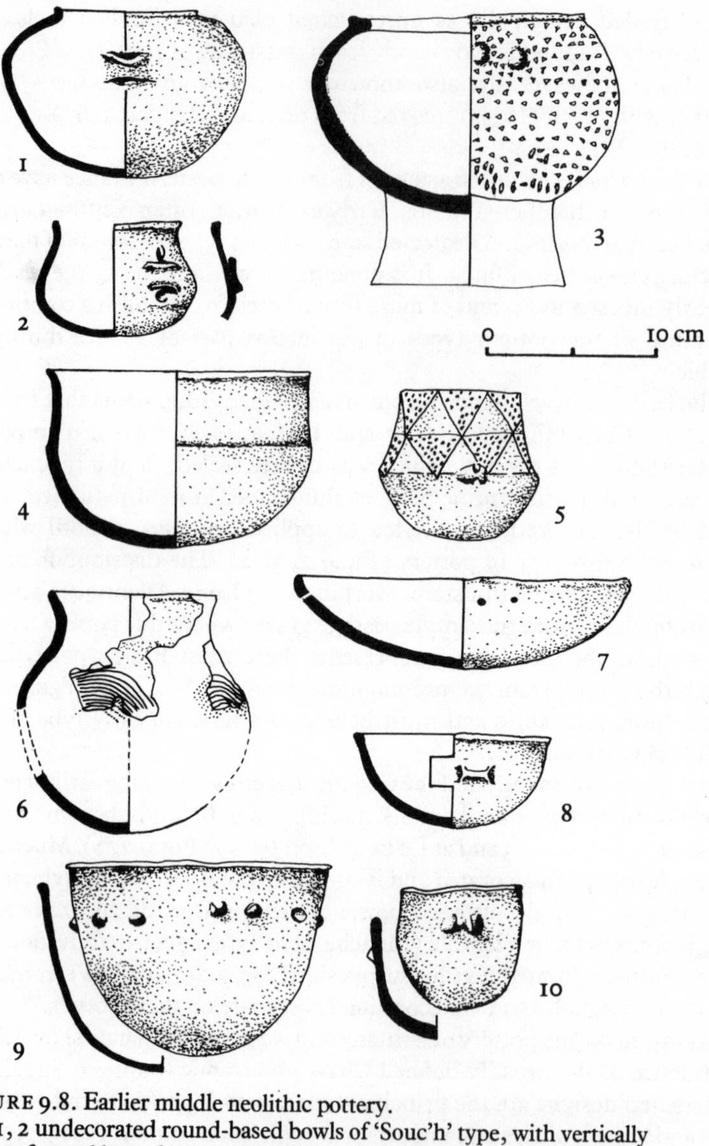

FIGURE 9.8. Earlier middle neolithic pottery.
1, 2 undecorated round-based bowls of 'Souc'h' type, with vertically perforated lugs, from (1) Mané Bras (Morbihan) and (2) Le Souc'h (Finistère); 3 Larcuste 2 (Morbihan): *vase à pied creux* with paired buttons and stab-decorated body; 4-10 Chasséen-influenced pottery: 4 carinated bowl from Mané Beg Portivy (Morbihan); 5 high-necked bowl with Chasséen-type geometric decoration, Mané Roh en Tallec (Morbihan); 6 round-based bowl with curvilinear decoration, Les Mousseaux (Loire-Atlantique); 7 low bowl with paired perforations, Larcuste 2 (Morbihan); 8 undecorated bowl with trumpet lug, Kervadel (Finistère); 9, 10 round-based bowls with paired buttons, Kerleven (Finistère). (1, 2, 4 after L'Helgouach, 1965; 3 after L'Helgouach, 1977c; 5-10 after Giot, L'Helgouach and Monnier, 1979.)

vases-supports of Brittany form a recognisable western variety, known as the *Er Lannic* type, and are typically cylindrical with triangular, elongated or circular perforations in the sides. A second concentration of vases-supports is found on Jersey, with outliers in the Cotentin area, and these clearly represent an insular development of types known in the Paris basin, with only circular perforations (L'Helgouach, 1965; Hawkes, 1939; Bailloud, 1974). Though found principally at Er Lannic and on Jersey, vases-supports have also been found in northern and southern Finistère and Loire-Atlantique, and an isolated example is known from Herquemoulin (Manche; Fig.9.9, 2; Verron, 1976). Most of the known vases-supports were discovered in clearly ritual contexts, though some were associated with the remains of domestic activities.

Localised pottery styles were current throughout the period of Chasséen influence in north-western France. *Castellic* grooved ware, with Chasséen-related shapes but a completely original style of decoration, has been found at sites in the littoral zone of southern Morbihan (Bailloud, 1975; L'Helgouach, 1971). Pottery of the type labelled *Souc'h* is found in the same area but also to the east and west in Finistère and Loire-Atlantique. Souc'h ware takes the form of round-bottomed bowls with very short necks and frequently with two perforated lugs (Fig.9.8, 1–2; L'Helgouach, 1965, 1971). An important variation are the *vases à pied creux* of *Colpo* type. These are similar in body to the vessels of the Souc'h type, but have an additional tall, concave base and are frequently decorated, though not on the foot (Fig.9.8, 3; L'Helgouach, 1977c).

By the middle of the 3rd millennium bc Chasséen influences on the pottery of north-western France are no longer so evident, and a new series of localised styles including the *Kerugou, lower Conguel* and *Rosmeur/Croh Collé* had arisen (L'Helgouach, 1965). Kerugou pottery (Fig.9.9, 4, 5) is found principally in southern Finistère. Flat-based or round-based bowls with decoration consisting of groups of vertical cordons on the neck and raised bosses on the shoulder are characteristic. The vessels of the lower Conguel and Rosmeur/Croh Collé types are more generally round-based and have decoration of groups of vertical, horizontal and arc-shaped lines, often in panels, on the neck (Fig.9.9, 6). Kerugou pottery was found in a context dated to 2480bc at the angled passage grave of Goërem (Morbihan). Pottery of *upper Conguel* type is a development from that of lower Conguel type and is probably rather later; at Conguel itself (Morbihan) it was associated with Beaker material (Giot *et al.*, 1979, 256–7; Bailloud, 1975; L'Helgouach, 1965, fig.39; 1970).

In central Brittany during the 3rd millennium bc pottery of SOM-related types is dominant, under the guise of a series of localised styles. The type known as *Quessoy* is typical of these and displays several SOM features, including flat bases and coarse fabrics (L'Helgouach and Le Roux, 1965; Fig.9.10, 3). A second localised style is the *Crec'h Quillé/Le Mélus* type, which again has tall flat-bottomed flower-pot vessels, alongside round-based forms (Fig.9.10, 1–2; Giot *et al.*, 1979, 277–9). A possible further indication of eastern influence at this period is provided by the 'collared bottles' (Fig.9.10, 5), which have a

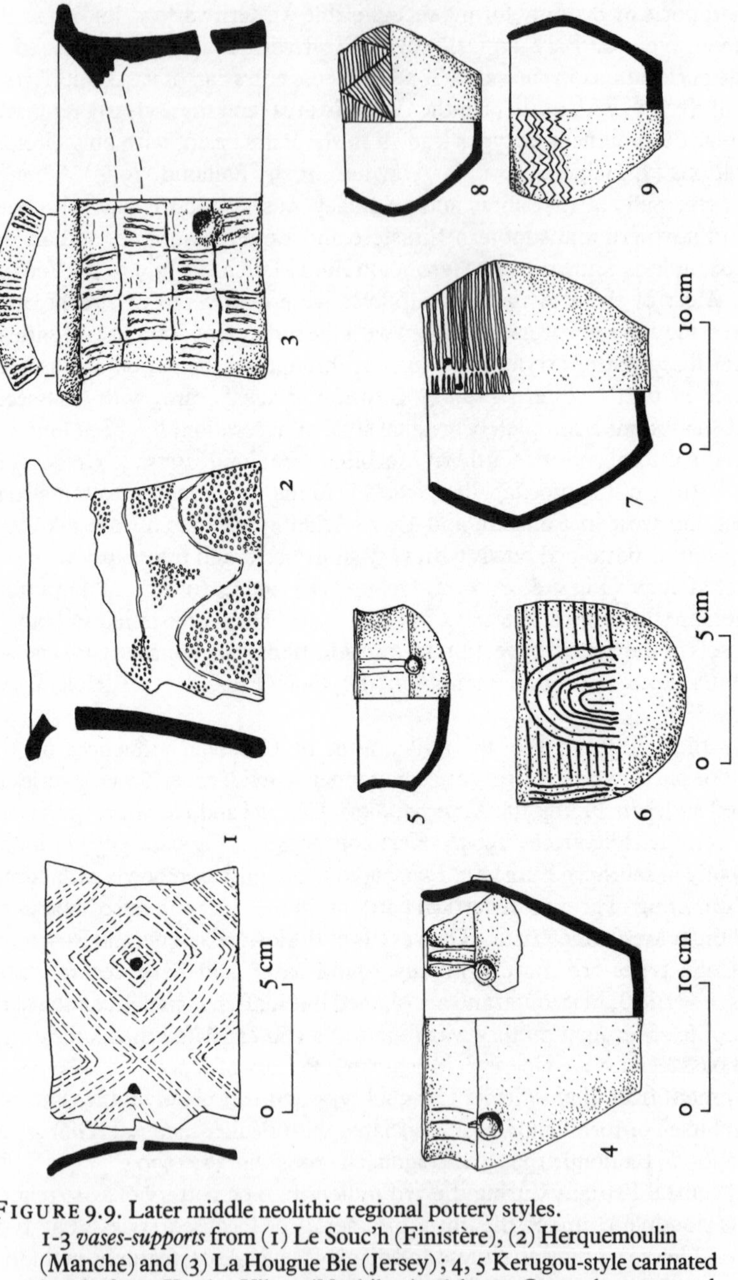

FIGURE 9.9. Later middle neolithic regional pottery styles.
1-3 *vases-supports* from (1) Le Souc'h (Finistère), (2) Herquemoulin (Manche) and (3) La Hougue Bie (Jersey); 4, 5 Kerugou-style carinated bowls from Kerdro-Vihan (Morbihan); 6 lower Conguel type round-based bowl with crude incised decoration, Conguel (Morbihan); 7-9 flat-based vessels of upper Conguel type from (8) Butten-er-Hah (Morbihan) and (7 and 9) Conguel. (1 after L'Helgouach, 1965; 2 after Verron, 1976; 3 after material now in the Museum of the Société Jersiaise; 5 after L'Helgouach, 1970; 6-9 after Giot, L'Helgouach and Monnier, 1979.)

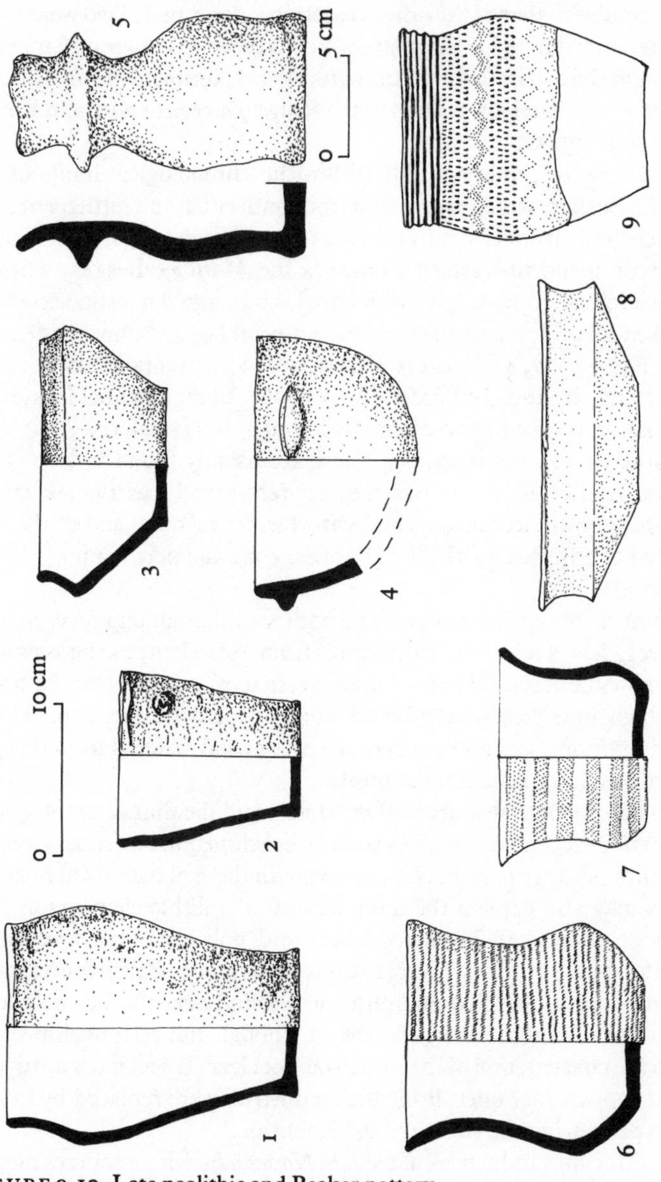

FIGURE 9.10. Late neolithic and Beaker pottery.
1, 2 Crec'h Quillé/Le Mélus pottery from Crec'h Quillé (Côtes-du-Nord); 3 high-necked bowl of Quessoy type, from Quessoy (Côtes-du-Nord); 4 round-based coarse ware bowl with horizontal lugs, Kerbannalec (Finistère); 5 *bouteille à collerette* from La Hoguette (Calvados); 6 all-over corded Beaker from Goërem (Morbihan); 7 comb-decorated Beaker from Kerbors (Côtes-du-Nord); 8 low carinated bowl of Beaker type, Kerbors; 9 Beaker-related 'Guernsey vase', La Varde (Guernsey). (1, 2, 4 after Giot, L'Helgouach and Monnier, 1979; 3 after L'Helgouach, 1965; 5 after Verron, 1976; 6-8 after Giot, Briard and Pape, 1979; 9 after material now in the Guernsey Museum.)

coarse fabric similar to that of the other vessels just described. Two were found in the SOM crematorium at La Hoguette which is dated to between 2870bc and 2350bc. Though the collared bottles of Brittany and Normandy form a distinct group, they may ultimately be related to the *Kragenflaschen* of northern Europe (Giot *et al.*, 1979, 279–81).

The final type of pottery to fall within the chronological limits of this chapter are the Beakers which are known from both ritual and settlement sites, as well as a few finds from rivers (Treinen, 1970; Verron, 1976). The dominant Beaker type in north-western France is the *Maritime* Beaker, which is frequently accompanied by a low, wide bowl, and large domestic vessels are also recognised as an integral part of these assemblages (Kinnes, 1982; Le Roux, 1981; Fig.9.10, 7, 8). Beakers with all-over cord decoration are found in southern Brittany, around Quiberon (Fig.9.10, 6). In the Channel Islands the Beaker material gave rise to two distinctive local vessel types, the *Jersey bowl* and the *Guernsey vase* (Fig.9.10, 9). These are usually found in association with Beakers. At Les Blanches Banques on Jersey and Les Fouaillages on Guernsey Jersey bowls were associated with Beaker material and at the later site were dated to 2050bc and 1880bc (Kinnes, 1982 and pers.comm.).

Lithic Artefacts

Objects of flint or other stone often had both a utilitarian and a ceremonial function. A very few, such as the jadeite axes from Morbihan, can be assigned a ritual function without regard to their context; in most cases it is the context of discovery which indicates what rôle an object should be ascribed. This is particularly important, since so much of the artefactual material from this part of France has come from chambered tombs.

Brittany has no natural sources of good flint and the flint assemblages are therefore based on secondary sources such as beach pebbles or small amounts of imported flint, and are poor in comparison with those of many other parts of France. This may also explain the discovery of microlithic elements in association with neolithic tranchet arrowheads and polished-stone axes at the settlement site of La Butte-aux-Pierres (Loire-Atlantique: Bellancourt, 1966). A large assemblage of over 800 microliths was found beneath the chambered tomb of Dissignac in the same *département*, though the relationship of the microliths to the construction of the tomb was not clear (L'Helgouach, 1976b). In general, it appears that microlithic flint industries were replaced by macrolithic stone types during the course of the Neolithic.

The neolithic flint industries of *western Normandy*, where sources of good quality flint are present, are rich and varied in comparison with those of Brittany. Some chambered tombs have yielded large assemblages (e.g. Vierville, Manche: 57 flint artefacts; Verron, 1975), and still larger assemblages have been recovered from settlement sites (e.g. Le Pinacle on Jersey, with a Campignien flint pick, 111 tranchet arrowheads and 925 simple scrapers; Godfray and Burdo, 1949).

The widespread trade in Grand Pressigny flint which began in the later 3rd millennium bc made a considerable impact on the flint industries of

Brittany, allowing the manufacture of large objects, including the flint dagger. The daggers and large blades were clearly luxury and display items. Recent evidence indicates that in the east of the region fine flints from Haute Normandie and the Paris basin were circulating alongside the Grand Pressigny flint in the same exchange networks (Kinnes, pers.comm.). Despite this evidence it is clear that throughout most of the neolithic period it was the trade in hardstone material from Brittany described in an earlier section rather than trade in flint from adjacent areas which was the principal form of raw material exchange.

ORNAMENTS. The high proportion of the neolithic material of north-western France which has come from ritual contexts makes it natural that ornaments should be well represented. These take a wide range of forms. At Vierville, perforated teeth and sea-shells, bone pendants, three steatite and one variscite (callaïs) bead, one amber bead and 35 cylindrical beads made from *Dentalium* shells (perhaps the remains of a necklace) were found (Verron, 1979). Large quantities of variscite beads were found in the long mounds of Morbihan, where they were associated with jadeite axes. 237 beads and 12 pendants of variscite were found at Tumiac, and 101 beads and 9 pendants of this material in the central cist of the Tumulus de Saint-Michel (L'Helgouach, 1971). 147 variscite beads came from the Kercado passage grave, in the same area. A possible source of the variscite has been located not far away at Pannecé in Loire-Atlantique (Forrestier *et al.*, 1973). In the west of Brittany schist appears to have replaced variscite as the principal material for the manufacture of fine stone ornaments.

Common types of ornament from middle and late neolithic contexts in north-western France are perforated arc-shaped pendants and miniature perforated axes. The former may in some cases be the reworked fragments of broken bracelets. Both are types which have a fairly wide currency in later neolithic France.

With the arrival of Beakers in north-western France, decorative artefacts become increasingly individualistic and sophisticated. Archer's wristguards and perforated V-shaped buttons are known, though the latter are prone to destruction in the predominantly acid soil conditions of the region. Gold and copper also appear at this time, the former principally in the form of small plaques, though there is also an object described as a 'diadem' from Kerouaren (Finistère) (L'Helgouach, 1970; Treinen, 1970). The gold and copper together with the other ornaments represent a major change in the nature of decorative artefacts, and suggest a change in the economic and social systems underlying display. There is indeed a close relationship between Beaker period display patterns and those of the Early Bronze Age, but the Armorican early bronze age 'Tumulus' series lies outside the scope of this survey.

MORTUARY RITUAL

The principal neolithic burial mode in north-western France was collective inhumation. The origin of this practice presumably lay in the mesolithic period, as it is represented at mesolithic Téviec and Hoëdic in the mid-5th millennium bc (Péquart *et al.*, 1937; Péquart and Péquart, 1954; Renfrew, 1976). The exact relationship between this mesolithic evidence and the ritual practised in the earliest chambered tombs of the region is not clear; neolithic collective inhumation is found throughout western Europe but the Breton manifestation is unlikely to be the result simply of local acculturation.

In most megalithic tombs, the evidence suggests that the bodies had been exposed elsewhere beforehand, and that the skeletons were finally deposited in the tomb in a disarticulated state. At Vierville (Manche) it was suggested that the bones had been put into bags (Verron, 1975), but the evidence varies, even between different chambers of the same monument. In chamber R at La Hogue (Calvados), articulated skeletons were arranged on a pavement overlying a level of black earth which contained disarticulated remains. In chamber N, Coutil (1918) noted a possible grave below a rectangular paved area, and in chamber P there was a square arrangement of stones surrounding a skull (Verron, 1977a). Human remains were also found in one of the passages of this monument, outside chamber X (Coutil, 1918).

At other sites the evidence suggests that much greater care was taken in the disposal of the remains. At Condé-sur-Ifs 1 (Calvados) 10 skeletons were arranged radially around the walls of the chamber, feet pointing towards the centre. The arrangement of the bodies at Condé-sur-Ifs 2 may have been similar (Bender, 1967; Dastugue and Torre, 1966). At La Hoguette (Calvados), 46 individuals were recognised in the six chambers, and 10 others recorded from areas of 19th century disturbance (Caillaud and Lagnel, 1972). In chamber VI the skeletons were laid on their sides in a crouching position, to the north of an internal partition, while in chamber IV skulls had been gathered together and placed in a hollow covered by a capstone. Careful attention seems to have been paid to the dead at Les Monts Grantez (Jersey), where six extended inhumations were each associated with shellfish, bones and carefully selected beach pebbles, while a seventh was arranged in a sitting position against one wall of the passage (Nicolle *et al.*, 1913).

Successive inhumations seem often to have been associated with the laying of a series of pavements. La Hogue, La Hoguette, and Condé-sur-Ifs 1 and 2 may be cited as examples. At La Varde (Guernsey) two pavements had mortuary deposits on them, and there were several layers of limpet shells which could also be interpreted as pavements (Lukis, 1847).

Bones of mammals, birds and fish were a common component of the mortuary deposits. Large numbers of limpet shells covered the capstones at La Hougue Bie (Jersey), and among the 80 bones or shells found at Vierville, there were many shellfish (Baal, 1925; Verron, 1977b). At La Hogue, chamber M, the bones of crow, water-rat, weasel, fox, pig and a bovid were associated with a small internal dolmen, and at Le Déhus (Guernsey) the deposit included the bones of swan, shag, razorbill and fulmar (Kendrick, 1928; Bender, 1967).

While inhumation seems to have been the general case, burnt bones are encountered fairly frequently, normally in association with unburnt bones.

PLATE 9.7. Engraving showing late neolithic artefacts and the multi-layered mortuary deposits found during excavation in 1838 within the chamber of the developed passage grave of La Varde (Guernsey). (From Lukis, 1853.)

Deliberate cremations are attested at Kercado and Mané Lud in Morbihan (L'Helgouach, 1965), but in most cases such burnt bones as are found are probably the result of accidental burning during ritual activities. The crematorium at La Hoguette is not directly associated with the megalithic monument and may be part of a different ritual. The mixing of ashes with burnt and unburnt bones is a particularly common feature of megalithic tombs on the Channel Islands, where it may represent an insular and late tradition (Hawkes, 1939).

The grouping of skeletons or groups of bones within internal subdivisions is a common feature of the megalithic tombs of north-western France. It is perhaps best represented on the Channel Islands. At Les Pourciaux 1 on Alderney five or six small cists were built against the wall and resting on a pavement, each enclosing a single skull (Lukis, 1865). Nine cists regularly spaced along the inside wall of the allée couverte of Ville ès Nouaux on Jersey contained whole Beakers, and were associated with an extended inhumation and a wristguard (Bellis and Cable, 1884). A particular feature of the tomb of La Varde (Guernsey) is the grouping of bones of several individuals around a vessel, usually a Guernsey vase, surrounded by a ring of beach pebbles (Lukis, 1844). At least 30 such groupings have been found, and they can be ascribed to the final phase of use of the monument at the end of the 3rd millennium bc (Plate 9.7).

Despite the rich and varied evidence at our disposal, it is not possible to reconstruct the rituals which were practised at these monuments. The variation in the treatment of the dead, both within and between chambers, may be the result of different families or other social groupings with distinct traditions, but the problems of quantifying the data preclude any detailed analysis of these differences. In addition, the remains found in the chambered tombs are clearly the end result of a sequence of activities, most of which have left no other material record. Despite our inability to interpret them, however, the activities connected with the dead and with the chambered tombs are, insofar as they have left traces, one of the most important sources of information we have about the Neolithic of this part of France.

The Role of Ritual Monuments

Ritual monuments are our main source of information on the Armorican Neolithic. This forces interpretations of the evidence to take into account structure and symbolism, neither of which are easily approachable through the archaeological record.

The ritual monuments of north-western France pose three principal questions: origin; function; and the processes that determined their variety of form and function and supported their continued development and use (L'Helgouach, 1973; Renfrew, 1976; Fleming, 1972, 1973).

The distribution of the sites is not markedly selective but is sprread over the whole range of geographical areas, while their chronology spans the whole of the neolithic period, with some related phenomena in the Mesolithic and the Bronze Age. Local sequences and comprehensive radiocarbon chronologies have been estabished for these sites (L'Helgouach, 1965; Verron, 1977a; Giot, 1971; Giot *et al.*, 1979). The sequence of early radiocarbon dates for the widespread types of simple passage grave and unchambered long mound (see list of dates at end of chapter) suggests that the Breton examples were amongst the earliest anywhere in Europe. The sites are well-constructed and architecturally complex and appear to have been associated with a developed, multi-stage ritual, which suggests that the initial development took place at an even earlier date. The megalithic and the later phases of the non-megalithic monuments may represent the final transformation of non-monumental ritual areas, which had been developing during the 5th millennium.

The collective burial rite at Téviec and Hoëdic (Morbihan) argues for a connection between mesolithic activities and the later, neolithic, ritual practice. Both these sites had inhumation graves, 10 at Téviec and 9 at Hoëdic, containing the remains of 23 and 14 bodies respectively. The graves were basically the same at both sites, consisting either of a stone-built cist with a hearth on top, and covered with more stones, or an antler structure of similar form. While some graves had only one burial, the larger collective graves had been used successively, the final body being articulated, while the previously buried skeletons had been disturbed to make room for each new burial. The excavators suggested that the covering stones would have been removed for each burial, and then replaced (Péquart *et al.*, 1937). At both sites the combination of domestic, ritual and grave-associated hearths argues for a complex, multi-stage ritual based on several discrete foci within a defined area. A variety of distinctive grave-goods was associated with the burials. Microlithic tools were common, and the occurrence of hammer stones and sometimes a core suggests that utilitarian manufacturing needs were considered to continue after death. Engraved bones, in particular a type of deer bone point which has been found only with these burials, suggests a non-functional, cultural component, also indicated by the presence of ochre and worked shells. The association of *Trivia* shells with male bodies and *Littoria* shells with female indicates a sexual differentiation in social and ritual organisation which continues into the neolithic period and beyond (Taborin, 1974).

Although these sites may be not representative of the social or ritual traditions of mesolithic Brittany as a whole, the presence of similar narrow-blade industries at La Torche (Finistère) and elsewhere, suggests that related groups were widely distributed. The date from La Torche is relatively late, 4020bc (Rozoy, 1978), but the traditions represented at Hoëdic (dated to 4625bc) could easily have survived until the end of the 5th millennium. At Dissignac microliths were associated with pottery and pollen evidence of a cleared landscape including traces of cereals (L'Helgouach, 1976b, 1979; Visset, 1974). The exact interrelationship of these elements is not clear, but radiocarbon determinations from the old land surface indicate an age of between 4300bc and 3830bc (L'Helgouach, 1977a). This suggests that mesolithic traditions survived into the early 4th millennium, and were not replaced by neolithic traditions but were absorbed. Neolithic groups, therefore, not only operated within similar economic and environmental contexts as mesolithic groups, but may also have incorporated elements derived from the earlier groups. Among the ritual traditions which may have been inherited can be included successive burial in collective tombs, the deposition of both functional and non-functional artefacts in graves, and the multi-stage ritual with which the inhumations were associated. These features are represented in the mesolithic burials of Téviec and Hoëdic and in the earliest passage graves and long mounds.

The changes in mortuary practice which the earliest neolithic monumental tombs represent may have been linked to changes in social organisation which may in turn have been related to changes in subsistence strategies. The concentration of mesolithic and early neolithic sites in littoral areas and on islands suggests that access to coastal resources was an important subsistence factor, and the continued use of sea-shells in neolithic mortuary deposits tends to confirm this view. If neolithic systems were flexible enough to integrate existing subsistence strategies, it is likely that conceptual systems were also flexible enough to absorb earlier concepts. The elaboration of subsistence strategies in the Neolithic, with the combination of agricultural and gathering practices, reflects the elaboration of the material expression of conceptual and ritual systems seen in the development of the neolithic ritual monument complex. With the adoption of more elaborate economic and ritual systems, and the realigned social relationships arising from this, there may have been a need for new mechanisms to articulate society. The material expression of these mechanisms may be seen in the construction of ritual monuments, themselves a combination of transforms of various traditions. The common idea expressed in these monuments would appear to be the use of an enclosed area to contain several smaller enclosed areas which served as the foci of successive ritual activities. This configuration is clearly seen in the long mound series, and is also present in the passage grave design, where the mound or cairn becomes the major enclosure, and internal subdivisions in the chamber take on the roles of the secondary foci. The elaboration of the designs in the middle neolithic is a reflection of the increasing stability of the groups responsible for the construction of the monuments. This type of monument can therefore be regarded as having arisen from the need felt by the early neolithic communities of north-western France to express social reorganisation. The same process may have been in operation in many other areas where ritual monuments are known, and may have been a common factor in the Neolithic of western Europe. There is however no reason to suppose that one area derived the form of its ritual complex directly from another.

The evidence of excavated sites in Armorica makes it clear that one of the primary, and continuous functions was the disposal of the dead. The continuous deposition of mortuary remains at ritual sites throughout the neolithic period indicates that whatever other functions were ascribed to the sites, ritual associated with burial remained important. The mortuary practices seen in the sites were, however, only part of a complex burial ritual. The presence of disarticulated skeletons and partly burnt bones in the chambers and passages of many Normandy passage graves suggests that other areas or enclosures played a part at different stages of the disposal procedure.

Convincing arguments have been put forward to explain the function of ritual monuments in social and economic terms (Renfrew, 1976; Fleming, 1972, 1973; Bloch, 1971). Within a non-centralised society there is a strong possibility of variation in social organisation arising under the influence of changing local conditions. The ritual monuments may therefore have had varying functions depending on the particular social and economic situation. However, these functions are likely to have been part of a developing process, and so subject to continuous change. The function of these sites must therefore be seen as having operated on two levels, an underlying, widespread, commonly recognised function on the one hand, and various specific functions, developed in response to local circumstances, and changing as those conditions changed, on the other.

The link between these two levels of function is the need to articulate relationships both within and between groups. For a group to articulate its own relationships, it requires a set of symbols shared by the members of the group. These need not, in their detail or material expression, be recognisable to members of other groups. Certain aspects of material culture, therefore, can be seen as group-specific, and the social, political and ritual relationships these reflect can also be assumed to be specific. In a non-centralised society, however, there is a need for articulation between groups, and communicating mechanisms to express this. The use of ritual monuments as widespread and recognisable symbols is one such mechanism. The building or use of a megalithic monument may have reinforced the corporate solidarity of a community, but at the same time it expressed the membership of the community in a wider network of relationships by expressing the commonly shared ideational system. This system need not have been explicit, nor need it have been imposed from outside the community. To judge from the variations in design, and from the development of monument types, such as menhirs, in which the concepts are expressed with extreme simplicity, the system was probably implicit. This implicit set of shared symbols and concepts seems to have allowed increasingly diversified groups to interact within the social and economic net-works which were necessary for the functioning of society.

The continued use of ritual monuments throughout the neolithic period suggests a continuity of concept. Developmental processes can, however, be recognised. Two clear trends in monument design can be distinguished, both of which reflect the movement towards the more regionalised expression of the underlying concepts. First, the formalised design of the early passage grave series, with the chamber and passage clearly differentiated, undergoes a series of transforms leading to the merging of the two elements in a more simple design. This process seems to result from emphasis being placed on the chamber at the expense of the passage, and is reflected in the local development of the trapezoidal, V-shaped and lateral entry tomb series. Secondly, there is a trend towards internal elaboration of the chamber, with free-standing orthostats, side chambers and transepts increasing in number and importance, ultimately at the expense of the chamber itself.

Both these trends can be identified in the earliest passage graves of the region. Chamber H at Barnenez, for instance, shows a less differentiated chamber and passage than the flanking chambers G, G′, I and J (Giot, 1970), and there are internal subdivisions within the chamber, defined by upstanding slabs and paving, at Vierville, La Hogue chambers M and N, La Hoguette, chamber IV and La Sergenté (Verron, 1977b; Nicolle, 1924). These internal foci were associated with specific ritual behaviour, often different from that in the rest of the chamber. At Ty Floc'h (dated to 3630bc), the 'lobster claw' chamber was further subdivided by orthostatic cists, in which were concentrated the bone and charcoal deposits, while at La Sergenté, the sub-division contained the only pottery found at the site (Le Roux and Lecerf, 1980; Nicolle, 1924). Channel Island tombs such as Les Monts Grantez, Mont Ubé and Faldouet (Jersey), Le Creux ès Fales and La Varde (Guernsey), illustrate the combination of simplified overall design and elaboration of the chamber, leading in the cases of Faldouet and Le Mont de la Ville (Jersey) to open chambers, reached by a passage, with cists set around the edge (Hawkes, 1939).

In the parallel-sided *allée couverte* series, the chamber and passage were structurally undifferentiated, though there was often a 'vestibule' defined by septal slabs or a 'porthole' entrance slab. The relationships between the various elements of the design (chamber, entrance-way, internal foci), however, are the same as in the passage graves.

Ultimately, the process of simplification and the more and more implicit expression of the system of ideas, led to the menhirs, alignments and stone circles. In these monuments, the concepts have become so implicit that they would have been recognisable only to the local community and they could no longer function as an articulating device between communities.

If these trends are correctly interpreted, an overall view of the ritual monument complex can now be reached. The introduction of neolithic influences into the region in the late 5th or early 4th millennium bc, together with a subsistence economy based on agriculture, may have been accompanied by new social systems. The existing pre-neolithic systems would have interacted with new subsistence strategies and this interaction may have involved the realignment of the social organisation. In this situation new structuring devices may have been necessary to allow the non-centralised communities to interact. The concepts linking these groups were expressed materially as a hierarchy of spatial areas, related to ritual, and more specifically to mortuary, practices, and formalised as ritual monuments in a complex ritual landscape of differing but related sites. Successive burial and multi-phase ritual activities had been features of the preceding mesolithic communities, and elements of these earlier concepts may have been adopted by the neolithic groups. The adoption of this articulating mechanism would have allowed social and economic networks to operate with an increased flexibility. There will have been some variation in social, political and economic organisation according to local circumstances, and while this will not have affected the basic concepts, monument design will have diversified in response to the particular needs of each group. With local perceptions influencing the transforms, the articulating or reinforcing functions would have continued to operate within the group, but as the concepts became more implicit, and hence less and less recognisable to other groups, articulation between groups would have become increasingly difficult. Because of the wide-ranging and complex networks for social and economic exchange, the effects of this change might not have become felt immediately. Regionalisation of monument design, however, related to the diversification of pottery styles, indicates that some form of collapse took place during the 4th millennium, and the elaboration of existing designs and the use of art in certain areas, suggest local attempts to develop a new set of symbols to assist articulation between communities at a sub-regional level.

The simplification of monument design and the use of internal foci for very specific activities will have enhanced the functioning of the ritual monuments at the group level, but only at the expense of their wider role. The adoption of the *allée couverte* design in the later 3rd millennium provided a widespread and acceptable alternative to the increasingly regionalised and

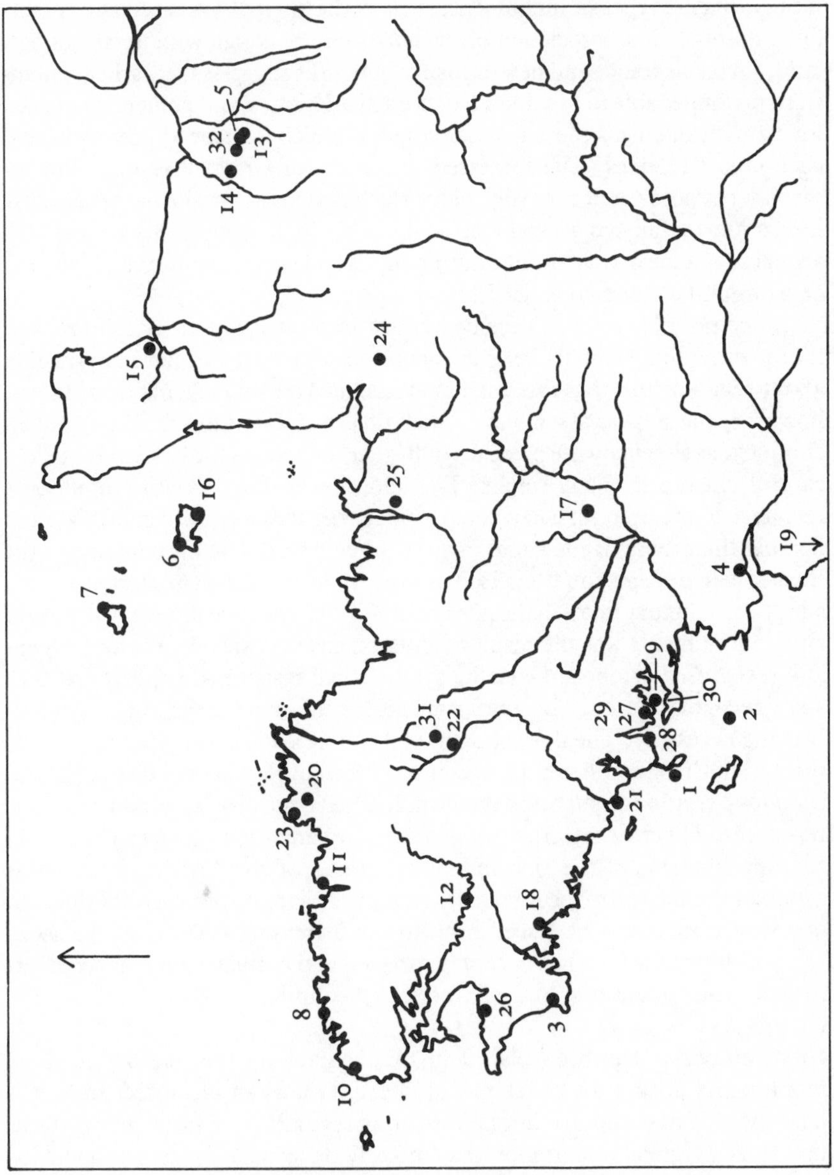

FIGURE 9.11. General map of sites, Brittany and Normandy.
1 Téviec; 2 Hoëdic; 3 Beg an Dorchenn; 4 Dissignac; 5 Brèche au Diable; 6 Le Pinacle; 7 Les Fouaillages; 8 Curnic; 9 Er Lannic; 10 Île Carn; 11 Barnenez; 12 Ty Floc'h; 13 La Hogue; 14 La Hoguette; 15 Vierville; 16 La Hougue Bie; 17 La Grée de Coujoux/Le Moulin; 18 Kerleven; 19 Les Mousseaux; 20 Crec'h Quillé; 21 Goërem; 22 Liscuis 1/2/3; 23 Prajou Menhir; 24 Sainte Symphorien; 25 Tressé; 26 Lesconil; 27 Tumiac; 28 Carnac; 29 Le Grand Menhir Brisé; 30 Gavrinis; 31 Sélédin; 32 La Fordelle.

locally diverse types of monument, such as the angled, V-shaped and trapezoidal designs. The association of the *allée couverte* design with uptake of new land, forest clearance and new exchange networks suggests that earlier systems were no longer able to provide adequate articulation, and that there was a need for new mechanisms the implementation of which demanded new social and economic strategies. The increased utilisation of Grand Pressigny flint for display purposes, and exchange networks based on luxury items, are an early indication of the replacement of communal ritual monuments by portable artefacts as a means of communicating status and group membership, with the concomitant changes in social relationships.

The portable artefact became of great importance in the late 3rd millennium, providing symbols flexible enough to contain the explicit information about relationships that the ritual monuments were no longer able to. It was, however, the Beaker assemblage which finally replaced the ritual monument complex, as shown by the presence of Beaker material as the last deposit before careful closure in many tombs. The adoption of Beakers was, in effect, a response to the need for a new set of articulating symbols more immediate and flexible than those of the ritual monument complex. The introduction of the Beaker assemblage thus finalised a process of replacement started by the adoption of luxury items in the late neolithic. The eventual decline of the use of ritual monuments was the result of an imbalance between locally and regionally recognised symbols. Once the symbols had become so implicit that they were recognisable only by the group using the monument, other symbols became necessary. The development of portable artefacts as symbols towards the end of the 3rd millennium encouraged the development of new social and economic relationships, based on the individual control of social and economic resources. The major restructuring of social organisation which can be seen in the development of the rich individual graves of the Armorican Tumulus group of the Early Bronze Age, marks a radical change from the Neolithic, but one whose roots can be traced back to the increasing inability of the social relationships based on the concepts expressed in the ritual monument complex to articulate the societies of the Armorican Neolithic.

Conclusion

Great emphasis has been placed in this chapter on the role of the ritual monuments during the development of the Armorican Neolithic, since it is here that the best opportunities for isolating regularities in behaviour patterns lie. It is of great importance that underlying general patterns should be distinguished from the more specific forms of behaviour, if the complexity and variety of information is not to become too bewildering, and this is especially true of the activities we associate with the ritual monument complex. Some form of reductionism is essential if we are not to lose sight of the fact that factors were in operation which invested the monuments with such importance that, in recognisable transforms, they retained a crucial role in the behaviour of neolithic groups over a wide geographical range and a period of 2000 years. For such a phenomenon to be maintained, the factors underlying it must have had a crucial effect on all aspects of activity. If we are properly to analyse the specific social and economic aspects of the Armorican Neolithic, therefore, a clear recognition of the role of ritual monuments, and the processes operating on and through them, is a prerequisite.

RADIOCARBON DATES

Mesolithic						
Pointe-Saint-Gildas, Préfailles (Loire-Atlantique)	5570±140bc	Gif-3531	Charcoal	Settlement	Hearth	Giot, L'Helgouach and Monnier, 1979, 153
Hoëdic (Morbihan)	4625±350bc	Gif-227	Charcoal	Settlement	Hearth	*Radiocarbon*, 8, 79
Le Curnic, Guissény (Finistère)	4030±150bc	Gsy-47B	Charcoal	Settlement	Hearth	*Radiocarbon*, 8, 134
Beg an Dorchenn, Plomeur (Finistère)	4020±80bc	GrN-2001	Charcoal	Settlement		*Radiocarbon*, 5, 176
Dissignac, Saint Nazaire (Loire-Atlantique)	4300±150bc	Gif-3823	Charcoal	Settlement	Pre-monument land surface	L'Helgouach, 1977a
	3990±150bc	Gif-3822	Charcoal	Settlement	Pre-monument land surface	L'Helgouach, 1977a
	3830±150bc	Gif-3820	Charcoal	Settlement	Pre-monument land surface	L'Helgouach, 1977a
Clearance Horizons						
Ile Carn, Ploudalmezeau (Finis.)	3820±150bc	Gif-766	Charcoal	Clearance	Pre-monument land surface	Morzadec-Kerfourn, 1974
Saint-Michel-de-Brasparts (Finistère)	3450±60bc	GrN-198	Charcoal	Clearance		*Radiocarbon*, 5, 199
	1820±55bc	GrN-217	Charcoal	Clearance		*Radiocarbon*, 5, 199
Fossé Catuélan, Erquy (Côtes-du-N)	2610±140bc	Gif-1118	Charcoal	Clearance	Old land surface beneath bank	*Radiocarbon*, 13, 216
Le Correjou, Plouguerneau (Finistère)	2285±250bc	Gif-282	Charcoal	Clearance	Base of pollen core	Morzadec-Kerfourn, 1974
Porsguen, Plouescat (Finistère)	2170±140bc	Gif-140	Charcoal	Clearance	Base of pollen core	Morzadec-Kerfourn, 1974
Juno-Bella, Berrien (Finistère)	2100±120bc	Gif-1545	Charcoal	Clearance	Pre-monument land surface	*Radiocarbon*, 16, 21

Kercado, Carnac (Morbihan)	3890±300bc	Sa-95	Charcoal	Passage grave		*Radiocarbon*, 6, 247
Île Guennoc III, Landeda (Finistère)	3850±300bc	Gif-165	Charcoal	Passage grave	Chamber C	*Radiocarbon*, 8, 76
	3125±140bc	Gif-1870	Charcoal	Passage grave	Chamber C	*Radiocarbon*, 16, 20
	2550±120bc	Gif-813	Charcoal	Passage grave	Chamber E	*Radiocarbon*, 13, 216
Barnenez, Plouézoc'h (Finistère)	3800±150bc	Gif-1309	Charcoal	Passage grave	Chamber G	*Radiocarbon*, 13, 215
	3600±140bc	Gif-1556	Charcoal	Passage grave	Chamber F	*Radiocarbon*, 13, 215
	3500±150bc	Gif-1310	Charcoal	Passage grave	Chamber A	*Radiocarbon*, 13, 215
	3150±140bc	Gif-1116	Charcoal	Passage grave	Chamber F	*Radiocarbon*, 13, 214
Ty Floc'h, Saint Thois (Finistère)	3630±120bc	Gif-5234	Charcoal	Passage grave	Floor of chamber B	Le Roux and Lecerf, 1980
	2720±120bc	Gif-5233	Charcoal	Passage grave	3rd phase of cairn	Le Roux and Lecerf, 1980
La Hoguette, Fontenay-le-Marmion (Calvados)	3610±150bc	Ly-131	Charcoal	Passage grave	Hearth, chamber IV	*Radiocarbon*, 15, 143
	3210±190bc	Ly-421	Bone	Passage grave	Chamber V	*Radiocarbon*, 15, 143
	3100±260bc	Ly-420	Bone	Passage grave	Chamber VII	*Radiocarbon*, 15, 143
	3050±130bc	Gif-1345	Charcoal	Passage grave	Hearth, chamber V	*Radiocarbon*, 14, 280
	2630±150bc	Ly-132	Charcoal	Passage grave	Hearth, outside chamber V	*Radiocarbon*, 15, 143
Île Carn, Ploudalmezeau (Finistère)	3440±150bc	Gif-1362	Charcoal	Passage grave	South chamber	*Radiocarbon*, 12, 431
	3390±250bc	Gif-414	Charcoal	Passage grave	Central chamber	*Radiocarbon*, 12, 431
	3280±75bc	GrN-1968	Charcoal	Passage grave	Central chamber	*Radiocarbon*, 12, 431
	2890±150bc	Gif-1363	Charcoal	Passage grave	North chamber	*Radiocarbon*, 12, 431
Tumulus de Mont-St-Michel, Carnac (Morbihan)	3770±300bc	Sa-96	Charcoal	Long mound	Mound body	*Radiocarbon*, 6, 247
	3030±150bc	Gsy-89	Charcoal	Long mound	Mound body	*Radiocarbon*, 6, 247
Le Grée de Coujoux, Saint-Just (Ille-et-Vilaine)	3710±120bc	Gif-5458	Charcoal	Long mound	Hearths beneath mound	Le Roux, 1981
	3630±120bc	Gif-5456	Charcoal	Long mound	Hearths beneath mound	Le Roux, 1981
	3600±120bc	Gif-5457	Charcoal	Long mound	Hearths beneath mound	Le Roux, 1981
Les Fouaillages, Vale (Guernsey)	3640±50bc	BM-1892	Charcoal	Long mound	Phase 2	Kinnes, 1982
	3560±60bc	BM-1893	Charcoal	Long mound	Phase 2	Kinnes, 1982
La Brèche-au-Diable (Calvados)	3830±150bc	Gif-2319	Charcoal	Settlement	Hearth below Chasséen levels	Edeine, 1972
Le Pinacle, Saint Ouen (Jersey)	3070±110bc	BM-370	Charcoal	Settlement	Hearth, cf. Bandkeramik	*Radiocarbon*, 13, 17

Middle Neolithic						
Larcuste II, Colpo (Morbihan)	3540±120bc	Gif-2826	Charcoal	Transepted pass. grave	Passage	Giot, L'Helgouach and Monnier, 1979, 249
	2660±110bc	Gif-2454	Charcoal	Transepted pass. grave	Cairn II	Giot, L'Helgouach and Monnier, 1979, 249
	2110±120bc	Gif-2827	Charcoal	Transepted pass. grave	Cairn II, façade	Giot, L'Helgouach and Monnier, 1979, 249
	2030±110bc	Gif-2453	Charcoal	Transepted pass. grave	Cairn II, façade	Giot, L'Helgouach and Monnier, 1979, 249
Colombiers-sur-Seulles (Calvados)	3200±130bc	Gif-1917	Charcoal	Long mound	Ground surface below mound	*Radiocarbon*, 16, 15
Liscuis 1, Laniscat (Côtes-du-Nord)	3190±110bc	Gif-3099	Charcoal	V-shaped passage grave	Chamber	Giot, L'Helgouach and Monnier, 1979, 320
Le Castellic, Carnac (Morbihan)	3075±300bc	Gif-198B	Charcoal	Long mound	West cist under mound	*Radiocarbon*, 8, 78
Dissignac, Saint Nazaire (Loire-Atlantique)	2990±140bc	Gif-3821	Charcoal	Passage grave	Entrance of chamber B, associated with Chasséen pot	L'Helgouach, 1977a
Kerleven, La Forêt Fouesnant (Finistère)	2875±125bc	Gsy-111	Charcoal	Passage grave	Chamber B	*Radiocarbon*, 8, 135
Mané Kernaplaye, Saint Philibert (Morbihan)	2635±200bc	Gsy-88	Charcoal	Passage grave		*Radiocarbon*, 8, 135
Beg an Dorchenn, Plomeur (Finistère)	3190±110bc	Gif-5063	Charcoal	Settlement	Hearth	Le Roux, 1981
Le Curnic, Guissény (Finistère)	3560±250bc	Gif-345	Charcoal	Settlement	Occupation levels	*Radiocarbon*, 12, 431
	3390±60bc	GrN-1966	Charcoal	Settlement	Occupation levels	*Radiocarbon*, 5, 186
	2650±200bc	Gsy-47A	Charcoal	Settlement	Occupation levels	*Radiocarbon*, 8, 134
La Brèche-au-Diable (Calvados)	2680±140bc	Gif-2320	Charcoal	Settlement	J 480	Edeine, 1972
Sélédin, Plussulien (Côtes-du-Nord)	3320±140bc	Gif-1877	Charcoal	Axe factory	Main working floor N2SW	*Radiocarbon*, 16, 18
	3200±140bc	Gif-1876	Charcoal	Axe factory	O1NW	*Radiocarbon*, 16, 18
	3200±140bc	Gif-1873	Charcoal	Axe factory	N1SW	*Radiocarbon*, 16, 18
	3150±140bc	Gif-1872	Charcoal	Axe factory	N1SW	*Radiocarbon*, 16, 18
	3125±140bc	Gif-1874	Charcoal	Axe factory	N1SW	*Radiocarbon*, 16, 18
	3010±110bc	Gif-1875	Charcoal	Axe factory	N1SE	*Radiocarbon*, 16, 18
	3010±110bc	Gif-2329	Charcoal	Axe factory	N1SE	*Radiocarbon*, 16, 18
	3010±110bc	Gif-2330	Charcoal	Axe factory	N1SE	*Radiocarbon*, 16, 18
	3000±140bc	Gif-1871	Charcoal	Axe factory	O0SE	*Radiocarbon*, 16, 18
	2990±115bc	Gif-2682	Charcoal	Axe factory	N1SE	*Radiocarbon*, 16, 18
	2990±115bc	Gif-2684	Charcoal	Axe factory	O2NE	*Radiocarbon*, 16, 18
	2980±130bc	Gif-1542	Charcoal	Axe factory	O0SE	*Radiocarbon*, 16, 17
	2840±110bc	Gif-2328	Charcoal	Axe factory	N1SE	*Radiocarbon*, 16, 17
	2780±110bc	Gif-4079	Charcoal	Axe factory		Giot, L'Helgouach and Monnier, 1979, 373

(Côtes-du-Nord)						
Tossen-Keler, Penvenan (Côtes-du-Nord)	2550±260bc	Gif-280	Charcoal	Allée couverte	Central hearth	Giot, L'Helgouach and Monnier, 1979, 320
Liscuis 2, Laniscat (Côtes-du-Nord)	2500±110bc	Gif-3944	Charcoal	Allée couverte	Remodelling of terminal cell	Le Roux, 1977
	2220±110bc	Gif-3585	Charcoal	Allée couverte	Entrance	Le Roux, 1977
Liscuis 3, Laniscat (Côtes-du-Nord)	2250±110bc	Gif-4076	Charcoal	Allée couverte	Hearth associated with SOM pot	Le Roux, 1977
	1730±110bc	Gif-4075	Charcoal	Allée couverte	Hearth	Le Roux, 1977
Goërem, Gâvres (Morbihan)	2480±140bc	Gif-1148	Charcoal	Angled passage grave	Primary level, 4th chamber	*Radiocarbon*, 12, 433
	2150±140bc	Gif-768	Charcoal	Angled passage grave	3rd chamber	*Radiocarbon*, 12, 433
	1910±200bc	Gif-329	Charcoal	Angled passage grave	Passage	*Radiocarbon*, 12, 433
Kermené, Guidel (Morbihan)	2440±140bc	Gif-1966	Charcoal	Allée couverte		*Radiocarbon*, 16, 22
	2080±100bc	Gsy-73	Charcoal	Allée couverte		*Radiocarbon*, 8, 135
Les Fouaillages, Vale (Guernsey)	2050±60bc	BM-1895	Charcoal	Long mound	Hearth in final mound	Kinnes, 1982
	1880±50bc	BM-1897	Charcoal	Settlement	Posthole, settlement	Kinnes, 1982
Le Grée de Coujoux, Saint-Just (Ille-et-Vilaine)	1990±80bc	Gif-5235	Charcoal	Long mound/alignment	Carbon associated with early bronze age urn	Le Roux, 1981
Le Castellic, Carnac (Morbihan)	1980±250bc	Gif-198A	Charcoal	Long mound	Hearth E	*Radiocarbon*, 8, 78
Le Champ Grosset, Quessoy (Côtes-du-Nord)	1870±200bc	Gif-283	Charcoal	Allée couverte		*Radiocarbon*, 8, 75
Kerleven, La Forêt Fouesnant (Finistère)	1850±120bc	Gif-809	Charcoal	Passage grave	Chamber C	*Radiocarbon*, 13, 214
Crec'h Quillé, Saint-Quay-Perros (Côtes-du-Nord)	1790±200bc	Gsy-344	Charcoal	Lateral entry tomb	Charcoal in blockage of passage	Giot, L'Helgouach and Monnier, 1979, 320
Kerivoelen, Plelauff (Finistère)	1730±110bc	Gif-3586	Charcoal	Allée couverte		Giot, L'Helgouach and Monnier, 1979, 320
	1690±110bc	Gif-3587	Charcoal	Allée couverte		Giot, L'Helgouach and Monnier, 1979, 320
Sélédin, Plussulien (Côtes-du-Nord)	2660±140bc	Gif-1538	Charcoal	Axe factory	N1SW	*Radiocarbon*, 16, 18
	2550±130bc	Gif-1541	Charcoal	Axe factory	N1SW	*Radiocarbon*, 16, 18
	2470±110bc	Gif-3098	Charcoal	Axe factory	O3NW	Giot, L'Helgouach and Monnier, 1979, 373
	2410±130bc	Gif-1543	Charcoal	Axe factory	O4SE	*Radiocarbon*, 16, 18
	2400±115bc	Gif-2683	Charcoal	Axe factory	N1SW	*Radiocarbon*, 16, 18
	2100±130bc	Gif-1539	Charcoal	Axe factory	N1SW	*Radiocarbon*, 16, 18

A Survey of the French Neolithic

CHRIS SCARRE

THE CHAPTERS in this volume have described the neolithic and chalcolithic material of France on a region-by-region basis, and have outlined some recent approaches to its interpretation. The arrangement has put the emphasis on development within individual regions, and less has been said about the broad similarities and differences *between* regions. This final chapter is intended to redress the balance by drawing some of the strands together and showing how the French Neolithic developed as a whole.

The Beginning of the Neolithic in France

The neolithic period, defined by the presence of pottery and agriculture, appears in France to have had dual origins, in the north-east and in the south (Fig.10.1). There is a considerable contrast between the processes by which neolithic features were introduced into the two areas. The earliest Neolithic of north-eastern France is represented by the Bandkeramik (discussed in this volume by Ilett), a group thought to have crystallised in the Great Hungarian Plain and characterised by a remarkable uniformity in material culture, despite its extensive distribution. The earliest radiocarbon dates for the Hungarian Bandkeramik, of about 4600bc, are little if at all older than those for similar material in the Low Countries, and indicate the astonishing rapidity with which the tradition spread across the loess lands of central Europe. Ammerman and Cavalli-Sforza (1971, 1973, 1979) have studied this spread in terms of a 'wave of advance' model of colonisation fuelled by population increase. The advance seems to have slowed a little on encountering the non-loessic landscape of north-eastern France, but Bandkeramik villages of fully agricultural character appear to have been established in the Paris basin before the end of the 5th millennium bc. The sites are located on gravel river terraces which would have supported light, well-drained soils, fertile and easy to cultivate, and not altogether dissimilar to the central European loess. Cereal remains and the abundance of grindstones testify to arable farming, though possibly fixed-plot horticulture rather than large-scale farming. Animal bones are not usually preserved at Bandkeramik settlements in central Europe owing to the acidic nature of the preferred loessic soils, but the non-loessic soils of the Paris basin Bandkeramik have left us some faunal assemblages, which indicate the importance of cattle in the economy. The Bandkeramik settlements are concentrated in small enclaves and most of the landscape of north-eastern France is in fact devoid of evidence of early neolithic farming communities. It is therefore

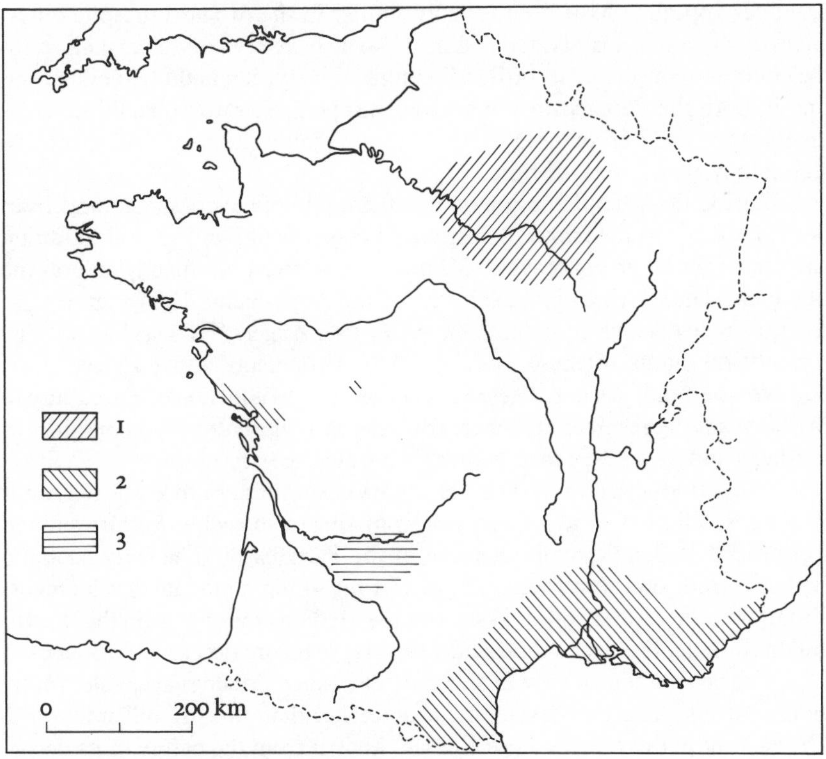

FIGURE 10.1. The Early Neolithic in France.
1 Bandkeramik; 2 Impressed Ware; 3 Roucadourien.

probable that non-farming mesolithic groups persisted for centuries if not millennia alongside the Bandkeramik communities, though little evidence for mesolithic-Bankeramik contact has been found in this region.

The Bandkeramik settlement of north-eastern France, like that of Germany and the Low Countries, is difficult to explain as other than the result of colonisation of the region by groups originating further east. The Paris basin marks the extreme western limit reached by this central European tradition. The colonists brought with them a village-based settlement system and a fully developed agricultural way of life. There is in north-eastern France no evidence for a preliminary phase of agriculture mixed with hunting and gathering, for the absorption of local mesolithic groups, or for extensive farming; the intensive fixed-plot horticulture developed further east appears to have been practised from the outset (Kruk, 1973, 1980; Bakels, 1978a). This may be a further reflection of the rigid conservatism of Bandkeramik society so well expressed by the house types and their orientation, by the pottery forms and decoration, and by other aspects of material culture. There were several important similarities between the material culture of Bandkeramik communities in Hungary and the Paris basin, and settlement locations and agricultural practices appear to have been broadly similar in the two areas despite differences of climate and landscape. While this may have been due at least in part to the inherent conservatism of Bandkeramik society, it should be pointed out that in both the Paris basin and central Europe these earliest neolithic settlements were sited on or near to what was probably the best land, given the technology available at the time.

During the 4th millennium bc Bandkeramik influences spread west from the Paris basin to the fringe of Brittany. Potsherds of Bandkeramik tradition have been found at Fontenay-le-Marmion in western Normandy and on the Channel Islands, while an assemblage of the Augy-Sainte-Pallaye group has recently been discovered in the Loire valley near Angers (Hibbs, chap.9). The agricultural status of these more westerly settlements is not always clear, however, and radiocarbon dates suggest that the introduction of agriculture to Brittany was the result of influences from the early agricultural communities of southern and western France, rather than from the Paris basin.

The introduction of neolithic elements in southern France was the result of a very different kind of process from that responsible for the sudden appearance of Bandkeramik material in the Paris basin. The early neolithic evidence from southern France suggests a much more gradual development. Pottery and sheep first appear at sites on the Mediterranean coast in the late 7th millennium bc, but over a thousand years elapse before the earliest evidence of a fully agricultural economy in this part of France becomes available. Mills, indeed, would date this development no earlier than the 4th millennium bc. The earliest pottery of southern France, known from the nature of its decoration as Impressed or Cardial Ware, is of a type found throughout the west Mediterranean basin. Its appearance on the island of Corsica demonstrates that sea-travel was taking place, and the fact that all the earliest sites, both here and on the mainland, are on or near the coast suggests that it was principally by sea-travel that the Impressed Ware was disseminated. The pottery bears some resemblance to contemporary ceramics from the east Mediterranean, indicating the possible extent of this network; the early domesticates (sheep, cereals) must ultimately have come from the Near East. Lewthwaite has recently suggested that Impressed Ware may have spread among interlinked coastal communities as a prestige object, rather like Beakers three or four millennia later (Lewthwaite, 1982). This argument gains some support from the fineness of the earliest Impressed Ware, and the decline in quality in the subsequent Epicardial phase. Other features, perhaps including domesticates, may have spread along the same networks. There is no evidence in this part of France of any 'colonisation' such as some earlier writers (e.g. Evans, 1956) proposed.

Several cave sequences illustrate the gradual nature of the introduction of neolithic elements in southern and south-western France. At the Grotte de l'Abeurador (Hérault), lentils and peas thought by some to be Near Eastern domesticates have been found in a pre-ceramic level of doubtful date (Vaquer, 1980). Apparently domestic sheep or goat appear in pre-neolithic (i.e. pre-pottery) levels at the Dourgne II, Gazel (Aude) and Balma Margineda (Andorra) caves, and at the Châteauneuf-les-Martigues rockshelter (Bouches-du-Rhône). Cereals and pottery seem to make their appearance at approximately the same time, but it is clear that while the pottery and domestic animals soon became of some importance to the inhabitants of these sites, arable farming was only slowly taken up on any scale. This apparent time-lag between the first appearance of cereals in southern France and the development of arable agriculture may, as Mills has suggested (p.132ff.), be in part a distortion resulting from the types of site from which most of the early neolithic evidence has come. Many of these sites have continuous sequences of occupation beginning in the mesolithic period (if not earlier), and most are in 'mesolithic' locations, well-situated for hunting, fishing and gathering, but not chosen for their agricultural potential; it is hardly surprising that they have yielded only slight evidence of agriculture. For agricultural settlements we must look to the lowlands and the river valleys, but unfortunately few sites are known from these areas. This no doubt is in part the consequence of millennia of sediment deposition, which must have buried many of them. The earliest lowland agricultural settlements known in Mediterranean France are the submerged site of Ile Corrège (Aude), dated to 4850bc, and Le Baratin (dated 4650bc) in the Rhône valley. These open-air Impressed Ware sites may have been substantial villages, comparable to the Bandkeramik settlements of the Paris basin and dependent like them on cereal agriculture. Similar sites probably lie buried beneath the valley sediments, including perhaps some of earlier date. At present, however, it seems that over a thousand years separates the first appearance of neolithic features in southern France and the first agriculturally-based villages. If the Bandkeramik settlements represent the movement of colonists into north-eastern France, the contrast suggests that in the Mediterranean zone it was a case of the slow spread and acceptance of neolithic features among indigenous mesolithic communities.

The introduction and early development of neolithic features is less well documented in Atlantic France than in the south or the north-east. Impressed Ware has been found at several sites on the coast of west-central France and at one cave site inland, but there is no direct geographical link with the similar material of southern France (Fig.10.1), and a derivation via the western seaways from Portugal is possible. At La Tranche (Vendée), Impressed Ware is associated with domestic animals and grindstones, indicating an agricultural base, and there are mid-5th millennium bc radiocarbon dates (Scarre, this volume). There is too little evidence from this region for more to be said at present. Between the Impressed Ware sites of west-central France and those of southern France lie the Roucadourien sites of Aquitaine, representing a separate early neolithic tradition. The coil-built pointed-based Roucadourien vessels can be paralleled in other peripheral early neolithic groups such as the Ertebølle of Jutland (Clark, 1975), the Narva of Poland (Dolukhanov, 1979) and the Swifterbant ware of Holland (Louwe-Kooijmans, 1980). These parallels are suggestive, but the pottery found at the French sites is probably best regarded as a local development. The possibility that the use of this pottery spread gradually among interlinked mesolithic communities of the Atlantic façade should not, however, be ruled out. Some Roucadourien sites have yielded remains suggestive of cultivation as well as bones of domestic animals but most, like the early Impressed Ware sites of southern France, are in 'mesolithic' locations not very suitable for arable farming. In Brittany, the earliest Neolithic is represented by the level underlying the burial mound of Dissignac (Loire-Atlantique), in which microliths and archaic pottery were found associated with cereal pollen and radiocarbon dates of c.4000bc (Giot, L'Helgouach and Monnier, 1979, 159). Here again there is insufficient evidence to allow the establishment and early development of the Neolithic usefully to be discussed. In both west-central France and Brittany, however, present information suggests that the neolithic features were adopted gradually, as in the south, rather than having been introduced as a package by colonists, as in the case of the Paris basin.

Chambered Tombs

Almost all the regional studies in this volume have made some mention of megalithic or dry-stone chambered tombs, which in most parts of France are perhaps the most impressive feature of the neolithic record (Fig. 10.2). Related to these are the rock-cut tombs which are known in some *départements*, notably the *hypogées* associated with the Seine-Oise-Marne group in the Paris basin and the series of rock-cut tombs near the mouth of the River Rhône which includes the famous 'Grotte des Fées'. Several chapters have commented on the difficulty of dating such monumental tombs. The remains within the chambers can provide a *terminus ante quem* for the date of construction, but the earliest deposits have in the majority of cases been severely disturbed by later activity and are not able to provide detailed information. Radiocarbon determinations are available for some tombs, but these suffer from the same difficulty. It is nevertheless possible to divide the chambered tombs of France in broad chronological terms into three groups (Giot, 1976, 1981; Fig. 10.2). The first of these includes all the early tombs datable to the 4th and early 3rd millennium bc, principally the passage graves and their derivatives. The second belongs to the Late Neolithic (later 3rd millennium bc) and includes the *allées couvertes* which are particularly well represented in the Paris basin but may also be found in Brittany and south-western France. The Seine-Oise-Marne *hypogées* belong to this group. Finally, there are the late neolithic and chalcolithic *dolmens simples* of the late 3rd and early 2nd millennium, which consist of a simple chamber with covering mound. Such tombs are very common in the Alps, the Pyrenees, and along the southern and western fringes of the Massif Central. The three groups of tombs are united by several common features – dry-stone or megalithic construction, chamber with covering mound, and funerary purpose – but are not necessarily parts of a single phenomenon, and there is no compelling reason to think that one type must have developed from another. The possibility of multiple independent origins should not be ruled out, and the chambered tombs may have possessed a very different significance and function depending upon their particular social and

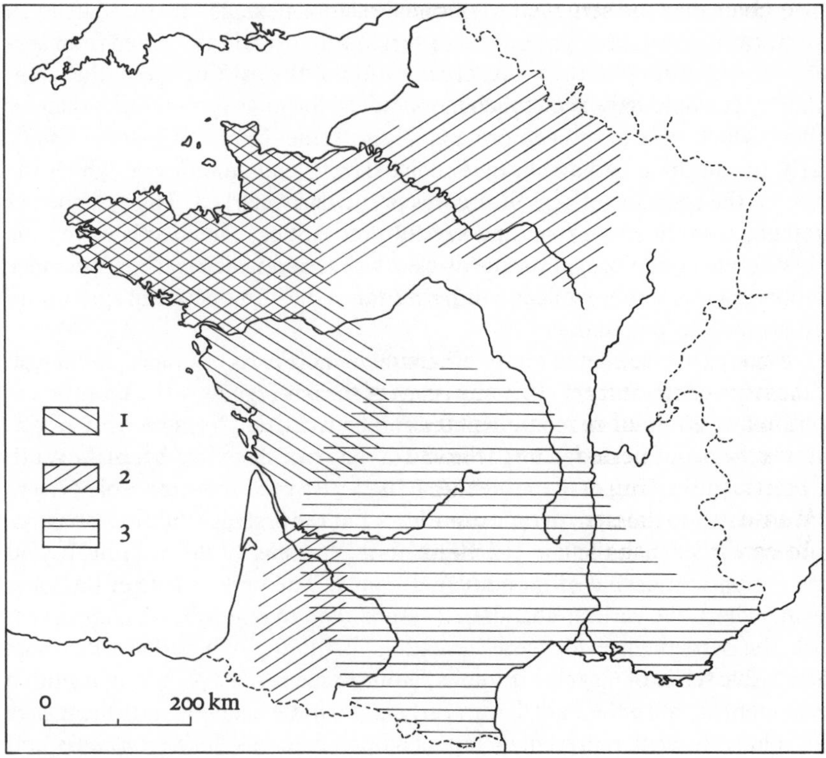

FIGURE 10.2. Distribution of the principal classes of neolithic chambered tomb in France.
1 Passage graves; 2 *Allées couvertes*; 3 *Dolmens simples*.
(After Giot, 1976.)

economic context.

In a much-quoted recent article, Renfrew has argued for the independent development of megalithic tombs in several parts of western Europe, including southern Scandinavia, Portugal and Brittany (Renfrew, 1976). The Breton evidence is particularly interesting, in that there are mesolithic collective burials at Téviec, surmounted by small cairns. Radiocarbon dates indicate that Breton chambered tombs are among the earliest in any part of Europe (see date-list at end of Chapter 9), and these early passage graves may have been a direct development of the local mesolithic tradition. Renfrew argues that it was the pressure exerted on Atlantic mesolithic communities by the westward expansion of agriculturalists from the Paris basin which stimulated the construction of the monumental tombs, perhaps as territorial markers or symbols of group solidarity. This hypothesis is difficult to evaluate. However, the fact that in Brittany the first monumental tombs are of approximately the same date as the earliest evidence of agriculture and other neolithic features such as pottery suggests that their appearance may in some way have been connected with the change in the structure of social relations entailed by the shift to an agricultural way of life. The impact of agriculture would have varied from area to area, depending on the social organisation of the existing mesolithic community. It would have been much more radical for some communities than for others which may have been pre-adapted to some degree (Wiessner, 1982). Early megaliths may have been associated with communities on which the effect of the adoption of agriculture was particularly marked. This, as much as pressure from nearby expanding agricultural groups, could explain why the transition to agriculture in the north-west was accompanied by the appearance of monumental tombs while in southern France the introduction of agriculture had no such accompaniment.

Groups of chambered tombs are found in most parts of France, but not all of them are contemporary. Brittany is one of the few regions with a more or less continuous tradition of monumental tomb construction from the very beginning of the neolithic period up to the end of the 3rd millennium bc. In the south of France the beginning of the Neolithic (defined by the appearance of pottery) may be dated to the late 7th millennium bc, but the first megalithic tombs were built no earlier than the late 3rd millennium; for most of the neolithic period this region was devoid of monumental tombs. The same is true of the Paris basin, where the earliest chambered tombs date to c.2500bc. A comparison with the settlement evidence is revealing. Brittany, with perhaps the most impressive series of megalithic tombs, is one of the regions poorest in neolithic settlement sites. In the Paris basin, early and middle neolithic settlement sites are relatively well represented but chambered tombs (*allées couvertes* and *hypogées*) do not appear until the Late Neolithic when the settlements known are only small and insubstantial (Howell's 'Expanded Village Pattern' (p.84ff.)). During the late neolithic and chalcolithic periods chambered tombs (*dolmens simples*) and settlements of dry-stone houses were founded on the Languedoc Garrigues of southern France, but their distributions are mutually exclusive: the settlements are associated with cultivable land, the *dolmens simples* with areas of pasture. Mills suggests (p.136) that the tombs may have served as territorial markers. In maritime west-central France the chambered tombs belong to the middle neolithic period, for which there is little settlement evidence, while with the appearance of substantial fortified settlements in the Late Neolithic the tombs seem largely to have fallen into disuse. Thus monumental chambered tombs may have been built so as to emphasise the durability of settlement or landholding where other indicators, such as substantial villages or fortified sites, were lacking.

Patterns of insubstantial or shifting settlement sites are characteristic of situations where new land is being colonised, and some of the groups of monumental tombs may have been associated with such a process. In west-central France, the few early neolithic settlements known are concentrated near the coast, and the middle neolithic chambered tombs appear to have been associated with the agricultural colonisation of the more inland parts of the region. Similarly, both the later groups of tombs (those of the Paris basin and the *dolmens simples* of the south and south-west) were associated with population expansion into hitherto marginal areas and a pattern of insubstantial or shifting settlements in which one role of the collective burial monument may have been as a territorial fixed point and a group focus. In the case of the Paris basin this was the colonisation of the plateau-interfluves using extensive farming methods (Howell, chap.4), while the *dolmens simples* seem to have been associated with the late neolithic and chalcolithic seasonal exploitation of the high pastures of the Pyrenees and the Grands Causses (Plate 7.5). The same association of monumental tombs with the opening-up of new areas may apply to the *allées couvertes* of Brittany, which unlike the earlier passage graves of the region are commonly found inland (Daniel, 1960; Renfrew, 1981; figs 9.4, 9.5).

In those areas and at those periods when there were no chambered tombs, and very likely alongside them also, other types of burial must have been practised. A few small groups of single graves with Bandkeramik material are known from north-eastern France, though no cemeteries comparable to that at Elsloo in the Netherlands (Modderman, 1970) have yet been found. In the south and south-west there are single cist-burials of middle neolithic date, and one must not forget the inhumations associated with the rather curious structures of Saint-Michel-du-Touch, nor those encountered in the ditches of the enclosures of north-eastern and west-central France. Overall, however, we are forced to admit that though the use of monumental collective tombs for successive interments must have accounted for a considerable number of burials, a substantial quantity must have been disposed of otherwise. The most conservative estimate of the population of Neolithic France shows that the burial data which we have are only a part, and perhaps a small part, of what there must once have been.

Neolithic Settlement Sites

The chambered tombs of France have been the subject of much interest and study on the part of prehistorians for over a century and a half, but rather less attention has been paid to the remains of the living sites of the neolithic period. This is due in part to the result of erosion, both natural and agricultural, which has in many cases reduced their remains to only slight traces, which have been unable to compete for attention with the spectacular megalithic monuments. Nevertheless, France boasts some impressive neolithic settlement sites, not least the enclosed and fortified sites whose numbers have been greatly increased and distribution greatly extended in recent years by aerial survey and photography (e.g. Agache, 1978; Dassié, 1978; Jalmain, 1970; Marsac and Scarre, 1979). At the same time, prehistorians have become more interested in settlements and settlement patterns and more prepared to devote time and effort to the investigation and interpretation of their less spectacular remains.

The nature of the evidence and the kind of study which has hitherto been carried out means that in no region is a full picture of the settlement pattern at present available for any part of the neolithic period. More intensive surveys of restricted areas are being attempted, however, and when coupled with an assessment of the effect which erosion and aggradation have had on the archaeological record it may become possible to reconstruct the settlement patterns of most areas. Some work of this kind in the relatively heavily-researched Mediterranean region has been described by Mills in these pages, and it is to be hoped that a beginning will soon be made in such other regions as maritime west-central France, Burgundy, and parts of the Paris basin.

The lack of adequate and representative samples means that the settlement evidence which we possess is heavily weighted towards the sites which are relatively conspicuous either because of their size or because of the ditches or ramparts by which they were enclosed. However, it is possible to derive from this evidence a picture which, though incomplete, and inaccurate in detail, probably reflects fairly well the broad nature and contrasts between the settlement patterns of the different parts of France.

In north-eastern France the Bandkeramik colonists appear to have introduced a fully developed village settlement pattern virtually at the outset. One of the earliest and best-known sites is Cuiry-lès-Chaudardes, which was of moderate size (6–7 longhouses at any one time) though apparently unenclosed (Fig.2.11). The earliest enclosed site yet known in this part of France is Berry-au-Bac in the Aisne valley (Fig.2.13), which dates to the Late Rössen period (second half of the 4th millennium bc). Ditched enclosures are a Late Bandkeramik feature of some settlements in the Rhineland, such as the famous site of Köln-Lindenthal. In the Paris basin the tradition of enclosed settlements continues into the middle neolithic period apparently without a break, despite major changes in certain other cultural aspects. The substantial early neolithic Berry-au-Bac enclosure (Fig.2.13) is clearly the forerunner of such middle neolithic sites as Noyen-sur-Seine (Fig.3.3). With the Middle Neolithic, an important distinction arises between the valley floor or river terrace settlements with complete circuits of defences such as Noyen-sur-Seine and L'Etoile, and the promontory sites (*éperons barrés*) on the edges of higher ground such as Fort Harrouard on the western side of the Paris basin or Chassey-le-Camp in Burgundy. The common choice of elevated, more easily defensible locations as the neolithic period progressed may reflect an increase in the amount of tension and inter-group hostility as all the best land was taken into use and expansion began into areas hitherto considered marginal. This is one of the recurring themes of the French Neolithic.

In Burgundy and the Franche-Comté promontory and substantial lakeside settlements continued to be occupied in the late neolithic period, but in the Paris basin the middle of the 3rd millennium bc sees an important change in the nature and distribution of settlement evidence. There appear to be no substantial or enclosed settlement sites of late neolithic date in this part of France. Howell's analysis (p.74ff.) suggests that extensive colonisation of the plateau-interfluves of the Paris basin took place in the later 3rd millennium bc and was associated with a dispersed pattern of insubstantial settlements. The opportunity for continued colonisation of new land in this region may have reduced the population pressure being experienced in other parts of France at this period and thus, perhaps, obviated the need for defended settlements. It may also have retarded, or even reversed, the trend towards more complex social organisation suggested by the early and middle neolithic evidence from the Paris basin.

In southern France neolithic settlement development followed a very different course. The earliest sites in this region with neolithic features were coastal caves and middens, in many cases with a history of occupation extending back into mesolithic times. Larger settlements located in positions where they could be dependent upon agriculture do not seem to have developed for more than a millennium after the first pottery made its appearance, though it is possible, as Mills suggests (p.134) that earlier agricultural sites in the valleys or on the coastal plain have been covered by more recent sediments and hence have not been found. The earliest dated settlements of any size known at present are in just such locations – Le Baratin in the Rhône valley, and Ile Corrège submerged beneath the waters of a coastal lagoon. Both sites are associated with Impressed Ware and belong to the first half of the 5th millennium bc. No substantial middle neolithic settlements are yet known from these areas, however, and hence it is not legitimate to present Le Baratin and Ile Corrège as standing at the head of an unbroken regional tradition of agriculturally dependent villages.

The most impressive neolithic settlements of the southern half of France lie outside the Mediterranean zone in the middle valley of the River Garonne, around Toulouse. Some of these are of considerable extent (e.g. Villeneuve-Tolosane 30ha; Saint-Michel-du-Touch (Fig.7.6) 20ha). They are associated with middle neolithic Chasséen material. The best investigated of these settlements are Villeneuve-Tolosane and Saint-Michel-du-Touch, where large numbers of cobble-floored structures which some have interpreted as hut floors have been found. Both these settlements were enclosed by interrupted ditches. Radiocarbon dates suggest that the principal period of occupation lay in the centuries following 3600bc, though there is one radiocarbon date from Saint-Michel-du-Touch of as early as 4100bc (see date-list at end of Chapter 7). Bahn (p.201ff.) has listed some of the conflicting interpretations which have been proposed for these sites, including the possibility that there was a seasonal or a ritual component in their occupation. The group of sites seems to have been abandoned in the middle of the 3rd millennium, as mysteriously as it was first established.

A new type of enclosed settlement made its appearance in the central and eastern parts of southern France in the second half of the 3rd millennium. These are relatively small in size and make use of dry-stone walling (Fig.5.10). The defensive works are not impressive, though they include what appear to have been towers (Mills; Plate 5.6). Some authors have suggested that they may have been little more than sheep corrals, though others have argued that they had at least some of the functions of central places. A substantial number of unenclosed settlements of later neolithic and chalcolithic date is also known from southern France, and though most are represented only by surface scatters, in some areas, notably on the limestone Garrigues of Languedoc, the remains of dry-stone longhouses grouped in hamlets or villages have been found (Fig.5.9; Plate 5.5). These indicate the scale of the evidence which has been lost in areas where more perishable materials were employed.

In western France the evidence of neolithic settlements is even poorer than in the regions we have been considering hitherto. This deficiency is particularly striking in the case of Brittany, which is so rich in remains of funerary and ritual monuments. In west-central France only a handful of settlement sites is known which can be assigned to the early or middle neolithic periods. Some 60 fortified settlement sites belonging to the Late Neolithic have however been found, though they are restricted in distribution to the maritime half of west-central France. There is a superficial resemblance between these enclosures and those of contemporary southern France in their use of dry-stonework and the provision of towers and gates (Fig.8.10; Plate 8.5), but those of west-central France are larger in size and much more strongly fortified, with rock-cut ditches of impressive proportions in addition to the dry-stone works. What evidence we have suggests domestic occupation in their interiors, and they may be regarded as fortified villages.

Finally, a brief mention must be made of Corsica, which like much of mainland France is relatively poor in prehistoric settlement sites prior to the 3rd millennium bc, when a series of fortified sites appear. Among the most striking of these are the 'proto-Torréen' sites of the later part of the millennium which have impressive dry-stone fortifications and are often in inaccessible locations (Plate 6.5). They resemble citadels in rocky fastnesses rather than defended villages, and cannot be regarded as closely related to any of the mainland groups of enclosures.

In this brief survey of neolithic settlement particular attention has been devoted to the evidence provided by the enclosed sites, not only because they are more impressive and on the whole better understood than the open settlements, but also because of their particular social and economic significance. Though the earliest of the enclosed sites are those of the north-east, it is not necessary to suppose that all the other groups of French neolithic enclosures must have derived from this tradition. The principal feature common to these sites is the enclosing ditch, which is insufficiently distinctive in itself to support the theory of a shared ancestry. The idea of surrounding a settlement with a ditch, to keep enemies out or to keep livestock in, is a very old one and was no doubt 'discovered' on numerous occasions as need arose. Each group of neolithic enclosures in France may thus have developed independently. More important are questions concerning the precise nature and function of the different groups of sites, and whether their appearance can be held to reflect the arrival of the communities of the different regions at a similar stage of socio-economic development. There is not the space for a full discussion here. Substantial settlements such as Villeneuve-Tolosane and elaborately fortified villages such as Peu-Richard must have been major elements in the settlement patterns of their respective regions. The fortified sites of west-central France appear to have been carefully sited so as to control valuable lowland pastures essential for the support of such centres of population, and the strength of the defensive works which these sites possess is testimony to the fierceness of the inter-community rivalry for control of these critical areas (see Scarre, 1982, and above p.253ff.). The construction of enclosed settlements, particularly those with elaborate defences, strongly suggests the presence of a central authority, which in some cases may have taken the form of a ruling élite or lineage. To this extent the appearance of a series of enclosed settlements may serve as an indication of increasing social differentiation in a region, though we must not expect circumstances to have been precisely equivalent in the different cases. For one thing, the scale of the defensive works varies considerably. However, population growth, leading to pressure on resources and competition between communities, might ultimately have been responsible for all the groups of defended settlements, as well as for the rise of the social élites which may have directed their construction. The lack of late neolithic enclosed settlements in the Paris basin which has already been remarked probably results from the continued availability of new land for colonisation and could be the reflection of a relatively non-hierarchical society in that region, as compared for example with contemporary west-central France.

In closing this discussion, it may be useful briefly to review the overall distribution of neolithic settlement evidence within France. Early neolithic villages are known in north-eastern and (less commonly) in southern France, and substantial middle neolithic settlements, enclosed and unenclosed, have been found in north-eastern, eastern and south-western France, but the first substantial settlements in the west-centre date to the Late Neolithic. Only a handful of settlements is known from Brittany, and these belong to the middle and late neolithic periods. Chances of discovery and survival may have contributed largely to this pattern, and new evidence may alter it considerably. However, at periods for which there is no evidence of large settlement sites in a region there are almost always scatters of material representing the remains of small settlements, perhaps hamlets or individual farmsteads, and it is likely that the settlement system sometimes consisted entirely of such small, dispersed sites. It has been suggested that this was the case in the Paris basin during the late neolithic period, and it may also have been true of west-central France prior to the 3rd millennium bc. In both instances the absence of substantial settlements coincides with a period of chambered tomb construction, providing further support for the link between chambered tombs and dispersed patterns of settlement which was proposed in the previous section.

The Development of the French Neolithic

The introduction of agriculture into France marked a radical change in economy and was accompanied by important social consequences, but further developments of no less importance took place during the following millennia. Burkill (this volume) has considered some of the changes which occurred in the Paris basin and Burgundy at the Early Neolithic–Middle Neolithic transition. The earliest Neolithic of these regions is represented by the Bandkeramik, a tradition strikingly uniform in terms of artefacts, house type and settlement organisation and location. The middle neolithic communities, on the other hand, appear to have had a greater variety in settlement organisation and location, pottery form and decoration, and burial rite. This change must reflect significant social developments. The Middle Neolithic is a period of diversification in all parts of the Bandkeramik distribution in central and western Europe, perhaps resulting from a breakdown of communication between the scattered Bandkeramik settlement cells. It may have been as much a relaxation of social constraints as economic pressure which led to the spread of settlements in the Paris basin from the typical river terrace locations of the Bandkeramik sites to the edges of the plateaux. This was the beginning of a long process of expansion of neolithic settlement in the Paris basin, culminating in the late neolithic period with the colonisation of the plateau-interfluves (Fig.4.6).

Hodder (1979) has sketched the development of the Neolithic of Mediterranean France in terms of economic and social pressures and their effects on material culture. He stresses the contrast between the Impressed Ware of the Early Neolithic, without marked regional differences or idiosyncracies, and the numerous late neolithic groups each with its own distinctive pottery decoration. Hodder's basic contention is that there was a continuous increase in the degree of social and economic stress in southern France during the Neolithic which, particularly towards the end of the period, caused communities to express their group affiliation and corporate solidarity to an increasing extent in their material culture. This is reflected in the flamboyance of late neolithic pottery decoration and its division into a number of local and regional styles. The principal source of stress may ultimately have been population pressure, perhaps stimulating the development of increasingly stratified societies. The gradual expansion of settlement onto the limestone uplands on the northern edge of the Mediterranean zone in the Middle and Late Neolithic could have been due to population increase. The appearance in the late 3rd millennium of dolmens on the upland pastures of the Pyrenees and in the interior of the Garrigues is an indication of this process.

Thus in both north-eastern and southern France there seems to have been a gradual expansion of the area of agricultural settlement during the neolithic period, beginning in the lowland and river valley niches in the Early Neolithic and spreading so as to cover the greater part of the landscape of these regions by the end of the 3rd millennium bc. There is evidence from west-central France and Brittany of a similar expansion. In Brittany, early settlement was concentrated around the coast and colonisation of the interior did not begin until towards the end of the 4th millennium. The expansion of settlement here is reflected in the comparative distributions of the predominantly 4th-millennium passage graves and the 3rd-millennium *allées couvertes*, as remarked earlier (Figs 9.4, 9.5).

As in most of Europe, the pottery is one of the principal means of identifying and dating neolithic sites in France, and the traditional division into cultures, despite its evident limitations, provides useful spatial and chronological units for analysis. The pottery can also throw some light on social organisation and communication. The earliest Impressed Ware of southern France and Corsica may have been a prestige ceramic exchanged between communities. Only towards the end of the Impressed Ware period, in the so-called Epicardial phase, does coarser, more utilitarian pottery appear. In contrast, the Bandkeramik settlers of north-eastern France brought with them a fully developed range of fine and domestic vessel types. The role of the earliest pottery in these two regions appears therefore to have been different, though as the range of types in use in the south increased, these differences probably became less significant. Organic containers may of course have been used by these and later neolithic communities, though only in rare circumstances have traces of them been preserved.

The middle neolithic period saw a complete change in the distribution and type of pottery in use. Ceramics spread into new areas, so that almost the whole of France could now have been said to be pottery-using. The most striking feature of this period is not however the spread of ceramics but the similarity of the vessels used in the different regions, with a similar range of forms and the same rarity or absence of decoration and (where it is present) the same motifs in all parts of France save perhaps Brittany. This is the so-called 'Chasséen' ceramic tradition. Pottery decoration is restricted in most of these assemblages to the rather enigmatic vases-supports (Figs 3.7, 8.5), in contrast to the fairly common use of decoration on early and late neolithic vessels of various types. It would be misleading to suggest, however, that middle neolithic pottery is poorly made or unattractive; thin walls and a glossy black surface are characteristic.

As Burkill has stressed in his account of the Middle Neolithic of eastern France, the Chasséen is not a tightly defined group and there are important regional and sub-regional differences that give rise to a complex terminology. The problem is particularly acute in the Paris basin, where the frequency with which Michelsberg features such as *plats-à-pain* appear has led some recent writers to propose the term 'Chasséo-Michelsberg' rather than 'Chasséen' for these assemblages (e.g. Louwe-Kooijmans, 1980). Other regional varieties can be distinguished in Burgundy (the 'Néolithique Moyen Bourguignon'), in the south (the 'Chasséen du Midi') and in the west (the 'Cous' and 'Roquefort' groups and the so-called 'Chasséen de Luxé'), all of which fall however within the same general family of pottery assemblages. The Chasséen of France must be regarded, therefore, as a series of linked groups having certain features in common, particularly in the pottery, rather than as a single uniform 'culture' covering the whole of middle neolithic France. It should also be borne in mind that it is one of a series of broadly similar west European middle neolithic pottery traditions, which includes the Michelsberg of Belgium and the Cortaillod of Switzerland.

Guilaine (1979b) has argued that the Chasséen ceramic assemblage developed from the late Impressed Ware of southern France, via the transitional

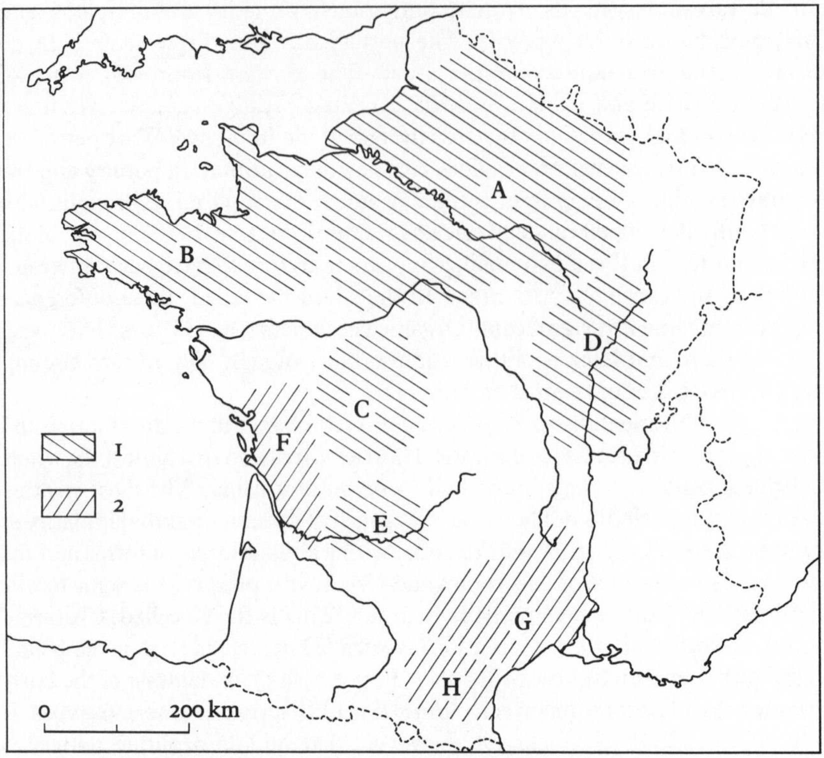

FIGURE 10.3. Late neolithic pottery groups in France.
1 Coarse ware groups: A Seine-Oise Marne; B coarse ware groups of Brittany and western Normandy (Seine-Oise-Marne influence); C Vienne-Charente; D Saône-Rhône; E Isle-Dordogne.
2 Decorated fine ware groups: F Peu-Richardien; G Ferrières-Fontbouisse and related groups; H Vérazien.

Montbolo group, and it is clear that an origin in the other early neolithic tradition, the Bandkeramik, is less likely. Pottery of the Chasséen tradition appears to have become established throughout France fairly rapidly, but the reason for its adoption over such a wide area is unclear. In the south of France the Middle Neolithic is a period of long-distance trade in high-quality flint, and Mills suggests (p. 136) that this may have been one of the factors behind the uniformity of the middle neolithic material of the region.

The beginning of the late neolithic period is marked by the appearance of a family of flamboyantly decorated wares in Mediterranean and west-central France and a series of coarse-ware traditions in northern and eastern France (Fig. 10.3), both very different from the middle neolithic assemblages. In the south and west the uniform middle neolithic pottery types were replaced by a number of highly decorated and regionally or locally specific groups such as Ferrières, Fontbouisse and Peu-Richardien. These may be related to foreign traditions such as the Millaran of Almerian Spain and the Ozieri of Sardinia.

The idea of a family of west European late neolithic channelled wares was originally put forward by the British prehistorian Jacquetta Hawkes in 1938. Her concept was rather more grandiose than that considered here, since in accordance with the diffusionist ideas then prevailing she included Breton, north British and Irish pottery in her group. There is nevertheless good reason to consider the late neolithic incised and channelled wares of Almeria, southern and western France and Sardinia as related series. The distribution of these types is strikingly reminiscent of that of the earlier west Mediterranean Impressed Ware, even to the inclusion of maritime west-central France within the area (compare Figs. 10.1 and 10.3). This suggests that the pattern of cultural contact around the northern side of the west Mediterranean basin and including part of the Atlantic coast of France remained much the same from mesolithic times until at least the end of the neolithic period.

In northern and eastern France the pottery assemblages of the Late Neolithic are dominated by coarse-ware vessels, especially those of the flat-based 'flower-pot' type. The principal groups are the Seine-Oise-Marne of the Paris basin, the Vienne-Charente of inland west-central France, the Saône-Rhône of Burgundy and the Horgen group of Switzerland. These groups are characterised by the absence of fine ware, though comparable coarse pottery types occur alongside fine ware in some of the late neolithic assemblages of western and southern France. The coarse ware may reflect innovations in storage, cooking and eating habits connected with a change such as the 'secondary products revolution' which Sherratt (1981) suggests occurred at around this time. The social significance of the northern pottery development must be very different from that of the flamboyantly decorated wares of the south and west. If the latter are an indication of the appearance of ranked societies at about this time, then the absence of such pottery styles from the Paris basin and adjacent areas may have in part been a consequence of the less highly stratified nature of late neolithic society in north-eastern France. One explanation may be that the opportunity for the continued colonisation of new areas which existed in the Paris basin reduced the stress caused by population pressure on land and thus removed one of the principal factors behind the increasing social stratification which was taking place in the south and west at this period. Such an interpretation is supported in west-central France by the evidence of fortified settlements discussed in the previous section of this chapter. Howell has suggested (p.88ff.) that social and economic circumstances prevented the Paris basin from entering into Beaker and early bronze age metal exchange networks, and prolonged its distinctive and rather retarded character into the Early or Middle Bronze Age. The failure of the region to develop a stratified society comparable to that which seems to be represented in southern and west-central France at this period may have been the principal cause of this.

Population pressure and agricultural intensification during the late neolithic period in southern and west-central France seem, in contrast to the north, to have led to the development of a stratified or ranked society of which the pottery, fortified sites and evidence of trade are a reflection. In the absence of single burials, however (since most of the late neolithic graves are collective tombs), it is difficult to study the details of the social ranking. Only at the very end of the 3rd millennium does the appearance of copper and gold objects in Beaker burial contexts provide the kind of evidence of a hierarchical society, perhaps based on wealth, which one might have expected earlier. The defensive works at some of the late neolithic sites of west-central France suggest the existence of a powerful co-ordinating authority by the middle of the 3rd millennium in that part of France, and it may be that we should envisage the development of a whole series of rival petty chiefdoms in the south and west at about this time.

The foregoing paragraphs have shown that the contrast between late neolithic material from southern and northern France was closely associated with social organisation, population pressure and the uptake of new land. It is possible, however, that it had its roots at a deeper level in basic differences in environmental constraints and agricultural strategies between the Temperate and Mediterranean zones of France. In the south, crop failure due to the dryness of the interfluves will have become an increasingly severe risk as population levels rose. Under these circumstances community autonomy and self-reliance may have been impossible to sustain. Seasonal movement of livestock between pastures, involving contact and co-operation between communities, would also have been necessary in this zone, and close inter-community relationships might have been developed to act as a buffer against the effects of occasional crop-failure and the consequent food shortages. Networks of trade and exchange would have helped to consolidate and maintain these essential relationships, which could eventually have led to the formation of small polities. In the more humid temperate environment of northern France, on the other hand, constraints of this kind were absent, and it may have been possible for individual farmsteads or groups of farmsteads to thrive without developing close relationships with their neighbours. Hence the non-hierarchical society, dispersed settlement pattern, and limited evidence of trade of the Paris basin Late Neolithic.

Evidence for trade becomes increasingly abundant as the French Neolithic progresses, and wider and wider exchange networks are represented. The first pottery probably reached the Mediterranean coast of France through exchange among maritime trading partners in the west Mediterranean basin. Obsidian may have followed the same paths, though it only becomes well represented in southern France in middle neolithic contexts (Courtin, 1967). The obsidian from this region is of Sardinian origin and indicates continuing contacts between southern France and the west Mediterranean islands up to and beyond the end of the neolithic period. Much neolithic trade was in functionally desirable materials or items. The sedimentary basins of France lacked the hard igneous rocks needed for the manufacture of polished-stone axes, and suitable material had to be imported from neighbouring volcanic regions such as Brittany (Fig.9.70) and the Massif Central. Many of the items traded, however, would today be thought of as non-functional (e.g. seashells). Between these two categories fall those materials which were undoubtedly functional, but were prized and traded perhaps largely because of their attractive appearance – Sardinian obsidian, jadeite from Brittany or the Alpine region, banded Douhet-Taillebourg flint from the west-centre, and honey-coloured flint from the mines at Le Grand Pressigny. Traded items travelled ever further as the period progressed, culminating in the Chalcolithic with the trade of Grand Pressigny flint to the Low Countries and the appearance of Beaker-related objects of Iberian origin in Brittany. These long-distance networks served as the basis for the still wider trade in metals of the Bronze Age.

The demand for exotic traded items in southern and western France in the 3rd millennium bc is probably a further reflection of the existence in those regions of a stratified society, with a social élite seeking to indicate its exclusiveness and superiority and to legitimate its power through the possession of exotic objects. The evidence from trade reinforces the conclusions reached on the basis of the settlement patterns, fortified sites and decorated pottery. The final stage in the development which concerns us here is marked by the appearance of Beaker pottery and Beaker-related objects in the last few centuries of the 3rd millennium bc. These are found principally in Atlantic and Mediterranean France, and are absent from conservative areas such as the Paris basin which remains in essence neolithic well into the Bronze Age. Beakers are particularly well represented in regions which had earlier been active in long-distance trade, such as Languedoc and the Vendée (Fig. 10.4). Several authors recently have discussed the prestige character of many of the elements of the so-called 'Beaker package', and the international exchange networks along which they seem to have travelled (e.g. Clarke, 1976; Harrison, 1980). The highly decorated Beakers and the rich objects which are associated with them have been shown to be the mark of social élites in some areas, for instance central Europe and southern Britain. In France, such an interpretation may be proposed for instance for the rich Beaker graves of the Vendée, with copper and gold objects and fine decorated Beakers. Hibbs argues (chap. 9) that the appearance of Beakers marks an important change in the direction of social development in Brittany, where the internationally recognised elements of the Beaker assemblage replace varieties of ritual monument (especially the chambered tombs) as one of the principal mechanisms of articulation between communities. This may reflect the change from a predominantly intra-regional perspective to a much more outward-looking attitude, and from this point it was only a short step to the 'princely' early bronze age burials of the Armorican Tumulus Culture.

Conclusions

Previous accounts of the French Neolithic have dealt with it largely in terms of explanatory models which are now outdated, in which the culture-people hypothesis and theories of invasion and migration play major roles. The chapters in this volume have attempted to re-interpret the material in the light of more recent theoretical perspectives, with emphasis placed on settlement

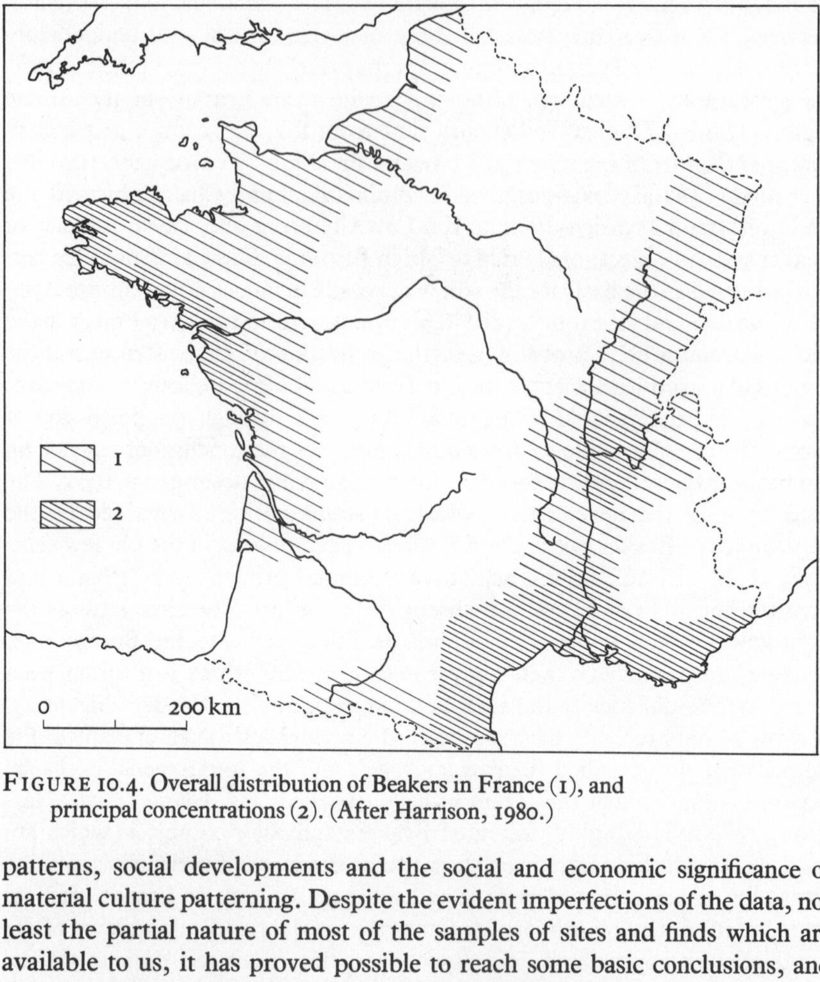

FIGURE 10.4. Overall distribution of Beakers in France (1), and principal concentrations (2). (After Harrison, 1980.)

patterns, social developments and the social and economic significance of material culture patterning. Despite the evident imperfections of the data, not least the partial nature of most of the samples of sites and finds which are available to us, it has proved possible to reach some basic conclusions, and these have allowed the presentation in this final chapter of a tentative interpretive framework for the French Neolithic. The principal points of this framework may be summarised as follows:

(1) The continuous nature of the development of the French Neolithic – the increasing size of the population, the continued gradual uptake of new land, increasingly widespread trade and increasingly complex social organisation in many parts of France.

(2) The contrast between developments in the north-east and in the south and south-west:

early neolithic Bandkeramik colonisation in the north-east; gradual adoption of neolithic traits by communities using Impressed Ware in the south and west;

late neolithic evidence for stratified societies associated with fairly wide-reaching trade networks in the south and south-west; a dispersed settlement pattern, relatively little trade, and a less highly stratified society in the north-east.

The contrast between late neolithic developments in the north and south may have been due to differences in the availability of new land for colonisation, and to basic differences in agricultural potential between the Temperate and Mediterranean zones of France.

(3) The link between different types of settlement pattern, chambered tombs and social organisation:

Monumental chambered tombs seem often to have been associated with patterns of small, dispersed settlements; in some cases these patterns represent a colonisation or settlement expansion phase;

in contrast to these are patterns of larger sites, including enclosed or fortified settlements, unassociated with chambered tombs, and which may reflect a more hierarchical social ordering.

These points are not altogether new, and it is expected that some will have to be modified considerably as fresh evidence emerges. It is hoped, however, that they may serve to stimulate further research on the Neolithic of France.

The British Museum Society

Bibliography

Abelanet, J. (1953) Ossuaires énéolithiques dans les Corbières Roussillonnaises. *Etudes Roussillonnaises*, 3, 7-14.

—— (1960) Ossuaires chalcolithiques des Pyrénées-Orientales. *Travaux de L'Inst. d'Art Préhist. Toulouse*, 3, 5-17.

—— (1970a) Une tombe néolithique: L'Arca de Calahons (Cattla, Pyr-Or), in *Les Civilisations Néolithiques du Midi de la France* (ed. J. Guilaine), 54-5. Carcassonne.

—— (1970b) Les Dolmens du Roussillon, in *Ibid.*, 74-9.

—— (1975) Le Roussillon, province méconnue du mégalithisme. *Archéologia*, 83, 16-21.

—— (1979) Premiers agriculteurs et pasteurs dans la plaine de Tautavel, in *L'Homme de Tautavel, Dossiers de l'Archéologie*, 36, 96-102.

—— (1980) Stations du Néolithique final du type de Véraza en Roussillon, in *Le Groupe de Véraza et la Fin des Temps Néolithiques dans le Sud de la France et la Catalogne* (ed. J. Guilaine), 55-60. Toulouse.

Abelanet, J. and Charles, R-P. (1964) Un site du Néolithique ancien en Roussillon: La Cova de l'Espérit (habitat et sépultures). *Cahiers Ligures*, 13, 177-206.

Acquaviva, L. (1976) *La Préhistoire du Niolu*. Pietra-Albertacce.

—— (1979) La Castellu de Marze à Corsica. *Archeologia Corsa*, 4, 93-8.

Agache, R. (1968) Circonscription de Nord et de Picardie. *Gallia Préhistoire*, 11, 267-309.

—— (1978) *La Somme préromaine et romaine*. Amiens.

Agache, R., Bourdier, F. and Petit, R. (1963) Le Quaternaire de la basse Somme: tentative de synthèse. *Bull. Soc. Géol. de France*, 7, 422-42.

Albrethsen, S. E. and Brinch-Petersen, E. (1976) Excavation of a mesolithic cemetery at Vedbaek, Denmark. *Acta Archaeologia*, 47, 1-28.

Allain, J. (1974) Circonscription du Centre. *Gallia Préhistoire*, 17, 465-85.

Aloisi, J. C., Monaco, A., Thommeret, J. and Thommeret, Y. (1975) Evolution paléogéographique du plateau continental languedocien dans le cadre du Golfe du Lion. *Revue de Géographie Physique et de Géologie Dynamique*, 2, 13-22.

Ambert, P. and Ambert, M. (1980) La stratigraphie de la grotte Tournié (Pardailhan, Hérault), in *Le Groupe de Véraza et la Fin des Temps Néolithiques dans le Sud de la France et la Catalogne* (ed. J. Guilaine), 20-1. Toulouse.

Ammerman, A. J. and Cavalli-Sforza, L. L. (1971) Measuring the rate of spread of early farming in Europe. *Man*, 6, 674-88.

—— (1973) A population model for the diffusion of early farming in Europe, in *The Explanation of Culture Change* (ed. C. Renfrew), 343-57. London.
—— (1979) The wave of advance model for the spread of agriculture in Europe, in *Transformations* (eds C. Renfrew and K. L. Cooke), 275-93. London.
Arambourou, R. (1979) La fin des temps glaciaires à Duruthy, cne de Sorde-l'Abbaye (Landes), in *La Fin des Temps Glaciaires en Europe* (ed. D. de Sonneville-Bordes), vol.2, 661-6. Paris.
—— (1981) Préhistoire des Landes: Les temps postglaciaires, in *Bull. Soc. de Borda*, 106, 443-65.
Arbos, P. (1922) *La Vie Pastorale dans les Alpes Françaises*. Paris.
Arnal, G. B. (1970) Le néolithique récent dans la stratigraphie de St Etienne de Gourgas, in *Les Civilisations Néolithiques du Midi de la France* (ed. J. Guilaine), 104-5. Carcassonne.
—— (1972) L'abri sous roche de St Etienne de Gourgas (Hérault). *Gallia Préhistoire*, 15, 261-308.
—— (1976) *La Céramique Néolithique dans le Haut-Languedoc*. Lodève.
Arnal, H. (1970) Le cailloutis calcaire de Vérargues (Hérault) et son altération pédologique au Quaternaire. *Bull. de l'Assoc. Fr. pour l'Etude du Quaternaire*, 2-3, 71-91.
Arnal, H., Barrière, J. and Bornaud, M. (1973) Les paléosols des terrasses fluviatiles du bassin rhodanien et du Languedoc. *9e Congrès International de l'INQUA*, 203-6. Christchurch.
Arnal, J. (1950) A propos de la 'néolithisation' de l'Europe occidentale. *Zephyrus*, 1, 23-7.
—— (1953) La structure néolithique française d'après les récentes stratigraphies. *Zephyrus*, 4, 311-44.
—— (1953-4) Presentacion de dolmenes y estaciones del departamento del Herault. *Ampurias*, 15-16, 67-115.
—— (1956) La grotte de la Madeleine. *Zephyrus*, 7, 33-79.
—— (1963) Les dolmens du département de l'Hérault. *Préhistoire*, 15.
—— (1973a) Le Lébous: un château préhistorique. *Archéologia*, 58, 38-51.
—— (1973b). Le Lébous à St Mathieu-de-Treviers. *Gallia Préhistoire*, 16, 131-200.
Arnal, J., Arnal, H. and Prades, H. (1977) L'implantation de terramares ou ports lagunaires sur la rive nord de l'étang de Maugio, Hérault, in *Ecologie de l'Homme Fossile* (eds H. Laville and J. Renault-Miskovsky), 377-82. Paris.
Arnal, J., Burnez, C. and Roussot-Larroque, J. (1967) Sauvetage de la station fontbuxienne du Gravas, St Mathieu-de-Treviers (Hérault). *Bull. Soc. Préhist. Fr.*, 64, 527-86.
Arnal, J., Bailloud, G. and Riquet, R. (1960) Les styles céramiques du néolithique Français. *Préhistoire*, 14.
Arnal, J., Majurel, R. and Prades, H. (1974) *Le Port de Lattuara*. Institut International d'Etudes Ligures. Collection des Monographies. Montpellier.
Ascari, M. C. (1939) L'Aspetto Etnico della Corsica. *Archivio Etorico di Corsica*, 15, 161-210.
Asquerino Fernandez (1977) Notas sobre Periodización del Neolitico Espanol: el proceso del Neolitización y el horizonte cardial. *Actas XIV Cong. Nac. Arqu.*, 231-40.

Assaillit, H. (1953) La vie domestique dans le 'Néolithique pyrénéen'. *Bull. Soc. Préhist. Ariège*, 8, 49-64.
Astre, G. (1935) Documents de géologie luchonnaise, III: Lac quaternaire et plaine de Luchon. *Bull. Soc. Hist. Nat. Toulouse*, 67, 281-315.
Atkinson, R. J. C. (1976) Lukis, Dryden and the Carnac Megaliths, in *To Illustrate the Monuments* (ed. J. V. S. Megaw), 112-24. London.
Atzeni, E. (1966) L'Abri sous Roche D' du village Préhistorique de Filitosa (Sollacaro-Corse). *Congr. Préhist. Fr.*, 18, 169-191.
—— (1975) *Nuovi Idoli della Sardegna Prenuragica*. Sassari.
Aubert, P. (1979) Essai sur la flèche asymetrique du Néolithique languedocien. *Bull. Soc. Préhist. Fr.*, 76, 87-90.
Audibert, J. (1958) La période chalcolithique dans le Languedoc oriental. *Gallia Préhistoire*, 1, 39-65.
—— (1962) *La Civilisation Chalcolithique du Languedoc Oriental*. Montpellier.
Audouze, F. and Leroi-Gourhan, A. (1981) France: a continental insularity. *World Archaeology*, 13, 170-89.
Baal, H. J. (1925) Report on the discovery of a prehistoric burial chamber at La Hougue Bie, with a description of the monument and an account of the examination of its floor. *Bull. Soc. Jers.*, 50, 178-229.
Bahn, P. G. (1979) *The French Pyrenees: an economic prehistory*. Unpublished Ph.D. Dissertation, University of Cambridge.
—— (1981) La Néolithisation dans les Pyrénées Atlantiques et Centrales, in *Le Néolithique Ancien Méditerranéen* (ed. R. Montjardin), 191-9. Montpellier.
—— (1982) La Paléoéconomie paléolithique et mésolithique du Béarn, in *Revue de Pau et du Béarn*, 10 (in press).
Bailloud, G. (1958) L'habitat néolithique et protohistorique des Roches, commune de Videlles (Seine-et-Oise). *Mémoires de la Soc. Préhist. Fr.*, 5, 192-214.
—— (1964) *Le Néolithique dans le Bassin Parisien* (1st ed.). Paris.
—— (1969) Fouille d'un Habitat Néolithique et Torréen à Basí (Serra-di-Ferro, Corse). *Bull. Soc. Préhist. Fr.*, 66, 67-84.
—— (1970) Discussion à propos du néolithique récent en Languedoc occidental, in *Les Civilisations Néolithiques du Midi de la France* (ed. J. Guilaine), 116. Carcassonne.
—— (1971) Le Néolithique danubien et le Chasséen dans le Nord et le centre de la France, in *Die Anfänge des Neolithikums vom Orient bis Nordeuropa*, Teil VI (Fundamenta A3), 201-45. Köln.
—— (1973) Les habitations chalcolithiques de Conquette (St Martin-de-Londres, Hérault), in *L'Homme Hier et Aujourd'Hui*, 493-504. Paris.
—— (1974) *Le Néolithique dans le Bassin Parisien* (2nd ed.). Paris.
—— (1975) Les céramiques 'cannelées' du néolithique Armoricain. *Bull. Soc. Préhist. Fr.*, 72, 343-67.
—— (1976) Le Néolithique en Picardie. *Revue Arch. de l'Oise*, 7, 10-28.
—— (1976a) Les civilisations neolithiques du Bassin Parisien et du Nord de la France, in *La Préhistoire Française, II: Les civilisations néolithiques et protohistoriques* (ed. J. Guilaine), 375-86. Paris.
—— (1976b) Les civilisations néolithique de la Champagne, in *Les civilisations néolithiques et protohistoriques* (ed. J. Guilaine), 415-21. Paris.

Bailloud, G. and Brézillon, M. (1968) L'hypogée de l'Homme-Mort à Tinqueux. *Bull. Soc. Préhist. Fr.*, 65, 479-504.

Bailloud, G. and Burnez, C. (1962) Le bronze ancien dans le Centre-Ouest de la France. *Bull. Soc. Préhist. Fr.*, 59, 515-24.

Bailloud, G. and Coiffard, P. (1967) Le locus 5 des Roches à Videlles (Essonne): 1. Etude archéologique. *Bull. Soc. Préhist. Fr.*, 64, 371-410.

Baills, H. (1980) Les rites funéraires sur le site de Can Pay (Montferrer, Pyr-Or), in *Le Groupe de Véraza et le Fin des Temps Néolithiques dans le Sud de la France et la Catalogne* (ed. J. Guilaine), 129-30. Toulouse.

Bakels, C. C. (1978a) Four Linearbandkeramik settlements and their environment: a palaeoecological study of Sittard, Stein, Elsloo and Hienheim. *Analecta Praehistorica Leidensia*, 11.

—— (1978b) Analyse des restes de plantes carbonisées. *Les Fouilles Protohistoriques dans la Vallée de l'Aisne*, 6, 261-3.

Barbier, A. *et al.* (1981) La grotte des Planches-près-Arbois (Jura). *Gallia Préhistoire*, 24, 145-200.

Barker, G. W. W. and Webley, D. (1978) Causewayed camps and early neolithic economies in central southern England. *Proc. Prehist. Soc.*, 44, 161-86.

Barrié, P. (1980) Vestiges d'agriculture vérazienne à la grotte des Cazals (Sallèles-Cabardès, Aude), in *Le Groupe de Véraza et la fin des temps néolithiques dans le Sud de la France et la Catalogne* (ed. J. Guilaine), 135-7. Paris.

Barrière, J., Bouteyre, G., Mazier, J., Rutten, P. and Vigneron, J. (1966). Interprétation géomorphologique et paléopédologique de la vallée de l'Orb dans la région de Maraussan (Hérault). *Comptes Rendues Sommaires des Séances de la Société Géologique de France*, 2, 68-9.

Baudouin, M. (1911) Les Haches plates en Vendée. *Mémoires de la Soc. Préhist. Fr.*, 1, 1-113.

Baumann, F. and Tarrête, J. (1979) La sépulture collective des Maillets à Germigny-l'Evêque (Seine-et-Marne). *Gallia Préhistoire*, 22, 143-202.

Beaulieu, J-L. de (1969) Analyses polliniques dans les Monts de l'Espinouse, Hérault. *Pollen et Spores*, 11, 83-96.

Beaulieu, J-L. de and Evin, J. (1972) Analyses polliniques et datages C14 dans les Monts de Lacaune (Tarn). *Comptes Rendus de l'Académie des Sciences de Paris*, Series D, 274, 3531-4.

Beaulieu, J-L. de and Gilot, E. (1972) Végétations holocènes du Mont Lozère: analyses polliniques et datages. *Comptes Rendus de l'Académie des Sciences de Paris*, Series D, 274, 46-9.

Bellancourt, G. (1966) Découverte au voisinage de l'estuaire de la Loire d'un habitat chasséen superposé à un néolithique à poteries non décorées. *Cong. Préhist. Fr.*, 18, 161-8.

Bellis, R. and Cable, E. K. (1884) Mont Cochon cromlech. *Bull. Soc. Jers.*, 9, 422-35.

Bender, M. B. (1967) *The neolithic cultures of North Western France*. Unpublished Ph.D. Thesis, London University.

Bender, B. and Phillips, P. (1972) The early farmers of France. *Antiquity*, 46, 97-105.

Bernabo Brea, L. (1946) *Gli Scavi nella Caverna delle Arene Candide. Part 1, Gli Strati con Ceramiche*, vol. 1. Bordighera.

Bernabo Brea, L. (1950) Il Neolitico a Ceramica Impressa e la sua Diffusione nel Mediterraneo. *Revue d'Etudes Ligures*, 16, 25-36.
—— (1956) *Gli Scavi nella Caverna delle Arene Candide. Part 1, Gli Strati con Ceramiche*, vol.2. Bordighera.
Bernard, J. (1972) Palynologie: Analyse pollinique du remplissage versilien de la grotte sous-marine de la Trémie (Cassis, Bouches-du-Rhône). *Comptes Rendues de l'Académie des Sciences de Paris*, Series D, 274, 58-64.
Bersu, G. (1936) Rössener Wohnhäuser vom Goldberg, OA. Neresheim, Württemberg. *Germania*, 20, 229-43.
Bertrand, J. P. and l'Homer, A. (1975) *Les Deltas de la Méditerranée du Nord*. IXme Congrès International de Sédimentologie. Nice. Excursion 16.
Bézier, P. (1883) *Inventaire des monuments mégalithiques du département d'Île et Vilaine*. Rennes.
Bigot, M. (1971 (1887)) *Paysans Corses en Communauté*. Bastia.
Billamboz, A. (1977) L'industrie du bois de cerf en Franche-Comté au Néolithique et au début de l'Age du Bronze. *Gallia Préhistoire*, 20, 91-176.
Bintliff, J. L. (1977) *Natural Environment and Human Settlement in Prehistoric Greece*. Oxford.
Birocheau, P. and Large, J.-M. (1982) Les fouilles 1981 aux Châtelliers du Vieil-Auzay (Vendée). *Bull. Groupe Vendéen d'Etudes Préhist.*, 7, 24-37.
Blair, A. and Rowlands, F. (1836) *Sketches at Carnac (Brittany) in 1834*. London.
Blanchard, R. (1914) Les Genres de Vie en Corse et Leur Evolution. *Rec. Trav. Inst. Alp. Grenoble*, 2, 187-238.
Blanchet, J.-C. (1974) Datations radiocarbones du Néolithique chasséen du Bassin parisien de Jonquières (Oise). *Bull. Soc. Préhist. Fr.*, 71, 107-8.
Blanchet, J.-C., Decormeille, A. and Marquis, P. (1980) Récentes découvertes du Néolithique danubien dans la moyenne vallée de l'Oise. *Préhistoire et Protohistoire en Champagne-Ardenne, 5-21. Châlons-sur-Marne.*
Blanchet, J. C., Martinez, R. and Méniel, P. (1982) Deux nouveaux sites chasséens dans l'Oise: le site fortifié de Boury-en-Vexin et l'habitat de Pont-Sainte-Maxence. Bull. Soc. Préhist. Fr., 79, 7-9.
Blanchet, J-C. and Petit, M. (1972) L'habitat néolithique de Jonquières (Oise): premiers résultats. *Bull. Soc. Préhist. Fr.*, 69, 389-407.
Blanchet, J-C. and Fitte, P. (1978) Le site archéologique de Moru, commune de Pontpoint (Oise). *Revue Arch. de l'Oise*, 11, 3-25.
Bloch, A. (1902) Considérations Anthropologiques Sur la Corse Actuelle, Ancienne et Préhistorique. *Bull Soc. Anth. Paris*, 5, 333-63.
Bloch, M. E. F. (1971) *Placing the dead: Tombs, ancestral villages and kinship organisation in Madagascar*. London.
Blot, J. (1974) Contribution à la Protohistoire en Pays Basque. Nouveaux vestiges mégalithiques en Pays Basque (I to VII). Collected work from *Bulletin du Musée Basque*.
Bocquet, A. (1974) Le village des Baigneurs à Charavines, Isère. *Archéologia*, 69, 44-9.
Boisaubert, J. L., Petrequin, P. and Schifferdecker, F. (1974) Les villages néolithiques de Clairvaux (Jura, France) at d'Auvernier

(Neuchâtel, Suisse). Problèmes d'interpretation des plans. *Bull. Soc. Préhist. Fr.*, 71, 355-82.

Bökönyi, S. (1974) *History of Domestic Mammals in Central and Eastern Europe*. Budapest.

Bonney, P. (1976) Early boundaries and estates in southern England, in *Medieval Settlement* (ed. P. H. Sawyer), 72-87. London.

Bonzom, H., Clottes, J. *et al.* (1981) Sauvetage à Villeneuve-Tolosane. *Archéologia*, 154, 71.

Bordreuil, M. (1974) Les mines de silex néolithiques dans le Gard. *Bull. Soc. Préhist. Fr.*, 71, 34.

Boureux, M. and Coudart, A. (1978) Implantations des premiers paysans sédentaires dans la vallée de l'Aisne. *Bull. Soc. Préhist. Fr.*, 75, 341-60.

Bousquet, N., Gourdiole, R. and Guiraud, R. (1966) La grotte de Labeil, près de Lauroux (Hérault). *Cahiers Ligures de Préhistoire et d'Archéologie*, 15, 79-166.

Bouteyre, G. (1971) Quelques réflexions sur les paléosols en Languedoc (France), in *Paleopedology – Origin, Nature, and Dating of Paleosols* (ed. D. H. Yaalon), 301-7. Jerusalem.

Bradley, R. (1978) *The Prehistoric Settlement of Britain*. London.

Bresson, P. and Gadé, B. (1980) Restes humains et poteries peu-richardiennes dans le fossé de pente à Champ Durand, commune de Nieul-sur-l'Autize (Vendée). *Bull. Groupe Vendéen d'Etudes Préhist.*, 4, 15-24.

Brezillon, M., Girard, C., Degros, J., Tarrête, J., Poulain, T., Girard, M. and Delibrias, G. (1973) La sépulture collective du Paradis à Noisy-sur-Ecole (Seine-et-Marne). *Cahiers du Centre de Recherches Préhistoriques, Université de Paris I*, 2.

Brouillet, P-A. (1862) Notes sur la tombelle de Brioux, commune de Pairé, canton de Couhé (Vienne). *Bull. Soc. Antiq. de l'Ouest*, 1862, 71-5.

Burgess, C. (1980) *The Age of Stonehenge*. London.

Burnez, C. (1965) La station de Soubérac à Gensac-la-Pallue (Charente). *Bull. Soc. Préhist. Fr.*, 62, 289-315.

—— (1976) *Le Néolithique et le Chalcolithique dans le Centre-Ouest de la France*. Paris.

Burnez, C. and Case, H. (1966) Les camps néolithiques des Matignons à Juillac-le-Coq (Charente). *Gallia Préhistoire*, 9, 131-245.

Burnez, C. and Morel, J. (1965) Contribution à la connaissance de la céramique préhistorique de la Saintonge. *Bull. Soc. Préhist. Fr.*, 62, 555-66.

Cahen, D. and van Berg, P-L. (1979) Un habitat danubien à Blicquy. I. Structures et industrie lithique. *Archaeologia Belgica*, 221.

—— (1980) Un habitat danubien à Blicquy. II. Céramique. *Archaeologia Belgica*, 225.

Cahen, D. and De Laet, S. (1980) Persistance de la Civilisation de Seine-Oise-Marne à l'age du Bronze dans certaines régions de la Belgique. *Helinium*, 20, 114-135.

Cahen, D., Demarez, L. and van Berg, P-L. (1979) Néolithique rubané de faciès omalien à Blicquy. *Archaeologia Belgica*, 123, 25-9.

Caillaud, R. and Lagnel, E. (1972) Le cairn et le crématoire néolithique de La Hoguette à Fontenay-le-Marmion (Calvados). *Gallia Préhistoire*, 15, 137-97.

Caillaud, R., Lagnel, E., Dastugue, J., and Torre, S. (1967) Sépulture collective de Bardouville (carrière de Beaulieu). *Annales de Normandie*, 17, 281-315.

Callot, G. (1971) *Etude pédologique du Bassin de la Charente non domaniale*. Montpellier.

Calvet, A. (1969) *Les Abris sous Roche de St Mitre à Reillane (Basses-Alpes)*. Manosque.

Camps, G. (1978) Aperçu sur la Préhistoire Corse et Ses Problèmes. *Bull. Soc. Etudes Recherches Préhist. Les Eyzies*, 28, 1-22.

—— (1979) La Préhistoire dans la région d'Aléria. *Archeologia Corsa*, 4, 5-21.

Camps-Fabrer, H. and D'Anna, A. (1980) Le gisement de Miouvin (Istres, Bouches-du-Rhône) et la question de Néolithique Final en Provence, in *Le Groupe de Véraza et la Fin des Temps Néolithiques dans le Sud de la France et la Catalogne* (ed. J. Guilaine), 165-70. Toulouse.

Canet, H. and Roudil, J-L. (1978) Le village chalcolithique de Cambous à Viols-en-Laval (Hérault). *Gallia Préhistoire*, 21, 143-88.

Carey Curtis, S. (1912) An account of the discovery and examination of a cist of a type novel to Guernsey in October and November, 1912. *Transactions de la Société Guernesiaise*, 6, 400-14.

Carré, H., Dousson, J. and Poulain, P. (1958) Habitat néolithique dans les alluvions Yonne et Cure de la plaine de Sainte-Pallaye. *Bull. Soc. Préhist. Fr.*, 55, 133-4.

Carré, H. and Thévenot, J-P. (1976) Les civilisations néolithiques de la Bourgogne, in *La Préhistoire Française, II: Les civilisations néolithiques et protohistoriques* (ed. J. Guilaine), 402-24. Paris.

Cartailhac, E. (1889) *La France Préhistorique, d'après les sépultures et les monuments*. Paris.

Cazalis de Fondouce, P. (1900) *L'Hérault au Temps Préhistoriques*. Montpellier.

Caziot, Cdt. (1897) Découvertes d'Objets Préhistoriques et Protohistoriques, Faites dans l'Ile de Corse. *Bull. Soc. Anth. Paris*, 4, 463-76.

Césari, J. and Jehasse, O. (1978) Le Site Archéologique de Castellucciu (Pila Canale-Corse du Sud). *Archeologia Corsa*, 3, 55-70.

Chauchat, C. (1968) *Les Industries Préhistoriques de la région de Bayonne, du Périgordien ancien à l'Asturien*. 2 vols. Thèse de doctorat de 3e cycle, Université de Bordeaux.

—— (1974) Datations concernant le site de Mouligna, Bidart (Pyr-Atl). *Bull. Soc. Préhist. Fr.*, 71, 140.

Chenet, G. (1926) Le village néolithique d'Ante (Marne). *Bull. Soc. Arch. Champenoise*, 4, 113-34.

Cherry, J. F. (1981) Pattern and Process in the Earliest Colonisation of the Mediterranean Islands. *Proc. Prehist. Soc.*, 47, 41-60.

Chertier, B. (1980) Le site néolithique de Larzicourt (Marne). Premiers résultats. *Préhistoire et Protohistoire en Champagne-Ardenne*, 51-67. Châlons-sur-Marne.

Childe, V. G. (1931) The continental affinities of British neolithic pottery. *Archaeol. J.*, 88, 37-66.

Childe, V. G. and Sandars, N. (1950) La Civilisation de Seine-Oise-Marne. *L'Anthropologie*, 54, 1-18.

Clark, J. G. D. (1952) *Prehistoric Europe: The Economic Basis*. London.

—— (1975) *The Earlier Stone Age Settlement of Scandinavia.* Cambridge.

Clarke, D. L. (1968) *Analytical Archaeology.* London.

—— (1970) *Beaker Pottery of Great Britain and Ireland.* Cambridge.

—— (1976a) Mesolithic Europe – The Economic Basis, in *Problems in Economic and Social Archaeology* (eds G. Sieveking, I. Longworth and K. Wilson), 449-81. London.

—— (1976b) The Beaker network – social and economic models, in *Glockenbecher Symposion, Oberried 1974* (eds J. M. Lanting and J. D. van der Waals), 459-77. Bussum/Haarlem.

Clottes, J. (1975) Circonscription de Midi-Pyrénées. *Gallia Préhistoire,* 18, 613-50.

—— (1977a) *Inventaire des Mégalithes de la France, 5: Lot.* Paris.

—— (1977b) Circonscription de Midi-Pyrénées. *Gallia Préhistoire,* 20, 517-59.

—— (1979) Circonscription de Midi-Pyrénées. *Gallia Préhistoire,* 22, 629-71.

—— (1981) Circonscription de Midi-Pyrénées. *Gallia Préhistoire,* 24, 525-688.

Clottes, J. and Costantini, G. (1976) Les civilisations néolithiques dans les Causses, in *La Préhistoire Française, II: Les civilisations néolithiques et protohistoriques* (ed. J. Guilaine), 279-91. Paris.

Clottes, J., Coularou, J., Giraud, J-P., Rouzaud, F. and Duday, H. (1980) Nouvelles découvertes à Villeneuve-Tolosane. *Archéologia,* 142, 61-2.

Clottes, J., Giraud, J-P., Rouzaud, F. and Vaquer, J. (1979) Le village néolithique de Villeneuve-Tolosane. *Archéologia,* 130, 6-13.

—— (1981) Le village chasséen de Villeneuve-Tolosane (Haute-Garonne). Fouilles 1978, in *La Préhistoire du Quercy dans le contexte de Midi-Pyrénées, 21e Congr. Préhist. Fr.,* Montauban-Cahors, 1979, vol.1, 116-28.

Clottes, J., Querre, J., Rouzaud, F. and Sarny, H. (1977) Les structures chasséennes de Frouzins (Hte-Gar). *Bull. Soc. Préhist. Fr.,* 74, 583-603.

Cogné, J. (1974) Le Massif Armoricain, in *Géologie de la France* (ed. J. Debelmas), 105-61. Paris.

Coles, J. M. (1976) Forest farmers: some archaeological, historical and experimental evidence relating to the prehistory of Europe, in *Acculturation and Continuity in Atlantic Europe* (ed. S. J. de Laet), 59-66. Bruges.

Colomer, A., Coularou, J., Gutherz, X. and Vallon, J. (1980) L'enceinte en pierres sèches de Boussargues (Argelliers, Hérault), in *Le Groupe de Véraza et la Fin des Temps Néolithiques dans le Sud de la France et la Catalogne* (ed. J. Guilaine), 257-62. Toulouse.

Combarnous, G. (1960) Un pays de dolmen au coeur du Bas-Languedoc. *Cahiers Ligures de Préhistoire et d'Archéologie,* 9, 3-93.

Conchon, O. (1977) Aperçu sur le recul glaciaire et les niveaux marins en Corse au Tardiglaciaire et au Postglaciaire, in *Approche Ecologique de l'Homme Fossile* (eds H. Laville and J. Renault-Miskovsky). Paris.

Constantin, C. (1976) La céramique néolithique et chalcolithique du Bassin Parisien et de la vallée de la Meuse, dégraissée à l'aide d'os pilés. *Les Fouilles Protohistoriques dans la Vallée de l'Aisne,* 4, 166-72.

Constantin, C. (1981) Neues zur Verbreitung der Limburger Keramik. *Archäologisches Korrespondenzblatt*, 10, 215-20.
—— (1982) *Le Néolithique le plus ancien dans le Bassin Parisien et le Hainaut* (unpublished doctoral thesis, Université de Paris I).
Constantin, C., Coudart, A. and Boureux, M. (1981). Céramique du Limbourg : vallée de l'Aisne. *Helinium*, 21, 161-75.
Constantin, C. and Demarez, L. (1981) Eléments non-rubanés du Néolithique Ancien entre les vallées du Rhin Inférieur et de la Seine. *Helinium*, 21, 136-226.
Constantin, C. and Demoule, J-P. (1982) Le groupe de Villeneuve-Saint-Germain. *Helinium*, 22, in press.
Constantin, C., Farruggia, J-P. and Demarez, L. (1980) Aubechies, site de la Céramique Linéaire en Hainaut occidental. *Bull. Soc. Préhist. Fr.*, 77, 367-84.
Constantin, C., Farruggia, J-P., Plateaux, M. and Demarez, L. (1978) Fouille d'un habitat néolithique à Irchonwelz (Hainaut occidental). *Revue Arch. de l'Oise*, 13, 3-20.
Coquerel, R. (1971) Les récentes découvertes archéologiques en Hautes-Pyrénées et les nouveaux enseignements qui en découlent. *94e Congr. Nat. Soc. Savantes*, Pau, avril 1969, 189-201.
Cordier, G. (1963) *Inventaire des Mégalithes de la France, 1: Indre-et-Loire*. Paris.
Costantini, G. (1967) Chalcolithique et céramique à triangles hachurés des Grands Causses. *Bull. Soc. Préhist. Fr.*, 64, 743-54.
—— (1970a) L'évolution du Chasséen caussenard, in *Les Civilisations Néolithiques du Midi de la France* (ed. J. Guilaine), 31-3. Carcassonne.
—— (1970b) L'évolution du Chalcolithique caussenard, in *Les Civilisations Néolithiques du Midi de la France* (ed. J. Guilaine), 95-8. Carcassonne.
—— (1970c) Inventaire des documents en cuivre pré-campaniformes de la région des Grands Causses, in *Les Civilisations Néolithiques du Midi de la France* (ed. J. Guilaine), 125-6. Carcassonne.
—— (1978) *Le Néolithique et le Chalcolithique des Grands Causses*. Millau.
Cotte, V. (1924) *Documents sur la Préhistoire de Provence*. Aix-en-Provence.
Coudart, A. (1982) A propos de la maison néolithique danubienne, in *Le Néolithique de l'Est de la France* (Société Archéologique de Sens, Cahier no. 1).
Coursaget, J., Giot, P-R. and Le Run, J. (1960) C14 Neolithic dates from France. *Antiquity*, 34, 147-8.
—— (1961) New radiocarbon dates from France. *Antiquity*, 35, 147-8.
Courtin, J. (1967) La grotte de l'Eglise à Baudinard (Var). *Gallia Préhistoire*, 10, 282-300.
—— (1967) Le problème de l'obsidienne dans le Néolithique du Midi de la France. *Rivista di Studi Liguri*, 33, 93-109.
—— (1970) Le néolithique récent de la Provence, in *Les Civilisations Néolithiques du Midi de la France* (ed. J. Guilaine), 121-3. Carcassonne.
—— (1974) Les habitats du plein air du Néolithique ancien cardial en Provence. *Revue d'Etudes Ligures*, 38, 227-43.
—— (1974) *Le Néolithique de la Provence*. Paris.

—— (1976) Les civilisations néolithiques en Provence, in *La Préhistoire Française, II : Les civilisations néolithiques et protohistoriques* (ed. J. Guilaine), 255-66. Paris.
—— (1977) Les animaux domestiques du néolithique provençal, in *L'Elevage en Méditerranée Occidentale*, 67-76. Marseille.
—— (1978) Quelques Etapes de Peuplement de la Région de l'Etang de Berre au Post-Glaciaire. *Bull. Arch. Prov.*, 1, 1-36.
Courtin, J. and Erroux, J. (1974) Aperçu sur l'agriculture préhistorique en Provence. *Bull. Soc. Préhist. Fr.*, 71, 321-34.
Courtin, J., Gagnière, S., Granier, J., Ledoux, J. C. and Onoratini, G. (1972). La grotte du Cap Ragnon, Commune du Rove (Bouches-du-Rhône). *Bull. Soc. Etudes des Sciences Naturelles de Vaucluse*, 1970-2, 113-70.
Courtin, J. and Onoratini, G. (1976) L'Habitat Campaniforme de 'Fortin-du-Saut', Châteauneuf-lès-Martigues (Bouches-du-Rhône). *Cong. Préh. Fr.*, 20, 130-6.
Courtin, J. and Pelouard, S. (1971) Un habitat Chasséen en Haute-Provence : la grotte de Baudinard (Var). *Bull. Soc. Préhist. Fr.*, 68, 540-66.
Couteaux, M. (1974) Présence de sols striés en région subméditerr-anéenne pedogenèse, végétation, et climat. *Bull. Soc. Languedocienne de Géographie*, 8, 233-40.
Coutil, L. (1894) Résumé des recherches préhistoriques : Département du Calvados. *Bull. Soc. Normandie d'Etudes Préhist.*, 2, 65-145.
—— (1895a) Inventaire des découvertes d'archéologie préhistorique de Normandie. Orne. *Bull. Soc. Normandie d'Etudes Préhist.*, 3, 37-100.
—— (1895b) Inventaire des découvertes d'archéologie préhistorique de Normandie. Département de la Manche. *Bull. Soc. Normandie d'Etudes Préhistoriques*, 3, 101-69.
—— (1907) Les monuments mégalithiques de la Normandie (Dolmens, allées couvertes, menhirs, polissoirs). *Cong. Préhist. Fr.*, 3, 481-500.
—— (1908) Les allées couvertes de Saint Symphorien du Teilleul (Manche). *Assoc. Fr. Avancement de Sciences*, Clermont-Ferrand, 654-7.
—— (1918) Le tumulus de La Hogue à Fontenay-le-Marmion (Calvados) (Etude des tumulus néolithiques du Calvados et de l'Orne), *Bull. Soc. Préhist. Fr.*, 15, 65-115.
Daguin, F. (1936) Sur les lignites de la plage de Mouligna, à Biarritz (Basses-Pyr). *Procès verbaux Soc. Linnéenne Bordeaux*, 88, 139-42.
Daniel, G. E. (1939a) On two long barrows near Rodez in the south of France. *Antiquaries J.*, 19, 157-65.
—— (1939b) The transepted gallery graves of western France. *Proc. Prehist. Soc.*, 5, 143-65.
—— (1941) The dual nature of the megalithic colonisation of prehistoric Europe. *Proc. Prehist. Soc.*, 7, 1-50.
—— (1955) The 'allées couvertes' of France. *Archaeol. J.*, 112, 1-19.
—— (1958) The chronology of the French collective tombs. *Proc. Prehist. Soc.*, 24, 1-23.
—— (1960) *The Prehistoric Chamber Tombs of France*. London.
D'Anna, A., Balac-Hebert, A. M. and Camps-Fabrer, H. (1977) Le gisement néolithique du Miouvin (Istres, Bouches-du-Rhône). *Bull. Soc. Préhist. Fr.*, 74, 376-89.

D'Anna, A. and Mills, N. T. W. (1981) L'occupation néolithique du bassin de Trets (Bouches-du-Rhône). *Bulletin Archéologique de Provence*, 8, 3-37.

Darvill, T. C. (1979) Distribution of passage graves and court cairns in Ireland. *Man*, 14, 311-27.

Dassié, J. (1978) *Manuel d'archéologie aérienne*. Paris.

Dastugue, J. and Torre, S. (1966) Les sépultures d'Ifs. Étude anthropologique. *Annales de Normandie*, 16, 323-32.

Decker, E. and Guillaume, C. (1980) Les sites du Rubané en Lorraine, in *Le Rubané d'Alsace et de Lorraine. Etat de recherches 1979* (Association d'Etudes préhistoriques et protohistoriques d'Alsace), 225-8. Strasbourg.

De Barandiarán, J-M. (1953) *El Hombre Prehistorico en el Pais Vasco*. Buenos Aires.

De Chasteigner, A. (1874) Fouilles dans la grotte de Bagnères-de-Luchon. *41e Congr. Arch. de France*, Toulouse-Agen, 241-2.

De Laet, S. (1967) Quelques problèmes du néolithique belge. *Palaeohistoria*, 12, 335-62.

—— (1974) *Prehistorische Kulturen in het Zuiden der Lage Landern*. Wetteren.

Delano-Smith, C. (1972) Late neolithic settlement and land-use, and *garrigue* in the Montpellier region, France. *Man*, 7, 397-407.

—— (1979) *Western Mediterranean Europe*. London.

Delattre, A. and Nicolardot, J-P. (1976) Nouvelles datations par le carbone 14 et analyse chimique des matériaux de l'habitat fortifié de Myard à Vitteaux (Côte-d'Or). *Bull. Soc. Préhist. Fr.*, 73, 51-7.

Delibrias, G., Evin, J. and Thommeret, Y. (1982) Sommaire des datations C14 concernant la préhistoire en France, II: Dates parues de 1974 a 1982. Chapitre VI: Néolithique de environ 7000BP à environ 4000BP. *Bull. Soc. Préhist. Fr.*, 79, 175-92.

Delibrias, G., Guillier, M-T., Evin, J., Thommeret, J. and Thommeret, Y. (1976) Datations absolues des dépôts post-glaciaires et des gisements pré et protohistoriques par la méthode du Carbone 14, in *La Préhistoire Française, II: Les civilisations néolithiques et protohistoriques* (ed. J. Guilaine), 859-99. Paris.

Delibrias, G. and Le Roux, C-T. (1975) Un example d'application des datations radio-carbon à l'interpretation d'une stratigraphie complexe; la fouille des ateliers de Plussulien (Côtes-du-Nord). *Bull. Soc. Préhist. Fr.*, 72, 78-82.

De Lumley, H. (1976) Les lignes de rivage, in *La Préhistoire Française, II: Les civilisations néolithiques et protohistoriques* (ed. J. Guilaine), 24-6. Paris.

Depéret, C. (1897) Etude de Quelques Gisements Nouveaux de Vertébrés Pléistocènes de l'Ile de Corse. *Ann. Soc. Linn. Lyon*, 111-28.

Desse, J. (1976) La faune du site archéologique de Cuiry-lès-Chaudardes (Aisne). Note préliminaire sur le matériel osseux de la campagne de fouille de 1973. *Les Fouilles Protohistoriques dans la Vallée de l'Aisne*, 4, 187-94.

Doazan, L. (1967) Documents Pré-et Protohistoriques aux Portes d'Ajaccio. *Corse Historique*, 27/8, 5-30.

Dohrn-Ihmig, M. (1973) Gruppen in der jüngeren nordwestlichen Linienbandkeramik. *Archäologisches Korrespondenzblatt*, 3, 279-87.

—— (1979) Bandkeramik an Mittel- und Niederrhein, in *Beiträge zur Urgeschichte des Rheinlandes III* (Rheinische Ausgrabungen 19), 191-362. Köln.
Dolukhanov, P. M. (1979) *Ecology and Economy in Neolithic Eastern Europe*. London.
Doranlo, R. (1951). Les ateliers de la Brèche au Diable et d'Olendon. Leur date. *Bull. Soc. Antiq. Norm.*, 51, 323-4.
Drewett, P. (1975) A burial mound at Alfriston. *Proc. Prehist. Soc.*, 41, 119-52.
—— (1977) The neolithic enclosure on Offham hill. *Proc. Prehist. Soc.*, 43, 201-42.
Dubouloz, J., Ilett, M. and Lasserre, M. (1982) Enceinte et maisons chalcolithiques de Berry-au-Bac, La Croix-Maigret (Aisne), in *Le Néolithique de l'Est de la France* (Société Archéologique de Sens, Cahier no. 1).
Du Châtellier, P. (1897) *La poterie aux époques préhistoriques et gauloise en Armorique*. Rennes.
—— (1907) *Les époques préhistoriques et gauloises dans la Finistère. Inventaire des monuments de ce département* (2nd edition). Quimper.
Ducos, P. (1958) Le gisement de Châteauneuf-les-Martigues (Bouches-du-Rhône). Les mammifères et les problèmes de domestication. *Bulletin du Musée d'Anthropologie Préhistorique de Monaco*, 5, 119-33.
—— (1976) Quelques documents sur les débuts de la domestication en France, in *La Préhistoire Française, II. Les civilisations néolithiques et protohistoriques* (ed. J. Guilaine), 165-7. Paris.
—— (1977) Le mouton de Châteauneuf-les-Martigues, in *L'Elevage en Méditerranée Occidentale*, 77-86. Marseille.
Duday, H. (1977) Difficultés d'une approche anthropologique de la néolithisation, in *Approche Ecologique de l'Homme Fossile* (eds H. Laville and J. Renault-Miskovsky), 367-70. Paris.
Duday, H. and Guilaine, J. (1975) Les rites funéraires en Languedoc et Roussillon du Néolithique au Premier Age du Fer. *Cahiers Ligures*, 24, 141-551.
—— (1980) Deux sépultures à la grotte Gazel, in *Les Premiers Paysans, Dossiers de l'Archéologie*, 44, 88-9.
—— (1980) Le niveau Vérazien de la grotte des chambres d'Alaric à Moux (Aude), in *Le Groupe de Véraza et la Fin des Temps Néolithiques dans le Sud de la France et la Catalogne* (ed. J. Guilaine), 42-6. Toulouse.
Dugrand, R. (1964) *La Garrigue Montpelliéraine*. Paris.
Durand, J-M. (1958) La Préhistoire dans la Haute-Vallée de l'Hers: 'Las-Morts'. *Bull. Soc. Préh. Ariège*, 13, 59-83.
—— (1968) La Préhistoire de l'Ariège du Néolithique I à la période de la Tène. *Bull. Soc. Sc. Lett. Arts Ariège*, 24.
Durand-Tullou, A. (1956) Vestiges de la culture des plateaux sur le Causse de Blandas. *Cahiers Ligures de Préhistoire et d'Archéologie*, 5, 52-80.
Edeine, B. (1960) Du site de la Brèche-au-Diable (dit aussi du Mont Joly), commune de Soument-Saint-Quentin. Datation d'un habitat néolithique chasséen. *Bull. Soc. Préhist. Fr.*, 57, 331-3.
—— (1962) Pic néolithique en bois de cerf découvert à Potigny (Calvados). *Bull. Soc. Préhist. Fr.*, 59, 576-8.

Edeine, B. (1965) Ce que les fouilles du site de la Brèche-au-Diable (Calvados) et de son contexte peuvent déjà apporter à la solution des problèmes posés par G. Bailloud dans son ouvrage 'Le Néolithique dans la Bassin Parisien'. *Bull. Soc. Préhist. Fr.*, 62, 328-49.

—— (1972) Nouvelles datations par le C14 concernant les sites de la Brèche-au-Diable (Mont-Joly) et des Longrais (Calvados). *Bull. Soc. Préhist. Fr.*, 69, 197-9.

Elhäi, H. (1963) *La Normandie occidentale entre la Seine et le golfe Normand-Breton*. Bordeaux.

Enjalbert, H. (1960) *Les pays aquitains: le modélé et les sols*. Bordeaux.

Erroux, J. (1976) Les débuts de l'agriculture en France: les céréales, in *La Préhistoire Française, II: Les civilisations néolithiques et protohistoriques* (ed. J. Guilaine), 186-91. Paris.

Escalon de Fonton, M. (1947) Découverte d'une station en plein air à la Couronne (Bouches-du-Rhône). *Mémoires de l'Institut Historique de Provence*, 12, 33-43.

—— (1956) Préhistoire de la Basse Provence. *Préhistoire*, 12.

—— (1965) Un tribu de pêcheurs préhistoriques dans les gorges de la Cèze. *Archéologia*, 6, 57-62.

—— (1966) Circonscription de Languedoc-Roussillon. *Gallia Préhistoire*, 9, 545-83.

—— (1968) Circonscription de Languedoc-Roussillon. *Gallia Préhistoire*, 11, 463-92.

—— (1970a) Circonscription de Languedoc-Roussillon. *Gallia Préhistoire*, 13, 513-49.

—— (1970b) Le Couronnien, in *Les Civilisations Néolithiques du Midi de la France* (ed. J. Guilaine), 119-21. Carcassonne.

—— (1976a) Circonscription de Provence-Alpes-Côte-d'Azur. *Gallia Préhistoire*, 19, 581-606.

—— (1976b) Village néolithique Courronien de la Couronne (Martigues, Bouches-du-Rhône), in *Provence et Languedoc Méditerranéen: Sites Paléolithiques et Néolithiques, Livret-Guide de l'Excursion C2* (ed. H. De Lumley), 69-76. Nice.

—— (1980) Circonscription de Provence-Alpes-Côte-d'Azur. *Gallia Préhistoire*, 23, 525-47.

Eschasseriaux, E. (1882) Le camp néolithique du Peurichard (Charente-Inférieure). *Matériaux*, 18, 505-19.

—— (1884) Le camp néolithique du Peurichard (Charente-Inférieure). *Recueil des Actes de la Commission des Arts et Monuments Historiques de la Charente-Inférieure et Société d'Archéologie de Saintes*, 3, 191-215.

Evans, J. D. (1956) Two Phases of Prehistoric Settlement in the Western Mediterranean. *Institute of Archaeology Annual Report, 1955-56*, 49-70.

Evin, J. (1979) Réflexions générales et données nouvelles sur la chronologie absolue C14 des industries de la fin du Paléolithique Supérieur et du début du Mésolithique, in *La Fin des Temps Glaciaires en Europe* (ed. D. de Sonneville-Bordes), vol.1, 5-13. Paris.

Fabre, G. (1943) Contribution à l'étude du Protohistorique du Sud-Ouest de la France (Dépts. des Basses-Pyrénées et des Landes). *Gallia Préhistoire*, 1, 43-79.

—— (1952) *Les Civilisations Protohistoriques de l'Aquitaine*. Paris.

Fel, A. (1975) Paysages Agraires et Civilisation Rurale de la Vieille Corse. *Boll.. Dep. Stor. Patr. Umbria (App.)*, 12, 183-95.

Ferrarese Ceruti, M. L. (1972-4) La Tomba XVI di su Crucitissu Mannu e la Cultura di Bonnanaro. *Bullettino di Paletnologia Italiana*, 81, 113-218.

Ferton, C. (1898) Sur l'Histoire de Bonifacio à l'Epoque Néolithique. *Actes. Soc. Linn. Bordeaux*, 53, 129-47.

—— (1899) Seconde Note sur l'Histoire de Bonifacio à l'Epoque Néolithique. *Actes. Soc. Linn. Bordeaux*, 54, 347-66.

Fiedler, L. (1979) Formen und Techniken neolithischer Steingeräte aus dem Rheinland, in *Beiträge zur Urgeschichte des Rheinlandes III* (Rheinische Ausgrabungen 19), 53-190. Köln.

Fleming, A. (1971) Territorial patterns in Bronze Age Wessex. *Proc. Prehist. Soc.*, 37, 138-66.

—— (1972) Vision and design: approaches to ceremonial monument typology. *Man*, 7, 57-73.

—— (1973) Tombs for the living. *Man*, 8, 171-93.

Forde, C. D. (1930) The early cultures of Atlantic Europe. *American Anthropologist*, 19, 19-100.

—— (1932) The typology of the Breton megalithic tombs. *Proc. First International Congress of Prehistoric and Protohistoric Sciences, London*, 114-17.

Forrestier, F. H., Lasnier, B. and L'Helgouach, J. (1973) A propos de la 'Callais'. Découverte d'un gisement de variscite à Pannacé (Loire Atlantique). Analyse de quelques 'perles vertes' néolithiques. *Bull. Soc. Préhist. Fr.*, 70, 173-80.

F.P.V.A. (1973-81) *Les Fouilles Protohistoriques dans la Vallée de l'Aisne*, 1-8 (Université de Paris I).

Freises, A., Montjardin, R. and Guilaine, J. (1976) Le gisement cardial de l'Ile Corrège à Port-Leucate (Aude). Note préliminaire. *Congr. Préhist. Fr.*, 20, 277-94.

Gabet, C. and Massaud, J. (1965) Le gisement Peu-Richardien de La Garenne 2, commune de Saint-Hippolyte (Charente-Maritime). *Bull. Soc. Préhist. Fr.*, 62, 159-95.

Gachina, J. (1979) Un poignard à deux rivets et une nouvelle pointe de Palmela récemment trouvés en Charente-Maritime. *Bull. Soc. Préhist. Fr.*, 76, 199-200.

Gachina, J., Gomez, J. and Coffyn, A. (1975) Supplément à l'inventaire des instruments perforés pour les départements de Charente, Charente-Maritime et Gironde. *Bull. Soc. Préhist. Fr.*, 72, 368-81.

Gagnière, S. (1968) Circonscription de Provence-Côte d'Azur-Corse. *Gallia Préhistoire*, 11, 524-8.

—— (1972) Circonscription de Provence-Côte d'Azur-Corse. *Gallia Préhistoire*, 15, 562-9.

Gagnière, S., Lanfranchi, F. de, Miskovsky, J-C., Prost, M., Renault-Miskovsky, J. and Weiss, M-C. (1969) L'Abri de Araguina-Sennola à Bonifacio (Corse). *Bull. Soc. Préhist. Fr.*, 66, 385-418.

Galan, A. (1967) La station néolithique de la Perte du Cros à Saillac (Lot). *Gallia Préhistoire*, 10, 1-60.

Gallay, A. (1977) *Le Néolithique Moyen du Jura et des Plaines de la Saône*. Basel.

Gallay, G. (1981) Ein verschollener Grabfund der Bandkeramik von Dijon (Dép. Côte-d'Or, Ostfrankreich). *Antike Welt*, 12, 36-43.

Galy, G-R. (1966) La mise en place de l'habitat dans les Pyrénées-Orientales. *Etudes Rurales*, 21, 82-98.

Garrigou, F. (1865) *Etude comparative des alluvions quaternaires anciennes et des cavernes à ossements des Pyrénées et de l'Ouest de l'Europe*. Toulouse/Paris.

—— (1871a) Sur des terramares et des palafittes des Pyrénées. *Congr. Int. d'Anth. et d'Arch. Préhist.*, 5, 218-21. Bologne.

—— (1871b) Habitations lacustres du Midi de la France (région pyrénéenne). *Comptes Rendus Acad. Sc. Paris*, 73, 1220-3.

—— (1872a) Sur les bois incisés du Lac Saint-Andéol. *Bull. Soc. Anth. Paris*, 2e série, 7, 347-62.

—— (1872b) Les habitations lacustres dans les Pyrénées. *Matériaux*, 180-1.

—— (1883) *Inauguration du Musée de l'Ariège: Conférence*. Toulouse.

Garrigou, F. and Filhol, H. (1866) *Age de la Pierre Polie dans les cavernes des Pyrénées Ariégeoises*. Paris/Toulouse.

Gasco, J. (1976) *La Communauté Paysanne de Fontbouisse*. Carcassonne.

—— (1979) Le Néolithique de l'abri Jean-Cros. Déterminations végétales et techniques de consommation possibles ou probables, in *L'Abri Jean Cros: essai d'approche d'un groupe humain du Néolithique ancien dans son environnement* (ed. J. Guilaine), 371-4. Toulouse.

—— (1980a) Les structures d'habitat de plein air du groupe de Véraza, in *Le Groupe de Véraza et la Fin des Temps Néolithiques dans le Sud de la France et la Catalogne* (ed. J. Guilaine), 103-8. Toulouse.

—— (1980b) Un habitat de plein air au néolithique récent: la Mort des Anes (Villeneuve-les-Maguelonne, Hérault), in *Le Groupe de Véraza et la Fin des Temps Néolithiques dans le Sud de la France et la Catalogne* (ed. J. Guilaine), 177-91. Toulouse.

—— (1980c) L'aménagement de l'espace domestique à Font-Juvénal, in *Les Premiers Paysans, Dossiers de l'Archéologie*, 44, 41-3.

—— (1980d) Les structures d'habitat vóraziennes de l'abri de Font-Juvénal (Conques, Aude)/Les méthodes de cuisson des aliments et les structures de combustion de l'abri de Font-Juvénal (Conques, Aude), in *Le Groupe de Véraza et la Fin des Temps Néolithiques dans le Sud de la France et la Catalogne* (ed. J. Guilaine), 109-12/113-14. Toulouse.

Gaucher, G. (1976) Les Civilisations de l'Age du Bronze dans le Bassin Parisien et le Nord de la France, in *La Préhistoire Française, II: Les civilisations néolithiques et protohistoriques* (ed. J. Guilaine), 575-84. Paris.

Gaussen, H. (1926) Végétation de la moitié orientale des Pyrénées. *Bull. Soc. Hist. Nat. Toulouse*, 55.

Gauthier, A. and Thibault, J. C. (1979) Les Vertébrés Terrestres Actuels Eteints en Corse. *Courrier Parc. Corse*, 32, 13-44.

Geddes, D. (1980a) De la chasse au troupeau: les débuts de l'élevage. *Les Premiers Paysans, Dossiers de l'Archéologie*, 44, 22-5.

—— (1980b) *De la Chasse au Troupeau en Mediterranée Occidentale: Les débuts de l'élevage dans la vallée de l'Aude*. Toulouse.

—— (1981) Les débuts de l'élevage dans la vallée de l'Aude. *Bull. Soc. Préhist. Fr.*, 78, 370-8.

Gennes, Brouillet and de Longuemar (1863) Compte rendu de quelques explorations archéologiques exécutées dans le courant d'août dernier. *Bull. Soc. Antiq. de l'Ouest*, 1863, 303-13.

Germond, G., Joussaume, R. and Bizard, M. (1978) Le tumulus du Montiou à Sainte-Soline (Deux-Sèvres). Premières campagnes de fouilles. Premier bilan. *Bull. Soc. Hist. et Sci. des Deux-Sèvres*, 9, 129-88.

Giglioli, G. Q. (1932) Stazzone, Stantare e Filarate. *Corsica Antica e Moderna*, 1, 203-22.

Giot, P-R. (1960) Une statue menhir en Bretagne (Ou le mystère archéologique de la femme coupée en morceaux . . .). *Bull. Soc. Préhist. Fr.*, 57, 317-30.

—— (1970) *Barnenez*. Rennes.

—— (1971) The impact of radiocarbon dating on the establishment of the prehistoric chronology of Brittany. *Proc. Prehist. Soc.*, 37, part 2, 208-17.

—— (1976) Dolmens et menhirs. Le phénomène mégalithique en France, in *La Préhistoire Française, II : Les civilisations néolithiques et protohistoriques* (ed. J. Guilaine), 202-10. Paris.

—— (1981) The Megaliths of France, in *Antiquity and Man* (eds J. D. Evans, B. Cunliffe and C. Renfrew), 82-93. London.

Giot, P-R., Briard, J. and Pape, L. (1979) *Protohistoire de la Bretagne*. Rennes.

Giot, P-R. and L'Helgouach, J. (1965) Le cairn de l'Île Carn en Ploudalmézeau. *Bull. Soc. Ant. Fin.*, 81, 53-62.

Giot, P-R., L'Helgouach, J. and Briard, J. (1960) *Brittany*. London.

—— (1965) Le site du Curnic en Guisseny. *Annales de Bretagne*, 72, 49-70.

Giot, P-R., L'Helgouach, J., Briard, J., Waterbolk, H., Van Zeist, W. and Müller-Wille, M. (1960) Une station du néolithique primaire Armoricain : Le Curnic en Guissény (Finistère). *Bull. Soc. Préhist. Fr.*, 57, 38-50.

Giot, P-R., L'Helgouach, J. and Monnier, J. L. (1979) *Préhistoire de la Bretagne*. Rennes.

Giraud, J. P. and Vaquer, J. (1981) Nouvelles structures de galets chauffés dans la Haute-Garonne, in *Bull. Soc. Méridionale de Spéléologie et de Préhist.*, 21, 35-50.

Giraux, L. (1914) Les Monuments Mégalithiques de la Région de Sartène (Corse). *Assoc. Fr. Avancement des Sciences*, Ajaccio, 1-28.

Godfray, A. B. D. and Burdo, C. (1949) Excavations at The Pinnacle, Parish of St. Ouen, Jersey (1930-1936). Part 1. *Bull. Soc. Jers.*, 74, 22-100.

—— (1950) Excavations at The Pinnacle, Parish of St. Ouen, Jersey (1930-1936). Part 2. *Bull. Soc. Jers.*, 75, 165-258.

Gomez, J. (1975) Le rempart artenacien du camp de Pierre-Dure à Voeuil-et-Giget (Charente). Quelques réflexions au sujet d'Artenac. *Bull. Soc. Préhist. Fr.*, 72, 117-24.

—— (1978) La stratigraphie chalcolithique et protohistorique de la grotte Quéroy à Chazelles (Charente). *Bull. Soc. Préhist. Fr.*, 75, 394-421.

—— (1980) *Les cultures de l'Age du Bronze dans le bassin de la Charente*. Périgueux.

—— (1982) Une pirogue monoxyle néolithique dans le lit de la Charente. *Bull. Soc. Préhist. Fr.*, 79, 61-3.

—— (1983) Le rempart chalcolithique et du bronze ancien du Fort des Anglais à Mouthiers-sur-Boëme, Charente. *Bull. Soc. Préhist. Fr.*, 80, 38-9.

Griegel, R. and Bogucki, P. (1981) Early Neolithic Sites at Brzesc Kujawski, Poland: Preliminary Report on the 1976-1979 Excavations. *J. Field Arch.*, 8, 9-27.

Grosjean, R. (1956) Le Niolo préhistorique. *Etudes Corses*, 7, 5-36.

—— (1961) Filitosa et son Contexte Archéologique. *Mon et Mém. Acad. Inscr. Belles Lettr. Fond. Piot*, 52, 1-100 (hors texte).

—— (1962) Le gisement torréen fortifié de Tappa, Porto-Vecchio (Corse). *Bull. Soc. Préhist. Fr.*, 59, 206-16.

—— (1964) Chronique d'Archéologie Préhistorique. *Corse Historique*, 9-10, 5-17.

—— (1966a) *La Corse Avant l'Histoire*. Paris.

—— (1966b) Recent Work in Corsica. *Antiquity*, 40, 190-8.

—— (1967) Classification Descriptive du Mégalithique Corse, *Bull. Soc. Préhist. Fr.*, 64, 707-42.

—— (1971a) La Préhistoire, in *Histoire de la Corse* (ed. P. Arrighi), 11-13. Toulouse.

—— (1971b) Diorama de la Civilisation Torréene, in *Mélanges d'Etudes Corses* (ed. F. Ettori), 165-94.

Grosjean, R. and Liégeois, J. (1964) Les Coffres mégalithiques de la Région de Porto-Vecchio. *L'Anthropologie*, 68, 527-48.

Grosjean, R., Liégeois, J. and Peretti, G. (1976) Les Civilisations de l'Age du Bronze Corse, in *La Préhistoire Française, II: Les civilisations néolithiques et protohistoriques* (ed. J. Guilaine), 644-53. Paris.

Gruet, M. (1967) *Inventaire des Mégalithes de la France, 2: Maine-et-Loire*. Paris.

Gruet, M. and Passini, B. (1982) Le dolmen angevin de la Bajoulière (Maine-et-Loire). *Bull. Groupe Vendéen d'Etudes Préhist.*, 7, 7-11.

De Guérin, T. W. M. (1921) List of dolmens, menhirs and sacred rocks; compiled from Guernsey place names, with legends, etc. *Trans. Soc. Guern.*, 9, 30-64.

Guilaine, J. (1963) Boutons perforés en V du Chalcolithique pyrénéen. *Bull. Soc. Préhist. Fr.*, 60, 813-25.

—— (1967) *La Civilisation du Vase Campaniforme dans les Pyrénées françaises*. Carcassonne.

—— (1970a) Les fouilles de la grotte de Gazel (Sallèles-Cabardes, Aude). *Bulletin de la Société d'Etudes Scientifiques de l'Aude*, 70, 61-73.

—— (ed.) (1970b) *Les Civilisations Néolithiques du Midi de la France*. Carcassonne.

—— (1970c) Le groupe de Bize, in *Les Civilisations Néolithiques du Midi de la France* (ed. J. Guilaine), 60-3. Carcassonne.

—— (1970d) Le groupe de Véraza (Vérazien), in *Les Civilisations Néolithiques du Midi de la France* (ed. J. Guilaine), 113-15. Carcassonne.

—— (1970e) Sur l'Epicardial languedocien, in *Les Civilisations néolithiques du Midi de la France* (ed. J. Guilaine), 13-14. Narbonne.

—— (1971) La Néolithisation du Bassin de l'Aude et des Pyrénées méditerranéennes françaises, in *Die Anfänge des Neolithikums vom Orient bis Nordeuropa*, Teil VI (Fundamenta A, 3), 100-21.

—— (1972) L'Age du Bronze en Languedoc Occidental, Roussillon, Ariège. *Mém. Soc. Préh. fr.*, 9.

—— (1974a) *La Balma de Montbolo, et le Néolithique de l'Occident Méditerranéen*. Toulouse.

Guilaine, J. (1974b) La chronologie absolue du Néolithique languedocien d'après les stratigraphies de la Grotte Gazel et de l'abri de Font-Juvénal. *Bull. Soc. Languedocienne de Géog.*, 8, 293-9.

—— (1975) Premiers Bergers et Paysans des Pyrénées méditerranéennes. *Archéologia*, 85, 13-19.

—— (1976a) *Premiers Bergers et Paysans de l'Occident Méditerranéen.* Paris.

—— (1976b) Les civilisations néolithiques dans les Pyrénées, in *La Préhistoire française, II: Les civilisations néolithiques et protohistoriques* (ed. J. Guilaine), 326-37. Paris.

—— (1976c) La civilisation des vases campaniformes dans le Midi de la France, in *Glockenbecher Symposion*, Oberried 1974 (eds J. N. Lanting and J. D. Van der Waals), 351-70. Bussum/Haarlem.

—— (ed.) (1976) *La Préhistoire Française, II: Les civilisations néolithiques et protohistoriques*. Paris.

—— *et al.* (1976) *L'abri de Font-Juvénal. Une stratigraphie néolithique en Languedoc*. Carcassonne.

—— (1977) Sur les débuts de l'élevage en Méditerranée Occidentale, in *L'Elevage en Méditerranée Occidentale*, Actes du Colloque Int. de l'Inst. de Recherches Médit., Sénanque, 39-48.

—— (1978) La Néolithisation du Languedoc et de la Catalogne. *Godišnjak* (Sarajevo), XVI (14), 81-92.

—— (ed.) (1979) *L'Abri Jean Gros: essai d'approche d'un groupe humain du Néolithique ancien dans son environnement.* Toulouse.

—— (1979) The earliest neolithic in the west Mediterranean: a new appraisal. *Antiquity*, 53, 22-30.

—— *et al.* (1980) L'abri de Font-Juvénal. Une stratigraphie néolithique, in *Les Premiers Paysans, Dossiers de l'Archéologie*, 44, 36-40.

—— (ed.) (1980) *Le Groupe de Véraza et la Fin des Temps Néolithiques dans le Sud de la France et la Catalogne*. Toulouse.

—— (1980) Problèmes Actuels de la Néolithisation et du Néolithique Ancien en Méditerranée Occidentale, in *Interaction and Acculturation in the Mediterranean* (eds J. Best and N. de Vries), 1, 3-29. Amsterdam.

—— (1981) *La France d'avant la France*. Paris.

Guilaine, J., Duday, H. and Lavergne, J. (1972) La Nécropole mégalithique de la Clape (Laroque-de-Fa, Aude). *Atacina*, 7.

Guilaine, J. and Martzluff, M. (1976) Sur le Néolithique ancien de la Cerdagne. *Cypsela*, 1, 34-5.

Guilaine, J. and Rigaud, L. (1968) Le foyer de Perairol (Cavanac, Aude) dans son contexte régional de la fin du Néolithique et du Chalcolithique. *Bull. Soc. Préhist. Fr.*, 65, 671-98.

Guilaine, J. and Roudil, J-L. (1976) Les civilisations néolithiques en Languedoc, in *La Préhistoire Française, II. Les civilisations néolithiques et protohistoriques* (ed. J. Guilaine), 267-78. Paris.

Guilaine, J., Thommeret, J., Thommeret, Y., Vaquer, J. and Barrie, P. (1974) Stratigraphie et datations C14 d'un gisement néolithique languedocien: l'abri de Font-Juvénal (Conques, Aude). *L'Anthropologie*, 78, 257-82.

Guilaine, J. and Vaquer, J. (1973) Le site Chasséen d'Auriac, commune de Carcassonne (Aude). *Bull. Soc. Préhist. Fr.*, 70, 367-84.

Guilaine, J. and Vaquer, J. (1979) Les débuts de la metallurgie et les groupes culturels de la fin du Néolithique dans le Sud de la France, in *Proceedings of the 5th Atlantic Colloquium* (ed. M. Ryan), 65-79. Dublin.

Guilaine, J., Vaquer, J. and Bouisset, P. (1976) Un vase-support chasséen à Ouveillan (Aude). *Bull. Soc. Préhist. Fr.*, 73, 83-90.

Guilaine, J., Vaquer, J., Gasco, J. and Barrie, P. (1976a) L'abri de Dourgne II (Fontanes-de-Sault, Aude), in *Provence et Languedoc Méditerranéen: Sites Paléolithiques et Néolithiques, Livret-Guide de l'Excursion C2* (ed. H. De Lumley), 312-15. Nice.

—— (1976b) Abri de Font Juvénal (Conques, Aude), in *Provence et Languedoc Méditerranéen: Sites Paléolithiques et Néolithiques, Livret-Guide de l'Excursion C2* (ed. H. De Lumley), 292-7. Nice.

Guillaume, P. and Chevallier, R. (1956) Les stations chalcolithiques de Nogent-l'Artaud (Aisne). *Cong. Préhist. Fr.*, 15, 545-55.

Guillien, Y. (1979) Les tufs calcaires d'Aigre et de Mainxe (Charente), in *Etudes Géographiques offertes à Louis Papy*, 343-51.

Gutherz, X. (1975) *La Culture de Fontbouisse*. Caveirac.

—— (1980) Le groupe de Ferrières, in *Le Groupe de Véraza et la Fin des Temps Néolithiques dans le Sud de la France et la Catalogne* (ed. J. Guilaine), 217-21. Toulouse.

—— (1982) Les enceintes en pierre sèche du Néolithique à l'age du Bronze dans le sud-est de la France. *Bull. Soc. Préhist. Fr.*, 79, 56-8.

Hallam, B. R., Warren, S. E. and Renfrew, C. (1976) Obsidian in the western Mediterranean: characterisation by neutron activation analysis and optical emission spectroscopy. *Proc. Prehist. Soc.*, 42, 85-110.

Halstead, P. L. J. (1981) Counting sheep in Neolithic and Bronze Age Greece, in *Pattern of the Past* (eds I. Hodder, G. Isaac and N. Hammond), 307-39. Cambridge.

Harrison, R. J. (1980) *The Beaker Folk*. London.

Hassan, F. A. (1981) *Demographic Archaeology*. New York and London.

Hawkes, J. (1934) Aspects of the Neolithic and Chalcolithic Periods in Western Europe. *Antiquity*, 8, 24-42.

—— (1938) The Significance of Channelled Ware in Neolithic Western Europe. *Archaeol. J.*, 95, 126-73.

—— (1939) *The Archaeology of the Channel Islands. Vol. 2, The Bailiwick of Jersey*. Jersey.

Hibbs, J. L. (forthcoming) Land use and the survival of megalithic monuments in the Channel Islands. *Proc. Conference on Channel Islands Archaeology, 1981*. Guernsey.

Hodder, I. (1979) Economic and social stress and material culture patterning. *American Antiquity*, 44, 446-54.

—— (1982a) Sequences of structural change in the Dutch Neolithic, in *Symbolic and Structural Archaeology* (ed. I. Hodder), 162-77. Cambridge.

—— (1982b) *Symbols in Action*. Cambridge.

Howell, J. M. (1982) Settlement and Economy in Neolithic Northern France. *Oxford J. Arch.*, 1, 115-18.

—— (1983) *Settlement and Economy in Neolithic Northern France*. Oxford.

Hurtrelle, J. and Piningre, J-F. (1978) Datation radiocarbone des Sablins à Etaples (Pas-de-Calais). *Bull. Soc. Préhist. Fr.*, 75, 83-6.

Hutchinson, Sir J. (1969) Erosion and land-use: the influence of agriculture on the Epirus region of Greece. *Agricultural History Review*, 17, 85-90.
Ilett, M. (1980) *Aspects of Neolithic settlement in north-west Europe and Britain* (unpublished Ph.D. dissertation, University of Cambridge).
Ilett, M., Constantin, C., Coudart, A. and Demoule, J-P. (in press) The Late Bandkeramik of the Aisne valley: environment and spatial organisation. *Analecta Praehistorica Leidensia*.
Ilett, M. and Plateaux, M. (in press) Analyse de la céramique de Cuiry-lès-Chaudardes (vallée de l'Aisne): résultats préliminaires, in *Actes du colloque interrégional sur le Néolithique, Le Puy 1981*.
Itten, M. (1970) *Die Horgener Kultur*. Zurich.
Jalmain, D. (1970) *Archéologie aérienne en île de France*. Paris.
Jalut, G. (1976a) Les débuts de l'agriculture en France: les défrichements, in *La Préhistoire française, II: Les civilisations néolithiques et protohistoriques* (ed. J. Guilaine), 180-5. Paris.
—— (1976b) Les tourbières du Donezan: les débues de l'agriculture, in *Provence et Languedoc Méditerranéen, Sites Paléolithiques et Néolithiques, Livret-Guide de l'Excursion C2*, 316. Nice.
—— (1977) *Végétation et Climat des Pyrénées Méditerranéennes depuis quinze mille ans*. Archives d'Ecologie Préhist. No.2, 2 vols. Toulouse.
Jehasse, J. (1974) Circonscription de la Corse. *Gallia Préhistoire*, 17, 701-9.
—— (1976) Circonscription de la Corse. *Gallia Préhistoire*, 19, 607-15.
—— (1978) Circonscription de la Corse. *Gallia Préhistoire*, 21, 723-34.
—— (1980) Circonscription de la Corse. *Gallia Préhistoire*, 23, 549-65.
Joffroy, R. (1968) Circonscription de Champagne-Ardennes. *Gallia Préhistoire*, 11, 337-41.
Joly, J. (1968) Circonscription de Bourgogne. *Gallia Préhistoire*, 11, 367-419.
—— (1970) Circonscription de Bourgogne. *Gallia Préhistoire*, 13, 411-58.
Jourdan, L. (1976) Les complexites de l'élevage et de l'alimentation au Mésolithique et au Néolithique ancien en Provence, in *La Préhistoire Française, II: Les civilisations néolithiques et protohistoriques* (ed. J. Guilaine), 168-71. Paris.
Joussaume, R. (1972) Les fouilles du Docteur Guérin sur l'éperon des Châtelliers-du-Vieil-Auzay (Vendée). *Bull. Soc. Préhist. Fr.*, 69, 417-29.
—— (1976a) Le dolmen angevin de Pierre-Folle à Thiré (Vendée). *Gallia Préhistoire*, 19, 1-37.
—— (1976b) Dolmen de Pierre-Levée à Nieul-sur-l'Autize (Vendée). *Bull. Soc. Préhist. Fr.*, 73, 398-421.
—— (1977) Datations par le carbone 14 de sites archéologiques vendéens. *Bull. Soc. Emulation de la Vendée*, 124, 124-5.
—— (1978) Le dolmen à couloir dit 'la Ciste des Cous' à Bazoges-en-Pareds (Vendée). *Bull. Soc. Préhist. Fr.*, 75, 579-96.
—— (1980) *Champ Durand à Nieul-sur-l'Autize (Vendée). Site préhistorique fortifié*. La Roche-sur-Yon.
—— (1981) *Le Néolithique de l'Aunis et du Poitou Occidental dans son cadre Atlantique*. Rennes.

Joussaume, R., Jauneau, J-M., Boiral, M., Robin, P. and Gachina, J. (1979) Néolithique ancien du Centre-Ouest. Note Préliminaire. *Bull. Soc. Préhist. Fr.*, 76, 173-83.
Joussaume, R. and Robin, P. (1980) Site chasséen de la plage des Sables-d'Olonne (Vendée). *Bull. Groupe Vendéen d'Etudes Préhist.*, 3, 47-50.
Jürgens, A. (1979) Die Rössener Siedlung von Aldenhoven, Kreis Düren, in *Beiträge zur Urgeschichte des Rheinlandes III* (Rheinische Ausgrabungen 19), 385-506. Köln.
Kapps, R. and Bailloud, G. (1960) Découverte fortuite d'une sépulture chalcolithique à la Ferme de Champagne, commune d'Augy (Yonne). *Bull. Soc. Préhist. Fr.*, 57, 476-9.
Kendrick, T. D. (1928) *The Archaeology of the Channel Islands. Vol. I, The Bailiwick of Guernsey*. London.
Kinnes, I. (1980) The art of the exceptional: the statues-menhir of Guernsey in context. *Archaeologia Atlantica*, 3, 9-33.
—— (1982) Les Fouaillages and megalithic origins. *Antiquity*, 56, 24-30.
—— (forthcoming, a) Megaliths in action: some aspects of the neolithic period in the Channel Islands. *Proc. Conference on Channel Islands Archaeology, 1981*. Guernsey.
—— (forthcoming, b) *British Long Mounds (British Museum Occasional Paper)*.
Kraybill, N. (1977) Pre-agricultural tools for the preparation of foods in the Old World, in *Origins of Agriculture* (ed. C. A. Reed), 485-521. The Hague.
Kruk, J. (1973) *Studia Osadnicze Nad Neoliten Wyzyn Lessowych*. Krakow.
—— (1980) *The Earlier Neolithic Settlement of Southern Poland* (eds J. M. Howell and N. J. Starling). Oxford.
De La Chénelière, G. (1880) Inventaire des monuments mégalithiques compris dans le département des Côtes-du-Nord. *Bull. et Mém. de la Soc. d'émulation des Côtes-du-Nord*, 17, 85-171.
—— (1883) *Deuxième inventaire des monuments mégalithiques dans le département des Côtes-du-Nord*. Saint-Brieuc.
Lanfranchi, F. de (1967) La Grotte Sépulcrale de Curacchiaghiu (Levie, Corse), *Bull. Soc. Préhist. Fr.*, 64, 587-612.
—— (1972a) Etude de Deux Sites Préhistoriques: Ville di Paraso et Grossa. *Bull. Soc. Sci. Hist. Nat. Corse*, 603, 19-66.
—— (1972b) Contribution à la Connaissance des Cultures qui Erigèrent les Coffres Mégalithiques du Sud de la Corse. *Trav. Inst. Arch. Préhist. Toulouse*, 14, 273-83.
—— (1974a) Le Néolithique Ancien Méditerranéen, Faciès Curacchiaghiu à Levie. *Cahiers Corsica*, 43, 39-43.
—— (1974b) L'Abri sous roche No. 2 de Curacchiaghiu (Levie, Corse). *Bull. Soc. Préhist. Fr.*, 71, 11-13.
—— (1976a) Destruction d'un Site Cardiale à Bonifacio (Corse). *Bull. Soc. Préhist. Fr.*, 73, 273-5.
—— (1976b) Le Néolithique Récent du Curacchiaghiu (Levie, Corse) et le Problème de l'Obsidienne importée en Corse au IIIe Millénaire Avant J.C. *Archeologia Corsa*, 1, 7-73.
—— (1978) *Capula. Quatre millenaires de survivances et de traditions*. Levie.

—— (1979) La station préhistorique de Compolaggia. *Archeologia Corsa*, 4, 49-51.

—— (1982) Le Castellu de Cucuruzzu. Etude paléoethnographique. *Archeologia Corsa*, 6.

Lanfranchi, F. de and Milleliri, J. (1972) Les Meules de Punta Campana. *Bull. Soc. Sci. Hist. et Mat. Corse*, 603, 67-71.

Lanfranchi, F. de and Weiss, M-C. (1973) *La Civilisation des Corses – les Origines*. Ajaccio.

—— (1977) Araguina-Sennola. *Archeologia Corsa*, 2.

—— (1979) Les Débuts de l'Elevage en Corse. *Courrier Parc Corse*, 32, 9-12.

Lanting, J. N., Mook, W. G. and Van der Waals, J. D. (1973) C14 chronology and the Beaker Problem. *Helinium*, 13, 38-58.

Lanting, J. N. and Van der Waals, J. D. (1976) Beaker culture relations in the Lower Rhine Basin, in *Glockenbecher Symposion, Oberried 1974* (eds J. N. Lanting and J. D. Van der Waals), 1-80. Bussum/Haarlem.

Laplace, G. (1953) Les couches à escargots des cavernes pyrénéennes et le problème de l'Arisien de Piette. *Bull. Soc. Préhist. Fr.*, 50, 199-211.

Large, J-M. (1981) *Les premiers peuples paysans en Vendée. Point des connaissances sur le Néolithique 1972-1980*. La Roche-sur-Yon.

L'Helgouach, J. (1956) La civilisation des allées couvertes en Armorique. *Cong. Préhist. Fr.*, 15, 692-706.

—— (1965) *Les Sépultures Mégalithiques en Armorique*. Rennes.

—— (1966) Les sépultures mégalithiques à entrée latérale en Armorique. *Palaeohistoria*, 12, 259-81.

—— (1967) Fouilles de l'allée couverte de Prajou-Menhir en Trébeurden (Côtes-du-Nord). *Bull. Soc. Préhist. Fr.*, 63, 312-42.

—— (1970) Le monument mégalithique du Goërem à Gâvres (Morbihan). *Gallia Préhistoire*, 13, 217-61.

—— (1971) Les débuts du néolithique en Armorique au quatrième millénaire et son développement au troisième millénaire, in *Die Anfänge des Neolithikums vom Orient bis Nordeurope*, Teil VI (Fundamenta A3), 178-200. Köln.

—— (1973) Les mégalithiques de l'Ouest de la France; Evolution et chronologie, in *Megalithic graves and ritual* (eds G. Daniel and P. Kjaerum), 203-19. Copenhagen.

—— (1976a) Les relations entre le groupe des vases campaniformes et les groupes néolithiques dans l'Ouest de la France, in *Glockenbecher Symposion Oberried 1974* (eds J. N. Lanting and J. D. Van der Waals), 439-51. Bussum/Haarlem.

—— (1976b) Le tumulus de Dissignac à Saint-Nazaire (Loire-Atlantique) et les problèmes du contact entre le phénomène mégalithique et les sociétés à industrie microlithique, in *Acculturation and Continuity in Atlantic Europe* (ed. S. J. De Laet), 142-9. Bruges.

—— (1977a) Circonscription des Pays de la Loire. *Gallia Préhistoire*, 20, 433-55.

—— (1977b) Le cairn des Mousseaux à Pornic (Loire Atlantique). Nouvelles fouilles et restaurations. *L'Architecture Mégalithique: Colloque du 150e anniversaire de la Soc. Polym. Morb.*, 161-72. Vannes.

L'Helgouach, J. (1977c) Les vases à pied creux du néolithique Armoricain. *Arch. Atlantica*, 2, 9-19.
——(1979) Circonscription des Pays de la Loire. *Gallia Préhistoire*, 22, 557-84.
——(1981) Circonscription des Pays de la Loire. *Gallia Préhistoire*, 24, 425-37.
L'Helgouach, J. and Lecornec, J. (1976) Le site mégalithique de Min Goh Ru, près de Larcuste à Colpo (Morbihan). *Bull. Soc. Préhist. Fr.*, 73, 370-97.
Lepage, L., Bouville, C. and Poulain, T. (1980) Le camp de la Vergentière à Cohons (Haute-Marne), in *Préhistoire et Protohistoire en Champagne-Ardenne*, 139-65. Châlons-sur-Marne.
Le Provost, F., Giot, P-R. and Onnée, Y. (1972) Prospections sur les collines de Saint-Nicolas-du-Pelem (Côtes du Nord), du Chalcolithique à la Protohistoire. *Annales de Bretagne*, 79, 39-48.
Leroi-Gourhan, A., Bailloud, G. and Brezillon, M. (1962) L'hypogée III des Mournouards (Mesnil-sur-Oger, Marne). *Gallia Préhistoire*, 5, 23-133.
Le Roux, C-T. (1971) A stone axe factory in Brittany. *Antiquity*, 45, 283-8.
—— (1976) Nécropole mégalithique de Liscuis, Laniscat (Côtes-du-Nord), in *Brétagne, Livret-Guide de l'Excursion A3* (ed. P. R. Giot), 56-62. Nice.
——(1977) Le tertre néolithique de Bilgroves à Arzon. Fouilles de 1976-1977. *Bull. Soc. Polym. Morb.*, 105, 60.
——(1979a) Stone axes of Brittany and the Marches, in *Stone Axe Studies* (eds T. McK. Clough and W. Cummins), 49-56. London.
—— (1979b) Circonscription de la Bretagne. *Gallia Préhistoire*, 22, 525-56.
——(1981) Circonscription de la Bretagne. *Gallia Préhistoire*, 24, 395-423.
Le Roux, C-T. and Lecerf, Y. (1980) Le cairn de Ty Floc'h à Saint-Thois (Fouilles de 1978-1979). *Bull. Soc. Arch. du Fin.*, 108, 27-49.
Le Roux, C-T. and L'Helgouach, J. (1967) Le cairn mégalithique avec sépultures à chambres compartimentées de Kerleven, commune de la Forêt-Fouesnant (Finistère). *Annales de Bretagne*, 74, 7-52.
Le Rouzic, Z. (1930) *Les cromlechs de Er Lannic, Arzon*. Vannes.
——(1932) *Tumulus du Mont-Saint-Michel: (1900-1906)*. Vannes.
——(1933) Morphologie et chronologie des sépultures préhistoriques du Morbihan. *L'Anthropologie*, 43, 225-65.
——(1934) Le mobilier des sépultures préhistoriques du Morbihan. *L'Anthropologie*, 44, 485-524.
——(1965) Inventaire des monuments mégalithiques de la région de Carnac (l'arrondissement de Lorient). Reprinted extract, *Bull. Soc. Polym. Morb.*
Le Rouzic, Z., Péquart, S-J. and Péquart, M. (1923) *Carnac: fouilles faites dans la région. Campagne 1922. Tumulus du Crucuny, tertre du Manio, tertre du Castellic*. Paris.
Leroy Ladurie, E. (1966) *Les Paysans de Languedoc*. Paris.
Letterle, F. (1976-7) Quelques traces d'occupation du néolithique de tradition danubienne dans le Vexin français. *Bulletin archéologique du Vexin français*, 12-13, 135-40.

Lewthwaite, J. (1981) Plains tails from the hills: transhumance in Mediterranean archaeology, in *Economic Archaeology* (eds A. Sheridan and G. Bailey), 57-66. Oxford.

—— (1982a) La Culture des Castelli de la Corse: dernier témoin d'un genre de vie ouest-Méditerranean d'autrefois? *Archeologia Corsa*, 6.

—— (1982b) Ambiguous First Impressions: a Survey of Recent Work on the Early Neolithic of the West Mediterranean. *Journal of Mediterranean Anthropology and Archaeology*, 1, 292-307.

—— (1982c) The art of Corse herding: archaeological insights from recent pastoral practises on the west Mediterranean islands, in *Animals in Archaeology* (eds C. Grigson and J. Clutton-Brock). Oxford.

—— (1982d) Acorns for the Ancestors: the Prehistoric Exploitation of Woodland in the West Mediterranean, in *Archaeological Aspects of Woodland Ecology* (eds S. Limbrey and M. Bell), 217-30. Oxford.

Lichardus, J. (1976) *Rössen-Gatersleben-Baalberge. Ein Beitrag zur Chronologie des mitteldeutschen Neolithikums and zur Enstehung der Tricherterbecher-Kulturen* (Saarbrücker Beiträge zur Altertumskunde 17). Bonn.

Lichardus-Itten, M. (1980) *Die Gräber der Grossgartacher Gruppe im Elsass* (Saarbrücker Beiträge zur Altertumskunde 25). Bonn.

Liégeois, J. and Peretti, G. (1976) Sites mégalithiques découverts par Roger Grosjean, in *Sites Préhistoriques et Protohistoriques de l'Isle de Corse* (eds J. Jehasse and R. Grosjean), 101-14. Paris.

Lilliu, G. (1966) Rapports entre la Culture 'Torréene' et les Aspects culturels pré et protonuraghique de la Sardaigne. *Congr. Préhist. Fr.*, 18, 295-320.

—— (1973) *La Civiltà dei Sardi*. Turin.

Löhr, H., Zimmermann, A. and Hahn, J. (1977) Feuersteinartefakte, in *Der bandkeramische Siedlungsplatz Langweiler 9* (Rheinische Ausgrabungen 18; eds R. Kuper, H. Löhr, J. Lüning, P. Stehli and A. Zimmermann), 131-265. Bonn.

Lorblanchet, M. (1965) Contribution à l'étude du peuplement des Grands Causses. *Bull. Soc. Préhist. Fr.*, 62, 667-712.

—— (1970) Le Rodezien, in *Les Civilisations Néolithiques du Midi de la France* (ed. J. Guilaine), 69-72. Carcassonne.

Louis, M. (1931) *Le Gard Préhistorique*. Nîmes.

—— (1932) *Le Néolithique dans le Gard*. Nîmes.

—— (1948) *Préhistoire du Languedoc Méditerranéen et du Roussillon*. Nîmes.

Louis, M., Peryolles, D. and Arnal, J. (1947) Les fonds de cabanes énéolithiques de Fontbouisse. *Gallia*, 5, 5-18.

Louwe Kooijmans, L. P. (1976) Local developments in a borderland, a survey of the Neolithic at the Lower Rhine. *Oudheidkundige Mededelingen Leiden*, 57, 227-97.

—— (1980) Archaeology and Coastal Change in the Netherlands, in *Archaeology and Coastal Change* (ed. F. H. Thompson), 106-33. London.

—— (1980) The Middle Neolithic Assemblage of Het Vomer near Wijchen and the Culture Pattern around the Southern North Sea, c.3000BC. *Oudheidkundige Mededelingen*, 61, 113-208.

Lücke, H. (1976) *Ostkorsika*. Mainz.

Lukis, F. C. (1844) Observations on the primeval antiquities of the Channel Islands. *Arch. J.*, 1, 142-51.
—— (1845) On the cromlech of Du Tus. *Journ. Brit. Arch. Assoc.*, 1, 25-9.
—— (1847) On the cromlech of l'Ancresse Common. *Journ. Brit. Arch. Assoc.*, 3, 342-50.
—— (1830-65) *Collectanea Antiquita*, 5 vols, unpublished. Guernsey Museum, Guernsey.
—— (1853) Observations on the Celtic Megaliths, and the contents of Celtic Tombs, chiefly as they remain in the Channel Islands. *Archaeologia*, 35, 232-58.
Lukis, W. C. (1868) On the various forms of monuments, commonly called dolmens, in Brittany, pointing out a progress in their architectural construction, with an attempt to reduce them to chronological order. *Inter. Congr. Prehist. Arch*, 218-23. Norwich.
de Lumley, H. (1976) Les Lignes de Rivage des Côtes Méditerranéennes de la France, in *La Préhistoire Française, II: Les civilisations néolithiques et protohistoriques* (ed. J. Guilaine), 24-6. Paris.
Lüning, J. (1981) *Eine Siedlung der Mittelneolithischen Gruppe Bischheim in Schernau, Ldkr. Kitzingen* (Bayerisches Landesamt für Denkmalpflege Abteilung für Vor- und Frühgeschichte 44).
Magdeleine, J. (1979) L'Occupation Préhistorique au Monte Grossu I et Monte Grossu II – commune de Biguglia – Haute Corse. *Archeologia Corsa*, 4, 23-42.
Mahé, J. (1825) *Antiquités de Morbihan*. Vannes.
Maluquer de Motes, J. (1965) La estratigrafía del covacho de Berroberría (Urdax, Navarra), in *Miscelánea en Homenaje al Abate H. Breuil*, vol. 2, 135-40. Barcelona.
—— (1974) Les Pyrénées avant l'Histoire, in *Les Pyrénées, de la Montagne à l'Homme* (ed. F. Taillefer), 71-102. Toulouse.
Maluquer de Motes, J. and Fusté, M. (1962) La prehistoria de Andorra. *Zephyrus*, 13, 5-15.
Mariezkurrena, K. (1979) Dataciones de radiocarbone existentes para la prehistoria vasca. *Munibe*, 31, 237-55.
Marigan, E. (1893) Carte préhistorique de la vallée basse du Vidourle dans le département du Gard et une partie de la Vaunage. *Bull. Soc. Etudes Nat. et Sci. de Nîmes*, 1-13.
Marsac, M. and Joussaume, R. (1973) Détection aérienne et sondage dans un fossé à Xanton-Chassenon (Vendée). *Bull. Soc. Emulation de la Vendée*, 120, 14-20.
Marsac, M., Riley, D. and Scarre, C. (1982) Recent Discoveries of Possible Neolithic Long Mounds in Western France, and their British Parallels. *Aerial Archaeology*, 8, 1-16.
Marsac, M. and Scarre, C. (1979) Recent Discoveries of Neolithic Ditched Camps in West-Central France. *Aerial Archaeology*, 4, 37-57.
Marsan, G. (1972) *Le Problème du Néolithique dans les Pyrénées Occidentales*. Thèse de Doctorat de 3e cycle, Univ. de Paris I, Panthéon-Sorbonne.
—— (1979) L'occupation humaine à Arudy (Pyr-Atl) pendant la préhistoire et le début de la protohistoire. *7e rencontre d'historiens sur la Gascogne méridionale et les Pyrénées Occidentales*, Univ. de Pau, oct. 1977, 51-98.

Martin, L., Nourrit, A., Durand-Tullou, A. and Arnal, G. B. (1964) Les grottes citernes des Causses. Le vase à eau et son utilisation. *Gallia Préhistoire*, 7, 107-77.

Masset, C. (1971) Une sépulture collective mégalithique à la Chaussée-Tirancourt (Somme). *Bull. Soc. Préhist. Fr.*, 68, 178-82.

Maury, J. (1967) *Les Etapes de Peuplement sur les Grands Causses.* Millau.

Meier-Arendt, W. (1966) *Die bandkeramische Kultur im Untermaingebiet.* Bonn.

—— (1972) Zur Frage der jüngerlinienbandkeramischen Gruppenbildung: Omalien, 'Plaidter', 'Kölner', 'Wetterauer' und 'Wormser' Typ; Hinkelstein, in *Die Anfänge des Neolithikums vom Orient bis Nordeuropa,* Teil Va (Fundamenta A3), 85-152. Köln.

—— (1975) *Die Hinkelstein-Gruppe. Der Ubergang vom Früh- zum Mittelneolithikum in Südwestdeutschland* (Römisch-Germanische Forschungen 35, Berlin).

Mérimée, P. (1976 (1840)) *Voyage en Corse.* Paris.

Méroc, L. (1953) La conquète des Pyrénées par l'Homme et le rôle de la frontière pyrénéenne au cours des temps préhistoriques. *1er Congr. Int. de Spéléologie,* Paris, tome IV, section IV, 33-51.

—— (1961) Circonscription de Toulouse. *Gallia Préhistoire,* 4, 243-73.

—— (1962) Le village et la sépulture chasséens de Villeneuve-Tolosane (Hte-Gar). *Zephyrus,* 13, 94-6.

—— (1963) Circonscription de Toulouse. *Gallia Préhistoire,* 6, 193-233.

—— (1967) Circonscription de Midi-Pyrénées. *Gallia Préhistoire,*, 10, 389-411.

—— (1969) Circonscription de Midi-Pyrénées. *Gallia Préhistoire,* 12, 485-503.

—— (1970) Le Cardial, dans la haute et moyenne vallée de la Garonne et de ses affluents pyrénéens, in *Les Civilisations Néolithiques du Midi de la France* (ed. J. Guilaine), 23-5. Carcassonne.

Méroc, L. and Simonnet, G. (1970) Le Chasséen de la haute et de la moyenne vallée de la Garonne, in *Les Civilisations Néolithiques du Midi de la France* (ed. J. Guilaine), 38-47. Carcassonne.

—— (1979) Les sépultures chasséennes de Saint-Michel-du-Touch, à Toulouse (Hte-Gar). *Bull. Soc. Préhist. Fr.*, 76, 379-407.

—— (1981) Objets mobiliers insolites en terre cuite et en os, du Néolithique chasséen de Saint-Michel-du-Touch, à Toulouse (Hte-Gar), in *La Préhistoire du Quercy dans le contexte de Midi-Pyrénées, 21e Congr. Préhist. Fr.*, Montauban-Cahors, 1979, vol. 1, 223-33.

Michel, J. and Tabary-Picavet, D. (1979) La Bosse de l'Tombe à Givry (Hainaut). Tumulus protohistorique et occupation néolithique epi-Roessen. *Bull. Soc. royale belge Anthrop. Préhist.*, 90, 5-61.

Mills, N. T. W. (1976) *Exploitation and Settlement Patterns in Western Provence 7500-2000 b.c.* Unpublished M.A. thesis, Sheffield University.

—— (1980) *Prehistoric Agriculture in Southern France – Case Studies from Provence and Languedoc.* Unpublished Ph.D. thesis, Sheffield University.

—— (forthcoming) The Dynamics of Agricultural Settlement in South-East France: A Long-Term View, in *Beyond Subsistence* (eds G. Barker and C. Gamble). London.

Modderman, P. J. R. (1970) Linearbandkeramik aus Elsloo und Stein. *Analecta Praehistorica Leidensia*, 3.

—— (1981) Céramique du Limbourg: Rhénanie-Westphalie, Pays-Bas, Hesbaye. *Helinium*, 21, 140-60.

Mohen, J-P. (1973a). Les remparts néolithiques de Semussac (Charente-Maritime). *Recueil de la Société d'Archéologie et d'Histoire de la Charente-Maritime*, 25, 5-9.

—— (1973b) Les tumulus de Bougon, nécropole mégalithique. *Bull. Soc. Hist. et Sci. des Deux-Sèvres*, 1973, 1-54.

—— (1977) Les tumulus de Bougon, 4000-2000 ans avant Jesus-Christ. *Bulletin de la Société Historique et Scientifique des Deux-Sèvres*, 1977, 1-48.

—— (1978) Tumulus des Pyrénées françaises, in *Els Pobles Pre-Romans del Pirineu*, 2 Colloqui Int. d'Arq. de Puigcerda, 1976, 97-108.

Monaco, A., Thommeret, J. and Thommeret, Y. (1972) L'age des dépôts quaternaires sur le plateau continental du Roussillon (Golfe du Lion). *Comptes Rendus de l'Académie des Sciences de Paris*, Series D, 274, 2280-3.

Montjardin, R. (1962) Le peuplement préhistorique d'un plateau de la Basse-Ardèche: Chauzon. *Cahiers Rhodaniens*, 9, 4-52.

—— (1965) Le Peuplement préhistorique de Chauzon (Suite). *Cahiers Rhodaniens*, 12, 13-33.

—— (1966a) Schéma des formes et décors céramiques du chalcolithique de la Basse-Ardèche. *Ogam*, 18, 17-22.

—— (1966b) Le gisement néolithique d'Escanin aux Baux de Provence (Bouches-du-Rhône). *Cahiers Rhodaniens*, 13, 5-99.

—— (1967) Schéma des formes et décors céramiques du Ferrières de la Basse-Ardèche. *Ogam*, 19, 101-8.

—— (1970) Ferrières, Fontbouisse, et Campaniforme. *Bull. Soc. Préhist. Fr.*, 67, 277-81.

—— (1975) *Problèmes du Chalcolithique et du Fontbouisse*. Unpublished roneotyped article.

Montjardin, J. (1979) Quelques commentaires relatifs à la faune d'Escanin 2 – Les Baux. *Archéologie en Languedoc*, 2, 31-8.

Moravetti, A. and Lo Schiavo, F. (1979) Notiziario – Sardegna. *Riv. Sci. Preist*, 34, 332-43.

Mordant, C. (1980) Position chronologique et culturelle des anneaux-disques et des bracelets en roches schisteuses dans le bassin de l'Yonne. *Préhistoire et Protohistoire en Champagne-Ardenne*, 81-7. Châlons-sur-Marne.

Mordant, C. and Mordant, D. (1970) Le site néolithique des Gours-aux-Lions à Marolles-sur-Seine (Seine-et-Marne). *Bull. Soc. Préhist. Fr.*, 67, 345-70.

—— (1972) L'enceinte néolithique de Noyen-sur-Seine (Seine-et-Marne). *Bull. Soc. Préhist. Fr.*, 69, 554-69.

—— (1977a) Le Bois des Refuges à Misy-sur-Yonne (Seine-et-Marne). *Bull. Soc. Préhist. Fr.*, 74, 420-62.

—— (1977b) Noyen-sur-Seine, habitat néolithique de fond de vallée alluviale. *Gallia Préhistoire*, 20, 229-69.

—— (1978) Les sépultures néolithiques de Noyen-sur-Seine (Seine-et-Marne). *Bull. Soc. Préhist. Fr.*, 75, 559-78.

Mordant, D. (1967) Le Néolithique du Gros-Bois à Balloy (Seine-et-Marne). *Bull. Soc. Préhist. Fr.*, 64, 347-66.

—— (1980) Rapports entre le Cerny et les groupes de l'Est de la France. *Préhistoire et Protohistoire en Champagne-Ardenne*, 89-93. Châlons-sur-Marne.
Mortillet, A. de (1892) Rapport sur les Monuments Mégalithiques de la Corse. *Nouv. Arch. Miss. Sci.*, 3, 49-83.
Morzadec-Kerfourn, M-T. (1969) Variations de la ligne de rivage au cours du Post-Glaciaire le long de la côte nord du Finistère. Analyses polliniques de tourbes et de dépôts organiques littoraux. *Bull. de l'Assoc. Fr. pour l'Etude du Quatern.*, 21, 283-318.
—— (1973) Le quaternaire du Massif Armoricain. *Ann. Scient. de l'Univers. de Besançon.*, 21.
—— (1974) Variations de la ligne de rivage armoricaine au Quaternaire. Analyses polliniques de dépôts organiques littoraux. *Mém. Soc. Géol. et Min. Bret.*, 17.
—— (1976) L'évolution de la végétation en Armorique à partir du néolithique, in *La Préhistoire Française, II: Les civilisations néolithiques et protohistoriques* (ed. J. Guilaine), 88-94. Paris.
Moulis, A. (1936) *Essai de Préhistoire Ariégeoise*. Foix.
Naroll, R. (1962) Floor area and settlement pattern. *American Antiquity*, 27, 587-9.
Naval Intelligence Division (1942) *France. Geographical handbook, Vol. I.* London.
Nicolardot, J-P. (1973) Structures et datations par mesures C14 du rempart de l'habitat néolithique du camp de Myard à Vitteaux (Côte-d'Or). *Bull. Soc. Préhist. Fr.*, 70, 68.
—— (1974) Structures d'habitats de hauteur à caractères défensifs dans le Centre-Est de la France. *Antiquités Nationales*, 6, 32-45.
Nicolle, E. (1924) The discovery of a bee-hive hut at La Sergenté, St Brelade. *Bull. Soc. Jers.*, 49, 67-71.
Nicolle, E., Warton, R. and Sinel, J. (1913) Report on the exploration of the dolmen at Les Monts Grantez, St Ouen, September 1912. *Bull. Soc. Jers.*, 38, 314-25.
Niederlender, A., Lacam, R. and Arnal, J. (1966) *Le gisement néolithique de Roucadour*. Paris.
Nouel, A. (1940) La station préhistorique de Préfontaines (Loiret). *Bull. Soc. Préhist. Fr.*, 37, 56-69.
Nouel, A., Dauvois, M., Bailloud, G., Riquet, R., Poulain-Josien, T., Planchais, N. and Horemans, P. (1965) L'ossuaire néolithique d'Eteauville, commune de Lutz-en-Dunois (Eure-et-Loir). *Bull. Soc. Préhist. Fr.*, 62, 576-648.
Nougier, L-R. (1950) *Le Peuplement Préhistorique: ses étapes entre Loire et Seine*. Le Mans.
—— (1952) La civilisation du 'Néolithique Pyrénéen' et ses rapports avec le Néolithique lacustre suisse. *Pallas (Annales Fac. Lett. Toulouse)*, 158-71.
—— (1954) Le Vase Polypode Pyrénéen en Europe Occidentale. *Pallas (Annales Fac. Lett. Toulouse)*, 2, 178-97.
—— (1959) *La Géographie Préhistorique Humaine*. Paris.
Nougier, L-R. and Robert, R. (1953) La Céramique de la grotte de Bédeilhac (Ariège). *Congr. Préhist. Fr.*, 14, 494-538.
—— (1956) Matériel lithique et osseux de la grotte de Bédeilhac (Ariège). *Congr. Préhist. Fr.*, 15, 760-80.
Octobon, E. (1937) Contribution à l'étude du Néolithique: le Néolithique de la grotte de Bédeilhac (Ariège). *Rev. Anth.*, 59-76.

Oldfield, F. (1960) The coastal mud-bed at Mouligna, Bidart, and the age of the Asturian industry in the Pays Basque. *Pollen et Spores*, 2, 57-70. Paris.

Oliver, S. P. (1870) Report on the present state and condition of prehistoric remains in the Channel Islands. *Journ. Ethnol. Soc.*, 2, 45-69.

Omnès, J. (1980) L'ossuaire de la grotte d'Artigaou à Esparros (Htes-Pyr) suivi d'un inventaire des grottes sépulcrales des Hautes-Pyrénées. *Revue de Comminges*, 93, 161-74.

—— (1981) Inventaire préhistorique de la commune de Lourdes. *Lavedan et Pays toy, Rev. arch., hist. et ethnog. de l'arrond. d'Argelès-Gazost*, 17-20.

Paepe, R. and Sommé, J. (1970) Les loess et la stratigraphie du Pleistocène récent dans le Nord de la France et en Belgique. *Ann. Soc. Géol. Nord*, 90, 191-201.

Parent, R. (1971) Le peuplement préhistorique entre la Marne et l'Aisne *Travaux de l'Institut d'Art préhistorique de l'Université de Toulouse*, 13.

Pasquet, A. (1979) Contribution à l'Atlas Préhistorique de la Région de Porto-Vecchio. *Archeologia Corsa*, 4, 53-81.

Passard, F. (1980) L'habitat au Néolithique et début de l'Age de Bronze en Franche-Comté. *Gallia Préhistoire*, 23, 37-114.

Passemard, E. (1925) Trois Gisements Néolithiques en Corse. *Bull. Soc. Préhist. Fr.*, 22, 221-5.

Patte, E. (1971) Quelques sépultures du Poitou, du Mésolithique au Bronze Moyen. *Gallia Préhistoire*, 14, 139-244.

Pautreau, J-P. (1976) Le Camp Allaric, commune d'Aslonnes (Vienne). Premiers résultats. *L'Anthropologie*, 80, 389-429.

—— (1979) *Le Chalcolithique et l'Age du Bronze en Poitou (Vendée, Deux-Sèvres, Vienne)*. Poitiers.

Pautreau, J-P., Façon, R., Gabet, C., Hesse, A. and Robert, P-P. (1974) *L'habitat peu-richardien de la Sauzaie, commune de Soubise (Charente-Maritime)*. Poitiers.

Pautreau, J-P. and Gendron, C. (1981) Liste des vases supports du Centre-Ouest de la France, in Pautreau, J-P.: Les sépultures mégalithiques I et II des Busserais à La Bussière (Vienne). *Gallia Préhistoire*, 24, 201-28.

Pautreau, J-P. and Robert, P-P. (1980) Le foyer néolithique ancien des Gouillauds, au Bois, Ile de Ré (Charente-Maritime). *Bull. Soc. Préhist. Fr.*, 77, 123-8.

Peek, J. (1975) *Inventaire des Mégalithes de la France, 4: Région Parisienne*. Paris.

Pellet, C., Dapoigny, C. and Delor, J-P. (1978) La nécropole rubanée de 'L'Etang David' à Chichery (Yonne). *Revue Archéologique de l'Est*, 111, 65-80.

Péquart, S-J., Péquart, M., Boule, M. and Vallois, H. (1937) Téviec: station nécropole mésolithique du Morbihan. *Archives de l'Institut de paléontologie humaine*, 18.

Péquart, S-J. and Péquart, M. (1954) *Hoëdic. Deuxième station nécropole mésolithique du Morbihan*. Anvers.

Peretti, G. (1966) Une sépulture campaniforme en rapport avec l'alignement des menhirs de Palaggiu (Sartène, Corse). *Congr. Préhist. Fr.*, 18, 230-42.

Pericot, L. (1950) *Los Sepulcros Megalíticos Catalanes y la Cultura Pirenaica*, 2nd ed. Barcelona.

Pernet, F. and Lenclud, C. (1977) *Berger en Corse*. Grenoble.

Petrequin, A. M. and Petrequin, P. (1978) Le phénomène Campaniforme-Cordée en Franche-Comté. Chronologie et rapports avec les groupes régionaux. *Bull. Soc. Préhist. Fr.*, 75, 361-93.

—— (1980) La céramique du niveau V de Clairvaux-les-Lacs (Jura) et le Néolithique moyen bourguignon, in *Préhistoire et Protohistoire en Champagne-Ardenne*, 119-28. Châlons-sur-Marne.

Petrequin, P. (1970a) La grotte de la Baume de Gonvillars. *Annales Litteraires de l'Université de Besancon*, 107.

—— (1970b) Le camp néolithique de Moulin Rouge à Lavans-lès-Dole (Jura). *Revue Archéologique de l'Est*, 21, 99-120.

—— (1972) La Grotte de la Tuilerie à Gondenans-les-Montby. *Annales Littéraires de l'Université de Besançon*, 137.

—— (1974) Interprétation d'un habitat néolithique en grotte : le niveau XI de Gonvillars (Haute-Saône). *Bull. Soc. Préhist. Fr.*, 71, 489-534.

Petrequin, P. and Piningre, J-P. (1976) Les sépultures collectives mégalithiques de Franche-Comté. *Gallia Préhistoire*, 19, 287-394.

Philippe, J. (1936) Le Fort Harrouard. *L'Anthropologie*, 46, 257-301.

—— (1937) Le Fort Harrouard. *L'Anthropologie*, 47, 542-612.

Phillips, P. (1973) Les caractères régionaux du Chasséen du Midi. *Bull. Soc. Préhist. Fr.*, 69, 538-53.

—— (1973) The evolutionary model of human society and its application to certain early farming populations of Western Europe, in *The Explanation of Culture Change: Models in Prehistory* (ed. C. Renfrew), 529-37. London.

—— (1975) *Early Farmers of West Mediterranean Europe*. London.

—— (1982) *The Middle Neolithic in Southern France, Chasséen Farming and Culture Process*. Oxford.

Phillips, P., Aspinall, A. and Feather, S. (1977) Stages of 'Neolithisation' in Southern France: supply and exchange of raw materials. *Proc. Prehist. Soc.*, 43, 303-16.

Pi, M. and Baills, H. (1980) Etude des histogrammes polliniques de la grotte de Can Pey (Montferrer, Pyr-Or), in *Le Groupe de Véraza et la Fin des Temps Néolithiques dans le Sud de la France et la Catalogne* (ed. J. Guilaine), 138-9. Toulouse.

Pierpoint, S. (1980) *Social Patterns in Yorkshire Prehistory 3500-750 B.C.* Oxford.

Piette, E. (1881) Note sur les Tumulus de Bartrès et d'Ossun. *Matériaux*, 522-40.

—— (1895) Etudes d'ethnographie préhistorique, I: Répartition stratigraphique des harpons dans les grottes des Pyrénées. *L'Anthropologie*, 6, 276-92.

—— (1896) Etudes d'ethnographie préhistorique, II: Les plantes cultivées de la période de transition au Mas d'Azil. *L'Anthropologie*, 7, 1-17.

Piette, J. (1973-4) Le site néolithique des Grèves de Frécul à Barbuise-Courtavant (Aube). *Bull. Groupe Archéol. du Nogentais*, 10, 3-18.

Piggott, S. (1953) Le Néolithique Occidental et le Chalcolithique de la France: Esquisse préliminaire (1). *L'Anthropologie*, 57, 401-43.

Piggott, S. (1954) Le Néolithique Occidental et le Chalcolithique de la France: Esquisse préliminaire (2). *L'Anthropologie*, 58, 1-28.

Piggott, S., Daniel, G. E. and McBurney, C. (eds) (1974) *France Before the Romans*. London.

Piningre, I. and Bréart, B. (1976) La sépulture collective de Vers-sur-Selle (Somme): Note préliminaire. *Cahiers Archéologiques de Picardie*, 3, 29-37.

Piningre, J-F. (1974) Un aspect de l'économie néolithique: le problème de l'aphanite en Franche-Comté et dans les régions limitrophes. *Annales Littéraires de l'Université de Besançon*, 158.

—— (1980) La stratigraphie du site néolithique de la 'Montagne de Lumbres'. Etat de recherches 1977-1978. *Préhistoire et Protohistoire en Champagne-Ardenne*, 109-17. Châlons-sur-Marne.

Piningre, J-F. and Hurtrelle, J. (1979) Préhistoire dans le Nord de la France. Premiers agriculteurs du néolithique. *Archéologia*, 137, 30-5.

Planchais, N. (1973) Premiers résultats d'analyse pollinique de sédiments versilien en Languedoc. *Bull. de l'Assoc. Fr. pour l'Etude du Quaternaire*, 36, 146-52.

Planchais, N., Renault-Miskovsky, J. and Vernet, J-L. (1977) Les facteurs d'évolution de la végétation dans le sud de la France (côte à moyenne montagne) depuis le tardiglaciaire d'après l'analyse pollnique et les charbons de bois, in *Ecologie de l'Homme Fossile* (eds H. Laville and J. Renault-Miskovsky), 373-75. Paris.

Planson, E. (1979) Le camp-refuge néolithique de Marcilly-sur-Tille. *Revue archéologique de l'Est*, 30, 47-56.

Plateaux, M. (1982) *Données sur l'industrie lithique (R.R.B.P.) de Cuiry-lès-Chaudardes* (mémoire de maitrise, Université de Paris I).

—— (forthcoming) Le lithique rubané de Cuiry-les-Chaudardes (Aisne), in *Actes du colloque interrégional sur le Néolithique, Compiègne 1982*.

Plog, S. (1980) *Stylistic variation in prehistoric ceramics*. New York.

Poingdestre, J. (1682) *Caesarea*. London.

Popescu, C. P., Quéré, J-P. and Franceschi, P. (1980) Observations Chromosomiques chez le Sanglier Français. *Ann. Génét. Sél. Anim.*, 12, 395-400.

Poplin, F. (1975) La faune danubienne d'Armeau (Yonne, France): ses données sur l'activité humaine, in *Archaeozoological Studies* (ed. A. T. Clason), 179-92. Amsterdam.

—— (1975) Restes de rostre d'Espadon trouvés dans un gisement néolithique de l'étang de Leucate (Aude). *Bull. Soc. Préhist. Fr.* 72, 69-70.

—— (1979) Origine du Mouflon de Corse dans une Nouvelle Perspective Palaéontologique: par Marronnage. *Ann. Génét. Sél. Anim.*, 11, 133-43.

Pothier, E. (1900) *Les Tumulus du Plateau de Ger*. Paris.

Pouech, Abbé (1872) Groupe de Dolmens et Demi-dolmens des environs du Mas d'Azil (Ariège). *Bull. Soc. Arch. de Tarn-et-Garonne*, 2, 41-56 & 70-86.

Poulain, T. (1973) Les animaux domestiques en France à l'époque néolithique, in *L'Homme et l'Animal* (eds R. Pujol and R. Laurens).

—— (1976) La faune, in *La Préhistoire Française, II: Les civilisations néolithiques et protohistoriques* (ed. J. Guilaine), 104-16. Paris.

Poulain-Josien, T. (1965) Etude de la faune du gisement de Soubérac, Gensac-la-Pallue (Charente). *Bull. Soc. Préhist. Fr.*, 62, 316-27.

—— (1966) Etude de la faune du gisement néolithique des Matignons, commune de Juillac-le-Coq (Charente). *Gallia Préhistoire*, 9, 210-41.

—— (1967) Camp néolithique de Semussac (Charente-Maritime). Etude de la faune de la fouille de 1965. *Bull. Soc. Préhist. Fr.*, 64, 483-500.

Prades, H. (1972) La colonisation antique des rivages du Languedoc. *Revue d'Etudes Ligures*, 33, 110-30.

Prévost, R. (1962) L'habitat néolithique de la Montagne de Lumbres. *Mémoires de la Commission Départementale des Monuments Historiques du Pas-de-Calais*, 11.

Reille, M. (1976) Histoire de la Végétation de la Montagne Corse depuis le Tardiglaciaire, in *La Préhistoire Française, II: Les civilisations néolithiques et protohistoriques* (ed. J. Guilaine), 52-8. Paris.

—— (1977) Quelques Aspects de l'Activité Humaine en Corse durant le Subatlantique et ses Conséquences sur la Végétation, in *Approche Ecologique de l'Homme Fossile* (eds H. Laville and J. Renault-Miskovsky), 329-42. Paris.

Renault-Miskovsky, J. (1972) Contribution à la paléoclimatologie du Midi méditerranéen pendant la dernière glaciation et le post-glaciaire d'après l'étude palynologique du remplissage des grottes et abris sous roche. *Bull. Musée d'Anthropol. et Préhist. de Monaco*, 18, 145-210.

—— (1976) Les flores quaternaires dans le bassin occidental de la Méditerranée, in *Chronologie et Synchronisme dans la Préhistoire Circum-Méditerranéenne* (ed. G. Camps), 50-76. Nice.

Renfrew, C. (1973) *Before Civilisation*. London.

—— (1976) Megaliths, Territories and Populations, in *Acculturation and Continuity in Atlantic Europe* (ed. S. J. De Laet), 198-220. Bruges.

—— (1977) Space, time and polity, in *The Evolution of Social Systems* (eds J. Friedman and M. J. Rowlands), 89-112. London.

—— (1981) The Megalith Builders of Western Europe, in *Antiquity and Man* (eds J. D. Evans, B. Cunliffe and C. Renfrew), 72-81. London.

Renouf, J. and Urry, J. (1976) *The First Farmers in the Channel Islands*. Jersey.

Ricq-de-Bouard, M. (1980) Echanges et commerce des objets de pierre polie. *Les Dossiers d'Archéologie*, 44, 56-9.

Rigaud, J-P. (1980) Circonscription d'Aquitaine. *Gallia Préhistoire*, 23, 391-426.

Riquet, R. (1953) Les styles céramiques néo-enéolithiques des pays de l'ouest. *Bull. Soc. Préhist. Fr.*, 50, 407-22.

Roberts, N. (1979) The Location and Environment of Knossos. *Ann. Brit. School Athens*, 74, 231-41.

Rodriguez, G. (1968) Le néolithique dans le Saintponais (Hérault). *Bull. Soc. Préhist. Fr.*, 65, 699-748.

—— (1970a) Grotte de Camprafaud (Hérault). Datations au C-14. *Bull. Soc. Préhist. Fr.*, 67, 210-11.

—— (1970b) Le Néolithique final, faciès de Saint-Pons (Saint-Ponien), *Les Civilisations Néolithiques du Midi de la France* (ed. J. Guilaine), 106-10. Carcassonne.

Rodriguez, G. (1976) Grotte de Camprafaud (Ferrières-Poussarou, Hérault), in *Provence et Languedoc Méditerranéen: Sites Paléolithiques et Néolithiques, Livret-Guide de l'Excursion C2* (ed. H. De Lumley), 253-5. Nice.
Roseville des Grottes (1911) Une cachette néolithique dans la grotte d'Espalungue (alias d'Izeste) en Arudy (Basses-Pyr). *L'Homme Préhistorique*, 9e année, 53-4.
Roubet, C. (1979) *Economie Pastorale Préagricole en Algérie Orientale: Le Néolithique de Tradition Capsienne*. Paris.
Roudil, J-L. (1963) La station de la Madeleine, Hérault. *Cahiers Ligures de Préhistoire et d'Archéologie*, 12, 230-2.
—— (1965) La station de la Madeleine, Hérault. *Cahiers Ligures de Préhistoire et d'Archéologie*, 14, 165-73.
—— (1978) Circonscription du Languedoc-Roussillon. *Gallia Préhistoire*, 21, 661-95.
—— (1980) Circonscription de Languedoc-Roussillon. *Gallia Préhistoire*, 23, 427-71.
Roudil, J-L. and Grimal, J. (1978) Découverte d'une nouvelle civilisation du néolithique ancien en Languedoc, Peiro Signado, Portiragnes. *Bull. Soc. Préhist. Fr.*, 75, 101-3.
Roudil, J. and Saumade, H. (1968) La grotte de Peyroche II à Auriolles (Ardèche). *Gallia Préhistoire*, 11, 147-203.
Roussot-Larroque, J. (1973) Quelques datations radio-carbone pour le Néolithique d'Aquitaine. *Bull. Soc. Préhist. Fr.*, 70, 38-9.
—— (1976) Les civilisations néolithiques en Aquitaine, in *La Préhistoire Française, II: Les civilisations néolithiques et protohistoriques* (ed. J. Guilaine), 338-50. Paris.
—— (1977) Néolithisation et Néolithique ancien d'Aquitaine. *Bull. Soc. Préhist. Fr.*, 74, 559-82.
Roux, I. (1967) Videlles (Essonne). Analyse Palynologique. *Bull. Soc. Préhist. Fr.*, 64, 425-38.
Roux, J. and Leroi-Gourhan, A. (1964) Les défrichements de la période atlantique. *Bull. Soc. Préhist. Fr.*, 61, 309-15.
Rowley-Conwy, P. (1981) Mesolithic Danish Bacon: Permanent and Temporary sites in the Danish Mesolithic, in *Economic Archaeology* (eds A. Sheridan and G. Bailey), 51-5. Oxford.
Rozoy, J-G. (1978) *Les Derniers Chasseurs*. Reims.
Ryder, M. (1981) A survey of European primitive breeds of sheep. *Ann. Génét. Sél. Anim.*, 13, 381-418.
Sacaze, J. (1887) Histoire ancienne de Luchon. *Revue de Comminges*, 3, 65-115.
Sakellaridis, M. (1979) *The Mesolithic and Neolithic of the Swiss Area*. Oxford.
Saussol, A. (1970) *L'Elevage Ovin en Languedoc Central et Oriental (Hérault, Gard, Lozère)*. Montpellier.
—— (1971) Les parcours pastoraux en Languedoc oriental. *Bulletin de la Société Languedocienne de Géographie*, 5, 429-54.
Sauze (1845) Rapport sur les fouilles faites à Bougon. *Mém. Soc. Stat. des Deux-Sèvres*, 9, 97-106.
Scarre, C. (1982) Settlement Patterns and Landscape Change: the Late Neolithic and the Bronze Age of the Marais Poitevin area of Western France. *Proc. Prehist. Soc.*, 48, 53-73.
Schietzel, K. (1965) *Müddersheim: eine Ansiedlung der jüngeren Bandkeramik im Rheinland* (Fundamenta A1). Köln.

Schmitt, G. (1974) La transition entre le Néolithique moyen et le Néolithique final en Basse-Alsace, I. *Revue Archéologique de l'Est*, 25, 277-364.

—— (1975) La transition entre le Néolithique moyen et lh Néolithique final en Basse-Alsace, II. *Revue Archéologique de l'Est*, 26, 69-94.

Schuldt, E. (1972) *Die Mecklenburgischen megalithgräber*. Berlin.

Schweitzer, J. (1980) Aperçu sur la céramique rubanée du Haut Rhin. *Préhistoire et Protohistoire en Champagne-Ardenne*, 33-44. Châlons-sur-Marne.

Sclafert, T. (1959) *Cultures en Haute Provence: Déboisements et Pâturages au Moyen Age*. Paris.

Shee Twohig, E. (1981) *The Megalithic Art of Western Europe*. Oxford.

Sherratt, A. G. (1979) Water, soil and seasonality in early cereal cultivation. *World Archaeology*, 11, 313-30.

—— (1981) Plough and pastoralism: aspects of the secondary products revolution, in *Pattern of the Past* (eds I. Hodder, G. Isaac and N. Hammond), 261-306. Cambridge.

Sielmann, B. (1972) Die Frühneolithische Besiedlung Mitteleuropas, in *Die Anfänge des Neolithikums vom Orient bis Nordeuropa*, Teil Va (Fundamenta A3), 1-65. Köln.

Simi, P. (1981) *Précis de Géographie Physique, Humaine, Economique, Régionale de la Corse*. Bastia.

Simonnet, G. (1976) Le village chasséen de Saint-Michel-du-Touch à Toulouse (Hte-Gar), in *Pyrénées, Livret-Guide de l'Excursion A5* (ed. J. Clottes), 15-34. Nice.

—— (1980a) La structure chasséenne 'V.T. 215' à Villeneuve-Tolosane (Hte-Gar). *Bull. Soc. Préhist. Fr.*, 77, 144-51.

—— (1980b) Les structures dites 'Fonds de Cabanes' du Néolithique Chasséen de Saint-Michel-du-Touch, à Toulouse (Hte-Gar). *Travaux de l'Inst. Art Préhist. Toulouse*, 22, 451-80.

Sire, P. M. (1938) Folklore préhistorique de l'Aude. *Folklore* (Aude), 5, 77-80.

Southwell Colucci, E. (1930) Un Insegne Scienziato Inglese Amico della Corsica: Dott. Ch. Forsyth Major. *Archivio Storico di Corsica*, 357-70.

Sprockhoff, E. (1938) *Die Nordische megalithkultur*. Berlin and Leipzig.

Stanley Price, N. (1977a) Khirokitia and the Initial Settlement of Cyprus. *Levant*, 9, 66-89.

—— (1977b) Colonization and continuity in the Early Prehistory of Cyprus. *World Archaeology*, 9, 27-41.

Strahm, C. and Thévenot, J. P. (1976) La Civilisation Saône-Rhône. *Revue Archéologique de l'Est*, 27, 331-420.

Sutton, K. (1977) Reclamation of wasteland during the 18th and 19th centuries, in *Themes in the Historical Geography of France* (ed. H. Clout), 247-300. London.

Taborin, Y. (1974) La parure en coquillage de l'épipaléolithique au bronze ancien en France. *Gallia Préhistoire*, 17, 101-79, 307-417.

Tanda, G. (1980) Il Neolitico Antico e Medico della Grotta Werde, Alghero. *Atti Biun Sci. Ist. Ital. Preist. Protost.*, 22, 45-94.

Tarrête, J. (1977) *Le Montmorencien*. Paris.

—— (1978) Les gravures de l'allée couverte de la Cave-aux-Fées à Breuil-en-Vexin (Yvelines). *Bull. Soc. Préhist. Fr.*, 75, 241-9.

—— (1981) Circonscription d'Ile de France. *Gallia Préhistoire*, 24, 291-328.

Ters, M. (1973) Les variations du niveau marin depuis 10,000 ans, le long du littoral Atlantique français, in *Le Quaternaire – géodynamique, stratigraphie et environnement. Travaux français récents. 9e Congrès International de l'INQUA*, 114-35. Paris.

Thaler, L. (1973) Namisme et Gigantisme Insulaires. *La Recherche*, 4, 741-59.

Thévenot, J-P. (1969) Eléments Chasséens de la Céramique de Chassey. *Revue Archéologique de l'Est*, 20, 7-95.

—— (1973) Le village protohistorique d'Ouroux-sur-Saône. *Travaux du Centre de Recherches de Solutré*, 1.

—— (1978) Circonscription de Bourgogne. *Gallia Préhistoire*, 21, 573-602.

Thom, A. and Thom, A. S. (1978) *Megalithic remains in Britain and Brittany*. Oxford.

Thommasset, J-J. (1927) Les poteries ornées du camp de Chassey. *L'Anthropologie*, 37, 459-72.

Todd, I. (1978) Vasilikos Valley Project: Second Preliminary Report, 1977. *J. Field. Arch.*, 55, 161-95.

Toupet, C. (1980) L'enceinte néolithique de Compiègne (Oise), in *Préhistoire et Protohistoire en Champagne-Ardenne*, 95-108. Châlons-sur-Marne.

Treinen, F. (1970) Les poteries campaniformes en France. *Gallia Préhistoire*, 13, 53-107, 261-332.

Treinen-Claustre, F., Guilaine, J. and Vaquer, J. (1981) Le Néolithique de la Catalogne du Nord, in *El Neolitic a Catalunya*, Taula Rodona de Montserrat, maig 1980; Publicacions de l'Abadia de Montserrat, 209-25.

Triat, H. (1973) Analyse pollinique de sédiments versiliens en Provence, in *9e Congrès International de l'INQUA*, 142-5. Christchurch.

—— (1978) *Contribution Pollenanalytique à l'Histoire Tardi et Postglaciaire de la Végétation de la Basse Vallée du Rhône*. Unpublished thesis (Docteur es Sciences), Marseille.

Trump, D. (1982) La Grotta Filiestru, Bonu Ighinu, Mara (Sardeigne), in *Le Néolithique Ancien Méditerranéen* (ed. R. Montjardin), 327-32. Montpellier.

Truffreau, A. (1974) La fosse chasséenne de Liévin (Pas de Calais). *Bull. Soc. Préhist. Fr.*, 67, 43-6.

Uerpmann, H. P. (1979) *Probleme der Neolithisierung der Mittelmeerraumes*. Tübingen.

Van der Waals, J. D. and Waterbolk, H. T. (1976) Excavations at Swifterbant – Discovery, Progress, Aims and Methods. *Helinium*, 16, 3-14.

Van Zeist, W. (1964) A paleobotanical study of some bogs in western Brittany (Finistère), France. *Palaeohistoria*, 10, 157-80.

Vaquer, J. (1975) *La Céramique Chasséenne du Languedoc*. Carcassonne.

—— (1976) Gisements néolithiques en Cerdagne. *Cypsela*, 1, 36-8.

—— (1980) De la cueillette à l'agriculture: la grotte de l'Abeurador. *Les Premiers Paysans, Dossiers de l'Archéologie*, 44, 18-19.

—— (1980a) Les villages chasséens du bassin supérieur de la Garonne. *Les Premiers Paysans, Dossiers de l'Archéologie*, 44, 52-55.

—— (1980b) Une empreinte d'épi de céréales à Ouveillan (Aude), in *Le Groupe de Véraza et la Fin des Temps Néolithiques dans le Sud de la France et la Catalogne* (ed. J. Guilaine), 140. Toulouse.

—— (1980c) Le groupe de Véraza, essai sur l'évolution de la culture matérielle, in *Ibid.*, 84-93.
—— (1980d) Le gisement de la Tuilerie de Grépiac (Haute-Garonne), in *Ibid.*, 61-3.
—— (1981) D'étranges fosses néolithiques. *La Recherche*, 12, 882-3.
Vernet, J-L. (1973) Etude sur l'Histoire de la Végétation du Sud-Est de la France au Quaternaire d'après les Charbons de Bois Principalement. *Paléobiologie Continentale*, 4, 1. Montpellier.
—— (1976) La flore et la végétation méditerranéennes : à propos de leur mise en place en Europe de l'ouest, in *Chronologie et Synchronisme dans la Préhistoire Circum-Méditerranéenne* (ed. G. Camps), 8-19. Nice.
Verron, G. (1973) Circonscription de Haute et Basse Normandie. *Gallia Préhistoire*, 16, 361-99.
—— (1975) Circonscription de Haute et Basse Normandie. *Gallia Préhistoire*, 18, 469-510.
—— (1976) Acculturation et continuité en Normandie durant le néolithique et les âges des métaux, in *Acculturation and Continuity in Atlantic Europe* (ed. S. J. De Laet), 261-83. Bruges.
—— (1976) Les civilisations néolithiques en Normandie, in *La Préhistoire Française, II : Les civilisations néolithiques et protohistoriques* (ed. J. Guilaine), 387-401. Paris.
—— (1977a) Un type de monuments funéraires classique dans le néolithique de Normandie. *Bull. Soc. Polym. Morb.*, 104, 187-219.
—— (1977b) Circonscription de Haute et Basse Norm ndie. *Gallia Préhistoire*, 20, 357-406.
—— (1979) Circonscription de Haute et Basse Normandie. *Gallia Préhistoire*, 22, 471-523.
—— (1981) Circonscription de Haute et Basse Normandie. *Gallia Préhistoire*, 24, 365-94.
Vézian, J. and Vallois, H. V. (1927) La grotte sépulcrale et les ossements humains de Quérénas (Ariège). *Rev. Anth.*, 336-45.
Vidal, P. (1922) *La Roussillon Préhistorique*. Perpignan.
Vigne, J. D. (1982) The beginning of sheep, goat and pig domestication in south Corsica (France), in *Animals in Archaeology* (eds C. Grigson and J. Clutton-Brock). Oxford.
Vigne, J. D. and Lanfranchi, F. de (1981) Nouvelles Données sur l'Origine du Cerf de Corse et de Sardaigne. *Bull. Soc. Préhist. Fr.*, 78, 105-6.
Vigne, J. D., Marinval-Vigne, M. C., Lanfranchi, F. de and Weiss, M-C. (1981) Consommation du 'Lapin-Rat' (*Prolagus Sardus* Wagner) au Néolithique Ancien Méditerranéen. *Bull. Soc. Préhist. Fr.*, 78, 222-4.
Virili, F. L. and Grosjean, J. (1979) *Guide des Sites Torréens de l'Age du Bronze Corse*. Paris.
Visset, L. (1974) Le tumulus de Dissignac à Saint Nazaire (Loire-Atlantique). Etude palynologique. *Bull. de la Soc. Scient. de Bretagne*, 48, 7-14.
Waldren, W. H. (1979) A Beaker workshop area in the rock shelter of Son Matge, Mallorca. *World Archaeology*, 11, 43-67.
Watté, J-P. (1976) L'habitat Seine-Oise-Marne du Grand-Epauville à Montivilliers (Seine-Maritime). *Bull. Soc. Préhist. Fr.*, 73, 196.
Wedgewood, W. and Mourant, A. (1954) The megalithic structures at the Jersey Gasworks. *Bull. Soc. Jers.*, 79, 148-60.

Weiss, M-C. (1966) Préhistoire de la Balagne Déserte. *Bull. Soc. Sci. Hist. Nat. Corse*, 581, 7-14.
—— (1973) Un gisement sur éperon de la vallée du Liamone. *Cahiers Corsica*, 29, 4-8.
—— (1976) Contribution à l'étude du Niolo Préhistorique. L'Abri Albertini à Albertacce. *Archeologia Corsa*, 1, 75-96.
Weiss, M-C. and Desneiges, C. (1971) Le Gisement du Monte-Lazzo à Tiuccia (Corse). *Bull. Soc. Préhist. Fr.*, 68, 417-29.
—— (1974) Inventaire, Etude et Typologie du Matériel de Broyage du Monte Lazzo. *Cahiers Corsica*, 43, 49-56.
Weiss, M-C. and Lanfranchi, F. de (1976) Les Civilisations Néolithiques en Corse, in *La Préhistoire Française, II: Les civilisations néolithiques et protohistoriques* (ed. J. Guilaine), 432-42. Paris.
Weissner, P. (1982) Beyond Willow Smoke and Dogs' Tails: A Comment on Binford's Analysis of Hunter-Gatherer Settlement Systems. *American Antiquity*, 47, 171-8.
Whittle, A. W. R. (1977) *The Earlier Neolithic of Southern England and its Continental Background*. Oxford.
Whittle, A. (1978) Resources and population in the British Neolithic. *Antiquity*, 52, 34-42.
Wobst, H. (1977) Stylistic Behavior and Information exchange. *Anthropological Papers of the Museum of Anthropology, University of Michigan*, 61, 317-42.

Acknowledgements

The idea of a volume such as this first arose out of discussions with James Lewthwaite in the summer of 1981. My grateful thanks go to him and to all the other contributors for their help in bringing the idea to realisation, and to the staff of the Edinburgh University Press, in particular Mr Archie Turnbull, for their expert guidance at all stages of this process. Professor Colin Renfrew gave much useful advice during the planning of the volume, and Professor Glyn Daniel provided help and encouragement in the at times laborious, apparently endless and seemingly thankless task of editing it. Thanks are also due to Gwil Owen for preparing several of the plates, including all those of Chapters 6 and 8, to Heather Wall and Phil and Deirdre Lee for help with the diagrams, and to Margaret Chapman and Thyrza Smith for help with typing.

Detailed acknowledgement is due as follows:

Chapter 2: Mike Ilett is grateful for the co-operation and advice in writing this chapter of his colleagues at the Centre de Recherches Protohistoriques, Université de Paris I, and to the Délégation Générale à la Recherche Scientifique et Technique (Ministère de la Recherche) for financial support.

Chapter 3: Mark Burkill would like to thank the following for their help during the research on which this chapter is based and during the writing of the chapter: Jean-Claude Blanchet, Anne-Marie and Pierre Petrequin, Mike Ilett, Ian Hodder, and the members of the URA 12 team, in particular A. Coudart. The plates were provided through the kind co-operation of Roger Agache and Pierre Delor.

Chapter 4: John Howell would like to acknowledge the help received from Gerard Bailloud, R. Parent, Andrew Sherratt and Guy Verron while carrying out the research on which this chapter is based. Thanks are due to John Peek and Claude Masset for providing the plates.

Chapter 5: Nigel Mills wishes to thank M. Escalon de Fonton and J-L. Roudil for permittting him to carry out research in their respective *circonscriptions*. He would also like to thank Jean Courtin, who first encouraged his research in this part of France, and who has now succeeded M. Escalon de Fonton as director of the Provence-Alpes-Côte-D'Azur *circonscription*. The detailed studies referred to in this chapter were carried out with help from A. D'Anna, G. Costantini, X. Gutherz and J-M. Roger, and the research was funded by grants from the Department of Education and Science, the Sidney Perry Foundation and the Sheffield University Research Fund, and by a French Government Scholarship.

Chapter 6: James Lewthwaite is grateful to many scholars for the gift of offprints, and for an invitation from the Société Archéologique de Haute Corse and a grant from Lord William Taylour's Mediterranean Trust which enabled him to travel to Corsica in June 1981 and discuss many issues at first hand with Corsican scholars including A. Amadei, J. Césari, J. L. and O. Jehasse, F. de Lanfranchi, J. Magdeleine, A. Milleliri and M-C. Weiss. Fred Hamond and Mrs Val Miller typed drafts of the chapter, John Howell drew the figures and Gwil Owen prepared the plates.

Chapter 7: This chapter was written during the tenure of a Research Fellowship in Prehistoric Archaeology at the University of Liverpool. The author would like to thank Jean Clottes, Jean Guilaine and Jean Vaquer for permission to copy drawings and to reproduce plates from their publications. Thanks are also due to David Geddes for access to unpublished information.

Chapter 8: Chris Scarre would like to thank the various French archaeologists without whose help and hospitality the research on which this chapter is based would not have been possible, in particular André Coffyn of the University of Bordeaux, Roger Joussaume, director of the excavations at Champ Durand, Jean-Pierre Mohen of the Musée des Antiquités Nationales, and Daniel Prigent, Archéologue-Géologue Départementale for Maine-et-Loire. Gwil Owen prepared the plates and Heather Wall helped with the figures.

Chapter 9: James Hibbs wishes to thank K. McBarron for help in preparing the illustrations and Anthony Harding for providing many of the plates. He would also like to thank Anthony Harding, Colin Haselgrove and C-T. Le Roux for their generous help and comments, H. Nowell for providing much encouragement, and Ian Kinnes for the benefit of many long and interesting discussions.

Chris Scarre

Index